Instructor's Guide to Text and Media

Human Anatomy & Physiology

Seventh Edition

Theresa Bissell
Ivy Tech State College

Laura Steele
Ivy Tech State College

PEARSON

Benjamin Cummings

San Francisco   Boston   New York
Cape Town   Hong Kong   London   Madrid   Mexico City
Montreal   Munich   Paris   Singapore   Sydney   Tokyo   Toronto

Editor-in-Chief: Serina Beauparlant
Editorial Assistant: Alex Streczyn
Managing Editor: Wendy Earl
Production Editor: Leslie Austin
Composition: Cecelia G. Morales
Proofreader: Martha Ghent
Senior Manufacturing Buyer: Stacey Weinberger
Executive Marketing Manager: Lauren Harp
Cover Designer: Frances Baca

ISBN: 0-8053-7379-

1 2 3 4 5 6 7 8 9 10—TCS—10 09 08 07 0

www.aw-bc.com

PREFACE

This Instructor's Guide to Text and Media has been updated and revised to accompany *Human Anatomy & Physiology*, Seventh Edition, by Elaine N. Marieb and Katja Hoehn. Each chapter has been outlined in a way that we hope benefits you in your use of the text and instruction of your classes. At the beginning of each chapter is a list of Objectives to guide you in deciding how to focus your teaching. A detailed Suggested Lecture Outline is provided for each chapter to aid you in developing your own course outline. Additionally, there are Cross References that point you to concepts in other chapters of the text to facilitate integration of other information. Each chapter contains Lecture Hints and Activities/Demonstrations that may be beneficial in presenting material in a way that makes it more meaningful for students. There are also Critical Thinking/Discussion Topics, as well as Library Research Topics, to be used in class discussion or as outside assignments that may help your students further understand the lectured material.

A number of resources are listed in the chapters of this instructor's guide that may be useful in making your presentations more engaging or effective. Histology Slides for the Life Sciences, Laboratory Correlations, Multimedia in the Classroom and Lab (including descriptive listings of videos and software as well as online resources for students), and Lecture Enhancement Materials (transparency acetates and Media Manager images) are available to coordinate with your lecture. A Suggested Reading list includes articles relevant to the system covered by the chapter. In addition, Answers to End-of-Chapter Short Essay Questions and Critical Thinking and Clinical Application Questions are provided with page references pointing to the main text.

New to this edition is a list of Online Resources for Students that shows the organization of the Chapter Guide page in both the Anatomy & Physiology Place (www.anatomyandphysiology.com) and MyA&P™ (www.myaandp.com). Each Chapter Guide organizes all the online media resources in one convenient location, with e-book links to each section of *Human Anatomy & Physiology*, Seventh Edition. Both sites provide access to other resources, such as *InterActive Physiology*®, PhysioEx 6.0™, Anatomy 360°, self-study quizzes, anatomy labeling activities, flashcards, a glossary, a new Histology Tutorial, and other study tools to help enhance students' understanding of A&P. For more information, please refer to the media preview section at the very front of your textbook.

Appendix A is a guide to audio-visual distributors and their contact information. Appendix B provides thumbnails of all the textbook images, including art, photos, and tables, organized by chapter. Appendix C contains InterActive Physiology® Exercise Sheets, created by Dr. Shirley Whitescarver and Brian Witz, for use with the *InterActive Physiology*® 9-System Suite. Answers to these Exercise Sheet questions can be found in Appendix D. Finally, Appendix E includes a Correlation Guide between selected review questions from the main text and the A.D.A.M.® Interactive Anatomy (AIA) CD-ROM, version 4.0. This helps students find the most relevant view to help them answer questions that require critical reasoning.

An electronic version of this guide and other instructor supplements are available to download at the Addison Wesley/Benjamin Cummings catalog page. Visit www.aw-bc.com and select instructor resources for *Human Anatomy & Physiology*, Seventh Edition, by Elaine Marieb and Katja Hoehn.

The Internet is a tremendous resource for you and your students to find additional information on A&P topics. For a general listing of A&P websites, search for "anatomy" or "physiology" on search engines such as Google or Yahoo. Here are a few websites that you might find useful, but keep in mind that we cannot guarantee that these links will remain active.

www.medtropolis.com   The Virtual Body includes interactive presentations on various body systems, including animations, narrations, and quizzes.

www.nlm.nih.gov   The U.S. National Library of Medicine includes general health information as well as the Visible Human Project, which creates anatomical images of the male and female human body.

www.nlm.nih.gov/medlineplus   Medline is a health database maintained by the National Institutes of Health's National Library of Medicine.

www.nih.gov   The National Institutes of Health is an excellent resource for general health information; a good source of research topics.

www.npac.syr.edu   The Northeast Parallel Architectures Center at Syracuse University has created the Visible Human Viewer (based on the Visible Human Project), which allows you to examine a cadaver layer by layer from different views.

Anatomy and physiology are fascinating disciplines that students are always enriched by. We hope that you find this guide a valuable partner in your teaching effort, and that the resources listed within allow you to present an effective and enjoyable learning experience for your students. Comments and suggestions are always welcome. They may be sent care of Benjamin Cummings, 1301 Sansome Street, San Francisco, CA, 94111.

THERESA BISSELL and LAURA STEELE
Ivy Tech State College, Ft. Wayne, IN

CONTENTS

11

Fundamentals of the Nervous System and Nervous Tissue   125

12

The Central Nervous System   138

13

The Peripheral Nervous System and Reflex Activity   155

14

The Autonomic Nervous System   166

29

Heredity 354

Appendices

The Human Body: An Orientation

Objectives

An Overview of Anatomy and Physiology

1. Define anatomy and describe the nature of different topics in anatomy.
2. Define physiology and describe the main focus of physiology.
3. Describe the principle of complementarity of structure and function. How does it unite the disciplines of anatomy and physiology?

Levels of Structural Organization

4. Name the different levels of structural organization and describe their relationships with each other.
5. List the organ systems of the body and the major structures within each system.

Maintaining Life

6. Describe the importance of each of the necessary life functions.
7. Describe the survival needs for human life and discuss the importance of each.

Homeostasis

8. Define homeostasis and list the components of a homeostatic control mechanism.

9. Distinguish between negative and positive feedback mechanisms. Describe the mechanics of each and their importance to the maintenance of homeostasis.

The Language of Anatomy

10. Describe the body's position in anatomical position. Why is this position important?
11. Define the directional terms as they relate to the human body.
12. Define the regional terms of the body. Which regions are found within other regions?
13. Identify the body planes and how they relate to sectioning terms and techniques.
14. Describe the body cavities and their relationships to each other. Which cavities are contained within other cavities?
15. Describe the membranes of the ventral cavity and their relationships to each other, the body wall, and the organs they are associated with.
16. Define the abdominopelvic regions and quadrants and describe how they are used by professionals.

Suggested Lecture Outline

I. An Overview of Anatomy and Physiology (pp. 2–3)

A. Anatomy is the study of the structure of body parts and their relationships to each other, and physiology is the study of the function of body parts (p. 2).

B. Topics of Anatomy (pp. 2–3)
1. Gross (macroscopic) anatomy is the study of structures large enough to be seen with the naked eye.
    a. Regional anatomy is the study of all body structures in a given body region.
    b. Systemic anatomy is the study of all structures in a body system.
    c. Surface anatomy is the study of internal body structures as they relate to the overlying skin.
2. Microscopic anatomy is the study of structures that are too small to be seen with the naked eye.
    a. Cytology is the study of individual cells.
    b. Histology is the study of tissues.
3. Developmental anatomy is the study of the change in body structures over the course of a lifetime.
4. Specialized Branches of Anatomy
    a. Pathological anatomy is the study of structural changes associated with disease.
    b. Radiographic anatomy is the study of internal structures using specialized visualization techniques.
    c. Molecular biology is the study of biological molecules.
C. Topics of Physiology (p. 3)
1. Physiology has several topics, most of which consider the function of specific organ systems.
2. Physiology often focuses on cellular and molecular events.
D. Complementarity of Structure and Function (p. 3)
1. The principle of complementarity of structure and function states that function is dependent on structure, and that the form of a structure relates to its function.

II. Levels of Structural Organization (pp. 3–4)

A. The chemical level is the simplest level of organization (Fig. 1.1).
1. Atoms, tiny building blocks of matter, combine to form molecules.
2. Molecules combine in specific ways to form organelles, which are the basic unit of living cells.
B. The cellular level is the smallest unit of life, and varies widely in size and shape according to the cells' function.
C. The tissue level is groups of cells having a common function.
D. The organ level is made up of discrete structures that are composed of at least two groups of tissues that work together to perform a specific function in the body.
E. The organ system level is a group of organs that work closely together to accomplish a specific purpose (Fig. 1.3).
F. The organismal level is the total of all structures working together to promote life.

III. Maintaining Life (pp. 4–8)

A. Necessary Life Functions (pp. 4–8; Fig. 1.2)

1. Maintaining boundaries allows an organism to maintain separate internal and external environments, or separate internal chemical environments.

2. Movement allows the organism to travel through the environment, and allows transport of molecules within the organism.

3. Responsiveness, or irritability, is the ability to detect changes in the internal or external environment and respond to them.

4. Digestion is the process of breaking down food into molecules that are usable by the body.

5. Metabolism includes all chemical reactions that occur in the body.

6. Excretion is the process of removing wastes.

7. Reproduction is the process of producing more cells or organisms.

8. Growth is an increase in size in body parts or the whole organism.

B. Survival Needs (p. 8)

1. Nutrients are consumed chemical substances that are used for energy and cell building.

2. Oxygen is required by the chemical reactions that release energy from foods.

3. Water, the most abundant chemical substance in the body, provides an environment for chemical reactions and a fluid medium for secretions and excretions.

4. Normal body temperature is required for the chemical reactions of the body to occur at the proper rate.

5. Atmospheric pressure must be within an appropriate range so that proper gas exchange occurs in the lungs.

IV. Homeostasis (pp. 8–12)

A. Homeostasis is the ability of the body to maintain a relatively constant internal environment, regardless of environmental changes (p. 9).

B. Homeostatic Control Mechanisms (pp. 9–12; Figs. 1.4–1.6)

1. Components

a. Variable: the regulated factor or event.

b. Receptor: structure that monitors changes in the environment and sends information to the control center.

c. Control center: structure that determines the set point for a variable, analyzes input, and coordinates an appropriate response.

d. Effector: struture that carries out the response directed by the control center.

2. Negative Feedback Mechanisms

a. Most homeostatic control mechanisms are negative feedback mechanisms.

b. A negative feedback mechanism causes the variable to change in a way that opposes the initial change.

c. Both the nervous system and the endocrine system are important to the maintenance of homeostasis.

   d. The goal of negative feedback mechanisms is to prevent sudden, severe changes in the body.

3. Positive Feedback Mechanisms

   a. A positive feedback mechanism causes the variable to change in the same direction as the original change, resulting in a greater deviation from the set point.

   b. Positive feedback mechanisms typically activate events that are self-perpetuating.

   c. Most positive feedback mechanisms are not related to the maintenance of homeostasis.

4. Homeostatic imbalance often results in disease.

V. The Language of Anatomy (pp. 12–22)

A. Anatomical Position and Directional Terms (p. 12; Table 1.1; Fig. 1.7)

   1. Anatomical position is a position in which the body is erect, palms face forward, and thumbs point away from the body.

      a. In anatomical position, right and left refer to the right and left sides of the person viewed.

      b. In anatomy, anatomical position is always assumed, regardless of the actual position of the body.

   2. Directional terms are used to explain exactly where one body part is in relation to another.

B. Regional Terms (pp. 12–14)

   1. There are two fundamental divisions of the body.

      a. The axial region includes the head, neck, and trunk.

      b. The appendicular region consists of the upper and lower limbs.

   2. Regional terms designate specific areas within the axial and appendicular divisions.

C. Body Planes and Sections (p. 15; Fig. 1.8)

   1. Body planes are flat surfaces that lie at right angles to each other.

      a. Sagittal plane: a vertical plane that separates the body into right and left parts.

         i. Median, or midsagittal plane: lies exactly along the body's midline.

         ii. Parasagittal plane: lies offset from the midline.

      b. Frontal plane: a vertical plane that separates the body into anterior and posterior parts.

      c. Transverse, or horizontal, plane: a plane that runs horizontally from right to left, and divides the body into superior and inferior parts.

   2. Sections are cuts made along specific planes.

      a. Transverse section, or cross section, is a cut made along the transverse plane.

      b. Oblique sections are cuts made at angles between the horizontal and vertical planes.

D. Body Cavities and Membranes (pp. 15–19; Figs. 1.9–1.13)

   1. Body cavities are spaces within the body that are closed to the outside and contain the internal organs.

2. The dorsal body cavity is the space that houses the central nervous system, and has two subdivisions: the cranial cavity and the vertebral cavity.

    a. The cranial cavity is within the skull, and houses the brain.

    b. The vertebral, or spinal, cavity is within the vertebral column, and houses the spinal cord.

3. The ventral body cavity is anterior to and larger than the dorsal cavity and has two main subdivisions: the thoracic cavity, and the abdominopelvic cavity.

    a. The thoracic cavity is a superior division of the ventral cavity that is further subdivided into the lateral pleural cavities that surround the lungs.

    b. The thoracic cavity also contains the medial mediastinum, which includes the pericardial cavity surrounding the heart and the space surrounding the other thoracic structures.

4. The ventral body cavity houses the body organs, or viscera.

5. Membranes in the Ventral Body Cavity

    a. Serous membranes, or serosae, cover the inner walls of the ventral cavity and the outer surfaces of organs.

    b. The parietal serosa lines the body cavity walls, and is named for the specific cavities it is associated with.

    c. The visceral serosa covers the outer surfaces of organs, and is named for the specific organs it is associated with.

    d. Serous membranes secrete and are separated by a thin layer of lubrication fluid called serous fluid, which allows organs to slide without friction along cavity walls and between each other.

6. Abdominopelvic Regions and Quadrants

    a. There are nine abdominopelvic regions used primarily by anatomists.

    b. There are four quadrants used primarily by medical personnel.

7. Other Body Cavities

    a. Oral and digestive cavities are continuous cavities that extend from the mouth through the digestive system to the anus.

    b. The nasal cavity is within and posterior to the nose.

    c. The orbital cavities house the eyes.

    d. The middle ear cavities are within the skull just medial to the eardrums, and house the bones that transmit sound vibrations to the inner ears.

    e. Synovial cavities are joint cavities lined with a lubricating fluid-secreting membrane associated with all movable joints.

Cross References

Additional information on the topics covered in Chapter 1 can be found in the chapters listed below.

1. Chapter 2: Basic chemical and physical principles
2. Chapter 3: Cellular level of structural organization
3. Chapter 4: Tissue level of structural organization
4. Chapter 16: Hormonal control as an example of feedback regulation
5. Chapter 22: Organs of the mediastinum
6. Chapter 23: Serous membranes of the abdominal cavity
7. Chapter 28: Example of positive feedback (see Fig. 28.16)

Laboratory Correlations

1. Marieb, E. N. *Human Anatomy & Physiology Laboratory Manual: Cat and Fetal Pig Versions*. Eighth Edition Updates. Benjamin Cummings, 2006.
   Exercise 1: The Language of Anatomy
   Exercise 2: Organ Systems Overview

2. Marieb, E. N. *Human Anatomy & Physiology Laboratory Manual: Main Version*. Seventh Edition Update. Benjamin Cummings, 2006.
   Exercise 1: The Language of Anatomy
   Exercise 2: Organ Systems Overview

Lecture Hints

1. *The Incredible Human Machine* is an excellent videotape that offers an exciting overview of many physiological functions. With the help of sophisticated photographic techniques, the wonders of the body's internal world are revealed. The videotape is inexpensive and available from numerous vendors, including Carolina Biological. Listed below are alternate methods for using the tape.
   a. Show the entire video during lecture or lab (60 minutes).
   b. Show selected sections of video during an introductory lecture or lab.
   c. Show selected sections as an introduction to each body system.
   d. Place the videotape on reserve in the library or video center and have students view it on their own. This could be required or optional (if optional, encourage viewing by adding bonus points).

2. In order to illustrate the principle of complementarity of structure and function, ask the students to consider the relatively similar structure of the human arm and a bird wing. Then ask them to consider the functional constraints placed on the limbs by their form, as well as the adaptive value of each form. Manual dexterity vs. flight is an excellent compare-and-contrast example.

3. Many students have a very poor concept of the dynamics of the human body and how it functions in the environment. Try to stress throughout this chapter the adaptive nature of the body and the interrelationship between environmental variables and system response.

4. The body organ systems are actually an artificial grouping of structures that work toward a common goal. Stress the interrelationship between organs and systems that make the body "work" as an entire unit.

5. At times, students might substitute the term *circulatory system* for *cardiovascular system*. Explain the difference and the relationship to the lymphatic system.

6. The role of negative and positive feedback systems in maintaining or disrupting homeostasis is basic to understanding many of the physiological processes covered throughout the text. Stress the importance of feedback systems throughout the course.

7. Students often equate the term *negative* in feedback systems to something disruptive. This misunderstanding is compounded by the term *positive* also used in feedback systems. Stress the differences and give an example; for example, describe how a thermostat controls house temperature.

8. To illustrate the different degrees of protection in the dorsal and ventral cavities, ask the questions:
   a. Why do you suppose that a dog instinctively curls up to protect its abdomen?

b. Two people have rapidly growing tumors: one in the dorsal cavity, the other in the ventral. Which one would develop symptoms first?

9. To encourage understanding of structure/function relationships, ask students to comment on the relationship between muscle and bone, and between the respiratory and circulatory systems.

Activities/Demonstrations

1. Audio-visual materials listed under Multimedia in the Classroom and Lab.

2. Ask the students to explain how scratching an itch can be considered an example of negative feedback.

3. Assume the anatomical position and ask why this particular position is important to the study of anatomy. Then relate that any position would be acceptable as long as it was the standard for anatomical description.

4. Place a chair center stage. Ask a student to indicate how the chair would be cut in the different planes of section. The answer should include why the other options were not selected.

5. Have students identify body regions on themselves or a lab partner. Stress the usage of directional terms in describing their positions relative to each other.

6. Arrange for the class to attend an autopsy (after the material in Chapter 1 has been covered).

7. Use a balloon to illustrate the two layers of a serous membrane.

8. Use a torso model and/or dissected animal model to exhibit body cavities, organs, and system relationships.

9. Use the thermostat found in the classroom (or one found in a home) to illustrate how a negative feedback system works.

Critical Thinking/Discussion Topics

1. Discuss how our intercellular environment can be described as the "sea within us."

2. List several embryonic features that form early in the developmental stages but are "lost" or converted to entirely new structures such as our "tail" (coccyx).

3. If an object were found on Mars that appeared to move and react to external stimuli, what other characteristics would be necessary to classify it as "live" and why?

4. Contrast the type of imagery obtained with X-ray machines, CT scans, DSR scans, and ultrasonics.

5. What differences are there between a free-living, single-celled organism such as a paramecium and a single human cell such as a ciliated cell of the respiratory tract?

Library Research Topics

1. Research the historical development of anatomy and physiology.

2. Review the current definitions of death and life.

3. Develop a rationale for the chemical basis of stress and how it can affect homeostasis.

4. Explore the current research on aging and describe the effect of aging on the genetic material of the cell.

Multimedia in the Classroom and Lab

Online Resources for Students

The
Anatomy & Physiology Place
www.anatomyandphysiology.com

MyA&P
www.myaandp.com

The following shows the organization of the Chapter Guide page in both the Anatomy & Physiology Place and MyA&P™. The Chapter Guide organizes all the chapter-specific online media resources for Chapter 1 in one convenient location, with e-book links to each section of the textbook. Please note that both sites also give you access to other general A&P resources, like InterActive Physiology®, PhysioEx 6.0™, Anatomy 360°, Flashcards, a Glossary, a Histology Tutorial, and much more.

> **Objectives**
>
> **Section 1.1 An Overview of Anatomy and Physiology (pp. 2–3)**
>
> **Section 1.2 Levels of Structural Organization (pp. 3–4)**
>
> **Section 1.3 Maintaining Life (pp. 4–8)**
>
> Memory: Major Systems of the Body
>
> **Section 1.4 Homeostasis (pp. 8–12)**
>
> Art Labeling Activity: The Elements of a Homeostatic Control System (Fig. 1.4, p. 9)
>
> **Section 1.5 The Language of Anatomy (pp. 12–19)**
>
> Art Labeling Activity: Regional Terms Used to Designate Specific Body Areas (Fig. 1.7a, p. 14)
>
> Art Labeling Activity: Regional Terms Used to Designate Specific Body Areas (Fig. 1.7b, p. 14)
>
> Art Labeling Activity: Dorsal and Ventral Body Cavities (Fig. 1.9, p. 17)
>
> Memory: Major Cavities of the Body
>
> **Chapter Summary**
>
> **Self-Study Quizzes**
>
> Art Labeling Quiz
>
> Matching Quiz
>
> Multiple-Choice Quiz (Level I)
>
> Multiple-Choice Quiz (Level II)
>
> True-False Quiz
>
> **Crossword Puzzles**
>
> Crossword Puzzle 1.1
>
> Crossword Puzzle 1.2

Media

See Guide to Audio-Visual Resources in Appendix A for key to AV distributors.

Video

1. *Systems Working Together* (WNS; 15 min., 1993). Animation, X rays, motion pictures, and micrographs help explain the workings of the human body. Students learn that some organs belong to more than one system, and that all of the systems must work together to support all of their activities.

2. *The Incredible Human Machine* (CBS; 60 min., 1992). Sophisticated photographic techniques show the wonders of the body's internal world.

3. *The Universe Within* (CBS; 60 min., 1995). NOVA takes viewers on an incredible voyage into the microworld of the human body. The coordination of muscles, bones, heart, and circulatory systems is revealed by microphotography.

Software

1. *A.D.A.M.® InterActive Anatomy® 4.0* (ADAM, BC; Win/Mac). Comprehensive, precise, and anatomically correct database of the human body gives the student an opportunity to explore human systems and structures within the context of the whole body.

2. *A.D.A.M.® MediaPro* (ADAM, BC; Win/Mac). Provides clinical illustrations for classroom curriculum and presentations. Contains more than 2000 images in JPEG format.

3. *Bodyworks* (WNS; Windows). An economical CD of anatomy and physiology, which includes lesson plans and quizzes that can be printed.

4. *Explorations in Human Biology* (WNS; Win/Mac). This CD contains a set of 15 animated, interactive lessons. It features clearly written topic information, colorful graphics, and animated illustrations.

5. *The Ultimate Human Body* (ED; Win/Mac). A blend of high-quality 3-D images, animation, sounds, and text. Students can explore the body through three search paths: "The Body Machine," "The Body Organs," and "The Body Systems."

6. *WARD's Radiographic Anatomy: A Gallery of Images CD-ROM* (WNS; Windows). This CD contains an extensive collection of images ideal for college-level study. Includes X rays, angiograms, CT scans, MRIs, and urograms. Each image is accompanied by descriptive text and identifying labels. The CD also includes a variety of testing methods.

Lecture Enhancement Material

To view thumbnails of all of the illustrations for Chapter 1, see Appendix B.

Transparencies Index/Media Manager

Figure 1.1	Levels of structural organization.
Figure 1.2	Examples of selected interrelationships among body organ systems.
Figure 1.3	Summary of the body's organ systems.
Figure 1.4	The elements of a homeostatic control system.
Figure 1.5	Regulation of room temperature by a negative feedback mechanism.
Figure 1.6	Summary of the positive feedback mechanism regulating blood clotting.
Figure 1.7	Regional terms used to designate specific body areas.
Figure 1.8	Planes of the body—frontal, transverse, and median (midsagittal) with corresponding magnetic resonance imaging (MRI) scans.
Figure 1.9	Dorsal and ventral body cavities and their subdivisions.
Figure 1.10	Serous membrane relationships.
Figure 1.11	The nine abdominopelvic regions.
Figure 1.12	The four abdominopelvic quadrants.
Figure 1.13	Other body cavities.
Table 1.1	Orientation and Directional Terms
A Closer Look	Medical Imaging: Illuminating the Body*

Indicates images that are on the Media Manager only.

Answers to End-of-Chapter Questions

Multiple Choice and Matching Question answers appear in Appendix G of the main text.

Short Answer Essay Questions

11. Since function (physiology) reflects structure, structure will determine and/or influence function. (p. 3)

12. See Fig. 1.3, which provides a summary of all the organ systems of the body.

13. Nutrients—the chemical substances used for energy and cell building; oxygen— used in the reactions that produce cellular energy; water—the liquid environment necessary for all chemical reactions; body temperature—to maintain the proper temperature for chemical reactions to proceed; and atmospheric pressure—to allow gas exchange to occur. (p. 8)

14. It is the ability to maintain relatively stable internal conditions even in the face of continuous change in the outside world. (p. 9)

15. Negative feedback mechanisms operate in the opposite direction to decrease the original stimulus and/or reduce its effects, thus returning the system back to normal. Examples include regulation of body temperature and blood sugar levels. (p. 10)

    Positive feedback mechanisms operate in the same direction to enhance the original stimulus such that the activity is accelerated. Examples include regulations of blood clotting and enhancement of labor contractions. (pp. 10–11)

16. The anatomical position requires the body being erect, the arms hanging at the sides, the palms forward, the thumbs pointing away from the body, and the feet flat to the ground. It is necessary to use this standard position because most directional terms refer to the body in this position, regardless of its actual position. The use of anatomical terms saves a great deal of description and is less ambiguous. (p. 12)

17. A plane refers to an imaginary line, and a section refers to a cut along that imaginary line. (p. 15)

18. a. arm—brachial

    b. thigh—femoral

    c. chest—thoracic

    d. fingers/toes—digits

    e. anterior aspect of knee—patellar (p. 14)

19. The elbow's olecranal region is proximal (superior) and posterior (dorsal) to the palm. (pp. 13–14)

20. See Figs. 1.11 and 1.12. The figures illustrate the regions and quadrants and list several organs for each.

Critical Thinking and Clinical Application Questions

1. a. Parietal and/or visceral pleural membranes.

   b. The membranes allow the organs to slide easily across the cavity walls and one another without friction.

   c. The organs and membranes stick together and grate against one another, creating friction, heat, and pain. (p. 17)

2. a. anterior aspect of elbow

   b. took off his shirt

   c. buttock (p. 14)

3. Of the procedures listed, MRI would be the best choice because dense structures (e.g., the skull) do not impair the view with this technique, and it is best at producing a high-resolution view of soft tissues, particularly neural tissue. Furthermore, MRI can provide information about chemical conditions in a tissue. Thus, once the suspected tumor is localized, MRI can perform a "metabolic biopsy" to determine if it is cancerous . . . all of this without surgery. (p. 20)

4. When we take a drink, body hydration increases and thirst declines—an example of a typical negative feedback system. If it were a positive feedback system, the body's need for water (and thirst) would increase after taking a drink. (pp. 10–11)

5. The carpal region is found at the wrist. (p. 14)

Suggested Readings

Lester, David S. and Olds, James L. "Biomedical Imaging: 2001 and Beyond." *The Anatomical Record* 265 (2001): 35–36.

Morris, D. *The Naked Ape: A Zoologist's Study of the Human Animal.* New York: Dell Publishing Co., 1999.

Raichle, M.E. "Visualizing the Mind." *Scientific American* 270 (April 1994): 58.

Sivitz, Laura B. "Beyond Imaging." *Science News* 159 (Jan. 2001): 12–13.

Weiss, Peter. "Magnetic Whispers." *Science News* 159 (Jan. 2001): 42–44.

Yonas, H., D.W. Johnson, and R. R. Pindzola. "Xenon-enhanced CT of Cerebral Blood Flow." *Scientific American* (Sept./Oct. 1995).

Chemistry Comes Alive

Objectives

PART 1: BASIC CHEMISTRY

Definition of Concepts: Matter and Energy

1. Define matter and energy. Differentiate between potential energy and kinetic energy.
2. Describe the major forms of energy.

Composition of Matter: Atoms and Elements

3. Define element. What four elements are responsible for the bulk of body matter?
4. Define atom. List the subatomic particles, their charges, relative sizes, and location in the atom.
5. Identify atomic number, atomic mass, atomic weight, isotope, and radioisotope.

How Matter Is Combined: Molecules and Mixtures

6. Define molecule. Differentiate between a molecule of an element and a molecule of a compound. Distinguish between a compound and a mixture.
7. Compare solutions, colloids, and suspensions.

Chemical Bonds

8. Define a chemical bond. Explain the role of electrons in chemical bonding and their importance in the octet rule.
9. Differentiate between ionic bonds, covalent bonds, and hydrogen bonds. Differentiate between a polar and a nonpolar molecule.

Chemical Reactions

10. Explain what happens in a chemical reaction and discuss the four patterns of chemical reactions.
11. Define exergonic and endergonic reactions.
12. Discuss the factors that influence the rate of chemical reactions.

PART 2: BIOCHEMISTRY

Inorganic Compounds

13. Discuss the importance of water and its special properties.
14. Describe salts.
15. Define acid, base, neutralization, and buffers. Explain the concept of pH.

Organic Compounds

16. Describe the building blocks, general structures, and functions of carbohydrates, lipids, and proteins.
17. Describe the four levels of protein structure.
18. Identify the role and function of enzymes.
19. Describe the function of molecular chaperones.
20. Describe, compare, and contrast DNA and RNA.
21. Explain the role of ATP in the body.

Suggested Lecture Outline

PART 1: BASIC CHEMISTRY

I. Definition of Concepts: Matter and Energy (pp. 25–27)

A. Matter is anything that occupies space and has mass (p. 25).

   1. Mass is equal to the amount of matter in the object.

   2. Mass remains constant regardless of gravity.

B. States of Matter (p. 25)

   1. Matter exists in one of three states: solid, liquid, or gas.

C. Energy (pp. 25–27)

   1. Energy is the capacity to do work, and it exists in two forms.

      a. Kinetic energy is the energy of motion.

      b. Potential energy is stored energy.

   2. Forms of Energy

      a. Chemical energy is energy stored in chemical bonds.

      b. Electrical energy results from the movement of charged particles.

      c. Mechanical energy is energy directly involved with moving matter.

      d. Radiant energy is energy that travels in waves.

   3. Energy is easily converted from one form to another.

II. Composition of Matter: Atoms and Elements (pp. 27–30)

A. Basic Terms (p. 27; Table 2.1)

   1. Elements are unique substances that cannot be broken down into simpler substances by ordinary chemical means.

   2. Four elements: carbon, hydrogen, oxygen, and nitrogen make up roughly 96% of body weight.

   3. Atoms are the smallest particles of an element that retain the characteristics of that element.

   4. Elements are designated by a one- or two-letter abbreviation called the atomic symbol.

B. Atomic Structure (pp. 27–29; Figs. 2.1–2.2)

   1. Each atom has a central nucleus with tightly packed protons and neutrons.

      a. Protons have a positive charge and weigh 1 atomic mass unit (amu).

      b. Neutrons do not have a charge and weigh 1 amu.

   2. Electrons are found moving around the nucleus, have a negative charge, and are weightless (0 amu).

   3. Atoms are electrically neutral and the number of electrons is equal to the number of protons.

   4. The planetary model is a simplified, two-dimensional model of atomic structure.

   5. The orbital model is a more accurate three-dimensional model talking about orbital regions instead of set orbital patterns.

C. Identifying Elements (pp. 28–29)

   1. Elements are identified based on their number of protons, neutrons, and electrons.

    D. Atomic Number (pp. 28–29)

        1. The atomic number of an element is equal to the number of protons of an element.

        2. Since the number of protons is equal to the number of electrons, the atomic number indirectly tells us the number of electrons.

    E. Mass Number and Isotopes (p. 29; Fig. 2.3)

        1. The mass number of an element is equal to the number of protons plus the number of neutrons.

        2. The electron is weightless and is ignored in calculating the mass number.

        3. Isotopes are structural variations of an atom. They have the same number of protons and neutrons of all other atoms of the element but differ in the number of neutrons the atom has.

    F. Atomic Weight (p. 29)

        1. The atomic weight is an average of the relative weights of all isotopes of an element, taking into account their relative abundance in nature.

    G. Radioisotopes are heavier, unstable isotopes of an element that spontaneously decompose into more stable forms (pp. 29–30).

        1. The time required for a radioactive isotope to lose one-half of its radioactivity is called the half-life.

III. How Matter Is Combined: Molecules and Mixtures (pp. 30–31)

    A. Molecules and Compounds (p. 30)

        1. A combination of two or more atoms is called a molecule.

        2. If two or more atoms of the same element combine it is called a molecule of that element.

        3. If two or more atoms of different elements combine it is called a molecule of a compound.

    B. Mixtures (pp. 30–31)

        1. Mixtures are substances made of two or more components mixed physically.

        2. Solutions are homogeneous mixtures of compounds that may be gases, liquids, or solids.

            a. The substance present in the greatest amounts is called the solvent.

            b. Substances present in smaller amounts are called solutes.

            c. Solutions may be described by their concentrations. These may be expressed as a percent or in terms of its molarity.

        3. Colloids or emulsions are heterogeneous mixtures.

        4. Suspensions are heterogeneous mixtures with large, often visible solutes that tend to settle out.

    C. Distinguishing Mixtures and Compounds (p. 31)

        1. The main difference between mixtures and compounds is that no chemical bonding occurs between molecules of a mixture.

        2. Mixtures can be separated into their chemical components by physical means; separation of compounds is done by chemical means.

        3. Some mixtures are homogeneous, while others are heterogeneous.

IV. Chemical Bonds (pp. 31–36)

   A. A chemical bond is an energy relationship between the electrons of the reacting atoms (p. 31).

      1. The Role of Electrons in Chemical Bonding (Fig. 2.4)

         a. Electrons occupy regions of space called electron shells that surround the nucleus in layers.

         b. Each electron shell represents a different energy level.

         c. Each electron shell holds a specific number of electrons, and shells tend to fill consecutively from the closest to the nucleus to the furthest away.

         d. The octet rule, or rule of eights, states that except for the first energy shell (stable with two electrons), atoms are stable with eight electrons in their outermost (valence) shell.

   B. Types of Chemical Bonds (pp. 33–36; Figs. 2.5–2.10)

      1. Ionic bonds are chemical bonds that form between two atoms that transfer one or more electrons from one atom to the other.

         a. Ions are charged particles.

         b. An anion is an electron acceptor carrying a net negative charge due to the extra electron.

         c. A cation is an electron donor carrying a net positive charge due to the loss of an electron.

         d. Crystals are large structures of cations and anions held together by ionic bonds.

      2. Covalent bonds form when electrons are shared between two atoms.

         a. Some atoms are capable of sharing two or three electrons between them, resulting in double covalent or triple covalent bonds.

         b. Nonpolar molecules share their electrons evenly between two atoms.

         c. In polar molecules, electrons spend more time around one atom thus providing that atom with a partial negative charge, while the other atom takes on a partial positive charge.

         d. A polar molecule is often referred to as a dipole due to the two poles of charges contained in the molecule.

      3. Hydrogen bonds are weak attractions that form between partially charged atoms found in polar molecules.

         a. Surface tension is due to hydrogen bonds between water molecules.

         b. Intramolecular bonds may form between partially charged atoms in a large molecule, and are important in maintaining the shape of that molecule.

V. Chemical Reactions (pp. 36–40)

   A. Chemical Reactions (pp. 36–37)

      1. Chemical reactions occur whenever bonds are formed, rearranged, or broken.

      2. Chemical Equations

         a. A chemical equation describes what happens in a reaction.

         b. Chemical reactions denote the kinds and number of reacting substances, called reactants; the chemical composition of the products; and the relative proportion of each reactant and product, if balanced.

    B. Patterns of Chemical Reactions (pp. 37–38; Fig. 2.11)

        1. In a synthesis (combination) reaction, larger molecules are formed from smaller molecules.

        2. In a decomposition reaction a molecule is broken down into smaller molecules.

        3. Exchange (displacement) reactions involve both synthesis and decomposition reactions.

        4. Oxidation-reduction reactions are special exchange reactions in which electrons are exchanged between reactants.

    C. Energy Flow in Chemical Reactions (pp. 38–39)

        1. Exergonic reactions release energy as a product, while endergonic reactions absorb energy.

    D. Reversibility of Chemical Reactions (p. 39)

        1. All chemical reactions are theoretically reversible.

        2. When the rate of the forward reaction equals the rate of the reverse reaction, the reactions have reached a chemical equilibrium.

    E. Factors Influencing the Rate of Chemical Reactions (pp. 39–40)

        1. Chemicals react when they collide with enough force to overcome the repulsion by their electrons.

        2. An increase in temperature increases the rate of a chemical reaction.

        3. Smaller particle size results in a faster rate of reaction.

        4. Higher concentration of reactants results in a faster rate of reaction.

        5. Catalysts increase the rate of a chemical reaction without taking part in the reaction.

PART 2: BIOCHEMISTRY

I. Inorganic Compounds (pp. 40–43)

    A. Water (pp. 40–41)

        1. Water is the most important inorganic molecule, and makes up 60–80% of the volume of most living cells.

        2. Water has a high heat capacity, meaning that it absorbs and releases a great deal of heat before it changes temperature.

        3. Water has a high heat of vaporization, meaning that it takes a great deal of energy (heat) to break the bonds between water molecules.

        4. Water is a polar molecule and is called the universal solvent.

        5. Water is an important reactant in many chemical reactions.

        6. Water forms a protective cushion around organs of the body.

    B. Salts (p. 41; Fig. 2.12)

        1. Salts are ionic compounds containing cations other than H^+ and anions other than the hydroxyl (OH^-) ion.

        2. When salts are dissolved in water they dissociate into their component ions.

    C. Acids and Bases (pp. 41–43; Fig. 2.13)

        1. Acids are also known as proton donors, and dissociate in water to yield hydrogen ions and anions.

        2. Bases are also called proton acceptors, and absorb hydrogen ions.

3. The relative concentration of hydrogen ions is measured in concentration units called pH units.
   a. The greater the concentration of hydrogen ions in a solution, the more acidic the solution is.
   b. The greater the concentration of hydroxyl ions, the more basic, or alkaline, the solution is.
   c. The pH scale extends from 0–14. A pH of 7 is neutral; a pH below 7 is acidic; a pH above 7 is basic or alkaline.
4. Neutralization occurs when an acid and a base are mixed together. They react with each other in displacement reactions to form a salt and water.
5. Buffers resist large fluctuations in pH that would be damaging to living tissues.

II. Organic Compounds (pp. 43–59)

A. Carbohydrates (pp. 44–46; Fig. 2.14)
   1. Carbohydrates are a group of molecules including sugars and starches.
   2. Carbohydrates contain carbon, hydrogen, and oxygen.
   3. The major function of carbohydrates in the body is to provide cellular fuel.
   4. Monosaccharides are simple sugars that are single-chain or single-ring structures.
   5. Disaccharides are formed when two monosaccharides are joined by a dehydration synthesis.
   6. Polysaccharides are long chains of monosaccharides linked together by dehydration synthesis.

B. Lipids (pp. 46–48; Table 2.2; Fig. 2.15)
   1. Lipids are insoluble in water but dissolve readily in nonpolar solvents.
   2. Triglycerides (neutral fats) are commonly known as fats when solid and oils when liquid.
   3. Phospholipids are diglycerides with a phosphorus-containing group and two fatty acid chains.
   4. Steroids are flat molecules made up of four interlocking hydrocarbon rings.
   5. Eicosanoids are a group of diverse lipids derived from arachidonic acid.

C. Proteins (pp. 48–54; Table 2.3; Figs. 2.16–2.21)
   1. Proteins compose 10–30% of cell mass.
      a. They are the basic structural material of the body.
      b. They also play vital roles in cell function.
   2. Proteins are long chains of amino acids connected by peptide bonds.
   3. Proteins can be described in terms of four structural levels.
      a. The linear sequence of amino acids is the primary structure.
      b. Proteins twist and turn on themselves to form a more complex secondary structure.
      c. A more complex structure is tertiary structure, resulting from protein folding upon itself to form a ball-like structure.
      d. Quaternary structure results from two or more polypeptide chains grouped together to form a complex protein.

       4. Fibrous and Globular Proteins

          a. Fibrous proteins are extended and strandlike. They are known as structural proteins and most have only secondary structure.

          b. Globular proteins are compact, spherical structures. They are water soluble, chemically active molecules, and play an important role in vital body functions.

          c. Fibrous proteins are stable but globular proteins are susceptible to denaturing, losing their shape due to breaking of their hydrogen bonds.

       5. Protein denaturation is a loss of the specific three-dimensional structure of a protein. It may occur when globular proteins are subjected to a variety of chemical and physical changes in their environment.

       6. Molecular chaperones, or chaperonins, are a type of globular protein that help proteins achieve their three-dimensional shape.

       7. Enzymes and Enzyme Activity

          a. Enzymes are globular proteins that act as biological catalysts.

          b. Enzymes may be purely protein, or may consist of two parts which are collectively called a holoenzyme.

          c. Each enzyme is chemically specific.

          d. Enzymes work by lowering the activation energy of a reaction.

D. Nucleic Acids (DNA and RNA) (pp. 54–57; Table 2.4; Fig. 2.22)

       1. Nucleic acids composed of carbon, oxygen, hydrogen, nitrogen, and phosphorus are the largest molecules in the body.

       2. Nucleotides are the structural units of nuleic acids.

       3. Each nucleotide consists of three components: a pentose sugar, phosphate group, and a nitrogen-containing base.

       4. There are five nitrogenous bases used in nucleic acids: Adenine (A), Guanine (G), Cytosine (C), Uracil (U), and Thymine (T).

       5. DNA, or Deoxyribonucleic Acid

          a. DNA is the genetic material of the cell, and is found within the nucleus.

          b. DNA replicates itself before cell division and provides instructions for making all of the proteins found in the body.

          c. The structure of DNA is a double-stranded polymer containing the nitrogenous bases A, T, G, and C, and the sugar deoxyribose.

          d. Bonding of the nitrogenous bases in DNA is very specific; A bonds to T, and G bonds to C.

          e. The bases that always bind together are known as complementary bases.

       6. RNA, or Ribonucleic Acid

          a. RNA is located outside the nucleus, and is used to make proteins using the instructions provided by the DNA.

          b. The structure of RNA is a single-stranded polymer containing the nitrogenous bases A, G, C, and U, and the sugar ribose.

          c. In RNA, G bonds with C, and A bonds with U.

E. ATP, or Adenosine Triphosphate (pp. 57–59; Figs. 2.23–2.24)

       1. ATP is the energy currency used by the cell.

       2. ATP is an adenine-containing RNA nucleotide that has two additional phosphate groups attached.

       3. The additional phosphate groups are connected by high energy bonds.

       4. Breaking the high energy bonds releases energy the cell can use to do work.

Cross References

Additional information on topics covered in Chapter 2 can be found in the chapters listed below.

1. Chapter 3: Phospholipids in the composition and construction of membranes; DNA replication and roles of DNA and RNA in protein synthesis; cellular ions; enzymes and proteins in cellular structure and function; hydrogen bonding
2. Chapter 9: Function of ATP in muscle contraction; role of ions in generating muscle cell contraction
3. Chapter 11: ATP, ions, and enzymes in the nervous impulse
4. Chapter 16: Steroid- and amino-acid based hormones
5. Chapter 22: Acid-base balance
6. Chapter 23: Digestive enzyme function; acid function of the digestive system; digestion of proteins, carbohydrates, and lipids
7. Chapter 24: Oxidation-reduction reaction; importance of ions (minerals) in life processes; metabolism of carbohydrates, lipids, and proteins; basic chemistry of life examples
8. Chapter 25: Renal control of electrolytes
9. Chapter 26: Acid-base balance, electrolytes, and buffers; sodium and sodium-potassium pump
10. Appendix E: Periodic table of the elements

Lecture Hints

1. *Introduction to Chemistry for Biology Students*, by George Sackheim, is an excellent aid for students who need a quick brushup in chemistry or for those that need extra help. The book is designed as a self-paced learning guide. Most students should be able to finish a review of the essentials for Marieb Chapter 2 in about 2 to 6 hours.
2. As an alternative to presenting the chemistry in Chapter 2 as a distinct block of material, you could provide the absolute minimum coverage of the topics at this time and expand topics later as areas of application are discussed.
3. Students often find the concept of isotopes confusing. A clear distinction between atomic mass and atomic weight will help clarify the topic.
4. In discussing radioisotopes it might be helpful to refer the students back to the discussion of PET scans in *A Closer Look* in Chapter 1.
5. Oxidation-reduction reactions involve the loss and gain of electrons. The reactant oxidized will lose electrons while the reactant reduced will gain electrons. One easy way to remember this is by using the phrase "Leo the lion goes ger." Leo stands for "loss of electrons is oxidation," and ger for "gain of electrons is reduction."
6. In biological oxidation-reduction reactions the loss and gain of electrons is often associated with the loss and gain of hydrogen atoms. Electrons are still being transferred since the hydrogen atom contains an electron.
7. The relationship between the terms *catalyst* and *enzyme* can be clarified by asking the students if all enzymes are catalysts and if all catalysts are enzymes.
8. Table 2.4 is an excellent summary of the differences between DNA and RNA. This information will be important when discussing protein synthesis.

9. The notion that ATP is the "energy currency" of the cell should be emphasized. Students should realize that without ATP, molecules cannot be synthesized or degraded, cells cannot maintain boundaries, and life processes cease.

10. The cycling back and forth between ATP and ADP is a simple but important concept often overlooked by students.

Activities/Demonstrations

1. Audio-visual materials listed under Multimedia in the Classroom and Lab.

2. Obtain and/or construct 3-D models of various types of biological molecules such as glucose, DNA, protein, and lipids.

3. Bring in materials or objects that are composed of common elements, e.g., a gold chain, coal, copper pipe, cast iron. Also provide examples of common compounds such as water, table salt, vinegar, and sodium bicarbonate. Solicit definitions of *atom, element,* and *compound,* and an explanation of how an atom and a molecule of a compound differ.

4. Ask students to name all the foods containing saturated fats and all those containing unsaturated fats that they have eaten in the past 24 hours.

5. Obtain a two-foot-long piece of thick string or cord. Slowly twist to exhibit primary, secondary, and tertiary levels of protein organization.

6. Obtain a Thompson-style vacuum tube with an internal frosted plate (to exhibit electrons), a direct current generator (Tesla coil), and bar magnet. Turn off room lights and charge one end of the tube to start an electron beam. Use a magnet to move the electron beam up and down. This experiment helps to illustrate electrons as particles.

7. Obtain an electrolyte testing system (light bulb setup connected to electrodes) and prepare a series of solutions such as salt, acid, base, glucose, etc. Place the electrodes into the solutions to illustrate the concept of electrolytes.

8. Prepare two true solutions (1% sodium chloride; 1% glucose) and two colloidal solutions (1% boiled starch, sol state; Jell-O, gel state). Turn off the room lights and pass a beam of light through each to demonstrate the Tyndall effect of colloids.

9. Obtain two strings of dissimilar "pop-it" beads. Put the beads together to demonstrate a synthesis reaction, and take them apart to demonstrate a decomposition reaction. Take a bead from each different chain and put them together to illustrate an exchange reaction.

10. Use a slinky to demonstrate denaturation of an enzyme. Tie colored yarn on the slinky at two sites that are widely separated, and then coil and twist the slinky upon itself to bring the two pieces of yarn next to each other. Identify the site where the yarn pieces are as the active site. Then remind students that when the hydrogen bonds holding the enzyme (or structural protein) in its specific 3-D structure are broken, the active site (or structural framework) is destroyed. Uncoil the slinky to illustrate this point.

Critical Thinking/Discussion Topics

1. Discuss how two polysaccharides, starch and cellulose, each having the same subunit (glucose), have completely different properties. Why can we digest starch but not cellulose?

2. How and why can virtually all organisms—plant, animal, and bacteria—use the exact same energy molecule, ATP?

3. How could a substance such as alcohol be a solvent under one condition and a solute under another? Provide examples of solid, liquid, and gaseous solutions.
4. Describe how weak bonds can hold large macromolecules together.
5. Why can we state that most of the volume of matter, such as the tabletop you are writing on, is actually empty space?
6. When you drive up your driveway at night you see the light from the headlights on the garage door, but not in the air between the car and the door. Why? What would be observed if the night were foggy?
7. Why are water molecules at the surface of a drop of water closer together than those in the interior?

Library Research Topics

1. Explore the use of radioisotopes in the treatment of cancers.
2. Study the mechanisms by which DNA can repair itself.
3. Locate the studies of Niels Bohr concerning the structure of atoms and the location of electrons. Determine why his work with hydrogen gas provided the foundation of our knowledge about matter.
4. How can a donut provide us with so much "energy"? Find out exactly where this energy is coming from.
5. Phospholipids have been used for cell membrane construction by all members of the "cellular" world. What special properties do these molecules have to explain this phenomenon?
6. Virtually every time an amino acid chain consisting of all 20 amino acids is formed in the cell, it twists into an alpha helix, then folds upon itself into a glob. Why?
7. What is the current status of the Human Genome Project? Who is directing the project? What are the expected benefits from the study?
8. What is DNA fingerprinting? Explore the applications of this technology.

Multimedia in the Classroom and Lab

Online Resources for Students

The Anatomy & Physiology Place
www.anatomyandphysiology.com

MyA&P
www.myaandp.com

The following shows the organization of the Chapter Guide page in both the Anatomy & Physiology Place and MyA&P™. The Chapter Guide organizes all the chapter-specific online media resources for Chapter 2 in one convenient location, with e-book links to each section of the textbook. Please note that both sites also give you access to other general A&P resources, like InterActive Physiology®, PhysioEx 6.0™, Anatomy 360°, Flashcards, a Glossary, a Histology Tutorial, and much more.

Objectives

PART ONE: BASIC CHEMISTRY

Section 2.1 Definition of Concepts: Matter and Energy (pp. 25–26)
Animation: Energy Concepts

Section 2.2 Composition of Matter: Atoms and Elements (pp. 27–30)
Animation: The Structure of Atoms

Media

See Guide to Audio-Visual Resources in Appendix A for key to AV distributors.

Video

1. *Basic Chemistry for Biology Students* (HRM; 21 min., 1993). Introduces students to the chemical concepts important to understanding life processes.
2. *Double Helix* (FHS; 107 min., 1998). Exceptional Hollywood-style film (starring Jeff Goldblum) that captures all the drama of the discovery of DNA.
3. *The Molecular Building Blocks of Life* (WNS; 19 min.). Nine modules explore life's molecular architecture—carbohydrates, fats, proteins, and an overview of nucleic acids.

Software

1. *Cell Biology* (CBS; Win/Mac). Provides the information necessary to cover the cell, presents the structure and function of organelles, and examines systems of cell motility.
2. *Cellular Respiration* (CBS; Win/Mac). Topics include Energy, Structure of ATP and ADP, the Krebs Cycle, and the Role of Food in the Production of Energy.
3. *The Chemistry of Life* (BC; Win/Mac). This tutorial aims at teaching chemistry through animation and interactive learning activities. Includes diagnostic quizzes and illustrated glossary.

4. *Inside the Cell* (CE, WNS; Win/Mac). Cells and their processes are detailed in three-dimensional illustrations, animation sequences, and electron micrographs.

Lecture Enhancement Material

To view thumbnails of all of the illustrations in Chapter 2, see Appendix B.

Transparencies Index/Media Manager

Indicates images that are on the Media Manager only.

Answers to End-of-Chapter Questions

Multiple Choice and Matching Question answers appear in Appendix G of the main text.

Short Answer Essay Questions

23. Energy is defined as the capacity to do work, or to put matter into motion. Energy has no mass, takes up no space, and can be measured only by its effects on matter. Potential energy is the energy an object has because of its position in relation to other objects. Kinetic energy is energy associated with a moving object. (p. 25)

24. According to the First Law of Thermodynamics, energy cannot be created or destroyed. Therefore, energy is not really lost, but may be released in another form such as heat or light. In this form, the energy may be partly unusable. (p. 27)

25. a. Ca, b. C, c. H, d. Fe, e. N, f. O, g. K, h. Na (Appendix E)

26. a. All three are carbon with six protons. (p. 29)
    b. All possess different numbers of neutrons and therefore have different atomic masses. (p. 29)
    c. Isotopes. (p. 29)
    d. See Fig 2.4b, which provides a drawing of a planetary model.

27. a. Add molecular weight of all atoms: 9×12 (C) + 8×1 (H) + 4×16 (O) = 180 g.
    b. Total molecular weight equals the number of grams in one mole, in this case 180.
    c. Divide the number of grams in the bottle by the number of grams in one mole of aspirin. This equals the total number of moles in the bottle.
    d. Answer = 2.5 moles (p. 31)

28. a. Covalent
    b. Covalent
    c. Ionic (pp. 33–34)

29. Hydrogen bonds are weak bonds that form when a hydrogen atom, already covalently linked to an electronegative atom, is attracted by another electronegative atom. Hydrogen bonding is common between water molecules, and in binding large molecules such as DNA and protein into specific three-dimensional shapes. (p. 36)

30. a. The reversibility of the reaction can be indicated by double reaction arrows pointed in opposing directions.
    b. When arrows are of equal length the reaction is at equilibrium.
    c. Chemical equilibrium is reached when, for each molecule of product formed, one product molecule breaks down, releasing the same reactants. (p. 39)

31. a. Primary structure—linear molecule formed by peptide bonds; second structure—coiling of primary structure into alpha helix or ß-pleated sheet; tertiary structure—folding of helical coils.
    b. Secondary level.
    c. Globular (functional) proteins achieve the tertiary level and tend to operate independently rather than in combination with others such as with structural proteins. (p. 50)

32. Dehydration refers to the joining together of two molecules by the removal of water. Monosaccharides are joined to form disaccharides and amino acids are joined to form dipeptides (and proteins) by this process. Hydrolysis refers to the breakdown of a larger molecule such as a disaccharide into small molecules or monosaccharides by the addition of water at the bond that joins them. (pp. 44, 49)

33. Enzymes are highly specific biological catalysts that help to increase the rate of reactions. The exact mechanism of how enzymes decrease activation energy is not known; however, they decrease the randomness of reactions by binding specifically and temporarily to the reacting molecules and, perhaps, holding them in the proper position(s) to interact. (p. 53)

34. Proteins that aid the folding of other proteins into their functional three-dimensional structures. They also inhibit incorrect folding. They are produced in great amounts when cells are damaged and proteins are denatured and must be replaced. (pp. 52–53)

35. The surface tension of water tends to pull water molecules into a spherical shape, and since the glass does not completely overcome this attractive force, water can elevate slightly above the rim of the glass. (p. 36)

36. Seawater is significantly hypertonic to our own body fluids. Drinking quantities of seawater raises the blood plasma osmolarity, leading to fluid imbalances between our intracellular and extracellular fluids. (p. 41)

Critical Thinking and Clinical Application Questions

1. In a freshwater lake, there are comparatively few electrolytes (salts) to carry a current away from a swimmer's body. Hence, the body would be a better conductor of the current and the chance of a severe electrical shock if lightning hit the water is real. (p. 41)

2. a. Some antibiotics compete with the substrate at the active site of the enzyme. This would tend to reduce the effectiveness of the reaction.

   b. Since the bacteria would be unable to catalyze the essential chemical reactions normally brought about by the "blocked" enzymes, the anticipated effect would be the inhibition of its metabolic activities. This would allow white blood cells to remove them from the system. However, some human cells would also be affected and this could cause them to cease their functions, hopefully only temporarily. (p. 54)

3. a. pH is defined as the measurement of the hydrogen ion concentration in a solution. The normal blood pH is 7.4.

   b. Severe acidosis is critical because blood comes in contact with nearly every body cell and can adversely affect the cell membranes, the function of the kidneys, muscle contraction, and neural activity. (pp. 42–43)

4. The blood pH is rising, thus becoming more basic or alkaline. This is due to the carbonic acid-bicarbonate buffer system that is at work within the blood. Changes in respiratory rate will cause a change in blood pH by altering the amount of carbonic acid in the blood. (pp. 42–43)

Suggested Readings

Ballew, et al. "Folding Proteins Caught in the Act." *Science* 273 (July 1996): 29–30.

Cech, T.R. "RNA as an Enzyme." *Scientific American* 255 (Nov. 1986): 64–75.

Doolittle, R.F. "Proteins." *Scientific American* 253 (Oct. 1985): 88–99.

Dressler, D.H., and H. Potter. *Discovering Enzymes*. New York: Scientific American Library, 1991.

Gorman, Jessica. "Getting Out the Thorn: Biomaterials Become Friendlier to the Body." *Science News* 161 (1) (Jan. 2002): 13–14.

Hartl, F. U. "Molecular Chaperones in Cellular Protein Folding." *Nature* 381 (June 1996): 571–580.

Horgan, J. "In the Beginning." *Scientific American* 264 (Feb. 1991): 116–125.

Karplus, M., and J.A. McCammon. "The Dynamics of Proteins." *Scientific American* 254 (Apr. 1986): 42–51.

Russo, S., and M. Silver. *Introductory Chemistry: A Conceptual Focus*. San Francisco: Benjamin Cummings, 2000.

Ruvkun, Gary. "Glimpses of a Tiny RNA World." *Science* 294 (5543) (Oct. 2001): 797–799.

Welch, W.J. "How Cells Respond to Stress." *Scientific American* 268 (May 1993): 56.

3 Cells: The Living Units

Objectives

Overview of the Cellular Basis of Life

1. Define cell. Discuss cell diversity.
2. Discuss a generalized cell. List the three main parts of a cell and their functions.

The Plasma Membrane: Structure

3. Discuss the fluid mosaic model of membrane structure.
4. List and describe the plasma membrane specializations.

The Plasma Membrane: Functions

5. Discuss membrane transport. Differentiate between active and passive transport.
6. Compare and contrast simple diffusion, facilitated diffusion, osmosis, and filtration.
7. Compare and contrast primary and secondary active transport.
8. Discuss the differences and similarities between the vesicular transport processes.
9. Define the resting membrane potential. How is it created and maintained?
10. Identify the different ways a cell interacts with its environment. Discuss cell adhesion molecules and the roles of membrane receptors.

The Cytoplasm

11. Discuss the cytoplasm and its components.

12. Discuss the functions of the cytoplasmic organelles. What conditions lead to a greater prevalence of a specific organelle?

The Nucleus

13. Define the characteristics and functions of the nucleus, nuclear envelope, and nucleoli.
14. Discuss chromatin structure and function.

Cell Growth and Reproduction

15. Identify the phases of cell growth and division, and describe what specific events occur within each phase.
16. Name the factors that influence cell division.
17. Define protein synthesis and the processes of transcription and translation.
18. Describe the types of RNA that are used in protein synthesis and their specific roles.
19. Discuss how proteins are degraded within the cytosol.

Extracellular Material

20. Define extracellular material and list its components.

Developmental Aspects of Cells

21. Discuss how cell development progresses, and what signals stimulate these changes.
22. Discuss the various theories of cell aging.

Suggested Lecture Outline

I. Overview of the Cellular Basis of Life (pp. 65–66)

A. The four concepts of the cell theory state (p. 65):

1. Cells are the basic structural and functional units of life.
2. The activity of an organism depends on the activities of its cells.
3. The biochemical activities of a cell are dictated by their organelles.
4. The continuity of life has a cellular basis.

B. Characteristics of Cells (pp. 65–66; Figs. 3.1–3.2)

1. Cells vary greatly in their size, shape, and function.
2. All cells are composed primarily of carbon, hydrogen, nitrogen, and oxygen.
3. All cells have the same basic parts and some common functions.
4. A generalized human cell contains the plasma membrane, the cytoplasm, and the nucleus.

II. The Plasma Membrane: Structure (pp. 67–69)

A. The Fluid Mosaic Model (pp. 67–68; Figs. 3.3–3.4)

1. The plasma membrane is composed of a double layer of phospholipids embedded with small amounts of cholesterol and proteins.
2. The phospolipid bilayer is composed of two layers of phospholipids lying tail to tail, with their polar heads exposed to water inside and outside the cell.
3. The inward-facing and outward-facing surfaces of the plasma membrane differ in the kinds and amounts of lipids they contain.
   a. Glycolipids are found only in the outer membrane.
   b. Lipid rafts are also found only in the outer membrane, and are assumed to function in cell signaling.
4. Integral proteins are firmly inserted into the plasma membrane.
   a. Most integral proteins are transmembrane proteins that span the entire width of the membrane and are involved with transport as channels or carriers.
5. Peripheral proteins are not embedded in the plasma membrane, but attach to integral proteins or to phospolipids.
   a. Peripheral proteins may function as enzymes or in mechanical functions of the cell.
6. The glycocalyx is the fuzzy, sticky, carbohydrate-rich area surrounding the cell.

B. Specializations of the Plasma Membrane (p. 69; Fig. 3.5)

1. Microvilli are fingerlike extensions of the plasma membrane that increase the surface area of the cell.
2. Most body cells are bound together using glycolipids, specialized interlocking regions, or specialized membrane junctions.
   a. Tight junctions are a type of membrane junction in which integral proteins on adjacent cells fuse together to form an impermeable junction in order to prevent molecules from passing through the extracellular space between cells.

      b. Desmosomes are mechanical couplings that are scattered along the sides of adjoining cells that prevent their separation and reduce the chance of tearing when a tissue is stressed.

      c. Gap junctions are a communication junction between cells that allows substances to pass between adjacent cells.

III. The Plasma Membrane: Functions (pp. 70–83)

A. Membrane Transport (pp. 69–81; Tables 3.1–3.2; Figs. 3.6–3.14)

    1. The plasma membrane is a selectively permeable barrier, regulating how substances pass into and out of the cell.

    2. Passive processes do not use energy and move substances down a concentration gradient.

        a. Diffusion is a process in which substances move directly through the plasma membrane from an area of higher concentration to an area of lower concentration.

        b. In facilitated diffusion substances are moved through the plasma membrane by binding to protein carriers in the membrane or by moving through channels.

        c. Osmosis is the diffusion of water through a selectively permeable membrane.

        d. Filtration is a pressure-driven process that forces water and solutes through a membrane or capillary wall.

    3. Active processes use energy (ATP) to move substances across a membrane.

        a. Active transport uses solute pumps to move substances against a concentration gradient. The two kinds of active transport are primary active transport and secondary active transport.

        b. Vesicular transport is the means by which large particles, macromolecules, and fluids are transported across the plasma membrane, or within the cell.

           i. Exocytosis is a process used to move substances from inside the cell to the extracellular environment.

        c. Endocytosis, transcytosis, and vesicular traffiking are vesicular transport processes that move molecules using protein-coated vesicles.

        d. Clathrin-coated vesicles are the main route for endocytosis and transcytosis of bulk solids.

        e. Non-clathrin-coated vesicles, or caveolae, are inpocketings of the cell membrane that capture specific molecules in vesicles lined with caveolin, not clathrin.

B. Generating and Maintaining a Resting Membrane Potential (pp. 81–83; Fig. 3.15)

    1. A membrane potential is a voltage across the cell membrane that occurs due to a separation of oppositely charged particles (ions).

    2. The resting membrane potential is a condition in which the inside of the cell membrane is negatively charged compared to the outside, and ranges in voltage from -5 to -100 millivolts.

        a. The resting membrane potential is determined mainly by the concentration gradient of potassium (K^+).

      b. Active transport pumps ensure that passive ion movement does not lead to an electrochemical equilibrium across the membrane, thus maintaining the resting membrane potential.

  C. Cell-Environmental Interactions (pp. 83–84)

    1. Cells can interact directly with other cells, respond to extracellular chemicals, and interact with molecules that direct migration.

    2. Roles of Cell Adhesion Molecules

      a. Cell adhesion molecules (CAMs) are glycoproteins that play roles in embryonic development, wound repair, and immunity.

    3. Roles of Membrane Receptors (Fig. 3.16)

      a. Membrane receptors are integral proteins and glycoproteins that serve as binding sites.

      b. Some membrane receptors function in contact signaling, electrical signaling, and chemical signaling.

    4. Nitric oxide, consisting of one atom of oxygen and one atom of nitrogen, is the first known gas to act as a biological messenger.

IV. The Cytoplasm (pp. 84–95)

  A. The cytoplasm is the cellular material between the cell membrane and the nucleus, and is the site of most cellular activity (p. 84).

    1. There are three major elements of the cytoplasm: cytosol, cytoplasmic organelles, and cytoplasmic inclusions.

  B. Cytoplasmic Organelles (pp. 84–95; Table 3.3; Figs. 3.17–3.27)

    1. Mitochondria are sausage-shaped membranous organelles that are the power plants of the cell, producing most of its ATP.

    2. Ribosomes are small staining granules consisting of protein and ribosomal RNA that are the site of protein synthesis.

    3. The endoplasmic reticulum is an extensive system of tubes and membranes enclosing fluid-filled cavities, called cisternae, that extend throughout the cytosol.

      a. The rough endoplasmic reticulum has ribosomes that manufacture all proteins that are secreted from cells.

      b. Smooth ER is a continuation of rough ER, consisting of a looping network of tubules. Its enzymes catalyze reactions involved in several processes.

    4. The Golgi apparatus is a series of stacked, flattened, membranous sacs associated with groups of membranous vesicles.

      a. The main function of the Golgi apparatus is to modify, concentrate, and package the proteins and lipids made at the rough ER.

      b. The Golgi apparatus creates vesicles containing lipids and transmembrane proteins for incorporation into the cell membrane.

      c. The Golgi apparatus packages digestive enzymes into lysosomes.

    5. Lysosomes are spherical membranous organelles that contain digestive enzymes.

      a. Lysosomes function best in acidic environments, can digest almost any kind of biological molecule, and are abundant in phagocytes.

      b. The membrane of the lysosome functions to allow products of digestion to be released to the cytosol, yet contain the acid hydrolases used to digest molecules.

6. The endomembrane system includes the ER, Golgi apparatus, secretory vesicles, lysosomes, and nuclear membrane.
   a. The endomembrane system functions together to produce, store, and export biological molecules, as well as degrade potentially harmful substances.
7. Peroxisomes are membranous sacs containing enzymes, such as oxidases and catalases, which are used to detoxify harmful substances such as alcohol, formaldehyde, and free radicals.
8. The cytoskeleton is a series of rods running through the cytosol, supporting cellular structures and aiding in cell movement.
   a. There are three types of rods in the cytoskeleton: microtubules, microfilaments, and intermediate filaments.
9. Centrosome and Centrioles
   a. The centrosome is a region near the nucleus in which a group of microtubules is anchored.
   b. The centrosome functions as a microtubule organizing center, and forms the mitotic spindle during cell division.
   c. Centrioles are small, barrel-shaped organelles associated with the centrosome, and also form the bases of cilia and flagella.
10. Cellular Extensions
    a. Cilia are whiplike, motile cellular extensions on the exposed surfaces of some cells.
    b. Flagella are long cellular projections that move the cell through the environment.

V. The Nucleus (pp. 95–97)

A. Basic Characteristics (p. 95; Fig. 3.28)
   1. The nucleus is the control center of the cell and contains the cellular DNA.
   2. Most cells have only one nucleus, but very large cells may be multinucleate.
   3. All body cells except mature red blood cells have nuclei.
   4. The nucleus is larger than the cytoplasmic organelles; it has three regions and protein-containing subcompartments.
B. Nuclear Envelope (p. 95)
   1. The nuclear envelope is a double-membrane barrier surrounding the nucleus.
      a. The outer membrane is continuous with the rough ER.
      b. The inner membrane is lined with a shape-maintaining network of protein filaments, the nuclear lamina.
   2. At various points, nuclear pores penetrate areas where the membranes of the nuclear envelope fuse.
      a. A complex of proteins, called a pore complex, lines each nuclear pore and regulates passage of large particles into and out of the nucleus.
   3. The nuclear envelope encloses the fluid and solutes of the nucleus, the nucleoplasm.
C. Nucleoli (p. 96)
   1. Nucleoli are dark-staining spherical bodies within the nucleus.
   2. There are typically one or two nucleoli per nucleus.
   3. Nucleoli are the sites of assembly of ribosomal subunits, and are large in actively growing cells.

D. Chromatin (p. 97; Fig. 3.29)

    1. Chromatin is roughly half DNA, the genetic material of the cell, and half histone proteins.

    2. Nucleosomes are the fundamental unit of chromatin, consisting of clusters of eight histone proteins connected by a DNA molecule.

    3. When a cell is preparing to divide, chromatin condenses into dense, rodlike chromosomes.

VI. Cell Growth and Reproduction (pp. 97–111)

A. The Cell Life Cycle (pp. 97–101; Figs. 3.30–3.32)

    1. The cell life cycle is a series of changes a cell goes through from the time it is formed to the time it reproduces.

    2. Interphase and cell division are the two main periods of the cell cycle.

    3. Interphase is the period from cell formation to cell division, and has three subphases.

        a. During G_1, or gap 1, subphase the cell is synthesizing proteins and actively growing.

        b. During the S phase, DNA is replicated.

        c. During the G_2, or gap 2, subphase enzyme and other proteins are synthesized and distributed throughout the cell.

        d. DNA replication takes place when the DNA helix uncoils, and the hydrogen bonds between its base pairs are broken. Then each nucleotide strand of the DNA acts as a template for the construction of a complementary nucleotide strand.

    4. Cell division is a process necessary for growth and tissue repair. There are three main events of cell division.

        a. Mitosis is the process of nuclear division in which cells contain all genes.

        b. Meiosis is the process of nuclear division found only in egg and sperm cells in which the cells have half the genes found in other body cells.

        c. Cytokinesis is the process of dividing the cytoplasm.

        d. Control of cell division depends on surface-volume relationships, chemical signaling, and contact inhibition.

B. Protein Synthesis (pp. 101–110; Figs. 3.33–3.38)

    1. DNA specifies the structure of protein molecules that act as structural or functional molecules.

    2. Proteins are composed of polypeptide chains made up of amino acids.

    3. Each gene is a segment of DNA that carries instructions for one polypetide chain, as well as exons that specify amino acid informational sequences and noncoding sequences called introns.

    4. Each sequence of three nucleotide bases of DNA is called a triplet, and specifies a particular amino acid.

    5. The role of RNA

        a. RNA exists in three forms that decode and carry out the instructions of DNA in protein synthesis: Transfer RNA (tRNA), Ribosomal RNA (rRNA), and Messenger RNA (mRNA).

        b. All three types of RNA are constructed on the DNA in the nucleus, then released from the DNA to migrate to the cytoplasm while the DNA recoils to its original form.

6. There are two main steps of protein synthesis: transcription and translation.
   a. Transcription is the process of transferring information from a gene's base sequence to a complementary mRNA molecule.
      i. To make the mRNA complement, the transcription factor mediates binding of RNA polymerase, an enzyme that directs the synthesis of mRNA.
      ii. The mRNA that initially results from transcription, called primary transcript, contains introns that must be removed.
   b. Translation is the process of converting the language of nucleic acids (nucleotides) to the language of proteins (amino acids).
7. Introns now appear to code for a variety of RNAs.
   a. Antisense RNAs, made from the complementary DNA strand, can prevent mRNA from being translated.
   b. Small RNAs, called microRNAs, can suppress some mRNAs.
   c. Folded RNAs, called microswitches, can turn its own protein synthesis on or off in response to environmental changes.

VII. Extracellular Materials (p. 111)

A. Extracellular materials are substances contributing to body mass that are found outside the cells (p. 111).
B. There are three classes of extracellular materials (p. 111).
   1. Body fluids consist mainly of interstitial fluid, blood plasma, and cerebrospinal fluid, and are important to transport and solute dissolution.
   2. Cellular secretions include substances aiding in digestion or functioning as lubrication.
   3. Extracellular matrix is a jellylike substance consisting of proteins and polysaccharides.

VIII. Developmental Aspects of Cells (pp. 111–112)

A. Embryonic and Fetal Development of Cells (p. 111)
   1. Embryonic cells are exposed to different chemical signals that cause them to follow different pathways in development.
   2. Chemical signals influence development by switching genes on and off.
   3. Cell differentiation is the process of cells developing specific and distinctive features.
   4. Apoptosis is the programmed cell death of stressed, surplus developing cells.
B. Development of Cells Through Adolescence (p. 111)
   1. Most organ systems are well formed and functional before birth.
   2. The body continues to form new cells throughout childhood and adolescence.
   3. During young adulthood, cell numbers remain relatively constant, but local changes in the rate of cell division are common.
C. Effect of Aging on Cells (p. 112)
   1. The wear and tear theory considers the cumulative effect of slight chemical damage and the production of free radicals.

2. Cell aging may also be a result of autoimmune responses and progressive weakening of the immune response.

3. The genetic theory of cell aging suggests that cessation of mitosis and cell aging are genetically programmed.

Cross References

Additional information on topics covered in Chapter 3 can be found in the chapters listed below.

1. Chapter 2: Phospholipids; kinetic energy; ions; adenosine triphosphate; protein; enzymes; deoxyribonucleic acid; ribonucleic acid; comparison of DNA and RNA; hydrogen bond

2. Chapter 8: Lysosomal rupture (autolysis) and self-digestion of cells

3. Chapter 9: Role of smooth ER in calcium ion storage and release; microfilaments as contractile elements

4. Chapter 11: Specialized forms of cytoskeletal elements; nervous system membrane potentials

5. Chapter 14: Membrane receptors and functions in the autonomic nervous system

6. Chapter 18: Cell junctions and cardiac function

7. Chapter 19: Cell junctions and movement of substances through capillary walls

8. Chapter 21: Function of lysozyme in protection of the body; function of cilia in innate defense of the body

9. Chapter 22: Diffusion of respiratory gases

10. Chapter 23: Microvilli and increased absorptive surface area in epithelial cells of the small intestine; membrane transport related to absorption of digested substances

11. Chapter 24: Examples of membrane transport

12. Chapter 25: Hydrostatic pressure and movement of fluid through membranes

13. Chapter 26: Membrane transport related to electrolyte and water balance

14. Chapter 27: Reproductive cell division and gamete production; tight junctions and the blood/testis barrier; functions of flagella and cilia; mitochondria and energy production in sperm cells

15. Chapter 29: Cell division in relation to hereditary process

16. Appendix C: mRNA codons and the amino acids they specify

Laboratory Correlations

1. Marieb, E. N. *Human Anatomy & Physiology Laboratory Manual: Cat and Fetal Pig Versions*. Eighth Edition Updates. Benjamin Cummings, 2006.

   Exercise 3: The Microscope

   Exercise 4: The Cell—Anatomy and Division

   Exercise 5: The Cell—Transport Mechanisms and Cell Permeability

2. Marieb, E. N. *Human Anatomy & Physiology Laboratory Manual: Main Version*. Seventh Edition Update. Benjamin Cummings, 2006.

   Exercise 3: The Microscope

   Exercise 4: The Cell—Anatomy and Division

   Exercise 5: The Cell—Transport Mechanisms and Cell Permeability

Histology Slides for the Life Sciences

Available through Benjamin Cummings, an imprint of Pearson Education, Inc. To order, contact your local Benjamin Cummings sales representative.

Slide 41   Mitosis—Late Prophase.

Slide 42   Mitosis—Early Telophase.

Lecture Hints

1. It is important to stress the distinction between passive and active processes.
2. Students will often equate bulk-phase endocytosis with "cell drinking" and forget that the importance of the process is taking in the dissolved solutes in the fluid rather than the solvent itself.
3. The generation and maintenance of a resting membrane potential can be covered now or postponed until the contraction of a skeletal muscle fiber is presented in Chapter 9.
4. Explain that the nuclear membrane is a double membrane and that each membrane is a phospholipid bilayer. Some students will equate phospholipid bilayer and double membrane.
5. As a method of review, the cellular organelles can be grouped as being either membranous, microtubular, or "other."
6. Clarify the distinction between centrioles and centromeres.
7. Clearly distinguish between mitosis and cytokinesis.
8. In order to reinforce the idea of complementary base pairing, point out that cytosine and thymine are pyrimidines (single-ring structures) and guanine and adenine are purines (double-ring structures). For proper spacing it is necessary to combine a purine with a pyrimidine for each step in the DNA "ladder" (a three-ring-wide step). Furthermore, point out that adenine-thymine form two hydrogen bonds and cytosine-guanine form three hydrogen bonds.
9. Note the similarity of G and C so that students may readily remember the complementary base pairing of cytosine-guanine.

Activities/Demonstrations

1. Audio-visual materials listed under Multimedia in the Classroom and Lab.
2. Set up models of DNA and RNA to illustrate complementary base pairing.
3. Extract DNA from a beaker of lysed bacterial cells using a glass rod to illustrate the fibrillar nature of the molecule.
4. Use models of chromosomes with detachable chromatids to illustrate mitotic phases.
5. Ask students to name examples of diffusion, osmosis, and filtration commonly found in daily life.
6. Secure a glass funnel containing filter paper over a beaker. Illustrate how greater fluid pressure (provided by more fluid in the funnel) leads to faster filtration.
7. Set up one or more of the following simple diffusion demonstrations:
   a. Place a large histological dye crystal on the center of an agar plate a few hours before lecture. A ring of color will appear radiating from the crystal. The plate can be displayed on an overhead projector.

b. Place a crystal of dye in a beaker of water and display on an overhead projector. This dramatic demonstration allows students to easily relate to the process involved.

c. Use a bottle of perfume (or other substance) to illustrate diffusion in the classroom. Don't announce its use until it has diffused.

8. A simple osmometer: Place a glucose solution in a dialysis sac and tie securely to a length of glass tubing. Secure the tubing with a stand and clamp so that the dialysis bag is immersed in distilled water. Have students observe the fluid level in the tube over time.

9. If a microscope/TV camera system is available (or a microprojector), set it up to show the effects of: (a) physiologic saline, (b) hypertonic saline, and (c) distilled water on red blood cells.

10. Use an animal cell model to demonstrate the various organelles and cell parts.

11. Use a set of transparencies or slides of electron micrographs to illustrate subcellular organelles.

12. Use a hypothetical Jell-O salad to illustrate a cell. The Jell-O represents the cytosol; an orange represents the nucleus; and nuts, raisins, or other fruits are the different organelles. The container represents the plasma membrane.

Critical Thinking/Discussion Topics

1. Cells tend to have a relatively small and uniform size. Why aren't cells larger? Discuss your answer.

2. What are the advantages and disadvantages of asexual reproduction? Is mitosis an asexual reproductive method?

3. What is the value of start and stop signals in mRNA?

4. Why have certain cells of the body, such as muscle and nerve cells, "lost" their ability to divide?

5. Why must each daughter cell produced by mitosis have mitochondria?

6. Use the mathematical equations for surface area and volume determination to show that volume increases faster than surface area.

7. Why is damage to the heart more serious than damage to the liver (or other organ)?

8. Start with a cell containing 24 (or any hypothetical number you wish) chromosomes, and in each stage of mitosis predict the number of chromosomes and chromatids present.

9. Why is precise division of chromosomes during mitosis so important?

10. What could be the evolutionary advantage of genetically programming cellular aging?

Library Research Topics

1. Receptor-mediated endocytosis is a highly selective mechanism of ingesting molecules. How could it be used to kill cancer cells?

2. Why do we age? What appears to initiate the aging process and do we have any cellular mechanisms that control or facilitate this process?

3. Are all cancers caused by carcinogens? What other substances can cause cancer?

4. How can hybridomas aid research techniques and facilitate our understanding of the immune system?

5. Many genetic diseases are caused by mutations that change the sequence of the nitrogen bases in the DNA. How many codons are changed in the genetic disease sickle-cell anemia? What amino acid is substituted in the hemoglobin because of this mutation?

6. During the past few years experimental implants of fetal tissue have been used for treatment of brain disorders such as Parkinson's disease. What is the current status of such experimentation? What are some of the moral, ethical, and legal concerns involving such experimentation?

7. How has the advent of recombinant DNA techniques aided in our understanding of proteins such as interferon, insulin, and interleukins?

8. Compare and contrast procaryotic and eucaryotic cells.

Multimedia in the Classroom and Lab

Online Resources for Students

The
Anatomy & Physiology Place   **MyA&P**
www.anatomyandphysiology.com   www.myaandp.com

The following shows the organization of the Chapter Guide page in both the Anatomy & Physiology Place and MyA&P™. The Chapter Guide organizes all the chapter-specific online media resources for Chapter 3 in one convenient location, with e-book links to each section of the textbook. Please note that both sites also give you access to other general A&P resources, like InterActive Physiology®, PhysioEx 6.0™, Anatomy 360°, Flashcards, a Glossary, a Histology Tutorial, *and much more.*

Objectives

Section 3.1 Overview of the Cellular Basis of Life (pp. 65–66)

Art Labeling Activity: Structure of a Generalized Cell (Fig. 3.2, p. 66)

Section 3.2 The Plasma Membrane: Structure (pp. 66–70)

Animation: Plasma Membrane Structure

Animations: Transport Proteins | Enzymes | Receptor Proteins | Structural Proteins

Animations: Tight Junctions | Desmosomes | Gap Junctions

Section 3.3 The Plasma Membrane: Functions (pp. 70–84)

Animations: Diffusion | Osmosis | Active Transport

PhysioEx: Cell Transport Mechanisms and Permeability

Activity: Selective Permeability

Activity: Passive Transport

InterActive Physiology®: The Membrane Potential

Animation: Signal Transduction

Section 3.4 The Cytoplasm (pp. 84–95)

Memory: Cellular Organelles

Animation: The Endomembrane System

Animation: Cilia and Flagella

Section 3.5 The Nucleus (pp. 95–98)

Section 3.6 Cell Growth and Reproduction (pp. 98–111)

Memory: Important Cellular Processes

Animations: DNA & RNA Structure | DNA Replication |

Animations: Prophase | Prometaphase |Metaphase | Anaphase | Mitosis and
  Cytokinesis

Case Study: Diabetes Mellitus

Section 3.7 Extracellular Materials (p. 111)

Section 3.8 Developmental Aspects of Cells (pp. 111–112)

Chapter Summary

Self-Study Quizzes

Art Labeling Quiz

Matching Quiz

Multiple-Choice Quiz (Level I)

Multiple-Choice Quiz (Level II)

True-False Quiz

Crossword Puzzles

Crossword Puzzle 3.1

Crossword Puzzle 3.2

Media

See Guide to Audio-Visual Resources in Appendix A for key to AV distributors.

Slides

1. *Onion Mitosis 35mm Slides Set* (CBS)

Video

1. *The Aging Process* (FHS; 19 min.). This program explains the effects of aging on
   the mind and body, explores the theories about why cells wear out.
2. *Cancer* (FHS; 23 min.). Provides a look at how cancers form and some of the
   weapons used in the fight against them. Some of the treatments demonstrated
   include: chemotherapy, radiation therapy, surgery, photochemotherapy, and monoclonal antibodies.
3. *An Introduction to the Living Cell* (CBS; 30 min.). This program takes students
   on a visual tour of a cell. Subcellular organelles are shown working together. Computer animation and microscopic images are used to visualize the complexities of
   the cell. This is an excellent program for lecture presentation.
4. *A Journey Through the Cell* (FHS; 25 min. each, 1997). Contains computer graphics and animations, includes presentations by scientists introducing ideas central to
   understanding cells.

Software

1. *Animal and Plant Mitosis SMARTSlides* (WNS; Win/Mac). Your classroom computer
   becomes a microscope with a library of 20 prepared slides. The program presents
   all phases of plant and animal mitosis.
2. *The Cell: Structure, Function, and Process* (HRM; Win/Mac). Introduces the microscopic world of the cell and explores various cell processes.
3. *The Genetic Basis of Cancer* (IM; Win/Mac). CD-ROM, focusing on breast and
   colon cancer, studies the genetic basis for cancer.
4. *Inside the Cell* (CBS, CE; Win/Mac). 3-D graphics illustrate cellular organization
   and recent advancements in cellular biology.
5. *Introduction to Cells: The Structure of the Cell* (IM; Win/Mac). Provides an
   introduction to the cell and describes cell structure and function.

6. *Osmosis Lab* (IM; Win/Mac). Studies osmosis by controlling numerous variables and discusses hypertonic, hypotonic, and isotonic solutions.
7. *The Plasma Membrane and Cellular Transport* (CE; Win/Mac). This CD provides a detailed study of membranes and cell motility. Introduces the fluid mosaic model. Students can explore cell biology at their own pace.

Lecture Enhancement Material

To view thumbnails of all of the illustrations for Chapter 3, see Appendix B.

Transparencies Index/Media Manager

Figure 3.1	Cell diversity.
Figure 3.2	Structure of the generalized cell.
Figure 3.3	Structure of the plasma membrane according to the fluid mosaic model.
Figure 3.4	Some functions of membrane proteins.
Figure 3.5	Cell junctions.
Figure 3.6	Diffusion.
Figure 3.7	Diffusion through the plasma membrane.
Figure 3.8	Influence of membrane permeability on diffusion and osmosis.
Figure 3.9	The effect of solutions of varying tonicities on living red blood cells.
Figure 3.10	Operation of the sodium-potassium pump, an antiport pump $(Na^+-K^+ATPase)$.
Figure 3.11	Secondary active transport.
Figure 3.12	Exocytosis.
Figure 3.13	Clathrin-mediated endocytosis.
Figure 3.14	Clathrin-coated versus caveolin-coated vesicles.
Figure 3.15	The role of K^+ in generating the resting membrane potential.
Figure 3.16	Model of the operation of a G protein–linked receptor.
Figure 3.17	Mitochondrion.
Figure 3.18	The endoplasmic reticulum (ER) and ribosomes.
Figure 3.19	The signal mechanism targets ribosomes to the ER for protein synthesis.
Figure 3.20	Golgi apparatus.
Figure 3.21	The sequence of events from protein synthesis on the rough ER to the final distribution of those proteins.
Figure 3.22	Lysosomes.
Figure 3.23	The endomembrane system.
Figure 3.24	Cytoskeleton.
Figure 3.25	Interaction of motor molecules (motor proteins) with cytoskeletal elements.
Figure 3.26	Centrioles.
Figure 3.27	Cilia structure and function.
Figure 3.28	The nucleus.
Figure 3.29	Chromatin and chromosome structure.
Figure 3.30	The cell cycle.
Figure 3.31	Replication of DNA.

Answers to End-of-Chapter Questions

Multiple Choice and Matching Question answers appear in Appendix G of the main text.

Short Answer Essay Questions

20. a. Mitochondria. (p. 85)

    b. Ribosomes, endoplasmic reticulum, and golgi bodies. (pp. 85–89)

    c. Lysosomes—digestive bag of hydrolytic enzymes for intracellular digestion. (p. 89) Peroxisomes—an organelle that detoxifies harmful and/or toxic substances, such as free radicals produced during metabolism. (p. 90)

21. Each daughter cell produced following mitosis is genetically identical to the mother cell. Because each cell contains part of the original cell, a portion of the very first original cell will always be found in each and every daughter cell. In terms of immortality, a cancer cell is truly immortal since it is not bounded by normal cellular constraints and does not actually "age." (p. 101)

22. Red blood cells, when mature, actually eject their nucleus. Without genetic material to guide repair processes (protein synthesis and metabolism), these cells cannot reproduce and will ultimately die. (p. 95)

23. The "sugar-coated" proteins are called glycoproteins and act as highly specific biological markers that aid cellular interactions (such as during embryonic development and in the immune response). (pp. 67–68) Other markers, the glycolipids, may serve similar functions as surface markers.

24. a. Body fluids, such as interstitial fluids, blood plasma, and cerebrospinal fluid, are important as transport and dissolving media. (p. 111)

    b. Cellular secretions, such as gastric and pancreatic fluids, aid in digestion, while others, such as saliva and mucus, act as lubricants. (p. 111)

    c. Extracellular matrix represents a jellylike substance that acts as a tissue "glue" in all tissues and helps to determine the characteristics of connective tissues. (p. 111)

25. The sodium-potassium pump acts to maintain a polarized state of the membrane by maintaining the diffusion gradient of sodium and potassium ions. The pump couples the transport of sodium and potassium ions so that with each "turn" of the pump, three sodium ions are ejected out of the cell and two potassium ions are carried back into the cell. (p. 77)

26. Primary active transport involves a change in the confirmation of the transport protein, which directly transports the bound solute across the membrane. Secondary active transport, on the other hand, is an indirect transport in which the solute is "dragged along" with another ion that is actively being pumped against its concentration gradient. This pumped ion is usually transported by a primary active transport system. (p. 77)

Critical Thinking and Clinical Application Questions

1. In each case, living cells have been immersed in a hypotonic solution which will result in water entry into the cells. In the case of celery, where the cells are also bounded by cell walls of cellulose, water entry makes the cell "stiff" due to hydrostatic pressure. In the case of skin cells, as water is absorbed, the cells swell causing the skin to take an undulating course to accommodate greater cell volume. (pp. 74–75)

2. By interfering with normal digestion and absorption of food material, the infectious agents are causing the intestinal cell membrane to become impermeable to solute (food) molecules in the intestines and the solute molecules within the cells. As a result of this situation, the effect of the difference between the intestinal cells' content osmolarity (compartment 1) and the intestinal content osmolarity (compartment 2) will not only prevent water reabsorption by the intestinal cell but will cause water to move rapidly from compartment 1 into compartment 2, resulting in diarrhea. (p. 74)

3. a. By damaging the mitotic spindle, vincristine will inhibit the proper formation of the microtubules used in pushing the centrioles toward the opposite poles of the cell. Failure to do this will result in the cell being unable to complete its mitotic division process, thus killing the cell. (p. 105)

   b. By binding to DNA and blocking mRNA synthesis, adriamycin effectively inhibits protein synthesis. Cessation of this process prevents the cell from replacing enzymes and other proteins required for cellular survival. (p. 104)

4. "G_1 to S" is actually the time between cell divisions and used to be referred to as the "resting stage" to differentiate it from cell division. Actually, gap 1 is the time when the cell is not dividing but is very metabolically active. It will stay in this phase until it is ready to divide, at which time it moves into S, or the synthetic phase. In the synthetic phase, DNA replicates itself in preparation for cell division. The length of G_1 varies greatly from cell to cell, ranging from several minutes or hours to the life of the cell, in cells that have ceased to divide. Therefore, cells prevented from moving from G_1 to S would not divide. (pp. 98, 102–103)

   "G_2 to M" represents the time frame between gap 2 (G_2), which is the time needed for synthesis of enzymes that are required for division to visible mitosis (M_1). Here cells would be prepared to divide, and have increased DNA, but would not go into actual mitosis. Chromosomes would not be identified under the light microscope, even though there would be an increase in DNA. Cells would be in prophase. (pp. 98, 102–103)

5. Peroxisomes are the cellular organelles that break down toxins. This organelle contains oxidases and catalases. Oxidases use molecular oxygen to detoxify many substances, such as alcohol and formaldehyde. (p. 90)

6. Both cilia and flagella are involved in movement. Cilia propel other substances across the cell's surface, whereas the flagella propel the cell itself. Lack of dynein would render both these structures dysfunctional. Hence the normal "sweeping out" of the respiratory tract provided by the cilia lining the lumen of this system

would be lost, leading to increased respiratory problems. Loss of a functioning flagella would render the sperm immobile and lead to sterility in males. (p. 93)

7. One of the functions of the smooth ER is detoxification of drugs, such as alcohol. Specific enzyme concentration on the smooth ER is need-based: the cell will produce more if the demand on the cell is greater. The high alcohol consumption typical of alcoholics stimulates the production of smooth ER that contains enzymes involved in elimination of alcohol, making the cells more efficient at this task. All other factors being equal, people who consume little or no alcohol have much less smooth ER because there is much less demand for its detoxification function. (pp. 86–87)

Suggested Readings

Anderson, Richard G. W. "The Caveolae Membrane System." *Annual Review of Biochemistry* 67 (1998): 199–225.

Bartek, Jiri and Lukas, Jiri. "Order From Destruction." *Science* 294 (5540) (Oct. 2001): 66–67.

Bird, Adrian. "Methylation Talk Between Histones and DNA." *Science* 294 (5549) (Dec. 2001): 2113–2115.

Chen, Yu A. and Scheller, Richard H. "Snare-Mediated Membrane Fusion." *Nature Reviews: Molecular Cell Biology* 2 (Feb. 2001): 98–106.

Dahlberg, Albert E. "The Ribosome in Action." *Science* 292 (5518) (May 2001): 868–869.

Finkel, Elizabeth. "The Mitochondrion: Is it Central to Apoptosis?" *Science* 292 (5516) (April 2001): 624–626.

Geiger, B. et al. "Transmembrane Extracellular Matrix—Cytoskeletal Crosstalk." *Nature Reviews: Molecular Cell Biology* 2 (11) (Nov. 2001): 793–805.

Gilooly, David, J. and Stenmark, Harald, A. "Lipid Oils the Endocytosis Machine." *Science* 291 (5506) (Feb. 2001): 993–994.

Gray, John A. and Roth, Bryan L. "A Last GA SP for GPCRs?" *Science* 297 (5581) (July 2002): 529–532.

Hentze, Matthias W. "Believe It or Not—Translation in the Nucleus." *Science* 293 (5532) (Aug. 2001): 1058–1059.

Hunot, Stephane and Flavell, Richard A. "Death of a Monopoly?" *Science* 292 (5518) (May 2001): 865–866.

Jesenberger, Veronika and Jentsch, Stefan. "Deadly Encounter: Ubiquitin Meets Apoptosis." *Nature Reviews: Molecular Cell Biology* 2 (3) (Feb. 2002): 112–120.

Keys, Andrew R. and Green, Michael R. "The Odd Coupling." *Nature* 413 (6856) (Oct. 2001): 583–585.

King, Ian F. and Kingston, Robert E. "Specifying Transcription." *Nature* 414 (6866) (Dec. 2001): 858–860.

Kirchhausen, Tomas. 'Three Ways to Make a Vesicle." *Nature Reviews: Molecular Cell Biology* 1 (3) (Dec. 2000): 187–198.

Marmorstein, Ronen. "Protein Molecules that Manipulate Histone Tails for Chromatin Regulation." *Nature: Molecular Cell Biology* 2 (6) (June 2001): 422–432.

Martinou, Jean-Claude and Green, Douglas R. "Breaking the Mitochondrial Barrier." *Nature Reviews: Molecular Cell Biology* 2 (1) (Jan. 2001): 63–71.

Marx, Jean, Caveolae. "A Once-Elusive Structure Gets Some Respect." *Science* 294 (5548) (Nov. 2001): 1862–1865.

Mayer, John R. "The Meteoric Rise of Regulated Intracellular Proteolysis." *Nature Reviews: Molecular Cell Biology* 1 (2) (Nov. 2000): 145–148.

Misteli, Tom. "Protein Dynamics: Implications for Nuclear Architecture and Gene Expression." *Science* 291 (5505) (Feb. 2001): 843–847.

Murray, Andrew W. "Centrioles at the Checkpoint." *Science* 291 (5508) (Feb. 2001): 1499–1502.

Nasmyth, Kim. "Segregating Sister Genomes: The Molecular Biology of Chromosome Separation." *Science* 297 (5581) (July 2002): 559–565.

Newman, Andy. "RNA Enzymes for RNA Splicing." *Nature* 413 (6857) (Oct. 2001): 695–696.

Nigg, Erich A. "Mitotic Kinases as Regulators of Cell Division and Its Checkpoints." *Nature Reviews: Molecular Cell Biology* 2 (1) (Jan. 2001): 21–32.

Pennisi, Elizabeth. "Closing in on the Centromere." *Science* 294 (5540) (Oct. 2001): 30–31.

Pennisi, Elizabeth. "Ribosome's Inner Workings Come Into Sharper View." *Science* 291 (5513) (March 2001): 2526–2527.

Razani, Babak and Lisanti, Michael P. "Caveolins and Caveolae: Molecular and Functional Relationships." *Experimental Cell Research* 271 (2001): 36–44.

Sheetz, Michael P. "Cell Control by Membrane-Cytoskeleton Adhesion." *Nature Reviews: Molecular Cell Biology* 2 (5) (May 2001): 392–396.

Shin, Jeoung-Sook and Abraham, Soman N. "Caveolae—Not Just Craters in the Cellular Landscape." *Science* 293 (5534) (Aug. 2001): 1447–1448.

Simons, Kai and Toomre, Derek. "Lipid Rafts and Signal Transduction." *Nature Reviews: Molecular Cell Biology* 1 (1) (Oct. 2000): 31–39.

Slepnev, Vladimir I. and De Camilli, Pietro. "Accessory Factors in Clathrin-Dependent Synaptic Vesicle Endocytosis." *Nature Reviews: Molecular Cell Biology* 1 (3) (Dec. 2000): 187–198.

Sprong, H. et al. "How Proteins Move Lipids and Lipids Move Proteins." *Nature Reviews: Molecular Cell Biology* 2 (July 2001): 504–513.

Travis, John. "What's in the Vault?" *Science News* 150 (4) (July 1996): 56–57.

Van Meer, Gerrit. "The Different Hues of Lipid Rafts." *Science* 296 (5569) (May 2002): 855–857.

Tissue: The Living Fabric

Objectives

Epithelial Tissue

1. Describe the special characteristics of epithelial tissue.
2. Discuss how epithelial tissue is named and classified.
3. List the types of epithelial tissues and give an example of each.
4. Define gland, and explain the difference between exocrine and endocrine glands.
5. Describe the three modes of exocrine secretions.

Connective Tissue

6. Describe the functions of connective tissue.
7. Discuss the similarities and differences between connective tissue types.
8. Explain the types of connective tissue found in the body and their characteristic functions.

Covering and Lining Membranes

9. Describe the structure and the function of cutaneous, mucous, and serous membranes.

Nervous Tissue

10. List the structure and function of nervous tissue.

Muscle Tissue

11. Compare and contrast the structure, location, and function of the three types of muscular tissue.

Tissue Repair

12. Discuss the process involved in normal tissue repair.

Developmental Aspects of Tissues

13. Discuss the embryonic origin of the different tissue types.
14. Explain the changes that occur in the tissues with age.

Suggested Lecture Outline

I. Introduction to Tissue (p. 118)

A. Tissues are groups of cells that are similar in structure and function.
B. There are four primary tissue types: epithelial (covering), connective (support), nervous (control), and muscular (movement).

II. Preparing Human Tissue for Microscopy (p. 118)

A. Tissue specimens must be fixed (preserved) and sectioned (sliced) thinly enough to allow light transmission.
B. Tissue sections must be stained with dyes that bind to different parts of the cell in slightly different ways so that anatomical structures are distinguished from one another.

III. Epithelial Tissue (pp. 118–126)

A. Features of Epithelia (p. 118)

    1. An epithelium is a sheet of cells that covers a body surface or lines a cavity.

    2. Epithelium occurs in the body as covering or lining epithelium, and as glandular epithelium.

B. Special Characteristics of Epithelium (pp. 118–119)

    1. Composed of closely packed cells with little extracellular material between.

    2. Adjacent epithelial cells are bound together by specialized contacts such as desmosomes and tight junctions.

    3. Exhibits polarity by having an apical surface (free) and a basal surface (attached).

    4. Supported by the underlying connective tissue.

    5. Innervated but avascular.

    6. Has a high regeneration capacity.

C. Classification of Epithelia (pp. 119–124; Figs. 4.1–4.2)

    1. Each epithelial tissue is given two names.

        a. The first name indicates the number of layers present, either simple (one) or stratified (more than one).

        b. The second name describes the shape of the cells.

    2. Simple epithelia are mostly concerned with absorption, secretion, and filtration.

        a. Simple squamous epithelium is a single layer of fish scale-shaped cells.

        b. Simple cuboidal epithelium is a single layer of cube-shaped cells forming the smallest ducts of glands and many kidney tubules.

        c. Simple columnar epithelium is a single layer of column-shaped cells that line the digestive tract.

        d. Pseudostratified columnar epithelium contains cells of varying heights giving the false impression of the presence of many layers.

    3. Stratified epithelia's main function is protection.

        a. Stratified squamous epithelium is composed of several layers with the cells on the free surface being squamous-shaped and the underlying cells being cuboidal or columnar in shape.

        b. Stratified cuboidal epithelium is rare, found mostly in the ducts of some of the larger glands.

        c. Stratified columnar epithelium is found in limited distribution with small amounts in the pharynx, male urethra, and lining some glandular ducts.

        d. Transitional epithelium forms the lining of the hollow organs of the urinary system that stretch as they fill.

D. Glandular Epithelia (pp. 124–126; Figs. 4.3–4.5)

    1. Endocrine glands are ductless glands that secrete hormones by exocytosis directly into the blood or lymph.

    2. Exocrine glands have ducts and secrete their product onto a surface or into body cavities.

        a. Exocrine glands may be unicellular or multicellular.

        b. Exocrine secretions in humans may be merocrine, which are products released through exocytosis, or holocrine, which are synthesized products released when the cell ruptures.

IV. Connective Tissue (pp. 126–138)

A. Functions of Connective Tissue (pp. 126–127)

  1. The major functions of connective tissue are binding and support, protection, insulation, and transportation.

B. Common Characteristics of Connective Tissue (p. 127)

  1. All connective tissue arises from an embryonic tissue called mesenchyme.

  2. Connective tissue ranges from avascular to highly vascularized.

  3. Connective tissue is composed mainly of nonliving extracellular matrix that separates the cells of the tissue.

C. Structural Elements of Connective Tissue (pp. 127–130; Fig. 4.3)

  1. Ground substance is the unstructured material that fills the space between the cells and contains the fibers.

  2. Fibers of the connective tissue provide support.

    a. Collagen fibers are extremely strong and provide high tensile strength to the connective tissue.

    b. Elastic fibers contain elastin, which allows them to be stretched and to recoil.

    c. Reticular fibers are fine, collagenous fibers that form networks.

  3. Each major class of connective tissue has a fundamental cell type that exists in immature and mature forms.

D. Types of Connective Tissue (pp. 131–139; Figs. 4.6, 4.9)

  1. Mesenchyme forms during the early weeks of embryonic development from the mesoderm layer and eventually differentiates into all other connective tissues.

  2. Loose connective tissue is one of the two subclasses of connective tissue proper.

    a. Areolar connective tissue serves to bind body parts together while allowing them to move freely over one another, wraps small blood vessels and nerves, surrounds glands, and forms the subcutaneous tissue.

    b. Adipose (fat) tissue is a richly vascularized tissue that functions in nutrient storage, protection, and insulation.

    c. Reticular connective tissue forms the internal framework of the lymph nodes, the spleen, and the bone marrow.

  3. Dense connective tissue is one of the two subclasses of connective tissue proper.

    a. Dense regular connective tissue contains closely packed bundles of collagen fibers running in the same direction and makes up tendons and ligaments.

    b. Dense irregular connective tissue contains thick bundles of collagen fibers arranged in an irregular fashion, and is found in the dermis.

  4. Cartilage lacks nerve fibers and is avascular.

    a. Hyaline cartilage is the most abundant cartilage providing firm support with some pliability.

    b. Elastic cartilage is found where strength and exceptional stretchability are needed, such as the external ear.

    c. Fibrocartilage is found where strong support and the ability to withstand heavy pressure are required, such as the intervertebral disks.

     5.   Bone (osseous tissue) has an exceptional ability to support and protect body structures due to its hardness, which is determined by the additional collagen fibers and calcium salts found in the extracellular matrix.

     6.   Blood is classified as a connective tissue because it developed from mesenchyme, and consists of blood cells and plasma proteins surrounded by blood plasma.

V. Nervous Tissue (p. 139; Fig. 4.10)

A.   Nervous tissue is the main component of the nervous system, which regulates and controls body functions.

B.   Nervous tissue is composed of two types of cells.

     1.   Neurons are specialized cells that generate and conduct electrical impulses.

     2.   Supporting cells are nonconductive cells that support, insulate, and protect the neurons.

VI. Muscle Tissue (pp. 139–141; Fig. 4.11)

A.   Muscle tissues are highly cellular, well-vascularized tissues responsible for movement.

B.   There are three types of muscular tissue:

     1.   Skeletal muscle attaches to the skeleton and produces voluntary body movement.

     2.   Cardiac muscle is responsible for the involuntary movement of the heart.

     3.   Smooth muscle is found in the walls of the hollow organs.

VII. Covering and Lining Membranes (pp. 141–143; Fig. 4.12)

A.   Cutaneous membrane, or skin, is an organ system consisting of a keratinized squamous epithelium firmly attached to a thick layer of dense irregular connective tissue (p. 138).

B.   Mucous membranes line body cavities that open to the exterior and contain either stratified squamous or simple columnar epithelia (pp. 141–142).

C.   Serous membranes consist of simple squamous epithelium resting on a thin layer of loose connective (areolar) tissue. (pp. 142–143)

VIII. Tissue Repair (pp. 143–145; Fig. 4.13)

A.   Tissue repair occurs in two ways: regeneration and fibrosis.

B.   Three steps are involved in the tissue repair process.

     1.   Inflammation prepares the area for the repair process.

     2.   Organization restores the blood supply.

     3.   Regeneration and fibrosis effect permanent repair.

C.   The generative capacity of tissues varies widely among the tissue types.

IX. Developmental Aspects of Tissues (pp. 145–148)

A.   Embryonic and Fetal Development of Tissues (Fig. 4.14)

     1.   Primary germ layer formation is one of the first events of embryonic development.

        a.   Ectoderm is the most superficial of the layers.

        b.   Mesoderm is the middle layer.

        c.   Endoderm is the deepest layer.

2. The primary germ layers specialize to form the four primary tissues.

B. With increasing age, epithelia become thin, the amount of collagen fibers in the body decreases, and bone, muscle, and nervous tissue atrophy.

Cross References

Additional information on topics covered in Chapter 4 can be found in the chapters listed below.

1. Chapter 1: The hierarchy of structural organization; divisions of the ventral body cavity

2. Chapter 5: The function of keratin in keratinized stratified squamous epithelium; cutaneous membrane (skin); function of the basement membrane in skin; role of connective tissues in the integument; exocrine glands found in the skin

3. Chapter 6: Osseous tissue and the structure and growth of bone; formation of osseous tissue; chondrocytes and cartilage in bone formation

4. Chapter 8: Connective tissues in ligaments and tendons; cartilage in joint formation

5. Chapter 9: Skeletal and smooth muscle; connective tissue coverings of muscles

6. Chapter 11: Nervous tissue

7. Chapter 13: Function of nervous tissue

8. Chapter 16: Ductless (endocrine) glands

9. Chapter 17: Blood

10. Chapter 18: Cardiac muscle; serous coverings of the heart, epithelium of the heart, and connective tissue in cardiac valves; function of nervous tissue

11. Chapter 19: Epithelial and connective tissue components of the blood vessels

12. Chapter 20: Interstitial fluid (generation and removal); reticular connective tissue support of lymphatic tissue

13. Chapter 21: Inflammatory and immune responses

14. Chapter 22: Cartilaginous support of respiratory structures; pseudostratified epithelium in the lining of the trachea

15. Chapter 23: Epithelial and secretory cells of the digestive tract

16. Chapter 25: Epithelial cell characteristics of filtration, secretion, and absorption

Laboratory Correlations

1. Marieb, E. N. *Human Anatomy & Physiology Laboratory Manual: Cat and Fetal Pig Versions*. Eighth Edition Updates. Benjamin Cummings, 2006.

   Exercise 6A: Classification of Tissues

2. Marieb, E. N. *Human Anatomy & Physiology Laboratory Manual: Main Version*. Seventh Edition Update. Benjamin Cummings, 2006.

   Exercise 6A: Classification of Tissues

Histology Slides for the Life Sciences

Available through Benjamin Cummings, an imprint of Pearson Education, Inc. To order, contact your local Benjamin Cummings sales representative.

Slides 1–39 Tissue Types—various titles.

Lecture Hints

1. The relationship between structure and function is important and can be readily illustrated by examples of epithelial tissues. Stress how the multilayered structure of stratified squamous epithelium is much better adapted for surfaces exposed to wear and tear, while simple squamous epithelium is better adapted for filtration.

2. Stratified squamous epithelium is usually the first of the multilayered epithelial tissues presented. Emphasize that only the surface cells are flattened. The student's first conception is often that the tissue is composed of multiple layers of thin flat cells.

3. Emphasize the uniqueness of the matrix when explaining the classification of the connective tissues. This will be helpful since this group of tissues seems so diverse to the students. Students may often lose sight of how and why such a diverse group is classified together. Also relate the type of matrix to the specific function of the tissue.

4. Students are sometimes confused about why collagen and elastic fibers are called white and yellow fibers respectively, even though under microscopic observation they appear to be pink and black respectively. This is because prepared specimens are stained, not natural, colors.

5. Point out that hyaline cartilage contains large numbers of collagen fibers even though they will not be visible on the slides observed in the lab.

6. Emphasize that cartilage is avascular and that this results in a slow repair or healing rate.

7. While presenting the information on bone (osseous tissue), stress that this is a living tissue that has a direct blood supply. Often the student conception of bone is that it is nonliving material (due to observations in the lab).

8. Mention that the "fibers" in blood are unique because they are composed of a soluble protein that becomes insoluble only during the process of clot formation.

9. Epithelial membranes are composed of epithelial and connective tissues. The best example to illustrate this is the skin (cutaneous membrane).

10. Stress that regeneration is not the same as repair.

Activities/Demonstrations

1. Audio-visual materials listed under Multimedia in the Classroom and Lab.

2. Ask the students to make a list of all the things the body could not do if connective tissue were absent.

3. Use moderate pressure to scrape a fingernail along the anterior surface of the forearm to demonstrate the beginnings of the inflammatory response (redness, swelling).

4. In the lab, cut a planaria transversely and follow the regeneration of the missing body region over the next few weeks.

5. Use 3-D models, such as a cube (for cuboidal), a fried egg (for squamous), or a drinking glass (for columnar), to illustrate the various types of epithelial tissues.

6. Obtain or prepare 2×2 slides of all the tissues used during the lecture presentation of histology.

7. Illustrate how tissues are sectioned to show how thin sections are made. Remind students that slides possess only a small, thin slice of tissue and that the slide may have more than one type of tissue.

8. Use models of epithelial, connective tissue, muscle cells, and a neuron to illustrate how the cells of the different tissue types are similar and dissimilar.

9. Cover your fist with a collapsed balloon to demonstrate the relationship between parietal and visceral layers of a serous membrane.

10. Use a human torso model to indicate the locations of mucous and serous membranes.

11. Use models of skeletal, cardiac, and smooth muscle to compare and contrast these tissue types.

Critical Thinking/Discussion Topics

1. What types of inflammations are there, and how do they differ from each other?

2. How are tissues prepared and sectioned to produce the various tissue slides seen in this textbook?

3. How can macrophages detect what is foreign and what is self (not foreign) in the body?

4. Of what medical significance is the entrance into the tissue spaces of the body of a microorganism that could degrade collagen? Name an example and describe the disease it causes.

5. If all cells of the body arise from the same embryonic cell (zygote), how can each cell take on specific roles? Could any of these differentiated cells revert to a different cell type?

6. In some cysts and tumors, bone, hair, and even teeth can be found. How can this happen?

7. Since cartilage is avascular, how is it supplied with the essentials of life?

8. Other than to reduce bleeding and prevent microbial invasion, why are wounds sutured?

9. There appears to be an inverse relationship between potential regeneration and level of specialization of tissues. Why might this be so?

Library Research Topics

1. Basement membranes provide the interface between epithelium and connective tissue. What is the chemical composition of this layer and why is this area of great interest to cell biologists?

2. What is the current status of cloning? Is it feasible for human cells?

3. What is suction lipectomy? Who can perform this procedure?

4. Why can some cells regenerate and others not? What advantages and disadvantages are there for either case?

5. Some nutritionists suggest that obesity later in life results from overfeeding during infancy and childhood. Review some of the articles that support or dispute this theory.

Multimedia in the Classroom and Lab

Online Resources for Students

The
Anatomy & Physiology Place   **MyA&P**
www.anatomyandphysiology.com   www.myaandp.com

The following shows the organization of the Chapter Guide page in both the Anatomy & Physiology Place and MyA&P™. The Chapter Guide organizes all the chapter-specific online media resources for Chapter 4 in one convenient location, with e-book links to each section of the textbook. Please note that both sites also give you access to other general A&P resources, like InterActive Physiology®, *PhysioEx 6.0™,* Anatomy 360°, *Flashcards, a Glossary, a Histology Tutorial, and much more.*

Histology Tutorial

   Objectives

   Section 4.1   Preparing Human Tissue for Microscopy (p. 118)

   Section 4.2   Epithelial Tissue (pp. 118–126)

   Art Labeling Activity: Types of Multicellular Exocrine Glands (Fig. 4.4, p. 126)

   Memory: Tissue Organization of the Body

   Section 4.3   Connective Tissue (pp. 126–139)

   Art Labeling Activity: Areolar Connective Tissue (Fig. 4.8, p. 130)

   Memory: Connective Tissue Proper

   Section 4.4   Nervous Tissue (p. 139)

   InterActive Physiology®: Nervous System Anatomy Review

   Section 4.5   Muscle Tissue (pp. 139–141)

   InterActive Physiology®: Skeletal Muscle Tissue Anatomy Review

   Section 4.6   Covering and Lining Membranes (pp. 141–143)

   Section 4.7   Tissue Repair (pp. 143–145)

   Case Study: Cirrhosis of the Liver

   Section 4.8   Developmental Aspects of Tissues (pp. 145, 148)

   Case Study: Congenital Defect

   Chapter Summary

   Self-Study Quizzes

   Art Labeling Quiz

   Matching Quiz

   Multiple-Choice Quiz (Level I)

   Multiple-Choice Quiz (Level II)

   True-False Quiz

   Crossword Puzzles

   Crossword Puzzle 4.1

   Crossword Puzzle 4.2

Media

See Guide to Audio-Visual Resources in Appendix A for key to AV distributors.

Slides

1. *Basic Epithelium Types Set* (CBS)
2. *Basic Human Histology Set* (CBS). Set of 100 transparencies that covers a broad spectrum of human histology.
3. *Connective Tissue Types Set* (CBS)
4. *Connective Tissue Set* (CBS)
5. *Human Muscle Tissues Set* (CBS)
6. *Skeletal Tissue Set* (CBS)

Video

1. *Organ Systems Working Together* (WNS; 14 min.). This program introduces students to the functions of the organ systems in the human body. An excellent overview of all the systems with a special animated sequence that shows how every organ system in the human body has developed from a single cell of a fertilized egg.

2. *Skin and Soft Tissue Infections* (FHS; 18 min., 1999). Discusses commonly occurring skin and soft tissue infections, including impetigo, necrotizing fasciitis, and burns.

Software

1. *Cross-Sectional Anatomy Tutor on CD-ROM* (FHS; Windows). Interactive, instructional program correlates normal cross-sectional anatomy with radiographic images from CT and MRI images.

2. *Interactive Histology Resource CD-ROM* (WNS; Win/Mac). Slides cover cytology of most major systems. Includes detailed text describing structures, form, and function. Printable quizzes included in the CD.

3. *The Pathology Atlas* (FHS; Win/Mac). Extensive database of pathology images with associated medical information.

4. *WARD's Epithelial Cells, SMARTSlides CD-ROM* (WNS; Win/Mac). Examples of cell specialization and organization are presented through guided lessons. Students can view various types of epithelial cells just as they are seen through a microscope. Text can be printed for further study. Can be used by an individual student for review or presented to an entire class.

5. *WARD's Histology Collection CD-ROM* (WNS; Win/Mac). A collection of microscopic slides that students can use to explore the microanatomy of the organ systems. The CD can be used for presentation or for individual review. Contains 384 images and a comprehensive text file.

Lecture Enhancement Material

To view thumbnails of all the illustrations for Chaper 4, see Appendix B.

Transparencies Index/Media Manager

Figure 4.1	Classification of epithelia.
Figure 4.2	Epithelial tissues.
Figure 4.3	Goblet cells (unicellular exocrine glands).
Figure 4.4	Types of multicellular exocrine glands.
Figure 4.5	Chief modes of secretion in human exocrine glands.
Figure 4.6	Major classes of connective tissue.
Figure 4.7	Proteoglycan aggregate in cartilage.
Figure 4.8	Areolar connective tissue: A prototype (model) connective tissue.
Figure 4.9	Connective tissues.
Figure 4.10	Nervous tissue.
Figure 4.11	Muscle tissues.
Figure 4.12	Classes of membranes.
Figure 4.13	Tissue repair of a nonextensive skin wound: regeneration and fibrosis.

Figure 4.14   Embryonic germ layers and the primary tissue types they produce.

A Closer Look   Development of colon cancer*

Indicates images that are on the Media Manager only.

Answers to End-of-Chapter Questions

Multiple Choice and Matching Question answers appear in Appendix G of the main text.

Short Answer Essay Questions

7. Groups of closely associated cells that are similar in structure and perform a common function. (p. 118)

8. Protection—stratified squamous; absorption—simple columnar; filtration—simple squamous; secretion—simple cuboidal. (pp. 118–124)

9. The covering and lining epithelia are classified on the basis of the shape of the cells and the number of cell layers present. The three common shapes are squamous, cuboidal, and columnar. The classes in terms of cell number are: simple (single layer) or stratified (multiple layers). In some cases, such as with endothelium, it is important to indicate their special location in the body. (p. 120)

10. Merocrine glands (sweat glands) secrete their products by exocytosis; holocrine glands (oil glands) release their products by lysis of the entire cell; apocrine (not believed to be present in humans) release their products by pinching off parts of the cell contents. (p. 126)

11. Binding—areolar; support—cartilage; protection—bone; insulation—adipose; and transportation—blood. (pp. 127, 131–133)

12. Fibroblast; chondroblast; osteoblast. (p. 129)

13. Ground substance—interstitial fluid, proteoglycans, and glycosaminoglycans; fibers—collagen, elastic, reticular. (pp. 127–129)

14. The matrix gets to its position due to secretion of its components by the undifferentiated (blast) cells located throughout the matrix. (p. 129)

15. a. areolar (p. 131)

    b. elastic cartilage (p. 137)

    c. elastic connective tissue (p. 135)

    d. mesenchyme (p. 131)

    e. fibrocartilage (p. 137)

    f. hyaline cartilage (p. 135)

    g. areolar connective tissue (p. 131)

16. The macrophage system is involved in overall body defenses. Its cells are phagocytic and act in the immune response. (p. 130)

17. Neurons are highly specialized cells that generate and conduct nerve impulses, whereas the supporting cells (neuroglial) are nonconducting cells that support, insulate, and protect the neurons. (p. 139)

18. See Fig. 4.11, which illustrates the location, function, and description of the three muscle types.

19. Tissue repair begins during the inflammatory response with organization, during which the blood clot is replaced by granulation tissue. If the wound is small and the damaged tissue is actively mitotic, the tissue will regenerate and cover the fibrous tissue forced to bridge the gap. When a wound is extensive or the damaged tissue amitotic, it is repaired only by using fibrous connective (scar) tissue. (pp. 143–145)

20. Ectoderm—epithelium and nervous; mesoderm—connective, muscle, and epithelium; endoderm—epithelium. (p. 145)
21. During development, skeletal muscle cells fuse with neighboring muscle cells, forming a single, multinucleate cell. (p. 139)

Critical Thinking and Clinical Application Questions

1. No. Cartilage heals slowly because it lacks the blood supply necessary for the healing process. (p. 135)
2. The skin is subjected to almost constant friction, which wears away the surface cells, and is charged with preventing the entry of damaging agents and with preventing water loss from the body. A stratified squamous epithelium with its many layers is much better adapted to stand up to abrasion than is simple epithelium (single layer cells); also the stratified epithelia regenerate more efficiently than simple epithelia. Finally, keratin is a tough waterproofing protein that fills the bill for preventing dessication and acting as a physical barrier to injurious agents. Since a mucosa is a wet membrane, it would be ineffective in preventing water loss from the deeper tissues of the body. (p. 119–120)
3. If ligaments contained more elastic fibers they would be more stretchy; thus joints would be more flexible. However, the function of the ligaments is to bond bones together securely so proper controlled joint movement can occur. More elastic ligaments would result in floppy joints in which the bones involved in the joint would be prone to misalignment and dislocation. (p. 135)
4. Epithelium, because epithelia remain mitotic throughout life. This is not the case for nervous and muscle tissue, and some forms of connective tissue. (p. 144)
5. Whereas "white" fat stores nutrients, "brown" fat uses its nutrient stores to produce heat, and actually weighs less than white fat. Brown fat occurs only in limited areas of the body, whereas white fat is found subcutanueosly anywhere in the body. Keep in mind that brown fat is found only in infants and can not be converted from white fat. (p. 133)
6. Beef tenderloin is skeletal muscle. Cow tripe is digestive smooth muscle. (pp. 139–141)

Suggested Readings

Cormack, D. H. *Essential Histology*. 2nd ed. New York: J. B. Lippincott Company, 2000.

Jones, Peter A. "Cancer: Death and Methylation." *Nature* 409 (6817) (Jan. 2001): 142–144.

McCormick, Frank. "New-age Drug Meets Resistance." *Nature* 412 (6844) (July 2001): 281–282.

Peto, Julian. "Cancer Epidemiology in the Last Century and the Next Decade." *Nature* 411 (6835) (May 2001): 390–395.

Strete, Dennis. *A Color Atlas of Histology*. San Francisco: Benjamin Cummings, 1995.

Travis, J. "Aging Cells May Promote Tumors Nearby." *Science News* 160 (14) (Oct. 2001): 214.

Van De Water, Livingston. "Tissue Engineering: Regulating the Wound Healing Response." *Science and Medicine* 7 (2) (May-Apr. 2000): 6–7.

Vogelstein, Bert and Kinzler, Kenneth W. "Achilles' Heel of Cancer?" *Nature* 412 (6850) (Aug. 2001): 865–866.

The Integumentary System

Objectives

The Skin

1. Discuss the location and functions of the hypodermis.
2. Describe the five cells and layers that make up the epidermis.
3. Discuss the two layers of the dermis.
4. List the factors that contribute to skin color.

Appendages of the Skin

5. Compare and contrast eccrine and apocrine glands.
6. Describe the types of modified sweat glands found in the body.
7. Discuss sebaceous glands. How do they differ from sudoriferous glands?
8. Describe the structure of a nail.

9. List the parts of a hair follicle and explain their functions.
10. Name the regions of a hair. Describe the types of hairs, their locations, and the changes hair goes through throughout life.

Functions of the Integumentary System

11. Discuss the functions of the skin.

Homeostatic Imbalances of Skin

12. Name the characteristics of the three main types of skin cancer.
13. Explain why a burn is life threatening. Discuss the classifications of burns.

Developmental Aspects of the Integumentary System

14. Identify the changes that occur in the skin from birth until death.

Suggested Lecture Outline

I. The Skin (pp. 152–157; Fig. 5.1)

A. The hypodermis, also called the superficial fascia, is subcutaneous tissue beneath the skin consisting mostly of adipose tissue that anchors the skin to underlying muscle, allows skin to slide over muscle, and acts as a shock absorber and insulator.

B. Epidermis (pp. 152–155; Fig. 5.2)

1. The epidermis is a keratinized stratified squamous epithelium.
2. Cells of the Epidermis
   a. The majority of epidermal cells are keratinocytes that produce a fibrous protective protein called keratin.
   b. Melanocytes are epithelial cells that synthesize the pigment melanin.
   c. Langerhans' cells, or epidermal dendritic cells, are macrophages that help activate the immune system.
   d. Merkel cells are associated with sensory nerve endings.

3. Layers of the Epidermis
    a. The stratum basale (basal layer) is the deepest epidermal layer and is the site of mitosis.
    b. The stratum spinosum (prickly layer) is several cell layers thick and contains keratinocytes, melanin granules, and the highest concentration of Langerhans' cells.
    c. The stratum granulosum (granular layer) contains keratinocytes that are undergoing a great deal of physical changes, turning them into the tough outer cells of the epidermis.
    d. The stratum lucidum (clear layer) is found only in thick skin and is composed of dead keratinocytes.
    e. The stratum corneum (horny layer) is the outermost protective layer of the epidermis composed of a thick layer of dead keratinocytes.

C. Dermis (pp. 155–157)
    1. The dermis is composed of strong, flexible connective tissue.
    2. The dermis is made up of two layers: the thin, superficial papillary layer is highly vascularized areolar connective tissue containing a woven mat of collagen and elastin fibers; and the reticular layer, accounting for 80% of the thickness of the dermis, is dense irregular connective tissue.

D. Skin color is determined by three pigments: melanin, hemoglobin, and carotene (p. 157).

II. Appendages of the Skin (pp. 158–163)

A. Sweat (Sudoriferous) Glands (p. 158; Fig. 5.3)
    1. Eccrine sweat glands, or merocrine sweat glands, produce true sweat, are the most numerous of the sweat glands, and are particularly abundant on the palms of the hands, soles of the feet, and forehead.
    2. Apocrine sweat glands are confined to the axillary and anogenital areas and produce true sweat with the addition of fatty substances and proteins.
    3. Ceruminous glands are modified sweat glands found lining the ear canal that secrete ear wax, or cerumen.
    4. Mammary glands are modified sweat glands found in the breasts that secrete milk.

B. Sebaceous (Oil) Glands (p. 159; Fig. 5.3)
    1. Sebaceous glands are simple alveolar glands found all over the body except the palms of the hands and soles of the feet that secrete sebum, an oily secretion.
    2. The sebaceous glands function as holocrine glands, secreting their product into a hair follicle or to a pore on the surface of the skin.
    3. Secretion by sebaceous glands is stimulated by hormones.

C. Hairs and Hair Follicles (pp. 159–163; Figs. 5.4–5.5)
    1. Hairs, or pili, are flexible strands produced by hair follicles that consist of dead, keratinized cells.
        a. The main regions of a hair are the shaft and the root.
        b. A hair has three layers of keratinized cells: the inner core is the medulla, the middle layer is the cortex, and the outer layer is the cuticle.
        c. Hair pigments (melanin of different colors) are made by melanocytes at the base of the hair follicle.

      2. Structure of a Hair Follicle

         a. Hair follicles fold down from the epidermis into the dermis and occasionally into the hypodermis.

         b. The deep end of a hair follicle is expanded, forming a hair bulb, which is surrounded by a knot of sensory nerve endings called a hair follicle receptor, or root hair plexus.

         c. The wall of a hair follicle is composed of an outer connective tissue root sheath, a thickened basement membrane called a glossy membrane, and an inner epithelial root sheath.

         d. Associated with each hair follicle is a bundle of smooth muscle cells called an arrector pili muscle.

      3. Types and Growth of Hair

         a. Hairs come in various sizes and shapes, but can be classified as vellus or terminal.

         b. Hair growth and density are influenced by many factors, such as nutrition and hormones.

         c. The rate of hair growth varies from one body region to another and with sex and age.

      4. Hair Thinning and Baldness

         a. After age 40 hair is not replaced as quickly as it is lost, which leads to hair thinning and some degree of balding, or alopecia, in both sexes.

         b. Male pattern baldness, which is a type of true, or frank, balding, is a genetically determined, sex-influenced condition.

   D. Nails (p. 163; Fig. 5.6)

      1. A nail is a scalelike modification of the epidermis that forms a clear, protective covering.

      2. Nails are made up of hard keratin and have a free edge, a body, and a proximal root.

III. Functions of the Integumentary System (pp. 163–165)

   A. Protection

      1. Chemical barriers include skin secretions and melanin.

      2. Physical or mechanical barriers are provided by the continuity of the skin, and the hardness of the keratinized cells.

      3. Biological barriers include the Langerhans' cells of the epidermis, the macrophages of the dermis, and the DNA itself.

   B. The skin plays an important role in body temperature regulation by using the sweat glands of the skin to cool the body, and constriction of dermal capillaries to prevent heat loss.

   C. Cutaneous sensation is made possible by the placement of cutaneous sensory receptors, which are part of the nervous system, in the layers of the skin.

   D. The skin provides the metabolic function of making vitamin D when it is exposed to sunlight.

   E. The skin may act as a blood reservoir by holding up to 5% of the body's blood supply, which may be diverted to other areas of the body should the need arise.

   F. Limited amounts of nitrogenous wastes are excreted through the skin.

IV. Homeostatic Imbalances of Skin (pp. 165–170)

   A. Skin Cancer (pp. 165–166; Fig. 5.7)

      1. Basal cell carcinoma is the least malignant and the most common skin cancer.

      2. Squamous cell carcinoma tends to grow rapidly and metastasize if not removed.

      3. Melanoma is the most dangerous of the skin cancers because it is highly metastatic and resistant to chemotherapy.

   B. Burns (pp. 166–170; Fig. 5.8)

      1. A burn is tissue damage inflicted by intense heat, electricity, radiation, or certain chemicals, all of which denature cell proteins and cause cell death to infected areas.

      2. The most immediate threat to a burn patient is dehydration and electrolyte imbalance due to fluid loss.

      3. After the first 24 hours has passed, the threat to a burn patient becomes infection to the wound site.

      4. Burns are classified according to their severity.

         a. First-degree burns involve damage only to the epidermis.

         b. Second-degree burns injure the epidermis and the upper region of the dermis.

         c. Third-degree burns involve the entire thickness of the skin.

V. Developmental Aspects of the Integumentary System (pp. 170–171)

   A. The epidermis develops from the embryonic ectoderm, and the dermis and the hypodermis develop from the mesoderm.

   B. By the end of the fourth month of development the skin is fairly well formed.

   C. During infancy and childhood, the skin thickens and more subcutaneous fat is deposited.

   D. During adolescence, the skin and hair become oilier as sebaceous glands are activated.

   E. The skin reaches its optimal appearance when we reach our 20s and 30s; after that time the skin starts to show the effects of cumulative environmental exposures.

   F. As old age approaches, the rate of epidermal cell replacement slows and the skin thins, becoming more prone to bruising and other types of injuries.

Cross References

Additional information on topics covered in Chapter 5 can be found in the chapters listed below.

1. Chapter 3: Desmosomes

2. Chapter 4: Stratified squamous epithelium, keratinized; basement membrane; loose (areolar) connective tissue; dense irregular connective tissue; fibers in matrix of connective tissue; simple coiled tubular glands; simple branched alveolar glands; merocrine glands; holocrine glands

3. Chapter 13: Cutaneous sensation and reflex activity

4. Chapter 15: Sebaceous and sudoriferous glands of the ear canal

5. Chapter 21: Organ and tissue transplants and prevention of rejection; mechanical and chemical nonspecific defense mechanisms
6. Chapter 23: Jaundice and the buildup of bilirubin
7. Chapter 24: Body temperature regulation
8. Chapter 28: Effects of androgens

Laboratory Correlations

1. Marieb, E. N. *Human Anatomy & Physiology Laboratory Manual: Cat and Fetal Pig Versions*. Eighth Edition Updates. Benjamin Cummings, 2006.

   Exercise 7: The Integumentary System
   Exercise 8: Classification of Covering and Lining Membranes

2. Marieb, E. N. *Human Anatomy & Physiology Laboratory Manual: Main Version*. Seventh Edition Update. Benjamin Cummings, 2006.

   Exercise 7: The Integumentary System
   Exercise 8: Classification of Covering and Lining Membranes

Histology Slides for the Life Sciences

Available through Benjamin Cummings, an imprint of Pearson Education, Inc. To order, contact your local Benjamin Cummings sales representative.

Slide 43   Meissner's Corpusle in a Dermal Papilla.
Slide 44   Free Dendritic Endings at the Dermal-Epidermal Junction.
Slide 45   Pacinian Corpuscle in the Hypodermis.

Lecture Hints

1. The strata basale and spinosum are often referred to collectively as the growing layers (stratum germinativum). Some authors consider the stratum germinativum to be only the stratum basale. Students are easily confused if terminology is not consistent between lecture, text, and lab test.
2. Stress that the hypodermis is not a skin layer, but is actually the superficial fascia beneath the skin. Point out that there is a deep fascia beneath the hypodermis under the skin that is covered later in Chapter 9.
3. The hypodermis (superficial fascia) is an important location of fat storage that insulates the body. This layer is more prominent in females than males, resulting in a softer feel to the touch. This softer skin is considered a secondary sex characteristic of the female.
4. Discuss the activity of melanocytes, melanin production, and degree of ultraviolet radiation. Point out the genetic basis of melanocyte activity and the geographic distribution of ancestral humans as an explanation for racial variation. Explain the effect of the degree of exposure to UV radiation and tanning in individuals.
5. During lab, students often try to locate and identify the stratum lucidum in all skin slides. Stress that this layer of the epidermis is present only in thick skin.
6. Explain that the skin plays a role in regulating body temperature by evaporation of sweat and by controlling blood flow through dermal blood vessels.
7. Some sebaceous glands are not associated with hair follicles and open directly onto the skin surface. Examples include the sebaceous glands of the skin, lips, and eyelids (tarsal glands).

8. Actual contact with the environment is through a layer of dead cells (rather than living). This specialization was critical for the evolution of life forms that could survive in a terrestrial environment.

Activities/Demonstrations

1. Audio-visual materials listed under Multimedia in the Classroom and Lab.
2. Show the students a picture of a heavily wrinkled person. Ask them to list all the factors that have contributed to the skin deterioration seen.
3. Provide small glass plates and instruct students to observe the change in the color of their skin while pressing the heel of their hand firmly against the glass. Ask them to explain the color change, and what would happen to the skin if the pressure were prolonged.
4. Have a small fan operating. As students file into the classroom, spray their arm or hand with water. Ask them to describe the sensation as the water evaporates from the skin, and to explain why evaporation of water (or sweat) is important to temperature homeostasis. Repeat the demonstration with alcohol and ask why the cooling effect is greater.
5. Use 3-D models of skin to illustrate layers and strata.
6. Use a microprojector and microscope slides of skin to illustrate layers. Use slides of skin from the scalp and palm to contrast the differences in the layers.

Critical Thinking/Discussion Topics

1. What role does the skin play in the regulation of body temperature?
2. Why exactly can animals with thick fur, such as Alaskan huskies, resist extremely cold temperatures?
3. Humans are often called the "naked apes." Since we have extensive hair follicles all over our body, why do you suppose we lack body hair?
4. If the skin acts as a barrier to most substances, how can it initiate an allergic response to such things as poison ivy?
5. Many organisms such as snakes, insects, and lobsters shed their "skin" periodically. How does this compare to the process taking place in humans?
6. The air is 80°F and the lake temperature is 70°F. Why do you first feel cold when you enter the water? Why do you feel chilled when exiting the water?
7. Why does axillary hair not grow as long as hair on the scalp? How long would scalp hair grow if it were not cut?
8. Discuss the advantages and disadvantages of using the drug minoxidil for stimulating hair regrowth in bald men.
9. Which structures located in the dermis are of epidermal origin?
10. When fair-skinned individuals go outside on a cold windy day, their skin turns "white" and after a time turns "red." Explain.
11. Nancy has a dry skin condition and prefers to take her bath in the evening. Would it be more effective for her to apply a skin care lotion such as Keri lotion in the morning or in the evening after taking a bath? Why?
12. Why is it more difficult to get a suntan during the winter months even though the sun is closer to the earth during this season?
13. Individuals living in Ohio may be able to go out into the sun for three hours and not burn, but if they go to Florida during spring break, they may get a sunburn after only two hours. Why?

14. Describe the difference between the A and B types of ultraviolet rays relative to skin damage.
15. Why does a suntan eventually fade?
16. Other than to reduce bleeding, why are wounds sutured together?

Library Research Topics

1. Explore the literature on the latest techniques and materials such as test-tube skin, synthetic skin, and heterograft skin used in skin grafting.
2. The long-term effects of sunburn seem to include severe wrinkling of the skin and skin cancer. What are the latest statistics on this problem and what has been done to correct it?
3. What are the latest therapies for baldness?
4. Although our skin is a "barrier" to microbes, prepare a list of microbes, such as bacteria, yeast, fungi, protozoans, and arthropods, that may reside on or in our skin.
5. Accutane (Isotretinoin) is a prescriptive drug approved in the early 1980s for treatment of severe cystic acne. Is this drug safe to use during pregnancy?
6. Student assignment: Look up the signs and symptoms of basal cell carcinoma, squamous cell carcinoma, and malignant melanoma for class discussion.

Multimedia in the Classroom and Lab

Online Resources for Students

The
Anatomy & Physiology Place
www.anatomyandphysiology.com

MyA&P
www.myaandp.com

The following shows the organization of the Chapter Guide page in both the Anatomy & Physiology Place and MyA&P™. The Chapter Guide organizes all the chapter-specific online media resources for Chapter 5 in one convenient location, with e-book links to each section of the textbook. Please note that both sites also give you access to other general A&P resources, like InterActive Physiology®, PhysioEx 6.0™, Anatomy 360°, Flashcards, a Glossary, a Histology Tutorial, and much more.

Objectives
Section 5.1 The Skin (pp. 152–158)
Art Labeling Activity: Skin Structure (Fig. 5.1, p. 153)
Memory: Cutaneous Membrane Components
Memory: Integumentary System Components
Section 5.2 Appendages of the Skin (pp. 158–163)
Art Labeling Activity: Structure of a Hair Follicle (Fig. 5.5, p. 161)
Art Labeling Activity: Structure of a Nail (Fig. 5.6, p. 163)
Section 5.3 Functions of the Integumentary System (pp. 163–165)
Section 5.4 Homeostatic Imbalances of Skin (pp. 165–167, 170)
Case Study: Burns
Case Study: Athlete's Foot
Case Study: Skin Cancer
Section 5.5 Developmental Aspects of the Integumentary System (pp. 170–171)

Chapter Summary
Self-Study Quizzes
Art Labeling Quiz
Matching Quiz
Multiple-Choice Quiz (Level I)
Multiple-Choice Quiz (Level II)
True-False Quiz
Crossword Puzzles
Crossword Puzzle 5.1
Crossword Puzzle 5.2

Media

See Guide to Audio-Visual Resources in Appendix A for key to AV distributors.

Slides

1. *Systems of the Human Body—The Skin and Its Function Set* (CBS)
2. *The Skin and Its Appendages Set* (CBS)
3. *Integument Types Set* (CBS)

Video

1. *Melanoma: Winning the Battle Against Skin Cancer* (FHS; 17 min., 1996). Examines the problem of skin cancer from its roots in overexposure to the sun to treatment that prevents recurrences.
2. *The New Living Body: Skin* (FHS; 20 min., 1995). Contains live action video with current imaging technology. Gives a glimpse into the inner workings of the human body. Provides an interesting and informative presentation for an entire class.
3. *Plastic and Reconstructive Surgery* (FHS; 19 min.). This video explains some of the more common cosmetic surgical procedures and the use of computer-generated models that aid in the design.
4. *The Senses: Skin Deep* (FHS; 26 min., 1984). Reviews sense receptors, taste buds, touch sensors, and olfactory cells. Written by a team of internationally recognized medical specialists. The complex world beneath the skin is recreated.
5. *Virtual Reality in Medicine* (FHS; 30 min., 1992). This program presents surgeons using virtual reality in training. It shows plastic surgeons using computers to reconstruct faces. Gives the student a glimpse of new technology in medicine.

Lecture Enhancement Material

To view thumbnails of all the illustrations for Chapter 5, see Appendix B.

Transparencies Index/Media Manager

Figure 5.1   Skin structure.
Figure 5.2   The main structural features in skin epidermis.
Figure 5.3   Cutaneous glands.
Figure 5.4   Hair shaft emerging from a follicle at the epidermal surface.
Figure 5.5   Structure of a hair and hair follicle.
Figure 5.6   Structure of a nail.
Figure 5.7   Photographs of skin cancers.

Figure 5.8   Estimating the extent and severity of burns.

A Closer Look   Wrinkle Wrinkle Go Away—Or I'll Shoot You (with Botox)*

Indicates images that are on the Media Manager only.

Answers to End-of-Chapter Questions

Multiple Choice and Matching Question answers appear in Appendix G of the main text.

Short Answer Essay Questions

14. Cells of the stratum spinosum are called prickle cells because of their spiky shape in fixed tissues; granules of keratohyalin and lamellated granules appear in the cells of the stratum granulosum. (p. 154)

15. Generally not. Most "bald" men have fine vellus hairs that look like peach fuzz in the "bald" areas. (p. 162)

16. Due to the lack of adipose tissue, there is a decrease in the skin's ability to act as an insulator. (p. 152)

17. The skin acts as a mechanical barrier to water and infectious agents and as a chemical barrier to absorb the UV light. (p. 164)

18. First-degree burns affect only the epidermis; second-degree burns affect down to the dermis; and third-degree burns affect down to the subcutaneous tissue and muscle. (p. 170)

19. Hair formation begins with an active growth phase, followed by a resting phase. After the resting phase a new hair forms to replace the old one. Factors that affect growth cycles include nutrition, hormones, local dermal blood flow, body region, gender, age, genetic factors, physical or emotional trauma, excessive radiation, and certain drugs. Factors that affect hair texture include hormones, body region, genetic factors, and age. (p. 162)

20. Cyanosis is a condition in which the skin of Caucasians turns blue due to improperly oxygenated hemoglobin. (p. 157)

21. Wrinkling is due to the loss of elasticity of the skin, along with the loss of the subcutaneous tissue, and is hastened by prolonged exposure to wind and sun. (p. 171)

22. a. A whitehead is formed by blockage of the duct of a sebaceous gland with sebum. When this sebum oxidizes, it produces a blackhead. When a blocked sebaceous gland becomes infected, it produces a pimple. (p. 159)

    b. Noninfectious dandruff is the normal shedding of the stratum corneum of the scalp. (p. 155)

    c. Greasy hair and a shiny nose both result from the secretion of sebum onto the skin. (p. 159)

    d. Stretch marks represent small tears in the dermis, as the skin is stretched by obesity or pregnancy. (p. 157)

    e. A freckle is a small area of pigmentation in the epidermis, caused by an accumulation of melanin. (p. 157)

    f. Fingerprints are films of sweat derived from sweat glands that open along the epidermal ridges of the palm. (p. 155)

23. (a) Porphyria. Porphyria victims lack the ability to form the heme of Hb. Buildup of intermediate by-products (porphyrins) in the blood cause lesions in sun-exposed skin. Dracula was said to have drunk blood and to have shunned the daylight. (p. 171)

24. Stratum corneum cells are dead. By definition, cancer cells are rapidly dividing cells. (p. 155)

25. Nail body: the visible attached portion of the nail. Nail root: the embedded portion of the nail. Nail bed: the epidermis that extends beneath the nail. Nail matrix: the proximal, thickened portion of the nail bed responsible for nail growth. Eponychium: the cuticle. If the matrix is damaged the nail may not grow back or may grow back distorted. In this case the nail probably will not grow back since everything including the matrix was lost. (p. 163; Fig. 5.6)

26. See Figure 5.8. (p. 167) (a) 18% posterior trunk + 4.5% (Right buttock*) + 4.5% (Left buttock) = 27%. *buttock is approximate only (b) Entire lower limb = 36% (c) Entire front (anterior) left upper limb = 4.5%

Critical Thinking and Clinical Application Questions

1. His long-term overexposure to ultraviolet radiation in sunlight is considered to be a risk factor for the development of skin cancer. In addition, moles or pigmented spots that show asymmetry (A), border irregularity (B), color variation (C), and a diameter greater than 6 mm (D) are all signs of a possible malignant melanoma. He should seek immediate medical attention. If it is a malignant melanoma, the chance for survival is not high, but early detection increases the survival rate. (p. 166)

2. The two most important problems encountered clinically with a victim of third-degree burns are a loss of body fluids resulting in dehydration and an electrolyte imbalance, and the risk of infection. Intact skin effectively blocks not only the diffusion of water and water-soluble substances out of the body, but acts as a barrier limiting the invasion of various microorganisms. (p. 167)

3. Chronic physical irritation or inflammation can lead to excessive hair growth in the region affected due to an increase in blood flow to the area. (p. 162)

4. The appendectomy incision ran parallel to the less dense "lines of cleavage" that separate bundles of collagen fiber in the dermis. The gallbladder incision cut across them. (p. 156)

5. As long as the second-degree burns were not too extensive, which might lead to infection, she should not need skin grafts, and should expect to be fully healed within a few weeks. (p. 170)

Suggested Readings

Christensen, Damaris. "Hair Today, Gone Tomorrow?" *Science News* 160 (16) (Oct. 2001): 254–255.

Glausiusz, Josie. "A Sunscreen for Our Delicate Genes." *Discover* 22 (3) (March 2001): 13.

Karow, Julia. "Skin So Fixed." *Scientific American* 284 (3) (March 2001): 21.

Kirchweger, Gina. "Black and White." *Discover* 22 (2) (Feb. 2001): 32–33.

Krueger, James G. "Treating Psoriasis with Biologic Agents." *Science and Medicine* 8 (3) (May/June 2002): 150–161.

Nizet, V. et al. "Innate Antimicrobial Peptide Protects the Skin from Invasive Bacterial Infection." *Nature* 414 (Nov. 2001): 454–457.

Pins, George D. "An Analog of the Basal Lamina." *Science and Medicine* 7 (3) (2000): 6–7.

Rusting, Ricki L. "Hair: Why it Grows, Why it Stops." *Scientific American* 284 (6) (Oct. 2001): 70–79.

Travis, J. "Human Sweat Packs a Germ-Killing Punch." *Science News* 160 (19) (Nov. 2001): 292.

Wright, Karen. "Skeeter Beaters." *Discover* 22 (8) (Aug. 2001): 20–21.

6

Bones
and Skeletal Tissues

Objectives

Skeletal Cartilages

1. Describe the structure of cartilage.
2. List the three types of skeletal cartilage, their functions, and locations.

Classification of Bones

3. Name the axial and appendicular groups of bones of the skeleton.
4. Describe the shape classes of bones, and give examples of each.

Functions of Bones

5. List the functions of bones.

Bone Structure

6. Name the various types of bone markings.
7. Describe the anatomical structure of typical long, short, flat, and irregular bones.
8. List the locations of red bone marrow in the bones of infants, children, and adults.
9. Describe the anatomy of compact and spongy bone. List all structural elements.
10. Explain the organic and inorganic composition of bone, and the function of each.

Bone Development

11. Describe the processes of intramembranous and endochondral ossification, and list the bones that are formed by each process.
12. Describe the processes of lengthwise bone growth and growth in width during postnatal development.

13. Discuss the effects of growth hormone, thyroxine, and sex hormones testosterone and estrogen on bone growth.

Bone Homeostasis: Remodeling and Repair

14. Discuss the uses and mechanisms of bone remodeling, bone depositions, and bone resorption in the body.
15. Explain the hormonal mechanism controlling bone remodeling.
16. Discuss the role of mechanical stress on bone remodeling.
17. List the types and characteristics of bone fractures.
18. Describe the events of bone repair.

Homeostatic Imbalances of Bone

19. Identify the causes and effects of bone disorders: osteomalacia, rickets, osteoporosis, and Paget's disease.
20. Discuss the role of hormones in the development of osteoporosis.

Developmental Aspects of Bone: Timing of Events

21. Explain the timing of primary and secondary ossification of the skeleton, and the role of epiphyseal plates in bone growth.
22. Describe the changes in bone deposition and bone resorption that occur during different stages of life.

Suggested Lecture Outline

I. Skeletal Cartilages (p. 176; Fig. 6.1)

A. Basic Structure, Types, and Locations (p. 176; Fig. 6.1)

1. Skeletal cartilages are made from cartilage, surrounded by a layer of dense irregular connective tissue called the perichondrium.
2. Hyaline cartilage is the most abundant skeletal cartilage, and includes the articular, costal, respiratory, and nasal cartilages.
3. Elastic cartilages are more flexible than hyaline, and are located only in the external ear and the epiglottis of the larynx.
4. Fibrocartilage is located in areas that must withstand a great deal of pressure or stretch, such as the cartilages of the knee and the intervertebral discs.

B. Growth of Cartilage (p. 176)

1. Appositional growth results in outward expansion due to the production of cartilage matrix on the outside of the tissue.
2. Interstitial growth results in expansion from within the cartilage matrix due to division of lacunae-bound chondrocytes and secretion of matrix.

II. Classification of Bones (pp. 176–178; Figs. 6.1–6.2)

A. There are two main divisions of the bones of the skeleton: the axial skeleton, consisting of the skull, vertebral column, and rib cage; and the appendicular skeleton, consisting of the bones of the upper and lower limbs, and the girdles that attach them to the axial skeleton (pp. 176–177; Fig. 6.1).

B. Shape (pp. 177–178; Fig. 6.2)

1. Long bones are longer than they are wide, have a definite shaft and two ends, and consist of all limb bones except patellas, carpals, and tarsals.
2. Short bones are somewhat cube-shaped and include the carpals and tarsals.
3. Flat bones are thin, flattened, often curved bones that include most skull bones, the sternum, scapulae, and ribs.
4. Irregular bones have complicated shapes that do not fit in any other class, such as the vertebrae and coxae.

III. Functions of Bones (pp. 178–179)

A. Bones support the body and cradle the soft organs, protect vital organs, allow movement, store minerals such as calcium and phosphate, and house hematopoietic tissue in specific marrow cavities.

IV. Bone Structure (pp. 179–184; Figs. 6.3–6.6; Table 6.1)

A. Gross Anatomy (pp. 179–181; Fig. 6.3, 6.4; Table 6.1)

1. Bone markings are projections, depressions, and openings found on the surface of bones that function as sites of muscle, ligament, and tendon attachment, as joint surfaces, and as openings for the passage of blood vessels and nerves.
2. Bone Textures: Compact and Spongy Bone
   a. All bone has a dense outer layer consisting of compact bone that appears smooth and solid.
   b. Internal to compact bone is spongy bone, which consists of honeycomb, needle-like, or flat pieces, called trabeculae.

3. Structure of a Typical Long Bone
    a. Long bones have a tubular bone shaft, consisting of a bone collar surrounding a hollow medullary cavity, which is filled with yellow bone marrow in adults.
    b. Epiphyses are at the ends of the bone, and consist of internal spongy bone covered by an outer layer of compact bone.
    c. The epiphyseal line is located between the epiphyses and diaphysis, and is a remnant of the epiphyseal plate.
    d. The external surface of the bone is covered by the periosteum.
    e. The internal surface of the bone is lined by a connective tissue membrane called the endosteum.
4. Structure of Short, Flat, and Irregular Bones
    a. Short, flat, and irregular bones consist of thin plates of periosteum-covered compact bone on the outside, and endosteum-covered spongy bone inside, which houses bone marrow between the trabeculae.
5. Location of Hematopoietic Tissue in Bones
    a. Hematopoietic tissue of bones, red bone marrow, is located within the trabecular cavities of the spongy bone in flat bones, and in the epiphyses of long bones.
    b. Red bone marrow is found in all flat bones, epiphyses, and medullary cavities of infants, but in adults, distribution is restricted to flat bones and the proximal epiphyses of the humerus and femur.
B. Microscopic Anatomy of Bone (pp. 181–182; Figs. 6.5, 6.6)
    1. The structural unit of compact bone is the osteon, or Haversian system, which consists of concentric tubes of bone matrix (the lamellae) surrounding a central Haversian canal that serves as a passageway for blood vessels and nerves.
        a. Perforating, or Volkmann's, canals lie at right angles to the long axis of the bone, and connect the blood and nerve supply of the periosteum to that of the central canals and medullary cavity.
        b. Osteocytes occupy lacunae at the junctions of the lamellae, and are connected to each other and the central canal via a series of hair-like channels, canaliculi.
        c. Circumferential lamellae are located just beneath the periosteum, extending around the entire circumference of the bone, while interstitial lamellae lie between intact osteons, filling the spaces in between.
    2. Spongy bone lacks osteons but has trabeculae that align along lines of stress, which contain irregular lamellae.
C. Chemical Composition of Bone (pp. 182–184)
    1. Organic components of bone include cells (osteoblasts, osteocytes, and osteoclasts) and osteoid (ground substance and collagen fibers), which contribute to the flexibility and tensile strength of bone.
    2. Inorganic components make up 65% of bone by mass, and consist of hydroxyapatite, a mineral salt that is largely calcium phosphate, which accounts for the hardness and compression resistance of bone.

V. Bone Development (pp. 184–187; Figs. 6.7–6.10)

A. Formation of the Bony Skeleton (pp. 184–186; Figs. 6.7, 6.8)

1. Intramembranous ossification forms membrane bone from fibrous connective tissue membranes, and results in the cranial bones and clavicles.

2. In endochondral ossification bone tissue replaces hyaline cartilage, forming all bones below the skull except for the clavicles.

   a. Initially, osteoblasts secrete osteoid, creating a bone collar around the diaphysis of the hyaline cartilage model.

   b. Cartilage in the center of the diaphysis calcifies and deteriorates, forming cavities.

   c. The periosteal bud invades the internal cavities and spongy bone forms around the remaining fragments of hyaline cartilage.

   d. The diaphysis elongates as the cartilage in the epiphyses continues to lengthen and a medullary cavity forms through the action of osteoclasts within the center of the diaphysis.

   e. The epiphyses ossify shortly after birth through the development of secondary ossification centers.

B. Postnatal Bone Growth (pp. 186–187; Figs. 6.9–6.10)

1. Growth in length of long bones occurs at the ossification zone through the rapid division of the upper cells in the columns of chondrocytes, calcification and deterioration of cartilage at the bottom of the columns, and subsequent replacement by bone tissue.

2. Growth in width, or thickness, occurs through appositional growth due to deposition of bone matrix by osteoblasts beneath the periosteum.

3. Hormonal Regulation of Bone Growth

   a. During infancy and childhood, the most important stimulus of epiphyseal plate activity is growth hormone from the anterior pituitary, whose effects are modulated by thyroid hormone.

   b. At puberty, testosterone and estrogen promote a growth spurt, but ultimately induct the closure of the epiphyseal plate.

VI. Bone Homeostasis: Remodeling and Repair (pp. 187–193; Figs. 6.10–6.13; Table 6.2)

A. Bone Remodeling (pp. 188–190; Figs. 6.10–6.12)

1. In adult skeletons, bone remodeling is balanced bone deposit and removal, bone deposit occurs at a greater rate when bone is injured, and bone resorption allows minerals of degraded bone matrix to move into the blood.

2. Control of Remodeling

   a. The hormonal mechanism is mostly used to maintain blood calcium homeostasis, and balances activity of parathyroid hormone and calcitonin.

   b. In response to mechanical stress and gravity, bone grows or remodels in ways that allow it to withstand the stresses it experiences.

B. Bone Repair (pp. 190–193; Fig. 6.13; Table 6.2)

1. Fractures are breaks in bones, and are classified by: the position of the bone ends after fracture, completeness of break, orientation of the break relative to the long axis of the bone, and whether the bone ends penetrate the skin.

2. Repair of fractures involves four major stages: hematoma formation, fibrocartilaginous callus formation, bony callus formation, and remodeling of the bony callus.

VII. Homeostatic Imbalances of Bone (pp. 193–198; Fig. 6.14)

A. Osteomalacia and Rickets (p. 193)

1. Osteomalacia includes a number of disorders in adults in which the bone is inadequately mineralized.

2. Rickets is inadequate mineralization of bones in children caused by insufficient calcium or vitamin D deficiency.

B. Osteoporosis refers to a group of disorders in which the rate of bone resorption exceeds the rate of formation (pp. 193–195, Fig. 6.14).

1. Bones have normal bone matrix, but bone mass is reduced and the bones become more porous and lighter increasing the likelihood of fractures.

2. Older women are especially vulnerable to osteoporosis, due to the decline in estrogen after menopause.

3. Other factors that contribute to osteoporosis include a petite body form, insufficient exercise or immobility, a diet poor in calcium and vitamin D, abnormal vitamin D receptors, smoking, and certain hormone-related conditions.

C. Paget's disease is characterized by excessive bone deposition and resorption, with the resulting bone abnormally high in spongy bone. It is a localized condition that results in deformation of the affected bone (pp. 195–198).

VIII. Developmental Aspects of Bones: Timing of Events (p. 198; Fig. 6.15)

A. The skeleton derives from embryonic mesenchymal cells, with ossification occurring at precise times. Most long bones have obvious primary ossification centers by 12 weeks gestation.

B. At birth, most bones are well ossified, except for the epiphyses, which form secondary ossification centers.

C. Throughout childhood, bone growth exceeds bone resorption; in young adults, these processes are in balance; in old age, resorption exceeds formation.

Cross References

Additional information on topics covered in Chapter 6 can be found in the chapters listed below.

1. Chapter 2: Calcium salts

2. Chapter 4: Bone (osseous tissue); chondroblasts; collagen fibers; fibroblasts; fibrocartilage; hyaline cartilage; proteoglycans

3. Chapter 7: Individual bones that make up the skeleton; identifying marks of individual bones

4. Chapter 8: Articular cartilage and joint structure

5. Chapter 16: Gigantism and dwarfism as related to bone growth and length; effects of parathyroid hormone and calcitonin on bone homeostasis

6. Chapter 17: Hematopoietic tissue

Laboratory Correlations

1. Marieb, E. N. *Human Anatomy & Physiology Laboratory Manual: Cat and Fetal Pig Versions*. Eighth Edition Updates. Benjamin Cummings, 2006.

   Exercise 9: Overview of the Skeleton—Classification and Structure of Bones and Cartilages

2. Marieb, E. N. *Human Anatomy & Physiology Laboratory Manual: Main Version*. Seventh Edition Update. Benjamin Cummings, 2006.

   Exercise 9: Overview of the Skeleton—Classification and Structure of Bones and Cartilages

Histology Slides for the Life Sciences

Available through Benjamin Cummings, an imprint of Pearson Education, Inc. To order, contact your local Benjamin Cummings sales representative.

Slide 23   Hyaline Cartilage, Trachea.

Slide 24   Fibrocartilage, Intervertebral Disk.

Slide 25   Bone (Osseous) Tissue, Ground Bone.

Slide 46   Cartilage-Bone Junction, Toe Bone.

Slide 47   Epiphyseal Plate of a Bone.

Slide 48   Endochondral Ossification.

Lecture Hints

1. Students often erroneously distinguish between long and short bones on the basis of size. Stress that the distinction is based on shape, not size.
2. Emphasize the difference between the epiphyseal plate and epiphyseal line.
3. Point out that the perichondrium does not cover the articular cartilages.
4. Emphasize the difference between red and yellow marrow.
5. Point out that osteocytes in Haversian systems are not isolated from each other, but tied together by canaliculi.
6. Compare and contrast location and function of osteocytes, osteoblasts, and osteoclasts.
7. Point out that long bone growth ends sooner in females (18 years) than males (21 years).
8. Emphasize that bones can be remodeled or grow appositionally, even after longitudinal growth has ceased.
9. Point out that greenstick fractures are more common in children, since their bones contain a higher proportion of organic matrix and are more flexible.
10. Distinguish between a simple (closed) and a compound (open) fracture.
11. Emphasize that bones must be mechanically stressed to remain healthy. Physical activity pulls on bones, resulting in increased structure. Inactivity results in bone atrophy.

Activities/Demonstrations

1. Audio-visual materials listed under Multimedia in the Classroom and Lab.
2. As an analogy, hold a bundle of uncooked spaghetti to illustrate the arrangement of osteons within compact bone.
3. Break a green twig to illustrate a greenstick fracture. Then contrast with a dry twig.
4. Obtain a sectioned long bone, such as a femur, to illustrate major parts of a bone. A fresh sectioned bone could be used to illustrate the periosteum and the difference between red and yellow marrow.
5. Obtain a fetal skeleton to illustrate early stages of bone development.

6. Illustrate the chemical nature of bone tissue by placing one chicken bone in nitric acid and another in the oven. The nitric acid will leach out the calcium salts and the oven will break down the organic matter.

7. Obtain X rays of young children, teenagers, and adults to illustrate changes in the epiphyseal plate.

8. Obtain X rays of various types of fractures. If possible, obtain X rays that illustrate healing stages following the fracture.

9. Obtain a 3-D model of a Haversian system to illustrate the microscopic characteristics of bone.

10. Obtain a cleared and stained pig embryo to show the development of osseous tissue (Carolina Biological).

Critical Thinking/Discussion Topics

1. Explore the statement, "Multiple pregnancies will result in the mother losing all the enamel from her teeth and calcium from her bones." Is this all true, all false, or only partly true?

2. Prepare a list of the hormonal abnormalities that can affect the growth of bones, both in children and in adults.

3. If air pollution becomes much worse, could it have an effect on bone development? Why?

4. Calcium plays an important role in bone formation. What other roles does calcium play in the body?

5. Full-contact sports seem to be a part of the curriculum for primary-school-age children. In the view of bone development, is this wise?

6. Prehistoric remains of animals consist almost exclusively of bones and teeth. Why?

7. If bone tissue is so hard, how can we move teeth from one location in the jaw to another?

8. Why are infections more common with compound fractures than simple fractures?

9. What would be the effect of extended weightlessness on the skeletal system? How can these effects be minimized or at least reduced?

10. Why does the meaty portion of a cooked chicken drumstick often come off while it is being eaten?

11. Why are greenstick fractures more common in children?

Library Research Topics

1. Research the latest technique, such as the Ilizarov procedure, used to lengthen bones damaged in accidents or illnesses.

2. What is involved in a bone marrow transplant, and is it a risky and difficult procedure?

3. What drugs or treatments are available to help correct conditions of gigantism and dwarfism and how do they work?

4. Explore the procedures used in bone tissue transplants where pieces of bone are removed from one part of the body and implanted into another.

5. What effect would steroid use have on the bone tissue and bone marrow?

6. How are electrical fields being used to stimulate bone growth and repair?

Multimedia in the Classroom and Lab

Online Resources for Students

The
Anatomy & Physiology Place
www.anatomyandphysiology.com

MyA&P
www.myaandp.com

*The following shows the organization of the Chapter Guide page in both the Anatomy &
Physiology Place and MyA&P™. The Chapter Guide organizes all the chapter-specific
online media resources for Chapter 6 in one convenient location, with e-book links to
each section of the textbook. Please note that both sites also give you access to other
general A&P resources, like InterActive Physiology®, PhysioEx 6.0™, Anatomy 360°,
Flashcards, a Glossary, a Histology Tutorial, and much more.*

Objectives

Section 6.1 Skeletal Cartilages (p. 176)

Section 6.2 Classification of Bones (pp. 176–178)

Section 6.3 Functions of Bones (pp. 178–179)

Section 6.4 Bone Structure (pp. 179–184)

Art Labeling Activity: Structure of a Long Bone (Fig. 6.3, p. 180)

Art Labeling Activity: Microscopic Anatomy of Compact Bone (Fig. 6.6, p. 183)

Activity: Bone Markings

Memory: The Architecture of Bone

Memory: Cartilage and Bone Structure

Section 6.5 Bone Development (pp. 184–187)

Section 6.6 Bone Homeostasis: Remodeling and Repair (pp. 187–193)

Activity: Common Types of Fractures

Section 6.7 Homeostatic Imbalances of Bone (pp. 193–195, 198)

Section 6.8 Developmental Aspects of Bones: Timing of Events (p. 198)

Chapter Summary

Self-Study Quizzes

Art Labeling Quiz

Matching Quiz

Multiple-Choice Quiz (Level I)

Multiple-Choice Quiz (Level II)

True-False Quiz

Crossword Puzzles

Crossword Puzzle 6.1

Crossword Puzzle 6.2

Media

See Guide to Audio-Visual Resources in Appendix A for key to AV distributors.

Slides

1. *General Connective Tissues Slide Set* (WNS)

Video

1. *Bone Marrow Transplants* (FHS; 28 min.). Provides a view of state-of-the-art procedures in bone marrow transplants. Viewers are taken to the University of Washington Medical Center, renowned for its work in bone marrow transplants.

2. *Bones and Joints* (FHS; 20 min., 1995). From *The New Living Body* series, this video introduces the topics of movement, the structure and function of joints, bone growth, and the effects of exercise on bones.
3. *The Human Skeletal System* (IM; 23 min., 2001). This video explains the functions and components of the human skeletal system.
4. *Our Bones: A Delicate Matter* (FHS; 26 min.). Topics include the causes, diagnosis, and treatment of osteoporosis. The program gives the viewers a look at the current research and insight on the prevention of osteoporosis.

Software

1. *WARD's Radiographic Anatomy* (WNS; Windows). Excellent collection of health-related images (CTs, MRIs, etc.).

Lecture Enhancement Material

To view thumbnails of all the illustrations for Chapter 6, see Appendix B.

Transparencies Index/Media Manager

Figure 6.1	The bones and cartilages of the human skeleton.
Figure 6.2	Classification of bones on the basis of shape.
Figure 6.3	The structure of a long bone (humerus of arm).
Figure 6.4	Structure of a flat bone.
Figure 6.5	A single osteon.
Figure 6.6	Microscopic anatomy of compact bone.
Figure 6.7	Intramembranous ossification.
Figure 6.8	Endochondral ossification in a long bone.
Figure 6.9	Growth in length of a long bone.
Figure 6.10	Long bone growth and remodeling during youth.
Figure 6.11	Hormonal controls of blood calcium levels.
Figure 6.12	Bone anatomy and stress.
Figure 6.13	Stages in the healing of a bone fracture.
Figure 6.14	Normal versus osteoporotic bone.
Figure 6.15	Fetal primary ossification centers at 12 weeks.
Table 6.1	Bone Markings
Table 6.2	Common Types of Fractures
Table 6.2	Common Types of Fractures (continued)
A Closer Look	Them Bones, Them Bones Goin' to Walk Around—Clinical Advances in Bone Repair*

*Indicates images that are on the Media Manager only.

Answers to End-of-Chapter Questions

Multiple Choice and Matching Question answers appear in Appendix G of the main text.

Short Answer Essay Questions

15. Cartilage has greater resilience because its matrix lacks bone salts, but its cells receive nutrients via diffusion from blood vessels that lie external to the cartilage. By contrast, bone has a beautifully engineered system of canaliculi for nutrient delivery, and for that reason its regeneration is much faster and more complete. (p. 176)

16. For this answer, please refer to pp. 185–186 of *Human Anatomy & Physiology*, Seventh Edition.

17. Macroscopic appearance of compact bone indicates it is dense, while the appearance of spongy bone indicates it is porous; microscopic appearance of compact bone indicates it possesses Haversian systems, while spongy bone lacks osteons; compact bone is located along the shaft, while spongy bone is located at the ends or within the shaft. (pp. 179–182)

18. The increase in thickness of compact bone on its superficial face is counteracted by the resorption of bone by osteoclasts on its internal surface. (p. 187)

19. An osteoid seam is an unmineralized band of bony matrix that is about 10–12 micrometers wide. Between this seam and older bone is an abrupt transition called a calcification front. The osteoid seam always stays the same width, indicating that osteoid tissue must mature before it can be calcified. This area then changes quickly from an unmineralized matrix to a mineralized matrix. (p. 188)

20. Two control loops regulate bone remodeling. One is a negative feedback hormonal mechanism that involves mechanical and gravitational forces acting on the skeleton and services the needs of the skeleton itself. (p. 188)

21. a. First decade is fastest; fourth decade is slowest. (p. 198)

    b. Elderly people usually experience bone loss, osteoporosis, and an increasing lack of blood supply. (p. 191)

    c. Children have proportionally more organic matrix. (p. 192)

22. This bone section is taken from the diaphysis of the specimen. The presence of an osteon, the concentric layers surrounding a central cavity, indicates compact bone found in the diaphysis. The epiphyseal plate, the site of active bone growth, lacks osteons. (pp. 181, 186)

Critical Thinking and Clinical Application Questions

1. A bony callus represents the conversion of the calcified fibrocartilagenous callus to a woven callus, indicating healing. (p. 191)

2. Rickets. Milk provides dietary calcium and vitamin D. Vitamin D is needed for its uptake by intestinal cells; the sun helps the skin synthesize vitamin D. Thick epiphyseal plates indicate poor calcification of the growing area. Because of this lack of sufficient calcium, the bones will be more pliable, and weight-bearing bones, like those in the leg, will bend. (p. 193)

3. The compact lamellar structure of dense bone produces structural units designed to resist twisting and other mechanical stresses placed on bones. In contrast, spongy bone is made up of trabeculae only a few cell layers thick containing irregularly arranged lamellae. (pp. 181–182)

4. According to Wolff's law, bone growth and remodeling occur in response to stress placed on such bones. With disuse, the bones in the limbs not being used will begin to atrophy. (p. 190)

5. Presumably the epiphyseal plate-bone junction has separated. The same would not happen to the boy's 23-year-old sister because by this age, epiphyseal plates have been replaced by bone and are no longer present. (p. 198)

6. No, it's not surprising. While the astronauts do exercise, it would be difficult for them to replicate any weight-bearing exercises because of the lack of gravity in space, resulting in reduced bone mass. (p. 195)

7. Paget's disease. (p. 195)

8. The size difference between the two arms of the tennis player would best be explained using Wolff's law. Wolff's law states that a bone will increase in size in response to stress placed on the bone. The serving arm of the tennis player is under much greater muscular stress than the nonserving arm. (p. 190)

Suggested Readings

Arron, Joseph R. and Choi, Yongwon. "Bone Versus Immune System." *Nature* 408 (6792) (July 2000): 535–536.

Hahn, B. H., and E. L. Mazzaferri. "Glucocorticoid-Induced Osteoporosis." *Hospital Practice* 30 (Aug. 1995): 45–56.

Kotz, Rainer I. et al. "A Self-extending Pediatric Leg Implant." *Nature* 406 (6792) (July 2000): 143.

Manolagas, S.C. "Birth and Death of Bone Cells: Basic Regulatory Mechanisms and Implications for the Pathogenesis and Treatment of Osteoporosis." *Endocrine Reviews* 21 (2000): 115–137.

Riggs, B. L. "A New Option for Treating Osteoporosis." *New England Journal of Medicine* 327 (July 1990): 124–125.

Rubin, C., Turner, A.S., Bain, S., Mallinckrodt, C. and McLeod, K. "Low Mechanical Signals Strengthen Long Bones." *Nature* 412 (6847) (Aug. 2001): 604.

Sarrel, P.M., et al. "Estrogen Actions in Arteries, Bone, and Brain." *Scientific American: Science and Medicine* (July/Aug. 1994): 44.

Seachrist, L. Y. "Diet, Exercise, Genes, Strengthen Bones." *Science News* 148 (July 1995): 23.

The Skeleton

Objectives

PART 1: THE AXIAL SKELETON

1. Name the parts of the axial skeleton and their functions.

The Skull

2. Name, describe, and identify the skull bones, their locations relative to each other, and their major markings.
3. Describe the overall form of the skull, and state the major types of bones that form various areas.
4. Name and describe the bones of the cranium, their major markings, and sutures.
5. List and describe the facial bones, their major markings, and articulations.
6. Name and describe the positions of the bones that construct the orbits and nasal cavity.
7. List the locations and functions of the paranasal sinuses.
8. Describe the location and structure of the hyoid bone.

The Vertebral Column

9. Explain the form and function of the vertebral column.
10. Name and describe the divisions and curvatures of the spine.
11. Discuss the location and function of the ligaments of the spine.
12. Identify the structure and functions of the intervertebral discs.
13. Describe general vertebral structure, and discuss special characteristics of each type of vertebrae.

The Thoracic Cage

14. Name and describe the elements of the thoracic cage.
15. List the bones and structures of the sternum.
16. Discuss the structure of the ribcage, distinguishing between true and false ribs, and discuss rib structure.

PART 2: THE APPENDICULAR SKELETON

17. Name the parts of the appendicular skeleton.

The Pectoral (Shoulder) Girdle

18. Identify the bones of the pectoral girdle, and describe their attachments to each other, and to the thorax.
19. Describe the features of the clavicles and scapulae.

The Upper Limb

20. Describe the features of the humerus, ulna, and radius, and how these bones articulate with each other.
21. List the bones of the wrist and hand, and describe how these bones articulate with each other.

The Pelvic (Hip) Girdle

22. Describe the pelvic girdle, how the coxa articulate, and describe the three bones that each coxa is formed from.
23. Explain the features of the ilium, ischium, and pubis.
24. Describe the differences in features of male and female pelvises, and the modifications of the pelvis for childbearing.

The Lower Limb

25. Describe the features of the femur, patella, tibia, and fibula, and how these bones articulate with each other.
26. List the bones of the ankle and foot, and describe how these bones articulate with each other.
27. Describe the arches of the foot.

Developmental Aspects of the Skeleton

28. Describe the bones and fontanels of a fetal skull, and the changes in relative proportions of the skull as an individual ages.
29. Describe the changes in the curvatures of the spine as a baby ages.
30. Describe the age-related changes in the skeleton as an individual progresses through childhood, adulthood, and old age.

Suggested Lecture Outline

PART 1: THE AXIAL SKELETON

I. The Skull (pp. 203–218; Figs. 7.1–7.12; Table 7.1)

A. The skull consists of 22 cranial and facial bones that form the framework of the face, contain cavities for special sense organs, provide openings for air and food passage, secure the teeth, and anchor muscles of facial expression (p. 203).

B. Except for the mandible, which is joined to the skull by a movable joint, most skull bones are flat bones joined by interlocking joints called sutures (p. 203).

C. Overview of Skull Geography (p. 203)

1. The anterior aspect of the skull is formed by facial bones, and the remainder is formed by a cranium, which is divided into the cranial vault, or calvaria, and cranial base.

2. The cavities of the skull include the cranial cavity (houses the brain), ear cavities, nasal cavity, and orbits (house the eyeballs).

3. The skull has about 85 named openings that provide passageways for the spinal cord, major blood vessels serving the brain, and the cranial nerves.

D. The cranium consists of eight strong, superiorly curved bones (pp. 203–211; Figs. 7.2–7.7).

1. The frontal bone articulates posteriorly with the parietal bones via the coronal suture, extends forward to the supraorbital margins, and extends posteriorly to form the superior wall of the orbits and most of the anterior cranial fossa.

2. The parietal bones are two large, rectangular bones on the superior and lateral aspects of the skull, which form the majority of the cranial vault.

   a. The four largest sutures of the skull are located where the parietal bones articulate with other bones: the coronal, sagittal, lambdoid, and squamous sutures.

3. The occipital bone articulates with the parietal, temporal, and sphenoid bones, forming most of the posterior wall and base of the skull.

   a. The foramen magnum, a large opening through which the brain connects to the spinal cord, is located in the base of the occipital bone.

4. The temporal bones articulate with the parietal bones and form the inferolateral aspects of the skull and parts of the cranial floor.

a. The temporal bone is characterized by the mandibular fossa, which forms part of the temporomandibular joint, and the external auditory meatus and petrous, which house the ear.

5. The sphenoid bone spans the width of the middle cranial fossa, and articulates with all other cranial bones.

6. The ethmoid bone lies between the sphenoid and nasal bones, and forms most of the bony area between the nasal cavity and the orbits.

7. Sutural, or Wormian, bones are groups of irregularly shaped bones or bone clusters located within sutures that vary in number and are not present on all skulls.

E. Facial Bones (pp. 211–213; Fig. 7.8)

1. The mandible, or lower jawbone, articulates with the mandibular fossae of the temporal bones via the mandibular condyles to form the temporo-mandibular joint.

2. The maxillary bones form the upper jaw and central portion of the face, articulating with all other facial bones except the mandible.

3. The zygomatic bones articulate with temporal, frontal, and maxillary bones, and form the prominences of the cheeks and parts of the inferolateral margins of the orbits.

4. The nasal bones form the bridge of the nose, and articulate with the frontal, maxillary, and ethmoid bones, along with the cartilages that form most of the skeleton of the external nose.

5. The lacrimal bones are located in the medial wall of the orbits, and articulate with the frontal, ethmoid, and maxillary bones.

6. The palatine bones consist of bony plates that complete the posterior portion of the hard palate, form part of the posterolateral walls of the nasal cavity, and small parts of the orbits.

7. The vomer lies in the nasal cavity, where it forms part of the nasal septum.

8. The inferior nasal conchae are thin, curved bones in the nasal cavity that project medially from the lateral walls of the nasal cavity.

F. Special Characteristics of the Orbits and Nasal Cavity (pp. 213–218; Figs. 7.9–7.10)

1. The orbits are bony cavities that contain the eyes, muscles that move the eyes, and tear-producing glands. They consist of the frontal, sphenoid, zygomatic, maxilla, palatine, lacrimal, and ethmoid bones.

2. The nasal cavity is constructed of bone and hyaline cartilage, and is formed by the ethmoid, maxillary, and palatine bones, as well as the inferior nasal conchae. It is divided into right and left parts by the nasal septum, which consists of portions of the ethmoid bone and vomer.

G. Paranasal sinuses are air-filled sinuses clustered around the nasal cavity that lighten the skull and enhance resonance of the voice (pp. 214, 218; Figs. 7.10–7.11).

H. The hyoid bone lies inferior to the mandible in the anterior neck. It is the only bone that does not articulate directly with any other bone (p. 218; Fig. 7.12).

II. The Vertebral Column (pp. 218–226; Figs. 7.13–7.18; Table 7.2)

A. General Characteristics (pp. 218–221; Figs. 7.13–7.14)

1. The vertebral column consists of 26 irregular bones, forming a flexible, curved structure extending from the skull to the pelvis that surrounds and protects the spinal cord. It provides attachment for ribs and muscles of the neck and back.

2. Divisions and Curvatures
    a. The vertebrae of the spine fall in five major divisions: seven cervical, twelve thoracic, five lumbar, five fused vertebrae of the sacrum, and four fused vertebrae of the coccyx.
    b. The curvatures of the spine increase resiliency and flexibility of the spine.
    c. The cervical and lumbar curvatures are concave posteriorly, and the thoracic and sacral curvatures are convex posteriorly.
3. The major supporting ligaments of the spine are the anterior and posterior longitudinal ligaments, which run as continuous bands down the front and back surfaces of the spine. They support the spine and prevent hyperflexion and hyperextension.
4. Intervertebral discs are cushionlike pads that act as shock absorbers and allow the spine to flex, extend, and bend laterally.

B. General Structure of Vertebrae (p. 221; Fig. 7.15)
    1. Each vertebra consists of an anterior body and a posterior vertebral arch that, together with the body, form the vertebral foramen through which the spinal cord passes.
    2. The vertebral arch consists of two pedicles and two laminae, which collectively give rise to several projections: a median spinous process, two lateral transverse processes, and paired superior and inferior articular processes.
    3. The pedicles have notches on their superior and inferior borders called intervertebral foramen, which provide openings for the passage of spinal nerves.

C. Regional Vertebral Characteristics (pp. 221–225; Figs. 7.16–7.18; Table 7.2)
    1. Cervical vertebrae are the smallest vertebrae. They typically have an oval body, a short, bifid spinous process, a large, triangular vertebral foramen, and a transverse foramen.
        a. The atlas has no body or spinous process. It has articular facets on the superior and inferior surface that articulate with the skull superiorly, and the second cervical vertebra, the axis, inferiorly.
        b. The second cervical vertebra has a body, spine, and other typical vertebral processes, as well as a knoblike dens, or odontoid process, projecting superiorly from the body.
    2. Thoracic vertebrae all articulate with ribs, and gradually transition between cervical structure at the top, and lumbar structure toward the bottom.
        a. Thoracic vertebrae have a roughly heart-shaped body, which bear two facets on each side for rib articulation: a circular vertebral foramen and superior and inferior articular processes.
    3. Lumbar vertebrae are large vertebrae that have kidney-shaped bodies, a triangular vertebral foramen, short, thick pedicles and laminae, and short, flat, hatchet-shaped spinous processes.
    4. The sacrum forms the posterior wall of the pelvis. It is formed by five, fused vertebrae in adults, and articulates with the fifth lumbar vertebra superiorly, the coccyx inferiorly, and the hip bones laterally via the sacroiliac joint.
        a. The vertebral canal continues through the sacrum, often ending at a large external opening, the sacral hiatus.
    5. The coccyx (tailbone) is a small bone consisting of four, fused vertebrae that articulate superiorly with the sacrum.

III. The Thoracic Cage (pp. 226–228; Figs. 7.19–7.20)

A. The thoracic cage consists of the thoracic vertebrae dorsally, the ribs laterally, and the sternum and costal cartilages anteriorly. It forms a protective cage around the organs of the thoracic cavity, and provides support for the shoulder girdles and upper limbs (p. 226; Fig. 7.19).

B. Sternum (pp. 226–227; Fig. 7.19)
   1. The sternum (breastbone) lies in the anterior midline of the thorax, and is a flat bone resulting from the fusion of three bones: the manubrium, body, and xiphoid process.
   2. The manubrium articulates with the clavicles and the first two pairs of ribs. The body articulates with the cartilages of ribs two through seven. The xiphoid process forms the inferior end, articulating only with the body.

C. Ribs (pp. 227–228; Fig. 7.20)
   1. The sides of the thoracic cage are formed by twelve pairs of ribs that attach posteriorly to the thoracic vertebrae and curve inferiorly toward the anterior body surface.
   2. The superior seven pairs of ribs are called true, or vertebrosternal, ribs. They attach directly to the sternum via individual costal cartilages.
   3. The lower five pairs of ribs are called false ribs. They either attach indirectly to the sternum or lack a sternal attachment entirely.

PART 2: THE APPENDICULAR SKELETON

IV. The Pectoral (Shoulder) Girdle (pp. 228–231; Figs. 7.21–7.22, 7.25; Table 7.3)

A. The pectoral (shoulder) girdle consists of the clavicle, which joins the sternum anteriorly, and the scapula, which is attached to the posterior thorax and vertebrae via muscular attachments (p. 229; Fig. 7.22).
   1. The pectoral girdles are very light and have a high degree of mobility due to the openness of the shoulder joint and the free movement of the scapula across the thorax.

B. The clavicles (collarbones) extend horizontally across the thorax, articulating medially with the sternum, and laterally with the scapula, bracing the arms and scapulae laterally (p. 229; Figs. 7.22, 7.25).

C. The scapulae (shoulder blades) are thin, flat bones that lie on the dorsal surface of the ribcage, articulating with the humerus via the glenoid cavity, and the clavicle via the acromion (pp. 229–231; Figs. 7.22, 7.25).

V. The Upper Limb (pp. 231–237; Figs. 7.23–7.26; Table 7.3)

A. Arm (pp. 231–232; Figs. 7.23, 7.25)
   1. The arm is the region extending from shoulder to elbow, and has one bone, the humerus.
   2. The humerus is the largest, longest bone of the upper limb. It articulates with the scapula at the shoulder, and with the radius and ulna at the elbow.

B. Forearm (pp. 232–233; Figs. 7.24–7.25)
   1. The forearm is the region between the elbow and wrist. It consists of two bones, the ulna and the radius.
   2. The ulna forms the elbow joint with the humerus. It articulates with the radius laterally at the proximal end, and articulates with the bones of the wrist via a cartilage disc at the distal end.

3. The radius articulates with the humerus and the ulna medially at the proximal end via a flattened head. It articulates with the carpals of the wrist and the ulna medially at the distal end.

C. Hand (pp. 233–237; Fig. 7.26)

1. The carpus (wrist) consists of eight short bones arranged in two irregular rows of four bones each: the scaphoid, lunate, triquetral, and pisiform proximally; and the trapezium, trapezoid, capitate, and hamate distally.

2. The metacarpus (palm) consists of five small, long bones numbering one through five from thumb to little finger. It articulates with the carpals proximally, and the proximal phalanges distally.

3. There are 14 phalanges of the fingers: the thumb (pollex) is digit 1, and has two phalanges. The other fingers, numbered 2–5 have three phalanges each.

VI. The Pelvic (Hip) Girdle (pp. 237–239; Figs. 7.27, 7.30; Tables 7.4–7.5)

A. The pelvic girdle attaches the lower limbs to the axial skeleton. It is formed by a pair of coxal bones, each consisting of three separate bones: the ischium, ilium, and pubis, that are fused in adults (p. 237).

B. The ilium forms the superior region of the coxal bone. It articulates with the sacrum, forming the sacroiliac joint, and also with the ischium and pubis anteriorly (p. 237).

C. The ischium forms the posteroinferior portion of the coxa (pp. 237–239).

D. The pubic bones form the anterior portion of the coxae. They are joined by a fibrocartilage disc, forming the midline pubic symphysis (p. 239).

E. Pelvic Structure and Childbearing (p. 239; Table 7.4)

1. The female pelvis is modified for childbearing. It tends to be wider, shallower, lighter, and rounder than the male pelvis.

2. The pelvis consists of a false pelvis, which is part of the abdomen and helps support the viscera, and a true pelvis, which is completely surrounded by bone and contains the pelvic organs.

VII. The Lower Limb (pp. 239–245; Figs. 7.28–7.32; Table 7.5)

A. Thigh (pp. 239–242; Figs. 7.28, 7.30)

1. The thigh is the region between the hip and knee. It has one bone, the femur.

2. The femur is the largest, longest, and strongest bone in the body. It articulates proximally with the hip via a ball-like head, and distally with the knee at the lateral and medial condyles.

3. The patella is a triangular sesamoid bone that articulates with the femur at the patellar surface.

B. Leg (pp. 242–244; Figs. 7.29–7.30)

1. The leg is the region between the knee and ankle. It has two bones, the tibia and fibula.

2. The tibia is the weight-bearing bone of the leg. It is characterized proximally by the medial and lateral condyles that articulate with the femur, and distally by the medial malleolus, an inferior projection on the medial aspect that articulates with the talus.

3. The fibula is a sticklike, non-weight-bearing bone. It has expanded ends that articulate proximally via the head and distally via the lateral malleolus with the lateral aspects of the tibia.

C. Foot (pp. 244–245; Figs. 7.31–7.32)

1. The tarsus consists of seven tarsal bones that make up the posterior half of the foot.

2. The metatarsus consists of five small, long bones called metatarsal bones which number 1 to 5 beginning on the medial side of the foot.

3. There are 14 phalanges of the toes: the great toe (hallux) is digit 1 and has two phalanges. The other toes, numbered 2–5, have three phalanges each.

4. The arches of the foot are maintained by interlocking foot bones, ligaments, and the pull of tendons during muscle activity.

VIII. Developmental Aspects of the Skeleton (pp. 246–248; Figs. 7.33–7.35)

A. Membrane bones of the skull begin to ossify late in the second month of development (p. 246).

B. At birth, skull bones are connected by fontanels, unossified remnants of fibrous membranes (p. 246; Fig. 7.33).

C. Changes in cranial-facial proportions and fusion of bones occur throughout childhood (p. 247).

1. At birth, the cranium is much larger than the face, and several bones are still unfused.

2. By nine months, the cranium is half the adult size due to rapid brain growth.

3. By age 8–9, the cranium has reached almost adult proportions.

4. Between ages 6–13, the jaws, cheekbones, and nose become more prominent, due to expansion of the nose, paranasal sinuses, and development of permanent teeth.

D. Curvatures of the Spine (p. 247).

1. The primary curvatures (thoracic and sacral curvatures) are convex posteriorly and are present at birth.

2. The secondary curvatures (cervical and lumbar curvatures) are convex anteriorly and are associated with the child's development.

3. The secondary curvatures result from reshaping the intervertebral discs.

E. Changes in body height and proportion occur throughout childhood (p. 248; Fig. 7.35).

1. At birth, the head and trunk are roughly 1 1/2 times the length of the lower limbs.

2. The lower limbs grow more rapidly than the trunk, and by age 10, the head and trunk are about the same length as the lower limbs.

3. During puberty, the female pelvis widens and the male skeleton becomes more robust.

F. Effects of old age on the skeleton (p. 248).

1. The intervertebral discs become thinner, less hydrated, and less elastic.

2. The thorax becomes more rigid, due to calcification of the costal cartilages.

3. All bones lose bone mass.

Cross References

Additional information on topics covered in Chapter 7 can be found in the chapters listed below.

1. Chapter 4: Fibrocartilage; hyaline cartilage
2. Chapter 6: Bone markings; classification of bones

3. Chapter 8: Joints; sutures
4. Chapter 10: Reinforcing muscles for the vertebral column; muscles of the face; muscles of the thorax; muscles of the upper extremity; muscles of the pelvic girdle; muscles of the lower extremity
5. Chapter 15: Bones of the middle ear cavity
6. Chapter 22: Bones of the skull that function in the respiratory system

Laboratory Correlations

1. Marieb, E. N. *Human Anatomy & Physiology Laboratory Manual: Cat and Fetal Pig Versions*. Eighth Edition Updates. Benjamin Cummings, 2006.
   Exercise 10: The Axial Skeleton
   Exercise 11: The Appendicular Skeleton
   Exercise 12: The Fetal Skeleton
2. Marieb, E. N. *Human Anatomy & Physiology Laboratory Manual: Main Version*. Seventh Edition Update. Benjamin Cummings, 2006.
   Exercise 10: The Axial Skeleton
   Exercise 11: The Appendicular Skeleton
   Exercise 12: The Fetal Skeleton

Histology Slides of the Life Sciences

Available through Benjamin Cummings, an imprint of Pearson Education, Inc. To order, contact your local Benjamin Cummings sales representative.

Slide 23   Hyaline Cartilage, Trachea.
Slide 24   Fibrocartilage, Intervertebral Disk.
Slide 25   Bone (Osseous) Tissue, Ground Bone.
Slide 46   Cartilage-Bone Junction, Toe Bone.
Slide 47   Epiphyseal Plate of a Bone.
Slide 48   Endochondral Ossification.

Lecture Hints

1. A good indicator of student comprehension of the spatial relationship among facial bones is the ability to list the bones making up the eye orbit.
2. Point out during the lecture that the styloid process of the temporal bone is often damaged during the preparation of a skeleton. As a result, skulls available in the lab may be lacking this fragile structure.
3. Students often have difficulty in identification of sphenoid and ethmoid bones. It would be helpful to show disarticulated specimens during lecture.
4. Point out that all facial bones (except mandible) articulate with the maxillae.
5. Remembering common meal times, 7 AM, 12 noon, and 5 PM, may help students to recall the number of bones in the three regions of the vertebral column.
6. "Atlas supports the world" can be used to help students remember that the atlas is first and axis second.
7. Point out that correct anatomical terminology specifies "arm" as the portion between shoulder and elbow; and "leg" refers to the portion between knee and ankle.
8. Although the obturator foramen is large, it is really closed by fibrous membrane in life.
9. In anatomical position the radius/ulna and fibula/tibia are in alphabetical order from the outside.

Activities/Demonstrations

1. Audio-visual materials listed under Multimedia in the Classroom and Lab.
2. The cranium is remarkably strong for its weight and the thinness of cranial bones. This is in part due to the curvature of the cranium, a "self-bracing" effect. To demonstrate this effect, attempt to break an egg by squeezing it in the palm of your (or a student's) hand.
3. Give a group of students a thoracic vertebra and a rib and ask them to articulate the two together.
4. Tie different colors of string around the lamina and pedicle of a vertebra and pass it around class.
5. Use an articulated skeleton to:
   a. indicate its protective and support aspects
   b. identify individual bones
6. Obtain a skull with its calvarium cut and a vertebral column to illustrate how these bones provide protection for the delicate neural tissues.
7. Obtain a skull that shows Wormian bones.
8. Use a Beauchene (disarticulated) skull to demonstrate the individual skull bones and to show the fragile internal structure of bones containing sinuses.
9. Use a disarticulated vertebral column to illustrate similarities/differences between vertebrae.
10. Point out that the superior articular surface of the atlas is elongated, matching the surface of the occipital condyle.
11. Obtain X rays that exhibit abnormal curvatures (scoliosis, lordosis, kyphosis).
12. Obtain different ribs and indicate how each is similar and different.
13. Point out differences between the male and female pelvis.
14. Obtain a sacrum to show fusion of the vertebrae.
15. Use a fetal skeleton to emphasize the changes in skull and body proportions that occur after birth, and to point out the fact that initially the skeleton is formed (mostly) of hyaline cartilage rather than bone.

Critical Thinking/Discussion Topics

1. List several skeletal landmarks that can be used to guide a nurse or physician in giving injections, locating areas for surgery, and assisting in the diagnosis of internal conditions.
2. What effect would exaggerated exercise or the complete lack of exercise have on bones such as the tibia, femur, and humerus if it occurred during childhood? During adulthood?
3. Numerous children are born with a congenital hip defect. Why is this area affected so often and what can be done to correct the defect?
4. Years ago, students used to carry large, heavy books on one arm or the other. Today, most students are using backpacks. What difference, if any, could be detected in the spinal column between then and now?
5. Various religious writings have suggested that a rib was taken from man to create woman. Are any ribs missing from the male rib cage? What could explain this discrepancy?
6. Humans have a short neck, but giraffes have a long one. Does the giraffe have more neck vertebrae to accommodate this extra length? What other similarities or variations can be found between human bone structure and other animals?

7. How is it possible to "taste" eye drops shortly after they are placed in the eye?

8. When a dentist injects novocaine near the mandibular foramen, why does the lower lip become numb?

9. At birth only two of the four spinal curvatures are present. The secondary curvatures (cervical and lumbar) do not develop until after birth. What is the role of these secondary curvatures, and why do they develop?

Library Research Topics

1. There is a new technique, known as percutaneous automated discectomy, that involves back surgery without stitches. How safe is it, and when can it be employed?

2. Temporomandibular joint disorders are very common and painful. What methods of treatment are there and how successful are they?

3. Spinal deviations such as scoliosis are very difficult to repair. What are the current methods of treatment, both invasive and noninvasive?

4. Paleontologists and archaeologists have unearthed many prehistoric skulls and bones of human-like creatures and animals. How can they reconstruct the soft features and tissues of these animals from only their skeletal remains?

5. Trace the origin of genetic disorders such as spina bifida and cleft palate, starting with the human embryo. What is the explanation for these defects?

6. In the surgical repair of a herniated disc it may be necessary to remove some of the nucleus pulposus. The removal may be by conventional surgery or by chemonucleosus. What are the advantages of the latter procedure?

Multimedia in the Classroom and Lab

Online Resources for Students

The
Anatomy & Physiology Place
www.anatomyandphysiology.com

MyA&P
www.myaandp.com

The following shows the organization of the Chapter Guide page in both the Anatomy & Physiology Place and MyA&P™. The Chapter Guide organizes all the chapter-specific online media resources for Chapter 7 in one convenient location, with e-book links to each section of the textbook. Please note that both sites also give you access to other general A&P resources, like InterActive Physiology®, PhysioEx 6.0™, Anatomy 360°, Flashcards, a Glossary, a Histology Tutorial, and much more.

Objectives

PART ONE: THE AXIAL SKELETON

Section 7.1 The Skull (pp. 203–216)

Art Labeling Activity: Anatomy of the Anterior Aspect of the Skull (Fig. 7.2a, p. 205)

Art Labeling Activity: Anatomy of the Posterior Aspect of the Skull (Fig. 7.2b, p. 205)

Art Labeling Activity: External Anatomy of the Lateral Aspect of the Skull (Fig. 7.3a, p. 206)

Art Labeling Activity: Internal Anatomy of the Left Side of the Skull (Fig. 7.3b, p. 206)

Art Labeling Activity: Inferior Superficial View of the Skull (Fig. 7.4a, p. 208)

Art Labeling Activity: Superior View of Floor of the Cranial Cavity (Fig. 7.4b, p. 208)

Bone Review: Skull

Media

See Guide to Audio-Visual Resources in Appendix A for key to AV distributors.

Video

1. *Anatomy of the Hand* (FHS; 15 min., 1999). This program demonstrates how the hand functions, spotlighting the opposable nature of the thumb.

2. *Anatomy of the Shoulder* (FHS; 18 min., 1999). This program presents the technical specifications of the shoulder: what muscles sheathe it, how it functions, and its range of motion. Various medical conditions are discussed.

3. *Artificial Body Parts* (FHS; 26 min., 1990). Recent strides in medical engineering are presented in this program. Shows the most recent information in research on blood vessel grafts and joint and limb replacement.

4. *Bones and Movement; The Ear; Ways of Looking* (FHS; 25 min., 1996). The first section of this program uses infrared technology to capture skeletal motion on film, catalogs the major bones, and investigates joint development.

5. *Bones and Muscles* (FHS; 15 min., 1999). This program provides a field trip to a pharmaceutical company to discuss new treatments for osteoporosis.

6. *Broken Bones and How They Mend* (FHS; 25 min., 1998). This program follows a young patient from a traumatic injury through recovery. Stunning 3-D computer animations of the subcutaneous mayhem caused by a broken radius. Illustrates how the body repairs itself.

7. *Our Flexible Frame—The Skeletal and Muscular Systems Video* (WNS; 20 min.). Animated graphics illustrate the essential functions of the skeletal system, such as protecting internal organs, producing blood cells, and providing places of attachment for muscles.

8. *Leg-Straightening Procedure* (FHS; 45 min.). Specialists explain the problems concerning the anatomical function of the patient's leg. They also discuss how the surgery will improve the patient's quality of life.

Software

1. *A.D.A.M.® Anatomy Practice 4.0* (ADAM, BC; Win/Mac, 1999). Allows students to review thousands of pinned structures within hundreds of anatomical images. The images and associated notes can be printed for review. Includes a testing mode with pinned images similar to lab practicals.

2. *A.D.A.M.® InterActive Anatomy®* (see p. 9 of this guide for full description).

3. *A.D.A.M.® MediaPro 4.0* (see p. 9 of this guide for full listing).

4. *Bodyworks* (see p. 9 of this guide for full listing).

5. *The Ultimate Human Body* (see p. 9 of this guide for full listing).

Lecture Enhancement Material

To view thumbnails of all of the illustrations for Chapter 7, see Appendix B.

Transparencies Index/Media Manager

Figure 7.1   Bones of the axial skeleton.
Figure 7.2   Anatomy of the anterior and posterior aspects of the skull.
Figure 7.3   Anatomy of the lateral aspects of the skull.
Figure 7.4   Anatomy of inferior portion of skull.
Figure 7.5   The temporal bone.
Figure 7.6   The sphenoid bone.
Figure 7.7   The ethmoid bone.
Figure 7.8   Detailed anatomy of (a) the mandible and (b) the maxilla.
Figure 7.9   Special anatomical characteristics of the orbits.
Figure 7.10   Special anatomical characteristics of the nasal cavity.
Figure 7.11   Paranasal sinuses.
Figure 7.12   The hyoid bone.
Figure 7.13   The vertebral column.
Figure 7.14   Ligaments and fibrocartilage discs uniting the vertebrae.
Figure 7.15   Structure of a typical vertebra.
Figure 7.16   The first and second cervical vertebrae.

Answers to End-of-Chapter Questions

Multiple Choice and Matching Question answers appear in Appendix G of the main text.

Short Answer Essay Questions

4. Cranial bones: parietal, temporal, frontal, occipital, sphenoid, and ethmoid. Facial bones: mandible, vomer, maxillae, zygomatics, nasals, lacrimals, palatines, and inferior conchae. Cranial bones provide sites for attachment and enclose and protect the brain. The facial bones form the framework of the face, hold eyes in position, provide cavities for organs of taste and smell, secure the teeth, and anchor facial muscles. (pp. 203–216; Table 7.1)

5. At birth, the skull is huge relative to the facial skeleton. During childhood and adolescence, the face grows out from the skull. By adulthood, the cranial and facial skeletons are the appropriate proportional size. (p. 247)

6. Normal curves are: cervical, thoracic, lumbar, and sacral. The thoracic and sacral are primary; the cervical and lumbar are secondary. (p. 219)

7. Cervical vertebrae possess transverse foramina, have small bodies and bifid spinous processes; thoracic vertebrae possess facets for the ribs and have circular vertebral foramina; lumbar vertebrae have massive bodies and blunt spines. (pp. 221–225; Table 7.2)

8. a. The discs act as shock absorbers and allow the spine to flex and extend (provide flexibility). (p. 220)

   b. The annulus fibrosis, composed of fibrocartilage, is more external and contains the nucleus pulposus. The nucleus is the semifluid substance enclosed by the annulus.

   c. The annulus provides strength and durability.

   d. The nucleus provides resilience.

   e. Disc herniation involves protrusion of the nucleus pulposus through the annulus. (pp. 220–221)

9. The thoracic cage includes the thoracic vertebrae, ribs, sternum, and costal cartilages. (p. 226)

10. a. True rib: attached at both ends directly; false rib: attached at vertebrae directly, sternum indirectly.

    b. A floating rib is a false rib.

    c. Floating ribs lack a costal cartilage connection. (pp. 227–228)

11. The pelvic girdle functions to attach and transfer the weight of the body to the lower limbs. The bones are large, strong, and securely attach the bones of the thigh to the axial skeleton. The pectoral girdle bones are light and quite mobile to provide flexibility at the expense of strength and stability. (pp. 237–239)

12. The female pelvis inlet and outlet are wider; the pelvis is shallower, lighter, and rounder than that of the male; and the ischial tuberosities are farther apart. (p. 239; Table 7.4)

13. The arches distribute the weight of the body. (p. 245)

14. Cleft palate: persistent opening in the palate interferes with sucking and can lead to aspiration of food into the lungs. Hip dysplasia: abnormality that allows the head of the femur to slip out of the acetabulum. (pp. 246–247)

15. In a young adult skeleton, the bone mass is dense, water content is normal in discs, the vertebral column is strong. In old age, the discs decline in water content and become thinner and less elastic, the spine shortens and becomes an arc, and all the bones lose mass. The thorax becomes more rigid with increasing age, mainly due to the ossification of costal cartilage. The cranial bones lose less mass with age than most bones, but the facial contours of the aged change. (pp. 247–248)

16. Peter was having a little fun with the obturator foramen, the large opening in the hip bone through which pass some blood vessels and nerves. (p. 239)

Critical Thinking and Clinical Application Questions

1. Justiniano is probably suffering from carpal tunnel syndrome, a nerve impairment common to persons who repeatedly flex their wrists and fingers, often at a computer keyboard. (p. 235)

2. A lateral curvature is scoliosis due to an uneven pull of muscles. Since muscles on one side of the body were nonfunctional, those on the opposite side exerted a stronger pull and forced the spine out of alignment. (p. 219)

3. The fracture of the neck of the femur is usually called a broken hip and is common in the elderly due to osteoporosis, which especially weakens the vertebrae and neck of the femur. (p. 241)

4. Mrs. Shea has developed soreness on her buttock in response to having her entire weight on her ischial tuberosity for three days. If she were to continue this activity for a few more days she would develop pressure sores called decubitus ulcers. (pp. 172, 239)

Suggested Readings

Agur, A.M. *Grant's Atlas of Anatomy*. 10th ed. Baltimore: Lippincott/Williams & Wilkins, 1999.

Chase, R.A. *The Bassett Atlas of Human Anatomy*. San Francisco: Benjamin Cummings, 1989.

Clemente, C.D. *Anatomy: A Regional Atlas of the Human Body*. 4th ed. Baltimore: Lippincott/Williams & Wilkins, 1998.

Gordon, K.R. "Adaptive Nature of Skeletal Design." *BioScience* 39 (Dec. 1989): 784–790.

Gray, H., et al. *Gray's Anatomy*. 38th ed. London: Churchill Livingstone, 1995.

Newschwander, G. E., et al. "Limb Lengthening with Llizaron External Fixator." *Orthopaedic Nursing* 8 (May-June 1989): 15–21.

8 Joints

Objectives

Classification of Joints

1. Explain how joints are classified structurally and functionally.

Fibrous Joints

2. Identify the three types of fibrous joints and give an example of each.

Cartilaginous Joints

3. Indicate the three types of cartilaginous joints and give an example of each.

Synovial Joints

4. Describe the general features of a synovial joint.

5. Define bursae and tendon sheaths.
6. Explain the three factors that influence the stability of a synovial joint.
7. Describe the movements allowed at synovial joints.
8. Examine the types of synovial joints.

Homeostatic Imbalances of Joints

9. Describe what happens in sprains, cartilage injuries, and dislocations.
10. Identify the inflammatory and degenerative conditions that target joints.

Developmental Aspects of Joints

11. Describe the fetal development of joints.
12. Explore the changes that occur to joints as one ages.

Suggested Lecture Outline

I. Introduction to Articulations (p. 253)

A. Sites where two or more bones meet are called joints or articulations.

B. Our joints give our skeleton mobility and hold it together.

II. Classification of Joints (p. 253; Table 8.1)

A. Structural classification focuses on the material binding the bones together and whether or not a joint cavity is present.

    1. In fibrous joints the bones are joined together by fibrous tissue and lack a joint cavity.

    2. In cartilaginous joints the bones are joined together by cartilage and they lack a joint cavity.

    3. In synovial joints, the articulating bones are separated by a fluid-containing joint cavity.

B. Functional classification is based on the amount of movement allowed at the joint.

    1. Synarthroses are immovable joints.

2. Amphiarthroses are slightly movable joints.

3. Diarthroses are freely movable joints.

III. Fibrous Joints (pp. 253–254; Fig. 8.1; Tables 8.1–8.2)

A. Sutures occur between bones of the skull and use very short connective tissue fibers to hold the bones together.

B. In syndesmoses, the bones are connected by a ligament, which is a cord or band of fibrous tissue.

C. A gomphosis is a peg-in-socket fibrous joint.

IV. Cartilaginous Joints (p. 254; Fig. 8.2; Tables 8.1–8.2)

A. Synchondroses involve a bar or plate of hyaline cartilage uniting the bones, such as the epiphyseal plate.

B. In symphyses, such as the pubic symphysis, the articular surfaces are covered with articular cartilage that is then fused to an intervening pad or plate of fibrocartilage.

V. Synovial Joints (pp. 255–272; Figs. 8.3–8.8, 8.10–8.13; Tables 8.1–8.2)

A. The general structure of a synovial joint contains five distinguishing features.

1. Articular cartilage covers the ends of the articulating bones.

2. The joint (synovial) cavity is a space that is filled with synovial fluid.

3. The two-layered articular capsule encloses the joint cavity.

4. Synovial fluid is a viscous, slippery fluid that fills all free space within the joint cavity.

5. Reinforcing ligaments cross synovial joints to strengthen the joint.

B. Bursae and tendon sheaths are bags of lubricant that reduce friction at synovial joints.

C. Factors Influencing the Stability of Synovial Joints

1. The shapes of the articular surfaces of bones found at a synovial joint determine the movements that occur at the joint, but play a minimal role in stabilizing the joint.

2. Ligaments at a synovial joint prevent excessive or unwanted movements and help to stabilize the joint; the greater the number of ligaments at the joint the greater the stability.

3. Muscle tone keeps tendons crossing joints taut, which is the most important factor stabilizing joints.

D. Movements Allowed by Synovial Joints

1. In gliding movements one flat, or nearly flat, bone surface glides or slips over another.

2. Angular movements increase or decrease the angle between two bones.

   a. Flexion decreases the angle of the joint and brings the articulating bones closer together.

   b. Extension increases the angle between the articulating bones.

   c. Dorsiflexion decreases the angle between the top of the foot (dorsal surface) and the anterior surface of the tibia.

   d. Plantar flexion decreases the angle between the sole of the foot (plantar surface) and the posterior side of the tibia.

   e. Abduction is the movement of a limb (or fingers) away from the midline body (or of the hand).

       f. Adduction is the movement of a limb (or fingers) toward the midline of the body (or the hand).

       g. Circumduction is moving a limb so that it describes a cone in the air.

   3. Rotation is the turning of a bone along its own long axis.

   4. Special Movements

       a. Supination is rotating the forearm laterally so that the palm faces anteriorly or superiorly.

       b. Pronation is rotating the arm medially so that the palm faces posteriorly or inferiorly.

       c. Inversion turns the sole of the foot so that it faces medially.

       d. Eversion turns the sole of the foot so that it faces laterally.

       e. Protraction moves the mandible anteriorly, juts the jaw forward.

       f. Retraction returns the mandible to its original position.

       g. Elevation means lifting a body part superiorly.

       h. Depression means to move an elevated body part inferiorly.

       i. Opposition occurs when you touch your thumb to the fingers on the same hand.

E. Types of Synovial Joints

   1. Plane joints have flat articular surfaces and allow gliding and transitional movements.

   2. Hinge joints consist of a cylindrical projection that nests in a trough-shaped structure, and allow movement along a single plane.

   3. Pivot joints consist of a rounded structure that protrudes into a sleeve or ring, and allow uniaxial rotation of a bone around the long axis.

   4. Condyloid, or ellipsoid, joints consist of an oval articular surface that nests in a complementary depression, and permit all angular movements.

   5. Saddle joints consist of each articular surface bearing complementary concave and convex areas, and allow more freedom of movement than condyloid joints.

   6. Ball-and-socket joints consist of a spherical or hemispherical structure that articulates with a cuplike structure. They are the most freely moving joints and allow multiaxial movements.

F. Selected Synovial Joints

   1. Knee Joint

       a. Enclosed in one joint cavity, the knee joint is actually three joints in one: the femoropatellar joint, the lateral and medial joints between the femoral condyles, and the menisci of the tibia, known collectively as the tibiofemoral joint.

       b. Many different types of ligaments stabilize and strengthen the capsule of the knee joint.

       c. The knee capsule is reinforced by muscle tendons such as the strong tendons of the quadriceps muscles and the tendon of the semimembranosus.

   2. Elbow Joint

       a. The elbow joint provides a stable and smoothly operating hinge joint that allows flexion and extension only.

       b. The ligaments involved in providing stability to the elbow joint are the annular ligament, the ulnar collateral ligament, and the radial collateral ligament.

       c. Tendons of several arm muscles, the biceps and the triceps, also provide additional stability by crossing the elbow joint.

  3. Shoulder (Glenohumeral) Joint

      a. Stability has been sacrificed to provide the most freely moving joint in the body.

      b. The ligaments that help to reinforce the shoulder joint are the coracohumeral ligament and the three glenohumeral ligaments.

      c. The tendons that cross the shoulder joint and provide the most stabilizing effect on the joint are the tendon of the long head of the biceps brachii and the four tendons that make up the rotator cuff.

  4. Hip (Coxal) Joint

      a. The hip joint is a ball-and-socket joint that provides a good range of motion.

      b. Several strong ligaments reinforce the capsule of the hip joint.

      c. The muscle tendons that cross the joint contribute to the stability and strength of the joint, but the majority of the stability of the hip joint is due to the deep socket of the acetabulum and the ligaments.

  5. Temporomandibular Joint

      a. The temporomandibular joint allows both hinge-like movement and side-to-side lateral excursion.

      b. The joint contains an articular disc that divides the synovial cavity into compartments that support each type of movement.

      c. The lateral aspect of the fibrous capsule contains a lateral ligament that reinforces the joint.

VI. Homeostatic Imbalances of Joints (pp. 272–275; Figs. 8.9, 8.13–8.14)

  A. Common Joint Injuries (pp. 272–273; Figs. 8.9, 8.13)

    1. Sprains and dislocations are the most common joint injuries.

  B. Inflammatory and Degenerative Conditions (pp. 272–276; Fig. 8.14)

    1. Bursitis, an inflammation of the bursa, is usually caused by a blow or friction; tendonitis is inflammation of the tendons, and is usually caused by overuse.

    2. Arthritis describes many inflammatory or degenerative diseases that damage the joints, resulting in pain, stiffness, and swelling of the joint.

      a. Osteoarthritis is the most common chronic arthritis. It is the result of breakdown of articular cartilage and subsequent thickening of bone tissue, which may restrict joint movement.

      b. Rheumatoid arthritis is a chronic inflammatory disorder that is an autoimmune disease.

      c. Gouty arthritis results when uric acid is deposited in the soft tissues of the joints.

VII. Developmental Aspects of Joints (p. 276)

  A. Joints develop at the same time as bones, resembling adult form by eight weeks gestation.

  B. At late middle age and beyond, ligaments and tendons shorten and weaken, intervertebral discs become more likely to herniate, and there is onset of osteoarthritis.

Cross References

Additional information on topics covered in Chapter 8 can be found in the chapters listed below.

1. Chapter 1: Planes of the body
2. Chapter 4: Ligaments and tendons (dense connective tissue); hyaline cartilage; fibrocartilage
3. Chapter 6: Epiphyseal plate; articular cartilage; periosteum
4. Chapter 7: Intervertebral discs; stability/flexibility of the pectoral (shoulder) girdle
5. Chapter 10: Role of synovial joints in the movement of the body
6. Chapter 23: Periodontal ligament

Laboratory Correlations

1. Marieb, E. N. *Human Anatomy & Physiology Laboratory Manual: Cat and Fetal Pig Versions.* Eighth Edition Updates. Benjamin Cummings, 2006.
   Exercise 13: Articulations and Body Movements
2. Marieb, E. N. *Human Anatomy & Physiology Laboratory Manual: Main Version.* Seventh Edition Update. Benjamin Cummings, 2006.
   Exercise 13: Articulations and Body Movements

Histology Slides for the Life Sciences

Available through Benjamin Cummings, an imprint of Pearson Education, Inc. To order, contact your local Benjamin Cummings sales representative.

Slide 20   Dense Irregular Connective Tissue, Tendon.
Slide 23   Hyaline Cartilage, Trachea.
Slide 24   Fibrocartilage, Intervertebral Disk.
Slide 46   Cartilage-Bone Junction, Toe Bone.
Slide 47   Epiphyseal Plate of a Bone.
Slide 72   Cross-section through the trachea showing psuedostratified ciliated epithelium, glands, and the supporting ring of hyaline cartilage.

Lecture Hints

1. Clearly distinguish between the two systems of joint classification (structural and functional).
2. Point out the difference between the joint of the first rib and sternum in contrast to ribs 2–10.
3. Emphasize that a muscle must cross a joint in order to cause movement.
4. Compare and contrast the size and shape of the glenoid cavity and acetabulum.
5. If only one synovial joint will be studied in detail, the best choice is the knee.
6. Stress the relationship between the shape of the articular surfaces of a joint, and the types of movements that are possible at that joint.

Activities/Demonstrations

1. Audio-visual materials listed under Multimedia in the Classroom and Lab.

2. Call on students to demonstrate the various types of body movements: abduction, adduction, flexion, extension, etc., occurring at specific joints (e.g., flex your knee, rotate your hand).

3. Obtain an articulated skeleton to exhibit joints such as sutures, syndesmoses, gomphoses, and others.

4. Obtain a 3-D model of a joint, such as the knee, to illustrate the relationship of ligaments, cartilage, and muscle. A fresh beef knee joint could also be used.

5. Obtain X rays of patients with gouty arthritis, osteoarthritis, and rheumatoid arthritis.

6. Obtain a video or request that a local orthopedic surgeon visit the class and describe the techniques and advantages of arthroscopic knee surgery.

7. Obtain an X ray showing a prosthetic joint.

Critical Thinking/Discussion Topics

1. Why are diarthroses found predominantly in the limbs while synarthroses and amphiarthroses are found largely in the axial skeleton?

2. What are the advantages of the shoulder joint being the most freely moving joint in the body?

3. Cortisone shots can readily reduce swelling that occurs in joints, such as the shoulder and knee, following athletic injuries. Why is it dangerous for athletes to continue getting these shots?

4. Physical therapists suggest various stretching exercises before proceeding with rigorous physical activity. Of what value are these exercises for the joint areas?

5. What does it mean to be "double-jointed"?

6. Most people can "crack" their knuckles. What does this term mean and what effect, if any, will this have on the knuckles in the future?

7. Bones appear to have numerous projections and protuberances. What do you suppose these are for?

Library Research Topics

1. Joints may often be injured during sports activities. What are the major joint injuries associated with football, basketball, baseball, and tennis?

2. Congenital dislocation of the hip is an orthopedic defect in which the acetabulum is too shallow and as a result the head of the femur has poor articulation. What is the current treatment for this defect?

3. The replacement of a damaged joint with an artificial one is becoming more common. Currently, which joints can be replaced?

4. Temporomandibular joint disorders are very painful. What methods of treatment are there and how successful are they? How do these joint disorders arise?

5. Much controversy surrounds the use of the drug dimethyl sulfoxide (DMSO). Why is the FDA so reluctant to provide full approval of this drug for use on humans when it's widely used for horses?

6. Contact an orthopedic surgeon in your area for information and/or videos on arthroscopic surgery.

7. Review the literature on the procedures and materials used for artificial joint replacements.

8. Rheumatoid arthritis appears to be an autoimmune disease. What are the current methods of treatment and what is the future prognosis for this disease and its cure?

9. What is the difference between the action of nonsteroidal anti-inflammatory drugs and steroidal anti-inflammatory drugs? What are the advantages and disadvantages of each?

Multimedia in the Classroom and Lab

Online Resources for Students

The Anatomy & Physiology Place
www.anatomyandphysiology.com

MyA&P
www.myaandp.com

The following shows the organization of the Chapter Guide page in both the Anatomy & Physiology Place and MyA&P™. The Chapter Guide organizes all the chapter-specific online media resources for Chapter 8 in one convenient location, with e-book links to each section of the textbook. Please note that both sites also give you access to other general A&P resources, like InterActive Physiology®, PhysioEx 6.0™, Anatomy 360°, Flashcards, a Glossary, a Histology Tutorial, and much more.

Objectives
Section 8.1 Classification of Joints (p. 253)
Section 8.2 Fibrous Joints (pp. 253–254)
Section 8.3 Cartilaginous Joints (p. 255)
Section 8.4 Synovial Joints (pp. 255–272)
Memory: Unique Movements
Memory: Classification of Joints
Section 8.5 Homeostatic Imbalances of Joints (pp. 272–274, 276)
Case Study: Articulations
Case Study: Craniosynotosis
Section 8.6 Developmental Aspects of Joints (p. 276)
Chapter Summary
Self-Study Quizzes
Art Labeling Quiz
Matching Quiz
Multiple-Choice Quiz (Level I)
Multiple-Choice Quiz (Level II)
True-False Quiz
Crossword Puzzles
Crossword Puzzle 8.1
Crossword Puzzle 8.2

Media

See Guide to Audio-Visual Resources in Appendix A for key to AV distributors.

Video

1. *Arthroscopic Knee Surgery* (FHS; 45 min., 1997). The physician presents the surgical procedure in detail. Each step is discussed, involving viewers in the medical and human drama. Bringing surgery procedures to the classroom setting provides a different perspective to understanding important concepts.

2. *Bones and Joints* (FHS; 20 min.). From *The New Living Body* series. Contains live-action video showing the human body in action, up-to-date imaging, and three-dimensional computer graphics. Students can actually observe how the parts work together to provide movement. Illustrations of difficult concepts greatly help the students understand. This is an excellent supplement to classroom presentation.

3. *Movements at Joints of the Body* (FHS; 40 min., 1997). This program, divided into three parts, demonstrates various body movements. The first part focuses on movement, the second part examines the actions of muscles, and the third part features a self-quiz.

4. *Moving Parts* (FHS; 26 min.). This program looks at the coordination of activity and balancing mechanisms. Shows how muscles, joints, and organs link up, and demonstrates the role of joints. Increases students' knowledge of how the parts of the body work together to produce movement.

Software

1. *A.D.A.M.® Anatomy Practice* (see p. 86 of this guide for full listing).
2. *A.D.A.M.® InterActive Anatomy® 4.0* (see p. 9 of this guide for full listing).
3. *A.D.A.M.® MediaPro* (see p. 9 of this guide for full listing).
4. *Bodyworks* (see p. 9 of this guide for full listing).
5. *The Interactive Hand* (LP; Win/Mac, 1997). This CD-ROM details the physiological structure and functions of the human hand using 3-D modeling. It examines the bones, joints, blood supply, nerve supply, and more.
6. *The Ultimate Human Body* (see p. 9 of this guide for full listing).

Lecture Enhancement Material

To view thumbnails of all of the illustrations for Chapter 8, see Appendix B.

Transparencies Index/Media Manager

Figure 8.1   Fibrous joints.
Figure 8.2   Cartilaginous joints.
Figure 8.3   General structure of a synovial joint.
Figure 8.4   Friction-reducing structures: Bursae and tendon sheaths.
Figure 8.5   Movements allowed by synovial joints.
Figure 8.6   Special body movements.
Figure 8.7   Types of synovial joints.
Figure 8.8   Knee joint.
Figure 8.9   A common knee injury.
Figure 8.10   The elbow joint.
Figure 8.11   The shoulder joint.
Figure 8.12   The hip joint.
Figure 8.13   The temporomandibular (jaw) joint.
Figure 8.14   Arthroscopic photograph of a torn medial meniscus
Figure 8.15   X ray of a hand deformed by rheumatoid arthritis.
Table 8.1   Summary of Joint Classes
Table 8.2   Structural and Functional Characteristics of Body Joints
Table 8.2   Structural and Functional Characteristics of Body Joints
A Closer Look   Joints: From Knights in Shining Armor to Bionic Humans*
*Indicates images that are on the Media Manager only.

Answers to End-of-Chapter Questions

Multiple Choice and Matching Question answers appear in Appendix G of the main text.

Short Answer Essay Questions

8. Joints are defined as sites where two or more bones meet. (p. 253)

9. Freely moveable joints provide mobility; slightly moveable joints provide strength with limited flexibility; immovable joints provide strong support, secure enclosures, and protection. (p. 253)

10. Bursae are synovial membrane-lined sacs that function to prevent friction, and are located where ligaments, muscles, skin, and/or muscle tendons overlie and rub against bone. In the latter case, the friction-reducing structures are called tendon sheaths. (p. 257)

11. Nonaxial movements mean slipping movements only, uniaxial movements mean movement in one plane, biaxial movements mean movement in two planes, and multiaxial movements mean movement in or around all three planes and axes. (p. 259)

12. Flexion and extension refer to decreasing or increasing the angle of a joint and bringing the two articulating bones together along the sagittal plane, while adduction and abduction refer to moving a limb closer to or away from the body midline along the frontal plane. (pp. 260–261)

13. Rotation means to turn a bone around its own long axis, while circumduction means to move a limb so that it describes a cone in space, an action that involves a variety of movements. (p. 261)

14. Uniaxial—hinge (elbow) and pivot (atlantoaxial and radioulnar); biaxial—condyloid (knuckle) and saddle (thumb); multiaxial—ball and socket (shoulder and hip). (p. 265)

15. The knee menisci deepen the articulating surface of the tibia to prevent side-to-side rocking of the femur on the tibia and to absorb shock transmitted to the knee joint. The cruciate ligaments prevent anterior/posterior displacement of the articulating bone and help to secure the joint. (pp. 265–267)

16. The knees must carry the total body weight and rely heavily on nonarticular factors for stability. The knees can absorb an upward force of great intensity; although they must also absorb direct blows and blows from the side, they are poorly designed to do so. (pp. 265–267)

17. Cartilages and ligaments are poorly vascularized and tend to heal very slowly. (p. 272)

18. Fibrous capsule: The fibrous capsule, composed of dense irregular connective tissue, is the external layer of the articular (joint) capsule, and strengthens the joint so that the bones are not pulled apart; synovial fluid: Synovial fluid occupies all free spaces within the joint capsule, including that within the articular cartilages, and serves to reduce friction between the cartilages. Synovial fluid also contains phagocyctic cells that rid the joint cavity of microbes or cellular debris; articular disc: Articular discs are wedges of fibrocartilage that separate the articular surfaces of the bones, thereby improving the fit between articulating bone ends and making the joint more stable. (pp. 255–256)

Critical Thinking and Clinical Application Questions

1. Most likely bursitis of the subcutaneous prepatellar bursa. It is a good guess that Sophie spends a good deal of time on her knees (perhaps scrubbing the floors). (p. 273)

2. a. Not really. The shape of the articular surfaces is not as enclosed as other joints, and has a greater degree of flexibility due to the fact that three bones, not two, create the joint. Also, there are relatively few strong muscles and ligaments that cross this joint, compared to other joints, such as the hip or knee. (p. 257)

   b. Ligaments.

   c. Returning bones back to position without an incision.

   d. Sprains heal slowly and need repair to stabilize joint.

   e. The examination of a joint by means of an endoscope.

   f. Using arthroscopic surgery, only small incisions are needed instead of an open surgical wound. There is less chance of infection and healing is considerably faster. (p. 272)

3. a. Probably gout, although it is more common in males.

   b. Caused by a deposition of uric acid crystals in soft tissues of joints. (p. 274)

4. The vector for the bacteria that causes Lyme disease is the deer tick, a very small tick carried by deer and other small mammals. (p. 276)

5. When Tony's mouth opened very wide, the mandibular condyle slid forward to the point that the joint dislocated. (p. 272)

Suggested Readings

Allman, W.F. "The Knee." *Science* 83 (Nov. 1983).

Fackelmann, K.A. "Chicken Cartilage Soothes Aching Joints." *Science News* 144 (Sept. 1993): 198.

Fackelmann, K.A. "The Nine-Month Arthritis Cure." *Science News* 144 (Oct. 1993): 144.

Germain, B.C. *Anatomy of Movement.* Eastland Press, 1993.

Gunn, C. *Bones and Joints: A Guide for Students.* 3rd ed. London: Churchill Livingstone, 1997.

Kantor, F.S. "Disarming Lyme Disease." *Scientific American* 271 (Sept. 1994): 34.

Matsumoto, I., et al. "Arthritis Provoked by Linked T and B Cell Recognition of a Glycolytic Enzyme." *Science* 286 (November 1999): 1732–1735.

Mayor, M.B., and J. Collier. "The Technology of Hip Replacement." *Scientific American: Science and Medicine* 1 (May/June 1994): 58–67.

Seppa, N. "Peptide Puts Mouse Arthritis Out of Joint." *Science News* 159 (18) (May 2001): 279.

Terkeltaub, R.A. "Gout: Fresh Insights Into an Ancient Disease." *Scientific American: Science and Medicine* 3 (July/Aug. 1996): 22.

Wang, L. "Fat Harbors Cells That Could Aid Joints." *Science News* 159 (9) (March 2001): 134.

Muscles and Muscles Tissue

Objectives

Overview of Muscle Tissues

1. Describe the properties of the three types of muscle tissue.
2. Identify the functional characteristics of muscle tissue.
3. Explain the functions of muscles.

Skeletal Muscle

4. Examine the gross anatomical features of skeletal muscle.
5. Describe the types of muscle attachments.
6. Explore the microscopic anatomy of skeletal muscle, and the specific arrangement of each element in relation to the others.
7. Describe the structural arrangement of the neuromuscular junction, and explain the mechanism of generation of an action potential across the sarcolemma.
8. Explain the sliding filament mechanism of muscle fiber contraction.
9. Define a motor unit, and explain the events of a muscle twitch.
10. Identify graded muscle response, and explain how factors affect graded responses.

11. Define muscle tone, and discuss in the context of isometric and isotonic contraction.
12. Describe the mechanisms through which muscles are supplied with ATP.
13. Discuss the factors that affect the force, velocity, and duration of muscle contraction.
14. Underscore the effects of exercise on muscles.

Smooth Muscle

15. Indicate the microscopic anatomy of smooth muscle cells, and compare to skeletal muscle cells.
16. Examine the mechanism and regulation of smooth muscle contraction.
17. Describe the types of smooth muscle and their locations in the body.

Developmental Aspects of Muscles

18. Identify the embryonic development of muscle tissue, and the changes in muscle tissue due to age.

Suggested Lecture Outline

I. Overview of Muscle Tissues (pp. 280–281; Table 9.3)

A. Types of Muscle Tissue (p. 280; Table 9.3)

1. Skeletal muscle is associated with the bony skeleton, and consists of large cells that bear striations and are controlled voluntarily.
2. Cardiac muscle occurs only in the heart, and consists of small cells that are striated and under involuntary control.

3. Smooth muscle is found in the walls of hollow organs, and consists of small elongated cells that are not striated and are under involuntary control.

B. Functional Characteristics of Muscle Tissue (p. 280)

1. Excitability, or irritability, is the ability to receive and respond to a stimulus.

2. Contractility is the ability to contract forcibly when stimulated.

3. Extensibility is the ability to be stretched.

4. Elasticity is the ability to resume the cells' original length once stretched.

C. Muscle Functions (pp. 280–281; Table 9.3)

1. Muscles produce movement by acting on the bones of the skeleton, pumping blood, or propelling substances throughout hollow organ systems.

2. Muscles aid in maintaining posture by adjusting the position of the body with respect to gravity.

3. Muscles stabilize joints by exerting tension around the joint.

4. Muscles generate heat as a function of their cellular metabolic processes.

II. Skeletal Muscle (pp. 281–309; Figs. 9.1–9.23; Tables 9.1–9.3)

A. Gross Anatomy of Skeletal Muscle (pp. 281–284; Figs. 9.1–9.2; Tables 9.1, 9.3)

1. Each muscle has a nerve and blood supply that allows neural control and ensures adequate nutrient delivery and waste removal.

2. Connective tissue sheaths are found at various structural levels of each muscle: endomysium surrounds each muscle fiber, perimysium surrounds groups of muscle fibers, and epimysium surrounds whole muscles.

3. Attachments span joints and cause movement to occur from the movable bone (the muscle's insertion) toward the less movable bone (the muscle's origin).

4. Muscle attachments may be direct or indirect.

B. Microscopic Anatomy of a Skeletal Muscle Fiber (pp. 284–288; Figs. 9.3–9.6; Tables 9.1, 9.3)

1. Skeletal muscle fibers are long cylindrical cells with multiple nuclei beneath the sarcolemma.

2. Myofibrils account for roughly 80% of cellular volume, and contain the contractile elements of the muscle cell.

3. Striations are due to a repeating series of dark A bands and light I bands.

4. Myofilaments make up the myofibrils, and consist of thick and thin filaments.

5. Ultrastructure and Molecular Composition of the Myofilaments

   a. There are two types of myofilaments in muscle cells: thick filaments composed of bundles of myosin, and thin filaments composed of strands of actin.

   b. Tropomyosin and troponin are regulatory proteins present in thin filaments.

6. The sarcoplasmic reticulum is a smooth endoplasmic reticulum surrounding each myofibril.

7. T tubules are infoldings of the sarcolemma that conduct electrical impulses from the surface of the cell to the terminal cisternae.

C. The sliding filament model of muscle contraction states that during contraction, the thin filaments slide past the thick filaments. Overlap between the myofilaments increases and the sarcomere shortens (pp. 288–289).

D. Physiology of a Skeletal Muscle Fiber (pp. 288–294; Figs. 9.7–9.11; Table 9.3)

1. The neuromuscular junction is a connection between an axon terminal and a muscle fiber that is the route of electrical stimulation of the muscle cell.

2. A nerve impulse causes the release of acetylcholine to the synaptic cleft, which binds to receptors on the motor end plate, triggering a series of electrical events on the sarcolemma.

3. Generation of an action potential across the sarcolemma occurs in response to acetylcholine binding with receptors on the motor end plate. It involves the influx of sodium ions, which makes the membrane potential slightly less negative.

4. Excitation-contraction coupling is the sequence of events by which an action potential on the sarcolemma results in the sliding of the myofilaments.

5. Ionic calcium in muscle contraction is kept at almost undetectable levels within the cell through the regulatory action of intracellular proteins.

6. Muscle fiber contraction follows exposure of the myosin binding sites, and follows a series of events.

E. Contraction of a Skeletal Muscle (pp. 295–300; Figs. 9.12–9.18)

1. A motor unit consists of a motor neuron and all the muscle fibers it innervates. It is smaller in muscles that exhibit fine control.

2. The muscle twitch is the response of a muscle to a single action potential on its motor neuron.

3. There are three kinds of graded muscle responses: wave summation, multiple motor unit summation (recruitment), and treppe.

4. Muscle tone is the phenomenon of muscles exhibiting slight contraction, even when at rest, which keeps muscles firm, healthy, and ready to respond.

5. Isotonic contractions result in movement occurring at the joint and shortening of muscles.

6. Isometric contractions result in increases in muscle tension, but no lengthening or shortening of the muscle occurs.

F. Muscle Metabolism (pp. 300–304; Figs. 9.19–9.20)

1. Muscles contain very little stored ATP, and consumed ATP is replenished rapidly through phosphorylation by creatine phosphate, glycolysis and anaerobic respiration, and aerobic respiration.

2. Muscles will function aerobically as long as there is adequate oxygen, but when exercise demands exceed the ability of muscle metabolism to keep up with ATP demand, metabolism converts to anaerobic glycolysis.

3. Muscle fatigue is the physiological inability to contract due to the shortage of available ATP.

4. Oxygen debt is the extra oxygen needed to replenish oxygen reserves, glycogen stores, ATP and creatine phosphate reserves, as well as conversion of lactic acid to pyruvic acid glucose after vigorous muscle activity.

5. Heat production during muscle activity is considerable. It requires release of excess heat through homeostatic mechanisms such as sweating and radiation from the skin.

G. Force of Muscle Contraction (pp. 304–305; Figs. 9.21–9.22)

1. As the number of muscle fibers stimulated increases, force of contraction increases.

2. Large muscle fibers generate more force than smaller muscle fibers.

3. As the rate of stimulation increases, contractions sum up, ultimately producing tetanus and generating more force.

4. There is an optimal length-tension relationship when the muscle is slightly stretched and there is slight overlap between the myofibrils.

H. Velocity and Duration of Muscle Contraction (pp. 305–307; Fig. 9.23; Tables 9.2–9.3)

1. There are three muscle fiber types: slow oxidative fibers, fast oxidative fibers, and fast glycolytic fibers.

2. Muscle fiber type is a genetically determined trait, with varying percentages of each fiber type in every muscle, determined by specific function of a given muscle.

3. As load increases, the slower the velocity and shorter the duration of contraction.

4. Recruitment of additional motor units increases velocity and duration of contraction.

I. Effect of Exercise on Muscles (pp. 307–309)

1. Aerobic, or endurance, exercise promotes an increase in capillary penetration, the number of mitochondria, and increased synthesis of myoglobin, leading to more efficient metabolism, but no hypertrophy.

2. Resistance exercise, such as weight lifting or isometric exercise, promotes an increase in the number of mitochondria, myofilaments and myofibrils, and glycogen storage, leading to hypertrophied cells.

III. Smooth Muscle (pp. 309–313; Figs. 9.24–9.26; Table 9.3)

A. Microscopic Structure of Smooth Muscle Fibers (pp. 309–311; Figs. 9.24–9.25; Table 9.3)

1. Smooth muscle cells are small, spindle-shaped cells with one central nucleus, and lack the coarse connective tissue coverings of skeletal muscle.

2. Smooth muscle cells are usually arranged into sheets of opposing fibers, forming a longitudinal layer and a circular layer.

3. Contraction of the opposing layers of muscle leads to a rhythmic form of contraction, called peristalsis, which propels substances through the organs.

4. Smooth muscle lacks neuromuscular junctions, but have varicosities instead, numerous bulbous swellings that release neurotransmitters to a wide synaptic cleft.

5. Smooth muscle cells have a less developed sarcoplasmic reticulum, sequestering large amounts of calcium in extracellular fluid within caveolae in the cell membrane.

6. Smooth muscle has no striations, no sarcomeres, a lower ratio of thick to thin filaments when compared to skeletal muscle, and has tropomyosin but no troponin.

7. Smooth muscle fibers contain longitudinal bundles of noncontractile intermediate filaments anchored to the sarcolemma and suurounding tissues via dense bodies.

B.   Contraction of Smooth Muscle (pp. 311–316; Figs. 9.26–9.27; Table 9.3)

   1.   Mechanism and Characteristics of Contraction

      a.   Smooth muscle fibers exhibit slow, synchronized contractions due to electrical coupling by gap junctions.

      b.   Like skeletal muscle, actin and myosin interact by the sliding filament mechanism. The final trigger for contraction is a rise in intracellular calcium level, and the process is energized by ATP.

      c.   During excitation-contraction coupling, calcium ions enter the cell from the extracellular space, bind to calmodulin, and activate myosin light chain kinase, powering the cross-bridging cycle.

      d.   Smooth muscle contracts more slowly and consumes less ATP than skeletal muscle.

   2.   Regulation of Contraction

      a.   Autonomic nerve endings release either acetylcholine or norepinephrine, which may result in excitation of certain groups of smooth muscle cells, and inhibition of others.

      b.   Hormones and local factors, such as lack of oxygen, histamine, excess carbon dioxide, or low pH, act as signals for contraction.

   3.   Special Features of Smooth Muscle Contraction

      a.   Smooth muscle initially contracts when stretched, but contraction is brief, and then the cells relax to accommodate the stretch.

      b.   Smooth muscle stretches more and generates more tension when stretched than skeletal muscle.

      c.   Hyperplasia, an increase in cell number through division, is possible in addition to hypertrophy, an increase in individual cell size.

C.   Types of Smooth Muscle (p. 316)

   1.   Single-unit smooth muscle, called visceral muscle, is the most common type of smooth muscle. It contracts rhythmically as a unit, is electrically coupled by gap junctions, and exhibits spontaneous action potentials.

   2.   Multiunit smooth muscle is located in large airways to the lungs, large arteries, arrector pili muscles in hair follicles, and the iris of the eye. It consists of cells that are structurally independent of each other, has motor units, and is capable of graded contractions.

IV. Developmental Aspects of Muscles (pp. 316–320)

A.   Nearly all muscle tissue develops from specialized mesodermal cells called myoblasts.

B.   Skeletal muscle fibers form through the fusion of several myoblasts, and are actively contracting by week 7 of fetal development.

C.   Myoblasts of cardiac and smooth muscle do not fuse but form gap junctions at a very early stage.

D.   Muscular development in infants is mostly reflexive at birth, and progresses in a head-to-toe and proximal-to-distal direction.

E.   Women have relatively less muscle mass than men due to the effects of the male sex hormone testosterone, which accounts for the difference in strength between the sexes.

F.   Muscular dystrophy is one of the few disorders that muscles experience, and is characterized by atrophy and degeneration of muscle tissue. Enlargement of muscles is due to fat and connective tissue deposit.

Cross References

Additional information on topics covered in Chapter 9 can be found in the chapters listed below.

1. Chapter 2: ATP; ions
2. Chapter 3: General cellular structural components; membrane transport; microfilaments; gap junctions; membrane potentials
3. Chapter 4: Connective tissues; muscle tissue
4. Chapter 6: Structure of bone tissue
5. Chapter 8: Joint stability as a function of skeletal muscle contraction
6. Chapter 10: Skeletal muscles of the body; interaction between muscle and bones
7. Chapter 11: General structure and function of synapses and neurotransmitters
8. Chapter 13: Sensory receptors located in skeletal muscle; motor neurons of the peripheral nervous system and the neuromuscular junction
9. Chapter 18: Function of cardiac tissue; example of the sliding filament mechanism of muscle contraction
10. Chapter 19: Smooth muscle utilization
11. Chapter 23: Smooth muscle utilization; single-unit smooth muscle function in relation to peristalsis
12. Chapter 24: Metabolic pathways of energy production (glycolysis, Kreb's cycle, and electron transport); shivering as a heat production mechanism
13. Chapter 27: Smooth muscle utilization

Laboratory Correlations

1. Marieb, E. N. *Human Anatomy & Physiology Laboratory Manual: Cat and Fetal Pig Versions*. Eighth Edition Updates. Benjamin Cummings, 2006.
   Exercise 14: Microscopic Anatomy and Organization of Skeletal Muscle
   Exercise 16: Skeletal Muscle Physiology
2. Marieb, E. N. *Human Anatomy & Physiology Laboratory Manual: Main Version*. Seventh Edition Update. Benjamin Cummings, 2006.
   Exercise 14: Microscopic Anatomy and Organization of Skeletal Muscle
   Exercise 16: Skeletal Muscle Physiology

Histology Slides for the Life Sciences

Available through Benjamin Cummings, an imprint of Pearson Education, Inc. To order, contact your local Benjamin Cummings sales representative.

Slide 20   Dense Irregular Connective Tissue, Tendon.
Slide 28   Skeletal Muscle Tissue, Cross Section, Tongue.
Slide 29   Skeletal Muscle Tissue, Longitudinal Section, Tongue.
Slide 30   Cardiac Muscle Tissue, Heart.
Slide 31   Smooth Muscle Tissue, Longitudinal Section, Uterus.
Slide 32   Smooth Muscle Tissue, Longitudinal and Cross Section, Uterus.
Slide 33   Thin Section of Cardiac Muscle.
Slide 34   Smooth Muscle.
Slide 49   Cardiac Muscle Tissue, Heart.
Slide 50   Neuromuscular Junction, Muscle Spread.
Slide 51   Skeletal Muscle.

Lecture Hints

1. The terminology used in the description of the functional characteristics of muscle is confusing to many students. Point out that "extend" is a root of the word extensibility, and it is easy to associate that stretching with extending. Elasticity (the ability to recoil) is the opposite of extensibility.

2. Since the prefixes endo-, epi-, and peri- are often used in anatomical terminology, emphasize the meanings and indicate that students will see these again.

3. A nice way to pull together the overall structure of muscle tissue from myofilaments to the entire muscle is by a cross-sectional diagram. Students are often confused by the similarity in the names of the structures, e.g., myofilaments vs. myofibril vs. myofiber. Use analogies to help students remember: filaments are like those in light bulbs, very thin, forming the basic structure for causing an action (light); in contrast, fibers are larger structures and, like nerve fibers, are cells; the term *fibril* is intermediate between the two.

4. In the description of the sliding filament mechanism, be sure to use several drawings (or diagrams) of the relationships between the thick and thin filaments during contraction. Students are easily confused by the series of static diagrams presented. Be sure to indicate the dynamic nature of contraction.

5. Students often have difficulty with "all or none" as applied to individual muscle fibers. Clearly point out the distinction between muscle cells (and motor units) vs. whole muscle. Use the analogy of a light switch control of all the lamps attached to it—either on or off, no in-between.

6. Emphasize that graded muscle contraction is achieved by increasing the frequency of stimulation of motor units or increasing the number of motor units activated.

7. As a way of introducing isometric and isotonic contractions, ask the class if muscle contraction always results in movement. Whatever their answer, illustrate the point by attempting to lift a fixed object in the classroom. Point out that although force is increasing, the object is not being lifted; therefore the muscle must remain the same length. Ask what system of measuring length is used in science. Someone will answer "metric," at which time the definition of the prefix iso- should be given. Use of real-life analogies will help students remember these very similar terms.

8. To illustrate length-tension relationships, ask the class to comment on the amount of force generated if myosin and actin do not overlap at all, so that the myosin heads do not cross-bridge with actin. Conversely, ask what would happen if myosin and actin were completely overlapped.

9. When explaining the differences between slow and fast (oxidative) fibers, it is helpful to give examples of different types of athletes and the types of muscle fibers that predominate as a result of specific exercises. Students remember these examples (and the principles) easily when they can relate to real-life experience.

10. Explain that all muscle types contain actin and myosin myofilaments, but that the arrangement (in part) accounts for the structural and functional differences.

11. Be sure to inform students that the terms *striated* and *skeletal muscle* are interchangeable, and that although cardiac muscle is striated, the term *striated* should not be used as a name for cardiac muscle.

Activities/Demonstrations

1. Audio-visual materials listed under Multimedia in the Classroom and Lab.

2. Demonstrate muscle contraction using a simple myograph or kymograph apparatus and the gastrocnemius muscle of a frog. A film loop showing these events might be used. It is important that students be able to visualize these events.

3. Ask students to demonstrate examples of isometric and isotonic contractions and explain how individual muscle cells and motor units are behaving to cause muscle contraction.

4. Set up a microscope with a slide of a motor unit for class viewing.

5. Use models that compare the three types of muscle tissue to point out the unique structural characteristics of each type.

6. Use an articulated skeleton to point out various origins and insertions; then ask students to specify the resulting movement.

7. Pick apart a piece of cooked chicken breast to demonstrate individual fascicles.

8. Obtain a 3-D model of a sarcomere to exhibit tubules and myofibrils.

9. Obtain or construct a 3-D model of a sarcomere that illustrates the sliding filament mechanism of muscle contraction.

10. Stress the importance of extracellular calcium ions to smooth muscle contraction, and distinguish this from skeletal muscle, which is more reliant on stored intracellular calcium ions.

11. Use a microprojector and microslides of skeletal, smooth, and cardiac muscle to illustrate their microscopic similarities and differences.

Critical Thinking/Discussion Topics

1. You are caught by a sudden snowstorm and you are without shelter or warm clothing. Why is it important for you to keep moving and exercising rather than sitting on the ground, motionless, waiting for rescue?

2. Muscles that are immobilized for long periods of time, as with a cast, frequently get smaller. Why? What is necessary to revitalize them?

3. Why do you suppose activities such as swimming and fast walking are so beneficial? Are there any negative attributes to activities such as racquetball and sprinting?

4. How can weight lifters have such enormous muscles, while long-distance runners have lean muscles?

5. What effect would there be on the body if intestinal peristaltic waves were stopped either by infection or injury?

6. Why do athletes "warm up" before a competitive event? Would you expect the warm-up period to make contraction more or less efficient? Why?

7. Visit a local gym frequented by body builders. Obtain information on the procedures used to build muscle mass and an explanation of how those procedures accomplish that goal.

8. If the number of myosin heads were doubled, what would be the effect on force production? ATP consumption?

9. What is a muscle spasm? How do you think it may be caused?

10. Are spasms and cramps related? Compare and contrast the different possible mechanisms of each.

11. Draw diagrams of different fascicle arrangements and describe what type of movement is characteristic of each (i.e., short range, powerful, etc.) Then have students apply these ideas to place the different fascicle types in logical locations on an articulated skeleton (e.g., the deltoid origin and insertion is a logical example of perfect use of a convergent pattern).

Library Research Topics

1. Why have muscle cells "lost" their ability to regenerate? What current research is being done in this area?

2. Investigate the long-term effect of anabolic steroid use on muscle tissue.

3. Why do you suppose the Olympic committees are so adamant against the use of "performance-enhancing" drugs such as anabolic steroids?

4. Trace the embryonic development of skeletal muscles, noting how they maintain constant contact with neural cells.

5. Explore the current theories for the etiology of muscular dystrophy.

6. What is the current status of the sliding filament model of muscle contraction? Do we know all there is to know?

7. Examine how biofeedback can reduce stress-induced muscle tension.

8. Describe several metabolic diseases of muscle (usually due to an enzyme or enzyme group deficiency).

9. Alcohol can induce a form of toxic myopathy. Describe the effects of alcohol on muscle tissue.

10. Define the term *myositis*. What causative agents could result in this form of muscle disease?

11. Are tumors (benign or malignant) associated with muscle tissue? Would cancer develop in the muscle cells themselves, or in the connective tissue coverings? Explore the possibilities.

Multimedia in the Classroom and Lab

Online Resources for Students

The
Anatomy & Physiology Place   MyA&P
www.anatomyandphysiology.com   www.myaandp.com

The following shows the organization of the Chapter Guide page in both the Anatomy & Physiology Place and MyA&P™. The Chapter Guide organizes all the chapter-specific online media resources for Chapter 9 in one convenient location, with e-book links to each section of the textbook. Please note that both sites also give you access to other general A&P resources, like InterActive Physiology®, PhysioEx 6.0™, Anatomy 360°, Flashcards, a Glossary, a Histology Tutorial, *and much more.*

Objectives

Section 9.1 Overview of Muscle Tissues (pp. 280–281)

InterActive Physiology®: Anatomy Review

Section 9.2 Skeletal Muscle (pp. 281–309, 314–315)

Art Labeling Activity: Connective Tissue Sheaths of Skeletal Muscle (Fig. 9.2, p. 283)

InterActive Physiology®: Muscle Metabolism

InterActive Physiology®: Neuromuscular Junction

InterActive Physiology®: Contraction of Motor Units

InterActive Physiology®: Sliding Filament Theory

InterActive Physiology®: Contraction of Whole Muscle

PhysioEx: Skeletal Muscle Physiology

Activity: Microscopic Anatomy of a Skeletal Fiber

Media

See Guide to Audio-Visual Resources in Appendix A for key to AV distributors.

Video

1. *Human Musculature Videotape* (BC; 23 min., 1999). Rose Leigh Vines, California State University. Offers a clear 23-minute anatomical tour of the muscles in the human body; an inexpensive alternative to cadaver dissection.
2. *Muscles and Joints: Muscle Power* (FHS; 26 min., 1984). Illustrates microscopic view of muscles and compares all three types of muscle.
3. *Muscles* (FHS; 20 min., 1989). From *The New Living Body* series. Introduces the nature of muscle tissue in the body and looks at the complex movements involved in exercise. Muscle is examined from gross structure to detailed microstructure.
4. *Muscular System: The Inner Athlete* (FHS; 25 min., 2000). From *The Human Body: Systems at Work* series, this program looks at the many roles played by muscle in our everyday lives.
5. *The Skeletal and Muscular Systems* (NIMCO; 24 min., 1997). Demonstrates how the skeletal and muscular systems work together to provide the structure and shape of the body.

Software

1. *Bodyworks* (see p. 9 of this guide for full listing).
2. *InterActive Physiology® 9-System Suite CD-ROM: Muscular System* (BC; Win/Mac, 2000). Offers lucid, interactive exploration of some of the more difficult concepts of muscle physiology.

Lecture Enhancement Material

To view thumbnails of all of the illustrations for Chapter 9, see Appendix B.

Transparencies Index/Media Manager

Figure 9.1   Photomicrograph of the capillary network surrounding skeletal muscle fibers.

Figure 9.2   Connective tissue sheaths of skeletal muscle.

Indicates images that are on the Media Manager only.

Answers to End-of-Chapter Questions

Multiple Choice and Matching Question answers appear in Appendix G of the main text.

Short Answer Essay Questions

15. The functions are: excitability—the ability to receive and respond to a stimulus; contractility—the ability to shorten; extensibility—the ability to be stretched; and elasticity—the ability to resume normal length after contraction or having been stretched. (p. 280)

16. a. In direct attachment, the epimysium of the muscle is fused to the periosteum of a bone, and in indirect attachment, the muscle connective tissue sheaths extend beyond the muscle as a tendon; the tendon anchors to the periosteum of a bone. (p. 284)

    b. A tendon is a ropelike mass of fibrous tissue; an aponeurosis is a flat, broad sheet. (p. 283)

17. a. A sarcomere is the region of a myofibril between two successive Z-lines and is the smallest contractile unit of a muscle cell. The myofilaments are within the sarcomere. (p. 284)

    b. The theory proposes that the thin filaments slide toward the center of the sarcomere through the rachetlike action of the myosin heads. The process is energized by ATP. (p. 288; Fig. 9.6)

18. AChE destroys the ACh after it is released. This prevents continued muscle fiber contraction in the absence of additional stimulation. (p. 289)

19. A slight, but smooth contraction involves rapid stimulation of a few motor units and affects only a few muscle fibers of the muscle, whereas a strong contraction would involve many (or all) motor units stimulated technically. (p. 298)

20. Excitation-contraction coupling is the sequence of events by which an action potential traveling along the sarcolemma leads to the contraction of a muscle fiber. (p. 291)

21. A motor unit is the motor neuron and all the muscle fibers it controls. (p. 296)

22. Table 9.2, p. 306, illustrates the structural and functional characteristics of the three types of skeletal muscle fibers.

23. False. Most body muscles contain a mixture of fiber types that allows them to exhibit a range of contractile speeds and fatigue resistance. However, certain muscle fiber types may predominate in specific muscles, e.g., white fibers predominate in the occular muscles. (p. 307)

24. Muscle fatigue is the state of physiological inability to contract. It occurs due to ATP deficit, lactic acid buildup, and ionic imbalance. (pp. 303–304)

25. Oxygen debt is defined as the additional amount of oxygen that must be taken in by the body to provide for restorative processes, and it represents the difference between the amount of oxygen needed for totally aerobic respiration during muscle activity and the amount that is actually used. (p. 304)

26. Contractile force is affected by (1) the number of muscle fibers contracting, (2) the relative size of the muscle, (3) frequency of stimulation, and (4) the degree of muscle stretch. Velocity and duration of contraction depend on both load and muscle fiber type. (pp. 304–305)

27. Smooth muscle is located within the walls of hollow organs and around blood vessels. The tissue is under involuntary control. These characteristics are essential since the vessels and hollow organs must respond slowly, fill and expand slowly, and avoid expulsive contractions. (pp. 309–310)

Critical Thinking and Clinical Application Questions

1. A strain is an excessively stretched or torn muscle, whereas a sprain is an injury to the ligaments reinforcing a joint. The symptoms are similar for both: pain and swelling. (pp. 272, 320)

2. Regular resistance exercise leads to increased muscle strength by causing muscle cells to hypertrophy or increase in size. The number of myofilaments increases in these muscles. (pp. 307, 309)

3. The reason for the tightness is rigor mortis. The myosin cross bridges are "locked on" to the actin because of the lack of ATP necessary for release. No, peak rigidity occurs at 12 hours and then gradually dissipates over the next 48 to 60 hours as biological molecules begin to degrade. (p. 294)

4. Chemical A. By blocking binding of ACh to the motor end plate, neural stimulation of the cell is blocked, and the muscle cell cannot depolarize. Chemical B would actually increase contraction of the muscle cell by increasing the availability of calcium ions that bind to troponin, contributing to actin-myosin cross bridging. (pp. 289, 293)

5. Eric is breathing heavily because he has incurred an oxygen debt. His breathing pattern is due to anaerobic metabolism involving glycolysis and lactic acid formation. The metabolic product that accounts for his sore muscles and his feeling of muscle weakness is lactic acid. (p. 304)

Suggested Readings

Barinaga, M. "Titanic Protein Gives Muscles Structure and Balance." *Science* 270 (Oct. 1995): 236.

Bers, D., and M. Fill. "Coordinated Feet and the Dance of Ryanodine Receptors." *Science* 281 (Aug. 1998): 790–791.

Block, S.M. "One Small Step for Myosin." *Nature* 378 (Nov. 1995): 132–133.

Campbell, K., and Crosbie, R. "Gene Therapy." *Science and Medicine* 4 (Nov. 1996): 6–7.

Conklin, W. *Nature Power Builders: Pros and Cons*. New York: St Martin's Press, 1999.

DeRosier, D. "The Changing Shape of Actin." *Nature* 347 (Sept. 1990): 21.

Fackelmann, K.A. "The Nine-Month Arthritis Cure." *Science News* 144 (Oct. 1993): 266.

Gautam, M., et al. "Failure of Postsynaptic Specialization to Develop at Neuromuscular Junctions of Rapsyn Deficient Mice." *Nature* 377 (Sept. 1995): 232–236.

Goldman, Y., and H. Higuchi. "Sliding Distance Between Actin and Myosin Filaments Per ATP Molecule Hydrolysed in Skin Muscle Fibers." *Nature* 352 (July 1991): 352.

Grady, D. "One Foot Forward." *Discover* 11 (Sept. 1990): 86–93.

Hartwig, J. S., et al. "Effect of ATP on Actin Filament Stiffness." *Nature* 347 (Sept. 1990): 95.

Huxley, A. "Crossbridge Tilting Confirmed." *Nature* 375 (June 1995): 631–632.

Jo, A.S., et al. "Neurgulins Are Concentrated at Nerve-Muscle Synapses and Activate ACh-Receptor Gene Expression." *Nature* 373 (Jan. 1995): 158–164.

Johnson, K. A., and F. Quiocho. "Twitching Worms Catch S100." *Nature* 380 (April 1996): 585.

Klein, M.G., et al. "Two Mechanisms of Quantized Calcium Release in Skeletal Muscle." *Nature* 379 (Feb. 1996): 455–458.

Labeit, S., and B. Kolmerer. "Titins: Giant Proteins in Charge of Muscle Ultrastructure and Elasticity." *Science* 270 (Oct. 1995): 293–296.

Lin, Weichun, et al. "Distinct Roles of Nerve and Muscle in Postsynaptic Differentiation of the Neuromuscular Synapse." *Nature* 410 (6832) (April 2001): 1057–1064.

Linari, M., V. Lombardi, and G. Piazzesi. "Rapid Regeneration of the Actin-Myosin Power Stroke in Contracting Muscle." *Nature* 355 (Feb. 1992): 638.

Nakai, J., et al. "Enhanced Dihydropyridine Receptor Channel Activity in the Presence of Ryanodine Receptor." *Nature* 380 (Mar. 1996): 72–75.

Pennisi, E. "3-D Atomic View of Muscle Molecule." *Science News* 144 (July 1993): 4.

Piazzesi, G., et al. "Mechanism of Force Generation by Myosin Heads in Skeletal Muscle." *Nature* 415 (6877) (Feb. 2002): 659–662.

Service, R.F. "Flexing Muscle with Just One Amino Acid." *Science* 271 (Jan. 1996): 31.

Somiyo, A.P., and A.V. Somiyo. "Signal Transduction and Regulation in Smooth Muscle." *Nature* 372 (Nov. 1994): 231–236.

Spudich, James A. "The Myosin Swinging Cross-Bridge Model." *Nature Reviews: Molecular Cell Biology* 2 (5) (May 2001): 387–392.

Travis, J. "Antibiotics for Muscular Dystrophy?" *Science News* 156 (Aug. 1999): 84.

The Muscular System

Objectives

Interactions of Skeletal Muscles in the Body

1. Explain the way muscles work in the body.
2. Describe prime movers, antagonists, synergists, and fixators.

Naming Skeletal Muscles

3. Identify the criteria used to name skeletal muscles.

Muscle Mechanics: Importance of Fascicle Arrangements and Leverage

4. Indicate the most common patterns of fascicle arrangement found in skeletal muscles.
5. Define a lever, fulcrum, and effort.
6. List the three types of lever systems and give examples of each in the body.

Major Skeletal Muscles of the Body

7. Name and identify the muscles described in Tables 10.1 to 10.17. State the action, origin, and insertion of each.

Suggested Lecture Outline

I. Interactions of Skeletal Muscles in the Body (p. 325)

A. Muscles only pull; they are not capable of pushing.
B. The muscle that provides the major force for the specific movement is called the prime mover or the agonist.
C. Muscles that oppose or reverse a particular movement are called the antagonists.
D. Synergists help the prime movers by adding extra force to the same movement, or by reducing undesirable or unnecessary movements.

II. Naming Skeletal Muscles (pp. 325–326)

A. Some muscle names indicate the bone or body region with which the muscle is associated.
B. Some muscles are named for their shape.
C. Terms such as maximus, minimus, longus, and brevis are often used in muscle names to indicate relative size of the muscle.
D. The names of some muscles indicate the direction in which their fibers run in relation to an imaginary line of the body, such as the midline.
E. The number of origins a muscle has may be indicated by the word biceps, triceps, or quadriceps in its name.

F. Some muscles are named according to the location of their origin and insertion.

G. A muscle may be named for its action by using a word such as flexor or extensor in its name.

III. Muscle Mechanics: Importance of Fascicle Arrangement and Leverage (pp. 326–330; Figs. 10.1–10.3)

A. In skeletal muscles the common arrangement of the fascicles varies, resulting in muscles with different shapes and functional capabilities. (p. 326; Fig. 10.1)

 1. The fascicular pattern is circular when the fascicles are arranged in concentric rings.

 2. A convergent muscle has a broad origin and its fascicles converge toward a single tendon of insertion.

 3. In a parallel arrangement, the long axis of the fascicles runs parallel to the long axis of the muscle.

 4. A spindle-shaped parallel arrangement of fascicles is sometimes classified as a fusiform muscle.

 5. In a pennate pattern of arrangement the fascicles are short and attach obliquely to a central tendon that runs the length of the muscle.

B. The operation of most skeletal muscles involves the use of leverage and lever systems, partnerships between the muscular and skeletal systems. (pp. 326–330; Figs. 10.2, 10.3)

 1. A lever is a rigid bar that moves on a fixed point, or a fulcrum, when a force is applied to it.

 2. The applied force, or effort is used to move a resistance or load.

 3. In your body, your joints act as the fulcrums, the bones as the levers, and the muscle contraction as the effort.

 4. There are three types of levers: first-class, second-class, and third-class.

IV. Major Skeletal Muscles of the Body (pp. 330–333; Figs. 10.4–10.25; Tables 10.1–10.17)

A. Muscles of the Head, Part I: Facial Expression (pp. 335–338; Fig. 10.6; Table 10.1)

 1. Muscles of the scalp include the epicranius consisting of the frontal belly and the occipital belly.

 2. Muscles of the face include corrugator supercilii, orbicularis oculi, zygomaticus, risorius, levator labii superioris, depressor labii inferioris, depressor anguli oris, orbicularis oris, mentalis, buccinator, and platysma.

B. Muscles of the Head, Part II: Mastication and Tongue Movement (pp. 338–339; Fig. 10.7; Table 10.2)

 1. Muscles of mastication include the masseter, temporalis, medial pterygoid, lateral pterygoid, and the buccinator.

 2. Muscles promoting tongue movements are the genioglossus, hyoglossus, and the styloglossus.

C. Muscles of the Anterior Neck and Throat: Swallowing (pp. 340–341; Fig. 10.8; Table 10.3)

 1. Suprahyoid muscles include digastric, stylohyoid, mylohyoid, and geniohyoid.

 2. Infrahyoid muscles include sternohyoid, sternothyroid, omohyoid, thyrohyoid, and the pharyngeal constrictor muscles (superior, middle, and inferior).

D. Muscles of the Neck and Vertebral Column: Head and Trunk Movements (pp. 342–345; Fig. 10.9; Table 10.4)
   1. Anterolateral neck muscles include the sternocleidomastoid, and scalenes (anterior, middle, and posterior).
   2. Intrinsic muscles of the back include splenius capitis, splenius cervicis, erector spinae (sacrospinalis), iliocostalis, longissimus, spinalis, semispinalis, and the quadratus lumborum.

E. Muscles of the Thorax: Breathing (pp. 346–347; Fig. 10.10; Table 10.5)
   1. Muscles of the thorax include the external intercostals, internal intercostals, and the diaphragm.

F. Muscles of the Abdominal Wall: Trunk Movements and Compression of Abdominal Viscera (pp. 348–349; Fig. 10.11; Table 10.6)
   1. Muscles of the anterolateral abdominal wall include the rectus abdominis, external oblique, internal oblique, and the transversus abdominis.

G. Muscles of the Pelvic Floor and Perineum: Support of Abdominopelvic Organs (pp. 350–351; Fig. 10.12; Table 10.7)
   1. Muscles of the pelvic diaphragm include the levator ani and the coccygeus.
   2. Muscles of the urogenital diaphragm include the deep transverse perineal muscle and the external urinary sphincter.
   3. Muscles of the superficial space include the ischiocavernosus, bulbospongiosus, and the superficial transverse perineal muscle.

H. Superficial Muscles of the Anterior and Posterior Thorax: Movements of the Scapula (pp. 352–353; Fig. 10.13; Table 10.8)
   1. Muscles of the anterior thorax include the pectoralis minor, serratus anterior, and the subclavius.
   2. Muscles of the posterior thorax include the trapezius, levator scapulae, and the rhomboids (major and minor).

I. Muscles Crossing the Shoulder Joint: Movements of the Arm (pp. 354–356; Fig. 10.14; Table 10.9)
   1. Muscles moving the arm include the pectoralis major, latissimus dorsi, deltoid, subscapularis, supraspinatus, infraspinatus, teres minor, teres major, and the coracobrachialis.

J. Muscles Crossing the Elbow Joint: Flexion and Extension of the Forearm (p. 357; Fig. 10.14; Table 10.10)
   1. Posterior muscles include the triceps brachii and the anconeus.
   2. Anterior muscles include the biceps brachii, brachialis, and the brachioradialis.

K. Muscles of the Forearm: Movements of the Wrist, Hand, and Fingers (pp. 358–361; Figs. 10.15, 10.16; Table 10.11)
   1. Anterior superficial muscles include the pronator teres, flexor carpi radialis, palmaris longus, flexor carpi ulnaris, and the flexor digitorum superficialis.
   2. Anterior deep muscles include the flexor pollicis longus, flexor digitorum profundus, and the pronator quadratus.
   3. Posterior superficial muscles include the brachioradialis, extensor carpi radialis longus, extensor carpi radialis brevis, extensor digitorum, and the extensor carpi ulnaris.
   4. Posterior deep muscles include the supinator, abductor pollicis longus, extensor pollicis brevis and longus, and the extensor pollicis indicis.

L. Summary of Actions of Muscles Acting on the Arm, Forehead, and Hand (pp. 362–363; Fig. 10.17; Table 10.12)

M. Intrinsic Muscles of the Hand: Fine Movements of the Fingers (pp. 364–366; Fig. 10.18; Table 10.13)

1. Thenar muscles in ball of thumb include the abductor pollicis brevis, flexor pollicis brevis, opponens pollicis, and the adductor pollicis.

2. Hypothenar muscles in ball of little finger include the abductor digiti minimi, flexor digiti minimi brevis, and the opponens digiti minimi.

3. Midpalmar muscles include the lumbricals, palmar interossei, and the dorsal interossei.

N. Muscles Crossing the Hip and Knee Joints: Movements of the Thigh and Leg (pp. 367–372; Figs. 10.19–10.20; Table 10.14)

1. Anteromedial muscles include the iliopsoas, which is composed of the iliacus and the psoas major, and the sartorius.

2. Muscles of the medial compartment of the thigh include the adductor group, which is made up of the adductor magnus, adductor longus and the adductor brevis, the pectineus, and the gracilis.

3. Muscles of the anterior compartment of the thigh include the quadriceps femoris group, which is made up of the rectus femoris, vastus lateralis, vastus medialis and vastus intermedius, and the tensor fasciae latae.

4. Posterior muscles are the gluteal muscles, which include the gluteus maximus, gluteus medius, and the gluteus minimus.

5. Lateral rotators include the piriformis, obturator externus, obturator internus, gemellus, and the quadratus femoris.

6. Muscles of the posterior compartment of the thigh include the hamstrings, which consists of the biceps femoris, semitendinosus, and the semimembranosus.

O. Muscles of the Leg: Movements of the Ankle and Toes (pp. 373–378; Figs. 10.21–10.23; Table 10.15)

1. Muscles of the anterior compartment include the tibialis anterior, extensor digitorum longus, fibularis (peroneus) tertius, and the extensor hallucis longus.

2. Muscles of the lateral compartment include the fibularis (peroneus) longus and the fibularis (peroneus) brevis.

3. Superficial muscles of the posterior compartment include the triceps surae, which is composed of the gastrocnemius and the soleus, and the plantaris.

4. Deep muscles of the posterior compartment include the popliteus, flexor digitorum longus, flexor hallucis longus, and the tibialis posterior.

P. Summary of Actions of Muscles Acting on the Thigh, Leg, and Foot (pp. 379–380; Fig. 10.24; Table 10.16)

Q. Intrinsic Muscles of the Foot: Toe Movement and Arch Support (pp. 381–383; Fig. 10.25; Table 10.17)

1. The muscle found on the dorsum of the foot is the extensor digitorum brevis.

2. Muscles on the sole of the foot found in the first layer are the flexor digitorum brevis, abductor hallucis, and the abductor digiti minimi.

3. Muscles on the sole of the foot found in the second layer are the flexor accessorius (quadratus plantae) and the lumbricals.

4. Muscles of the sole of the foot found in the third layer include the flexor hallucis brevis, adductor hallucis, and the flexor digiti minimi brevis.

5. Muscles of the sole of the foot found in the fourth layer include the plantar and the dorsal interossei.

Cross References

Additional information on topics covered in Chapter 10 can be found in the chapters listed below.

1. Chapter 7: Bones of the skull; facial bones; bones of the vertebral column; the bony thorax; pectoral bones; upper extremity; pelvic girdle; lower extremity
2. Chapter 8: Synovial joints
3. Chapter 9: Skeletal muscle tissue
4. Chapter 22: Abdominal muscles involved in respiration
5. Chapter 23: Muscles of mastication and tongue movement
6. Chapter 25: Muscles involved in controlling micturition
7. Chapter 27: Male and female perineum as related to reproductive anatomy; muscles of the pelvic floor

Laboratory Correlations

1. Marieb, E. N. *Human Anatomy & Physiology Laboratory Manual: Cat and Fetal Pig Versions*. Eighth Edition Updates. Benjamin Cummings, 2006.
   Exercise 15: Gross Anatomy of the Muscular System
2. Marieb, E. N. *Human Anatomy & Physiology Laboratory Manual: Main Version*. Seventh Edition Update. Benjamin Cummings, 2006.
   Exercise 15: Gross Anatomy of the Muscular System

Histology Slides for the Life Sciences

Available through Benjamin Cummings, an imprint of Pearson Education, Inc. To order, contact your local Benjamin Cummings sales representative.

Slide 20   Dense Irregular Connective Tissue, Tendon.
Slide 28   Skeletal Muscle Tissue, Cross Section, Tongue.
Slide 29   Skeletal Muscle Tissue, Longitudinal Section, Tongue.
Slide 30   Cardiac Muscle Tissue, Heart.
Slide 31   Smooth Muscle Tissue, Longitudinal Section, Uterus.
Slide 32   Smooth Muscle Tissue, Longitudinal and Cross Section, Uterus.
Slide 33   Thin Section of Cardiac Muscle.
Slide 34   Smooth Muscle.
Slide 49   Cardiac Muscle Tissue, Heart.
Slide 50   Neuromuscular Junction, Muscle Spread.
Slide 51   Skeletal Muscle.

Lecture Hints

1. It is easy for students to treat the muscular (or any other) system as an individual unit, without relating it to the rest of the body. Stress that students should associate any specific muscle (and its associated synergists, antagonists, etc.) with its fascicle arrangement, origin and insertion sites, and bones involved to "keep sight of the whole picture."
2. Be sure that students understand that motion is achieved by muscle pulling and shortening, never by muscle pushing.

3. Students often do not readily grasp the idea of the compromise between power and range of movement when discussing the relationship between origin and exact site of insertion (e.g., biceps brachii into radial tuberosity). Ask the class what would happen to power and range of movement if the biceps inserted several centimeters distal (or proximal) to the actual site.

4. When describing different muscles of the body, try coaxing names from the class by carefully indicating locations, properties, etc. For example, point to a diagram (or model) displaying transverse abdominis and ask the class which way the fibers are running. They should answer: "transversely." Then ask: "What general area of the body is this muscle located in?" Answer: "abdominal." Finally, ask: "What would be a logical name for this muscle?" One can apply this type of logic in many instances, all of which help students master the information rather than simply memorizing it.

Activities/Demonstrations

1. Audio-visual materials listed under Multimedia in the Classroom and Lab.

2. Select a volunteer and have him/her contract an arm or leg. Have students record: prime mover, synergists, and antagonists.

3. Obtain a dissected, preserved animal such as a cat or a fetal pig and exhibit the major muscle groups.

4. Have students work in pairs as follows: One should attempt to contract a particular muscle, while the second student provides resistance to prevent that movement. In this way the muscle will produce its maximal "bulge." Muscles being examined should be palpated in the relaxed and contracted states by both students. For example, the "demonstrator" can attempt to flex his/her elbow while the person providing the resistance holds the forearm to prevent its movement. The biceps brachii on the anterior arm will bulge and be easily palpated.

5. As muscles are being described, project 2 × 2 slides of cadaver dissection so that students can readily see "the real thing" as material is being presented in lecture. The microprojector can be running during the entire lecture, with cues placed in lecture notes on when to display specific slides.

6. Obtain a 3-D model or chart to illustrate the major human muscle groups.

7. Obtain implements such as scissors, a wheelbarrow, and forceps to illustrate the three types of lever systems.

8. Obtain a human cadaver to illustrate the major human muscle groups.

Critical Thinking/Discussion Topics

1. Why is it necessary for pregnant women to strengthen their "pelvic floor"?

2. What do bones possess that allow them to act as effective levers?

3. What are the most appropriate modes of therapy for a pulled hamstring muscle or pulled groin muscle?

4. Injections are often made directly into the muscle tissue. What are the advantages and disadvantages?

5. If a prime mover muscle such as the pectoralis major is surgically removed, how will the actions provided by that muscle be replaced?

6. How would one design an upper appendage so that it would operate with a relatively higher degree of mechanical advantage than presently exists?

Library Research Topics

1. Since muscle cells do not regenerate, what methods of treatment are available if a major group of muscles are lost? What is the status of skeletal muscle transplants?

2. What effect does old age have on skeletal muscle? What type of research is underway concerning this topic?

3. Different types of athletics require different training methods. Compare and contrast the training methods used by athletes in different types of sports.

4. Some muscle groups, such as the triceps surae, have individual muscles with predominantly different types of fibers. In order to build these muscles equally, the group must be exercised using combination isometric-isotonic exercises. Find out how these exercises work.

Multimedia in the Classroom and Lab

Online Resources for Students

The
Anatomy & Physiology Place   **MyA&P**
www.anatomyandphysiology.com   www.myaandp.com

The following shows the organization of the Chapter Guide page in both the Anatomy & Physiology Place and MyA&P™. The Chapter Guide organizes all the chapter-specific online media resources for Chapter 10 in one convenient location, with e-book links to each section of the textbook. Please note that both sites also give you access to other general A&P resources, like InterActive Physiology®, PhysioEx 6.0™, Anatomy 360°, Flashcards, a Glossary, a Histology Tutorial, and much more.

Muscle Review

Objectives

Section 10.1 Interactions of Skeletal Muscles in the Body (p. 325)

Section 10.2 Naming Skeletal Muscles (pp. 325–326)

Section 10.3 Muscle Mechanics: Importance of Fascicle Arrangement and Leverage (pp. 326–330)

Section 10.4 Major Skeletal Muscles of the Body (pp. 330–383)

Art Labeling Activity: Superficial Muscles, Anterior View, Photo (Fig. 10.4a, p. 330)

Art Labeling Activity: Superficial Muscles, Anterior View (Fig. 10.4b, p. 331)

Art Labeling Activity: Superficial Muscles, Posterior View, Photo (Fig. 10.5a, p. 332)

Art Labeling Activity: Superficial Muscles, Posterior View (Fig. 10.5b, p. 333)

Art Labeling Activity: Muscles of the Scalp, Face, and Neck, Lateral View (Fig. 10.6, p. 337)

Art Labeling Activity: Muscles of the Anterior Neck and Throat, Anterior and Lateral Views (Fig. 10.8a, p. 341)

Art Labeling Activity: Deep Muscles of the Back (Fig. 10.9d, p. 345)

Art Labeling Activity: Muscles of the Abdominal Wall (Fig. 10.11a, p. 349)

Art Labeling Activity: Hand Muscles (Fig. 10.18a, p. 365)

Art Labeling Activity: Deep Muscles of the Pelvis and Superficial Muscles of the Right Thigh (Fig. 10.19a, p. 368)

Art Labeling Activity: Posterior Muscles of the Hip and Thigh (Fig. 10.20, p. 371)

Art Labeling Activity: Anterior Compartment Muscles of the Right Leg (Fig. 10.21a, p. 374)

Art Labeling Activity: Lateral Compartment Muscles of the Right Leg (Fig. 10.22a, p. 375)

Art Labeling Activity: Posterior Compartment Muscles of the Right Leg (Fig. 10.23a–b, p. 377)

Art Labeling Activity: Deep Posterior Compartment Muscles of the Right Leg (Fig. 10.23c, p. 378)

Art Labeling Activity: Actions of Muscles of the Thigh (Fig. 10.24a, p. 380)

Art Labeling Activity: Actions of Muscles of the Leg (Fig. 10.24b, p. 380)

Art Labeling Activity: Muscles of the Foot (Fig. 10.25a–b, p. 382)

Art Labeling Activity: Muscles of the Foot, Plantar Aspect (Fig. 10.25d, p. 383)

Memory: Identification of Skeletal Muscles

Memory: Dissected Skeletal Muscle Identification

Chapter Summary

Self-Study Quizzes

Art Labeling Quiz

Matching Quiz

Multiple-Choice Quiz (Level I)

Multiple-Choice Quiz (Level II)

True-False Quiz

Crossword Puzzles

Crossword Puzzle 10.1

Crossword Puzzle 10.2

Media

See Guide to Audio-Visual Resources in Appendix A for key to AV distributors.

Slides

1. *Human Muscle Tissues Set* (CBS). This collection of 6 slides provides coverage of all 3 muscle types.

Video

1. *Human Musculature Videotape* (BC; 23 min., 1999). Rose Leigh Vines, California State University. Offers a clear 23-minute anatomical tour of the muscles in the human body; an inexpensive alternative to cadaver dissection.

2. *Muscular Dystrophy* (FHS; 26 min., 1990). From *The Doctor Is In*, this program looks at how muscular dystrophy sufferers deal with the disease.

3. *The Skeletal and Muscular Systems* (NIMCO; 24 min., 1997). Demonstrates how the skeletal and muscular systems work together to provide the structure and shape of the body.

Software

1. *A.D.A.M.® InterActive Anatomy® 4.0* (see p. 9 of this guide for full listing).

2. *A.D.A.M.® MediaPro* (see p. 9 of this guide for full listing).

3. *A.D.A.M.®Anatomy Practice* (see p. 86 of this guide for full listing).

4. *Bodyworks* (see p. 9 of this guide for full listing).

5. *The Ultimate Human Body* (see p. 9 of this guide for full listing).

6. *Interactive Physiology® 9-System Suite CD-ROM: Muscular System* (see p. 109 of this guide for full listing).

Lecture Enhancement Material

To view thumbnails of all of the illustrations for Chapter 10, see Appendix B.

Transparencies Index/Media Manager

Figure 10.1	Relationship of fascicle arrangement to muscle structure.
Figure 10.2	Lever systems operating at a mechanical advantage and a mechanical disadvantage.
Figure 10.3	Lever systems.
Figure 10.4	Anterior view of superficial muscles of the body.
Figure 10.5	Posterior view of superficial muscles of the body.
Figure 10.6	Lateral view of muscles of the scalp, face, and neck.
Figure 10.7	Muscles promoting mastication and tongue movements.
Figure 10.8	Muscles of the anterior neck and throat that promote swallowing.
Figure 10.9	Muscles of the neck and vertebral column causing movements of the head and trunk.
Figure 10.10	Muscles of respiration.
Figure 10.11	Muscles of the abdominal wall.
Figure 10.12	Muscles of the pelvic floor and perineum.
Figure 10.13	Superficial muscles of the thorax and shoulder acting on the scapula and arm.
Figure 10.14	Muscles crossing the shoulder and elbow joint, respectively causing movements of the arm and forearm.
Figure 10.15	Muscles of the anterior compartment of the forearm acting on the right wrist and fingers.
Figure 10.16	Muscles of the posterior compartment of the right forearm acting on the wrist and fingers.
Figure 10.17	Summary of actions of muscles of the arm and forearm.
Figure 10.18	Hand muscles, ventral view of right hand.
Figure 10.19	Anterior and medial muscles promoting movements of the thigh and leg.
Figure 10.20	Posterior muscles of the right hip and thigh.
Figure 10.21	Muscles of the anterior compartment of the right leg.
Figure 10.22	Muscles of lateral compartment of the right leg.
Figure 10.23	Muscles of the posterior compartment of the right leg.
Figure 10.24	Summary of actions of muscles of the thigh and leg.
Figure 10.25	Muscles of the right foot, plantar and medial aspects.
Table 10.1	Muscles of the Head, Part I: Facial Expression (Figure 10.6)
Table 10.2	Muscles of the Head, Part II: Mastication and Tongue Movement (Figure 10.7)
Table 10.3	Muscles of the Anterior Neck and Throat: Swallowing (Figure 10.8)
Table 10.4	Muscles of the Neck and Vertebral Column: Head and Trunk Movements (Figure 10.9)
Table 10.5	Muscles of the Thorax: Breathing (Figure 10.10)
Table 10.6	Muscles of the Abdominal Wall: Trunk Movements and Compression of Abdominal Viscera (Figure 10.11)
Table 10.7	Muscles of the Pelvic Floor and Perineum: Support of Abdominopelvic Organs (Figure 10.12)
Table 10.8	Superficial Muscles of the Anterior and Posterior Thorax: Movements of the Scapula (Figure 10.13)

Answers to End-of-Chapter Questions

Multiple Choice and Matching Question answers appear in Appendix G of the main text.

Short Answer Essay Questions

17. Student answers will vary. (pp. 325–326)
    a. Location of the muscle—frontalis, occipitalis, zygomaticus
    b. Shape of the muscle—rhomboids, serratus anterior, quadratus lumborum
    c. Relative size of the muscle—pectoralis major and minor, peroneus longus and brevis
    d. Direction of muscle fibers—rectus abdominus, external oblique, superficial transverse perineus
    e. Number of origins—triceps brachii, biceps femoris
    f. Location of the origin/insertion—stylohyoid, sternothyroid, coracobrachialis
    g. Action of the muscle—levator scapulae, pronator teres, flexor carpi radialis, adductor longus

18. First class: effort—fulcrum—load
    Second class: fulcrum—load—effort
    Third class: fulcrum—effort—load (p. 328)

19. When the load is far from the fulcrum and the effort is applied near the fulcrum, the effort applied must be greater than the load to be moved. This type of leverage can be advantageous because it allows the load to be moved rapidly through a large distance, with only minimal muscle shortening. (p. 328)

20. Pharyngeal constrictor muscles (p. 340)

21. To shake your head "no"—sternocleidomastoid. (p. 342) To nod "yes"—sternocleidomastoid and splenius muscles. (p. 343)

22. a. Rectus abdominus, external oblique, internal oblique, transversus abdominus (p. 348)
    b. Each pair is arranged at cross-directions to each other which provides strength, just as the different grain directions in plywood make a thin piece of wood strong for its thickness. (p. 348)

    c. External oblique and internal oblique (p. 348)

    d. Rectus abdominus (p. 348)

23. Flexion of the humerus: pectoralis major and deltoid

    Extension of the humerus: latissimus dorsi and deltoid

    Abduction of the humerus: deltoid

    Adduction of the humerus: pectoralis major, latissimus dorsi

    Circumduction of the humerus: combination of all above

    Rotation of the humerus laterally: infraspinatus and teres minor

    Rotation of the humerus medially: subscapularis (pp. 352–355)

24. a. Extensor carpi radialis longus and brevis (p. 360)

    b. Flexor digitorum profundus (p. 359)

25. Piriformis, obturator externus and internus, gemellus, and quadratus femoris (pp. 370–372)

26. Adductors, pectineus, and gracilis (p. 369)

27. a. Deltoid, vastus lateralis, gluteus maximus, gluteus medius (pp. 355, 370)

    b. Vastus lateralis is used in infants because their hip and arm muscles are poorly developed. (p. 369)

28. a. Opponens pollicis, flexor pollicis, brevis (p. 364)

    b. Supinator, abductor pollicis longus (p. 360)

    c. Flexor pollicis longus, flexor digitorum profundus (p. 359)

    d. Biceps brachii, brachialis (p. 357)

    e. Hyoglossus, styloglossus (p. 339)

    f. Flexor hallucis brevis, adductor hallucis (p. 383)

Critical Thinking and Clinical Application Questions

1. When the forearm is pronated, the biceps brachii, a prime mover of forearm flexion, is unable to act. (p. 357)

2. Levator ani, coccygeus, and sphincter urethrae (p. 350)

3. There was a rupture of the Achilles or calcaneous tendon. (p. 376) The calf appears swollen because the gastrocnemius muscle is no longer anchored to the calcaneus.

4. Peter was pleased by Sue's performance. He winked at her and gave her an okay sign. (pp. 335; 364)

5. a. second class lever

    b. third class lever

    c. first class lever (p. 328)

6. Chao injured her adductors. This condition is called a pulled groin. (p. 369)

Suggested Readings

Agur, A.M. *Grant's Atlas of Anatomy.* 10th ed. Baltimore: Lippincott, Williams & Wilkins, 1999.

Clemente, C.D. *Anatomy: A Regional Atlas of the Human Body.* 4th ed. Baltimore: Lippincott, Williams & Wilkins, 1998.

Gray, H., et al. *Gray's Anatomy.* 38th ed. London: Churchill Livingstone, 1995.

Yokochi, C., and J.W. Rohen. *Photographic Anatomy of the Human Body.* 3rd ed. (paperback) Tokyo, New York: Igaku-Shoin, Ltd., 1989.

Fundamentals of the Nervous System and Nervous Tissue

Objectives

Organization of the Nervous System

1. List the structural and functional divisions of the nervous system, and describe their relationship to each other.

Histology of Nervous Tissue

2. Describe the types of glial cells, their function, and location in the nervous system.
3. Explain the physiological characteristics of mature neurons.
4. Discuss the anatomy of a neuron, and the function of each structure.
5. Describe the anatomy and function of the myelin sheath, and differentiate between myelinated and unmyelinated neurons.
6. Define the structural and functional categories of neurons, and compare how the structural class of a neuron relates to its functional class.

Neurophysiology

7. Define the terms voltage, potential difference, and current, and describe how electrical current travels in the body.
8. Name the various types of membrane channels, and the signals that control each type.
9. Explain the resting membrane potential and how it is generated.
10. Identify how changes in membrane potentials act as signals, and relate each type of signal to the generation of action potentials.
11. Discuss the mechanism of generation of an action potential, and the three phases of an action potential.
12. Describe a threshold stimulus. Discuss how it relates to the graded potentials generated on dendrites, and the all-or-none behavior of axons.
13. Define the absolute and relative refractory periods, and describe the events that occur during each.
14. Identify the effects of axon diameter and myelination on conduction velocity of axons.
15. Define a synapse, name the two types, and describe how synaptic transmission occurs at a chemical synapse.
16. Define EPSP and IPSP. Describe what causes them and how they are summated by the postsynaptic cell.
17. List the chemical and functional classes of neurotransmitters, members of each class, and the types of receptors for neurotransmitters.

Basic Concepts of Neural Integration

18. Describe neuronal pools and their function.
19. Name the various types of circuits.
20. Compare and contrast serial and parallel processing.

Developmental Aspects of Neurons

21. Describe the major events of development, growth, and refinement of the nervous system.

Suggested Lecture Outline

I. Organization of the Nervous System (pp. 388–389; Figs. 11.1–11.2)

A. The central nervous system consists of the brain and spinal cord, and is the integrating and command center of the nervous system (p. 388; Figs. 11.1–11.2).

B. The peripheral nervous system is outside the central nervous system (pp. 388–389; Fig. 11.2).

1. The sensory, or afferent, division of the peripheral nervous system carries impulses toward the central nervous system from sensory receptors located throughout the body.

2. The motor, or efferent, division of the peripheral nervous system carries impulses from the central nervous system to effector organs, which are muscles and glands.

  a. The somatic nervous system consists of somatic nerve fibers that conduct impulses from the CNS to skeletal muscles, and allow conscious control of motor activities.

  b. The autonomic nervous system is an involuntary system consisting of visceral motor nerve fibers that regulate the activity of smooth muscle, cardiac muscle, and glands.

II. Histology of Nervous Tissue (pp. 389–397; Figs. 11.3–11.5; Table 11.1)

A. Neuroglia, or glial cells, are closely associated with neurons, providing a protective and supportive network (pp. 389–391; Fig. 11.3).

1. Astrocytes are glial cells of the CNS that regulate the chemical environment around neurons and exchange between neurons and capillaries.

2. Microglia are glial cells of the CNS that monitor health and perform defense functions for neurons.

3. Ependymal cells are glial cells of the CNS that line the central cavities of the brain and spinal cord and help circulate cerebrospinal fluid.

4. Oligodendrocytes are glial cells of the CNS that wrap around neuron fibers, forming myelin sheaths.

5. Satellite cells are glial cells of the PNS whose function is largely unknown. They are found surrounding neuron cell bodies within ganglia.

6. Schwann cells, or neurolemmocytes, are glial cells of the PNS that surround nerve fibers, forming the myelin sheath.

B. Neurons are specialized cells that conduct messages in the form of electrical impulses throughout the body (pp. 391–397; Figs. 11.4–11.5; Table 11.1).

1. Neurons function optimally for a lifetime, are mostly amitotic, and have an exceptionally high metabolic rate requiring oxygen and glucose.

  a. The neuron cell body, also called the perikaryon or soma, is the major biosynthetic center containing the usual organelles except for centrioles.

  b. Dendrites are cell processes that are the receptive regions of the cell.

  c. Each neuron has a single axon that generates and conducts nerve impulses away from the cell body to the axon terminals.

  d. The myelin sheath is a whitish, fatty, segmented covering that protects, insulates, and increases conduction velocity of axons.

2. There are three structural classes of neurons.

  a. Multipolar neurons have three or more processes.

  b. Bipolar neurons have a single axon and dendrite.

      c. Unipolar neurons have a single process extending from the cell body that is associated with receptors at the distal end.

   3. There are three functional classes of neurons.

      a. Sensory, or afferent, neurons conduct impulses toward the CNS from receptors.

      b. Motor, or efferent, neurons conduct impulses from the CNS to effectors.

      c. Interneurons, or association neurons, conduct impulses between sensory and motor neurons, or in CNS integration pathways.

III. Neurophysiology (pp. 397–421; Figs. 11.6–11.22; Tables 11.2–11.3)

  A. Basic Principles of Electricity (pp. 397–398)

   1. Voltage is a measure of the amount of difference in electrical charge between two points, called the potential difference.

   2. The flow of electrical charge from point to point is called current, and is dependent on voltage and resistance (hindrance to current flow).

   3. In the body, electrical currents are due to the movement of ions across cellular membranes.

  B. The Role of Membrane Ion Channels (pp. 393–399; Fig. 11.6)

   1. The cell has many gated ion channels.

      a. Chemically gated (ligand gated) channels open when the appropriate chemical binds.

      b. Voltage gated channels open in response to a change in membrane potential.

      c. Mechanically gated channels open when a membrane receptor is physically deformed.

   2. When ion channels are open, ions diffuse across the membrane, creating electrical currents.

  C. The Resting Membrane Potential (pp. 399–400; Figs. 11.7–11.8)

   1. The neuron cell membrane is polarized, being more negatively charged inside than outside. The degree of this difference in electrical charge is the resting membrane potential.

   2. The resting membrane potential is generated by differences in ionic makeup of intracellular and extracellular fluids, and differential membrane permeability to solutes.

  D. Membrane Potentials That Act as Signals (pp. 400–409; Figs. 11.9–11.17)

   1. Neurons use changes in membrane potential as communication signals. These can be brought on by changes in membrane permeability to any ion, or alteration of ion concentrations on the two sides of the membrane.

   2. Changes in membrane potential relative to resting membrane potential can either be depolarizations, in which the interior of the cell becomes less negative, or hyperpolarizations, in which the interior of the cell becomes more negatively charged.

   3. Graded potentials are short-lived, local changes in membrane potentials. They can either be depolarizations or hyperpolarizations, and are critical to the generation of action potentials.

   4. Action potentials, or nerve impulses, occur on axons and are the principle way neurons communicate.

      a. Generation of an action potential involves a transient increase in Na^+ permeability, followed by restoration of Na^+ impermeability, and then a short-lived increase in K^+ permeability.

      b. Propagation, or transmission, of an action potential occurs as the local currents of an area undergoing depolarization cause depolarization of the forward adjacent area.

      c. Repolarization, which restores resting membrane potential, follows depolarization along the membrane.

   5. A critical minimum, or threshold, depolarization is defined by the amount of influx of Na^+ that at least equals the amount of efflux of K^+.

   6. Action potentials are an all-or-none phenomena: they either happen completely, in the case of a threshold stimulus, or not at all, in the event of a subthreshold stimulus.

   7. Stimulus intensity is coded in the frequency of action potentials.

   8. The refractory period of an axon is related to the period of time required so that a neuron can generate another action potential.

E. Influence of Axon Diameter and the Myelin Sheath on Conduction Velocity (p. 407; Fig. 11.16)

   1. Axons with larger diameters conduct impulses faster than axons with smaller diameters.

   2. Unmyelinated axons conduct impulses relatively slowly, while myelinated axons have a high conduction velocity.

F. The Synapse (pp. 408–411; Figs. 11.17–11.18)

   1. A synapse is a junction that mediates information transfer between neurons or between a neuron and an effector cell.

   2. Neurons conducting impulses toward the synapse are presynaptic cells, and neurons carrying impulses away from the synapse are postsynaptic cells.

   3. Electrical synapses have neurons that are electrically coupled via protein channels and allow direct exchange of ions from cell to cell.

   4. Chemical synapses are specialized for release and reception of chemical neurotransmitters.

   5. Neurotransmitter effects are terminated in three ways: degradation by enzymes from the postsynaptic cell or within the synaptic cleft; reuptake by astrocytes or the presynaptic cell; or diffusion away from the synapse.

   6. Synaptic delay is related to the period of time required for release and binding of neurotransmitters.

G. Postsynaptic Potentials and Synaptic Integration (pp. 411–413; Figs. 11.19–11.20; Table 11.2)

   1. Neurotransmitters mediate graded potentials on the postsynaptic cell that may be excitatory or inhibitory.

   2. Summation by the postsynaptic neuron is accomplished in two ways: temporal summation, which occurs in response to several successive releases of neurotransmitter, and spatial summation, which occurs when the postsynaptic cell is stimulated at the same time by multiple terminals.

   3. Synaptic potentiation results when a presynaptic cell is stimulated repeatedly or continuously, resulting in an enhanced release of neurotransmitter.

   4. Presynaptic inhibition results when another neuron inhibits the release of excitatory neurotransmitter from a presynaptic cell.

   5. Neuromodulation occurs when a neurotransmitter acts via slow changes in target cell metabolism, or when chemicals other than neurotransmitter modify neuronal activity.

H. Neurotransmitters and Their Receptors (pp. 413–421; Figs. 11.21–11.22; Table 11.3)

1. Neurotransmitters are one of the ways neurons communicate, and they have several chemical classes.

2. Functional classifications of neurotransmitters consider whether the effects are excitatory or inhibitory, and whether the effects are direct or indirect.

3. There are two main types of neurotransmitter receptors: channel-linked receptors mediate direct transmitter action and result in brief, localized changes; and G protein-linked receptors mediate indirect transmitter action resulting in slow, persistent, and often diffuse changes.

IV. Basic Concepts of Neural Integration (pp. 421–423; Figs. 11.23–11.24)

A. Organization of Neurons: Neuronal Pools (p. 421; Fig. 11.24)

1. Neuronal pools are functional groups of neurons that integrate incoming information from receptors or other neuronal pools and relay the information to other areas.

B. Types of Circuits (pp. 421–422; Fig. 11.25)

1. Diverging, or amplifying, circuits are common in sensory and motor pathways. They are characterized by an incoming fiber that triggers responses in ever-increasing numbers of fibers along the circuit.

2. Converging circuits are common in sensory and motor pathways. They are characterized by reception of input from many sources, and a funneling to a given circuit, resulting in strong stimulation or inhibition.

3. Reverberating, or oscillating, circuits are characterized by feedback by axon collaterals to previous points in the pathway, resulting in ongoing stimulation of the pathway.

4. Parallel after-discharge circuits may be involved in complex activities, and are characterized by stimulation of several neurons arranged in parallel arrays by the stimulating neuron.

C. Patterns of Neural Processing (pp. 422–423; Fig. 11.25)

1. Serial processing is exemplified by spinal reflexes, and involves sequential stimulation of the neurons in a circuit.

2. Parallel processing results in inputs stimulating many pathways simultaneously, and is vital to higher level mental functioning.

V. Developmental Aspects of Neurons (pp. 423–426)

A. The nervous system originates from a dorsal neural tube and neural crest, which begin as a layer of neuroepithelial cells that ultimately become the CNS.

B. Differentiation of neuroepithelial cells occurs largely in the second month of development.

C. Growth of an axon toward its target appears to be guided by older "pathfinding" neurons and glial cells, nerve growth factor and cholesterol from astrocytes, and tropic chemicals from target cells.

D. The growth cone is a growing tip of an axon. It takes up chemicals from the environment that are used by the cell to evaluate the pathway taken for further growth and synapse formation.

E. Unsuccessful synapse formation results in cell death, and a certain amount of apoptosis occurs before the final population of neurons is complete.

Cross References

Additional information on topics covered in Chapter 11 can be found in the chapters listed below.

1. Chapter 2: Enzymes and enzyme function
2. Chapter 3: Passive and active membrane transport processes; membrane potential; cytoskeletal elements; cell cycle
3. Chapter 4: Nervous tissue
4. Chapter 9: Synapse (neuromuscular junction)
5. Chapter 13: Membrane potentials; neural integration
6. Chapter 14: Cholinergic and adrenergic receptors and other neurotransmitter effects; autonomic synapses
7. Chapter 15: Receptors for the special senses; synapses involved in the special senses; neurotransmitters in the special senses
8. Chapter 16: Nervous system modulation of endocrine function
9. Chapter 18: Membrane potential and the electrical activity of the heart
10. Chapter 19: Baroreceptors and chemoreceptors in blood pressure and flow regulation
11. Chapter 22: Chemoreceptors and stretch receptors related to respiratory function
12. Chapter 23: Sensory receptors and control of digestive processes
13. Chapter 24: Examples of receptors

Laboratory Correlations

1. Marieb, E. N. *Human Anatomy & Physiology Laboratory Manual: Cat and Fetal Pig Versions*. Eighth Edition Updates. Benjamin Cummings, 2006.

   Exercise 17: Histology of Nervous Tissue
   Exercise 18: Neurophysiology of Nerve Impulses

2. Marieb, E. N. *Human Anatomy & Physiology Laboratory Manual: Main Version*. Seventh Edition Update. Benjamin Cummings, 2006.

   Exercise 17: Histology of Nervous Tissue
   Exercise 18: Neurophysiology of Nerve Impulses

Histology Slides for the Life Sciences

Available through Benjamin Cummings, an imprint of Pearson Education, Inc. To order, contact your local Benjamin Cummings sales representative.

Slide 73   Myelinated Nerve Cross Section—Myelin Sheaths.
Slide 74   Myelinated Nerve, Longitudinal Section—Nodes of Ranvier.
Slide 75   Efferent (Motor) Neuron

Lecture Hints

1. By this time the class has been exposed to only a few systems (integumentary, skeletal, and muscular), but enough information has been given so that students can understand the basics of nervous system function from the beginning of this section. Ask students questions such as: (1) When you touch something hot, how do you react? (2) Do you have to consciously think about pulling your hand away? The idea for these basic questions is to get students to come up with the idea that

a neural pathway consists of a sensory structure, some means of conveying information to the brain, and some means of causing motor response. If you get students to come up with these "solutions," they will remember the logic used to derive the answers.

2. Emphasize strongly the three basic functions of the nervous system: sensory, integration, and motor. Students should "burn this into the brain," since it will be seen again and again in all systems.

3. Stress that although we discuss the nervous system in segments, it is actually tightly integrated.

4. Present a general introduction of the entire nervous system near the beginning of nervous system discussion so that students will be able to see the entire picture. In this way, they will better understand the relationships as material is covered.

5. Point out the similarities between skeletal muscle cells and neurons. It is also possible to introduce the electrical characteristics of cardiac pacemaker cells (modified muscle cells) and note the similarities to neuron function. Mention that although function is totally different (muscle = contractile, nervous = impulse generation, propagation), the structural basis of each is a slight modification of a basic cellular blueprint.

6. Bring a model (or overheads, 2 × 2 slides) of a neuron to lecture to visually demonstrate the anatomy of a nerve cell.

7. Many students have difficulty understanding the difference between the myelin sheath and the neurilemma (sheath of Schwann). Use a diagram (blackline master) to point out that both are parts of the same cell.

8. Emphasize the difference in myelination between the CNS and PNS. Point out the regeneration capabilities of each.

9. Many students have trouble relating ion movements with electrical current. One way to approach neurophysiology is to (loosely) compare a 1.5-V battery to the cell membrane. The electrical potential between the positive and negative poles is analogous to the outside and inside of a cell. When a connection is made between positive and negative poles (ion gates opened), current is delivered.

10. Clearly distinguish the difference between graded potentials and action potentials. It helps to use a full-page acetate of a neuron to demonstrate the positive feedback nature of the action potential.

11. Most introductory physiology students will experience difficulty with the idea of saltatory conduction. Draw (or project) diagrams of myelinated vs. unmyelinated fibers and electrical propagation.

12. Draw a diagram of a synapse, then use root word dissection to emphasize the distinction between pre- and postsynaptic neurons. This is a good introduction to the synapse and establishes a reference point upon which students can build.

13. Use absolute numbers as an introductory example for summation. For example: If three presynaptic neurons each simultaneously deliver a one-third threshold stimulus, will the postsynaptic neuron fire? Use several examples to emphasize the difference between spatial and temporal summation.

14. Use diagrams when describing the different types of circuits.

Activities/Demonstrations

1. Audio-visual materials listed under Multimedia in the Classroom and Lab.

2. Obtain a microprojector and microscope slides of neurons, neuroglia, and peripheral nerves to illustrate the histology of the tissue.

3. Obtain an oscilloscope and a neurophysiology kit to illustrate how an action potential can be registered.
4. Obtain 3-D models of motor and sensory neurons to illustrate their similarities and differences.
5. Use a match to illustrate how an EPSP can work and how a graded potential will be intense at the receptor end and decrease thereafter; then use a fuse wire to illustrate how an action potential is carried down the wire.

Critical Thinking/Discussion Topics

1. How can drugs, such as novocaine, effectively block the transmission of pain impulses? Why don't they block motor impulses—or do they?
2. What effect does alcohol have on the transmission of electrical impulses?
3. How can rubbing one's nose decrease the possibility of a sneeze? Discuss in terms of EPSPs and IPSPs.
4. Acetylcholine has long been recognized as a neurotransmitter. Why has it been so difficult to identify other neurotransmitters?
5. How can some people eat extremely hot peppers without experiencing the same pain that others normally have?
6. What would happen at a synapse if an agent was introduced that blocked the activity of chemically gated Na^+ channels? K^+ channels?

Library Research Topics

1. Of what value is the development of recombinant DNA technology to our study of protein-based neurotransmitters?
2. What is the status of research on the repair and/or regeneration of nervous tissue of the CNS?
3. Why do most tumors of nervous tissue develop in neuroglia rather than neurons?
4. Could we use neurotransmitters to enhance our memory capacity?
5. How are experiments performed to test the anatomy and physiology of plasma membrane ion gates and channels?

Multimedia in the Classroom and Lab

Online Resources for Students

The
Anatomy & Physiology Place   **MyA&P**
www.anatomyandphysiology.com   www.myaandp.com

The following shows the organization of the Chapter Guide page in both the Anatomy & Physiology Place and MyA&P™. The Chapter Guide organizes all the chapter-specific online media resources for Chapter 11 in one convenient location, with e-book links to each section of the textbook. Please note that both sites also give you access to other general A&P resources, like InterActive Physiology®, PhysioEx 6.0™, Anatomy 360°, Flashcards, a Glossary, a Histology Tutorial, and much more.

Objectives

Section 11.1 Organization of the Nervous System (pp. 388–389)

InterActive Physiology®: Nervous I: Orientation

InterActive Physiology®: Nervous I: Anatomy Review (Neurons)

Section 11.2 Histology of Nervous Tissue (pp. 389–397)

InterActive Physiology®: Nervous I: Ion Channels

Memory: Neural System

Section 11.3 Neurophysiology (pp. 397–421)

InterActive Physiology®: Nervous I: Membrane Potential

InterActive Physiology®: Nervous I: Action Potential

InterActive Physiology®: Nervous II: Anatomy Review (Synapses)

InterActive Physiology®: Nervous II: Synaptic Potentials and Cellular Integration

InterActive Physiology®: Nervous II: Ion Channels

InterActive Physiology®: Nervous II: Synaptic Transmission

PhysioEx: Neurophysiology of Nerve Impulses

Memory: Action Potential Propagation

Case Study: Nervous Tissue

Section 11.4 Basic Concepts of Neural Integration (pp. 421–423)

Section 11.5 Developmental Aspects of Neurons (pp. 423–425)

Case Study: Congenital Defect

Chapter Summary

Self-Study Quizzes

Art Labeling Quiz

Matching Quiz

Multiple-Choice Quiz (Level I)

Multiple-Choice Quiz (Level II)

True-False Quiz

Crossword Puzzles

Crossword Puzzle 11.1

Crossword Puzzle 11.2

Media

See Guide to Audio-Visual Resources in Appendix A for key to AV distributors.

Slides

1. *Human Nervous Tissue Set* (CBS). A collection of 25 slides provides complete coverage of the nervous system.

Video

1. *Decision* (FHS; 28 min., 1984). This exceptional program from *The Living Body* series shows how the brain coordinates functions to make a simple but lifesaving decision.

2. *The Human Nervous System: The Brain and Cranial Nerves Videotape* (BC; 28 min., 1997). This video by Rose Leigh Vines and Rosalee Carter, California State University, Sacramento, links nervous system structures and functions.

3. *The Human Nervous System: The Spinal Cord and Nerves Videotape* (BC; 29 min., 1997). Illustrations and figures help students learn the organization of the spinal nerves into complicated plexuses. Major nerves arising from these plexuses are traced on the cadaver as they course through the upper and lower extremities.

4. *The Nervous System* (IM; 24 min., 1993). Details the job of the nervous system, revealing its control over all bodily activity.

5. *The Nervous System: The Ultimate Control Center* (KV; 20 min., 2001). Explores the structural and functional classifications of the brain and addresses homeostatic imbalances such as Parkinson's disease and strokes.

6. *The Peripheral Nervous System* (UL; 29 min., 1997). This three-part series illustrates how the human body senses and responds to its internal and external environments.

7. *Reflexes and Synaptic Transmission* (UL; 29 min., 1997). Investigates the physiology of the reflex arc.

8. *Wired* (LM; 27 min., 2001). Through an examination of "phantom limb syndrome," this video explores the biology and function of the body's nervous system.

Software

1. *InterActive Physiology 9-System Suite CD-ROM: Nervous System I and II* (BC; Win/Mac, 2006). Presents in-depth information on neurons, resting membrane potential, and the generation/propagation of the action potential within the nervous system. Topics covered include ion channels, membrane potential, and action potential.

2. *SylviusPRO: 3D Dissector and Atlas of the Human Central Nervous System* (SIN; Win/Mac). Uses color graphics, animation, and cross-sectional diagrams to examine the anatomy of the brain.

Lecture Enhancement Material

To view thumbnails of all of the illustrations for Chapter 11, see Appendix B.

Transparencies Index/Media Manager

Figure 11.1	The nervous system's functions.
Figure 11.2	Levels of organization in the nervous system.
Figure 11.3	Neuroglia.
Figure 11.4	Structure of a motor neuron.
Figure 11.5	Relationship of Schwann cells to axons in the PNS.
Figure 11.6	Operation of gated channels.
Figure 11.7	Measuring membrane potential in neurons.
Figure 11.8	The basis of the resting membrane potential.
Figure 11.9	Depolarization and hyperpolarization of the membrane.
Figure 11.10	The mechanism of a graded potential.
Figure 11.11	Changes in membrane potential produced by a depolarizing graded potential.
Figure 11.12	Phases of the action potential and the role of voltage-gated ion channels.
Figure 11.13	Propagation of an action potential (AP).
Figure 11.14	Relationship between stimulus strength and action potential frequency.
Figure 11.15	Refractory periods in an AP.
Figure 11.16	Saltatory conduction in a myelinated axon.
Figure 11.17	Synapses.
Figure 11.18	Events at a chemical synapse in response to depolarization.
Figure 11.19	Postsynaptic potentials.

Indicates images that are on the Media Manager only.

Answers to End-of-Chapter Questions

Multiple Choice and Matching Question answers appear in Appendix G of the main text.

Short Answer Essay Questions

13. Anatomical division includes the CNS (brain and spinal cord) and the PNS (nerves and ganglia). Functional division includes the somatic and autonomic motor divisions of the PNS. The autonomic division is divided into sympathetic and parasympathetic subdivisions. (pp. 388–389)

14. a. The cell body is the biosynthetic and metabolic center of a neuron. It contains the usual organelles, but lacks centrioles. (p. 391)

    b. Dendrites and axons both function to carry electrical current. Dendrites differ in that they are short, transmit toward the cell body, and function as receptor sites. Axons are typically long, are myelinated, and transmit away from the cell body. Only axons can generate action potentials, the long distance signals. (p. 393)

15. a. Myelin is a whitish, fatty, phospholipid-insulating material (essentially the wrapped plasma membranes of oligodendrocytes or Schwann cells).

    b. CNS myelin sheaths are formed by flaplike extensions of oligodendrocytes and lack a neurilemma. Each oligodendrocyte can help to myelinate several fibers. PNS myelin is formed by Schwann cells; the wrapping of each Schwann cell forms the internode region. The sheaths have a neurilemma, and the fibers they protect are capable of regeneration. (p. 394)

16. Multipolar neurons have many dendrites, one axon, and are found in the CNS (and autonomic ganglia). Bipolar neurons have one axon and one dendrite, and are found in receptor end organs of the special senses such as the retina of the eye and olfactory mucosa. Unipolar neurons have one process that divides into an axon and a dendrite and is a sensory neuron with the cell body found in a dorsal root ganglion or cranial nerve ganglion. (p. 395)

17. A polarized membrane possesses a net positive charge outside, and a net negative charge inside, with the voltage across the membrane being at -70 mv. Diffusion of Na^+ and K^+ across the membrane establishes the resting potential because the membrane is slightly more permeable to K^+. The $Na^+ - K^+$ pump, an active transport mechanism, maintains this polarized state by maintaining the diffusion gradient for Na^+ and K^+. (p. 399)

18. a. The generation of an action potential involves: (1) an increase in sodium permeability and reversal of the membrane potential; (2) a decrease in sodium permeability; and (3) an increase in potassium permeability and repolarization. (pp. 402–404)

    b. The ionic gates are controlled by changes in the membrane potential and activated by local currents.

    c. The all-or-none phenomenon means that the local depolarizing current must reach a critical "firing" or threshold point before it will respond, and when it responds, it will respond completely by conducting the action potential along the entire length of its axon. (pp. 402–405)

19. The CNS "knows" a stimulus is strong when the frequency or rate of action potential generation is high. (p. 406)

20. a. An EPSP is an excitatory (depolarizing) postsynaptic potential that increases the chance of a depolarization event. An IPSP is an inhibitory (hyperpolarizing) postsynaptic potential that decreases the chance of a depolarization event. (See Table 11.2, pp. 411–412.)

    b. It is determined by the type and amount of neurotransmitter that binds at the postsynaptic neuron and the specific receptor subtype it binds to. (pp. 411–413)

21. Each neuron's axon hillock keeps a "running account" of all signals it receives via temporal and spatial summation. (p. 413)

22. The neurotransmitter is quickly removed by enzymatic degradation or reuptake into the presynaptic axon. This ensures discrete limited responses. (p. 411)

23. a. A fibers have the largest diameter and thick myelin sheaths and conduct impulses quickly; B fibers are lightly myelinated, have intermediate diameters, and are slower conductors. (p. 408)

    b. Absolute refractory period is when the neuron is incapable of responding to another stimulus because the sodium gates are still open or are inactivated. (p. 406)

    c. A node of Ranvier is an interruption of the myelin sheath between the wrappings of individual Schwann cells or of the oligodendrocyte processes. (p. 394)

24. In serial processing, the pathway is constant and occurs through a definite sequence of neurons; the response is predictable and stereotyped. In parallel processing, impulses reach the final CNS target by multiple pathways. Parallel processing allows for a variety of responses. (pp. 422–423)

25. First, they proliferate; second, they migrate to proper position; third, they differentiate. (p. 423)

26. Development of the axon is due to the chemical signals neurotropin and NGF that interact with receptors on the developing axon to support and direct its growth. (p. 424)

Critical Thinking and Clinical Application Questions

1. The resting potential would decrease, that is, become less negative, because the concentration gradient causing net diffusion of K^+ out of the cell would be smaller. Action potentials would be fired more easily, that is, in response to smaller stimuli, because the resting potential would be closer to threshold. Repolarization would occur more slowly because repolarization depends on net K^+ diffusion from the cell and the concentration gradient driving this diffusion is lower. Also, the after hyperpolarization would be smaller. (pp. 399–404)

2. Local anesthetics such as novocaine and sedatives affect the neural processes usually at the nodes of Ranvier, by reducing the membrane permeability to sodium ions. (p. 408)

3. The bacteria remain in the wound; however, the toxin produced travels via axonal transport to reach the cell body. (pp. 393–394)

4. In MS, the myelin sheaths are destroyed. Loss of this insulating sheath results in shunting of current and eventual cessation of neurotransmission. (pp. 407–408)

5. Glycine is an inhibitory neurotransmitter that is used to modulate spinal cord transmission. Strychnine blocks glycine receptors in the spinal cord, leading to unregulated stimulation of muscles, and spastic contraction to the point where the muscles cannot relax. (p. 416)

Suggested Readings

Aldrich, Richard W. "Fifty Years of Inactivation." *Nature* 411 (6838) (June 2001): 643–644.

Barres, Ben A. and Smith, Stephen J. "Cholesterol—Making or Breaking the Synapse." *Science* 294 (5545) (Nov. 2001): 1296–1297.

Bertram, John S. "Cellular Communication Via Gap Junctions." *Science and Medicine* 7 (2) (March/April 2000): 18–27.

Brown, Anthony. "Slow Axonal Transport: Stop and Go Traffic in the Axon." *Nature Reviews: Molecular Cell Biology* 1 (2) (Nov. 2000): 153–156.

Fernandez-Chacon, Rafael, et al. "Synaptotagmin I Functions as a Calcium Regulator of Release Probability." *Nature* 410 (6824) (March 2001): 41–48.

Gallo, Vittoria and Chittajallu, Ramesh. "Unwrapping Glial Cells from the Synapse: What Lies Inside?" *Science* 292 (5518) (May 2001): 872–873.

Haydon, Philip G. "Glia: Listening and Talking to the Synapse." *Nature Reviews: Neuroscience* 2 (3) (March 2001): 185–192.

Helmuth, Laura. "Glia Tell Neurons to Build Synapses." *Science* 291 (5504) (Jan. 2001): 569–570.

Kast, Ben. "The Best Supporting Actors." *Nature* 412 (6848) (Aug. 2001): 674–676.

Khakh, Baljit S. "Molecular Physiology of P2X Receptors and ATP Signaling at Synapses." *Nature Reviews: Neuroscience* 2 (3) (March 2001): 165–174.

Magee, Jeffery C. "Dendritic Integration of Excitatory Synaptic Input." *Nature Reviews: Neuroscience* 1 (3) (Dec. 2000): 181–190.

McBain, Chris J. and Fisahn, Andre. "Interneurons Unbound." *Nature Reviews: Neuroscience* 2 (1) (Jan. 2001): 11–22.

Miller, Christopher. "See Potassium Run." *Nature* 414 (6859) (Nov. 2001): 23–24.

Nestler, Eric J. "Total Recall—The Memory of Addiction." *Science* 292 (5525) (June 2001): 2266–2267.

Rash, John et al. "Mixed Synapses Discovered and Mapped Throughout Mammalian Spinal Cord." *Proceedings National Academy Sciences* 93 (April 1996): 4235–4239.

Schmitz, Dietmar, et al. "Axo-Axonal Coupling: A Novel Mechanism for Ultrafast Neuronal Communication." *Neuron* 31 (Sept. 2001): 831–840.

Spruston, Nelson. "Axonal Gap Junctions Send Ripples Through the Hippocampus." *Neuron* 31 (Sept. 2001): 669–675.

Stix, Gary. "Saying Yes to NO." *Scientific American* 285 (5) (Nov. 2001): 34.

The Central Nervous System

Objectives

The Brain

1. Describe the development of the brain, and relate embryonic regions to the structures of the fully developed brain.
2. Explain the arrangement of gray and white matter in the brain.
3. Identify the ventricles of the brain, and the interconnections between ventricles.
4. Describe the anatomy of the cerebral hemispheres, and the location of functional areas of the cerebral cortex.
5. Name the structures and functions of cerebral white matter.
6. List the structures and functions of the diencephalon and brain stem.
7. Describe the anatomy of the cerebellum, its functional areas, and the mechanism of cerebellar processing.
8. Describe the distribution and function of functional brain systems.

Higher Mental Functions

9. Explain what EEGs measure, and discuss normal brain wave patterns and uses of EEGs.
10. Define consciousness, and discuss how various levels of consciousness are defined.
11. Describe sleep, and discuss the patterns and importance of NREM and REM sleep.
12. Define memory, and discuss the differences between short- and long-term memory, and fact and skill memory.
13. Discuss the physical effects of learning on the brain.

Protection of the Brain

14. Describe the structural and functional relationships of meninges, cerebrospinal fluid, and the blood-brain barrier to the brain.
15. Identify the causes and effects of homeostatic imbalances of the brain.

The Spinal Cord

16. Discuss the embryonic development of the spinal cord.
17. Indicate the anatomy of the spinal cord and its meninges within the vertebral column.
18. Explain the anatomy of gray matter, white matter, and spinal nerves of the spinal cord.
19. Describe the anatomy and function of the spinal tracts within the spinal cord.
20. List the causes and effects of spinal traumas and disorders.

Diagnostic Procedures for Assessing CNS Dysfunction

21. Name the techniques used to assess CNS function, and what each technique tests for.

Developmental Aspects of the Central Nervous System

21. Discuss the changes that occur throughout the prenatal period of growth and development.
22. Describe how gender-specific areas develop in the brain.
23. Identify the causes and effects of congenital brain disorders.
24. Explain the age-related changes in brain function.

Suggested Lecture Outline

I. The Brain (pp. 431–456; Figs. 12.1–12.19)

A. Embryonic Development (pp. 431–433; Figs. 12.2–12.3)

1. At three weeks' gestation, the ectoderm forms the neural plate, which invaginates, forming the neural groove, flanked on either side by neural folds.

2. By the fourth week of pregnancy, the neural groove fuses, giving rise to the neural tube, which rapidly differentiates into the CNS.

3. The neural tube develops constrictions that divide the three primary brain vesicles: the prosencephalon (forebrain), mesencephalon (midbrain), and rhombencephalon (hindbrain).

B. Regions and Organization (p. 433; Fig. 12.4)

1. The basic pattern of the CNS consists of a central cavity surrounded by a gray matter core, external to which is white matter.

2. In the brain, the cerebrum and cerebellum have an outer gray matter layer, which is reduced to scattered gray matter nuclei in the spinal cord.

C. Ventricles (pp. 433–434; Fig. 12.5)

1. The ventricles of the brain are continuous with one another, and with the central canal of the spinal cord. They are lined with ependymal cells, and are filled with cerebrospinal fluid.

   a. The paired lateral ventricles lie deep within each cerebral hemisphere, and are separated by the septum pellucidum.

   b. The third ventricle lies within the diencephalon, and communicates with the lateral ventricles via two interventricular foramina.

   c. The fourth ventricle lies in the hindbrain and communicates with the third ventricle via the cerebral aqueduct.

D. Cerebral Hemispheres (pp. 434–443; Figs. 12.6–12.11; Table 12.1)

1. The cerebral hemispheres form the superior part of the brain, and are characterized by ridges and grooves called gyri and sulci.

2. The cerebral hemispheres are separated along the midline by the longitudinal fissure, and are separated from the cerebellum along the transverse cerebral fissure.

3. The five lobes of the brain separated by specific sulci are: frontal, parietal, temporal, occipital, and insula.

4. The cerebral cortex is the location of the conscious mind, allowing us to communicate, remember, and understand.

5. The cerebral cortex has several motor areas located in the frontal lobes, which control voluntary movement.

   a. The primary motor cortex allows conscious control of skilled voluntary movement of skeletal muscles.

   b. The premotor cortex is the region controlling learned motor skills.

   c. Broca's area is a motor speech area that controls muscles involved in speech production.

   d. The frontal eye field controls eye movement.

6. There are several sensory areas of the cerebral cortex that occur in the parietal, temporal, and occipital lobes.

   a. The primary somatosensory cortex allows spatial discrimination and the ability to detect the location of stimulation.

        b. The somatosensory association cortex integrates sensory information and produces an understanding of the stimulus being felt.

        c. The primary visual cortex and visual association area allow reception and interpretation of visual stimuli.

        d. The primary auditory cortex and auditory association area allow detection of the properties and contextual recognition of sound.

        e. The olfactory cortex allows detection of odors.

        f. The gustatory cortex allows perception of taste stimuli.

        g. The vestibular cortex is responsible for conscious awareness of balance.

    7. Several association areas are not connected to any sensory cortices.

        a. The prefrontal cortex is involved with intellect, cognition, recall, and personality, and is closely linked to the limbic system.

        b. The language areas involved in comprehension and articulation include Wernicke's area, Broca's area, the lateral prefrontal cortex, and the lateral and ventral parts of the temporal lobe.

        c. The posterior association area receives input from all sensory areas, integrating signals into a single thought.

        d. The visceral association area is involved in conscious visceral sensation.

    8. There is lateralization of cortical functioning, in which each cerebral hemisphere has unique abilities not shared by the other half.

        a. One hemisphere (often the left) dominates language abilities, math, and logic, and the other hemisphere (often the right) dominates visual-spatial skills, intuition, emotion, and artistic and musical skills.

    9. Cerebral white matter is responsible for communication between cerebral areas and the cerebral cortex and lower CNS centers.

    10. Basal nuclei consist of a group of subcortical nuclei, which play a role in motor control and regulating attention and cognition.

E. The diencephalon is a set of gray matter areas, and consists of the thalamus, hypothalamus, and epithalamus (pp. 443–447; Figs. 12.11–12.15; Table 12.1).

    1. The thalamus plays a key role in mediating sensation, motor activities, cortical arousal, learning, and memory.

    2. The hypothalamus is the control center of the body, regulating ANS activity such as emotional response, body temperature, food intake, sleep-wake cycles, and endocrine function.

    3. The epithalamus includes the pineal gland, which secretes melatonin and regulates the sleep-wake cycle.

F. The brain stem, consisting of the midbrain, pons, and medulla oblongata, produces rigidly programmed, automatic behaviors necessary for survival (pp. 447–451; Figs. 12.15–12.16; Table 12.1).

    1. The midbrain is comprised of the cerebral peduncles, corpora quadrigemina, and substantia nigra.

    2. The pons contains fiber tracts that complete conduction pathways between the brain and spinal cord.

    3. The medulla oblongata is the location of several visceral motor nuclei controlling vital functions such as cardiac and respiratory rate.

G. Cerebellum (pp. 451–454; Fig. 12.17; Table 12.1)

    1. The cerebellum processes inputs from several structures and coordinates skeletal muscle contraction to produce smooth movement.

a. There are two cerebellar hemispheres consisting of three lobes each. Anterior and posterior lobes coordinate body movements and the flocculonodular lobes adjust posture to maintain balance.

b. Three paired fiber tracts, the cerebellar peduncles, communicate between the cerebellum and the brain stem.

2. Cerebellar processing follows a functional scheme in which the frontal cortex communicates the intent to initiate voluntary movement to the cerebellum, the cerebellum collects input concerning balance and tension in muscles and ligaments, and the best way to coordinate muscle activity is relayed back to the cerebral cortex.

H. Functional brain systems consist of neurons that are distributed throughout the brain but work together (pp. 454–456; Figs. 12.18–12.19).

1. The limbic system is involved with emotions, and is extensively connected throughout the brain, allowing it to integrate and respond to a wide variety of environmental stimuli.

2. The reticular formation extends through the brain stem, keeping the cortex alert via the reticular activating system, and dampening familiar, repetitive, or weak sensory inputs.

II. Higher Mental Functions (pp. 456–463; Figs. 12.20–12.23)

A. Brain Wave Patterns and the EEG (pp. 456–457; Fig. 12.20)

1. Normal brain function results from continuous electrical activity of neurons, and can be recorded with an electroencephalogram, or EEG.

2. Patterns of electrical activity are called brain waves, and fall into four types: alpha, beta, theta, and delta waves.

B. Consciousness encompasses conscious perception of sensations, voluntary initiation and control of movement, and capabilities associated with higher mental processing (pp. 457–458).

C. Sleep and Sleep-Awake Cycles (pp. 458–460; Fig. 12.21; Table 12.2)

1. Sleep is a state of partial unconsciousness from which a person can be aroused, and has two major types that alternate through the sleep cycle.

a. Non-rapid eye movement (NREM) sleep has four stages.

b. Rapid eye movement (REM) sleep is when most dreaming occurs.

2. Sleep patterns change throughout life, and are regulated by the hypothalamus.

3. NREM sleep is considered to be restorative, and REM sleep allows the brain to analyze events or eliminate meaningless information.

D. Memory is the storage and retrieval of information (pp. 460–463; Figs. 12.22–12.23).

1. Short-term memory, or working memory, allows the memorization of a few units of information for a short period of time.

2. Long-term memory allows the memorization of potentially limitless amounts of information for very long periods.

3. Transfer of information from short-term to long-term memory can be affected by a high emotional state, repetition, association of new information with old, or the automatic formation of memory while concentrating on something else.

4. Declarative memory entails learning explicit information, is often stored with the learning context, and is related to the ability to manipulate symbols and language.

5. Nondeclarative memory usually involves motor skills, is often stored without details of the learning context, and is reinforced through performance.

6. Learning causes changes in neuronal RNA, dendritic branching, deposition of unique proteins at LTM synapses, increase of presynaptic terminals, increase of neurotransmitter, and development of new neurons in the hippocampus.

III. Protection of the Brain (pp. 463–470; Figs. 12.24–12.27)

A. Meninges are three connective tissue membranes that cover and protect the CNS, protect blood vessels and enclose venous sinuses, contain cerebrospinal fluid, and partition the brain (pp. 463–465; Figs. 12.24–12.25).

1. The dura mater is the most durable, outermost covering that extends inward in certain areas to limit movement of the brain within the cranium.

2. The arachnoid mater is the middle meninx that forms a loose brain covering.

3. The pia mater is the innermost layer that clings tightly to the brain.

B. Cerebrospinal Fluid (pp. 465–467; Figs. 12.26–12.27)

1. Cerebrospinal fluid (CSF) is the fluid found within the ventricles of the brain and surrounding the brain and spinal cord.

2. CSF gives buoyancy to the brain, protects the brain and spinal cord from impact damage, and is a delivery medium for nutrients and chemical signals.

C. The blood-brain barrier is a protective mechanism that helps maintain a protective environment for the brain (p. 467).

D. Homeostatic Imbalances of the Brain (pp. 467–470)

1. Traumatic head injuries can lead to brain injuries of varying severity: concussion, contusion, and subdural or subarachnoid hemorrhage.

2. Cerebrovascular accidents (CVAs), or strokes, occur when blood supply to the brain is blocked resulting in tissue death.

3. Alzheimer's disease is a progressive degenerative disease that ultimately leads to dementia.

4. Parkinson's disease results from deterioration of dopamine-secreting neurons of the substantia nigra, and leads to a loss in coordination of movement and a persistent tremor.

5. Huntington's disease is a fatal hereditary disorder that results from deterioration of the basal nuclei and cerebral cortex.

IV. The Spinal Cord (pp. 470–481; Figs. 12.28–12.35; Tables 12.2–12.3)

A. Embryonic Development (p. 470)

1. The spinal cord develops from the caudal portion of the neural tube.

2. Axons from the alar plate form white matter, and expansion of both the alar and ventral plates gives rise to the central gray matter of the cord.

3. Neural crest cells form the dorsal root ganglia, and send axons to the dorsal aspect of the cord.

B. Gross Anatomy and Protection (pp. 470–472; Figs. 12.28–12.29)

1. The spinal cord extends from the foramen magnum of the skull to the level of the first or second lumbar vertebrae. It provides a two-way conduction pathway to and from the brain and serves as a major reflex center.

2. Fibrous extensions of the pia mater anchor the spinal cord to the vertebral column and coccyx, preventing excessive movement of the cord.

3. The spinal cord has 31 pairs of spinal nerves along its length that define the segments of the cord.

4. There are cervical and lumbar enlargements for the nerves that serve the limbs, and a collection of nerve roots (cauda equina) that travel through the vertebral column to their intervertebral foramina.

C. Cross-Sectional Anatomy (pp. 472–478; Figs. 12.30–12.35; Tables 12.2–12.3)

1. Two grooves partially divide the spinal cord into two halves: the anterior and posterior median fissures.

2. Two arms that extend posteriorly are dorsal horns, and the two arms that extend anteriorly are ventral horns.

3. In the thoracic and superior lumbar regions, there are also paired lateral horns that extend laterally between the dorsal and ventral horns.

4. Afferent fibers from peripheral receptors form the dorsal roots of the spinal cord.

5. The white matter of the spinal cord allows communication between the cord and brain.

6. All major spinal tracts are part of paired multineuron pathways that mostly cross from one side to the other, consist of a chain of two or three neurons, and exhibit somatotropy.

7. Ascending pathways conduct sensory impulses upward through a chain of three neurons.

   a. Nonspecific ascending pathways receive input from many different types of sensory receptors, and make multiple synapses in the brain.

   b. Specific ascending pathways mediate precise input from a single type of sensory receptor.

   c. Spinocerebellar tracts convey information about muscle and tendon stretch to the cerebellum.

8. Descending pathways involve two neurons: upper motor neurons and lower motor neurons.

   a. The direct, or pyramidal, system regulates fast, finely controlled, or skilled movements.

   b. The indirect, or extrapyramidal, system regulates muscles that maintain posture and balance, control coarse limb movements, and head, neck, and eye movements involved in tracking visual objects.

D. Spinal Cord Trauma and Disorders (pp. 478–481)

1. Any localized damage to the spinal cord or its roots leads to paralysis (loss of motor function) or paresthesias (loss of sensory function).

2. Poliomyelitis results from destruction of anterior horn neurons by the polio virus.

3. Amyotrophic lateral sclerosis (ALS), or Lou Gehrig's, disease is a neuro-muscular condition that involves progressive destruction of anterior horn motor neurons and fibers of the pyramidal tract.

V. Diagnostic Procedures for Assessing CNS Dysfunction (p. 481)

A. Pneumoencephalography is used to diagnose hydrocephalus, and allows X-ray visualization of the ventricles of the brain.

B. A cerebral angiogram is used to assess the condition of cerebral arteries to the brain in individuals that have suffered a stroke or TIA.

    C. CT scans and MRI scanning techniques allow visualization of most tumors, intracranial lesions, multiple sclerosis plaques, and areas of dead brain tissue.

    D. PET scans can localize brain lesions that generate seizures and diagnose Alzheimer's disease.

VI. Developmental Aspects of the Central Nervous System (pp. 481–485; Fig. 12.36)

    A. The brain and spinal cord grow and mature throughout the prenatal period due to influence from several organizer centers.

    B. Gender-specific areas of the brain and spinal cord develop depending on the presence or absence of testosterone.

    C. Lack of oxygen to the developing fetus may result in cerebral palsy, a neuromuscular disability in which voluntary muscles are poorly controlled or paralyzed as a result of brain damage.

    D. Age brings some cognitive decline but losses are not significant until the seventh decade.

Cross References

Additional information on topics covered in Chapter 12 can be found in the chapters listed below.

1. Chapter 13: Spinal nerves and peripheral nervous system function; the relationship between the peripheral nervous system and gray and white matter of the spinal cord; different brain areas and neural integration

2. Chapter 14: Spinal nerves and peripheral nervous system function; the relationship between the peripheral nervous system and gray and white matter of the spinal cord

3. Chapter 15: Role of the thalamus in the special senses; role of the cerebral cortex and cerebellum in integration of sensory information

4. Chapter 16: Hypothalamus and hormone production

5. Chapter 18: Role of the medulla in cardiac rate regulation

6. Chapter 19: Capillaries of the brain (blood-brain barrier); medulla and regulation of blood vessel diameter (vasomotor center); hypothalamus and blood pressure regulation

7. Chapter 22: Respiratory centers in the medulla and pons; cortical and hypothalamic involvement in respiration

8. Chapter 23: Central nervous system involvement in the reflex activity controlling digestive processes

9. Chapter 24: Role of the hypothalamus in body temperature regulation

10. Chapter 26: Role of the hypothalamus in regulation of fluid electrolyte balance

11. Chapter 27: Testosterone and development of the brain

Laboratory Correlations

1. Marieb, E. N. *Human Anatomy & Physiology Laboratory Manual: Cat and Fetal Pig Versions.* Eighth Edition Updates. Benjamin Cummings, 2006.

    Exercise 19: Gross Anatomy of the Brain and Cranial Nerves

    Exercise 20: Electroencephalography

    Exercise 21: Spinal Cord, Spinal Nerves, and the Autonomic Nervous System

2. Marieb, E. N. *Human Anatomy & Physiology Laboratory Manual: Main Version.* Seventh Edition Update. Benjamin Cummings, 2006.

   Exercise 19: Gross Anatomy of the Brain and Cranial Nerves

   Exercise 20: Electroencephalography

   Exercise 21: Spinal Cord, Spinal Nerves, and the Autonomic Nervous System

Histology Slides for the Life Sciences

Available through Benjamin Cummings, an imprint of Pearson Education, Inc. To order, contact your local Benjamin Cummings sales representative.

Slide 73   Myelinated Nerve Cross Section—Myelin Sheaths.

Slide 74   Myelinated Nerve Longitudinal Section—Nodes of Ranvier.

Slide 75   Efferent (Motor) Neuron.

Slide 76   Spinal Cord Bottom, Stained for Axons.

Lecture Hints

1. Study of the central nervous system is difficult for most students. The complexity of the material can overwhelm practically anyone. Present the material from an overall conceptual perspective, then progress into greater levels of detail. In this way, students are less likely to get lost.

2. When discussing the ventricles, draw a rough diagram on the board (or on acetate) that shows a schematic representation of the chambers and connecting passageways. As students comprehend the serial nature of CSF flow, translate the sketches to actual cross-sectional photographs or accurate diagrams.

3. Students often have difficulty understanding how the cerebellum is involved in the control of motor activity. Try using a physical activity such as golf to illustrate cerebellar interaction. I.e., we all know how to swing a club, but only well-developed cerebellar coordination of muscle group action allows a "pro" to place the ball exactly where it should be.

4. Emphasize that the meningeal protection of the brain and spinal cord is continuous, but that the spinal cord has an epidural space, whereas the brain does not.

Activities/Demonstrations

1. Audio-visual materials listed under Multimedia in the Classroom and Lab.

2. Project or set up microslides to demonstrate cross-sectional anatomy of the spinal cord at several different levels to show how gray and white matter changes with each level in the cord.

3. Obtain a 3-D model of a human brain and compare it to a real human brain and/or a dissected sheep brain.

4. Acquire a 3-D model of a spinal cord, both longitudinal section and cross section, to illustrate its features.

5. Obtain stained sections of brain tissue to illustrate the differences between gray and white matter and to show internal parts.

6. Use a 3-D model or cast of the ventricles of the brain.

7. Obtain a sheep brain with the cranium and/or meninges still intact.

Critical Thinking/Discussion Topics

1. Discuss the difference between encephalitis and meningitis.
2. Prefrontal lobotomies have been used in psychotherapy along with electrical shock. How and why have these techniques been used?
3. Since a right-handed person's left hemisphere appears to dominate in cerebral functions, what could be done to increase the use of the left hemisphere?
4. Anencephalic children will usually die soon after birth. There is currently a desire among some medical groups to use the organs of these children to help others. What are the pros and cons of this type of organ transplantation?
5. If a needle is used to deliver or remove fluids from the spaces surrounding the spinal cord, where is the best location (along the length of the cord) to perform the procedure? Why?
6. Trace the complete path of CSF from formation to reabsorption and examine the consequences if choroid plexus function were altered, or an obstruction developed in the path of CSF flow.

Library Research Topics

1. What techniques are currently used to localize and treat tumors of the brain?
2. How has the human brain changed in size and shape over millions of years of evolution? Explore the development of the human nervous system.
3. What drugs are being used to enhance memory? Where and how do they work?
4. The sensory and motor areas of the cerebral cortex around the pre- and postcentral gyrus have been carefully mapped out. How was this done?
5. What methods of experimentation have been used to study the limbic system? What research has been done to determine whether some habitual criminals have defects in this system?
6. Describe the latest techniques used to examine structure/function of the CNS.
7. How can fetal tissues be used to repair adult CNS dysfunctions?

Multimedia in the Classroom and Lab

Online Resources for Students

The
Anatomy & Physiology Place   MyA&P
www.anatomyandphysiology.com   www.myaandp.com

The following shows the organization of the Chapter Guide page in both the Anatomy & Physiology Place and MyA&P™. The Chapter Guide organizes all the chapter-specific online media resources for Chapter 12 in one convenient location, with e-book links to each section of the textbook. Please note that both sites also give you access to other general A&P resources, like InterActive Physiology®, PhysioEx 6.0™, Anatomy 360°, Flashcards, a Glossary, a Histology Tutorial, and much more.

Objectives
Section 12.1 The Brain (pp. 431–456)

Art Labeling Activity: Lobes and Fissures of the Cerebral Hemispheres (Fig. 12.6, p. 435)

Art Labeling Activity: Functional and Structural Areas of the Cerebral Cortex (Fig. 12.8a, p. 437)

Art Labeling Activity: Basal Nuclei (Fig. 12.11, p. 444)

Art Labeling Activity: Midsagittal Section of the Brain, Part 1 (Fig. 12.12, p. 445)

Art Labeling Activity: Midsagittal Section of the Brain, Part 2 (Fig. 12.12, p. 445)

Art Labeling Activity: Selected Structures of the Diencephalon (Fig. 12.13, p. 445)

Art Labeling Activity: Relationship of the Brain Stem and the Diencephalon, Ventral View (Fig. 12.15a, p. 448)

Art Labeling Activity: Relationship of the Brain Stem and the Diencephalon, Left Lateral View (Fig. 12.15b, p. 448)

Art Labeling Activity: Relationship of the Brain Stem and the Diencephalon, Dorsal View (Fig. 12.15c, p. 448)

Art Labeling Activity: Important Brain Stem Nuclei, Midbrain (Fig. 12.16a, p. 450)

Art Labeling Activity: Important Brain Stem Nuclei, Pons (Fig. 12.16b, p. 450)

Art Labeling Activity: Important Brain Stem Nuclei, Medulla Oblongata (Fig. 12.16c, p. 450)

Memory: Brain Structure

Section 12.2 Higher Mental Functions (pp. 456–463)

Section 12.3 Protection of the Brain (pp. 463–470)

Art Labeling Activity: Meninges (Fig. 12.24a, p. 464)

Art Labeling Activity: Location and Circulatory Patterns of CSF (Fig. 12.26, p. 466)

Case Study: Cerebrovascular Accident

Case Study: Parkinson's Disease

Section 12.4 The Spinal Cord (pp. 470–481)

Art Labeling Activity: Anatomy of the Spinal Cord, Cross Section (Fig. 12.31a, p. 473)

Art Labeling Activity: Anatomy of the Spinal Cord, Three-Dimensional View (Fig. 12.31b, p. 473)

Memory: Major Nerves of the Central Nervous System

Case Study: Nervous System

Section 12.5 Diagnostic Procedures for Assessing CNS Dysfunction (p. 481)

Section 12.6 Developmental Aspects of the Central Nervous System (pp. 481–484)

Chapter Summary

Self-Study Quizzes

Art Labeling Quiz

Matching Quiz

Multiple-Choice Quiz (Level I)

Multiple-Choice Quiz (Level II)

True-False Quiz

Crossword Puzzles

Crossword Puzzle 12.1

Crossword Puzzle 12.2

Media

See Guide to Audio-Visual Resources in Appendix A for key to AV distributors.

Video

1. *The Addicted Brain* (FHS; 26 min., 1987). Documentary explores drug use and the effects on the brain. Shows the latest developments and research in the biochemistry of addiction and addictive behavior. For classroom discussion.

2. *Anatomy of the Human Brain* (FHS; 35 min., 1997). Neuropathologist Dr. Marco Rossi dissects and examines a normal human brain.

3. *Decision* (FHS; 28 min., 1984). This exceptional program from *The Living Body* series shows how the brain coordinates functions to make a simple but lifesaving decision.

4. *The Human Brain in Situ* (FHS; 19 min., 1997). Neurobiologist Susan Standring conducts a basic anatomical examination of the human brain and its connections in the skull. Standring identifies parts of the brain and skull.

5. *The Human Nervous System: The Brain and Cranial Nerves Videotape* (BC; 28 min., 1997). This video by Rose Leigh Vines and Rosalee Carter, California State University, Sacramento, links nervous system structures and functions.

6. *The Human Nervous System: The Spinal Cord and Nerves Videotape* (BC; 29 min., 1997). Illustrations and figures help students learn the organization of the spinal nerves into complicated plexuses. Major nerves arising from these plexuses are traced on the cadaver as they course through the upper and lower extremities.

7. *Inside Information: The Brain and How it Works* (FHS; 58 min., 1990). This program explains research on the brain's processes. Includes interviews with the foremost researchers in the field.

8. *Men, Women, and the Brain* (FHS; 57 min., 1998). In this program, specialists from the National Institute of Child Health and Human Development, and other institutions define and explore differences between the brains of men and women. These differences can affect aging, reading ability, spatial skills, aggression, depression, schizophrenia, and sexuality.

9. *Pathology Examples in the Human Brain* (FHS; 24 min., 1997). Neuropathologist Dr. Marco Rossi examines different human brain specimens and presents evidence of trauma or disease.

10. *The Seven Ages of the Brain* (FHS; 58 min., 1994). This program focuses on how a brain grows from a fertilized egg and how our brains change with age.

11. *Spinal Surgery* (FHS; 45 min., 1995). In this program, spinal surgery is performed on a 15-year-old gymnast who has popped a vertebra out of place, leaving her neck unstable.

12. *Stress, Trauma, and the Brain* (FHS; 57 min., 1999). In section one of this program, doctors from Harvard Medical School and other institutions study the stress of modern living in light of the innate fight-or-flight mechanism. In section two, a pioneer in brain imaging technology and experts from MIT describe revolutionary imaging techniques and their application to brain tumor surgery. In the third section medical professionals investigate brain trauma.

Software

1. *A.D.A.M.® InterActive Anatomy® 4.0* (see p. 9 of this guide for full listing).

2. *A.D.A.M.® MediaPro* (see p. 9 of this guide for full listing).

3. *A.D.A.M.® Anatomy Practice* (see p. 86 of this guide for full listing).

4. *Bodyworks* (see p. 9 of this guide for full listing).

5. *Interactive Nervous System* (IM; Windows). This two CD-ROM set explores the structure, functions, and processes of the nervous system. It studies reaction to stimuli, neurons, reflexes, and senses.

6. *The Ultimate Human Body* (see p. 9 of this guide for full listing).

Lecture Enhancement Material

To view thumbnails of all of the illustrations for Chapter 12, see Appendix B.

Transparencies Index/Media Manager

Indicates images that are on the Media Manager only.

Answers to End-of-Chapter Questions

Multiple Choice and Matching Question answers appear in Appendix G of the main text.

Short Answer Essay Questions

12. See Fig. 12.2 for a diagram of the primary embryonic brain vesicles and the resulting brain structure.

13. a. Convolutions increase the cortical surface area, which allows more neurons to occupy the limited space. (p. 433)

    b. Sulci and fissures; gyri (p. 434)

    c. Median longitudinal fissure (p. 434)

    d. Central sulcus; lateral sulcus (pp. 434–436)

14. a. See Fig. 12.8 for a drawing of the functional areas of the brain.

    b. Primary motor cortex—All voluntary somatic motor responses arise from this region. (p. 438)

    Premotor cortex—This region controls learned motor skills of a repetitious or patterned nature. (p. 439)

    Somatosensory association area—Acts to integrate and analyze different somatosensory inputs, such as temperature, touch, pressure, and pain. (pp. 439–440)

    Primary somatosensory cortex—Receives all somatosensory information from receptors located in the skin and from proprioceptors in muscles; identifies the body region being stimulated. (p. 439)

    Visual area—Receives information that originates in the retinas of the eyes. (p. 440)

    Auditory area—Receives information that originates in the hearing receptors of the inner ear. (p. 440)

    Prefrontal cortex—Mostly involved with elaboration of thought, intelligence, motivation, and personality. It also associates experiences necessary for the production of abstract ideas, judgment, planning, and conscience, and is important in planning motor activity. (p. 441)

    Wernicke's area—Speech area involved in the comprehension of language, especially when the word needs to be sounded out or related. (p. 441)

    Broca's area—Previously called the motor speech area; now known to be active in many other activities as well. (p. 439)

15. a. Specialization of cortical functions. The "dominant" hemisphere excels at language and mathematical skills. The nondominant hemisphere is better at visual-spatial skills, intuition, emotion, and appreciation of art and music. (p. 441)

b. Both hemispheres have perfect and instant communication with each other so there is tremendous integration; therefore neither side is better at everything. However, each hemisphere does have unique abilities not shared by its partner. (pp. 441–443)

16. a. Initiate slow and sustained movement; help to coordinate and control motor activity. (p. 443)

    b. The putamen and globus pallidus (p. 443)

    c. Caudate nucleus (p. 443)

17. a. Three paired fiber tracts (cerebellar peduncles) connect it to the brain stem. (p. 448)

    b. The cerebellum has a convoluted surface with gray matter on the outside and white on the inside with deeply situated nuclei. It has two hemispheres with overlapping functions. (pp. 452–454)

18. The cerebellum acts like an automatic pilot by initiating and coordinating the activity of skeletal muscle groups. (A step-by-step discussion is given on p. 454.)

19. a. Medial aspect of each cerebral hemisphere. (p. 454)

    b. Cingulate gyrus, parahippocampal gyrus, hippocampus, regions of the hypothalamus, mammillary bodies, septal nuclei, amygdaloid nucleus, anterior thalamic nuclei, and fornix. (p. 454)

    c. Acts as our emotional or affective (feeling) brain. (p. 455)

20. a. It extends through the central core of the medulla, pons, and midbrain. (p. 455)

    b. RAS means reticular activating system, which is our cortical arousal mechanism. It helps to keep the cerebral cortex alert while filtering out unimportant inputs. (p. 456)

21. An aura is a sensory hallucination that occurs just before a seizure, such as a taste, smell, or flashes of light. (p. 457)

22. REM sleep occupies about 50% of the total sleeping time in infants, but then declines with age to stabilize at 25%. Stage 4 sleep declines steadily from birth and disappears completely in those over 60 years. (pp. 459–460)

23. STM is fleeting memory that serves as a sort of temporary holding bin for data and is limited to seven or eight chunks of data. LTM seems to have unlimited capacity for storage and is very long-lasting unless altered. (p. 460)

24. a. Emotional state, rehearsal, association of new information with information already stored, and automatic memory. (p. 461)

    b. Memory consolidation involves fitting new facts into the network of preexisting consolidated knowledge stored in the cerebral cortex. (p. 461)

25. Fact memory is the ability to learn explicit information and is related to our conscious thoughts and our ability to manipulate symbols and language. Skill memory is concerned with motor activities acquired through practice. (p. 461)

26. The CNS is protected by: the bony cranium, meninges, cerebrospinal fluid, and blood-brain barrier. (p. 463)

27. a. CSF is formed by the choroid plexus via a secretory process involving both active transport and diffusion and is drained by the arachnoid villi. See Fig. 12.25 for the circulatory pathway. (pp. 464–465)

    b. A condition called hydrocephalus can develop. In children, the fontanels allow expansion without brain damage, but in adults, the inability of the skull to expand may cause severe damage due to brain compression. (p. 467)

28. The blood-brain barrier is formed mainly by capillaries with endothelial cells joined by tight junctions. This characteristic makes them highly selective, ensuring that only certain substances can gain access to the neural tissue. (p. 467)

29. Scalp, cranial bone, periosteal layers of the dura mater, subdural space, arachnoid, subarachnoid space, pia mater, brain tissue. (pp. 463–464)

30. a. A concussion occurs when brain injury is slight and the symptoms are mild and transient. Contusions occur when marked tissue destruction takes place. (p. 468)

    b. Due to injury of the RAS. (p. 468)

31. a. The spinal cord is enclosed in the vertebral column and extends from the foramen magnum of the skull to the first or second lumbar vertebra, inferior to the ribs. It is composed of both gray and white matter. The gray matter consists of a mixture of neuron cell bodies, their unmyelinated processes, and neuroglia. In cross section, it looks like a butterfly. White matter is composed of myelinated and unmyelinated nerve fibers that run in three directions: ascending, descending, and transversely. Ascending and descending tracts make up most of the white matter. The spinal roots of the spinal cord are of two kinds: ventral and dorsal, and they fuse laterally to form the spinal nerves, which are part of the peripheral nervous system. (pp. 469–479)

32. c (pp. 474–476)

33. a. The lateral spinothalamic tract transmits pain, temperature, and course touch impulses, and they are interpreted eventually in the somatosensory cortex. If cut, our sensory perception of the occurrence of a stimulus, as well as our ability to detect the magnitude of the stimulus and identify the site or pattern of the stimulation or its specific texture, shape, or quality, e.g., sweet or sour, would be impaired. (pp. 474–476)

    b. The anterior and posterior spinocerebellar tracts convey information from proprioceptors (muscle or tendon stretch) to the cerebellum, which uses this information to coordinate skeletal muscle activity. Cerebellar damage can cause equilibrium problems and speech difficulties. (p. 476)

    c. The tectospinal tract transmits motor impulses from the midbrain, which are important for coordinated movement of the head and eyes toward visual targets. If cut, problems of locomotion could occur. (p. 477)

34. Spastic paralysis—due to damage to upper motor neurons of the primary motor cortex. Muscles can respond to reflex arcs initiated at spinal cord level. (p. 479)

    Flaccid paralysis—damage to ventral root or anterior horn cells. Muscles do not respond because they receive no stimuli. (p. 479)

35. Paraplegia—damage to cord (lower motor neurons) between T_1 and L_1 that causes paralysis of both lower limbs. (p. 479)

    Hemiplegia—damage, usually in the brain, that causes paralysis of one side of the body. (p. 479)

    Quadriplegia—damage to cord in cervical area affecting all four limbs. (p. 479)

36. a. CVA, also known as stroke, occurs when blood circulation to a brain area is blocked and vital brain tissue dies. A new hypothesis targets the release of glutamate by oxygen-starved neurons (and subsequent entry of excess Ca^{2+}) as the culprit. (pp. 467–468)

    b. Any event that kills brain tissue due to a lack of oxygen; includes blockage of a cerebral artery by a blood clot, compression of brain tissue by hemorrhage or edema, and arteriosclerosis. Consequences include paralysis, sensory deficits, language difficulties, and speech problems. (pp. 467–468)

37. a. Continued myelination of neural tissue accounts for growth and maturation of the nervous system.

    b. There is a decline in brain weight and volume with age. (pp. 480–481)

Critical Thinking and Clinical Application Questions

1. a. The only likely diagnosis is hydrocephalus. (p. 466)

   b. CT or sonograms, but most importantly pneumoencephalography. (p. 480)

   c. Lateral and third ventricles enlarge; fourth ventricle, central canal, and subarachnoid space are not affected. If arachnoid villi are obstructed, all CSF areas will be enlarged. (pp. 464–466)

2. Alzheimer's disease. (p. 468)

3. Probably the frontal lobes, specifically the prefrontal cortex, which mediates personality and moral behavior. (p. 441)

4. In myelomeningocele, a cyst containing parts of the spinal cord, nerve roots, and meninges protrudes from the spine. Pressure during vaginal delivery could cause the cyst to rupture, leading to infection and further damage. A C-section is preferable. (p. 481)

5. a. Parkinson's disease.

   b. Neurons of the substantia nigra; deficiency of the neurotransmitter dopamine.

   c. Combination drug therapy with L-dopa, carbidopa, and a dopamine agonist. (p. 468)

6. Cynthia's waist-down paralysis is a result of damage to nonspecific and specific ascending pathways, which causes a loss of sensory input to the brain from the extremities, and damage to the upper, but not lower, motor neurons of the descending pathways. All of this results in loss of voluntary control of muscle movements, but leaves reflexive movements intact. Therefore, bedsores would be an issue, since Cynthia will be immobilized for long periods, and cannot feel the localized compressions that lead to them. As a consequence of both sensory and voluntary motor loss, she is prone to bladder infections and incomplete and infrequent voiding because she lacks the inability to feel when her bladder is full, allowing it to become overfull. Muscle spasms result from the reflexive contractions directed by the lower motor neurons that are still intact. (p. 479)

7. The left side of the brain was affected. The specific area of the brain affected was Broca's area. Broca's area is usually found on the left side of the brain and controls thinking, preparing for speech and the muscles involved with speech. (p. 439)

8. The needle will be inserted in the lumbar area of the vertebral column below L2. The needle will be inserted into the subarachnoid space to withdraw cerebrospinal fluid to be tested for the presence of pathogens. (p. 470)

Suggested Readings

Birmingham, Karen. "Future of Neuroprotective Drugs in Doubt." *Nature Medicine* 8 (1) (Jan. 2002): 5.

Bower, B. "Brain May Forge Some Memories in Waves." *Science News* 160 (19) (Nov. 2001): 294.

Bucciantini, Monica et al. "Inherent Toxicity of Aggregates Implies a Common Mechanism for Protein Misfolding Diseases." *Nature* 416 (6880) (April 2002): 507–511.

Calder, A. J. et al. "Neurophysiology of Fear and Loathing." *Nature Reviews: Neurophysiology* 2 (5) (May 2001): 352–363.

Check, Erica. "Parkinson's Patients Show Positive Response to Implants." *Nature* 416 (6882) (April 2002): 666.

Dunnett, S. B. et al. "Cell Therapy in Parkinson's Disease—Stop or Go?" *Nature Reviews: Neuroscience* 2 (5) (May 2001): 365–368.

Eichenbaum, Howard. "A Cortical-Hippocampal System for Declarative Memory." *Nature Reviews: Neuroscience* 1 (1) (Oct. 2000): 41–50.

Fricker-Gater, Rosemary A. and Dunnett, Stephen B. "Rewiring the Parkinsonian Brain." *Nature Medicine* 8 (2) (Feb. 2002): 105–106.

Gross, Charles G. "Neurogenesis in the Adult Brain: Death of a Dogma." *Nature Reviews: Neuroscience* 1 (1) (Oct. 2000): 67–72.

Hansel, D. E. et al. "Neuropeptide Y Functions as a Neuroproliferative Factor." *Nature* 410 (6831) (April 2001): 940–944.

Helmuth, Laura. "Redrawing the Brain's Map of the Body." *Science* 296 (5573) (May 2002): 1587–1588.

Macklis, Jeffrey D. "New Memories from New Neurons." *Nature* 410 (6826) (March 2001): 314–315.

Manabe, Toshiya. "Does BDNF Have Pre- or Postsynaptic Targets?" *Science* 295 (5560) (March 2002): 1651–1652.

Maquet, Pierre. "The Role of Sleep in Learning and Memory." *Science* 294 (5544) (Nov. 2001): 1048–1051.

Marx, Jean. "New Leads on the 'How' of Alzheimer's." *Science* 293 (5538) (Sept. 2001): 2192–2194.

Miller, Earl K. "The Prefrontal Cortex and Cognitive Control." *Nature Reviews: Neuroscience* 1 (1) (Oct. 2000): 59–65.

Nathanson, Neal and Fine, Paul. "Poliomyelitis Eradication—A Dangerous Endgame." *Science* 296 (April 2002): 269–270.

Shi, Song-Hai. "AMPA Receptor Dynamics and Synaptic Plasticity." *Science* 294 (5548) (Nov. 2001): 1851–1852.

Siegel, Jerome M. "The REM Sleep-Memory Consolidation Hypothesis." *Science* 294 (5544) (Nov. 2001): 1058–1063.

Stern, Claudio. "Initial Patterning of the Central Nervous System: How Many Organizers?" *Nature Reviews: Neuroscience* 2 (2) (Feb. 2001): 92–98.

Svitil, Kathy A. "Fire in the Brain: Can Programmable Implants Help Epileptics Detect the Onset of Seizures?" *Discover* 23 (5) (May 2002): 51–50.

The Peripheral Nervous System and Reflex Activity

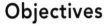

Objectives

1. Define peripheral nervous system and identify its components.

PART 1: SENSORY RECEPTORS AND SENSATION

Sensory Receptors

2. Classify general sensory receptors by structure, stimulus detected, and body location.

Overview: From Sensation to Perception

3. Outline the events that lead to sensation and perception.
4. Explore the levels of neural integration in the somatosensory system.
5. Identify the main aspects of sensory perception.

PART 2: TRANSMISSION LINES: NERVES AND THEIR STRUCTURE AND REPAIR

Nerves and Associated Ganglia

6. Define nerve and ganglion and indicate the general body location of ganglia.
7. Describe the general structure of a nerve and follow the process of nerve regeneration.

Cranial Nerves

8. Name the 12 pairs of cranial nerves; indicate the body regions and structures innervated by each.

Spinal Nerves

9. Describe the general features of spinal nerves and the distribution of their rami.

10. Define plexus. Name the major plexuses and describe the distribution and function of the peripheral nerves arising from each plexus.

PART 3: MOTOR ENDINGS AND MOTOR ACTIVITY

Peripheral Motor Endings

11. Compare and contrast the motor endings of somatic and autonomic nerve fibers.

Overview of Motor Integration: From Intention to Effect

12. Outline the three levels of the hierarchy of motor control.
13. Compare the roles of the cerebellum and basal nuclei in controlling motor activity.

PART 4: REFLEX ACTIVITY

The Reflex Arc

14. Name the components of a reflex arc and distinguish between autonomic and somatic reflexes.

Spinal Reflexes

15. Compare and contrast stretch, flexor, crossed extensor, and superficial reflexes.

Developmental Aspects of the Peripheral Nervous System

16. List changes that occur in the sensory system with aging.
17. Describe the developmental relationship between the segmented arrangement of the peripheral nerves, skeletal muscles, and skin dermatomes.

Suggested Lecture Outline

PART 1: SENSORY RECEPTORS AND SENSATION

I. Sensory Receptors (pp. 491–494; Fig. 13.1; Table 13.1)

A. Sensory receptors are specialized to respond to changes in their environment called stimuli (pp. 491–494).

1. Receptors may be classified according to the activating stimulus.

2. Receptors may be classified based on their location or the location of the activating stimulus.

3. Receptors may be classified based on their overall structural complexity.

B. Free, or naked, nerve endings are present everywhere in the body and respond primarily to pain and temperature. (p. 492)

C. Encapsulated Dendritic Endings (pp. 492–494; Table 13.1)

1. Meissner's corpuscles are receptors for discriminatory and light touch in hairless areas of the body.

2. Pacinian, or lamellated, corpuscles, are stimulated when deep pressure is first applied.

3. Ruffini endings respond to deep and continuous pressure.

4. Muscle spindles detect when a muscle is being stretched and initiate a reflex that resists the stretch.

5. Golgi tendon organs are stimulated when the associated muscle stretches the tendon.

6. Joint kinesthetic receptors monitor the stretch in the articular capsules of synovial joints.

II. Overview: From Sensation to Perception (pp. 494–498; Fig. 13.2)

A. The somatosensory system, the part of the sensory system serving the body wall and limbs, involves the receptor level, the circuit level, and the perceptual level.

1. Processing at the receptor level involves a stimulus that must excite a receptor in order for sensation to occur.

2. Processing at the circuit level is involved with delivery of impulses to the appropriate region of the cerebral cortex for stimulus localization and perception.

3. Processing at the perceptual level involves interpretation of sensory input in the cerebral cortex.

PART 2: TRANSMISSION LINES: NERVES AND THEIR STRUCTURE AND REPAIR

I. Nerves and Associated Ganglia (pp. 498–500; Figs. 13.3–13.4)

A. A nerve is a cordlike organ consisting of parallel bundles of peripheral axons enclosed by connective tissue wrappings.

B. Ganglia are collections of neuron cell bodies associated with nerves in the PNS.

C. If damage to a neuron occurs to the axon and the cell body remains intact, cut or compressed axons can regenerate.

II. Cranial Nerves (pp. 500–508; Fig. 13.5; Table 13.2)

A. Olfactory nerves are responsible for smell.

B. Optic nerves are responsible for vision.

C. Oculomotor nerves play a role in eye movement.

D. Trochlear nerves play a role in eye movement.

E. Trigeminal nerves are general sensory nerves of the face.

F. Abducens nerves play a role in eye movement.

G. Facial nerves function as the chief motor nerves of the face.

H. Vestibulocochlear nerves are responsible for hearing and equilibrium.

I. Glossopharyngeal nerves innervate part of the tongue and pharynx.

J. Vagus nerves innervate the heart, lungs, and the abdominal organs.

K. Accessory nerves move structures associated with the head and neck.

L. Hypoglossal nerves are mixed nerves that arise from the medulla and serve the tongue.

III. Spinal Nerves (pp. 508–518; Figs. 13.6–13.12; Tables 13.3–13.6)

A. Thirty-one pairs of mixed spinal nerves arise from the spinal cord and serve the entire body except the head and neck.

B. Innervation of Specific Body Regions

1. Each spinal nerve connects to the spinal cord by a dorsal root and a ventral root.

2. Rami lie distal to and are lateral branches of the spinal nerves that carry both motor and sensory fibers.

3. The back is innervated by the dorsal rami with each rami innervating the muscle in line with the point of origin from the spinal column.

4. Only in the thorax are the ventral rami arranged in a simple segmental pattern corresponding to that of the dorsal rami.

5. The cervical plexus is formed by the ventral rami of the first four cervical nerves.

6. The brachial plexus is situated partly in the neck and partly in the axilla and gives rise to virtually all the nerves that innervate the upper limb.

7. The sacral and lumbar plexuses overlap and because many fibers of the lumber plexus contribute to the sacral plexus via the lumbosacral trunk, the two plexuses are often referred to as the lumbosacral plexus.

8. The area of skin innervated by the cutaneous branches of a single spinal nerve is called a dermatome.

9. Hinton's law states that any nerve serving a muscle that produces movement at a joint also innervates the joint and the skin over the joint.

PART 3: MOTOR ENDINGS AND MOTOR ACTIVITY

I. Peripheral Motor Endings (p. 519)

A. Peripheral motor endings are the PNS element that activates effectors by releasing neurotransmitters.

B. The terminals of the somatic motor fibers that innervate voluntary muscles form elaborate neuromuscular junctions with their effector cells and they release the neurotransmitter acetylcholine.

C. The junctions between autonomic motor endings and the visceral effectors involve varicosities and release either acetylcholine or epinephrine as their neurotransmitter.

II. Overview of Motor Integration: From Intention to Effect (pp. 519–521; Fig. 13.13)

A. Levels of Motor Control

1. The segmental level is the lowest level on the motor control hierarchy and consists of the spinal cord circuits.

2. The projection level has direct control of the spinal cord.

3. The precommand level is made up of the cerebellum and the basal nuclei and is the highest level of the motor system hierarchy.

PART 4: REFLEX ACTIVITY

I. The Reflex Arc (pp. 521–522; Fig. 13.14)

A. Reflexes are unlearned, rapid, predictable motor responses to a stimulus, and occur over highly specific neural pathways called reflex arcs (pp. 521–522; Fig. 13.14).

II. Spinal Reflexes (pp. 522–527; Figs. 13.15–13.19)

A. Spinal reflexes are somatic reflexes mediated by the spinal cord (pp. 522–527; Figs. 13.15–13.19).

1. In the stretch reflex the muscle spindle is stretched and excited by either an external stretch or an internal stretch.

2. The Golgi tendon reflex produces muscle relaxation and lengthening in response to contraction.

3. The flexor, or withdrawal, reflex is initiated by a painful stimulus and causes automatic withdrawal of the threatened body part from the stimulus.

4. The crossed extensor reflex is a complex spinal reflex consisting of an ipsilateral withdrawal reflex and a contralateral extensor reflex.

5. Superficial reflexes are elicited by gentle cutaneous stimulation.

III. Developmental Aspects of the Peripheral Nervous System (p. 527)

A. The spinal nerves branch from the developing spinal cord and adjacent neural crest and exit between the forming vertebrae. Each nerve becomes associated with the adjacent muscle mass.

B. Cranial nerves innervate muscles of the head in a similar way.

C. Sensory receptors atrophy to some degree with age, and there is a decrease in muscle tone in the face and neck; reflexes occur a bit more slowly.

Cross References

Additional information on topics covered in Chapter 13 can be found in the chapters listed below.

1. Chapter 3: Membrane functions

2. Chapter 4: Nervous tissue

3. Chapter 5: Cutaneous sensation and sensory receptors

4. Chapter 9: Neuromuscular junction

5. Chapter 11: Membrane potentials; neural integration; serial and parallel processing; synapses; neurotransmitters

6. Chapter 12: Ascending and descending tracts of the spinal cord; spinal roots; gray and white matter of the spinal cord

7. Chapter 15: Sensory receptors for the special senses and generator potentials; cranial nerves associated with their special senses; reflex activity of the special senses

8. Chapter 23: Reflex activity and control of digestive secretions; nerve plexuses involved in digestion; function of the vagus nerve in parasympathetic control

9. Chapter 25: Spinal reflex control of micturition

10. Chapter 27: Spinal reflexes and the physiology of the sexual response

Laboratory Correlations

1. Marieb, E. N. *Human Anatomy & Physiology Laboratory Manual: Cat and Fetal Pig Versions.* Eighth Edition Updates. Benjamin Cummings, 2006.

   Exercise 22: Human Reflex Physiology

2. Marieb, E. N. *Human Anatomy & Physiology Laboratory Manual: Main Version.* Seventh Edition Update. Benjamin Cummings, 2006.

   Exercise 22: Human Reflex Physiology

Histology Slides for the Life Sciences

Available through Benjamin Cummings, an imprint of Pearson Education, Inc. To order, contact your local Benjamin Cummings sales representative.

Slide 73   Myelinated Nerve Cross Section—Myelin Sheaths.

Slide 74   Myelinated Nerve Longitudinal Section—Nodes of Ranvier.

Slide 75   Efferent (Motor) Neuron.

Slide 76   Spinal Cord Bottom, Stained for Axons.

Lecture Hints

1. Emphasize the distinction between the central and peripheral nervous system, but stress that the nervous system functions as a continuous unit, even though we like to study its anatomy in bits and pieces. Students often treat each section as if it operates autonomously, without regard to what may be happening in other parts of the nervous system.

2. Many students will have difficulty with the difference between receptor potentials, generator potentials, and action potentials. It is worth taking time to be sure the distinction is clear.

3. As the anatomy of the nerve is discussed, point out the similarity between the basic structure of muscle tissue and nervous tissue. Also bring to the students' attention the similarity in nomenclature. Point out that by knowing the structure of muscle, they already know nerve anatomy (with slight changes in names).

4. Students often have problems with neuron regeneration and myelination (i.e., understanding why, since CNS and PNS neurons are both myelinated, a regeneration occurs in the PNS and not in the CNS). Spend time explaining the difference or refer the class to Chapter 11 to review myelination, the sheath of Schwann, and oligodendrocytes.

5. Draw a diagram (cross section) of the spinal cord indicating the dorsal and ventral roots and an extension into a short section of the spinal nerve. Draw arrows in these pathways indicating the direction of information flow. Remind the class that the brain must always receive information from an area in order to effect a change (the reason for two-way traffic in each level of the cord). Students are more likely to remember the anatomical relationship between these structures since they can logically relate material from a previous chapter to the material presented in this chapter.

6. Try asking specific questions of the class in order to promote student involvement. This technique holds their attention and, more importantly, enforces the logical thought processes necessary in order to thoroughly comprehend physiological concepts. The reflex arc is an excellent tool to employ this strategy, since by this time the class has a general knowledge of all the components necessary to construct a generalized arc. After a brief introduction to the reflex arc and what its general function is, ask questions such as: "If we wanted to construct a reflex arc, what could we use to convert a stimulus to a nervous impulse?" Lead the class by a series of questions to the complete construction of the basic reflex arc, then go into the modifications of the basic blueprint to describe specific arc types and their functions. Students will not forget the reflex arc since they have constructed it themselves.

Activities/Demonstrations

1. Audio-visual materials listed under Multimedia in the Classroom and Lab.
2. Select a student to help in the illustration of reflexes such as patellar, plantar, and abdominal.
3. Obtain a skull to illustrate the locations, exits, and entrances of several cranial nerves, such as the olfactory, optic, and trigeminal.
4. Obtain a sheep brain with the cranial nerves intact to illustrate their locations.
5. Use a 3-D model of the peripheral nervous system to illustrate the distribution of the spinal nerves.
6. Obtain a 3-D model of a spinal cord cross section to illustrate the five components of a reflex arc and to illustrate terms such as *ipsilateral*, *contralateral*, and *monosynaptic*.

Critical Thinking/Discussion Topics

1. How can the injection of novocaine into one area of the lower jaw anesthetize one entire side of the jaw and tongue?
2. How can seat belts for both the front and back seat passengers of a car prevent serious neurological damage? How can using only lap belts cause severe damage?
3. Some overly eager parents swing their newborn infants around by the hands. What damage could this cause?
4. Pregnant women often experience numbness in their fingers and toes. Why?
5. Animals have considerably more reflexive actions than humans. Why?

Library Research Topics

1. How does acupuncture relate to the distribution of spinal nerves?
2. Will all victims of polio be rendered paralyzed? What different forms are there?
3. How has microsurgery been used to reconnect severed peripheral nerves?
4. What techniques can be employed to increase our reflexive actions?

Multimedia in the Classroom and Lab

Online Resources for Students

The
Anatomy & Physiology Place   MyA&P
www.anatomyandphysiology.com   www.myaandp.com

The following shows the organization of the Chapter Guide page in both the Anatomy & Physiology Place and MyA&P™. The Chapter Guide organizes all the chapter-specific online media resources for Chapter 13 in one convenient location, with e-book links to each section of the textbook. Please note that both sites also give you access to other general A&P resources, like InterActive Physiology®, PhysioEx 6.0™, Anatomy 360°, Flashcards, a Glossary, a Histology Tutorial, and much more.

Media

See Guide to Audio-Visual Resources in Appendix A for key to AV distributors.

Video

1. *The Peripheral Nervous System* (UL; 29 min., 1997). This video illustrates how the human body senses and responds to its internal and external environments. Describes the structures and functions of the peripheral nervous system, examines current research on nerve regeneration.

2. *Reflexes and Synaptic Transmission* (UL; 29 min, 1997). This video investigates the physiology of the reflex arc through experiments on the papillary and patellar reflexes. Examines the transmission of an impulse across the synapse and at the neurotransmitters and chemicals that affect impulse transmission.

3. *Spinal Impact* (FHS; 51 min., 1999). This program explores the most promising scientific breakthroughs in the treatment of spinal cord injuries, including nerve regeneration and electrical stimulation devices.

4. *Spinal Injuries: Recovery of Function* (FHS; 18 min., 1994). Shows the most up-to-date advances in rehabilitation. Gives an overview from diagnosis of spinal injury to the different levels of treatment. Excellent for class discussion and presentation.

Software

1. *A.D.A.M.® InterActive Anatomy® 4.0* (see p. 9 of this guide for full listing).
2. *A.D.A.M.® MediaPro* (see p. 9 of this guide for full listing).
3. *A.D.A.M.®Anatomy Practice* (see p. 86 of this guide for full listing).
4. *Bodyworks* (see p. 9 of this guide for full listing).
5. *InterActive Physiology® 9-System Suite CD-ROM: Nervous System I and II* (see p. 134 of this guide for full listing).
6. *The Ultimate Human Body* (see p. 9 of this guide for full listing).

Lecture Enhancement Material

To view thumbnails of all of the illustations for Chapter 13, see Appendix B.

Transparencies Index/Media Manager

Figure 13.1	Place of the PNS in the structural organization of the nervous system.
Figure 13.2	General organization of the somatosensory system.
Figure 13.3	Structure of a nerve.
Figure 13.4	Regeneration of a nerve fiber in a peripheral nerve.
Figure 13.5	Location and function of cranial nerves.
Figure 13.6	Distribution of spinal nerves.
Figure 13.7	Formation of spinal nerves and rami distribution.
Figure 13.8	The cervical plexus.
Figure 13.9	The brachial plexus.
Figure 13.10	The lumbar plexus.
Figure 13.11	The sacral plexus.
Figure 13.12	Dermatomes.
Figure 13.13	Hierarchy of motor control.
Figure 13.14	The basic components of all human reflex arcs.
Figure 13.15	Anatomy of the muscle spindle and Golgi tendon organ.

Answers to End-of-Chapter Questions

Multiple Choice and Matching Question answers appear in Appendix G of the main text.

Short Answer Essay Questions

12. The PNS enables the CNS to receive information and carry out its decisions. (p. 490)

13. The PNS includes all nervous tissue outside the CNS, that is, the sensory receptors, the peripheral nerves (cranial or spinal), the ganglia, and motor nerve endings. The peripheral nerves transmit sensory and motor impulses, the ganglia contain cell bodies of sensory or autonomic nerve fibers, the sensory receptors receive stimuli, and the motor end plates release neurotransmitters that regulate the activity of the effectors. (p. 490)

14. Sensation is simply the awareness of a stimulus, whereas perception also understands the meaning of the stimulus. (p. 493)

15. a. Central pattern generators (CPGs) control locomotion and motor activities that are repeated often.

    b. The precommand center, the cerebellum and basal nuclei, modify and control the activity of the CPG circuits. (p. 520)

16. See Figure 13.13.

17. The direct (pyramidal) system control muscles in the distal extremities, regulating fast or fine movements. The indirect (extrapyramidal) system acts more widely in skeletal muscles. It regulates muscle tone, supports against gravity, mediates visual head movements, and controls the CPGs of the spinal cord during locomotion or other rhythmic activities. (p. 520)

18. a. The lateral spinothalamic tract transmits pain, temperature, and course touch impulses, and they are interpreted eventually in the somatosensory cortex. If cut, our sensory perception of the occurrence of a stimulus, as well as our ability to detect the magnitude of the stimulus and identify the site or pattern of the stimulation or its specific texture, shape, or quality, e.g., sweet or sour, would be impaired. (pp. 474–476)

    b. The anterior and posterior spinocerebellar tracts convey information from proprioceptors (muscle or tendon stretch) to the cerebellum, which uses this information to coordinate skeletal muscle activity. Cerebellar damage can cause equilibrium problems and speech difficulties. (p. 476)

    c. The tectospinal tract transmits motor impulses from the midbrain, which are important for coordinated movement of the head and eyes toward visual targets. If cut, problems of locomotion could occur. (p. 477)

19. The cerebellum and basal nuclei coordinate a response, but the cerebral cortex controls whether or not the action is performed, so the true command center lies beyond the precommand center. (p. 520)

20. In the PNS, macrophages and Schwann cells aid the regeneration process physically and chemically. Macrophages fail to aid the process in the CNS. Further, oligodendrocytes die and thus do not aid fiber regeneration. (p. 499)

21. a. Spinal nerves form from dorsal and ventral roots that unite distal to the dorsal root ganglion. Spinal nerves are mixed. (See Fig. 13.6.)

    b. The ventral rami, with the exception of those in the thorax that form the intercostal nerves, contribute to large plexi that supply the anterior and posterior body trunk and limbs. The dorsal rami supply the muscles and skin of the back (posterior trunk). (pp. 508–509)

22. a. A plexus is a branching nerve network formed by roots from several spinal nerves that ensures that any damage to one nerve root will not result in total loss of innervation to that part of the body. (p. 510)

    b. See Figs. 13.8 to 13.11, and Tables 13.3 to 13.6, pp. 511–516, for detailed information about each of the four plexuses.

23. Ipsilateral reflexes involve a reflex initiated on and affecting the same side of the body (p. 524); contralateral reflexes involve a reflex that is initiated on one side of the body and affects the other side. (p. 526)

24. The flexor or withdrawal reflex is a protective mechanism to withdraw from a painful stimulus. (p. 525)

25. Flexor reflexes are protective ipsilateral, polysynaptic, and prepotent reflexes. Crossed extensor reflexes consist of an ipsilateral withdrawal reflex and a contralateral extensor reflex that usually aids in balance. (pp. 525–526)

26. The sensory input of a crossed extensor reflex illustrates parallel processing, an ipsolateral response to a stimulus. The serial processing phase consists of motor activity, the contralateral response that activates the extensor muscles on the opposite side of the body. (pp. 525–526)

27. Reflex tests assess the condition of the nervous system. Exaggerated, distorted, or absent reflexes indicate degeneration or pathology of specific regions of the nervous system often before other signs are apparent. (p. 522)

28. Dermatomes are related to the sensory innervation regions of the spinal nerves. The spinal nerves correlate with the segmented body plan, as do the muscles (at least embryologically). (p. 518)

Critical Thinking and Clinical Application Questions

1. Precise realignment of cut, regenerated axons with their former effector targets is highly unlikely. Coordination between nerve and muscle will have to be relearned. Additionally, not all damaged fibers regenerate. (p. 499)

2. He would have problems dorsiflexing his right foot, and his knee joint would be unstable (more rocking of the femur from side-to-side on the tibia). (p. 516)

3. Damage to the brachial plexus occurred when he suddenly stopped his fall by grabbing the branch. (p. 512)

4. The left trochlear nerve (IV), which innervates the superior oblique muscle responsible for this action. (p. 503)

5. The region of motor and sensory loss follows the course of the sciatic nerves (and

their divisions); hence they must have been severely damaged by the shooting accident. (p. 516)

6. The specific ascending pathways of the fasciculus cuneatus carry discriminatory touch information from the upper limbs to the cortex. You must use feature abstraction and possibly pattern recognition to identify a specific pattern feature such as the teeth of a key or the fur of a rabbit's foot.

7. The right facial nerve was affected. This condition is called Bell's Palsy and is commonly caused by a herpes simplex 1 viral infection. (p. 505)

Suggested Readings

Gillespie, P. G. and Walker, R. G. "Molecular Basis of Mechanosensory Transduction." *Nature* 413 (6852) (Sept. 2001): 194–202.

Hunt, Stephen P. and Mantyh, Patrick W. "The Molecular Dynamics of Pain Control." *Nature Reviews: Neuroscience* 2 (2) (Feb. 2001): 83–91.

Julius, D. and Basbaum, A. I. "Molecular Mechanisms of Nociception." *Nature* 413 (6852) (Sept. 2001): 203–210.

Kirkpatrick, Peter. "A Touchy Subject." *Nature Reviews: Neuroscience* 2 (4) (April 2001): 227.

Raineteau, Oliver and Schwab, Martin E. "Plasticity of Motor Systems After Incomplete Spinal Cord Injury." *Nature Reviews: Neuroscience* 2 (4) (April 2001): 263–273.

Yang, Jay and Wu, Christopher L. "Gene Therapy for Pain." *American Scientist* 89 (2) (March/April 2001): 126–135.

Zuker, Charles S. "A Cool Ion Channel." *Nature* 416 (6876) (March 2002): 27–28.

14 The Autonomic Nervous System

Objectives

Introduction

1. Define autonomic nervous system and explain its relationship to the peripheral nervous system.
2. Compare the somatic and autonomic nervous systems relative to effectors, efferent pathways, and neurotransmitters released.
3. Compare and contrast the roles of the parasympathetic and sympathetic divisions.

ANS Anatomy

4. Describe the site of CNS origin, location of ganglia, and general fiber pathways for the parasympathetic and sympathetic divisions.

ANS Physiology

5. Define cholinergic and adrenergic fibers, and list the different types of their receptors.

6. Explain the clinical importance of drugs that mimic or inhibit adrenergic or cholinergic effects.
7. Underscore the effects of the parasympathetic and sympathetic divisions on the following organs: heart, blood vessels, gastrointestinal tract, lungs, adrenal medulla, and external genitalia.
8. Identify the autonomic nervous system controls of the spinal cord, brain stem, hypothalamus, and cerebral cortex.

Homeostatic Imbalances of the ANS

9. Correlate the relationship of some types of hypertension, Raynaud's disease, and the mass reflex reaction to disorders of autonomic functioning.

Developmental Aspects of the ANS

10. Describe some effects of aging on the autonomic nervous system.

Suggested Lecture Outline

I. Introduction (pp. 533–535, Figs. 14.1–14.2)

A. Comparison of the Somatic and Autonomic Nervous System (pp. 533–535)
   1. The somatic nervous system stimulates skeletal muscles, while the ANS innervates cardiac and smooth muscle and glands.
   2. In the somatic nervous system, the cell bodies of the neurons are in the spinal cord and their axons extend to the skeletal muscles they innervate. The ANS consists of a two-neuron chain.
   3. The neurotransmitter released by the somatic motor neurons is acetylcholine, which always has an excitatory effect; the neurotransmitters

released by the ANS are epinephrine and acetylcholine, and both may have either an excitatory or an inhibitory effect.

4. There is overlap between the somatic and autonomic nervous systems, and most body responses to changing internal and external stimuli involve both skeletal muscle activity and visceral organ responses.

B. Divisions of the Autonomic Nervous System (p. 535)

1. The parasympathetic division keeps body energy use as low as possible while directing digestion and elimination activities.

2. The sympathetic division prepares the body to respond to an emergency or threatening situation (or vigorous exercise).

II. ANS Anatomy (pp. 535–542; Figs. 14.3–14.7; Tables 14.1–14.2)

A. Parasympathetic (Craniosacral) Division (pp. 536–538; Fig. 14.4)

1. The preganglionic axons extend from the CNS nearly all the way to the structures to be innervated where they synapse with ganglionic neurons in the terminal ganglia.

2. The cranial outflow consists of preganglionic fibers that run in the oculomotor, facial, glossopharyngeal, and vagus cranial nerves.

3. The rest of the large intestine and the pelvic organs are served by the sacral outflow, which arises from neurons located in the lateral gray matter of spinal cord segments S_2–S_4.

B. Sympathetic (Thoracolumbar) Division (pp. 538–542; Figs. 14.5–14.6; Table 14.2)

1. The sympathetic division supplies the visceral organs in the internal body cavities but also all visceral structures in the somatic part of the body.

2. When synapses are made in chain ganglia, the postganglionic axons enter the ventral (or dorsal) ramus of the adjoining spinal nerves by way of communicating branches called gray rami communicantes.

3. The preganglionic fibers from T_5 down synapse in collateral ganglia; thus these fibers enter and leave the sympathetic chains without synapsing.

4. Some fibers of the thoracic splanchnic nerves terminate by synapsing with the hormone producing medullary cells of the adrenal cortex.

C. The visceral sensory neurons are the first link in autonomic reflexes by sending information concerning chemical changes, stretch, and irritation of the viscera. (p. 542; Fig. 14.7)

III. ANS Physiology (pp. 543–550, Tables 14.3–14.5)

A. Neurotransmitters and Receptors (pp. 543–544; Fig. 14.8; Table 14.3)

1. Cholinergic receptors, such as nicotinic and muscarinic receptors, bind acetylcholine.

2. Adrenergic receptors alpha and beta bind to epinephrine.

B. Knowing the locations of the cholinergic and adrenergic receptor subtypes allows specific drugs to be prescribed to obtain desired inhibitory or stimulatory effects on target organs (pp. 543–544; Table 14.4).

C. Interactions of the Autonomic Divisions (pp. 544–547; Table 14.5)

1. Most visceral organs receive dual innervation by both ANS divisions, allowing for a dynamic antagonism to exist between the divisions and precise control of visceral activity.

    2. The sympathetic division will increase heart and respiratory rates during a fight-or-flight situation and decrease activity of digestive and elimination organs.

    3. Sympathetic tone occurs in the vascular system, and parasympathetic tone occurs in the digestive and urinary tracts.

    4. The parasympathetic and sympathetic divisions may work together to achieve a common purpose. For example, the parasympathetic division controls erection while the sympathetic division controls ejaculation.

    5. The sympathetic division mediates reflexes that regulate body temperature, release renin from the kidneys, and promote metabolic effects.

    6. The parasympathetic division exerts short-lived, localized control over its effectors, while the sympathetic division responds in a diffuse and interconnected way to cause a body-wide mobilization.

  D. Control of Autonomic Functioning (pp. 547–550, Fig. 14.9)

    1. The brain stem appears to exert the most direct influence over autonomic functions.

    2. The hypothalamus is the main integration center for the autonomic nervous system.

    3. Cortical or voluntary control of the autonomic nervous system does appear to be possible.

IV. Homeostatic Imbalances of the ANS (pp. 550–551)

  A. Hypertension, or high blood pressure, may result from an overactive sympathetic vasoconstrictor response due to continuous high levels of stress.

  B. Raynaud's disease is characterized by intermittent attacks causing the skin of the fingers and the toes to become pale, then cyanotic and painful.

  C. Mass reflex reaction is a life-threatening condition involving uncontrolled activation of both somatic and autonomic motor neurons.

V. Developmental Aspects of the ANS (p. 551)

  A. Embryonic and fetal development of the autonomic nervous system

    1. ANS preganglionic neurons and somatic motor neurons derive from the embryonic neural tube.

    2. ANS structures found in the PNS (ganglionic neurons, adrenal medulla, and all autonomic ganglia) derive from the neural crest.

    3. Nerve growth factor is a protein secreted by target cells of the postganglionic axons.

  B. In old age the efficiency of the ANS begins to decline, partly due to structural changes of some preganglionic axonal terminals.

Cross References

Additional information on topics covered in Chapter 14 can be found in the chapters listed below.

1. Chapter 3: Membrane functions; membrane receptors
2. Chapter 4: Nervous tissue
3. Chapter 11: Membrane potentials; neuronal integration; serial and parallel processing; synapses; neurotransmitters

4. Chapter 12: Ascending and descending tracts of the spinal cord; spinal roots; gray and white matter of the spinal cord

5. Chapter 18: The role of the sympathetic and parasympathetic pathways (as well as epinephrine and norepinephrine) in medullary control of cardiac rate

6. Chapter 19: Sympathetic control of blood vessel diameter

7. Chapter 23: Sympathetic and parasympathetic control of digestive processes

8. Chapter 25: Sympathetic control of blood vessels to the kidney; parasympathetic pelvic splanchnic nerves and the urinary system

9. Chapter 27: Sympathetic and parasympathetic effects in human sexual response

Laboratory Correlations

1. Marieb, E. N. *Human Anatomy & Physiology Laboratory Manual: Cat and Fetal Pig Versions.* Eighth Edition Updates. Benjamin Cummings, 2006.

   Exercise 21: Spinal Cord, Spinal Nerves, and Autonomic Nervous System

2. Marieb, E. N. *Human Anatomy & Physiology Laboratory Manual: Main Version.* Seventh Edition Update. Benjamin Cummings, 2006.

   Exercise 21: Spinal Cord, Spinal Nerves, and Autonomic Nervous System

Histology Slides for the Life Sciences

Available through Benjamin Cummings, an imprint of Pearson Education, Inc. To order, contact your local Benjamin Cummings sales representative.

Slide 73   Myelinated Nerve Cross Section—Myelin Sheaths.

Slide 74   Myelinated Nerve Longitudinal Section—Nodes of Ranvier.

Slide 75   Efferent (Motor) Neuron.

Slide 76   Spinal Cord Bottom, Stained for Axons.

Lecture Hints

1. Since the autonomic nervous system is more complex than the somatic nervous system, it is worthwhile to spend some time comparing and contrasting the anatomy of each.

2. Figure 14.4 is a good 3-D representation of parasympathetic pathways; however, as an initial introduction during lecture, it might be useful to use the enlarged transparency Figure 14.3, or to draw a 2-D schematic diagram of sympathetic and parasympathetic pathways, so that the class can follow the construction of the circuit logically and understand how it is "wired." Then refer students to the overall construction presented in Figure 14.4, p. 536.

3. Emphasize that somatic efferent pathways consist of a motor neuron cell body in the CNS whose axon extends out through the PNS to directly innervate the skeletal muscle effector. In contrast, autonomic efferent pathways follow the same general plan, but consist of two motor neurons in series.

4. Point out that in many cases sympathetic and parasympathetic synapses use different neurotransmitters, an essential characteristic in the dual nature of autonomic function. This will be illustrated when discussing fight/flight and rest/digest responses.

5. Many students have difficulty with the idea of neurotransmitter/receptor function. Point out that many substances similar in chemical construction to the actual

neurotransmitter are capable of generating the same response. Emphasize that it is the binding of a substance to a receptor that generates the cellular response.

6. To illustrate sympathetic tone, use the example of vasomotor control. Point out that dilation (to decrease blood pressure) is not a muscle contraction response, but that relaxation of the smooth muscle in the wall of the blood vessel is the actual cause. To vasoconstrict, increase sympathetic stimulation. Therefore, in order for dilation to be possible, there must be a certain amount of constant sympathetic stimulation (tone) even during a relaxed state.

7. Emphasize that there is a constant level of parasympathetic stimulation (tone) to many visceral organs and that there is just enough sympathetic stimulation to keep systems in homeostasis. To probe the students ask, "What would happen to resting heart rate if parasympathetic stimulation were cut?"

Activities/Demonstrations

1. Audio-visual materials listed under Multimedia in the Classroom and Lab.
2. Set up a live, exposed frog or turtle heart demonstration to illustrate the effects of acetylcholine and epinephrine.
3. Without announcing what you will be doing, walk quietly into the lecture room, set your notes down, and yell very loudly (to startle the students). Then, have each student prepare a list of all those organs that were affected and what the effects were.
4. Obtain a preserved cat and dissect it to illustrate the sympathetic nerve trunk, celiac ganglia, splanchnic nerves, and other portions of the ANS.
5. Obtain a 3-D model of a spinal cord cross section and longitudinal section that illustrate the parts of the ANS and especially the sympathetic, gray, and white rami.

Critical Thinking/Discussion Topics

1. Describe the role of beta blockers in treating certain types of visceral disorders.
2. At certain times when people are very excited or are shocked suddenly, their bowels and/or urinary sphincters lose control. In terms of the role of the ANS, why does this happen?
3. Some individuals, following a very stressful event such as final exams, frequently come down with colds. Is there any relationship between the ANS, stress, and the onset of an illness? Discuss.
4. Most people feel very tired after they eat a big meal. Why?
5. How can biofeedback be used to reduce effects of constant pain and stress?
6. Why is sympathetic action diffuse and long-lasting while parasympathetic is local and short-lived? What would happen to body systems during a stressful situation if these characteristics were reversed? How would anatomy have to be changed?

Library Research Topics

1. Do all animals have an autonomic nervous system? If so, is it more or less advanced than ours?
2. The ANS regulates peristaltic waves of the GI tract. If the ganglia and/or fibers controlling this activity were damaged, what would happen? What bacterial agents or type of trauma could cause this?

3. Ulcers seem to occur in hypertensive individuals. What are the causes of this problem and what treatment is available?

4. Nicotine and muscarine are substances that bind at specific receptors. What exactly do these receptors look like? Draw a cell membrane and illustrate how the receptors might look.

Multimedia in the Classroom and Lab

Online Resources for Students

The
Anatomy & Physiology Place   MyA&P
www.anatomyandphysiology.com   www.myaandp.com

The following shows the organization of the Chapter Guide page in both the Anatomy & Physiology Place and MyA&P™. The Chapter Guide organizes all the chapter-specific online media resources for Chapter 14 in one convenient location, with e-book links to each section of the textbook. Please note that both sites also give you access to other general A&P resources, like InterActive Physiology®, PhysioEx 6.0™, Anatomy 360°, Flashcards, a Glossary, a Histology Tutorial, and much more.

Objectives
Section 14.1 Introduction (pp. 533–535)
Section 14.2 ANS Anatomy (pp. 535–543)
Memory: Autonomic Pathways
Memory: The Major Ganglia of the Autonomic Nervous System
Section 14.3 ANS Physiology (pp. 543–547, 550)
Section 14.4 Homeostatic Imbalances of the ANS (pp. 550–551)
Case Study: Nervous Tissues
Case Study: Cardiac Arrhythmia
Section 14.5 Developmental Aspects of the ANS (p. 551)
Chapter Summary
Self-Study Quizzes
Art Labeling Quiz
Matching Quiz
Multiple-Choice Quiz (Level I)
Multiple-Choice Quiz (Level II)
True-False Quiz
Crossword Puzzles
Crossword Puzzle 14.1
Crossword Puzzle 14.2

Media

See Guide to Audio-Visual Resources in Appendix A for key to AV distributors.

Video

1. *Biologix: The Neuroendocrine System* (IM, UL; 29 min., 1997). This video compares the nervous and endocrine system by describing how each responds to situations of physical activity, changes in body temperature, eating, and stress.

2. *Brain and Nervous System: Your Information Superhighway* (FHS; 25 min., 2000). This program explores the brain and nervous system using the analogy of computers and the Internet.

3. *Managing Stress* (FHS; 19 min.). Demonstrates the difference between positive stress, which strengthens the immune system, and negative stress, which can increase the likelihood of illness. Excellent aid to encourage class understanding of complicated concepts.

4. *Nerve Impulse Conduction* (IM; 29 min., 1997). This video explores the electrochemical nature of nerve impulse conduction and transmission. It uses simulations to analyze the different stages of membrane potential and presents research on how chemicals affect membrane potential.

5. *The Nervous System: The Ultimate Control Center* (KV; 20 min., 2001). This video explores voluntary and autonomic functions, the central nervous system, and the network of nerves and other structures that make up the peripheral nervous system.

6. *Stress and Immune Function* (FHS; 26 min., 1986). Presents an in-depth examination of the relationship between stress and illness. Encourages class discussion.

Software

1. *A.D.A.M.® InterActive Anatomy® 4.0* (see p. 9 of this guide for full listing).
2. *A.D.A.M.® MediaPro* (see p. 9 of this guide for full listing).
3. *A.D.A.M.® Anatomy Practice* (see p. 86 of this guide for full listing).
4. *Bodyworks* (see p. 9 of this guide for full listing).
5. *InterActive Physiology 9-System Suite CD-ROM: Nervous System I and II* (see p. 148 for full listing).
6. *The Ultimate Human Body* (see p. 9 of this guide for full listing).

Lecture Enhancement Material

To view thumbnails of all of the illustrations for Chapter 14, see Appendix B.

Transparencies Index/Media Manager

Figure 14.1   Place of the ANS in the structural organization of the nervous system.
Figure 14.2   Comparison of somatic and autonomic nervous systems.
Figure 14.3   Overview of the subdivisions of the ANS.
Figure 14.4   Parasympathetic (craniosacral) division of the ANS.
Figure 14.5   Sympathetic (thoracolumbar) division of the ANS.
Figure 14.6   Sympathetic trunks and pathways.
Figure 14.7   Visceral reflexes.
Figure 14.8   Referred pain.
Figure 14.9   Levels of ANS control.
Table 14.1   Anatomical and Physiological Differences Between the Parasympathetic and Sympathetic Divisions
Table 14.2   Segmental Sympathetic Supplies
Table 14.3   Cholinergic and Adrenergic Receptors
Table 14.4   Selected Drug Classes That Influence the Activity of the Autonomic Nervous System
Table 14.5   Effects of the Parasympathetic and Sympathetic Divisions on Various Organs

Answers to End-of-Chapter Questions

Multiple Choice and Matching Question answers appear in Appendix G of the main text.

Short Answer Essay Questions

6. Involuntary nervous system is used to reflect its subconscious control; emotional-visceral system reflects the fact that the hypothalamus is the major regulatory center for both the emotional (limbic) response and visceral controls. The term visceral also indicates the location of most of its effectors. (p. 533)

7. White rami contain myelinated preganglionic fibers that leave the spinal nerve to enter the paravertebral ganglion; gray rami represent axons of postganglionic neurons, are unmyelinated, and enter the spinal nerve to travel to their ultimate destination. (p. 541)

8. Sweat glands—increase the production of sweat; eye pupils—enlarge (dilate); adrenal medulla—releases norepinephrine and epinephrine; heart—increase in rate and force of contraction; lungs—bronchodilation; liver—glycogenolysis and the release of glucose to the blood; blood vessels to the skeletal muscles—dilation; blood vessels to digestive viscera—constriction; salivary glands—constriction of blood vessels supplying the gland, causing a decrease in saliva production. (p. 546)

9. All except the effects on the adrenal medulla, liver, and blood vessels. (p. 546)

10. All preganglionic fibers and postganglionic fibers of the parasympathetic division secrete acetylcholine. Some postganglionic sympathetic fibers secrete acetylcholine. Only postganglionic fibers of sympathetic division release norepinephrine. (p. 543)

11. Sympathetic tone means that the vascular system is under a partial state of contraction. Parasympathetic tone maintains the tone of the digestive organs and keeps heart rate at the lowest level that maintains homeostasis. (p. 545)

12. Acetylcholine—nicotinic and muscarinic; norepinephrine—alpha 1, alpha 2, ß1, ß2. See Table 14.3 for major locations. (p. 544)

13. The reticular formation nuclei in the brain stem, particularly those in the medulla. (p. 550)

14. The hypothalamus is the main integration center that coordinates heart rate, blood pressure, and body temperature. (p. 550)

15. The premise of biofeedback training is that we do not routinely exert voluntary controls over our visceral activities because we have little conscious awareness of our internal environment. The training allows subjects to become aware of the body's signals and subsequently make subtle internal changes to help them control such things as migraine headaches and stress. (p. 550)

16. Elderly people often complain of constipation and dry eyes, and faintness when they change position, e.g., stand up abruptly after sitting. (p. 551)

17. The cell body of the preganglionic neuron resides in the CNS, whereas the ganglionic neuron's cell body lies *in* the autonomic ganglion, not distal ("post") to the ganglion. However, its axon does lie distal to the ganglion, therefore, the term postganglionic axon is correct. (p. 538)

Critical Thinking and Clinical Application Questions

1. Parasympathetic stimulation of the bladder via the release of acetylcholine increases bladder tone and releases the urinary sphincters, a result which will be reproduced by bethanechol. He will probably experience dizziness due to low blood pressure (decreased heart rate), deficient tear formation, wheezing, diarrhea, cramping, and undesirable erection of the penis—all parasympathetic effects. (p. 545)

2. Referred pain is the sensation of pain that appears to originate from a site other than that of the painful stimulus. Damage to the heart gives rise to pain impulses that enter the spinal cord in the thoracic region, and also receives impulses from the left chest and arm. (p. 543)

3. Raynaud's disease. Smoking causes vasoconstriction, i.e., the nicotine mimics the affects of acetylcholine on sympathetic nicotinic receptors of the skin blood vessels. (p. 551)

4. Tiffany may temporarily experience light-headedness, blurred vision, dry mouth, constipation, and difficulty urinating or incontinence.

5. The smell stimulates the olfactory nerves and carries the information to the CNS. The response is parasympathetic activation, which stimulates increased salivary gland secretion (mouth watering) and increased secretory activity and motility of the stomach (stomach rumbling). (pp. 545–546)

6. Raynaud's disease. The fingertips turn cyanotic (blue) and once blood flow has been restored to them they turn red. (p. 551)

Suggested Readings

Herbert, W. "Punching the Biological Timeclock." *Science* News 122 (July 1982).

House, M.A. "Cocaine." *American Journal of Nursing* 90 (Apr. 1990): 40–45.

Kalin, N.H. "The Neurobiology of Fear." *Scientific American* 268 (May 1993): 94.

Revkin, A. "Hunting Down Huntington's." *Discover* (Dec. 1993): 100.

Simpson, S. "Pain, Pain, Go Away." *Science News* 155 (Feb. 1999): 108–110.

15

The Special Senses

Objectives

The Eye and Vision

1. List and explain the structure and function of the accessory eye structures.
2. Describe the structure and function of the three tunics of the eyeball.
3. Examine the internal chambers of the eye.
4. Discuss refraction and the focusing of light in the eyeball. Relate this to focusing for distance vision and focusing for close vision.
5. Identify the photoreceptors. Be sure to include stimulation, anatomy, chemistry, and light transduction.
6. Explain the visual pathways to the brain.
7. Discuss visual processing.
8. List and discuss homeostatic disorders of the eye and vision.

The Chemical Senses: Taste and Smell

9. Describe the location, structure and afferent pathways for the taste and smell receptors.

10. Explain activation of taste and smell receptors.

The Ear: Hearing and Balance

11. Explore the structure of the outer, middle, and inner ear.
12. Describe the physiology of sound.
13. Explain the auditory pathway to the brain.
14. Define tinnitus and Ménière's syndrome.
15. Discuss the sense of equilibrium; identify where the receptors are located and what they respond to.
16. Examine the equilibrium pathway to the brain.

Developmental Aspects of the Special Senses

17. List and discuss developmental accomplishments and aging concerns for hearing, vision, taste, and smell.

Suggested Lecture Outline

I. The Eye and Vision (pp. 556–578; Figs. 15.1–15.20)

A. Vision is our dominant sense with 70% of our body's sensory receptors found in the eye.

B. Accessory Structures of the Eye (pp. 556–559; Figs. 15.1–15.3)

   1. Eyebrows are short, coarse hairs overlying the supraorbital margins of the eye that shade the eyes and keep perspiration out.

   2. Eyelids (palpebrae), eyelashes, and their associated glands help to protect the eye from physical danger as well as from drying out.

3. Conjunctiva is a transparent mucous membrane that lines the eyelids and the whites of the eyes. It produces a lubricating mucus that prevents the eye from drying out.

4. The lacrimal apparatus consists of the lacrimal gland, which secretes a dilute saline solution that cleanses and protects the eye as it moistens it, and ducts that drain excess fluid into the nasolacrimal duct.

5. The movement of each eyeball is controlled by six extrinsic eye muscles that are innervated by the abducens and trochlear nerves.

C. Structure of the Eyeball (pp. 559–565; Figs. 15.4–15.9)

   1. Three layers form the wall of the eyeball.

     a. The fibrous tunic is the outermost coat of the eye and is made of a dense avascular connective tissue with two regions: the sclera and the cornea.

     b. The vascular tunic (uvea) is the middle layer and has three regions: the choroid, the ciliary body, and the iris.

     c. The inner layer (retina) is the innermost layer made up of two layers: the outer pigmented layer absorbs light; the inner neural layer contains millions of photoreceptors (rods and cones) that transduce light energy.

   2. Internal Chambers and Fluids

     a. Posterior segment (cavity) is filled with a clear gel called vitreous humor that transmits light, supports the posterior surface of the lens, holds the retina firmly against the pigmented layer, and contributes to intraocular pressure.

     b. Anterior segment (cavity) is filled with aqueous humor that supplies nutrients and oxygen to the lens and cornea while carrying away wastes.

   3. The lens is an avascular, biconcave, transparent, flexible structure that can change shape to allow precise focusing of light on the retina.

D. Physiology of Vision (pp. 565–578; Figs. 15.10–15.20)

   1. Overview: Light and Optics

     a. Electromagnetic radiation includes all energy waves from long waves to short waves, and includes the visible light that our eyes see as color.

     b. Refraction of a light ray occurs when it meets the surface of a different medium at an oblique angle rather than a right angle.

   2. Focusing of Light on the Retina

     a. Light is bent three times: as it enters the cornea and on entering and leaving the lens.

     b. The far point of vision is that distance beyond which no change in lens shape is required (about 6 m or 20 ft.).

     c. Focusing for close vision demands that the eye make three adjustments: accommodation of the lens, constriction of the pupils, and convergence of the eyeballs.

     d. Myopia, or nearsightedness, occurs when objects focus in front of the retina and results in seeing close objects without a problem but distance objects are blurred.

     e. Hyperopia or farsightedness occurs when objects are focused behind the retina and results in seeing distance objects clearly but close objects are blurred.

   3. Photoreception is the process by which the eye detects light energy.

     a. Photoreceptors are modified neurons that structurally resemble tall epithelial cells.

   b. Rods are highly sensitive and are best suited to night vision. Cones are less sensitive to light and are best adapted to bright light and colored vision.

   c. Photoreceptors contain a light-absorbing molecule called retinal.

4. Stimulation of the Photoreceptors

   a. The visual pigment of rods is rhodopsin and is formed and broken down within the rods.

   b. The breakdown and regeneration of the visual pigments of the cones is essentially the same as for rhodopsin.

5. Exposure of the photoreceptors to light causes pigment breakdown, which hyperpolarizes the receptors inhibiting the release of neurotransmitter conveying the information.

6. Light adaptation occurs when we move from darkness into bright light. Retinal sensitivity decreases dramatically and the retinal neurons switch from the rod to the cone system.

7. Dark adaptation occurs when we go from a well-lit area into a dark one. The cones stop functioning and the rhodopsin starts to accumulate in the rods increasing retinal sensitivity.

8. Visual Pathway to the Brain

   a. The retinal ganglion cells merge in the back of the eyeball to become the optic nerve, which crosses at the optic chiasma to become the optic tracts.

   b. The optic tracts send their axons to neurons within the lateral geniculate body of the thalamus.

   c. Axons from the thalamus project through the internal capsule to form the optic radiation of fibers in the cerebral white matter. These fibers project to the primary visual cortex in the occipital lobes.

9. Visual processing occurs when the action of light on photoreceptors hyperpolarizes them, which causes the bipolar neurons from both the rods and cones to ultimately send signals to their ganglion cells.

II. The Chemical Senses: Taste and Smell (pp. 578–583; Figs. 15.21–15.24)

A. The receptors for taste and smell are chemoreceptors that respond to chemicals in solution.

B. The Olfactory Epithelium and the Sense of Smell (pp. 578–580; Figs. 15.21–15.22)

   1. The olfactory epithelium is the organ of smell located in the roof of the nasal cavity.

   2. The olfactory receptors are bipolar neurons with a thin apical dendrite that terminates in a knob with several olfactory cilia.

   3. To smell a particular odorant, it must be volatile and it must be dissolved in the fluid coating the olfactory epithelium which stimulates the olfactory receptors.

   4. In olfactory transduction, an odorant binds to the olfactory receptor, a G protein, and the secondary messenger of cyclic AMP.

   5. Axons of the olfactory receptor cells synapse in the olfactory bulbs sending impulses down the olfactory tracts to the thalamus, the hypothalamus, amygdala, and other members of the limbic system.

C. Taste Buds and the Sense of Taste (pp. 580–582; Figs. 15.23–15.24)

   1. Taste buds, the sensory receptor organs for taste, are located in the oral cavity with the majority located on the tongue.

2. Taste sensations can be grouped into one of five basic qualities: sweet, sour, bitter, salty, and umami.

3. Physiology of taste
   a. For a chemical to be tasted it must be dissolved in saliva, move into the taste pore, and contact a gustatory hair.
   b. Each taste sensation appears to have its own special mechanism for transduction.

4. Afferent fibers carrying taste information from the tongue are found primarily in the facial nerve and glossopharyngeal cranial nerves.

5. Taste impulses from the few taste buds found on the epiglottis and the lower pharynx are conveyed via the vagus nerve.

6. Taste is strongly influenced by smell and stimulation of thermoreceptors, mechanoreceptors, and nociceptors.

D. Homeostatic Imbalances of the Chemical Senses
   1. Anosmias are olfactory disorders resulting from head injuries that tear the olfactory nerves, nasal cavity inflammation, or aging.
   2. Uncinate fits are olfactory hallucinations.
   3. Taste disorders are less common but may be caused by respiratory tract infections, head injuries, chemicals, medications, or head and neck radiation.

III. The Ear: Hearing and Balance (pp. 583–599; Figs. 15.25–15.38)

A. Structure of the Ear (pp. 583–589; Figs. 15.25–15.27)
   1. The external ear consists of the auricle (pinna) and the external auditory canal, which is lined with skin bearing hairs, sebaceous glands, and ceruminous glands.
   2. The middle ear, or tympanic cavity, is a small, air-filled, mucosa-lined cavity in the petrous portion of the temporal bone. It is spanned by the auditory ossicles.
   3. The internal ear has two major divisions: the bony labyrinth and the membranous labyrinth.
      a. The vestibule is the central cavity of the bony labyrinth with two membranous sacs suspended in the perilymph, the saccule and the utricle.
      b. The semicircular canals project from the posterior aspect of the vestibule, each containing an equilibrium receptor region called a crista ampullaris.
      c. The spiral, snail-shaped cochlea extends from the anterior part of the vestibule and contains the cochlear duct, which houses the spiral organ (of Corti), the receptors for hearing.

B. Physiology of Hearing (pp. 587–593; Figs. 15.28–15.34)
   1. Properties of Sound
      a. Sound is a pressure disturbance produced by a vibrating object and propagated by the molecules of the medium.
      b. Frequency is the number of waves that pass a given point in a given time.
      c. Amplitude, or height, of the wave reveals a sound's intensity (loudness).
   2. Airborne sound entering the external auditory canal strikes the tympanic membrane and sets it vibrating.
   3. The resonance of the basilar membrane processes sound signals mechanically before they ever reach the receptors.

4. Transduction of sound stimuli occurs after the trapped stereocilia of the hair cells are deflected by localized movements of the basilar membrane.

5. Impulses generated in the cochlea pass through the spiral ganglion, along the afferent fibers of the cochlear nerve to the cochlear nuclei of the medulla, to the superior olivary nucleus, to the inferior colliculus, and finally to the auditory cortex.

6. Auditory processing involves perception of pitch, detection of loudness, and localization of sound.

C. Homeostatic Imbalances of Hearing (pp. 593–594)

1. Deafness is any hearing loss, no matter how slight.

2. Tinnitus is a ringing or clicking sound in the ears in the absence of auditory stimuli.

3. Ménière's syndrome is a labyrinth disorder that causes a person to suffer repeated attacks of vertigo, nausea, and vomiting.

D. Mechanisms of Equilibrium and Orientation (pp. 593–598; Figs. 15.35–15.38)

1. The equilibrium sense responds to various head movements and depends on input from the inner ear, vision, and information from stretch receptors of muscles and tendons.

2. The sensory receptors for static equilibrium are the maculae.

3. The receptor for dynamic equilibrium is the crista ampullaris, found in the ampulla of the semicircular canals and activated by head movement.

4. Information from the balance receptors goes directly to reflex centers in the brain stem, rather than to the cerebral cortex.

IV. Developmental Aspects of the Special Senses (pp. 598–599)

A. Embryonic and Fetal Development of the Senses

1. Smell and taste are fully functional at birth.

2. The eye begins to develop by the fourth week of embryonic development; vision is the only special sense not fully functional at birth.

3. Development of the ear begins in the fourth week of fetal development; at birth the newborn is able to hear but most responses to sound are reflexive.

B. Effects of Aging on the Senses

1. Around age 40 the sense of smell and taste diminishes due to a gradual loss of receptors.

2. Also around age 40 presbyopia begins to set in and with age the lens loses its clarity and discolors.

3. By age 60 a noticeable deterioration of the organ of Corti has occurred; the ability to hear high-pitched sounds is the first loss.

Cross References

Additional information on topics covered in Chapter 15 can be found in the chapters listed below.

1. Chapter 4: Epithelia; exocrine glands; connective tissues
2. Chapter 5: Sebaceous and sudoriferous glands
3. Chapter 8: Synovial joints
4. Chapter 10: Skeletal muscle naming
5. Chapter 11: Synapses; neurotransmitters

6. Chapter 12: Cerebral cortex; thalamus; CSF formation (similar to formation of aqueous humor)
7. Chapter 13: Receptor and generator potentials; cranial nerves; reflex activity; chemoreceptors
8. Chapter 21: Inflammation
9. Chapter 22: Relationship between the auditory tube and the respiratory system
10. Chapter 23: Secretion of saliva and gastric juice; salivary reflex; papillae and taste buds

Laboratory Correlations

1. Marieb, E. N. *Human Anatomy & Physiology Laboratory Manual: Cat and Fetal Pig Versions.* Eighth Edition Updates. Benjamin Cummings, 2006.
   Exercise 24: Special Senses: Vision
   Exercise 25: Special Senses: Hearing and Equilibrium
   Exercise 26: Special Senses: Olfaction and Taste
2. Marieb, E. N. *Human Anatomy & Physiology Laboratory Manual: Main Version.* Seventh Edition Update. Benjamin Cummings, 2006.
   Exercise 24: Special Senses: Vision
   Exercise 25: Special Senses: Hearing and Equilibrium
   Exercise 26: Special Senses: Olfaction and Taste

Histology Slides for the Life Sciences

Available through Benjamin Cummings, an imprint of Pearson Education, Inc. To order, contact your local Benjamin Cummings sales representative.

Slide 77   Cochlea and the Organ of Corti, Inner Ear.
Slide 78   Retina of the Eye.
Slide 79   Taste Buds, Rabbit Tongue.
Slide 80   Cutaneous Receptors, Pacinian Corpuscle.
Slide 81   Olfactory Epithelium.
Slide 82   The Organ of Corti.
Slide 85   Section of a Monkey Eye.

Lecture Hints

1. Emphasize that each taste sensation is not localized to a specific area, but that there is significant overlap of the different sensation areas. Students often assume that a particular point on the tongue responds to a single type of substance.
2. Point out the importance of other sensations (especially smell) on the perception of taste.
3. During the lecture on olfactory anatomy, ask the class what would happen to olfaction if mucus glands below the olfactory epithelium were absent.
4. Emphasize that olfactory receptors are the only renewable neurons in the body and are therefore the one exception to the rule that neurons do not replicate.
5. There is often confusion in the terminology of the chambers of the eye. Point out that the anterior segment is divided into anterior and posterior chambers by the iris.

6. Initially, it is difficult for even the sharpest students to grasp the concept of ciliary muscle contraction leading to lens thickening (for close focus). Intuitively, most think of the process of stretching the lens as a consequence of muscle contraction, not relaxation. Spend some time reinforcing this concept.

7. Have students try out focusing on objects at night. Explain that they should not look directly at the object, but slightly to one side, and the object should appear brighter. Relate this exercise to the distribution of rods and cones in the eye.

8. As a point of interest, mention that the ossicles are joined by the smallest synovial joints in the body.

9. Emphasize the difference between static and dynamic equilibrium by comparing and contrasting the anatomy of each type of equilibrium.

Activities/Demonstrations

1. Audio-visual materials listed under Multimedia in the Classroom and Lab.

2. Select four volunteers and spray a different strong cologne on their wrists. Then determine how long it takes for each to "adapt" to the cologne.

3. Bring a convex lens to class and have students hold the glass up and focus on a distant object. They will notice that it is upside down and reversed. Then explain that the human eye is also a single-lens system. The question should arise: "Why don't we see things upside down?"

4. Obtain a 3-D model of an eye and ear to illustrate the various anatomical parts of each.

5. Dissect a fresh (or preserved, if fresh is not available) beef eye to illustrate the anatomical structure and nature of the tissues and fluids.

6. Obtain a skull to illustrate the locations of any bony structures associated with the senses.

7. Obtain a set of ear ossicles to illustrate how tiny they are.

Critical Thinking/Discussion Topics

1. Most people with sinus infections can't smell or taste. Why?

2. Wine tasting can be a real art. Why are some people more adept at tasting than others? What effect does smoking, alcohol, and/or sweets have on wine tasting? Why is it useful to swirl a glass of wine and then sniff it?

3. Certain types of sunglasses can cause more harm than good. What could be wrong with inexpensive sunglasses?

4. What would happen to gustatory and olfactory sensations if the receptors for taste and smell were specific to a single substance?

5. Since the sclera is avascular, why do we see blood vessels in the white of the eye?

6. How is it possible that the cornea is transparent and the sclera is opaque when they are both constructed of the same material and continuous with each other?

7. Examine the consequences to the anatomy of the eye and vision if aqueous humor drainage exceeded production.

8. Explain why depth perception is lost if one eye is not functioning.

9. If the number of cones feeding into a single ganglion cell was increased tenfold, what would be the consequence to color visual acuity?

10. Examine the consequences to sound perception if the tympanic membrane increased twofold in surface area. What would happen if the oval window had increased surface area? Would sounds be perceived if the round window became rigid?

Library Research Topics

1. How successful are cochlear implants? What surgical techniques are employed?

2. Some permanently deaf individuals have been helped by means of computers and electrical probes connected to certain areas of the brain. How is this possible and what is the current research in this area?

3. Contact lenses have long been used to correct vision problems. What is the status of contact lens implants and why do ophthalmologists hesitate to perform them?

4. What substances are found in wines such as cabernet, chardonnay, chenin blanc, and others that provide the tremendous variety of tastes and smells?

5. If hearts, lungs, and livers can be transplanted, why not eyes? What would be some of the technical difficulties?

Multimedia in the Classroom and Lab

Online Resources for Students

The
Anatomy & Physiology Place   **MyA&P**
www.anatomyandphysiology.com   www.myaandp.com

The following shows the organization of the Chapter Guide page in both the Anatomy & Physiology Place and MyA&P™. The Chapter Guide organizes all the chapter-specific online media resources for Chapter 15 in one convenient location, with e-book links to each section of the textbook. Please note that both sites also give you access to other general A&P resources, like InterActive Physiology®, PhysioEx 6.0™, Anatomy 360°, Flashcards, a Glossary, a Histology Tutorial, and much more.

> **Objectives**
> **Section 15.1 The Eye and Vision (pp. 556–578)**
> Art Labeling Activity: The Eye and Associated Accessory Structures (Fig. 15.1b, p. 557)
> Art Labeling Activity: Internal Structures of the Eye (Fig. 15.4a, p. 560)
> Case Study: Special Senses: Vision
> **Section 15.2 The Chemical Senses: Taste and Smell (pp. 578–583)**
> Memory: Eyesight Factors and the Art of Smelling
> **Section 15.3 The Ear: Hearing and Balance (pp. 583–598)**
> Art Labeling Activity: Structure of the Ear, Part 1 (Fig. 15.25a, p. 584)
> Art Labeling Activity: Structure of the Ear, Part 2 (Fig. 15.25b, p. 584)
> Memory: Sensory Organs
> **Section 15.4 Developmental Aspects of the Special Senses (pp. 598–599)**
> **Chapter Summary**
> **Self-Study Quizzes**
> Art Labeling Quiz
> Matching Quiz
> Multiple-Choice Quiz (Level I)
> Multiple-Choice Quiz (Level II)
> True-False Quiz
> **Crossword Puzzles**
> Crossword Puzzle 15.1
> Crossword Puzzle 15.2

Media

See Guide to Audio-Visual Resources in Appendix A for key to AV distributors.

Video

1. *The Eye: Vision and Perception* (IM; 29 min., 1997). Highlights the structures and functions of the mammalian eye and illustrates how visual sensory receptors relay messages to the brain.
2. *How Sweet It Is: Tastes and Tasting* (NIMCO; 22 min., 2001). From the *Understanding our Five Senses* series. Provides an introduction to the sense of taste, shows how gustation works, and addresses the role that smell plays in tasting.
3. *The Nose Knows: Smelling and the Nose* (NIMCO; 23 min., 2001). From the *Understanding our Five Senses* series. Explores the olfactory organs, and discusses the molecular structure of odors and how the brain interprets smells.
4. *Sense Organs* (IM; 24 min., 1994). Explores the anatomy and mechanism of the five senses.
5. *The Senses* (FHS; 20 min., 1995). From *The New Living Body* series, this program demonstrates how the senses of sight and balance operate, as well as how they interact with each other.
6. *Understanding the Senses* (FHS; 56 min., 2000). Explores the beauty and complexity of visual, audial, chemosensory, and tactile perception.

Software

1. *A.D.A.M.® InterActive Anatomy® 4.0* (see p. 9 of this guide for full listing).
2. *A.D.A.M.® MediaPro* (see p. 9 of this guide for full listing).
3. *A.D.A.M.® Anatomy Practice* (see p. 86 of this guide for full listing).
4. *Bodyworks* (see p. 9 of this guide for full listing).
5. *Exploring Perception* (TM; Win/Mac). Explores such phenomena as apparent movement, pitch perception, sensory adaptation, and visual and auditory illusions.
6. *The Ultimate Human Body* (see p. 9 of this guide for full listing).

Lecture Enhancement Material

To view thumbnails of all of the illustrations for Chapter 15, see Appendix B.

Transparencies Index/Media Manager

Figure 15.1   The eye and associated accessory structures.
Figure 15.2   The lacrimal apparatus.
Figure 15.3   Extrinsic eye muscles.
Figure 15.4   Internal structure of the eye (sagittal section).
Figure 15.5   Pupil dilation and constriction, anterior view.
Figure 15.6   Microscopic anatomy of the retina.
Figure 15.7   Part of the posterior wall (fundus) of the right eye as seen with an ophthalmoscope.
Figure 15.8   Circulation of aqueous humor.
Figure 15.9   Photograph of a cataract due to a clouded lens.
Figure 15.10   The electromagnetic spectrum and photoreceptor sensitivities.
Figure 15.11   A spoon standing in a glass of water appears to be broken at the water-air interface.

Answers to End-of-Chapter Questions

Multiple Choice and Matching Question answers appear in Appendix G of the main text.

Short Answer Essay Questions

30. The five basic tastes are sweet, sour, salty, bitter, umami. The sense of taste is served by the facial (VII), glossopharyngeal (IX), and vagus (X) nerves. (p. 582)

31. The receptors are located in the roof of each nasal cavity. The site is poorly suited because air entering the nasal cavities must make a hairpin turn to stimulate the receptors. (p. 578)

32. The nasolacrimal duct empties into the nasal cavity. (p. 557)

33. Rods are dim-light visual receptors, while cones are for bright-light and high-acuity color vision. (p. 563)

34. The fovea lies lateral to the optic disk. It contains only cones and provides detailed color vision for critical vision. (p. 563)

35. Retinal changes to the all-*trans* form; the retinal-opsin combination breaks down, separating retinal and opsin (bleaching). The net effect is to "turn off" sodium entry into the cell, effectively hyperpolarizing the rod. (p. 572)

36. Each cone responds maximally to one of these colors of light, but there is overlap in their absorption spectra that accounts for the other hues. (p. 572)

37. With age, the lens enlarges, loses its crystal clarity and becomes discolored, and the dilator muscles of the iris become less efficient. Atrophy of the organ of Corti reduces hearing acuity, especially for high-pitched sounds. The sense of smell and taste diminish due to a gradual loss of receptors, thus appetite is diminished. (pp. 598–599)

38. False. Each olfactory receptor cell is believed to have only one type of receptor protein (odorant binding protein) that, however, responds to several different odorant molecules. (pp. 578–579)

Critical Thinking and Clinical Application Questions

1. Papilledema—a nipplelike protrusion of the optic disc into the eyeball, which is caused by conditions that increase intracranial pressure. A rise in cerebrospinal fluid pressure caused by an intracranial tumor will compress the walls of the central vein resulting in its congestion and bulging of the optic disc. (p. 600)

2. Pathogenic microorganisms spread from the nasopharynx through the pharyngotympanic tube into the tympanic cavity. They may then spread posteriorly into the mastoid air cells via the mastoid antrum resulting in mastoiditis, and medially to the inner ear, causing secondary labyrinthitis. If unchecked, the infection may spread to the meninges, causing meningitis and possibly an abscess in the temporal lobe of the brain or in the cerebellum. They may also invade the blood, causing septicemia. The cause of her dizziness and loss of balance is a disruption of the equilibrium apparatus due to the labyrinthitis. (pp. 584–585)

3. Conjunctivitis. The foreign object probably would be found in the conjunctival sac near the orifice of the lacrimal canals. (p. 557)

4. This is known as a detached retina. The condition is serious, but the retina can be reattached surgically using lasers before permanent damage occurs. (p. 563)

5. The inability to hear high-pitched sounds is called presbycusis, a type of sensorineural deafness. It is caused by the gradual loss of hearing receptors throughout life, but is accelerated if one is exposed to loud rock music for extended periods. (p. 599)

6. Blindness, because visual impulses will be blocked from reaching the optic disk. (p. 575)

7. Albinism involves a hereditary inability for melanocytes to synthesize tyrosinase, an enzyme that is needed for the production of melanin, a light-absorbing pigment that is normally present in the choroid and the pigmented layer of the retina. A lack of melanin allows light scattering and reflection within the eye, which causes visual confusion. (p. 569)

8. Jan had tinnitus. (p. 594)

9. This condition might be retinal detachment. (p. 563)

10. The chemotherapy could affect his sense of taste. (p. 583)

Suggested Readings

Barinaga, Marcia. "Smell's Course Is Predetermined." *Science* 294 (5545) (Nov. 2001): 1269–1271.

Berson, David M. "Phototransduction by Retinal Ganglion Cells that Set the Circadian Clock." *Science* 295 (5557) (Feb. 2002): 1070–1073.

Cerio, Gregory. "Artificial Sight." *Discover* 22 (8) (Aug. 2001): 50–54.

Daugman, John. "Iris Recognition." *American Scientist* 89 (4) (July/August 2001): 326–333.

Firestein, Stuart. "How the Olfactory System Makes Sense of Scents." *Nature* 413 (6852) (Sept. 2001): 211–218.

Gagescu, Raluca. "Hear, Hear." *Nature Reviews: Molecular Cell Biology* 2 (8) (Aug. 2001): 565.

Hattar, S. et al. "Melanopsin-Containing Retinal Ganglion Cells: Architecture, Projections, and Intrinsic Photosensitivity." *Science* 295 (5557) (Feb. 2002): 1065–1070.

Lindemann, B. "Receptors and Transduction in Taste." *Nature* 413 (6852) (Sept. 2001): 219–225.

Nirenberg, S. M. et al. "Retinal Ganglion Cells Act Largely as Independent Encoders." *Nature* 411 (6838) (June 2001): 698–701.

Oliver, Dominik, et al. "Intracellular Anions as the Voltage Sensor of Prestin, the Outer Hair Cell Motor Protein." *Science* 292 (5525) (June 2001): 2340–2343.

Pichaud, Franck and Desplan, Claude. "A New View of Photoreceptors." *Nature* 416 (6877) (March 2002): 139–140.

Stevens, David R. et al. "Hyperpolarization-Activated Channels HCN1 and HCN4 Mediate Responses to Sour Stimuli." *Nature* 413 (6856) (Oct. 2001): 1753–1754.

Sun, Hui and Nathans, Jeremy. "The Challenge of Macular Degeneration." *Scientific American* 285 (4) (Oct. 2001): 69–75.

Weiss, Giselle. "Why Is a Soggy Potato Chip Unappetizing?" *Science* 293 (5536) (Sept. 2001): 1753–1754.

Wood, Heather. "Sweet Sensation." *Nature Reviews: Neuroscience* 2 (6) (June 2001): 382.

The Endocrine System

16

Objectives

The Endocrine System: An Overview

1. Define an endocrine gland, and list the major endocrine glands of the body and their locations.

Hormones

2. Define a hormone, and describe the chemical categories of hormones.
3. Explain the relationship of hormones to target cells, and the types of changes that result in target cells in response to hormone stimulation.
4. Describe the second messenger systems used by amino acid-based hormones.
5. Explain the mechanism of intracellular activation used by steroid hormones and thyroid hormone.
6. Examine the factors that determine target cell activation, and compare how the cell uses up-regulation and down-regulation to alter its responsiveness to hormones.
7. Identify the factors that affect circulating hormone concentration, and the differences in the time required for the effects of hormones to be seen in target cells.

8. Underscore the three types of hormone interaction on target cells.
9. Discuss the three types of stimuli that promote or inhibit the release of hormones, and the effect of nervous system modulation.

Major Endocrine Organs

10. List the hormones produced by the major endocrine organs, the factors controlling their release, and their effects on target cells.

Other Hormone-Producing Structures

11. Name the hormones produced by other organs of the body, their source, and effects.

Developmental Aspects of the Endocrine System

12. Indicate the embryonic origins of endocrine glands and the chemical classes of hormones produced by each embryonic tissue.
13. Describe environmental effects on hormone secretion or activity.
14. Explain the age-related changes that occur to endocrine organ structure or secretion.

Suggested Lecture Outline

I. The Endocrine System: An Overview (pp. 605–606; Fig. 16.1)

A. Endocrine glands are ductless glands that produce and release hormones to the blood through diffusion.

B. Endocrine glands may be strictly endocrine, such as the pituitary, thyroid, parathyroid, adrenal, pineal and thymus; or they may be organs that have hormone production as one of many functions, such as the pancreas, gonads, hypothalamus, and others.

II. Hormones (pp. 606–612; Figs. 16.2–16.5)

A. Chemistry of Hormones (p. 606)

1. Hormones are long-distance chemical signals that are secreted by the cells to the extracellular fluid and regulate the metabolic functions of other cells.

2. Most hormones are amino acid based, but gonadal and adrenocortical hormones are steroids, derived from cholesterol.

B. Mechanisms of Hormone Action (pp. 606–610; Figs. 16.2–16.4)

1. Hormones typically produce changes in membrane permeability or potential, stimulate synthesis of proteins or regulatory molecules, activate or deactivate enzymes, induce secretory activity, or stimulate mitosis.

2. Water-soluble hormones (all amino acid-based hormones except thyroid hormone) exert their effects through an intracellular second messenger that is activated when a hormone binds to a membrane receptor.

3. Lipid-soluble hormones (steroids and thyroid hormone) diffuse into the cell, where they bind to intracellular receptors, migrate to the nucleus, and activate specific target sequences of DNA.

4. Second messenger systems, activated when a hormone binds to a plasma membrane receptor, activate G-proteins within the cell that alter enzyme activity.

5. Direct gene activation occurs when a hormone binds to an intracellular receptor, which activates a specific region of DNA, causing the production of mRNA, and intitiation of protein synthesis.

C. Target Cell Specificity (p. 610)

1. Cells must have specific membrane or intracellular receptors to which hormones can bind.

2. Target cell response depends on three factors: blood levels of the hormone, relative numbers of target cell receptors, and affinity of the receptor for the hormone.

3. Target cells can change their sensitivity to a hormone by changing the number of receptors.

D. Half-Life, Onset, and Duration of Hormone Activity (p. 610)

1. The concentration of a hormone reflects its rate of release, and the rate of inactivation and removal from the body.

2. The half-life of a hormone is the duration of time a hormone remains in the blood, and is shortest for water-soluble hormones.

3. Target organ response and duration of response vary widely among hormones.

E. Interaction of Hormones at Target Cells (p. 611)

1. Permissiveness occurs when one hormone cannot exert its full effect without another hormone being present.

2. Synergism occurs when more than one hormone produces the same effects in a target cell, and their combined effects are amplified.

3. Antagonism occurs when one hormone opposes the action of another hormone.

F. Control of Hormone Release (pp. 611–612; Fig. 16.5)

1. Most hormone synthesis and release is regulated through negative feedback mechanisms.

2. Endocrine gland stimuli may be humoral, neural, or hormonal.

3. Nervous system modulation allows hormone secretion to be modified by the nervous stimulation in response to changing body needs.

III. Major Endocrine Organs (pp. 612–636; Figs. 16.6–16.19; Tables 16.1–16.3)

    A. The Pituitary Gland (Hypophysis) (pp. 612–619; Figs. 16.6–16.7; Table 16.1)

        1. The pituitary gland is connected to the hypothalamus via a stalk, the infundibulum, and consists of two lobes: the anterior pituitary, or adenohypophysis, and the posterior pituitary, or neurohypophysis.

        2. There are six adenohypophyseal hormones and one prohormone.

           a. Growth hormone (GH) stimulates body cells to increase in size and divide.

           b. Thyroid stimulating hormone (TSH) is a tropic hormone that stimulates normal development and secretion of the thyroid gland.

           c. Adrenocorticotropic hormone (ACTH) stimulates the adrenal cortex to release corticosteroid hormones.

           d. Follicle-stimulating hormone (FSH) stimulates gamete production.

           e. Leutinizing hormone (LH) promotes ovulation in females and production of gonadal hormones.

           f. Prolactin stimulates milk production in females, and may enhance testosterone in males.

           g. Pro-opiomelanocortin (POMC) is a prohormone that is the source of adrenocorticotropic hormone and two opiates.

        3. Two neurohormones are synthesized by the hypothalamus and secreted by the posterior pituitary.

           a. Oxytocin acts on the smooth muscle of the uterus and breast to cause uterine contractions during childbirth and milk let-down during nursing.

           b. Antidiuretic hormone (ADH) acts on kidney tubules to promote increased water reabsorption.

    B. The Thyroid Gland (pp. 620–624; Figs. 16.8–16.10; Table 16.2)

        1. The thyroid gland consists of hollow follicles with follicle cells that produce thyroglobulin, and parafollicular cells that produce calcitonin.

        2. Thyroid hormone consists of two amine hormones: thyroxine (T_4) and triiodothyronine (T_3), that act on all body cells to increase basal metabolic rate and body heat production.

        3. Calcitonin is a peptide hormone that lowers blood calcium by inhibiting osteoclast activity, and stimulates Ca^{2+} uptake and incorporation into the bone matrix.

    C. The Parathyroid Glands (pp. 624–625; Figs. 16.11–16.12)

        1. The parathyroid glands contain chief cells that secrete parathyroid hormone, or parathormone.

    D. The Adrenal (Suprarenal) Glands (pp. 626–632; Figs. 16.13–16.16; Table 16.3)

        1. The adrenal glands, or suprarenal glands, consist of two regions: an inner adrenal medulla and an outer adrenal cortex.

        2. The adrenal cortex produces corticosteroids from three distinct regions: the zona glomerulosa, the zona fasciculata, and the zona reticularis.

           a. Mineralocorticoids, mostly aldosterone, are essential to regulation of electrolyte concentrations of extracellular fluids.

   b. Aldosterone secretion is regulated by the renin-angiotensin mechanism, fluctuating blood concentrations of sodium and potassium ions, and secretion of ACTH.

   c. Glucocorticoids are released in response to stress through the action of ACTH.

   d. Gonadocorticoids are mostly weak androgens, which are converted to testosterone and estrogens in the tissue cells.

3. The adrenal medulla contains chromaffin cells that synthesize epinephrine and norepinephrine.

E. The Pancreas (pp. 632–634; Figs. 16.17–16.19)

1. The pancreas is a mixed gland that contains both endocrine and exocrine gland cells.

   a. Glucagon targets the liver where it promotes glycogenolysis, gluconeogenesis, and release of glucose to the blood.

   b. Insulin lowers blood sugar levels by enhancing membrane transport of glucose into body cells.

F. The Gonads (pp. 634–635)

1. The ovaries produce estrogens and progesterone.

2. The testes produce testosterone.

G. The Pineal Gland (pp. 635–636)

1. Secretes melatonin, a hormone derived from serotonin, in a diurnal cycle.

2. Indirectly receives input from the visual pathways in order to determine the timing of day and night.

H. The Thymus (p. 636)

1. The thymus produces thymopoietin, thymic factor, and thymosin, which are essential for the development of T lymphocytes and the immune response.

IV. Other Hormone-Producing Structures (pp. 636–638; Table 16.4)

A. The atria of the heart contain specialized cells that secrete atrial natriuretic factor resulting in decreased blood volume, blood pressure, and blood sodium concentration.

B. The gastrointestinal tract contains enteroendocrine cells throughout the mucosa that secrete hormones to regulate digestive functions.

C. The placenta secretes estrogens, progesterone, and human chorionic gonadotropin, which act on the uterus to influence pregnancy.

D. The kidneys produce erythropoietin, which signals the bone marrow to produce red blood cells.

E. The skin produces cholecalciferol, an inactive form of vitamin D_3.

F. Adipose tissue produces leptin, which acts on the CNS to produce a feeling of satiety, and resistin, an insulin antagonist.

V. Developmental Aspects of the Endocrine System (p. 639)

A. Endocrine glands derived from mesoderm produce steroid hormones; those derived from ectoderm or endoderm produce amines, peptides, or protein hormones.

B. Environmental pollutants have been demonstrated to have effects on sex hormones, thyroid hormone, and glucocorticoids.

C. Old age may bring about changes in rate of hormone secretion, breakdown, excretion, and target cell sensitivity.

Cross References

Additional information on topics covered in Chapter 16 can be found in the chapters listed below.

1. Chapter 1: Negative feedback
2. Chapter 2: Steroids; amino acids
3. Chapter 3: General cellular function
4. Chapter 4: Endocrine glands
5. Chapter 6: Bone homeostasis; epiphyseal plate
6. Chapter 11: Enkephalin and beta-endorphin; norepinephrine and epinephrine
7. Chapter 12: Hypothalamus
8. Chapter 14: Norepinephrine and epinephrine
9. Chapter 19: Hepatic portal system; blood pressure control; atrial natriuretic factor and blood pressure regulation
10. Chapter 21: Effect of thymic hormones
11. Chapter 23: Gastrin and secretin (hormones of the digestive system)
12. Chapter 24: Insulin and glucagon effects; hormone function related to general body metabolism
13. Chapter 25: Antidiuretic hormone function; aldosterone effects on renal tissue; rennin-angiotensin mechanism of blood pressure regulation; role of atrial natriuretic factor and fluid-electrolyte balance
14. Chapter 26: Antidiuretic hormone function; aldosterone effects on renal tissue; rennin-angiotensin mechanism of blood pressure regulation; role of parathyroid hormone and calcium balance related to development; role of atrial natriuretic factor and fluid-electrolyte balance; estrogen and glucocorticoid function in fluid and electrolyte balance
15. Chapter 27: Function of gonadotropins; testosterone production; role of FSH and LH related to reproduction; role of relaxin and inhibin in reproduction; ovarian physiology; brain-testicular axis
16. Chapter 28: Stimulation of milk production by the mammary gland (due to prolactin secretion); results of oxytocin and prolactin release; role of parathyroid hormone and calcium balance related to development; functions of human placental lactogen and human chorionic thyrotropin; prostaglandins and reproductive physiology; role of relaxin

Laboratory Correlations

1. Marieb, E. N. *Human Anatomy & Physiology Laboratory Manual: Cat and Fetal Pig Versions.* Eighth Edition Updates. Benjamin Cummings, 2006.

   Exercise 27: Functional Anatomy of the Endocrine Gland

   Exercise 28: Hormonal Action

2. Marieb, E. N. *Human Anatomy & Physiology Laboratory Manual: Main Version.* Seventh Edition Update. Benjamin Cummings, 2006.
   Exercise 27: Functional Anatomy of the Endocrine Glands
   Exercise 28: Hormonal Action

Histology Slides for the Life Sciences

Available through Benjamin Cummings, an imprint of Pearson Education, Inc. To order, contact your local Benjamin Cummings sales representative.

Slide 100 Adrenal Cortex and Medulla.

Slide 101 Parathyroid Gland Principal and Oxyphil Cells, Endocrine Organs.

Slide 102 Thyroid Gland, Endocrine Organs.

Slide 103 Pancreatic Islet, Pancreas.

Slide 104 Seminiferous Tubules, Monkey Testis.

Slide 105 Thyroid Gland.

Slide 106 Pancreatic islet stained differentially to allow identification of alpha and beta cells.

Slide 107 Histologically Distinct Regions of the Adrenal Gland.

Slide 108 Vesicular Follicle of the Ovary.

Slide 109 Parts of two seminiferous tubules and the intervening connective tissue.

Lecture Hints

1. A flowchart structure is an ideal method to condense a large volume of complex material into a compact package. Suggest to the class that on a single, large sheet of butcher paper, they map the entire endocrine system, flowchart style. Have them start at the top with the hypophysis and trace the path of each hormone to its target tissue. If students are able to see the entire picture on a single sheet, they will easily master the concepts of endocrine function.

2. Emphasize that minute quantities of hormone are all that is necessary to have rather large effects in the body.

3. Students are often confused regarding the actual site of neurohypophyseal hormone production. Point out that the hypothalamus is the actual production site and that the axons from the hormone-producing neurons terminate in the neurohypophysis (where the neurohormones are released).

4. Point out the importance of receptor regulation in non-insulin-dependent diabetes.

5. The mechanism of hormone action is an ideal way to introduce some critical thought questions for the class. Ask the class: "Knowing the properties of steroids and proteins, how should these hormones be carried in the blood, and which mechanism (second messenger or intracellular receptor) demands what class of hormone?"

6. Some hormones are also neurotransmitters. Using an example such as norepinephrine, stress to students that there is no difference between the hormone and the neurotransmitter; the difference lies in the source of the chemical.

7. Use root word definitions to emphasize function of the parts of the pituitary: adeno = gland; neuro = nervous.

8. Point out the advantage of a portal system (like that in the digestive system) for the direct delivery of releasing and inhibiting hormones from hypothalamus to hypophysis.

9. Wherever possible, point out antagonistic hormone pairs (glucagon-insulin, calcitonin-parathyroid hormone) and indicate direct control vs. control by regulating factors (hormones).

Activities/Demonstrations

1. Audio-visual materials listed under Multimedia in the Classroom and Lab.

2. Use a torso model and/or dissected animal model to exhibit endocrine glands.

3. Use photographs to demonstrate various endocrine disorders such as goiter, gigantism, cretinism, acromegaly, etc.

Critical Thinking/Discussion Topics

1. Discuss how the negative feedback mechanism controls hormonal activity and yet allows hypo- and hypersecretion disorders to occur.

2. Study why the pancreas, ovaries, testes, thymus gland, digestive organs, placenta, kidney, and skin are considered to have endocrine function. Relate the endocrine functions to their non-endocrine functions.

3. Discuss the role of the endocrine system in stress and stress responses.

4. Explain the basis of the fact that nervous control is rapid but of short duration, while hormonal control takes time to start but the effects last a long time. How would body function change if the rate of hormone degradation increased? Decreased?

5. On the basis of their chemical properties, why do protein-based and steroid-based hormones utilize, respectively, second messenger and intracellular receptor mechanisms of action?

6. Examine the consequences of increasing receptor number, decreasing receptor number, and increasing or decreasing rates of hormone release.

7. Give students the following scenario: You have just finished a large meal and are relaxing when suddenly threatened by a mugger. Have students explain autonomically and hormonally what occurs in the body. Encourage them to think in logical terms and to be as complete as possible.

Library Research Topics

1. Research the role of hormones in treatment of non-hormone-related disorders.

2. Study the inheritance aspect of certain hormones (such as diabetes mellitus, and certain thyroid gland disorders).

3. Research the role of prostaglandins in treatment of homeostatic imbalances.

4. Identify the various circadian rhythms in the body.

5. Research the methods used to test the levels of hormones in blood.

6. Define diabetes insipidus. How is this type of diabetes related to insulin-related diabetes?

7. Research the various diseases of the pituitary, and discuss what body effects will be produced.

Multimedia in the Classroom and Lab

Online Resources for Students

The
Anatomy & Physiology Place   **MyA&P**
www.anatomyandphysiology.com   www.myaandp.com

The following shows the organization of the Chapter Guide page in both the Anatomy & Physiology Place and MyA&P™. The Chapter Guide organizes all the chapter-specific online media resources for Chapter 16 in one convenient location, with e-book links to each section of the textbook. Please note that both sites also give you access to other general A&P resources, like InterActive Physiology®, PhysioEx 6.0™, Anatomy 360°, Flashcards, a Glossary, a Histology Tutorial, and much more.

Objectives

Section 16.1 The Endocrine System: An Overview (pp. 605–606)

Art Labeling Activity: Major Endocrine Glands (Fig. 16.1, p. 605)

InterActive Physiology®: Orientation

InterActive Physiology®: Endocrine System Review

Section 16.2 Hormones (pp. 606–612)

InterActive Physiology®: Biochemistry, Secretion, and Transport of Hormones

InterActive Physiology®: The Actions of Hormones on Target Cells

Activity: Anterior Pituitary Hormones: Regulation and Effects

Section 16.3 Major Endocrine Organs (pp. 612–636)

InterActive Physiology®: The Hypothalamic-Pituitary Axis

InterActive Physiology®: Response to Stress

PhysioEx: Endocrine System Physiology

Case Study: Endocrine System

Case Study: Diabetes Mellitus

Memory: Endocrine Structure and Function

Memory: Endocrine-Related Regulatory Processes

Activity: Regulation of Blood Sugar Levels by Insulin and Glucagon

Section 16.4 Other Hormone-Producing Structures (pp. 636–638)

Section 16.5 Developmental Aspects of the Endocrine System (p. 639)

Chapter Summary

Self-Study Quizzes

Art Labeling Quiz

Matching Quiz

Multiple-Choice Quiz (Level I)

Multiple-Choice Quiz (Level II)

True-False Quiz

Crossword Puzzles

Crossword Puzzle 16.1

Crossword Puzzle 16.2

Media

See Guide to Audio-Visual Resources in Appendix A for key to AV distributors.

Slides

1. *Gland Types Set* (CBS). Offers scanning electron micrographs of organization, zona glomerulosa, zona fasciculata, and zona reticularis.

Video

1. *Diagnosing and Treating Diabetes* (FHS; 22 min., 1998). Explores the manifestation, diagnostic testing, treatment, and biochemistry of diabetes mellitus.
2. *The Endocrine System* (IM, WNS; 17 min., 1998). Shows how eight glands of the endocrine system make and release hormones.
3. *Hormonal Control* (FHS; 10 min.) This program takes a look at the role played by hormones in maintaining homeostasis. The program illustrates how hormone production stimulates reactions and, in turn, how hormone production is monitored.
4. *Hormonally Yours* (FHS; 50 min., 2000). From the *Body Chemistry: Understanding Hormones* series, this program examines the role of hormones on gender and sexuality.
5. *Hormone Heaven!* (FHS; 50 min., 2000). From the *Body Chemistry: Understanding Hormones* series, this program strives to answer questions related to the role of hormones in maintaining youthful vigor.
6. *Hormone Hell* (FHS; 50 min., 2000). From the *Body Chemistry: Understanding Hormones* series, this program examines the ways in which hormones affect different stages of life.
7. *Hormones: Messengers* (FHS; 27 min., 1984). From *The Living Body* series, this exceptional program covers a number of body processes that are controlled and coordinated by hormones.
8. *Selected Actions of Hormones and Other Chemical Messengers* (BC; 25 min., 1994). Provides a survey of the actions of selected hormones.

Software

1. *A.D.A.M.® InterActive Anatomy® 4.0* (see p. 9 of this guide for full listing).
2. *A.D.A.M.® MediaPro* (see p. 9 of this guide for full listing).
3. *A.D.A.M.® Anatomy Practice* (see p. 86 of this guide for full listing).
4. *Bodyworks* (see p. 9 of this guide for full listing).
5. *Interactive Physiology® 9-System Suite CD-ROM* (BC; Win/Mac). The Endocrine System section of this interactive program covers the identification of major glands and their target tissues as well as the classification and functions of hormones.
6. *The Ultimate Human Body* (see p. 9 of this guide for full listing).

Lecture Enhancement Material

To view thumbnails of all of the illustrations for Chapter 16, see Appendix B.

Transparencies Index/Media Manager

Figure 16.1   Location of the major endocrine organs of the body.
Figure 16.2   Cyclic AmP second-messenger mechanisms of amino acid-based hormones.
Figure 16.3   The PIP second-messenger mechanism of amino acid-based hormones.
Figure 16.4   Direct gene activation mechanism of steroid hormones.
Figure 16.5   Three types of endocrine gland stimuli.

Answers to End-of-Chapter Questions

Multiple Choice and Matching Question answers appear in Appendix G of the main text.

Short Answer Essay Questions

15. Hormone—a chemical substance, secreted by cells into the extracellular fluids, that regulates the metabolic functions of specific body cells. (p. 606)

16. Binding of a hormone to intracellular receptors would result in the most long-lived response, because extracellular receptors activate second messenger systems that are degraded rapidly by intracellular enzymes. (p. 608)

17. The anterior pituitary is connected to the hypothalamus by a stalk of tissue called the infundibulum. It produces the following hormones: growth hormone, thyroid-stimulating hormone, adrenocorticotropic hormone, follicle-stimulating hormone, luteinizing hormone, and prolactin. (pp. 613–614)

    The pineal gland hangs from the roof of the third ventricle within the diencephalon. Melatonin is its major secretory product. (pp. 635–636)

    The pancreas is located partially behind the stomach in the abdomen. The pancreatic islets produce glucagon and insulin, as well as small amounts of somatostatin. (p. 632)

    The ovaries are located in the female's abdominopelvic cavity. They produce estrogens and progesterone. (p. 634)

    The male testes are located in an inferior extra-abdominal skin pouch called the scrotum. They produce androgens, most importantly the hormone testosterone. (p. 635)

    The adrenal glands are perched atop the kidneys. The adrenal glands produce the adrenocortical hormones mineralocorticoids, glucocorticoids, and gonadocorticoids; and the adrenal medullary hormones epinephrine and norepinephrine. (pp. 626–627)

18. Endocrine regions that are important in stress response are the adrenal medulla and adrenal cortex. The adrenal medulla produces hormones that mimic the effects of neurotransmitters of the sympathetic division of the autonomic nervous system. The adrenal cortex produces the glucocorticoids (and mineralocorticoids) important in stress response. The adrenal medulla hormones function in the alarm reaction; the adrenal cortex hormones, in the resistance stage. (pp. 627–629)

19. The release of anterior pituitary hormones is controlled by hypothalamic-releasing (and hypothalmic-inhibiting) hormones. (pp. 613–614)

20. The posterior pituitary gland is composed largely of glial cells and nerve fibers. It releases ready-made neurohormones that it receives via nerve fibers from the hypothalamus. It serves as a hormone storage area. (p. 617)

21. A lack of iodine (required to make functional T_3 and T_4) causes a colloidal, or endemic, goiter. (p. 623)

22. Problems that elderly people might have as a result of decreasing hormone production include the following:

    a. chemical or borderline diabetes

    b. lessening of basal metabolic rate

    c. increase in body fat

    d. osteoporosis (p. 639)

23. Skeletal muscle cells, when stimulated by growth hormone (GH), produce and release insulin-like growth factor 1, which mediates the effects of GH. (p. 614) Two hormones secreted by neurons are norepinephrine and epinephrine. This comes about as a result of the sympathetic nervous system stimulation of the adrenal medulla during periods of stress. (p. 611)

24. Insulin enhances the uptake of glucose by cells, thus preventing hyperglycemia. It also promotes fat storage, thus decreasing its level in the blood and preventing lipidemia. Lack of the insulin gene, and thus, absence of insulin, would lead to both hyperglycemia and lipidemia. (pp. 632–634)

Critical Thinking and Clinical Application Questions

1. It is not unusual to find them in other regions of the neck or even the thorax. The adjacent neck regions should be checked first. (p. 624)

2. Insulin should be administered because symptoms are indicative of diabetic shock. (p. 634)

3. The hypersecreted hormone is growth hormone. The disorder is gigantism. The enlarging pituitary is pressing on his optic chiasma (or other parts of the visual pathway). (p. 615)

4. a. Hyposecretion of aldosterone would lead to decreased reabsorption of sodium ions from the urine. Since sodium reabsorption is tied to potassium secretion, less potassium ions would be secreted to the urine, and plasma levels would be elevated.

    b. An ACTH stimulation test will allow the clinician to differentiate between a pituitary insufficiency of ACTH secretion, or an adrenal insensitivity or insufficiency.

    c. If ACTH does not cause a normal elevation of cortisol, then the problem originates from the adrenals, and is likely Addison's disease.

    d. If ACTH does cause an elevation of cortisol secretion, then likely a problem such as a tumor or malignancy exists within the anterior pituitary. (p. 630)

5. Mr. Proulx is suffering from Cushing's disease, brought on by high levels of his prednisone. His overall lousy feeling is due to muscle weakness and possible hyperglycemia, the swelling is due to water and salt retention, and the anti-inflammatory effect of the drug plays a role in suppression of immune-related defense mechanisms, increasing his susceptibility to colds. (pp. 629–630)

Suggested Readings

Birnbaum, Morris J. "Dialogue Between Muscle and Fat." *Nature* 409 (6821) (Feb. 2001): 672–673.

Mathis, D. et al. "B-Cell Death During Progression to Diabetes." *Nature* 414 (6865) (Dec. 2001): 792–799.

Moller, D. E. "New Drug Targets for Type 2 Diabetes and the Metabolic Syndrome." *Nature* 414 (6865) (Dec. 2001): 821–827.

Rabinovitch, Alex. "Autoimmune Diabetes Mellitus." *Science and Medicine* 7 (3) (May/June 2002): 18–27.

Raloff, Janet. "Can Childhood Diets Lead to Diabetes?" *Science News* 159 (7) (Feb. 2001): 111.

Saltiel, A. R. and Kahn, C. R. "Insulin Signaling and the Regulation of Glucose and Lipid Metabolism." *Nature* 414 (6865) (Dec. 2001): 799–807.

Slight, Simon H. "Cardiovascular Steroidogenesis." *Science and Medicine* 8 (1) (Jan./Feb. 2002): 36–45.

Blood

Objectives

Overview: Blood Composition and Functions

1. Describe the components of blood and their relative proportions. Define the blood hematocrit.
2. List the physical characteristics of blood. Indicate the normal volumes for males and females.
3. Discuss the functions of blood.

Blood Plasma

4. Define blood plasma and list the components and their functions.

Formed Elements

5. Indicate the formed elements of the blood, their structure, function, and development.
6. Explain the fate and destruction of erythrocytes.
7. Examine the disorders of too many and too few of each type of formed element.

Hemostasis

8. Define hemostasis.
9. Identify the events of platelet plug formation.

10. List the events of the coagulation phase of hemostasis. Differentiate between the intrinsic and extrinsic pathways of prothrombin formation.
11. Explain the mechanism and function of clot retraction and tissue repair.
12. Discuss the factors that limit clot formation.

Transfusion and Blood Replacement

13. List the reasons for transfusion of whole blood, plasma, and blood volume expanders.
14. Discuss the basis for human blood groups. Identify what factor determines each blood group.
15. Explain the results of a transfusion reaction, and how blood typing is used to avoid such a problem.

Diagnostic Blood Tests

16. Indicate how the various types of diagnostic blood tests are used.

Developmental Aspects of Blood

17. List the structures involved in formation of fetal blood.
18. Compare fetal and adult hemoglobin.

Suggested Lecture Outline

I. Overview: Blood Composition and Functions (pp. 647–648; Fig. 17.1)

A. Components (pp. 647–648; Fig. 17.1)
   1. Blood is a specialized connective tissue consisting of living cells, called formed elements, suspended in a nonliving fluid matrix, blood plasma.

    2. Blood that has been centrifuged separates into three layers: erythrocytes, the buffy coat, and plasma.

    3. The blood hematocrit represents the percentage of erythrocytes in whole blood.

  B. Physical Characteristics and Volume (p. 648)

    1. Blood is a slightly basic (pH = 7.35–7.45) fluid that has a higher density and viscosity than water, due to the presence of formed elements.

    2. Normal blood volume in males is 5–6 liters, and 4–5 liters for females.

  C. Functions (p. 648)

    1. Blood is the medium for delivery of oxygen and nutrients, removal of metabolic wastes to elimination sites, and distribution of hormones.

    2. Blood aids in regulating body temperature, body fluid pH, and fluid volume within fluid compartments.

    3. Blood protects against excessive blood loss through the clotting mechanism, and from infection through the immune system.

II. Blood Plasma (pp. 648–649; Table 17.1)

  A. Blood plasma consists of mostly water (90%), and solutes including nutrients, gases, hormones, wastes, products of cell activity, ions, and proteins.

  B. Plasma proteins account for 8% of plasma solutes, mostly albumin, which function as carriers.

III. Formed Elements (pp. 649–662; Figs. 17.2–17.12; Table 17.2)

  A. Erythrocytes (pp. 649–656; Figs. 17.3–17.8)

    1. Erythrocytes, or red blood cells, are small cells that are biconcave in shape. They lack nuclei and most organelles, and contain mostly hemoglobin.

      a. Hemoglobin is an oxygen-binding pigment that is responsible for the transport of most of the oxygen in the blood.

      b. Hemoglobin is made up of the protein globin bound to the red heme pigment.

    2. Production of Erythrocytes

      a. Hematopoiesis, or blood cell formation, occurs in the red bone marrow.

      b. Erythropoiesis, the formation of erythrocytes, begins when a myeloid stem cell is transformed to a proerythroblast, which develops into mature erythrocytes.

      c. Erythrocyte production is controlled by the hormone erythropoietin.

      d. Dietary requirements for erythrocyte formation include iron, vitamin B_{12} and folic acid, as well as proteins, lipids, and carbohydrates.

      e. Blood cells have a short life span due to the lack of nuclei and organelles; destruction of dead or dying blood cells is accomplished by macrophages.

    3. Erythrocyte Disorders

      a. Anemias are characterized by a deficiency in RBCs.

      b. Polycythemia is characterized by an abnormal excess of RBCs.

  B. Leukocytes (pp. 656–662; Figs. 17.9–17.11)

    1. Leukocytes, or white blood cells, are the only formed elements that are complete cells and make up less than 1% of total blood volume.

    2. Leukocytes are critical to our defense against disease.

3. Granulocytes are a main group of leukocytes characterized as large cells with lobed nuclei and visibly staining granules; all are phagocytic.

    a. Neutrophils are the most numerous type of leukocyte. They are chemically attracted to sites of inflammation and are active phagocytes.

    b. Eosinophils are relatively uncommon and attack parasitic worms.

    c. Basophils are the least numerous leukocyte and release histamine to promote inflammation.

4. Agranulocytes are a main group of lymphocytes that lack visibly staining granules.

    a. T lymphocytes directly attack viral-infected and tumor cells; B lymphocytes produce antibody cells.

    b. Monocytes become macrophages and activate T lymphocytes.

5. Production and Life Span of Leukocytes

    a. Leukopoiesis, the formation of white blood cells, is regulated by the production of interleukins and colony-stimulating factors (CSF).

    b. Leukopoiesis involves differentiation of hemocytoblasts along two pathways: lymphoid and myeloid stem cells.

6. Leukocyte Disorders

    a. Leukopenia is an abnormally low white blood cell count.

    b. Leukemias are clones of a single white blood cell that remain unspecialized and divide out of control.

    c. Infectious mononucleosis is a disease caused by the Epstein-Barr virus.

C. Platelets (p. 662; Fig. 17.12)

  1. Platelets are not complete cells, but fragments of large cells called megakaryocytes.

  2. Platelets are critical to the clotting process, forming the temporary seal when a blood vessel breaks.

  3. Formation of platelets involves repeated mitoses of megakaryocytes without cytokinesis.

IV. Hemostasis (pp. 663–668; Figs. 17.13–17.14; Table 17.3)

A. A break in a blood vessel stimulates hemostasis, a fast, localized response to reduce blood loss through clotting. (p. 663)

B. Vascular spasms are the immediate vasoconstriction response to blood vessel injury. (pp. 663–665)

C. Platelet Plug Formation (p. 665; Fig. 17.13)

  1. When endothelium is damaged, platelets become sticky and spiky, adhering to each other and the damaged vessel wall.

  2. Once attached, other platelets are atracted to the site of injury, activating a positive feedback loop for clot formation.

D. Coagulation, or blood clotting, is a multi-step process in which blood is transformed from a liquid to a gel. (pp. 665–666; Figs. 17.13–17.14)

  1. Factors that promote clotting are called clotting factors, or procoagulants; those that inhibit clot formation are called anticoagulants.

  2. The clotting process involves: formation of prothrombin activator, conversion of prothrombin to thrombin, and the formation of fibrin mesh from fibrinogen in the plasma.

E. Clot Retraction and Repair (p. 666)

1. Clot retraction is a process in which the contractile proteins within platelets contract and pull on neighboring fibrin strands, squeezing plasma from the clot and pulling damaged tissue edges together.

2. Repair is stimulated by platelet-derived growth factor (PDGF).

F. Fibrinolysis removes unneeded clots through the action of the fibrin-digesting enzyme plasmin. (p. 666)

G. Factors Limiting Clot Growth or Formation (pp. 666–667)

1. Rapidly moving blood disseminates clotting factors before they can initiate a clotting cascade.

2. Thrombin that is not bound to fibrin is inactivated by antithrombin III and protein C, as well as heparin.

H. Disorders of Hemostasis (pp. 667–668)

1. Thromboembolytic disorders result from conditions that cause undesirable clotting, such as roughening of vessel endothelium, slow-flowing blood, or blood stasis.

2. Disseminated intravascular coagulation is a situation leading to widespread clotting throughout intact vessels, and may occur as a complication of pregnancy, septicemia, or incompatible blood transfusions.

3. Bleeding disorders arise from abnormalities that prevent normal clot formation, such as a deficiency in circulating platelets, lack of synthesis of procoagulants, or hemophilia.

V. Transfusion and Blood Replacement (pp. 668–671; Fig. 17.15; Table 17.4)

A. Transfusion of whole blood is routine when blood loss is substantial, or when treating thrombocytopenia. (pp. 668–670; Fig. 17.15; Table 17.4)

1. Humans have different blood types based on specific antigens on RBC membranes.

2. ABO blood groups are based on the presence or absence of two types of agglutinogens.

3. Preformed antibodies (agglutinins) are present in blood plasma and do not match the individual's blood.

4. The Rh factor is a group of RBC antigens that are either present in Rh^+ blood, or absent in Rh^- blood.

5. A transfusion reaction occurs if the infused donor blood type is attacked by the recipient's blood plasma agglutinins, resulting in agglutination and hemolysis of the donor cells.

B. Plasma and blood volume expanders are given in cases of extremely low blood volume. (p. 671)

VI. Diagnostic Blood Tests (pp. 671–672)

A. Changes in some of the visual properties of blood can signal diseases such as anemia, heart disease, and diabetes.

B. Differential white blood cell counts are used to detect differences in relative amounts of specific blood cell types.

C. Prothrombin time, which measures the amount of prothrombin in the blood, and platelet counts evaluate the status of the hemostasis system.

D. SMAC, SMA12–60, and complete blood count (CBC) give comprehensive values of the condition of the blood.

VII. Developmental Aspects of Blood (pp. 672–673)

    A. Prior to birth, blood cell formation occurs within the fetal yolk sac, liver, and spleen, but by the seventh month, red bone marrow is the primary site of hematopoiesis.

    B. Fetal blood cells form hemoglobin-F, which has a higher affinity for oxygen than adult hemoglobin, hemoglobin-A.

Cross References

Additional information on topics covered in Chapter 17 can be found in the chapters listed below.

1. Chapter 3: Diffusion; osmosis
2. Chapter 4: Tissue repair
3. Chapter 6: Hematopoietic tissue
4. Chapter 18: Role of the heart in blood delivery
5. Chapter 19: Vasoconstriction as a mechanism of blood flow control; general overview of arteries, capillaries, and veins
6. Chapter 20: Role of the spleen in the removal of old red blood cells; macrophages
7. Chapter 21: Granulocyte function in nonspecific resistance; lymphocyte function (T and B cells) in specific immune response; role of monocytes (macrophages) in the immune response; AIDS; antigen-antibody interaction; diapedesis; chemotaxis
8. Chapter 22: Gas exchange between blood, lungs, and tissues; respiratory gas transport
9. Chapter 23: Vitamin B_{12} absorbance; production of vitamin K in the large intestine
10. Chapter 24: Role of blood in body temperature regulation
11. Chapter 25: Erythropoietin related to renal function; plasma filtration
12. Chapter 26: Control of water and ion balance; acid-base balance

Laboratory Correlations

1. Marieb, E. N. *Human Anatomy & Physiology Laboratory Manual: Cat and Fetal Pig Versions.* Eighth Edition Updates. Benjamin Cummings, 2006.
   Exercise 29: Blood
2. Marieb, E. N. *Human Anatomy & Physiology Laboratory Manual: Main Version.* Seventh Edition Update. Benjamin Cummings, 2006.
   Exercise 29: Blood

Histology Slides for the Life Sciences

Available through Benjamin Cummings, an imprint of Pearson Education, Inc. To order, contact your local Benjamin Cummings sales representative.

Slide 86   Red Blood Cells, White Blood Cells, Platelets—Blood (Vascular).

Slide 95   Monocyte.

Slide 96   Neutrophils.

Slide 97   Eosinophil.

Slide 98   Lymphocyte.

Slide 99   Basophil.

Lecture Hints

1. Emphasize that the hematocrit is an indirect measurement of the O_2 carrying capacity of the blood. More red blood cells mean more O_2 carried by the same volume of blood.

2. Emphasize that simple diffusion gradients cause the loading and unloading of respiratory gases and other substances. It may be of benefit to ask the students pointed questions about respiratory gas diffusion during the lecture to be sure the class has mastered this concept.

3. As a point of interest, mention that well-oxygenated blood is bright red; normal deoxygenated blood (at the tissue level) is dark red; and that under hypoxic conditions, hemoglobin becomes blue.

4. Spend some time with the feedback loop involved in erythropoiesis. This is a typical negative feedback mechanism that allows the application of critical thought processes.

5. Mention that serum is essentially plasma without clotting proteins.

6. Point out the delicate balance between clotting and prevention of unwanted clotting. We want to be sure that hemorrhage is arrested, but at the same time, we need to prevent clot formation in unbroken blood vessels.

7. Emphasize that ABO incompatibility does not require sensitization by a previous blood transfusion, while Rh incompatibility does.

8. The regulation of hemostasis is often difficult for students. Areas to clarify include: the continuous presence of various clotting factors circulating in the blood in an inactive form; the production of activating and inhibiting stimuli; and the importance of rapid blood flow in the prevention of spontaneous clot formation.

9. Students often have difficulty with the concepts of blood antigens and antibodies, and relating them to the terms agglutinogens and agglutinins. Stress the location of each in the blood.

Activities/Demonstrations

1. Audio-visual materials listed under Multimedia in the Classroom and Lab.

2. Display equipment used to perform a hematocrit, sedimentation rate, and cell counts. Describe how these tests are performed and the information they yield. Run a hematocrit so that students can see the difference in volume of plasma and formed elements.

3. Provide blood-typing sera and have the students type their own blood. All lancets and disposable items are to be placed immediately in a disposable autoclave bag after use, and used slides should be placed in a solution of freshly prepared 10% bleach and soaked for at least two hours. Both the autoclave bag and the slides are to be autoclaved for 15 min. at 121°C, 15 lbs. pressure to ensure sterility. After autoclaving, the autoclave bag may be discarded in any disposable container; the glass slides may be washed with laboratory detergent and reprepared for use.

4. Provide a sample of centrifuged animal blood so that students can examine consistency, texture, and color of plasma. Have pH paper available so that students can determine its pH. Use this activity as a lead-in to a discussion about the composition and importance of plasma.

5. Use models to exhibit blood cells.

6. Set up a stained blood smear to illustrate as many types of white blood cells as possible.

Critical Thinking/Discussion Topics

1. Discuss the fears and facts associated with blood donation, transfusion, and AIDS.
2. Explore the problems associated with IV drug use (i.e., hepatitis, AIDS, necrosis of tissue, and other blood-related disorders).
3. Discuss the procedure of autologous transfusion.
4. Discuss why gamma globulin injections are painful.
5. Why do red blood cells lack a nucleus? Why is this an advantage?
6. How can you explain that an incompatible ABO blood group will generate a transfusion reaction the first time a transfusion is given, while Rh incompatibility creates a problem the second time a transfusion is given?

Library Research Topics

1. Research the blood disorders associated with IV street drug use.
2. Study the role of blood in the AIDS epidemic.
3. Investigate inherited blood disorders.
4. Explore the blood antigens other than A, B, and Rh.
5. Research the various blood immunoglobulins, their functions, and how they are made (i.e., stimulus required).
6. Examine the various uses of donated blood; i.e., packed red cells, platelets, etc.
7. Research which diseases are transmitted by blood and why these diseases are increasing in incidence. Why is careful handling of blood in the clinical agency vitally important?

Multimedia in the Classroom and Lab

Online Resources for Students

The
Anatomy & Physiology Place   MyA&P
www.anatomyandphysiology.com   www.myaandp.com

The following shows the organization of the Chapter Guide page in both the Anatomy & Physiology Place and MyA&P™. The Chapter Guide organizes all the chapter-specific online media resources for Chapter 17 in one convenient location, with e-book links to each section of the textbook. Please note that both sites also give you access to other general A&P resources, like InterActive Physiology®, PhysioEx 6.0™, Anatomy 360°, Flashcards, a Glossary, a Histology Tutorial, and much more.

Objectives
Section 17.1 Overview: Blood Composition and Functions (pp. 647–648)
Section 17.2 Blood Plasma (pp. 648–649)
Memory: Blood Cells
Section 17.3 Formed Elements (pp. 649–662)
InterActive Physiology®: Respiratory System: Gas Transport
Memory: Identifying the Formed Elements of Blood
Case Study: Iron Deficiency Anemia
Case Study: Sickle Cell Anemia
Section 17.4 Hemostasis (pp. 663–668)
Section 17.5 Transfusion and Blood Replacement (pp. 668–671)

Media

See Guide to Audio-Visual Resources in Appendix A for key to AV distributors.

Slides

1. *Human Blood Smear, Wright's Stain* (FSE). Slide clearly differentiates between erythrocytes and leukocytes.

Video

1. *Bleeding and Coagulation* (FHS; 31 min., 2000). Scrutinizes the body's mechanism of coagulation through the use of case studies.
2. *Blood* (FHS; 20 min., 1995). From *The New Living Body* series, this video explains blood and circulation through the story of a sickle-cell sufferer.
3. *Blood is Life* (FHS; 45 min., 1995). Award-winning video that provides a thorough introduction to human blood.
4. *Diseases of the Blood: Issues and Answers* (FHS; 24 min., 2001). Explores breakthroughs in treatments for multiple myeloma and chronic lymphocytic leukemia.

Software

1. *Blood and Immunity* (CE, LP; Win/Mac). Teaches the components of blood, blood types, and the processes of blood. Includes information on HIV.
2. *Blood and the Circulatory System NEO/LAB* (LP; Win/Mac). Provides interactive exercises on blood typing, morphology, and genetics.
3. *InterActive Physiology® 9-System Suite CD-ROM* (BC; Win/Mac). Interactive software that explores the physiology of the cardiovascular system.

Lecture Enhancement Material

To view thumbnails of all of the illustrations for Chapter 17, see Appendix B.

Transparencies Index/Media Manager

Figure 17.1   The major components of whole blood.
Figure 17.2   Photomicrograph of a human blood smear stained with Wright's stain.
Figure 17.3   Structure of erythrocytes.
Figure 17.4   Structure of hemoglobin.
Figure 17.5   Erythropoiesis: genesis of red blood cells.

Indicates images that are on the Media Manager only.

Answers to End-of-Chapter Questions

Multiple Choice and Matching Question answers appear in Appendix G of the main text.

Short Answer Essay Questions

11. a. The formed elements are living blood cells. The major categories of formed elements are erythrocytes, leukocytes, and platelets.

    b. The least numerous of the formed elements are the leukocytes.

    c. The buffy coat in a hematocrit tube comprises the white blood cells and platelets. (pp. 647–648)

12. Hemoglobin is made up of the protein globin bound to the pigment heme. Each molecule contains four polypeptide chains (globins) and four heme groups, each bearing an atom of iron in its center. Its function is to bind oxygen to each iron atom. When oxygen is loaded (bound to hemoglobin), the hemoglobin becomes bright red. When oxygen is unloaded from the iron, the hemoglobin becomes dark red. (p. 650)

13. With a high hematocrit, you would expect the hemoglobin determination to be high, since the hematocrit is the percent of blood made up of RBCs. (p. 648)

14. In addition to carbohydrates for energy and amino acids needed for protein synthesis, the nutrients needed for erythropoiesis are iron and certain B vitamins. (p. 652)

15. a. In the process of erythropoiesis, a hemocytoblast is transformed into a proerythroblast, which gives rise to early, then late erythroblasts, normoblasts, and reticulocytes.

    b. The immature cell type released to the circulation is the reticulocyte.

    c. The reticulocyte differs from a mature erythrocyte in that it still contains some rough ER. (pp. 651–652)

16. The physiological attributes which contribute to the function of white blood cells in the body include the ability to move by amoeboid action, exhibition of positive chemotaxis enabling them to pinpoint areas of tissue damage, diapedesis (moving through capillary walls), and the ability to participate in phagocytosis. (p. 657)

17. a. With a severe infection, the WBC count would be closest to 15,000 WBC/mm^3 of blood.

    b. This condition is called leukocytosis. (p. 657)

18. a. Platelets appear as small discoid fragments of large, multinucleated cells called megakaryocytes. They are essential for the clotting process and work by clumping together to form a temporary plug to prevent blood loss.

    b. Platelets should not be called "cells" because they are only fragments of cells. (p. 662)

19. a. Literally, hemostasis is "blood standing still" because it refers to clotted blood. It encompasses the steps that prevent blood loss from blood vessels. (p. 663)

    b. The three major steps of coagulation include the formation of prothrombin activator by a cascade of activated procoagulants, the use of prothrombin activator enzymatically to release the active enzyme thrombin from prothrombin, and the use of thrombin to cause fibrinogen to form fibrin strands. (pp. 663–665)

    c. The intrinsic pathway depends on substances present in (intrinsic to) blood. It has many more steps and intermediates, and is slower. The extrinsic mechanism bypasses the early steps of the intrinsic mechanism and is triggered by tissue factor (thromboplastin) released by injured cells in the vessel wall or in surrounding tissues. (pp. 665–666)

    d. Calcium is essential to virtually all stages of coagulation. (p. 664)

20. a. Fibrinolysis is the disposal of clots when healing has occurred.

    b. The importance of this process is that without it, blood vessels would gradually become occluded by clots that are no longer necessary. (p. 666)

21. a. Clot overgrowth is usually prevented by rapid removal of coagulation factors and inhibition of activated clotting factors. (pp. 666–667)

    b. Two conditions that may lead to unnecessary (and undesirable) clot formation are roughening of the vessel wall endothelium and blood stasis. (p. 667)

22. Bleeding disorders occur when the liver cannot synthesize its usual supply of procoagulants. (p. 668)

23. a. A transfusion reaction involves agglutination of foreign RBCs, leading to clogging of small blood vessels, and lysis of the donated RBCs. It occurs when mismatched blood is transfused.

    b. Possible consequences include disruption of oxygen-carrying capacity, fever, chills, nausea, vomiting, general toxicity, and renal failure. (pp. 669–670)

24. Among other things, poor nutrition can cause iron-deficiency anemia due to inadequate intake of iron-containing foods or to pernicious anemia due to deficiency of vitamin B_{12}. (p. 655)

25. The most common blood-related problems for the aged include chronic types of leukemias, anemias, and thromboembolytic disease. (p. 672)

Critical Thinking and Clinical Application Questions

1. Hemopoiesis is a process involving fairly rapid cell production. Since chemotherapeutics simply target cells exhibiting rapid turnover (rather than other specific properties of cancer cells), hemopoiesis is a target of chemotherapeutic drugs and must be carefully monitored. (pp. 651–652)

2. a. The woman would probably be given a whole blood transfusion. It is essential that she maintain sufficient O_2 carrying capacity to serve fetal needs and blood volume to maintain circulation.

   b. The blood tests that would be performed include tests for ABO and Rh group antigen and cross matching. (pp. 669–670)

3. a. Polycythemia accounts for his higher erythrocyte count because of the need to produce more RBCs to increase his O_2 binding and transport ability in the high altitude (thinner air) environment of the Alps. Enhanced production of RBCs was prompted by an increased production of erythropoietin.

   b. His RBC count will not stay higher than normal because the excess production of RBCs will depress erythropoietin production by the kidneys when adequate levels of O_2 are being transported in the blood. (p. 656)

4. Janie's leukocytes are immature or abnormal and are incapable of defending her body in the usual way. (p. 660)

5. Red bone marrow is the site of hemopoiesis, and if it is destroyed by benzene, hemocytoblasts will not be produced, which will reduce the production of megakaryocytes (the progenitor cells of platelets, which are involved in clotting). (p. 651)

6. Tyler is turning out a high rate of reticulocytes (immature red blood cells), which accounts for his high hematocrit. (p. 652)

7. An analysis of the clotting process described in the text should reveal that the two blood proteins are thrombin and fibringen. (p. 665)

8. An elevated RBC count could be related to smoking, due to the frequent hypoxia that results from inhalation of oxygen-poor cigarette smoke. (p. 652)

9. Aspirin is a mild anticoagulant, which could cause excessive bleeding during or after surgery. (p. 667)

Suggested Readings

Becker, R. "Antiplatelet Therapy." *Scientific American: Science and Medicine* 3 (July/Aug. 1996): 12–21.

Cooper, M.D. "B Lymphocytes: Normal Development and Function." *The New England Journal of Medicine* 317 (Dec. 1987): 1452–1456.

Eaton, W., and J. Hofrichter. "The Biophysics of Sickle Cell Hydroxyurea Therapy." *Science* 268 (May 1995): 1142–1143.

Fackelmann, K.A. "Blood Substances Linked to Heart Risk." *Science News* 144 (Nov. 1993).

Gareau, R., et al. "Erythropoietin Abuse in Athletes." *Nature* 380 (Mar. 1996): 113.

Gratzer, Walter. "The Wright Stuff." *Nature* 416 (6878) (March 2002): 275–277.

Hardison, R. "The Evolution of Hemoglobin." *American Scientist* 87 (Mar/Apr. 1999): 126–137.

Lin, L. "Psoralen Photochemical Treatment of Platelets." *Science and Medicine* 5 (Jan/Feb. 1998): 54–63.

Loupe, D.E. "Breaking the Sickle Cycle." *Science News* 136 (Dec. 1989): 360–362.

Luzzatto, Lucio and Notaro, Rosario. "Haemoglobin's Chaperone." *Nature* 417 (6890) (June 2002): 703–705.

Nucci, M.L., and A. Abuchowski. "The Search for Blood Substitutes." *Scientific American* 278 (Feb. 1998): 72–77.

Oliwenstein, L. "Liquid Assets." *Discover* 14 (Sept. 1993): 34.

Pickrell, J. "Globin Family Grows." *Science News* 161 (15) (April 2002): 230.

Radetsky, P. "The Mother of All Blood Cells." *Discover* 16 (Mar. 1995): 86–93.

Roos, Dirk and Winterbourn, Christine C. "Lethal Weapons." *Science* 296 (5568) (April 2002): 669–670.

Shivdasani, R., et al. "Transcription Factor NF-E2 Is Required for Platelet Formation Independent of the Actions of Thrombopoietin/MGDF in Megakaryocyte Development." *Cell* 81 (June 1995): 695–705.

Winslow, R.M. "Blood Substitutes." *Science and Medicine* 4 (Mar/Apr 1997): 54–63.

Ziegler, B.L., et al. "KDR Receptor: A Key Marker Defining Hematopoietic Stem Cells." *Science* 285 (Sept. 1999): 1553.

The Cardiovascular System: The Heart

Objectives

Heart Anatomy

1. Describe the size, location, and orientation of the heart.
2. Identify structures of the pericardium.
3. Define the endocardium, myocardium, and epicardium.
4. Compare the function of the atria and the ventricles, and describe the difference between the function of the right and left ventricles.
5. Discuss the need for coronary circulation, and name the vessels that play a role in it.
6. Indicate the function and location of the atrioventricular valves and aortic and pulmonary valves.

Properties of Cardiac Muscle Fibers

7. Describe the microscopic anatomy and control of cardiac muscle cells, and compare to skeletal muscle cells.
8. Name the energetic requirements of cardiac muscle and how these requirements are met.

Heart Physiology

9. Describe the structures and activities of the intrinsic conduction system.
10. Draw a typical ECG. Label and define the three phases.
11. Discuss the cardiac cycle in terms of relative pressure in each set of chambers.
12. Explain the normal heart sounds and how the sounds relate to closure of specific valves and systole or diastole of the ventricles.
13. Define cardiac output, stroke volume, and heart rate. Calculate cardiac output and cardiac reserve.
14. List the factors that affect stroke volume of the heart.
15. Describe the effects of the divisions of the autonomic nervous system on the heart.

Developmental Aspects of the Heart

16. Describe the events of development of the heart from two separate tubes to a finished structure.
17. Explain age-related changes that occur in the heart. Discuss possible changes in heart function due to these changes.

Suggested Lecture Outline

I. Heart Anatomy (pp. 678–689; Figs. 18.1–18.10)

    A. Size, Location, and Orientation (p. 678; Fig. 18.1)

        1. The heart is the size of a fist and weighs 250–300 grams.

        2. The heart is found in mediastinum and two-thirds lies left of the midsternal line.

        3. The base is directed toward the right shoulder and the apex points toward the left hip.

   B. Coverings of the Heart (p. 678; Fig. 18.2)

      1. The heart is enclosed in a doubled-walled sac called the pericardium.

      2. Deep to pericardium is the serous pericardium.

      3. The parietal pericardium lines the inside of the pericardium.

      4. The visceral pericardium, or epicardium, covers the surface of the heart.

   C. Layers of the Heart Wall (pp. 678–680; Fig. 18.3)

      1. The myocardium is composed mainly of cardiac muscle and forms the bulk of the heart.

      2. The endocardium lines the chambers of the heart.

   D. Chambers and Associated Great Vessels (pp. 680–684; Fig. 18.4)

      1. The right and left atria are the receiving chambers of the heart.

      2. The right ventricle pumps blood into the pulmonary trunk; the left ventricle pumps blood into the aorta.

   E. Pathway of Blood Through the Heart (pp. 684–685; Fig. 18.5)

      1. The right side of the heart pumps blood into the pulmonary circuit; the left side of the heart pumps blood into the systemic circuit.

   F. Coronary Circulation (pp. 685–686; Fig. 18.7)

      1. The heart receives no nourishment from the blood as it passes through the chamber.

      2. The coronary circulation provides the blood supply for the heart cells.

      3. In a myocardial infarction, there is prolonged coronary blockage that leads to cell death.

   G. Heart Valves (pp. 686–689; Figs. 18.8–18.10)

      1. The tricuspid and bicuspid valves prevent backflow into the atria when the ventricles contract.

      2. When the heart is relaxed the AV valves are open, and when the heart contracts the AV valves close.

      3. The aortic and pulmonary valves are found in the major arteries leaving the heart. They prevent backflow of blood into the ventricles.

      4. When the heart is relaxed the aortic and pulmonary valves are closed, and when the heart contracts they are open.

II. Properties of Cardiac Muscle Fibers (pp. 689–692; Figs. 18.11–18.12)

   A. Microscopic Anatomy (pp. 689–690; Fig. 18.11)

      1. Cardiac muscle is striated and contraction occurs via the sliding filament mechanism.

      2. The cells are short, fat, branched, and interconnected by intercalated discs.

   B. Mechanism and Events of Contraction (pp. 690–692; Fig. 18.12)

      1. Some cardiac muscle cells are self-excitable.

      2. The heart contracts as unit or not at all.

      3. The heart's absolute refractory period is longer than a skeletal muscle's, preventing tetanic contractions.

   C. Energy Requirements (p. 692)

      1. The heart relies exclusively on aerobic respiration for its energy demands.

      2. Cardiac muscle is capable of switching nutrient pathways to use whatever nutrient supply is available.

III. Heart Physiology (pp. 692–705; Figs. 18.13–18.23)

A. Electrical Events (pp. 692–697; Figs. 18.13–18.18)

1. Intrinsic conduction system is made up of specialized cardiac cells that initiate and distribute impulses, ensuring that the heart depolarizes in an orderly fashion.

2. The autorhythmic cells have an unstable resting potential, called pacemaker potentials, that continuously depolarizes.

3. Impulses pass through the autorhythmic cardiac cells in the following order: sinoatrial node, atrioventricular node, atrioventricular bundle, right and left bundle branches, and Purkinje fibers.

4. The autonomic nervous system modifies the heartbeat: the sympathetic center increases rate and depth of the heartbeat, and the parasympathetic center slows the heartbeat.

5. An electrocardiograph monitors and amplifies the electrical signals of the heart and records it as an electrocardiogram (ECG).

B. Heart Sounds (pp. 697–698; Fig. 18.19)

1. Normal

a. The first heart sound, lub, corresponds to closure of the AV valves, and occurs during ventricular systole.

b. The second heart sound, dup, corresponds to the closure of the aortic and pulmonary valves, and occurs during ventricular diastole.

2. Abnormal

a. Heart murmurs are extraneous heart sounds due to turbulent backflow of blood through a valve that does not close tightly.

C. Mechanical Events: The Cardiac Cycle (pp. 698–700; Fig. 18.20)

1. Systole is the contractile phase of the cardiac cycle and diastole is the relaxation phase of the cardiac cycle.

2. Cardiac Cycle

a. Ventricular Filling: Mid-to-Late Diastole

b. Ventricular Systole

c. Isovolumetric Relaxation: Early Diastole

D. Cardiac Output (pp. 700–705; Figs. 18.21–18.23)

1. Cardiac output is defined as the amount of blood pumped out of a ventricle per beat, and is calculated as the product of stroke volume and heart rate.

2. Regulation of Stroke Volume

a. Preload: the Frank-Starling law of the heart states that the critical factor controlling stroke volume is the degree of stretch of cardiac muscle cells immediately before they contract.

b. Contractility: contractile strength increases if there is an increase in cytoplasmic calcium ion concentration.

c. Afterload: ventricular pressure that must be overcome before blood can be ejected from the heart.

3. Regulation of Heart Rate

a. Sympathetic stimulation of pacemaker cells increases heart rate and contractility, while parasympathetic inhibition of cardiac pacemaker cells decreases heart rate.

      b. Epinephrine, thyroxine, and calcium influence heart rate.

      c. Age, gender, exercise, and body temperature all influence heart rate.

    4. Homeostatic Imbalance of Cardiac Output

      a. Congestive heart failure occurs when the pumping efficiency of the heart is so low that blood circulation cannot meet tissue needs.

      b. Pulmonary congestion occurs when one side of the heart fails, resulting in pulmonary edema.

IV. Developmental Aspects of the Heart (pp. 705–709; Figs. 18.24–18.25)

  A. Embryological Development (pp. 705–708; Figs. 18.24–18.25)

    1. The heart begins as a pair of endothelial tubes that fuse to make a single heart tube with four bulges representing the four chambers.

    2. The foramen ovale is an opening in the interatrial septum that allows blood returning to the pulmonary circuit to be directed into the atrium of the systemic circuit.

    3. The ductus arteriosus is a vessel extending between the pulmonary trunk to the aortic arch that allows blood in the pulmonary trunk to be shunted to the aorta.

  B. Aging Aspects of the Heart (pp. 708–709)

    1. Sclerosis and thickening of the valve flaps occurs over time, in response to constant pressure of the blood against the valve flaps.

    2. Decline in cardiac reserve occurs due to a decline in efficiency of sympathetic stimulation.

    3. Fibrosis of cardiac muscle may occur in the nodes of the intrinsic conduction system, resulting in arrhythmias.

    4. Atherosclerosis is the gradual deposit of fatty plaques in the walls of the systemic vessels.

Cross References

Additional information on topics covered in Chapter 18 can be found in the chapters listed below.

1. Chapter 1: Ventral body cavity; mediastinum
2. Chapter 3: Cell junctions
3. Chapter 4: Serous membranes; cardiac muscle; squamous epithelium; collagen
4. Chapter 9: Sliding filament mechanisms
5. Chapter 11: Membrane potential
6. Chapter 12: Medullary control of cardiac rate
7. Chapter 13: Vagus nerve
8. Chapter 14: Neurotransmitters and cardiac rate; general sympathetic and parasympathetic function
9. Chapter 19: Atherosclerosis; hydrostatic pressure and fluid movement; cardiac output and regulation of blood pressure; vasomotor centers and control of blood pressure; function of baroreceptors and chemoreceptors in blood pressure control; blood volume and pressure control; blood flow to the heart
10. Chapter 22: Function of pulmonary arteries and veins
11. Chapter 28: Fetal circulation and modifications that occur during birth

Laboratory Correlations

1. Marieb, E. N. *Human Anatomy & Physiology Laboratory Manual: Cat and Fetal Pig Versions*. Eighth Edition Updates. Benjamin Cummings, 2006.

   Exercise 30: Anatomy of the Heart

   Exercise 31: Conduction System of the Heart and Electrocardiography

2. Marieb, E. N. *Human Anatomy & Physiology Laboratory Manual: Main Version*. Seventh Edition Update. Benjamin Cummings, 2006.

   Exercise 30: Anatomy of the Heart

   Exercise 31: Conduction System of the Heart and Electrocardiography

Histology Slides for the Life Sciences

Available through Benjamin Cummings, an imprint of Pearson Education, Inc. To order, contact your local Benjamin Cummings sales representative.

Slide 30   Cardiac Muscle Tissue, Heart.

Lecture Hints

1. Point out that the visceral layer of the pericardium (epicardium) is the same as the outermost layer of the heart wall.

2. Display a single diagram of both pericardium and heart wall so that students get an overall perspective of construction.

3. Clearly distinguish between atrium and auricle.

4. Point out that blood flow through the right and left side of the heart occurs simultaneously, and that the direction of flow in both sides progresses from atrium to ventricle, with both sides of the heart pumping the same volume of blood.

5. Describe the construction differences between the atrioventricular valves and the semilunar valves, and why the construction of each type of valve works best in its location. Stress that the valves are not rigid structures, but flimsy.

6. Compare ion movement, depolarization, and repolarization in cardiac muscle to that of skeletal muscle. Emphasize why a long repolarization phase is important to cardiac muscle function.

7. Emphasize that the pacemaker cells are cardiac muscle cells, just modified so that they spontaneously depolarize.

8. Clearly distinguish between the basic rate set by the conduction system of the heart and the acceleratory or inhibitory controls (sympathetic and parasympathetic) set by the medulla.

9. Emphasize that the ECG is the measurement of the total electrical activity of the heart at the surface of the body. Students often wonder why the ECG does not look like an action potential.

10. When discussing ventricular systole and diastole, reinforce the definitions of root words so that students can think critically about meanings rather than memorize terminology, e.g., isovolumetric means "same volume."

11. Stress the relationship between pressure changes in the heart chambers and flow of blood through the heart. The concepts of pressure gradients and flow are often new to students.

12. Note that while the ventricles have both a passive and active phase to filling, the atria only fill passively.

13. Relate the heart sounds to specific points in the discussion of the cardiac cycle, so that students integrate these ideas.
14. Clearly differentiate between preload as a function of mechanical stretch, and contractility as a function of strength of stimulation of contraction.
15. Discuss the importance of most blood volume bypassing fetal lungs, and the role of the foramen ovale and ductus arteriosus. Stress the significance of the closure of these structures after birth.

Activities/Demonstrations

1. Audio-visual materials listed under Multimedia in the Classroom and Lab.
2. Play a recording of normal and abnormal heart sounds to accompany your presentation of valve function and malfunction. ("Interpreting Heart Sounds" is available on free loan from local chapters of the American Heart Association.)
3. Obtain tracings of normal and abnormal ECGs. Determine what is malfunctioning with the cardiac conduction system to yield the abnormal tracings.
4. Record the heart rates of student volunteers as they stand quietly and run in place for a few minutes. Using a standard stroke volume, calculate the change in cardiac output.
5. Use heart models and dissected specimens to show the anatomy of the heart and its position within the chest cavity.
6. Using dissected animal specimens, compare fetal heart structures with adult structures.

Critical Thinking/Discussion Topics

1. Relate the functioning of the heart to the functioning of a water pump. Include problems associated with low blood pressure going to the heart and high pressure leaving the heart.
2. Discuss the signs of impending heart attack.
3. Compare the significance of ventricular fibrillation as opposed to atrial fibrillation.
4. Discuss the role of cardiac muscle in ejecting blood from the ventricles as opposed to ejecting blood from the atria.
5. How would heart function change if cells of the AV node depolarized at a faster rate than SA node cells?
6. What would happen to the heart (and the rest of the body) over a period of time if a partial blockage of the aortic semilunar valve occurred?
7. Discuss the symptoms and potential problems in a person with mitral valve prolapse.
8. Examine the action of digoxin as a therapy for heart murmurs.
9. Identify long-term stress and its role in hypertensive disorders of the heart.

Library Research Topics

1. Research the role of antihypertensive drugs on the action of the heart.
2. Study the alternatives to coronary bypass operations.
3. Investigate the known effects of street drugs on heart activity.
4. Research the effect of smoking on the heart and its function.
5. Examine the criteria used for heart transplants and their success rate.

6. Research the effect of exercise on heart function.
7. Identify the use of pacemakers and what specific problems they are designed to correct.
8. Explore the status of artificial hearts or external heart pumps. Identify advances and problems.
9. Study fetal heart defects and outline advances in treatment.
10. Research the diagnostic tests done to measure heart health, and what they are designed to show.

Multimedia in the Classroom and Lab

Online Resources for Students

The Anatomy & Physiology Place
www.anatomyandphysiology.com

MyA&P
www.myaandp.com

The following shows the organization of the Chapter Guide page in both the Anatomy & Physiology Place and MyA&P™. The Chapter Guide organizes all the chapter-specific online media resources for Chapter 18 in one convenient location, with e-book links to each section of the textbook. Please note that both sites also give you access to other general A&P resources, like InterActive Physiology®, PhysioEx 6.0™, Anatomy 360°, Flashcards, a Glossary, a Histology Tutorial, and much more.

Objectives

Section 18.1 Heart Anatomy (pp. 678–689)
InterActive Physiology®: Anatomy Review: The Heart
Art Labeling Activity: Gross Anatomy of the Heart, External View (Fig. 18.4b, p. 681)
Art Labeling Activity: Gross Anatomy of the Heart, Internal View (Fig. 18.4e, p. 683)
Memory: The Structure of the Heart

Section 18.2 Properties of Cardiac Muscle Fibers (pp. 689–692)
InterActive Physiology®: Cardiac Action Potential

Section 18.3 Heart Physiology (pp. 692–705)
InterActive Physiology®: Intrinsic Conduction System
InterActive Physiology®: Cardiac Cycle
InterActive Physiology®: Cardiac Output
PhysioEx: Frog Cardiovascular Physiology
Case Study: Coronary Stenosis
Case Study: Cardiac Arrhythmia
Memory: The Cardiovascular System
Activity: Sequence of Excitation of the Heart

Section 18.4 Developmental Aspects of the Heart (pp. 705–709)

Chapter Summary

Self-Study Quizzes
Art Labeling Quiz
Matching Quiz
Multiple-Choice Quiz (Level I)
Multiple-Choice Quiz (Level II)
True-False Quiz

Crossword Puzzles
Crossword Puzzle 18.1
Crossword Puzzle 18.2

Media

See Guide to Audio-Visual Resources in Appendix A for key to AV distributors.

Video

1. *The Circulatory System: Two Hearts That Beat as One* (FHS; 28 min., 1989). From *The Living Body* series, this program describes the structure and functioning of the heart.
2. *Diagnosing Heart Disease* (FHS; 18 min., 1994). Discusses heart disease, the warning signs of heart attack, electrocardiograms, and cardio-catheterization. Helps students visualize the various tests used in the diagnosis of heart problems.
3. *Heart Attack* (FHS; 50 min., 2000). From *The Body Invaders* series, this program looks at the causes, symptoms, and treatment of atherosclerosis.
4. *Heart Valves: Repairing the Heart* (FHS; 19 min.). Discusses the symptoms and treatment of aortic valve stenosis. Covers the functions of angioplasty, the uses of a pacemaker, and an implantable defibrillator.
5. *The Human Cardiovascular System: The Heart Videotape* (BC; 25 min., 1995). A sheep heart is utilized to illustrate structure and function of the heart, along with dissected human specimen and the cadaver to show the heart coronary and great vessels. Excellent for a laboratory demonstration as a supplement to dissection.
6. *Pumping Life—The Heart and Circulatory System* (WNS; 20 min.). Explains the structure and function of the heart. Uses animation and live action. Discusses heart problems and the importance of preventive maintenance.

Software

1. *A.D.A.M.® InterActive Anatomy® 4.0* (see p. 9 of this guide for full listing).
2. *A.D.A.M.® MediaPro* (see p. 9 of this guide for full listing).
3. *A.D.A.M.® Anatomy Practice* (see p. 86 of this guide for full listing).
4. *Bodyworks* (see p. 9 of this guide for full listing).
5. *LOGAL Explorer™: Cardiovascular System™ CD-ROM* (RIL; Win/Mac). This program illustrates the role the heart plays in the function of the human body. Investigates the heart as well as its function, the effect of drugs, cardiac fitness, and various heart disorders.
6. *InterActive Physiology® 9-System Suite CD-ROM: Cardiovascular System* (BC; Win/Mac 2006). Presents topics related to heart and blood vessel physiology, such as blood pressure, cardiac output, intrinsic conduction system, cardiac action potential, and cardiac cycle.
7. *The Ultimate Human Body* (see p. 9 of this guide for full listing).

Lecture Enhancement Material

To view thumbnails of all of the illustrations for Chapter 18, see Appendix B.

Transparencies Index/Media Manager

Figure 18.1	Location of the heart in the mediastinum.
Figure 18.2	The pericardial layers and layers of the heart wall.
Figure 18.3	The circular and spiral arrangement of cardiac muscle bundles in the myocardium of the heart.
Figure 18.4	Gross anatomy of the heart.
Figure 18.5	The systemic and pulmonary circuits.

Answers to End-of-Chapter Questions

Multiple Choice and Matching Question answers appear in Appendix G of the main text.

Short Answer Essay Questions

10. The heart is enclosed within the mediastinum. It lies anterior to the vertebral column and posterior to the sternum. It tips slightly to the left. (p. 678)

11. The pericardium has two layers, a fibrous and a serous layer. The outer fibrous layer is a fibrous connective tissue that protects the heart and anchors it to surrounding structures. The inner serous layer (squamous epithelial cells) lines the fibrous layer as the parietal serous pericardium and at the base of the heart continues over the heart surface as the visceral serous pericardium. The visceral serous pericardium is the outermost layer of the heart wall, i.e., the epicardium. (p. 678)

12. Blood that enters the right atrium on its way to the left atrium is in the pulmonary circuit. The path is as follows: right atrium, right ventricle, pulmonary trunk, right and left pulmonary arteries, lungs, pulmonary veins, left atrium. This circuit is called the pulmonary circuit. (p. 684)

13. a. The coronary arteries are actively delivering blood to the myocardium when the heart is relaxed. The coronary vessels are compressed and ineffective in blood delivery when the ventricles are contracting. (pp. 685–686)

    b. The major branches of the coronary arteries and the areas they serve are as follows. The left coronary artery runs toward the left side of the heart and divides into the anterior interventricular artery and the circumflex artery. The anterior interventricular artery supplies blood to the interventricular septum and anterior walls of both ventricles, and the circumflex artery serves the left atrium and the posterior walls of the left ventricle. The right coronary artery splits to the right side of the heart, where it divides into the marginal artery and the posterior interventricular artery. The marginal artery serves the myocardium of the lateral part of the right side of the heart and the posterior interventricular artery, which runs to the heart apex and supplies the posterior ventricular walls. (pp. 685–686)

14. A longer refractory period of cardiac muscle is desirable because it prevents the heart from going into prolonged or tetanic contractions which would stop its pumping action. (p. 691)

15. a. The elements of the intrinsic conduction system of the heart, beginning with the pacemaker, are: the SA node or pacemaker, AV node, AV bundle, right and left bundle branches, and Purkinje fibers. (p. 693)

    b. This system functions to initiate and distribute impulses throughout the heart so that the myocardium depolarizes and contracts in an orderly, sequential manner from atria to ventricles. (p. 694)

16. See Figure 18.16. The P wave results from impulse conduction from the SA node through the atria. The QRS complex results from ventricular depolarization and precedes ventricular contraction. Its shape reveals the different size of the two ventricles and the time required for each to depolarize. The T wave is caused by ventricular repolarization. (p. 696)

17. The cardiac cycle includes all events associated with the flow of blood through the heart during one complete heartbeat. One cycle includes a period of ventricular filling (mid-to-late diastole at the end of which atrial systole occurs), ventricular systole, and isovolumetric relaxation (early diastole). (p. 698)

18. Cardiac output is the amount of blood pumped out by each ventricle in one minute. It can be calculated by the following equation: cardiac output = heart rate × stroke volume. (p. 700)

19. The Frank-Starling Law explains that the critical factor controlling stroke volume is the degree of stretch of the cardiac muscle cells just before they contract. The important factor in the stretching of cardiac muscle is the amount of blood returning to the heart and distending its ventricles. (pp. 700–701)

20. In a fetus, the common function of the foramen ovale and the ductus arteriosus is to allow blood to bypass the pulmonary circulation. If these shunts remain patent after birth, the opening prevents adequate gas exchange, O_2 loading and CO_2 unloading, in the pulmonary circulation. (pp. 706–707)

Critical Thinking and Clinical Application Questions

1. Cardiac tamponade is compression of the heart due to accumulation of blood or inflammatory fluid in the pericardial sac. Such compression reduces the ability of the heart to beat and act as an effective pump, leading to inadequate blood delivery (which results in ischemia and cyanosis), and ultimately cardiogenic shock. (p. 678)

2. a. To auscultate the aortic valve, place the stethoscope over the second intercostal space at the right sternal margin. To auscultate the mitral valve, place the stethoscope over the heart apex, in the fifth intercostal space in line with the middle of the clavicle. (p. 697)

    b. These abnormal sounds would be heard most clearly during ventricular diastole for the aortic valve and during atrial systole for the mitral valve. (pp. 697–698)

   c. An incompetent valve has a swishing sound after the valve has supposedly
      closed. A stenosed valve has a high-pitched sound when blood is being forced
      through its constricted opening during systole just before valve closure. (p. 698)

3. Failure of the left ventricle (which pumps blood to the body) can result in chest
   pain due to dying or dead ischemic cardiac cells; pale, cold skin due to lack of circulation of blood from blocked ventricular contraction; and moist sounds in the lower
   lungs due to high pressure and pooling of blood in the pulmonary circulation
   because of nonfunction of the left ventricle. (pp. 704–705)

4. Oxygen-deficient blood returning from the systemic circulation to the right heart
   will pass repeatedly around the systemic circuit, while oxygenated blood returned
   from the lungs is continually recycled through the pulmonary circuit. (p. 681)

5. Gabriel, being a user of an injectable drug, probably was infected by a bacteria-
   contaminated ("dirty") needle used to administer heroin. (p. 709)

6. The synonyms are as follows: (a) coronary sulcus, (b) right AV valve, (c) left AV or
   mitral valve, and (d) bundle of His. (pp. 681, 686, 693)

Suggested Readings

Anversa, P. and Nadal-Ginard, B. "Myocyte Renewal and Ventricular Remodelling."
   Nature 415 (6868) (Jan. 2002): 240–243.

Bers, D. M. "Cardiac Excitation-Contraction." *Nature* 415 (6868) (Jan. 2002): 198–205.

Bonetta, Laura. "New Study on Aging Heart." *Nature Medicine* 8 (3) (March 2002):
   201.

Dajer, Tony. "Plumbing the Depths." *Discover* 23 (3) (March 2002): 22–25.

Gottlieb, Roberta A. and Kitsis, Richard N. "Seeing Death in the Living." *Nature Medicine* 7 (12) (Dec. 2001): 1277–1278.

Harder, B. "Vitamin Void." *Science News* 161 (7) (Feb. 2002): 161.

Hoffman-Kim, Diane. "Tissue Engineering: Heart Valves." *Science and Medicine* 8
   (March/April 2002): 62–64.

Isner, J. M. "Myocardial Gene Therapy." *Nature* 415 (6868) (Jan. 2002): 234–239.

Marban, E. "Cardiac Channelopathies." *Nature* 415 (6868) (Jan. 2002): 213–218.

Nattel, S. "New Ideas About Atrial Fibrillation 50 Years On." *Nature* 415 (6868) (Jan.
   2002): 219–226.

Rockman, H. A., Koch, W. J., Lefkowitz, R. J. "Seven-Transmembrane-Spanning Receptors and Heart Function." *Nature* 415 (6868) (Jan. 2002): 206–212.

Towbin, J. A. and Bowles, N. E. "The Failing Heart." *Nature* 415 (6868) (Jan. 2002):
   227–233.

Vane, John R. "Back to an Aspirin a Day?" *Science* 296 (5567) (April 2002): 474–475.

19

The Cardiovascular System: Blood Vessels

Objectives

PART 1: OVERVIEW OF BLOOD VESSEL STRUCTURE AND FUNCTION

1. Define the direction of flow and oxygenation state of blood in arteries and veins.

2. Describe the structural arrangement and composition of the layers of blood vessels.

3. State the function of each type of blood vessel.

4. List the types of capillary endothelium and the functional applications of each.

5. Explain the pathway of blood flow through capillary beds, and the role of precapillary sphincters.

PART 2: PHYSIOLOGY OF CIRCULATION

6. Define blood flow, blood pressure, and resistance, and describe the factors that affect each.

7. State the relationship between flow, pressure, and resistance.

8. Discuss systemic blood pressure in terms of pressure gradients and characteristics in each type of vessel.

9. Define systolic and diastolic pressure, pulse pressure, and mean arterial pressure.

10. Explain the mechanisms used to regulate blood pressure.

11. Define hypertension and hypotension, and identify contributing factors.

12. Explain how blood flow is regulated by the body.

13. Identify the types and causes of circulatory shock.

PART 3: CIRCULATORY PATHWAYS: BLOOD VESSELS OF THE BODY

14. List the major blood vessels of the body and the areas and organs they serve.

15. Describe the major differences between arteries and veins.

Developmental Aspects of Blood Vessels

16. Explain how the vascular system develops during fetal development.

17. Discuss special structural adaptations of the fetal circulation.

18. Identify the changes that occur in the vascular system as a consequence of age.

Suggested Lecture Outline

I. *Part 1: Overview of Blood Vessel Structure and Function (pp. 714–723; Figs. 19.1–19.4; Table 19.1)*

A. Structure of Blood Vessel Walls (p. 714; Fig. 19.1; Table 19.1)

1. The walls of all blood vessels except the smallest consist of three layers: the tunica intima, tunica media, and tunica externa.

2. The tunica intima reduces friction between the vessel walls and blood; the tunica media controls vasoconstriction and vasodilation of the vessel; and the tunica externa protects, reinforces, and anchors the vessel to surrounding structures.

B. Arterial System (pp. 716–722; Figs. 19.2–19.4)

1. Elastic, or conducting, arteries contain large amounts of elastin, which enables these vessels to withstand and smooth out pressure fluctuations due to heart action.

2. Muscular, or distributing, arteries deliver blood to specific body organs, and have the greatest proportion of tunica media of all vessels, making them more active in vasoconstriction.

3. Arterioles are the smallest arteries and regulate blood flow into capillary beds through vasoconstriction and vasodilation.

4. Capillaries are the smallest vessels and allow for exchange of substances between the blood and interstitial fluid.

   a. Continuous capillaries are most common and allow passage of fluids and small solutes.

   b. Fenestrated capillaries are more permeable to fluids and solutes than continuous capillaries.

   c. Sinusoidal capillaries are leaky capillaries that allow large molecules to pass between the blood and surrounding tissues.

5. Capillary beds are microcirculatory networks consisting of a vascular shunt and true capillaries, which function as the exchange vessels.

6. A cuff of smooth muscle, called a precapillary sphincter, surrounds each capillary at the metarteriole and acts as a valve to regulate blood flow into the capillary.

C. Venous System (pp. 722–723)

1. Venules are formed where capillaries converge and allow fluid and white blood cells to move easily between the blood and tissues.

2. Venules join to form veins, which are relatively thin-walled vessels with large lumens containing about 65% of the total blood volume.

D. Vascular anastomoses form where vascular channels unite, allowing blood to be supplied to and drained from an area even if one channel is blocked (p. 723).

II. Part 2: Physiology of Circulation (pp. 723–742; Figs. 19.5–19.17; Table 19.2)

A. Introduction to Blood Flow, Blood Pressure, and Resistance (pp. 723–724)

1. Blood flow is the volume of blood flowing through a vessel, organ, or the entire circulation in a given period, and may be expressed as ml/min.

2. Blood pressure is the force per unit area exerted by the blood against a vessel wall, and is expressed in millimeters of mercury (mm Hg).

3. Resistance is a measure of the friction between blood and the vessel wall, and arises from three sources: blood viscosity, blood vessel length, and blood vessel diameter.

4. Relationship Between Flow, Pressure, and Resistance

   a. If blood pressure increases, blood flow increases; if peripheral resistance increases, blood flow decreases.

   b. Peripheral resistance is the most important factor influencing local blood flow, because vasoconstriction or vasodilation can dramatically alter local blood flow, while systemic blood pressure remains unchanged.

B. Systemic Blood Pressure (pp. 724–726; Figs. 19.5–19.6)

1. The pumping action of the heart generates blood flow; pressure results when blood flow is opposed by resistance.

2. Systemic blood pressure is highest in the aorta, and declines throughout the pathway until it reaches 0 mm Hg in the right atrium.

3. Arterial blood pressure reflects how much the arteries close to the heart can be stretched (compliance, or distensibility), and the volume forced into them at a given time.

   a. When the left ventricle contracts, blood is forced into the aorta, producing a peak in pressure called systolic pressure (120 mm Hg).

   b. Diastolic pressure occurs when blood is prevented from flowing back into the ventricles by the closed semilunar valve, and the aorta recoils (70–80 mm Hg).

   c. The difference between diastolic and systolic pressure is called the pulse presssure.

   d. The mean arterial pressure (MAP) represents the pressure that propels blood to the tissues.

4. Capillary blood pressure is low, ranging from 40–20 mm Hg, which protects the capillaries from rupture, but is still adequate to ensure exchange between blood and tissues.

5. Venous blood pressure changes very little during the cardiac cycle, and is low, reflecting cumulative effects of peripheral resistance.

C. Maintaining Blood Pressure (pp. 726–733; Figs. 19.7–19.11; Table 19.2)

1. Blood pressure varies directly with changes in blood volume and cardiac output, which are determined primarily by venous return and neural and hormonal controls.

2. Short-term neural controls of peripheral resistance alter blood distribution to meet specific tissue demands, and maintain adequate MAP by altering blood vessel diameter.

   a. The vasomotor center is a cluster of sympathetic neurons in the medulla that controls changes in the diameter of blood vessels.

   b. Baroreceptors detect stretch and send impulses to the vasomotor center, inhibiting its activity and promoting vasodilation of arterioles and veins.

   c. Chemoreceptors detect a rise in carbon dioxide levels of the blood, and stimulate the cardioacceleratory and vasomotor centers, which increases cardiac output and vasoconstriction.

   d. The cortex and hypothalamus can modify arterial pressure by signaling the medullary centers.

3. Chemical controls influence blood pressure by acting on vascular smooth muscle or the vasomotor center.

   a. Norepinephrine and epinephrine promote an increase in cardiac output and generalized vasoconstriction.

   b. Atrial natriuretic peptide acts as a vasodilator and an antagonist to aldosterone, resulting in a drop in blood volume.

   c. Antidiuretic hormone promotes vasoconstriction and water conservation by the kidneys, resulting in an increase in blood volume.

   d. Angiotensin II acts as a vasoconstrictor, as well as promoting the release of aldosterone and antidiuretic hormone.

   e. Endothelium-derived factors promote vasoconstriction, and are released in response to low blood flow.

   f. Nitric oxide is produced in response to high blood flow or other signaling molecules, and promotes systemic and localized vasodilation.

g. Inflammatory chemicals, such as histamine, prostacyclin, and kinins, are potent vasodilators.

h. Alcohol inhibits antidiuretic hormone release and the vasomotor center, resulting in vasodilation.

4. Long-Term Mechanisms

a. The direct renal mechanism counteracts an increase in blood pressure by altering blood volume, which increases the rate of kidney filtration.

b. The indirect renal mechanism is the renin-angiotensin mechanism, which counteracts a decline in arterial blood pressure by causing systemic vasoconstriction.

5. Monitoring circulatory efficiency is accomplished by measuring pulse and blood pressure; these values together with respiratory rate and body temperature are called vital signs.

a. A pulse is generated by the alternating stretch and recoil of elastic arteries during each cardiac cycle.

b. Systemic blood pressure is measured indirectly using the ascultatory method, which relies on the use of a blood pressure cuff to alternately stop and reopen blood flow into the brachial artery of the arm.

6. Alterations in blood pressure may result in hypotension (low blood pressure) or transient or persistent hypertension (high blood pressure).

D. Blood Flow Through Body Tissues: Tissue Perfusion (pp. 733–742; Figs. 19.12–19.17)

1. Tissue perfusion is involved in delivery of oxygen and nutrients to, and removal of wastes from, tissue cells; gas exchange in the lungs; absorption of nutrients from the digestive tract; and urine formation in the kidneys.

2. Velocity or speed of blood flow changes as it passes through the systemic circulation; it is fastest in the aorta, and declines in velocity as vessel diameter decreases.

3. Autoregulation: Local Regulation of Blood Flow

a. Autoregulation is the automatic adjustment of blood flow to each tissue in proportion to its needs, and is controlled intrinsically by modifying the diameter of local arterioles.

b. Metabolic controls of autoregulation are most strongly stimulated by a shortage of oxygen at the tissues.

c. Myogenic control involves the localized response of vascular smooth muscle to passive stretch.

d. Long-term autoregulation develops over weeks or months, and involves an increase in the size of existing blood vessels and an increase in the number of vessels in a specific area, a process called angiogenesis.

4. Blood Flow in Special Areas

a. Blood flow to skeletal muscles varies with level of activity and fiber type.

b. Muscular autoregulation occurs almost entirely in response to decreased oxygen concentrations.

c. Cerebral blood flow is tightly regulated to meet neuronal needs, since neurons cannot tolerate periods of ischemia, and increased blood carbon dioxide causes marked vasodilation.

d. In the skin, local autoregulatory events control oxygen and nutrient delivery to the cells, while neural mechanisms control the body temperature regulation function.

     e. Autoregulatory controls of blood flow to the lungs are the opposite of what happens in most tissues: low pulmonary oxygen causes vasoconstriction, while higher oxygen causes vasodilation.

     f. Movement of blood through the coronary circulation of the heart is influenced by aortic pressure and the pumping of the ventricles.

  5. Blood Flow Through Capillaries and Capillary Dynamics

     a. Vasomotion, the slow, intermittent flow of blood through the capillaries, reflects the action of the precapillary sphincters in response to local autoregulatory controls.

     b. Capillary exchange of nutrients, gases, and metabolic wastes occurs between the blood and interstitial space through diffusion.

     c. Hydrostatic pressure (HP) is the force of a fluid against a membrane.

     d. Colloid osmotic pressure (OP), the force opposing hydrostatic pressure, is created by the presence of large, nondiffusible molecules that are prevented from moving through the capillary membrane.

     e. Fluids will leave the capillaries if net HP exceeds net OP, but fluids will enter the capillaries if net OP exceeds net HP.

  6. Circulatory shock is any condition in which blood volume is inadequate and cannot circulate normally, resulting in blood flow that cannot meet the needs of a tissue.

     a. Hypovolemic shock results from a large-scale loss of blood, and may be characterized by an elevated heart rate and intense vasoconstriction.

     b. Vascular shock is characterized by a normal blood volume, but extreme vasodilation, often related to a loss of vasomotor tone, resulting in poor circulation and a rapid drop in blood pressure.

     c. Transient vascular shock is due to prolonged exposure to heat, such as while sunbathing, resulting in vasodilation of cutaneous blood vessels.

     d. Cardiogenic shock occurs when the heart is too inefficient to sustain normal blood flow, and is usually related to myocardial damage, such as repeated myocardial infarcts.

III. Part 3: Circulatory Pathways: Blood Vessels of the Body (pp. 742–743; Figs. 19.18–19.29; Tables 19.3–19.13)

  A. Two distinct pathways travel to and from the heart: pulmonary circulation runs from the heart to the lungs and back to the heart; systemic circulation runs to all parts of the body before returning to the heart. (pp. 742–743; Figs. 19.18–19.20; Tables 19.3–19.4)

  B. There are some important differences between arteries and veins.

    1. There is one terminal systemic artery, the aorta, but two terminal systemic veins: the superior and inferior vena cava.

    2. Arteries run deep and are well protected, but veins are both deep, which run parallel to the arteries, and superficial, which run just beneath the skin.

    3. Arterial pathways tend to be clear, but there are often many interconnections in venous pathways, making them difficult to follow.

    4. There are at least two areas where venous drainage does not parallel the arterial supply: the dural sinuses draining the brain, and the hepatic portal system draining from the digestive organs to the liver before entering the main systemic circulation.

C. Four paired arteries supply the head and neck. (pp. 748–749; Fig. 19.21; Table 19.5)

D. The upper limbs are supplied entirely by arteries arising from the subclavian arteries. (pp. 750–751; Fig. 19.22; Table 19.6)

E. The arterial supply to the abdomen arises from the aorta. (pp. 752–755; Fig. 19.23; Table 19.7)

F. The internal iliac arteries serve mostly the pelvic region; the external iliacs supply blood to the lower limb and abdominal wall. (pp. 756–757; Fig. 19.24; Table 19.8)

G. The venae cavae are the major tributaries of the venous circulation. (pp. 758–759; Fig. 19.25; Table 19.9)

H. Blood drained from the head and neck is collected by three pairs of veins. (pp. 760–761; Fig. 19.26; Table 19.10)

I. The deep veins of the upper limbs follow the paths of the companion arteries. (pp. 762–763; Fig. 19.27; Table 19.11)

J. Blood draining from the abdominopelvic viscera and abdominal walls is returned to the heart by the inferior vena cava. (pp. 764–765; Fig. 19.28; Table 19.12)

K. Most deep veins of the lower limb have the same names as the arteries they accompany. (p. 766; Fig. 19.29; Table 19.13)

IV. Developmental Aspects of the Blood Vessels (p. 743)

A. The vascular endothelium is formed by mesodermal cells that collect throughout the embryo in blood islands, which give rise to extensions that form rudimentary vascular tubes.

B. By the fourth week of development, the rudimentary heart and vessels are circulating blood.

C. Fetal vascular modifications include shunts to bypass fetal lungs (the foramen ovale and ductus arteriosus), the ductus venosus that bypasses the liver, and the umbilical arteries and veins, which carry blood to and from the placenta.

D. At birth, the fetal shunts and bypasses close and become occluded.

E. Congenital vascular problems are rare, but the incidence of vascular disease increases with age, leading to varicose veins, tingling in fingers and toes, and muscle cramping.

F. Atherosclerosis begins in youth, but rarely causes problems until old age.

G. Blood pressure changes with age: the arterial pressure of infants is about 90/55, but rises steadily during childhood to an average 120/80, and finally increases to 150/90 in old age.

Cross References

Additional information on topics covered in Chapter 19 can be found in the chapters listed below.

1. Chapter 3: Tight junctions; diffusion; osmosis
2. Chapter 4: Simple squamous epithelium; dense connective tissue; elastic connective tissue
3. Chapter 9: Smooth muscle
4. Chapter 12: Blood-brain barrier; medulla; hypothalamus
5. Chapter 13: Sensory receptors

6. Chapter 14: Sympathetic control; epinephrine and norepinephrine
7. Chapter 16: Atrial natriuretic factor
8. Chapter 17: Blood characteristics
9. Chapter 18: Cardiac output; cardioinhibitory and cardioacceleratory centers
10. Chapter 20: Relationship between blood capillaries and lymphatic capillaries; factors affecting fluid movement through capillary membranes; factors that aid venous return are the same as factors that aid lymph return
11. Chapter 23: Splanchnic circulation
12. Chapter 24: Blood flow regulation in the control of body temperature
13. Chapter 25: Antidiuretic hormone and aldosterone function in blood pressure control; effect of alcohol on antidiuretic hormone (and therefore blood pressure); function of fenestrated capillaries and arterioles in glomerular filtration; example of vascular resistance and autoregulation of blood flow; specific body example of capillary dynamics (filtration); renin-angiotensin mechanism
14. Chapter 26: Edema; renal mechanism of electrolyte balance
15. Chapter 28: Varicose veins and effects on the pregnant mother

Laboratory Correlations

1. Marieb, E. N. *Human Anatomy & Physiology Laboratory Manual: Cat and Fetal Pig Versions.* Eighth Edition Updates. Benjamin Cummings, 2006.
   Exercise 32: Anatomy of Blood Vessels
   Exercise 33: Human Cardiovascular Physiology
   Exercise 34: Frog Cardiovascular Physiology
2. Marieb, E. N. *Human Anatomy & Physiology Laboratory Manual: Main Version.* Seventh Edition Update. Benjamin Cummings, 2006.
   Exercise 32: Anatomy of Blood Vessels
   Exercise 33: Human Cardiovascular Physiology
   Exercise 34: Frog Cardiovascular Physiology

Histology Slides for the Life Sciences

Available through Benjamin Cummings, an imprint of Pearson Education, Inc. To order, contact your local Benjamin Cummings sales representative.

Slide 87   Artery and Vein, In Muscle.
Slide 88   Artery and Vein, In Mesentery.

Lecture Hints

1. Emphasize the smooth transition in wall structure from artery, to arteriole, to capillary, to venule, to vein.
2. Rather than strictly lecturing about muscular and elastic arteries, capillaries, etc., try giving basic wall structure and ask the class what the logical functions of these vessels could be, given their construction.
3. Stress the differences in permeability between capillary types, and the specific functions these different types are designed to perform.
4. When discussing blood flow, introduce each factor (pressure, resistance, etc.), then relate all together logically so that students can see the dynamic nature of blood transport. Students often treat the vascular system as being a rigid set of tubes.

5. Spend some time with a series of diagrams depicting the muscular pump as a factor aiding venous return. Students are often confused as to how this mechanism works.

6. Work through the respiratory factor aiding venous return in conjunction with the split of the second heart sound. Students will grasp the concept more easily if the two ideas are related together.

7. Emphasize the importance of vasomotor tone. Students should be made aware that if the arteries were not in a constant state of partial contraction (during normal activity), there would be no mechanism to allow for vasodilation.

8. Since hypertension and its risks are of interest to most individuals, use a discussion of this topic to bring together important concepts regarding cardiac and vascular function, and mechanisms of blood pressure control.

9. Students often have difficulty with the idea that capillaries have more total cross-sectional area than arteries. It often helps to diagram a single artery about 5 mm in diameter and 10–20 capillaries about 1 mm in diameter to show the relationship between total area and the total number of vessels.

10. A discussion of the pulmonary circulation is a good place to recall the relative size of the left and right heart. Point out the short-distance, low-pressure route from right ventricle to left atrium.

11. It is difficult for some students to recognize that coronary circulation is highest when cardiac muscle is in diastole. Emphasize the elastic recoil of the aorta as the driving force—that is, the aorta stores the force of ventricular contraction in its elastic connective tissue.

12. A thorough understanding of fluid movement at the capillary level is crucial for a complete understanding of how other systems function. Refer students to Chapter 3 for a review on osmosis and emphasize that this topic will be seen again in future systems.

13. Emphasize that arteries always carry blood away from the heart and veins always return blood to the heart.

14. The function of the cardiovascular system is simple to master if schematic diagrams are used. Test student knowledge by asking what possible consequences are likely if partial blockages occur in different parts of the system. Students should be able to describe reduced blood flow to the systemic circulation, LV hypertrophy and eventual failure, bicuspid failure, pulmonary edema, eventual venous congestion, etc. This is an excellent exercise in demonstrating the circular nature of this closed system, and that effects at one point in the system are likely to go full circle if not checked.

Activities/Demonstrations

1. Audio-visual materials listed under Multimedia in the Classroom and Lab.

2. Demonstrate the auscultatory method of determining arterial blood pressure, and provide the necessary equipment (sphygmomanometers and stethoscopes) so that students can practice on each other.

3. Use a model of human vasculature or an unlabeled acetate and ask students to call out the names of the vessels indicated.

4. Use a torso model, circulatory system model, and/or dissected animal model to exhibit major circulatory pathways.

5. Use a short piece of soaker hose to illustrate a capillary as the functional unit of the circulatory system.

6. Use a long, not completely blown up, balloon to illustrate the effect of altering pressure in a closed system.

Critical Thinking/Discussion Topics

1. Discuss the need for blood pressure monitoring in regard to hyper- or hypotension.
2. Examine the significance of proper diet in maintaining normal blood flow.
3. Discuss why some coronary bypass surgeries have to be repeated.
4. Explain how an artery loses its elasticity.
5. In terms of the mechanics of blood flow, discuss why a pulse is evident on the arterial side but not the venous side of circulation.
6. Describe the factors that retard venous return.
7. Explain why water and dissolved solutes leave the bloodstream at the arteriole end of the capillary bed and enter the bloodstream at the venous end.
8. Discuss why the elasticity of the large arteries is so important (or why arteriosclerosis is such a threat).

Library Research Topics

1. Research the role of diet in the clearance or obstruction of blood vessels.
2. Study the possible congenital defects of circulation resulting from the differences in the fetal and adult circulation.
3. Investigate the effect of untreated hypertension on kidney function.
4. Research the procedures and types of valves currently used in valve replacement surgery.
5. Explore the various types of heart blockages and their significance.
6. Examine the risk factors implicated in heart disease and what can be done to minimize the risk.

Multimedia in the Classroom and Lab

Online Resources for Students

The
Anatomy & Physiology Place
www.anatomyandphysiology.com

MyA&P
www.myaandp.com

The following shows the organization of the Chapter Guide page in both the Anatomy & Physiology Place and MyA&P™. The Chapter Guide organizes all the chapter-specific online media resources for Chapter 19 in one convenient location, with e-book links to each section of the textbook. Please note that both sites also give you access to other general A&P resources, like InterActive Physiology®, PhysioEx 6.0™, Anatomy 360°, Flashcards, a Glossary, a Histology Tutorial, and much more.

Objectives

PART ONE: OVERVIEW OF BLOOD VESSEL STRUCTURE AND FUNCTION (PP. 714–723)

InterActive Physiology®: Anatomy Review: Blood Vessel Structure and Function
Memory: Arteries and Veins

PART TWO: PHYSIOLOGY OF CIRCULATION (PP. 723–742)

InterActive Physiology®: Measuring Blood Pressure
InterActive Physiology®: Factors that Affect Blood Pressure
InterActive Physiology®: Blood Pressure Regulation
InterActive Physiology®: Autoregulation and Capillary Dynamics
PhysioEx: Cardiovascular Dynamics

Case Study: Septic Shock

PART THREE: CIRCULATORY PATHWAYS: BLOOD VESSELS OF THE BODY (PP. 744–766)

Art Labeling Activity: Major Systemic Arteries (Fig. 19.20b, p. 747)

Art Labeling Activity: Arteries of the Abdomen (Fig. 19.23b, p. 753)

Art Labeling Activity: Major Systemic Veins (Fig. 19.25b, p. 759)

Chapter Summary

Self-Study Quizzes

Art Labeling Quiz

Matching Quiz

Multiple-Choice Quiz (Level I)

Multiple-Choice Quiz (Level II)

True-False Quiz

Crossword Puzzles

Crossword Puzzle 19.1

Crossword Puzzle 19.2

Media

See Guide to Audio-Visual Resources in Appendix A for key to AV distributors.

Video

1. *Circulation* (IM; 20 min., 1994). Examines the detailed workings of the heart and compares the various functions of the arteries, veins, and capillaries that make up the body's intricate network of blood vessels.

2. *The Circulatory System* (IM; 23 min., 1997). This video examines the workings of the heart, blood, and blood vessels. It shows how the heart pumps blood throughout the veins and arteries, nourishing and cleansing the body.

3. *Life Under Pressure* (FHS; 26 min., 1984). This program follows the journey of a red blood cell around the circulatory system to demonstrate the efficient and elegant design of oxygen and food delivery to all parts of the body. It shows how veins and arteries are structured to perform their tasks.

4. *Pumping Life—The Heart and Circulatory System* (WNS; 20 min.). Explains the structure and function of the heart. Uses animation and live action. Discusses heart problems and the importance of preventive maintenance.

5. *William Harvey and the Circulation of Blood* (FHS; 29 min.). This program provides an introduction to the life and work of William Harvey, the English physician and physiologist who discovered the circulation of blood in the human body in 1628. The program describes the way in which Harvey formulated his revolutionary new theories of cardiac action and of the motion of the blood through the heart, arteries, and veins.

Software

1. *A.D.A.M.® InterActive Anatomy® 4.0* (see p. 9 of this guide for full listing).

2. *A.D.A.M.® MediaPro* (see p. 9 of this guide for full listing).

3. *A.D.A.M.® Anatomy Practice* (see p. 86 of this guide for full listing).

4. *Bodyworks* (see p. 9 of this guide for full listing).

5. *DynaPulse™ 200 M* (WNS; Windows). Details cardiovascular function by combining medical instrumentation with colorful, interactive software and graphics. Features clinical-grade systolic, diastolic, MAP, and heart rate measurements. An excellent hands-on tool that students can use to study cardiovascular function.

6. *LOGAL Explorer™: Cardiovascular System™ CD-ROM* (see p. 218 of this guide for full listing).

7. *InterActive Physiology® 9-System Suite CD-ROM: Cardiovascular System* (BC; Win/Mac). Presents topics related to heart and blood vessel physiology, such as blood pressure, cardiac output, intrinsic conduction system, cardiac action potential, and cardiac cycle.

8. *The Ultimate Human Body* (see p. 9 of this guide for full listing).

9. *WARD'S Blood Physiology and the Circulatory System CD-ROM* (WNS; Win/Mac). Learn about the components of blood, as well as the inner workings of the human heart. Comprehensive simulations of clinical techniques such as hematocrit counts, taking blood pressure, and more.

Lecture Enhancement Material

To view thumbnails of all of the illustrations for Chapter 19, see Appendix B.

Transparencies Index/Media Manager

Figure 19.1	Generalized structure of arteries, veins, and capillaries.
Figure 19.2	Overview of vascular components and blood distribution.
Figure 19.3	Capillary structure.
Figure 19.4	Anatomy of a capillary bed.
Figure 19.5	Blood pressure in various blood vessels of the systemic circulation.
Figure 19.6	The muscular pump.
Figure 19.7	Major factors enhancing cardiac output.
Figure 19.8	Baroreceptor reflexes that help maintain blood pressure homeostasis.
Figure 19.9	Direct and indirect (hormonal) mechanisms for renal control of blood pressure.
Figure 19.10	Factors causing an increase in MAP.
Figure 19.11	Body sites where the pulse is most easily palpated.
Figure 19.12	Distribution of blood flow at rest and during strenuous exercise.
Figure 19.13	Relationship between blood flow velocity and total cross-sectional area in various blood vessels of the systemic circulation.
Figure 19.14	Summary of control of arteriolar smooth muscle in the systemic circulation.
Figure 19.15	Capillary transport mechanisms.
Figure 19.16	Fluid flows at capillaries.
Figure 19.17	Events and signs of compensated (nonprogressive) hypovolemic shock.
Figure 19.18	Pulmonary circulation.
Figure 19.19	Schematic flowchart showing an overview of the systemic circulation.
Figure 19.20	Major arteries of the systemic circulation.
Figure 19.21	Arteries of the head, neck, and brain.
Figure 19.22	Arteries of the right upper limb and thorax.
Figure 19.23	Arteries of the abdomen.
Figure 19.24	Arteries of the right pelvis and lower limb.
Figure 19.25	Major veins of the systemic circulation.
Figure 19.26	Venous drainage of the head, neck, and brain.
Figure 19.27	Veins of the right upper limb and shoulder.
Figure 19.28	Veins of the abdomen.

Answers to End-of-Chapter Questions

Multiple Choice and Matching Question answers appear in Appendix G of the main text.

Short Answer Essay Questions

16. Capillary anatomy is suited to the exchange of material between blood and interstitial fluid because its walls are very thin and devoid of muscle and connective tissue. (p. 720)

17. Elastic arteries are the large, thick-walled arteries close to the heart. They have generous amounts of elastic tissue in all tunics, but especially in the tunica media. This elastic tissue enables them to withstand large pressure fluctuations by expanding when the heart contracts, forcing blood into them. They recoil as blood flows forward into the circulation during heart relaxation. They also contain substantial amounts of smooth muscle but are relatively inactive in vasoconstriction. (p. 716)

    Muscular arteries are medium- and smaller-sized arteries, farther along in the circulatory pathway, that carry blood to specific body organs. Their tunica media contains proportionately more smooth muscle and less elastic tissue than that of elastic arteries, but they typically have an elastic lamina on each face of the media. They are more active in vasoconstriction and are less distensible. (pp. 716–717)

    Arterioles are the smallest of the arterial vessels. The smallest—terminal arterioles—feed directly into the capillary beds. The larger arterioles exhibit all three tunics and their tunica media is chiefly smooth muscle with a few scattered elastic fibers. The walls of the smaller arterioles are little more than smooth muscle cells that coil around the tunica intima lining. When arterioles constrict, the tissues served are largely bypassed; when the arterioles dilate, blood flow into the local capillaries increases dramatically. (p. 717)

18. The equation showing the relationship between peripheral resistance, blood flow, and blood pressure is as follows: blood flow equals a change in blood pressure between two points in the circulation divided by the resistance. (p. 724)

19. a. Blood pressure is the force per unit area exerted on the wall of a blood vessel by its contained blood. Systolic pressure is the pressure that occurs during systole when the aortic pressure reaches its peak. Diastolic pressure is the pressure that occurs during diastole when aortic pressure drops to its lowest level. (pp. 724–725)

    b. The normal blood pressure for a young adult is between 110 and 140 mm Hg systolic and between 75 and 80 mm Hg diastolic. (p. 725)

20. The neural controls responsible for controlling blood pressure operate via reflex arcs chiefly involving the following components: baroreceptors and the associated afferent fibers, the vasomotor center of the medulla, vasomotor (efferent) fibers, and vascular smooth muscle. The neural controls are directed primarily at maintaining adequate systemic blood pressure and altering blood distribution to achieve specific functions. (pp. 727–729)

21. Changes in the velocity in different regions of the circulation reflect the cross-sectional area of the vascular tubes to be filled. Since the cross-sectional area is least in the aorta and greatest in the capillaries, the blood flow is fastest in the aorta and slowest in the capillaries. (p. 734)

22. Nutrient blood flow to the skin is controlled by autoregulation in response to the need for oxygen; whereas blood flow for regulating body temperature is controlled by neural intervention, i.e., the sympathetic nervous system. (pp. 737–738)

23. When one is fleeing from a mugger, blood flow is diverted to skeletal muscles from other body systems not in direct need of large volumes of blood. Blood flow increases in response to acetylcholine release by sympathetic vasodilator fibers and/or epinephrine binding to beta receptors of vascular smooth muscles in the skeletal muscles, and virtually all capillaries open to accommodate the increased flow. Systemic adjustments, mediated by the sympathetic vasomotor center, occur to ensure that increased blood volume reaches the muscles. Strong vasoconstriction of the digestive viscera diverts blood away from those regions temporarily, ensuring that an increased blood supply reaches the muscles. Blood-borne epinephrine enhances blood glucose levels, alertness, and metabolic rate. The major factor determining how long muscles can continue vigorous activity is the ability of the cardiovascular system to deliver adequate oxygen and nutrients. (p. 737)

24. Nutrients, wastes, and respiratory gases are transported to and from the blood and tissue spaces by diffusion. (pp. 738–739)

25. a. The veins draining the digestive viscera contribute to the formation of the hepatic portal circulation. The most important of these are the superior and inferior mesenteric veins and the splenic veins.

    b. The function of the hepatic portal circulation is to deliver blood laden with nutrients from the digestive organs to the liver.

    c. The portal circulation is a "strange" circulation because it consists of veins draining into capillaries which drain into veins again. (pp. 764–765)

26. a. The text states that postcapillary venules function "more like capillaries" (p. 722), meaning that exchanges of small molecules between the blood and the surrounding tissue fluid occur across these venules. Furthermore, inflammatory fluid and leukocytes leave the postcapillary venules just as they exit the capillaries.

    b. Whereas capillaries consist only of an endothelium, postcapillary venules have scattered fibroblasts on their endothelium layer.

Critical Thinking and Clinical Application Questions

1. The compensatory mechanisms of Mrs. Johnson induce an increase in heart rate and an intense vasoconstriction, which allows blood in various blood reservoirs to be rapidly added to the major circulatory channels. (pp. 735–736)

2. If the sympathetic nerves are severed, vasoconstriction in the area will be reduced and vasodilation will occur. Therefore, blood flow to the area will be enhanced. (p. 714)

3. An aneurysm is a balloonlike outpocketing of a blood vessel that places the vessel at risk for rupture. In this case, the aneurysm was so large that it was pressing on the brain stem and cranial nerves, threatening to interfere with the functions of these structures. The surgeons removed the ballooned section of the artery and sewed a section of strong tubing in its place. (p. 767)

4. Harry's condition suggests that this is a case of transient vascular shock. Marching in the severe heat of the day caused the cutaneous blood vessels to dilate, which resulted in an increased blood volume pooling in the lower limbs (because of gravity). A subsequent decrease in blood flow to the heart caused Harry's blood pressure to drop, and his dizziness and fainting was an indication that the brain was not receiving enough blood flow (hence, oxygen). (pp. 740–742)

5. Blood distribution is adjusted by a short-term neural control mechanism to meet specific demands. During exercise, blood is shunted temporarily from the digestive organs to the skeletal muscles in order to enhance heat loss from the body. (p. 737)

6. (1) Mrs. Taylor's liver is no longer producing enough plasma proteins to maintain adequate colloid osmotic pressure in the blood vessels. (p. 739)

   (2) The capillary hydrostatic pressure would be increased causing more fluid to flow out of the capillaries. (p. 739)

   (3) The interstitial fluid hydrostatic pressure would be increased due to the increase in plasma proteins. This would cause more fluid to flow out from the capillaries. (p. 739)

   (4) The lymphatic vessels can no longer drain the right arm so fluid pools in the arm causing swelling. The compression sleeve would increase the interstitial fluid hydrostatic pressure and would decrease the amount of fluid leaking from the capillaries in the right arm. (p. 739)

Suggested Readings

Carmeliet, Peter. "Creating Unique Blood Vessels." *Nature* 412 (6850) (Aug. 2001): 868–869.

Christensen, Damaris. "Things Just Mesh: Making Stents Even Better at Keeping Arteries Open." *Science News* 160 (21) (Nov. 2001): 328–330.

Corder, R. et al. "Endothelin-1 Synthesis Reduced by Red Wine." *Nature* 414 (6866) (Dec. 2001): 863.

Gross, Steven S. "Targeted Delivery of Nitric Oxide." *Nature* 409 (6820) (Feb. 2001): 577–578.

Harder, B. "Even High-Normal Blood Pressure is Too High." *Science News* 160 (18) (Nov. 2001): 277.

LeCouter, J. et al. "Identification of an Angiogenic Mitogen Selective for Endocrine Gland Endothelium." *Nature* 412 (6850) (Aug. 2001): 877–884.

Marx, Jean. "Possible New Path for Blood Pressure Control." *Science* 293 (5532) (Aug. 2001): 1030.

Miller, Greg. "Nerves Tell Arteries to Make Like a Tree." *Science* 296 (5571) (June 2002): 2121.

Schubert, C. "Vitamin A Calibrates a Heart Clock, 24-7." *Science* News 160 (2) (July 2001): 22.

Seydel, Caroline. "Organs Await Blood Vessels' Go Signal." *Science* 293 (5539) (Sept. 2001): 2365.

Swain, David P. "The Water-Tower Analogy of the Cardiovascular System." *Advances in Physiology Education* 24 (1) (Dec. 2000): 43–50.

Taubes, Gary. "Does Inflammation Cut to the Heart of the Matter?" *Science* 296 (5566) (April 2002): 242–245.

Travis, J. "Blood Vessels (Sans Blood) Shape Organs." *Science News* 160 (13) (Sept. 2001): 198.

Wang, L. "Radiation Therapy Keeps Arteries Clear." *Science News* 159 (4) (Jan. 2001): 184.

Zhu, Yan et al. "Abnormal Vascular Function and Hypertension in Mice Deficient in Estrogen Receptor Beta." *Science* 295 (5554) (Jan. 2002): 505–508.

20 The Lymphatic System

Objectives

Lymphatic Vessels

1. Describe the function of the lymphatic system.
2. Explain the structure, distribution, and adaptations of the lymph vessels.

Lymphoid Cells and Tissues

3. Identify the different types of lymphoid cells found in the body.
4. Describe lymphoid tissue.

Lymph Nodes

5. Examine the structure and function of the lymph nodes.

Other Lymphoid Organs

6. List the additional lymphoid organs and explain their structure and function.

Developmental Aspects of the Lymphatic System

7. Trace the development of the lymphatic system in the developing fetus, and indicate the structures that are fully formed and functional at birth.

Suggested Lecture Outline

I. Lymphatic Vessels (pp. 774–777; Figs. 20.1–20.2)

A. The lymphatic vessels form a one-way system in which lymph flows only toward the heart.

1. The lymphatic transport system starts with the lymph capillaries, found between the tissue cells and blood capillaries, in the loose connective tissue.
2. The lymph capillaries flow into the lymphatic collecting vessels and carry the lymph to the lymphatic trunks.
3. The lymphatic trunks drain fairly large areas of the body and eventually empty the lymph back into the circulatory system via the thoracic duct or the right lymphatic duct.

B Lymphatic vessels are low-pressure vessels that use the same mechanisms as veins to return the lymph to the circulatory system.

II. Lymphoid Cells and Tissues (p. 777; Fig. 20.3)

A. Lymphoid Cells

1. Lymphocytes arise in the red bone marrow and mature into one of two immunocompetent cells: T lymphocytes (T cells) or B lymphocytes (B cells).

2. Macrophages play an important role in body protection and in activating T lymphocytes.

3. Dendritic cells, found in lymphoid tissue, also play a role in T lymphocyte activation.

4. Reticular cells produce the stroma, which is the network that supports the other cell types in the lymphoid tissue.

B. Lymphoid tissues house and provide a proliferation site for lymphocytes, and furnish an ideal surveillance site for lymphocytes and macrophages.

III. Lymph Nodes (pp. 778–779; Fig. 20.4)

A. The principle lymphoid organs in the body are the lymph nodes, which act as filters to remove and destroy microorganisms and other debris for the lymph before it is transported back to the bloodstream.

B. Each lymph node is surrounded by a dense fibrous capsule with an internal framework, or stroma, of reticular fibers that supports the lymphocytes.

C. Lymph enters the convex side of a lymph node through afferent lymphatic vessels, and exists via a fewer number of efferent vessels after passing through several sinuses.

IV. Other Lymphoid Organs (pp. 779–782; Figs. 20.5–20.9)

A. The spleen is the largest lymphoid organ, located in the left side of the abdominal cavity directly below the diaphragm.

1. The spleen's main function is to remove old and defective RBCs and platelets as well as foreign matter and debris from the blood. It also provides a site for lymphocyte proliferation and immune surveillance.

2. The spleen is surrounded by a fibrous capsule and contains both lymphocytes found in white pulp, and macrophages found in red pulp.

B. Thymus

1. The thymus secretes hormones that cause T lymphocytes to become immunocompetent.

2. The thymus is made up of thymic lobules containing an outer cortex and an inner medulla.

C. Tonsils are the simplest lymphoid organs and form a ring of lymphoid tissue around the opening to the pharynx. They appear as swellings of the mucosa that gather and remove many of the pathogens entering the pharynx in food or inhaled air.

D. Clusters of lymphoid follicles are found in the wall of the distal portion of the small intestine, Peyer's patches, and in the appendix.

V. Developmental Aspects of the Lymphatic System (p. 783)

A. By the fifth week of embryonic development, the beginnings of the lymphatic vessels and the main clusters of lymph nodes are apparent and develop from the budding of lymph sacs from the developing veins.

B. The thymus is an endodermal derivative, while the rest of the lymphoid organs derive from the mesoderm.

C. Except for the spleen and the tonsils, the lymphoid organs are poorly developed at birth.

Cross References

Additional information on topics covered in Chapter 20 can be found in the chapters listed below.

1. Chapter 3: Interstitial fluid
2. Chapter 4: Reticular connective tissue
3. Chapter 16: Thymus gland and hormone production
4. Chapter 17: Agranulocytes; granulocytes; leukocyte production and life span
5. Chapter 19: Blood capillaries; hydrostatic and osmotic pressure related to fluid movement; factors that aid venous return
6. Chapter 21: Function of lymphatic organs in immunity; relationship of the thymus to cell-mediated immunity
7. Chapter 22: Tonsils
8. Chapter 23: Lacteal function; palatine tonsils; lymphatic tissue related to the digestive system (Peyer's patches)

Histology Slides for the Life Sciences

Available through Benjamin Cummings, an imprint of Pearson Education, Inc. To order, contact your local Benjamin Cummings sales representative.

Slide 89   Thymic Corpuscles.
Slide 90   Thymus, Young Individual.
Slide 91   Spleen.
Slide 93   Lymph Node.
Slide 94   Lymph Node and Lymph Vessel.

Lecture Hints

1. Emphasize the difference between lymphatic capillaries and blood capillaries. Students often raise the question: "Since both are capillaries, why does interstitial fluid flow from blood capillary to lymphatic capillary?"
2. Point out that the same factors that help venous return also aid lymph movement. Since both are structurally similar, and follow the same general pathways, logic dictates that factors affecting fluid movements should also be similar.
3. Mention that bubos (inflamed lymph nodes) are the "swollen glands" seen in infectious processes.
4. Point out that the structure and locations of lymph nodes are ideal for filtering the interstitial fluid (containing tissue proteins, metabolic wastes, and pathogenic microorganisms) flushed from tissue spaces.

Activities/Demonstrations

1. Audio-visual materials listed under Multimedia in the Classroom and Lab.
2. Use a torso model and/or dissected animal model to exhibit lymph organs.
3. Use a visual aid that shows a person with elephantiasis to illustrate the edema that results from obstruction of the lymphatic vessels.
4. Survey the class to determine how many students have had their palatine tonsils removed. Explain that in the 1950s, tonsillectomy was a routine operation, and almost 100% of the children in North America had their tonsils taken out. In the 1960s, this operation was recognized to be largely unnecessary.

Critical Thinking/Discussion Topics

1. Explain why and how lymphedema occurs after a modified radical mastectomy or other such surgery.
2. Indicate the reason why a physician checks for swollen lymph nodes in the neck when examining a patient who shows respiratory symptoms.
3. Examine the ramifications of spleen removal.
4. Explore the ramifications of tonsillar tissue removal.
5. Describe, briefly, the role of the thymus gland in the body's immune response.

Library Research Topics

1. Research the causes, effects, and treatment of lymphedema.
2. Study the differences between lymph nodes swollen due to disease, such as a viral infection, and those swollen due to cancer.
3. Research the changes that appear in the thymus gland with age and relate those changes to the body's immune response.

Multimedia in the Classroom and Lab

Online Resources for Students

The
Anatomy & Physiology Place
www.anatomyandphysiology.com

MyA&P
www.myaandp.com

The following shows the organization of the Chapter Guide page in both the Anatomy & Physiology Place and MyA&P™. The Chapter Guide organizes all the chapter-specific online media resources for Chapter 20 in one convenient location, with e-book links to each section of the textbook. Please note that both sites also give you access to other general A&P resources, like InterActive Physiology®, PhysioEx 6.0™, Anatomy 360°, *Flashcards, a Glossary, a Histology Tutorial, and much more.*

Objectives
Section 20.1 Lymphatic Vessels (pp. 774–777)
Art Labeling Activity: Regional Lymph Nodes (Fig. 20.2, p. 776)
Section 20.2 Lymphoid Cells and Tissues (p. 777)
Section 20.3 Lymph Nodes (pp. 778–779)
Art Labeling Activity: Lymph Node (Fig. 20.4, p. 778)
Section 20.4 Other Lymphoid Organs (pp. 779–782)
Art Labeling Activity: Lymphoid Organs (Fig. 20.5, p. 779)
Memory: The Immune System
Memory: Important Components of the Immune System
Section 20.5 Developmental Aspects of the Lymphatic System (p. 783)
Case Study: Genetic Immunodeficiency
Chapter Summary
Self-Study Quizzes
Art Labeling Quiz
Matching Quiz
Multiple-Choice Quiz (Level I)

Multiple-Choice Quiz (Level II)

True-False Quiz

Crossword Puzzles

Crossword Puzzle 20.1

Crossword Puzzle 20.2

Media

See Guide to Audio-Visual Resources in Appendix A for key to AV distributors.

Video

1. *Internal Defenses* (FHS; 26 min.). From *The Living Body* series, this program deals with events when the body is under attack. It shows the roles of the spleen, the lymphatic system and the WBCs, and explains the body's production of antibodies.
2. *Organ Systems Working Together Video* (WNS; 14 min.). Presents a view of the body's systems and how they work together. The program proceeds through each of the body's systems, including the lymphatic system. Introduces the student to the functions of the human body.

Software

1. *A.D.A.M.® InterActive Anatomy® 4.0* (see p. 9 of this guide for full listing).
2. *A.D.A.M.® MediaPro* (see p. 9 of this guide for full listing).
3. *A.D.A.M.® Anatomy Practice* (see p. 86 of this guide for full listing).
4. *Bodyworks* (see p. 9 of this guide for full listing).
5. *The Ultimate Human Body* (see p. 9 of this guide for full listing).

Lecture Enhancement Material

To view thumbnails of all of the illustrations for Chapter 20, see Appendix B.

Transparencies Index/Media Manager

Figure 20.1   Distribution and special structural features of lymphatic capillaries.

Figure 20.2   The lymphatic system.

Figure 20.3   Reticular tissue in a human lymph node.

Figure 20.4   Lymph node.

Figure 20.5   Lymphoid organs.

Figure 20.6   The spleen.

Figure 20.7   The thymus.

Figure 20.8   Histology of the palatine tonsil.

Figure 20.9   Peyer's patches.

Answers to End-of-Chapter Questions

Multiple Choice and Matching Question answers appear in Appendix G of the main text.

Short Answer Essay Questions

10. Blood, the carrier of nutrients, wastes, and gases, circulates within blood vessels through the body, exchanging materials with the interstitial fluid. Interstitial fluid, formed by filtration from blood, is the fluid surrounding body cells in the tissue spaces and is essential to proteinless plasma. Lymph is the protein-containing fluid

that enters the lymphatic capillaries (from the tissue spaces); hence, its composition is the same as that of the interstitial fluid. (p. 774)

11. Lymph nodes are very small bean-shaped structures consisting of both a medulla and cortex, which act as filters to cleanse lymph before it is allowed to reenter the blood. Each node is surrounded by a dense fibrous capsule from which connective tissue strands called trabeculae extend inward to divide the node into a number of compartments. The basic internal framework or stroma is an open network of reticular fibers that physically support lymphocytes and macrophages. The outer cortex contains densely packed spherical collections of lymphocytes called follicles, which frequently have lighter-staining centers called germinal centers. Cordlike extensions of the cortex, called medullary cords, invade the medulla. Macrophages are located throughout the node but are particularly abundant lining the sinuses of the medulla. (pp. 778–779)

The spleen is the largest lymphoid organ. It functions to remove aged or defective blood cells, platelets, and pathogens from the blood and to store some of the breakdown products of RBCs or release them to the blood for processing by the liver. The spleen is surrounded by a fibrous capsule, and has trabeculae. It contains lymphocytes, macrophages, and huge numbers of erythrocytes. Venous sinuses and other regions that contain red blood cells and macrophages and process blood are referred to as red pulp, whereas areas composed mostly of lymphocytes suspended on reticular fibers are called white pulp. The white pulp clusters around small branches of the splenic artery within the organ and serves the immune functions of the organ. (pp. 779–780)

12. a. The anatomical characteristic that ensures slow passage of lymph through a lymph node is the fact that there are fewer efferent vessels draining the node than afferent vessels feeding it. (pp. 778–779)

b. This feature is desirable to allow time for the lymphocytes and macrophages to perform their protective functions. (p. 779)

13. Lymph is generated in the body tissues and only flows back toward the heart, so there is no need for arteries to carry lymph away from the heart. (pp. 774–775)

Critical Thinking and Clinical Application Questions

1. a. With removal of the lymphatic vessels, fluid has built up in the tissues and drains very slowly back to the bloodstream.

b. Yes, she can expect to have relief since lymphatic drainage is eventually reestablished by regrowth of the lymphatic vessels. (p. 776)

2. Her swollen "glands" are inflamed cervical lymph nodes. Bacteria have spread from lymph vessels that drain the region of the cut in her face, and have lodged in the lymph nodes of the neck, infecting these nodes. (See Fig. 20.2.)

3. These lymphoid organs play a role in educating, monitoring and strengthening the immune response. (pp. 779–780, 781–782)

Suggested Readings

Mayerson, H. S. "The Lymphatic System." *Scientific American* (June 1963): 158.

Sprent, J., and Tough, D. F. "Lymphocyte Life-Span and Memory." *Science* 265 (Sept. 1994): 1395–1400.

Thorbecke, G. J., et al. "Biology of Germinal Centers in Lymphoid Tissue." *FASEB Journal* 8 (Aug. 1994): 832–840.

Waldmann, T. A. "T-Cell Receptors for Cytokines: Targets for Immunotherapy of Leukemia/Lymphoma." *Annals of Oncology* 11, Supplement 1 (2000): 101–106.

Whitman, M. "Preventing Lymphedema, an Unwelcome Sequel to Breast Cancer." *Nursing* 93 (Dec. 1993): 36–39.

Yang, K., et al. "Do Germinal Centers Have a Role in the Generation of Lymphomas?" *Current Topics in Microbiology and Immunology* 246 (1999): 53–62.

The Immune System: Innate and Adaptive Body Defenses

Objectives

Surface Barriers: Skin and Mucosae

1. Explain the roles of the skin and mucous membranes in the innate defense.
2. List and discuss the secretions of the skin and mucous membranes.

Internal Defenses: Cells and Chemicals

3. Describe the different types of phagocytes.
4. Identify the role of natural killer cells.
5. Explain the inflammatory response.
6. Discuss complement, interferon, and fever.

Antigens

7. Define antigen and differentiate between self and nonself.
8. Compare a complete and incomplete antigen.

Humoral Immune Response

9. Examine the clonal selection and differentiation of B cells.
10. Compare the primary immune response and the secondary immune response.

11. Discuss active and passive immunities, both naturally acquired and artificially acquired.
12. Explain the structure of an antibody.
13. List the five classes of antibodies and their functions.
14. Identify the ways antibodies function.

Cell-Mediated Immune Response

15. Discuss clonal selection and differentiation of T cells.
16. Explain how T cells are activated.
17. List the types of T cells and their roles.
18. Describe the different types of tissue grafts involved in organ transplants.

Homeostatic Imbalances of Immunity

19. Examine immunodeficiencies, auto-immune diseases, and hypersensitivities.

Developmental Aspects of the Immune System

20. Identify the events of embryonic development and the effects of aging on the immune system.

Suggested Chapter Outline

I. Innate Defenses (pp. 789–798; Figs. 21.1–21.6; Tables 21.1–21.2)

A. Surface Barriers: Skin and Mucosae

   1. Skin, a highly keratinized epithelial membrane, represents a physical barrier to most microorganisms and their enzymes and toxins.
   2. Mucous membranes line all body cavities open to the exterior and function as an additional physical barrier.
   3. Secretions of the epithelial tissues include acidic secretions, sebum, hydrochloric acid, saliva, and mucus.

B. Internal Defenses: Cells and Chemicals

    1. Phagocytes confront microorganisms that breach the external barriers.

       a. Macrophages are the main phagocytes of the body.

       b. Neutrophils are the first responders and become phagocytic when they encounter infectious material.

       c. Eosinophils are weakly phagocytic but are important in defending the body against parasitic worms.

       d. Mast cells have the ability to bind with, ingest, and kill a wide range of bacteria.

    2. Natural killer cells are able to lyse and kill cancer cells and virally infected cells before the adaptive immune system has been activated.

    3. Inflammation occurs any time the body tissues are injured by physical trauma, intense heat, irritating chemicals, or infection by viruses, fungi, or bacteria.

       a. The four cardinal signs of acute inflammation are redness, heat, swelling, and pain.

       b. Chemicals cause dilation of surrounding blood vessels to increase blood flow to the area and increase permeability, which allows fluid containing clotting factors and antibodies to enter the tissues.

       c. Soon after inflammation the damaged site is invaded by neutrophils and macrophages.

    4. Antimicrobial proteins enhance the innate defenses by attacking microorganisms directly or by hindering their ability to reproduce.

       a. Interferons are small proteins produced by virally infected cells that help protect surrounding healthy cells.

       b. Complement refers to a group of about 20 plasma proteins that provide a major mechanism for destroying foreign pathogens in the body.

    5. Fever, or an abnormally high body temperature, is a systemic response to microorganisms.

II. Adaptive Defenses (pp. 798–803; Figs. 21.7–21.9)

A. Aspects of the Adaptive Immune Response

    1. The adaptive defenses recognize and destroy the specific antigen that initiated the response.

    2. The immune response is a systemic response; it is not limited to the initial infection site.

    3. After an initial exposure the immune response is able to recognize the same antigen and mount a faster and stronger defensive attack.

    4. Humoral immunity is provided by antibodies produced by B lymphocytes present in the body's "humors" or fluids.

    5. Cellular immunity is associated with T lymphocytes and has living cells as its protective factor.

B. Antigens are substances that can mobilize the immune system and provoke an immune response.

    1. Complete antigens are able to stimulate the proliferation of specific lymphocytes and antibodies, and to react with the activated lymphocytes and produced antibodies.

2. Haptens are incomplete antigens that are not capable of stimulating the immune response, but if they interact with proteins of the body they may be recognized as potentially harmful.

3. Antigenic determinates are a specific part of an antigen that are immunogenic and bind to free antibodies or activated lymphocytes.

C. Cells of the Adaptive Immune System: An Overview

1. Lymphocytes originate in the bone marrow and when released become immunocompetent in either the thymus (T cells) or the bone marrow (B cells).

2. Antigen-presenting cells engulf antigens and present fragments of these antigens on their surfaces where they can be recognized by T cells.

III. Humoral Immune Response (pp. 804–810; Figs. 21.10–21.14; Table 21.3)

A. The immunocompetent but naive B lymphocyte is activated when antigens bind to its surface receptors.

1. Clonal selection is the process of the B cell growing and multiplying to form an army of cells that are capable of recognizing the same antigen.

2. Plasma cells are the antibody-secreting cells of the humoral response; most clones develop into plasma cells.

3. The clones that do not become plasma cells develop into memory cells.

B. Immunological Memory

1. The primary immune response occurs on first exposure to a particular antigen with a lag time of about 3–6 days.

2. The secondary immune response occurs when someone is reexposed to the same antigen. It is faster, more prolonged, and more effective.

C. Active and Passive Humoral Immunity

1. Active immunity occurs when the body mounts an immune response to an antigen.

   a. Naturally acquired active immunity occurs when a person suffers through the symptoms of an infection.

   b. Artificially acquired active immunity occurs when a person is given a vaccine.

2. Passive immunity occurs when a person is given preformed antibodies.

   a. Naturally acquired passive immunity occurs when a mother's antibodies enter fetal circulation.

   b. Artificially acquired passive immunity occurs when a person is given preformed antibodies that have been harvested from another person.

D. Antibodies or immunoglobulins are proteins secreted by plasma cells in response to an antigen that are capable of binding to that antigen.

1. The basic antibody structure consists of four looping polypeptide chains linked together by disulfide bonds.

2. Antibodies are divided into five classes based on their structure: IgM, IgG, IgA, IgD, and IgE.

3. Embryonic cells contain a few hundred gene segments that are shuffled and combined to form all of the different B cells that are found in the body.

4. Antibody Targets and Functions

   a. Complement fixation and activation occurs when complement binds to antibodies attached to antigens, and leads to lysis of the cell.

     b. Neutralization occurs when antibodies block specific sites on viruses or bacterial exotoxins, causing them to lose their toxic effects.

     c. Agglutination occurs when antibodies cross-link to antigens on cells, causing clumping.

     d. Precipitation occurs when soluble molecules are cross-linked into large complexes that settle out of solution.

    5. Monoclonal antibodies are commercially prepared antibodies specific for a single antigenic determinant.

IV. Cell-Mediated Immune Response (pp. 810–820; Figs. 21.15–21.20; Table 21.4)

A. The stimulus for clonal selection and differentiation of T cells is binding of antigen, although their recognition mechanism is different from B cells.

    1. T cells must accomplish a double recognition process: they must recognize both self (an MHC protein of a body cell) and nonself (antigen) at the same time.

    2. T Cell Activation

     a. Step 1: T cell antigen receptors (TCRs) bind to antigen-MHC complex on the surface of a body cell.

     b. Step 2: A T cell must recognize one or more co-stimulatory signals.

     c. Once activated, a T cell enlarges and proliferates to form a clone of cells that differentiate and perform functions according to their T cell class.

    3. Cytokines include hormonelike glycoproteins released by activated T cells and macrophages.

B. Specific T Cell Roles

    1. Helper T cells stimulate proliferation of other T cells and B cells that have already become bound to antigen.

    2. Cytotoxic T cells are the only T cells that can directly attack and kill other cells displaying antigen to which they have been sensitized.

    3. Regulatory T cells release cytokines that suppress the activity of both B cells and other types of T cells.

    4. Gamma delta T cells are found in the intestine and are more similar to NK cells than other T cells.

    5. Without helper T cells there is no adaptive immune response because the helper T cells direct or help complete the activation of all other immune cells.

C. Organ Transplants and Prevention of Rejection

    1. Grafts

     a. Autografts are tissue grafts transplanted from one body site to another in the same person.

     b. Isografts are grafts donated to a patient by a genetically identical individual such as an identical twin.

     c. Allografts are grafts transplanted from individuals that are not genetically identical but belong to the same species.

     d. Xenografts are grafts taken from another animal species.

    2. Transplant success depends on the similarity of the tissues because cytotoxic T cells, NK cells, and antibodies work to destroy foreign tissues.

V. Homeostatic Balances of Immunity (pp. 820–825; Fig. 21.21)

A. Immunodeficiencies are any congenital or acquired conditions that cause immune cells, phagocytes, or complement to behave abnormally.

1. Severe combined immunodeficiency (SCID) is a congenital condition that produces a deficit of B and T cells.

2. Acquired immune deficiency syndrome (AIDS) cripples the immune system by interfering with helper T cells.

B. Autoimmune diseases occur when the immune system loses its ability to differentiate between self and nonself and ultimately destroys itself.

C. Hypersensitivities, or allergies, are the result of the immune system causing tissue damage as it fights off a perceived threat that would otherwise be harmless.

1. Immediate hypersensitivities begin within seconds after contact and last about half an hour.

2. Subacute hypersensitivities take 1–3 hours to occur and last 10–15 hours.

3. Delayed hypersensitivity reactions take 1–3 days to occur and may take weeks to go away.

VI. Developmental Aspects of the Immune System (pp. 825–826)

A. Embryologic Development

1. Stem cells of the immune system originate in the liver and spleen during weeks 1–9 of embryonic development; later the bone marrow takes over this role.

2. In late fetal life and shortly after birth the young lymphocytes develop self-tolerance and immunocompetence.

B. Later in life the ability and efficiency of our immune system declines.

Cross References

Additional information on topics covered in Chapter 21 can be found in the chapters listed below.

1. Chapter 2: Protein structure
2. Chapter 3: Cilia; lysosomes
3. Chapter 5: Mechanical and chemical protection of the skin; Langerhans' cells
4. Chapter 15: Lysozyme
5. Chapter 16: Thymus
6. Chapter 17: Granulocytes; agranulocytes; chemotaxis; diapedesis
7. Chapter 22: Inflammatory processes involving respiratory tissues
8. Chapter 23: Protection of the mucous barrier in the stomach; role of saliva in protection of mucous barriers; Kupffer cells
9. Chapter 24: Body temperature regulation
10. Chapter 28: Antibody protection of the fetus due to maternal antibodies

Laboratory Correlations

1. Marieb, E. N. *Human Anatomy & Physiology Laboratory Manual: Cat and Fetal Pig Versions.* Eighth Edition Updates. Benjamin Cummings, 2006.

Exercise 35: The Lymphatic System and Immune Response

2. Marieb, E. N. *Human Anatomy & Physiology Laboratory Manual: Main Version.* Seventh Edition Update. Benjamin Cummings, 2006.
   Exercise 35: The Lymphatic System and Immune Response

Lecture Hints

1. Although specific and nonspecific defense mechanisms are treated as separate entities, emphasize that there is much overlap of function. For example, in antibody-mediated complement lysis, formation of the antibody that labels a cell is due to specific processes, but the actual lysis of that cell is accomplished nonspecifically by complement fixation.

2. Point out that the body has several lines of defense—mechanical, chemical, and cellular. It is helpful to orient students toward the idea that even with all of its complexity, the immune system has one underlying theme: rid the body of unwanted substances/life forms.

3. Students often have problems deciding what mechanisms are specific and which are nonspecific. Stress that the immune system tailors its response to each individual antigen, while the nonspecific mechanisms respond to cues that are much more broad.

4. Emphasize the logic behind the four cardinal signs of inflammation. For example, to bring the large quantities of oxygen and nutrients for repair processes, blood supply to an area must be increased. Redness results as vasodilation increases; heat, as warm blood is delivered; swelling as capillary walls become more permeable; pain as pressure due to swelling is transmitted to nerve endings.

5. Point out that neutrophils are seen early in an infection, but that macrophages are characteristic of chronic infection.

6. To illustrate the action of pyrogens on the hypothalamus, use the example of resetting the thermostat to a higher temperature in a home. As always, relating a physiological concept to something familiar to students will help reinforce the idea.

7. Mention that cytotoxic T cells must come in contact with the invader, but that B cells send out antibodies from sometimes remote locations to target specific antigens.

8. Emphasize the difference between antigens and haptens, and that size is the cause of the distinction between the two. Essentially, one can think of a hapten as an antigenic determinant if it is bound to a carrier molecule; alternatively, if an antigenic determinant were not part of a large molecule, it would be a hapten.

9. To reinforce the idea of clonal selection, point out that a single B cell could not possibly produce enough antibody to neutralize a large quantity of antigen.

10. Stress the difference between active and passive immunity, and that the body does not care where antibodies come from. If the students understand the concept, the question should arise: "Why don't the foreign antibodies generate a response in the recipient?" If no one asks, ask this of the class to generate discussion.

11. In the discussion of complement, ask the class, "What would happen if an antibody bound to a completely normal body cell?" Use this as a lead-in to the topic of complement recognition of the constant region of the antibody.

12. It is often difficult for students to grasp the concept of somatic recombination in the generation of antibody diversity. Ask plenty of questions during lecture to reinforce concepts.

13. Clearly distinguish between different types of allergies. As the material is being covered, ask students which arm of the immune system is responsible for what type of

hypersensitivity—immediate, subacute, or delayed. Students should be able to make the connection that a cell-mediated response will take time (delayed hypersensitivity).

Activities/Demonstrations

1. Audio-visual materials listed under Multimedia in the Classroom and Lab.
2. To open a discussion of the inflammatory process, ask if anyone has a cut or injury that is in the process of healing. If so, have the class members observe it, describe all obvious signs, and provide the underlying reason for the signs seen.
3. Ask students to come prepared to discuss the following questions during a subsequent lecture:
   a. Explain why vaccination provides long-term protection against a particular disease while passive immunization provides only temporary protection.
   b. What is the important difference between natural killer cells and cytotoxic T cells?
   c. Why can T helper cells be called the "managers" of the immune system?
4. Use a lock and several keys (with only one that fits the lock) to demonstrate the specificity of antigens and antibodies.

Critical Thinking/Discussion Topics

1. Discuss the pros and cons surrounding the use of immunizations for mumps, measles, etc.
2. Explore the autoimmune diseases, how they occur, symptoms, prognosis, and treatment.
3. Discuss why some individuals are sensitive (allergic) to drugs from one source, but are not so sensitive to drugs from another source.
4. Discuss the social implications of immunity disorders such as AIDS, ARC, SCID, etc.
5. Identify the role of the Epstein-Barr virus in immunity and immunity disorders.
6. Discuss the effects of AIDS both immunologically and socially.
7. Explain why we need specific resistance mechanisms even though nonspecific resistance mechanisms attack all foreign substances (i.e., why is specific resistance necessary at all?).
8. Explain what the body's immune response is to an antitoxin or other passive immunization.
9. Discuss why chemotherapeutics attached to monoclonal antibodies are an advantage over injection of the chemical agent alone. Could there be any drawbacks to this therapy?

Library Research Topics

1. Research some of the opportunistic diseases that often accompany AIDS.
2. Study the difficulties involved in transplant surgeries.
3. Explore the causes of several known autoimmune diseases.
4. Examine the signs, symptoms, and treatment of anaphylactic shock.
5. Investigate the possible side effects of vaccines.

Multimedia in the Classroom and Lab

Online Resources for Students

The
Anatomy & Physiology Place   MyA&P
www.anatomyandphysiology.com   www.myaandp.com

The following shows the organization of the Chapter Guide page in both the Anatomy & Physiology Place and MyA&P™. The Chapter Guide organizes all the chapter-specific online media resources for Chapter 21 in one convenient location, with e-book links to each section of the textbook. Please note that both sites also give you access to other general A&P resources, like InterActive Physiology®, PhysioEx 6.0™, Anatomy 360°, *Flashcards, a Glossary, a Histology Tutorial, and much more.*

Objectives

PART ONE: INNATE DEFENSES

Section 21.1 Surface Barriers: Skin and Mucosae (pp. 789–790)

Section 21.2 Internal Defenses: Cells and Chemicals (pp. 790–798)

Art Labeling Activity: Phagocytosis (Fig. 21.2, p. 791)

Art Labeling Activity: Phagocyte Mobilization (Fig. 21.4, p. 794)

PART TWO: ADAPTIVE DEFENSES

Section 21.3 Antigens (pp. 799–800)

Section 21.4 Cells of the Adaptive Immune System: An Overview (pp. 800–803)

Section 21.5 Humoral Immune Response (pp. 804–810)

Art Labeling Activity: Mechanisms of Antibody Actions (Fig. 21.14, p. 809)

PhysioEx: Serological Testing

Section 21.6 Cell-Mediated Immune Response (pp. 810–820)

Memory: The Immune Response, Part 1

Memory: The Immune Response, Part 2

Section 21.7 Homeostatic Imbalances of Immunity (pp. 820–825)

Case Study: Genetic Immunodeficiency

Section 21.8 Developmental Aspects of the Immune System (pp. 825–826)

Chapter Summary

Self-Study Quizzes

Art Labeling Quiz

Matching Quiz

Multiple-Choice Quiz (Level I)

Multiple-Choice Quiz (Level II)

True-False Quiz

Crossword Puzzles

Crossword Puzzle 21.1

Crossword Puzzle 21.2

Media

See Guide to Audio-Visual Resources in Appendix A for key to AV distributors.

Video

1. *AIDS: A Biological Perspective* (FHS; 30 min., 1995). Award-winning video that explores many of the difficult questions surrounding AIDS, including why a vaccine has been so difficult to find.

2. *Basic Immunology* (IM; 37 min., 1994). A highly recommended video that examines the anatomy and physiology of the immune system. It illustrates the system's tissues, organs, and cellular and soluble components.

3. *The Body Against Disease Video* (WNS; 48 min.). Presents a detailed picture of how the body defends itself against disease. Students are shown an in-depth analysis of the immune system, stressing the many ways in which it protects the body against disease.

4. *Cell Wars* (FHS; 22 min.). This program explains the role of antibodies in vaccinations and allergies, and shows the uses of monoclonal antibodies in the diagnosis and treatment of a variety of different types of tumors, as well as the immune system deficiency syndrome AIDS.

5. *Human Immune System* (IM; 20 min., 2002). Explains how the immune system defends the body against foreign invaders.

6. *Immunizations* (FHS; 20 min., 1994). Explains the need for vaccinations against disease and identifies the recommended pediatric immunization schedule.

7. *Your Immune System* (FHS; 20 min., 2001). Maps out the human immune system and what it does to keep the body healthy.

Software

1. *Blood and Immunity* (see p. 199 of this guide for full listing).

2. *Immunology* (IM; Win/Mac). Provides in-depth coverage of the principles of immunology.

3. *InterActive Physiology® 9-System Suite CD-ROM* (BC; Win/Mac). Interactive software that explores the physiology of the immune system.

Lecture Enhancement Material

To view thumbnails of all of the illustrations for Chapter 21, see Appendix B.

Transparencies Index/Media Manager

Figure 21.1   Overview of innate and adaptive defenses.
Figure 21.2   Phagocytosis.
Figure 21.3   Flowchart of events in inflammation.
Figure 21.4   Phagocyte mobilization.
Figure 21.5   The interferon mechanism against viruses.
Figure 21.6   Complement activation.
Figure 21.7   Antigenic determinants.
Figure 21.8   Lymphocyte traffic.
Figure 21.9   T cell selection in the thymus.
Figure 21.10   Clonal selection of a B cell.
Figure 21.11   Primary and secondary humoral responses.
Figure 21.12   Types of acquired immunity.
Figure 21.13   Antibody structure.
Figure 21.14   Mechanisms of antibody action.
Figure 21.15   Major types of T cells based on displayed cell differentiation glycoproteins (CD4, CD8).
Figure 21.16   MHC proteins, and antigen processing and display.
Figure 21.17   Clonal selection of T_H and T_C cells involves simultaneous recognition of self and nonself.

Indicates images that are on the Media Manager only.

Answers to End-of-Chapter Questions

Multiple Choice and Matching Question answers appear in Appendix G in the main text.

Short Answer Essay Questions

13. Mucosae are found on the outer surface of the eye and in the linings of all body cavities open to the exterior, i.e., the digestive, respiratory, urinary, and reproductive tracts. The epidermis is the outermost covering of the body surface. Mucus provides a sticky mechanical barrier that traps pathogens.

    Lysosyme, an enzyme that destroys bacteria, is found in saliva and lacrimal fluid.

    Keratin, a tough waterproofing protein in epithelial membranes, presents a physical barrier to microorganisms on the skin. It is resistant to most weak acids and bases and to bacterial enzymes and toxins.

    The acid pH of skin secretions inhibits bacterial growth. Vaginal secretions and urine (as a rule) are also very acidic. Hydrochloric acid is secreted by the stomach mucosa and acts to kill pathogens.

    Cilia of the upper respiratory tract mucosae sweep dust and bacteria-laden mucus superiorly toward the mouth, restraining it from entering the lower respiratory passages. (pp. 789–790)

14. Attempts at phagocytosis are not always successful because to accomplish ingestion, the phagocyte must first adhere to the particle. Complement proteins and antibodies coat foreign particles, providing binding sites to which phagocytes can attach, making phagocytosis more efficient. (p. 790)

15. The term *complement* refers to a heterogenous group of at least 20 plasma proteins that normally circulate in an inactive state. Complement is activated by one of two pathways (classical or alternative) involving the plasma proteins. Each pathway involves a cascade in which complement proteins are activated in an orderly sequence leading to the cleavage of C3. Once C3b is bound to the target cell's surface, it enzymatically initiates the remaining steps of complement activation, which incorporates C5 through C9 (MAC) into the target cell membrane, ensuring lysis of the target cell.

    Other roles of complement include opsonization, inflammatory actions such as stimulating mast cells and basophils to release histamine (which increases vascular permeability), and attracting neutrophils and other inflammatory cells to the area. (pp. 796–798)

16. Interferons are secreted by virus-infected cells. They diffuse to nearby cells where they interfere with the ability of viruses to multiply within these cells. Cells that form interferon include macrophages, lymphocytes, and other leukocytes. (pp. 795–796)

17. Humoral immunity is provided by the antibodies in the body's fluids. Cell-mediated immunity is provided by non–antibody-producing lymphocytes, i.e., T cells. (p. 799)

18. Cytokines released by Helper T cells help to amplify and regulate both the humoral and cellular immune response as well as the nonspecific defense responses. (pp. 814–815)

19. Immunocompetence is the ability of the immune system's cells to recognize foreign substances (antigens) in the body by binding to them. Acquisition is signaled by the appearance of a single, unique type of cell surface receptor protein on each T or B cell that enables the lymphocyte to recognize and bind to a specific antigen. (p. 800)

20. Helper T cell activation involves a double recognition: a simultaneous recognition of the antigen and an MHC II membrane glycoprotein of an antigen-presenting cell (macrophage). One or more costimulators also appear necessary. (pp. 813–814)

21. A primary immune response results in cellular proliferation, differentiation of mature effector and memory lymphocytes, and the synthesis and release of antibodies—a series of events that takes 3 to 6 days. The secondary immune response results in huge numbers of antibodies flooding into the bloodstream within hours after recognition of the antigen, as well as an amplified cellular attack. Secondary responses are faster because the immune system has been primed to the antigen and sizable numbers of sensitized memory cells are already in place. (p. 805)

22. An antibody is a soluble protein secreted by sensitized B cells and plasma cell offspring of B cells in response to an antigen. (pp. 806–807; Fig. 21.13)

23. The variable regions of an antibody combine to form an antigen-binding site that is shaped to "fit" a specific antigenic determinant or an antigen. The constant regions of an antibody determine what class of antibody will be formed, how the antibody class will carry out its immune roles in the body, and with which cell types or chemicals the antibody will bind. (pp. 807–808)

24. The antibody classes and their probable locations in the body include the following:

    Class IgD—virtually always attached to B cells; B cell receptor

    Class IgM—monomer attached to B cells; pentamer free in plasma (during primary response)

    Class IgG—in plasma

    Class IgA—some in plasma, most in secretions such as saliva, tears, intestinal juice, and milk

    Class IgE—secreted by plasma cells in skin, mucosae of gastrointestinal and respiratory tracts and tonsils (pp. 807–808; Table 21.3)

25. Antibodies help defend the body by complement fixation, neutralization, agglutination, and precipitation. Complement fixation and neutralization are most important in body protection. (pp. 808–810)

26. Vaccines produce active humoral immunity because most contain dead or extremely weakened pathogens which have the antigenic determinants necessary to stimulate the immune response but are generally unable to cause disease. Passive immunity is less than satisfactory because neither active antibody production nor immunological memory is established. (pp. 805–806)

27. Helper T cells function to chemically or directly stimulate the proliferation of other T cells and of B cells that have already become bound to antigen. Suppressor T cells function to temper the normal immune response by dampening the activity of both T cells and B cells by releasing cytokines that suppress their activity. Cytotoxic T cells function to kill virus-invaded body cells and cancer cells and are involved in rejection of foreign tissue grafts. (pp. 814–817)

28. Cytokines are soluble glycoproteins released by activated T cells. They enhance the defensive activity of T cells, B cells, and macrophages. Specific cytokines and their role in the immune response are summarized in Table 21.4.

29. Hypersensitivity is an antigen-induced state that results in abnormally intense immune responses to an innocuous antigen. Immediate hypersensitivities include anaphylaxis and atopy. Subacute hypersensitivities include cytotoxic and immune complex hypersensitivities. All of these involve antibodies. Delayed hypersensitivities include allergic contact dermatitis and graft rejection. These hypersensitivities involve T cells. (pp. 822–825)

30. Autoimmune disease results from changes in the structure of self-antigens, ineffective or inefficient lymphocyte programming, and by cross-reaction of antibodies produced against foreign antigens with self-antigens. (pp. 821–822)

31. Declining efficiency of the immune system with age probably reflects genetic aging. (p. 826)

Critical Thinking and Clinical Application Questions

1. a. Jenny has severe combined immunodeficiency disease (SCID) in which T cells and B cells fail to develop. At best there are only a few detectable lymphocytes. Bone marrow transplant is the treatment of choice; however, this is unsuccessful in some cases. The transplanted cells may not survive, or may mount an immune response against the recipient's tissues (graft versus host response).

    b. Jenny's brother has the closest antigenic match since both children are from the same parents.

    c. Bone marrow transplant using umbilical cord stem cells is the next best chance for survival. It is hoped that by replacing marrow stem cells, the populations of T cells and B cells would approach normal.

    d. Epstein-Barr virus is the etiologic agent of infectious mononucleosis, usually a self-limiting problem with recovery in a few weeks. Rarely, the virus causes the formation of cancerous B cells—Burkitt lymphoma.

    e. SCID is a congenital defect in which there is a lack of the common stem cell that develops into T cells and B cells. AIDS is the result of an infectious process by a virus that selectively incapacitates the CD4 (helper) T cells. Both result in a severe immunodeficiency that leaves the individual open to opportunistic pathogens and body cells that have lost normal control functions (cancerous). (p. 820)

2. IgA is found primarily in mucus and other secretions that bathe body surfaces. It plays an important role in preventing pathogens from entering the body. Lack of IgA would result in frequent major/minor infections of the sinuses or respiratory tract infections. (p. 808)

3. The mechanisms for the cardinal signs of acute inflammation involve the entire inflammatory process. The inflammatory process begins as a host of inflammatory chemicals are released into the extracellular fluid. They promote local vasodilation, allowing more blood to flow into the area, causing a local hyperemia that accounts for the redness and heat of an inflamed area. The liberated chemicals also increase the permeability to local capillaries and large amounts of exudate seep from the bloodstream into the tissue space, causing local edema or swelling. The excessive fluid in the extracellular space presses on adjacent nerve endings, contributing to a sensation of pain. (pp. 791–795)

4. Costanza was exhibiting the typical signs of anaphylaxis, an immediate hypersensitivity response. This typical inflammatory response (redness, edema, etc.) at the site of exposure to the allergen (in this case, the sting) is triggered any time the

body tissues are injured. He would benefit from a topical cream containing an anti-histamine drug. (p. 822–823)

5. The HIV virus is transferred from the mother to the baby through the placenta. Caroline's Helper T cells are infected. This is so devastating to the immune response because of the role of the Helper T cells in activating both the humoral immune response of the B cells and the activation of the T cytotoxic cells. Caroline is taking medications to control the infection and slow the progression of the disease to full-blown AIDS. She is taking a combination of drugs from three categories of action: reverse transcriptase inhibitors, protease inhibitors, and fusion inhibitors. (p. 821)

Suggested Readings

Brown, Phyllida. "Cinderella Goes to the Ball." *Nature* 410 (6832) (April 2001): 1018–1020.

Casellas, Rafael, et al. "Contribution of Receptor Editing to the Antibody Repertoire." *Science* 291 (5508) (Feb. 2001): 1541–1544.

Check, Erika. "The Virtue of Tolerance." *Nature* 418 (6896) (July 2002): 364–366.

Dove, Alan. "New Class of HIV Drugs Shows Promise." *Nature Medicine* 7 (12) (Dec. 2001): 1265.

DuClos, Terry. K. "C-Reactive Protein and the Immune Response." *Science and Medicine* 8 (2) (March/April 2002): 108–117.

Gura, Trisha. "Innate Immunity: Ancient System Gets New Respect." *Science* 291 (5511) (March 2002): 2068–2071.

King, Leslie B. and Monroe, John G. "B Cell Receptor Rehabilitation—Pausing to Reflect." *Science* 291 (5508) (Feb. 2001): 1503–1506.

Kloetzel, Peter M. "Antigen Processing by the Proteasome." *Nature Reviews: Molecular Cell Biology* 2 (3) (March 2001): 179–193.

Marshall, Eliot. "Lupus: Mysterious Disease Holds its Secrets Tight." *Science* 296 (5568) (April 2002): 689–691.

McCune, Joseph N. "The Dynamics of C D 4+ T-Cell Depletion." *Nature* 410 (6831) (April 2001): 1002–1007.

Medzhitov, Rusian and Janeway Jr. Charles A. "Decoding the Patterns of Self and Non-self by the Innate Immune System." *Science* 296 (5566) (April 2002): 298–300.

Murphy, William J. "Natural Killer Cells Alloreactivity in Bone Marrow Transplantation." *Science and Medicine* 8 (3) (May/June 2002): 162–171.

Nabel, Gary J. "Challenges and Opportunities for Development of an AIDS Vaccine." *Nature* 410 (6831) (April 19): 1002–2007.

Piot, Peter, et al. "The Global Impact of HIV/AIDS." *Nature* 410 (6831) (April 2001): 974–979.

Rudd, Pauline M. et al. "Glycosylation and the Immune System." *Science* 291 (5512) (March 2001): 2370–2376.

Taniguchi, Tadatsugu and Takaoka, Akinori. "A Weak Signal for Strong Responses: Interferon-alpha/beta Revisited." *Nature Reviews: Molecular Cell Biology* 2 (5) (May 2001): 378–386.

Vinuesa, Carola G. and Goodnow, Christopher C. "DNA Drives Immunity." *Nature* 416 (6881) (April 2002): 595–598.

Vivier, Eric and Biron, Christine A. "A Pathogen Receptor on Natural Killer Cells." *Science* 296 (5571) (May 2002): 1248–1249.

The Respiratory System

Objectives

Functional Anatomy of the Respiratory System

1. List the structures and functions of the nose, nasal cavity, and paranasal sinuses.

2. Describe the structures of the pharynx, larynx, and trachea.

3. Explain the structure of the lungs and the vascular and neural networks that supply them.

4. Discuss the relationship of the pleurae to the lungs and thoracic wall, and their functional importance.

Mechanics of Breathing

5. Define intrapulmonary and intrapleural pressure.

6. Describe pulmonary ventilation and the relationships between pressure and volume changes as they apply to the lungs.

7. Identify the events of quiet and forced inspiration, and passive and forced expiration.

8. Discuss the effects of airway resistance, alveolar surface tension, and lung compliance on pulmonary ventilation.

9. List and define the respiratory volumes and capacities.

10. Distinguish between obstructive and restrictive respiratory disorders, and describe the role of pulmonary function tests in distinguishing between them.

11. Name the nonrespiratory air movements.

Basic Properties of Gases

12. Define Dalton's law of partial pressures, and relate it to atmospheric gases.

13. Explain Henry's law, and describe its importance to gas exchange in the lungs.

Composition of Alveolar Gas

14. Compare the composition of alveolar gases to atmospheric gases.

Gas Exchanges Between the Blood, Lungs, and Tissues

15. Define external respiration and pulmonary gas exchange, and describe the factors that affect exchange.

Transport of Respiratory Gases by Blood

16. Describe how oxygen and carbon dioxide are carried in the blood, and explain the role of hemoglobin.

Control of Respiration

17. List the neural structures that control respiration, and the factors that affect rate and depth of respiration.

Respiratory Adjustments

18. Explain the adjustments to respiration that occur in response to exercise and increased altitude.

Homeostatic Imbalances of the Respiratory System

19. Identify the characteristics of chronic obstructive pulmonary disorders, asthma, tuberculosis, and lung cancer.

Developmental Aspects of the Respiratory System

20. Describe the events of development and growth of the respiratory system.

21. List the changes that occur in the respiratory system with age.

Suggested Lecture Outline

I. Functional Anatomy of the Respiratory System (pp. 831–846; Figs. 22.1–22.11; Table 22.1)

A. The Nose and Paranasal Sinuses (pp. 831–835; Figs. 22.1–22.3)

1. The nose provides an airway for respiration; moistens, warms, filters, and cleans incoming air; provides a resonance chamber for speech; and houses olfactory receptors.

2. The nose is divided into the external nose, which is formed by hyaline cartilage and bones of the skull, and the nasal cavity, which is entirely within the skull.

3. The nasal cavity consists of two types of epithelium: olfactory mucosa and respiratory mucosa.

4. The nasal cavity is surrounded by paranasal sinuses within the frontal, maxillary, sphenoid, and ethmoid bones that serve to lighten the skull, warm and moisten air, and produce mucus.

B. The Pharynx (p. 835; Fig. 22.3)

1. The pharynx connects the nasal cavity and mouth superiorly to the larynx and esophagus inferiorly.

a. The nasopharynx serves as only an air passageway, and contains the pharyngeal tonsil, which traps and destroys airborne pathogens.

b. The oropharynx is an air and food passageway that extends inferiorly from the level of the soft palate to the epiglottis.

c. The laryngopharynx is an air and food passageway that lies directly posterior to the epiglottis, extends to the larynx, and is continuous inferiorly with the esophagus.

C. The Larynx (pp. 835–838; Figs. 22.3–22.5)

1. The larynx attaches superiorly to the hyoid bone, opening into the laryngopharynx, and attaches inferiorly to the trachea.

2. The larynx provides an open airway, routes food and air into the proper passageways, and produces sound through the vocal cords.

3. The larynx consists of hyaline cartilages: thyroid, cricoid, paired arytenoid, corniculate, and cuneiform; and the epiglottis, which is elastic cartilage.

4. Vocal ligaments form the core of mucosal folds, the true vocal cords, which vibrate as air passes over them to produce sound.

5. The vocal folds and the medial space between them are called the glottis.

6. Voice production involves the intermittent release of expired air and the opening and closing of the glottis.

7. Valsalva's maneuver is a behavior in which the glottis closes to prevent exhalation and the abdominal muscles contract, causing intra-abdominal pressure to rise.

D. The trachea, or windpipe, descends from the larynx through the neck into the mediastinum, where it terminates at the primary bronchi (pp. 838–840; Fig. 22.6).

E. The Bronchi and Subdivisions: The Bronchial Tree (pp. 840–842; Figs. 22.7–22.8)

        1. The conducting zone consists of right and left primary bronchi that enter each lung and diverge into secondary bronchi that serve each lobe of the lungs.

        2. Secondary bronchi branch into several orders of tertiary bronchi, which ultimately branch into bronchioles.

        3. As the conducting airways become smaller, the supportive cartilage changes in character until it is no longer present in the bronchioles.

        4. The respiratory zone begins as the terminal bronchioles feed into respiratory bronchioles that terminate in alveolar ducts within clusters of alveolar sacs, which consist of alveoli.

           a. The respiratory membrane consists of a single layer of squamous epithelium, type-I cells, surrounded by a basal lamina.

           b. Interspersed among the type-I cells are cuboidal type-II cells that secrete surfactant.

           c. Alveoli are surrounded by elastic fibers, contain open alveolar pores, and have alveolar macrophages.

    F. The Lungs and Pleurae (pp. 842–846; Figs. 22.9–22.11)

        1. The lungs occupy all of the thoracic cavity except for the mediastinum; each lung is suspended within its own pleural cavity and connected to the mediastinum by vascular and bronchial attachments called the lung root.

        2. Each lobe contains a number of bronchopulmonary segments, each served by its own artery, vein, and tertiary bronchus.

        3. Lung tissue consists largely of air spaces, with the balance of lung tissue, its stroma, comprised mostly of elastic connective tissue.

        4. There are two circulations that serve the lungs: the pulmonary network carries systemic blood to the lungs for oxygenation, and the bronchial arteries provide systemic blood to the lung tissue.

        5. The lungs are innervated by parasympathetic and sympathetic motor fibers that constrict or dilate the airways, as well as visceral sensory fibers.

        6. The pleurae form a thin, double-layered serosa.

           a. The parietal pleura covers the thoracic wall, superior face of the diaphragm, and continues around the heart between the lungs.

           b. The visceral pleura covers the external lung surface, following its contours and fissures.

II. Mechanics of Breathing (pp. 846–854; Figs. 22.12–22.16; Tables 22.2–22.3)

    A. Pressure Relationships in the Thoracic Cavity (pp. 846–847; Fig. 22.12)

        1. Intrapulmonary pressure is the pressure in the alveoli, which rises and falls during respiration, but always eventually equalizes with atmospheric pressure.

        2. Intrapleural pressure is the pressure in the pleural cavity. It also rises and falls during respiration, but is always about 4 mm Hg less than intrapulmonary pressure.

    B. Pulmonary Ventilation: Inspiration and Expiration (pp. 847–849; Figs. 22.13–22.14)

        1. Pulmonary ventilation is a mechanical process causing gas flow into and out of the lungs according to volume changes in the thoracic cavity.

           a. Boyle's law states that at a constant temperature, the pressure of a gas varies inversely with its volume.

2. During quiet inspiration, the diaphragm and intercostals contract, resulting in an increase in thoracic volume, which causes intrapulmonary pressure to drop below atmospheric pressure, and air flows into the lungs.

3. During forced inspiration, accessory muscles of the neck and thorax contract, increasing thoracic volume beyond the increase in volume during quiet inspiration.

4. Quiet expiration is a passive process that relies mostly on elastic recoil of the lungs as the thoracic muscles relax.

5. Forced expiration is an active process relying on contraction of abdominal muscles to increase intra-abdominal pressure and depress the ribcage.

C. Physical Factors Influencing Pulmonary Ventilation (pp. 849–851; Fig. 22.15)

1. Airway resistance is the friction encountered by air in the airways; gas flow is reduced as airway resistance increases.

2. Alveolar surface tension due to water in the alveoli acts to draw the walls of the alveoli together, presenting a force that must be overcome in order to expand the lungs.

3. Lung compliance is determined by distensibility of lung tissue and the surrounding thoracic cage, and alveolar surface tension.

D. Respiratory Volumes and Pulmonary Function Tests (pp. 851–854; Fig. 22.16; Tables 22.2–22.3)

1. Respiratory volumes and specific combinations of volumes, called respiratory capacities, are used to gain information about a person's respiratory status.

   a. Tidal volume is the amount of air that moves in and out of the lungs with each breath during quiet breathing.

   b. The inspiratory reserve volume is the amount of air that can be forcibly inspired beyond the tidal volume.

   c. The expiratory reserve volume is the amount of air that can be evacuated from the lungs after tidal expiration.

   d. Residual volume is the amount of air that remains in the lungs after maximal forced expiration.

   e. Inspiratory capacity is the sum of tidal volume and inspiratory reserve volume, and represents the total amount of air that can be inspired after a tidal expiration.

   f. Functional residual capacity is the combined residual volume and expiratory reserve volume, and represents the amount of air that remains in the lungs after a tidal expiration.

   g. Vital capacity is the sum of tidal volume, inspiratory reserve and expiratory reserve volumes, and is the total amount of exchangeable air.

   h. Total lung capacity is the sum of all lung volumes.

2. The anatomical dead space is the volume of the conducting zone conduits, which is a volume that never contributes to gas exchange in the lungs.

3. Pulmonary function tests evaluate losses in respiratory function using a spirometer to distinguish between obstructive and restrictive pulmonary disorders.

4. Nonrespiratory air movements cause movement of air into or out of the lungs, but are not related to breathing (coughing, sneezing, crying, laughing, hiccups, and yawning).

III. Gas Exchanges Between the Blood, Lungs, and Tissues (pp. 854–858; Figs. 22.17–22.20)

A. Gases have basic properties, as defined by Dalton's law of partial pressures and Henry's law. (pp. 854–855)

   1. Dalton's law of partial pressures states that the total pressure exerted by a mixture of gases is the sum of the pressures exerted by each gas in the mixture.

   2. Henry's law states that when a mixture of gases is in contact with a liquid, each gas will dissolve in the liquid in proportion to its partial pressure.

B. The composition of alveolar gas differs significantly from atmospheric gas, due to gas exchange occurring in the lungs, humidification of air by conducting passages, and mixing of alveolar gas that occurs with each breath. (p. 855)

C. External Respiration: Pulmonary Gas Exchange (pp. 855–858; Figs. 22.17–22.19)

   1. External respiration involves O_2 uptake and CO_2 unloading from hemoglobin in red blood cells.

      a. A steep partial pressure gradient exists between blood in the pulmonary arteries and alveoli, and O_2 diffuses rapidly from the alveoli into the blood, but carbon dioxide moves in the opposite direction along a partial pressure gradient that is much less steep.

      b. The difference in the degree of the partial pressure gradients of oxygen and carbon dioxide reflects the fact that carbon dioxide is much more soluble than oxygen in the blood.

      c. Ventilation-perfusion coupling ensures a close match between the amount of gas reaching the alveoli and the blood flow in the pulmonary capillaries.

      d. The respiratory membrane is normally very thin, and presents a huge surface area for efficient gas exchange.

D. Internal Respiration: Capillary Gas Exchange in the Body Tissues (p. 858; Fig. 22.17)

   1. The diffusion gradients for oxygen and carbon dioxide are reversed from those for external respiration and pulmonary gas exchange.

   2. The partial pressure of oxygen in the tissues is always lower than the blood, so oxygen diffuses readily into the tissues, while a similar but less dramatic gradient exists in the reverse direction for carbon dioxide.

IV. Transport of Respiratory Gases by Blood (pp. 853–863; Figs. 22.20–22.23)

A. Oxygen Transport (pp. 858–861; Figs. 22.20–22.22)

   1. Since molecular oxygen is poorly soluble in the blood, only 1.5% is dissolved in plasma, while the remaining 98.5% must be carried on hemoglobin.

      a. Up to four oxygen molecules can be reversibly bound to a molecule of hemoglobin—one oxygen on each iron.

      b. The affinity of hemoglobin for oxygen changes with each successive oxygen that is bound or released, making oxygen loading and unloading very efficient.

   2. At higher plasma partial pressures of oxygen, hemoglobin unloads little oxygen, but if plasma partial pressure falls dramatically, i.e. during vigorous exercise, much more oxygen can be unloaded to the tissues.

3. Temperature, blood pH, P_{CO2}, and the amount of BPG in the blood all influence hemoglobin saturation at a given partial pressure.

4. Nitric oxide (NO), secreted by lung and vascular endothelial cells, is carried on hemoglobin to the tissues where it causes vasodilation and enhances oxygen transfer to the tissues.

B. Carbon Dioxide Transport (pp. 861–863; Figs. 22.22–22.23)

1. Carbon dioxide is transported in the blood in three ways: 7–10% is dissolved in plasma, 20% is carried on hemoglobin bound to globins, and 70% exists as bicarbonate, an important buffer of blood pH.

2. The Haldane effect encourages CO_2 exchange in the lungs and tissues: when plasma partial pressure of oxygen and oxygen saturation of hemoglobin decrease, more CO_2 can be carried in the blood.

3. The carbonic acid–bicarbonate buffer system of the blood is formed when CO_2 combines with water and dissociates, producing carbonic acid and bicarbonate ions that can release or absorb hydrogen ions.

V. Control of Respiration (pp. 863–869; Figs. 22.24–22.27)

A. Neural Mechanisms and Generation of Breathing Rhythm (pp. 863–865; Figs. 22.24–22.25)

1. The medulla oblongata contains the dorsal respiratory group, or inspiratory center, with neurons that act as the pacesetting respiratory group, and the ventral respiratory group, which functions mostly during forced breathing.

2. The pontine respiratory group within the pons modifies the breathing rhythm and prevents overinflation of the lungs through an inhibitory action on the medullary respiration centers.

3. It is likely that reciprocal inhibition on the part of the different respiratory centers is responsible for the rhythm of breathing.

B. Factors Influencing Breathing Rate and Depth (pp. 865–869; Figs. 22.25–22.27)

1. The most important factors influencing breathing rate and depth are changing levels of CO_2, O_2, and H^+ in arterial blood.

   a. The receptors monitoring fluctuations in these parameters are the central chemoreceptors in the medulla oblongata, and the peripheral chemoreceptors in the aortic arch and carotid arteries.

   b. Increases in arterial P_{CO2} cause CO_2 levels to rise in the cerebrospinal fluid, resulting in stimulation of the central chemoreceptors, and ultimately leading to an increase in rate and depth of breathing.

   c. Substantial drops in arterial P_{O2} are required to cause changes in respiration rate and depth, due to the large reserves of O_2 carried on the hemoglobin.

   d. As H^+ accumulates in the plasma, rate and depth of breathing increase in an attempt to eliminate carbonic acid from the blood through the loss of C_{O2} in the lungs.

2. Higher brain centers alter rate and depth of respiration.

   a. The limbic system, strong emotions, and pain activate the hypothalamus, which modifies respiratory rate and depth.

   b. The cerebral cortex can exert voluntary control over respiration by bypassing medullary centers and directly stimulating the respiratory muscles.

3. Pulmonary irritant reflexes respond to inhaled irritants in the nasal passages or trachea by causing reflexive bronchoconstriction in the respiratory airways.

4. The inflation, or Hering-Breuer, reflex is activated by stretch receptors in the visceral pleurae and conducting airways, protecting the lungs from over-expansion by inhibiting inspiration.

VI. Respiratory Adjustments (pp. 869–870)

A. Adjustments During Exercise (pp. 869–870)

1. During vigorous exercise, deeper and more vigorous respirations, called hyperpnea, ensure that tissue demands for oxygen are met.

2. Three neural factors contribute to the change in respiration: psychic stimuli, cortical stimulation of skeletal muscles and respiratory centers, and excitatory impulses to the respiratory areas from active muscles, tendons, and joints.

B. Adjustments at High Altitude (p. 870)

1. Acute mountain sickness (AMS) may result from a rapid transition from sea level to altitudes above 8000 feet.

2. A long-term change from sea level to high altitudes results in acclimatization of the body, including an increase in ventilation rate, lower than normal hemoglobin saturation, and increased production of erythropoietin.

VII. Homeostatic Imbalances of the Respiratory System (pp. 870–873; Fig. 22.28)

A. Chronic obstructive pulmonary diseases (COPD) are seen in patients that have a history of smoking, and result in progressive dyspnea, coughing and frequent pulmonary infections, and respiratory failure. (pp. 871–872)

1. Obstructive emphysema is characterized by permanently enlarged alveoli and deterioration of alveolar walls.

2. Chronic bronchitis results in excessive mucus production, as well as inflammation and fibrosis of the lower respiratory mucosa.

B. Asthma is characterized by coughing, dyspnea, wheezing, and chest tightness, brought on by active inflammation of the airways. (p. 872)

C. Tuberculosis (TB) is an infectious disease caused by the bacterium *Mycobacterium tuberculosis* and spread by coughing and inhalation. (p. 872)

D. Lung Cancer (pp. 872–873)

1. In both sexes, lung cancer is the most common type of malignancy, and is strongly correlated with smoking.

2. Squamous cell carcinoma arises in the epithelium of the bronchi, and tends to form masses that hollow out and bleed.

3. Adenocarcinoma originates in peripheral lung areas as nodules that develop from bronchial glands and alveolar cells.

4. Small cell carcinoma contains lymphocyte-like cells that form clusters within the mediastinum and rapidly metastasize.

VIII. Developmental Aspects of the Respiratory System (pp. 873–875; Fig. 22.29)

A. By the fourth week of development, the olfactory placodes are present and give rise to olfactory pits that form the nasal cavities.

B. The nasal cavity extends posteriorly to join the foregut, which gives rise to an outpocketing that becomes the pharyngeal mucosa.

C. By the eighth week of development, mesoderm forms the walls of the respiratory passageways and stroma of the lungs.

D. As a fetus, the lungs are filled with fluid, and vascular shunts are present that divert blood away from the lungs; at birth, the fluid drains away, and rising plasma P_{CO_2} stimulates respiratory centers.

E. Respiratory rate is highest in newborns, and gradually declines to adulthood; in old age, respiratory rate increases again.

F. As we age, the thoracic wall becomes more rigid, the lungs lose elasticity, and the amount of oxygen we can use during aerobic respiration decreases.

G. The number of mucus glands and blood flow in the nasal mucosa decline with age, as does ciliary action of the mucosa, and macrophage activity.

Cross References

Additional information on topics covered in Chapter 22 can be found in the chapters listed below.

1. Chapter 1: Mediastinum
2. Chapter 2: Acids and bases
3. Chapter 3: Diffusion
4. Chapter 4: Hyaline and elastic cartilage; squamous, cuboidal, and pseudostratified epithelium; serous and mucous glands
5. Chapter 7: Bones of the skull
6. Chapter 10: Muscles of respiration
7. Chapter 12: Medulla and pons; cortex
8. Chapter 13: Chemoreceptors, proprioceptors
9. Chapter 14: Sympathetic effects
10. Chapter 15: Auditory tube; lysozyme
11. Chapter 18: Great vessels
12. Chapter 19: Autoregulation of blood flow; pulmonary circulation
13. Chapter 20: Tonsils
14. Chapter 21: Inflammation; macrophages
15. Chapter 26: Acid-base balance of the blood
16. Chapter 28: Role of acidosis in initiating fetal respirations

Laboratory Correlations

1. Marieb, E. N. *Human Anatomy & Physiology Laboratory Manual: Cat and Fetal Pig Versions.* Eighth Edition Updates. Benjamin Cummings, 2006.
   Exercise 36: Anatomy of the Respiratory System
   Exercise 37: Respiratory System Physiology

2. Marieb, E. N. *Human Anatomy & Physiology Laboratory Manual: Main Version.* Seventh Edition Update. Benjamin Cummings, 2006.
   Exercise 36: Anatomy of the Respiratory System
   Exercise 37: Respiratory System Physiology

Histology Slides for the Life Sciences

Available through Benjamin Cummings, an imprint of Pearson Education, Inc. To order, contact your local Benjamin Cummings sales representative.

Slide 8   Pseudostratified Ciliated Columnar Epithelium, Nasal Mucosa.

Slide 69   Respiratory Bronchiole Alveoli Blood Vessel—Lung Interior.

Slide 70   Terminal Bronchiole, Respiratory Bronchiole, Alveolar Ducts—Lung.

Slide 71   Part of the lung showing alveoli and alveolar ducts and sacs.

Slide 72   Cross section through the trachea showing the pseudostratified ciliated epithelium, glands, and the supporting ring of hyaline cartilage.

Lecture Hints

1. Stress the difference between ventilation and respiration.

2. Show slides or acetates of the bones of the skull to illustrate the relationship between bony and soft tissue structures.

3. The conducting airways of the head are usually the most confusing of the respiratory structures. Spend some time with diagrams and photographs reinforcing the three-dimensional anatomy of the upper airway structures.

4. Point out the characteristics of the epithelia that line the conducting airways, and why those epithelia are the correct choice for that particular area. This will reinforce epithelial types and gradually establish an intuitive sense in the students so they can predict epithelia for any location in the body.

5. During a discussion of the trachea, ask students why the cartilage rings are C-shaped rather than continuous.

6. Be sure the class does not confuse the respiratory membrane with subcellular level membrane structures (plasma membrane, etc.).

7. Remind students that pulmonary vessels are exceptions to the rule that arteries = oxygenated blood and veins = deoxygenated blood. Students should not confuse the bronchial artery (oxygenated blood) with the pulmonary artery (deoxygenated blood).

8. Stress the development and importance of the slightly negative intrapleural pressure to normal inspiration.

9. Emphasize elastic recoil as the main mechanism of normal expiration.

10. A complete understanding of diffusion is necessary for comprehension of respiratory gas movement at lung and body tissue levels. Refer the class in advance to the section on diffusion in Chapter 3.

11. Mention that cellular respiration is not the same as internal or external respiration, but that cellular respiration involves the pathways of glucose catabolism.

12. Emphasize the increasing difficulty with which successive oxygens are removed from a hemoglobin molecule. This explains why hemoglobin is not unsaturated when returned to the lungs.

13. Point out that the carbon dioxide transport (bicarbonate buffering) system is the most important mechanism of maintaining pH of the blood.

14. Students often have the misconception that oxygen level is the principal stimulant of respiration. Emphasize that carbon dioxide level is the most important factor.

Activities/Demonstrations

1. Audio-visual materials listed under Multimedia in the Classroom and Lab.

2. Provide stethoscopes so that students can listen to respiratory (breathing) sounds over various regions of a partner's thorax. For example, bronchial sounds are produced by air rushing through the large passages (trachea and bronchi), whereas the more muffled vesicular breathing sounds are heard over the smallest airways and alveoli.

3. Using handheld spirometers, have students measure their respiratory volumes, particularly tidal volume and vital capacity.

4. Provide straws, beakers of water, and pH paper. Have students use the straws to blow into the water in the beakers. Since exhaled air contains a significant amount of CO_2, the water should become acidic. Have them measure the pH of the water at intervals to follow the pH change.

5. Provide tape measures so that students can measure the circumference of the rib cage before and after inspiration.

6. Use a torso model, respiratory system model, and/or dissected animal model to exhibit the respiratory system and related organs.

7. Use two glass slides with water between them to demonstrate the cohesive effect of the serous fluid between the chest cavity wall and the lungs via the pleura and its parts. (Note: Due to this force, chest cavity movement results in lung movement since the lungs cannot pull away from the chest wall under normal conditions.)

8. Use an open-ended bell jar with balloons inside to demonstrate the changing pressures as the diaphragm contracts and relaxes. (Note: Top of bell jar should have a one-hole stopper with a glass Y tube extending into the jar; to the Y tube will be attached two small balloons; the bottom of the jar will be covered with a flexible elastic sheeting.)

9. Use a stringed instrument to demonstrate the effect of vibration and thickness on sound production.

10. Add laundry detergent to a glass of water and immerse some cloth to demonstrate the role of surfactant in the lungs for reducing water surface tension and as attraction for other water molecules.

11. Use a freshly opened soft drink to demonstrate and explain Henry's law.

12. Demonstrate the location of the sinuses using a complete or Beauchene's skull.

13. Obtain a fresh lamb or calf pluck (lungs plus attached trachea and heart) from a slaughterhouse. Insert a rubber hose snugly into the trachea and attach the hose to a source of compressed air. Alternately inflate the lungs with air and allow them to deflate passively to illustrate the huge air capacity and elasticity of the lungs.

14. Obtain some animal blood and bubble air through the blood via a small section of tubing to demonstrate the color change that occurs when blood is well oxygenated.

Critical Thinking/Discussion Topics

1. Discuss why athletes would want to train at high altitudes if their competition was to be at a high altitude (relate to USA's Olympic training site, Denver, Colorado), or even if their competition was to be at a lower altitude.

2. Explore the changes in respiratory volumes with obstructive or congestive disorders.

3. Examine the relationship between oxygen debt and muscle fatigue and an elevated respiratory rate after exercise.

4. Discuss the logic behind the structure of the conducting airways. Why are cartilage rings necessary? Why is smooth muscle in the walls of the conducting tubes necessary?

5. Discuss the relationship between intrapulmonary pressure and intrapleural pressure. What happens to intrapulmonary pressure relative to intrapleural pressure when Valsalva's maneuver is performed?

6. Why are only slightly higher atmospheric levels of carbon monoxide gas dangerous?

Library Research Topics

1. Research and list the respiratory diseases caused by inhalation of toxic particles associated with occupations such as coal mining, etc.

2. Study the incidence of cancer in smokers versus nonsmokers, and in individuals working in respiratory hazard areas versus individuals working in relatively safe respiratory areas.

3. Examine the current status of heart-lung transplants, and why such a transplant would be considered.

4. Investigate the causes, known and supposed, of sudden infant death syndrome.

5. Research the respiratory problems a premature infant might face.

6. Research the emergence and incidence of respiratory ailments such as Severe Acute Respiratory Syndrome (SARS).

Multimedia in the Classroom and Lab

Online Resources for Students

The
Anatomy & Physiology Place
www.anatomyandphysiology.com

MyA&P
www.myaandp.com

The following shows the organization of the Chapter Guide page in both the Anatomy & Physiology Place and MyA&P™. The Chapter Guide organizes all the chapter-specific online media resources for Chapter 22 in one convenient location, with e-book links to each section of the textbook. Please note that both sites also give you access to other general A&P resources, like InterActive Physiology®, PhysioEx 6.0™, Anatomy 360°, Flashcards, a Glossary, a Histology Tutorial, and much more.

Objectives

Section 22.1 Functional Anatomy of the Respiratory System (pp. 831–846)

InterActive Physiology®: Anatomy Review

Art Labeling Activity: Upper Respiratory Tract (Fig. 22.3, p. 834)

Art Labeling Activity: The Larynx (Fig. 22.4, p. 836)

Memory: The Respiratory System (Art)

Memory: The Respiratory System (Cadaver)

Section 22.2 Mechanics of Breathing (pp. 846–854)

InterActive Physiology®: Pulmonary Ventilation

PhysioEx: Respiratory System Mechanics

Section 22.3 Gas Exchanges Between the Blood, Lungs, and Tissues (pp. 854–858)

InterActive Physiology®: Gas Exchange

Media

See Guide to Audio-Visual Resources in Appendix A for key to AV distributors.

Slides

1. *Human Lung* (CBS). Slides show bronchioles with pseudostratified ciliated columnar epithelium.

Video

1. *Breath of Life* (NIMCO; 30 min., 1994). This video traces the path of an oxygen molecule through the respiratory system and into the bloodstream.

2. *Breathing* (FHS; 20 min., 1995). From the award-winning *The New Living Body* series, this video looks at the typical day in the life of a cystic fibrosis sufferer, and problems encountered by individuals with that hereditary disease.

3. *The Human Respiratory System Videotape* (BC; 25 min., 1998). This video provides an excellent overview of the functions of the human respiratory system.

4. *Respiration* (FHS; 15 min., 1996). From *The World of Living Organisms* series, this video describes external and internal respiration and explains how energy for bodily functions is produced.

5. *Respiratory System: Intake and Exhaust* (FHS; 25 min., 2000). From *The Human Body: Systems at Work* series, this program uses the analogy of an automobile's system of fuel intake and exhaust to explore the makeup and functions of the respiratory system.

Software

1. *A.D.A.M.*® *InterActive Anatomy*® *4.0* (see p. 9 of this guide for full listing).

2. *A.D.A.M.*® *MediaPro* (see p. 9 of this guide for full listing).

3. *A.D.A.M.*® *Anatomy Practice* (see p. 86 of this guide for full listing).

4. *Bodyworks* (see p. 9 of this guide for full listing).

5. *LOGAL® Gateways™: The Human Respiratory System CD-ROM* (RIL; Win/Mac). Students can conduct complete, simulated physiology experiments on the human respiratory system without expensive equipment. Students set variables; generate, collect, and analyze data; form hypotheses; and develop models.

6. *InterActive Physiology® 9-System Suite CD-ROM* (BC; Win/Mac). Interactive software with a section on the respiratory system that explores the physiology of that system.

7. *Respiratory System* (NIMCO; Win/Mac). Simulates the mechanical and physiological workings of the human respiratory system.

8. *Spirocomp™ Human Spirometry System* (WNS; Windows). Includes a computerized spirometry system. Consists of hardware and software designed to allow quick and easy measurement of standard lung volumes. Can be used in a lab setting with students.

9. *The Ultimate Human Body* (see p. 9 of this guide for full listing).

Lecture Enhancement Material

To view thumbnails of all of the illustrations for Chapter 22, see Appendix B.

Transparencies Index/Media Manager

Figure 22.1	The major respiratory organs shown in relation to surrounding structures.
Figure 22.2	The external nose.
Figure 22.3	The upper respiratory tract.
Figure 22.4	The larynx.
Figure 22.5	Movements of the vocal cords.
Figure 22.6	Tissue composition of the tracheal wall.
Figure 22.7	Conducting zone passages.
Figure 22.8	Respiratory zone structures.
Figure 22.9	The respiratory membrane.
Figure 22.10	Anatomical relationships of organs in the thoracic cavity.
Figure 22.11	A cast of the bronchial tree.
Figure 22.12	Intrapulmonary and intrapleural pressure relationships.
Figure 22.13	Changes in thoracic volume during inspiration (top) and expiration (bottom).
Figure 22.14	Changes in intrapulmonary and intrapleural pressures during inspiration and expiration.
Figure 22.15	Resistance in respiratory passageways.
Figure 22.16	Respiratory volumes and capacities.
Figure 22.17	Partial pressure gradients promoting gas movements in the body.
Figure 22.18	Oxygenation of blood in the pulmonary capillaries.
Figure 22.19	Ventilation-perfusion coupling.
Figure 22.20	Oxygen-hemoglobin dissociation curve.
Figure 22.21	Effect of temperature, P_{CO_2}, and blood pH on the oxygen-hemoglobin dissociation curve.
Figure 22.22	Transport and exchange of CO_2 and O_2.
Figure 22.23	The Haldane effect.
Figure 22.24	Locations of respiratory centers and their postulated connections.

Indicates images that are on the Media Manager only.

Answers to End-of-Chapter Questions

Multiple Choice and Matching Question answers appear in Appendix G of the main text.

Short Answer Essay Questions

17. The route of air from the external nares to an alveolus and the organs involved are as follows: conducting zone structures—external nares, nasal cavity, pharynx (nasopharynx, oropharynx, laryngopharynx), larynx, trachea, and right and left primary bronchi, secondary bronchi, tertiary bronchi and successive bronchi orders, bronchioles, and terminal bronchioles; respiratory zone structures—respiratory bronchioles, alveolar ducts, alveolar sacs, and alveoli. (pp. 831–842)

18. a. The trachea is reinforced with cartilage rings to prevent the trachea from collapsing and to keep the airway patent despite the pressure changes that occur during breathing. (p. 839)

    b. The advantage of the rings not being complete posteriorly is that the esophagus is allowed to expand anteriorly during swallowing. (p. 839)

19. The adult male larynx as a whole is larger and the vocal cords are longer than those of women or boys. These changes occur at puberty under the influence of rising levels of testosterone. (p. 837)

20. a. The elastic tissue is essential both for normal inspiration and expiration; expiration is almost totally dependent on elastic recoil of the lungs when the inspiratory muscles relax. (p. 849)

    b. The passageways are air conduits used to warm, moisten, and transport air. (p. 840)

21. The volume of gas flow to and from the alveoli is directly proportional to the difference in pressure between the external atmosphere and the alveoli. Very small differences in pressure are sufficient to produce large volumes of gas flow. When intrapulmonary pressure decreases as thoracic volume increases, air flows into the lungs to equalize the pressure. When the lungs recoil, intrapulmonary pressure increases, and gases flow out of the lungs. (p. 848)

22. The walls of the alveoli are composed of a single layer of squamous epithelium surrounded by a flimsy basal lamina fused to the endothelium of the pulmonary capillaries. The thinness of the respiratory membrane allows gas diffusion to occur very rapidly across the membrane. (p. 842)

23. Pulmonary ventilation is influenced by airway resistance in that gas flow is equal to the pressure gradient divided by the resistance. Gas flow changes inversely with resistance. Lung compliance is assessed by measuring the increase in lung volume resulting from an increase in intrapulmonary pressure. The greater the volume increase for a given rise in pressure, the greater the compliance. The ability of lung tissue to distend and recoil, called lung elasticity, is essential for normal lung compliance. Surfactant reduces the surface tension of alveolar fluid, so less energy is needed to overcome surface tension forces to expand the lungs. (pp. 849–859)

24. a. Minute respiratory volume is the total amount of gas that flows into and out of the respiratory tract in one minute. Alveolar ventilation rate takes into account the amount of air wasted in dead space areas and provides a measurement of the concentration of fresh gases in the alveoli at a particular time. (p. 853)

    b. Alveolar ventilation rate provides a more accurate measure of ventilatory efficiency because it considers only the volume of air actually participating in gas exchange. (p. 853)

25. Dalton's law of partial pressure states that the total pressure exerted by a mixture of gases is the sum of the pressure exerted independently by each gas in the mixture. Henry's law states that when a mixture of gases is in contact with a liquid, each gas will dissolve in the liquid in proportion to its partial pressure and its solubility in the liquid. (p. 854)

26. a. Hyperventilation is deep breathing that flushes carbon dioxide rapidly out of the blood.

    b. When you hyperventilate, you expel more carbon dioxide.

    c. Hyperventilation increases blood pH. (p. 866)

27. Age-related changes include a loss of elasticity in the lungs and a more rigid chest wall. These factors result in a slowly decreasing ability to ventilate the lungs. Accompanying these changes is a decrease in blood oxygen levels and a reduced sensitivity to the stimulating effects of carbon dioxide. (pp. 874–875)

Critical Thinking and Clinical Application Questions

1. Hemoglobin is almost completely (98%) saturated with oxygen in arterial blood at normal conditions. Hence, hyperventilation will increase the oxygen saturation very little, if at all. However, hyperventilation will flush CO_2 out of the blood, ending the stimulus to breathe and possibly causing (1) cerebral ischemia due to hypocapnia, and (2) O_2 decrease to dangerously low levels, resulting in fainting. (p. 866)

2. a. The lung penetrated by the knife collapsed because the intrapleural pressure became equal to the atmospheric pressure, allowing the pleural membranes to separate.

    b. Only the penetrated lung collapsed because it is isolated from the remaining mediastinal structures (and the other lung) by the pleural membranes. (p. 846)

3. Adjacent bronchopulmonary segments are separated from one another by partitions of dense connective tissue, which no major vessels cross. Therefore, it is possible for a surgeon to dissect adjacent segments away from one another. The only vessels that had to be cauterized were the few main vessels to each bronchopulmonary segment. (p. 842)

4. Mary Ann is suffering from decompression sickness, brought on by the rapid ascent in the plane. During the week of diving, she accumulated nitrogen gas in her tissues that at normal altitudes leaves her tissues slowly and unnoticed. However,

on the flight, cabin pressure decreased quickly enough to allow residual nitrogen gas to leave more rapidly, causing her symptoms. The return to a lower altitude with a higher atmospheric pressure upon landing alleviates her symptoms. (pp. 868–869)

Suggested Readings

Beall, Cynthia M., et al. "Pulmonary Nitric Oxide in Mountain Dwellers." *Nature* 414 (Nov. 2001): 411–412.

Christensen, Damaris. "The Persistent Problem of Cystic Fibrosis." *Science News* 161 (4) (Jan. 2002): 59–60.

Floyd, Katherine, et al. "Resources Required for Global Tuberculosis Control." *Science* 295 (5562) (March 2002): 2040–2046.

Lipson, Stuart A. "Nitric Oxide and Respiration." *Nature* 413 (6852) (Sept. 2001): 118–121.

Okada, Yasumasa, Chen, Zibin, and Kuwana, Shun-ici. "Cyto-Architecture of Central Chemoreceptors in the Mammalian Ventral Medula." *Respiration Physiology* 129 (Dec. 2001): 13–23.

O'Toole, George A. "A Resistance Switch." *Nature* 416 (6882) (April 2002): 695–696.

Russel, David G. "Mycobacterium Tuberculosis: Here Today, and Here Tomorrow." *Nature Reviews: Molecular Biology* 2 (8) (Aug. 2001): 569–577.

Vogel, Gretchen. "Missing Gene Takes Mice's Breath Away." *Science* 295 (5553) (Jan. 2002): 253.

Wiemann, Martin and Bingmann, Dieter. "Ventrolateral Neurons of Medullary Organotypic Cultures: Intracellular pH Regulation and Bioelectric Activity." *Respiration Physiology* 129 (Dec. 2001): 57–70.

23 The Digestive System

Objectives

Suggested Lecture Outline

I. Part 1: Overview of the Digestive System (pp. 883–889; Figs. 23.1–23.6)

A. Digestive system organs fall into two main groups: the alimentary canal and the accessory organs. (pp. 883–884; Fig. 23.1)

    1. Alimentary canal, or the gastrointestinal (GI) tract, is the continuous muscular digestive tube that winds through the body digesting and absorbing foodstuff; its organs include: the mouth, pharynx, esophagus, stomach, small intestine, and large intestine.

2. Accessory digestive organs aid digestion physically and produce secretions that break down foodstuff in the GI tract; the organs involved are the teeth, tongue, gallbladder, salivary glands, liver, and pancreas.

B. Digestive Processes (pp. 884–885; Figs. 23.2–23.3)

1. Ingestion is the simple act of putting food into the mouth.

2. Propulsion moves food through the alimentary canal and includes both swallowing and peristalsis.

3. Mechanical digestion is the physical process of preparing the food for chemical digestion and involves chewing, mixing, churning, and segmentation.

4. Chemical digestion is a series of catabolic steps in which complex food molecules are broken down to their chemical building blocks by enzymes.

5. Absorption is the passage of digested end products from the lumen of the GI tract through the mucosal cells into the blood or lymph.

6. Defecation eliminates indigestible substances from the body via the anus as feces.

C. The digestive system creates an optimal internal environment for its functioning in the lumen of the GI tract, an area that is technically outside of the body. (pp. 885–886; Fig. 23.4)

1. Digestive activities within the GI tract are triggered by mechanical and chemical stimuli.

2. Controls of the digestive activity are both extrinsic and intrinsic (nervous and hormonal).

D. Digestive System Organs: Relationship and Structural Plan (pp. 886–889; Figs. 23.5–23.6)

1. Relationship of Digestive Organs to the Peritoneum

a. The visceral peritoneum covers the external surfaces of most of the digestive organs, and the parietal peritoneum lines the body wall of the abdominopelvic cavity.

b. Peritoneal cavity is located between the visceral and parietal peritoneums and is filled with serous fluid.

c. Mesentery is a double layer of peritoneum that extends to the digestive organs from the body wall. It allows blood vessels, lymphatics, and nerves to reach the digestive organs, and holds the organs in place as well as stores fat.

d. Retroperitoneal organs are found posterior to the mesentery, lying against the dorsal abdominal wall.

2. The splanchnic circulation serves the digestive system and includes those arteries that branch off the abdominal aorta to serve the digestive organs and the hepatic portal circulation.

3. Histology of the Alimentary Canal

a. Mucosa is the innermost, moist, epithelial membrane that lines the entire digestive tract. It secretes mucus, digestive enzymes, and hormones; absorbs digestive end products into the blood; and protects against infectious disease.

b. Submucosa is a moderately dense connective tissue layer containing blood and lymphatic vessels, lymphoid follicles, and nerve fibers.

c. Muscularis externa typically consists of smooth muscle and is responsible for peristalsis and segmentation.

d. Serosa, the protective outer layer of the intraperitoneal organs, is the visceral peritoneum.

4. The alimentary canal has its own nerve supply made up of enteric neurons that communicate widely with each other to regulate digestive activity.

II. **Part 2: Functional Anatomy of the Digestive System (pp. 889–927; Figs. 23.7–23.32; Tables 23.1–23.3)**

   A. Mouth, Pharynx, and Esophagus (pp. 889–897; Figs. 23.7–23.12)

      1. The mouth is a stratified squamous epithelial mucosa-lined cavity with boundaries of the lips, cheeks, palate, and tongue.

         a. The lips and cheeks have a core of skeletal muscle covered externally by skin that helps to keep food between the teeth when we chew and plays a small role in speech.

         b. The palate forms the roof of the mouth and has two parts: the hard palate anteriorly and the soft palate posteriorly.

         c. The tongue is made of interlacing bundles of skeletal muscle and is used to reposition food when chewing, mix food with saliva, initiate swallowing, and help form consonants for speech.

         d. Salivary glands produce saliva, which cleanses the mouth, dissolves food chemicals for taste, moistens food, and contains chemicals that begin the breakdown of starches.

         e. The teeth tear and grind food, breaking it into smaller pieces.

      2. The pharynx (oropharynx and laryngopharynx) provides a common passageway for food, fluids, and air.

      3. The esophagus provides a passageway for food and fluids from the laryngopharynx to the stomach where it joins at the cardiac orifice.

   B. Digestive Processes Occurring in the Mouth, Pharynx, and Esophagus (pp. 897–902; Figs. 23.13–23.15)

      1. Mastication, or chewing, begins the mechanical breakdown of food and mixes the food with saliva.

      2. Deglutition, or swallowing, is a complicated process that involves two major phases.

         a. The buccal phase is voluntary and occurs in the mouth where the bolus is forced into the oropharynx.

         b. The pharyngeal-esophageal phase is involuntary and occurs when food is squeezed through the pharynx and into the esophagus.

   C. The stomach is a temporary storage tank where the chemical breakdown of proteins is initiated and food is converted to chyme. (pp. 902–908; Figs. 23.16–23.19; Table 23.1)

      1. The adult stomach varies from 15–25 cm long, but its diameter and volume vary depending on the amount of food it contains.

         a. The major regions of the stomach include the cardiac region, fundus, body, and the pyloric region.

         b. The convex lateral surface of the stomach is its greater curvature, and its convex medial surface is its lesser curvature.

         c. Extending from the curvatures are the lesser omentum and the greater omentum, which help to tie the stomach to other digestive organs and the body wall.

      2. Microscopic Anatomy

         a. The surface epithelium of the stomach mucosa is a simple columnar epithelium composed of goblet cells, which produce a protective two-layer coat of alkaline mucus.

b. The gastric glands of the stomach produce gastric juice, which may be composed of a combination of mucus, hydrochloric acid, intrinsic factor, pepsinogen, and a variety of hormones.

3. Digestive Processes Occurring in the Stomach

   a. Gastric secretion is controlled by both neural and hormonal mechanisms and acts in three distinct phases: the cephalic phase, the gastric phase, and the intestinal phase.

   b. The reflex-mediated relaxation of the stomach muscle and the plasticity of the visceral smooth muscle allow the stomach to accommodate food and maintain internal pressure.

   c. The interstitial cells of Cajal establish the stomach's basic electrical rhythm of peristaltic waves.

   d. The rate at which the stomach empties is determined by both the contents of the stomach and the processing that is occurring in the small intestine.

D. Small Intestine and Associated Structures (pp. 908–918; Figs. 23.20–23.27)

   1. The small intestine is the site of the completion of digestion and absorption of nutrients.

      a. It extends from the pyloric sphincter to the ileocecal valve where it joins the large intestine. It has three subdivisions: the duodenum, the jejunum, and the ileum.

      b. It is highly adapted for absorption with three microscopic modifications: plicae circulares, villi, and microvilli.

      c. The intestinal crypts, or the crypts of Lieberkühn, secrete intestinal juice that serves as a carrier fluid for absorbing nutrients from chyme.

   2. The liver and gallbladder are accessory organs associated with the small intestine.

      a. The liver is the largest gland in the body and has four lobes.

      b. The liver is composed of liver lobules, which are made of plates of liver cells (hepatocytes).

      c. The digestive function of the liver is to produce bile, which is a fat emulsifier.

      d. Bile is a yellow-green, alkaline solution containing bile salts, bile pigments (primarily bilirubin), cholesterol, neutral fats, phospholipids, and a variety of electrolytes.

      e. The gallbladder stores and concentrates bile that is not needed immediately for digestion.

      f. Bile does not usually enter the small intestine until the gallbladder contracts when stimulated by cholecystokinin.

   3. The pancreas is an accessory gland that is retroperitoneal.

      a. Pancreatic juice consists mainly of water and contains enzymes that break down all categories of foodstuffs and electrolytes.

      b. Secretion of pancreatic juice is regulated by local hormones and the parasympathetic nervous system.

E. Digestive Processes Occurring in the Small Intestine (pp. 919–922; Fig. 23.28; Tables 23.2–23.3)

   1. Food takes 3 to 6 hours to complete its digestive path through the small intestine, the site of virtually all nutrient absorption.

2. Most substances required for chemical digestion within the small intestine are imported from the pancreas and the liver.

3. Optimal digestive activity in the small intestine depends on a slow, measured delivery of chyme from the stomach.

4. Segmentation is the most common motion of the small intestine.

F. The large intestine absorbs water from indigestible food residues and eliminates them as feces. (pp. 922–927; Figs. 23.29–23.32)

1. The large intestine exhibits three unique features: teniae coli, haustra, and epiploic appendages, and has the following subdivisions: cecum, appendix, colon, rectum, and anal canal.

2. The mucosa of the large intestine is thick and has crypts with a large number of mucus-producing goblet cells.

3. Bacteria entering the colon via the small intestine and anus colonize the colon and ferment some of the indigestible carbohydrates.

4. Digestive Processes Occurring in the Large Intestine

a. The movements seen in the large intestine include haustral contractions and mass movements.

b. Feces forced into the rectum by mass movements stretch the rectal wall and initiate the defecation reflex.

III. Part 3: Physiology of Chemical Digestion and Absorption (pp. 927–933; Figs. 23.33–23.36)

A. Chemical digestion is a catabolic process in which large food molecules are broken down to chemical building blocks (monomers), which are small enough to be absorbed by the GI tract lining. (pp. 927–931; Figs. 23.33–23.35)

1. Chemical digestion is accomplished by enzymes, secreted by intrinsic and accessory glands of the alimentary canal, used in hydrolysis reactions.

2. Carbohydrates

a. Monosaccharides are simple sugars that are absorbed immediately (glucose, galactose, and fructose).

b. Disaccharides are composed of two monosaccharides bonded together (maltose, lactose, and sucrose).

c. The digestible polysaccharide found in the diet is starch; other polysaccharides, such as cellulose, are not able to be broken down by humans.

d. Chemical digestion of carbohydrates begins in the mouth where salivary amylase breaks large polysaccharides into smaller fragments.

3. Proteins digested into amino acids in the GI tract include not only dietary proteins but also enzyme proteins secreted into the GI tract lumen.

a. Pepsin, secreted by the chief cells, begins the chemical digestion of proteins in the stomach.

b. Rennin is produced in infants and breaks down milk proteins.

c. Pancreatic enzymes, such as trypsin and chymotrypsin, further break down proteins in the small intestine.

d. The brush border enzymes carboxypeptidase, aminopeptidase, and dipeptidase work on freeing single amino acids in the small intestine.

4. The small intestine is the sole site for lipid digestion.

   a. Lipases are secreted by the pancreas and are the enzymes that digest fats after they have been pretreated with bile.

5. Nucleic acids (both DNA and RNA) are hydrolyzed to their nucleotide monomers by pancreatic nucleases present in pancreatic juice.

B. Absorption occurs along the entire length of the small intestine, and most of it is completed before the chyme reaches the ileum. (pp. 931–933; Fig. 23.36)

   1. Absorption of Specific Nutrients

      a. Glucose and galactose are transported into the epithelial cells by common protein carriers and are then moved by facilitated diffusion into the capillary blood.

      b. Several types of carriers transport the different amino acids before entering the capillary blood by diffusion.

      c. Monoglycerides and free fatty acids of lipid digestion become associated with bile salts and lecithin to form micelles, which are necessary for lipid absorption.

      d. Pentose sugars, nitrogenous bases, and phosphate ions are transported actively across the epithelium by special transport carriers in the villus epithelium.

      e. The small intestine absorbs dietary vitamins, while the large intestine absorbs vitamins B and K.

      f. Electrolytes are actively absorbed along the entire length of the small intestine, except for calcium and iron which are absorbed in the duodenum.

      g. Water is the most abundant substance in chyme and 95% of it is absorbed in the small intestine by osmosis.

   2. Malabsorption of nutrients can result from anything that interferes with the delivery of bile or pancreatic juices, as well as factors that damage the intestinal mucosa.

IV. Developmental Aspects of the Digestive System (pp. 933–937; Fig. 23.37)

A. Embryonic Development (pp. 933, 936; Fig. 23.37)

   1. The epithelial lining of the developing alimentary canal forms from the endoderm with the rest of the wall arising from the mesoderm.

   2. The anteriormost endoderm touches the depressed area of the surface ectoderm where the membranes fuse to form the oral membrane and ultimately the mouth.

   3. The end of the hindgut fuses with an ectodermal depression, called the proctodeum, to form the cloacal membrane and ultimately the anus.

   4. By week 8 the alimentary canal is a continuous tube stretching from the mouth to the anus.

B. Aging (pp. 936–937)

   1. GI tract motility declines, digestive juice production decreases, absorption is less efficient, and peristalsis slows resulting in less frequent bowel movements and often constipation.

   2. Diverticulosis, fecal incontinence, and cancer of the GI tract are fairly common problems in the elderly.

Cross References

Additional information on topics covered in Chapter 23 can be found in the chapters listed below.

1. Chapter 1: Serous membranes
2. Chapter 2: Enzyme function; acids and bases; carbohydrates, lipids, proteins, and nucleic acids
3. Chapter 3: Microvilli; membrane transport
4. Chapter 4: Simple columnar epithelium; areolar connective tissue; serous and mucous glands
5. Chapter 9: Smooth muscle
6. Chapter 10: Mastication and tongue movement
7. Chapter 12: Brain stem centers
8. Chapter 13: Receptors; reflex activity; nerve plexuses
9. Chapter 14: Sympathetic and parasympathetic controls
10. Chapter 15: Papillae and taste buds
11. Chapter 16: Hormones
12. Chapter 17: Pernicious anemia
13. Chapter 20: Lymphatic tissue; lacteals; palatine tonsils
14. Chapter 21: Macrophages
15. Chapter 24: Hepatic metabolism and detoxification; role of chylomicrons in lipid metabolism; bile formation; cholesterol and lipid transport in the blood
16. Chapter 26: Electrolyte balance

Laboratory Correlations

1. Marieb, E. N. *Human Anatomy & Physiology Laboratory Manual: Cat and Fetal Pig Versions.* Eighth Edition Updates. Benjamin Cummings, 2006.

   Exercise 38: Anatomy of the Digestive System

   Exercise 39: Chemical and Physical Processes of Digestion

2. Marieb, E. N. *Human Anatomy & Physiology Laboratory Manual: Main Version.* Seventh Edition Update. Benjamin Cummings, 2006.

   Exercise 38: Anatomy of the Digestive System

   Exercise 39: Chemical and Physical Processes of Digestion

Histology Slides for the Life Sciences

Available through Benjamin Cummings, an imprint of Pearson Education, Inc. To order, contact your local Benjamin Cummings sales representative.

Slide 56   Esophagus Wall.

Slide 57   Stomach Gastric Pits and Glands, Fundic Portion.

Slide 58   Submaxillary Gland.

Slide 59   Wall of Duodenum, Small Intestine.

Slide 60   Wall of Large Intestine, Colon.

Slide 61   Intestinal Glands, Jejunum.

Slide 62   Liver Lobule, Pig Liver.

Slide 63　Liver Lobule Central Vein, Monkey Liver Cell with Glycogen.

Slide 64　Pancreatic Islet, Pancreas.

Slide 65　Detailed Structure of the Gastric Glands and Pits.

Slide 66　Gastroesophageal Junction of Simple Columnar Epithelium (Stomach) and Stratified Squamous Epithelium (Esophagus).

Slide 67　Sublingual Salivary Glands.

Slide 68　Pancreas Tissue—Exocrine and Endocrine Areas Clearly Visible.

Lecture Hints

1. Emphasize that the digestive system is not only the alimentary (gastrointestinal) canal but all organs and tissues that aid in the process of digestion.

2. Point out that the gastrointestinal tract is formed of the same basic four layers through its length, but that each area is modified for the specific task involved.

3. Digestion is the process of breaking large particles into small particles. Emphasize that the overall function of the digestive system is the mechanical and chemical breakdown of ingested substances followed by the absorption of those substances and elimination of undigestible materials.

4. Most students have difficulty with the serous coverings of the abdominal viscera. Use diagrams and photographs of actual tissue to reinforce descriptions of the relatively complex folded nature of these membranes.

5. Spend some time with the hepatic portal system. This is another example of blood entering a capillary bed, feeding into a vein, then into another capillary bed before being returned to general circulation.

6. When discussing the histology of the tract, ask the class: "What is the logical epithelial choice for the mouth? For the esophagus?" Point out that the choice of columnar epithelium for the mucosal layer of the gastrointestinal tract is ideally suited to its function.

7. Emphasize that the esophagus is not covered by serosa, but instead has an adventitia as its outermost coat.

8. Emphasize that the lower esophageal sphincter (gastroesophageal) is not a true sphincter.

9. As a point of interest, mention that heartburn is actually acid reflux into the lower portion of the esophagus.

10. Point out the modification of the muscularis externa in the stomach as it relates to the function of the stomach.

11. Have students note the difference between the way the mucosa in the stomach has a relatively low surface area structure as compared to the small intestine. Ask the students why this is so.

12. Intrinsic factor is a stomach secretion necessary for vitamin B_{12} absorption; however, actual absorption of this vitamin does not occur in the stomach, but much later in the large intestine.

13. As each cell of the stomach mucosa is described, relate the logical function of each type to the overall function of the stomach.

14. Mention that the three areas of the small intestine are distinguishable histologically by examination of the mucosal structure.

15. Use diagrams or black line masters to demonstrate the three structural modifications of the small intestine that greatly increase the surface area for absorption.

16. When introducing the digestive function of the small intestine, lead into the topic by asking the class: "What functions must occur as chyme enters the initial part of the small intestine?" Using carefully led questioning, the class should respond: acid neutralization, further digestion of carbohydrates and proteins, and initiation of lipid digestion.

17. Students have difficulty with the pathways of flow in the liver lobule. Use two-dimensional cross sections of a lobule and indicate the directions of blood flow and bile flow. Stress the difference between the hepatic portal vein and the hepatic vein.

18. Ask the class why the hepatic artery is necessary, since the liver is already supplied by the portal vein. They should be able to respond that portal blood is "used" blood from the digestive tract.

19. Emphasize that the pancreas is a dual function/structure gland, endocrine and exocrine.

20. *Taenia coli* are best explained by using a cross-sectional diagram followed by a longitudinal section.

21. Emphasize that the amount of time the contents of the large intestine are in contact with the mucosa determines fecal water content. Too little time in the large intestine means a watery stool, and too much time results in constipation.

22. Point out the logical names of digestive enzymes: the prefix usually indicates the substrate, and the suffix "-ase" means enzyme. An exception, trypsin, was named before universal acceptance of the "-ase" convention.

23. Spend time on fat digestion and absorption, from emulsification to movement through the bloodstream. Point out that carbohydrates and proteins take a different (vascular) path to the liver than do the lipids.

Activities/Demonstrations

1. Audio-visual materials listed under Multimedia in the Classroom and Lab.

2. Have students calculate their total caloric intake over a 24-hour period by using a simple caloric guide available in any drugstore. Have students analyze their diet with attention to what improvements could (and should) be made in their eating habits.

3. Demonstrate the emulsification action of bile: first mix oil and water together and allow the layers to separate out. Then add bile salts and shake vigorously. Point out that the layer of oil has been dispersed into hundreds of tiny fat spheres by the action of the bile salts.

4. Use a torso model and/or dissected animal model to exhibit digestive organs.

5. Use gallstones obtained from a surgeon to exhibit as you discuss the liver and gallbladder.

6. Use a long balloon, not quite fully blown up, to demonstrate peristalsis.

7. Use a human skull or dentition models to demonstrate the different tooth shapes, types, and numbers.

8. Demonstrate molecular models of carbohydrate, fat, and protein.

Critical Thinking/Discussion Topics

1. Discuss symptoms, treatment, and prognosis of a hiatal hernia.

2. Explain why it is important to chew food properly.

3. Explore the importance of the liver.

4. Discuss the cause, treatment, and prevention of ulcers.

5. Talk about why it is necessary for someone with ulcer-like symptoms to consult a physician rather than to just use antacids.

6. Discuss the reasons why elderly individuals should be checked for colorectal cancer.

7. Examine the reasons for treatment and prognosis of a colostomy.

8. If a high-salt meal is ingested, why is a large amount of water not lost in the feces?

9. Discuss how people on low-carbohydrate diets have relatively constant glucose levels.

Library Research Topics

1. Research the causes and treatment of ulcers.

2. Study the benefits of fiber in the diet.

3. Research liver transplants in terms of rationale for the transplant, procedure, and prognosis.

4. Explore inherited metabolic disorders.

5. Research the congenital disorders that affect a newborn's ability to survive in the first days after birth.

6. Investigate the latest causes and treatments of hepatitis. What are the consequences of liver inflammation/infection?

7. What are malabsorption syndromes? Their causes? Their treatments?

8. Study the different types of motility disorders associated with the digestive tract. Include possible secondary complications and suggested treatments.

9. What are the common cancers of the digestive system? Are cancers limited to the gastrointestinal tract? Are they limited to the accessory structures?

Multimedia in the Classroom and Lab

Online Resources for Students

The
Anatomy & Physiology Place   MyA&P
www.anatomyandphysiology.com   www.myaandp.com

The following shows the organization of the Chapter Guide page in both the Anatomy & Physiology Place and MyA&P™. The Chapter Guide organizes all the chapter-specific online media resources for Chapter 23 in one convenient location, with e-book links to each section of the textbook. Please note that both sites also give you access to other general A&P resources, like InterActive Physiology®, PhysioEx 6.0™, Anatomy 360°, *Flashcards, a Glossary, a Histology Tutorial, and much more.*

Objectives

PART ONE: OVERVIEW OF THE DIGESTIVE SYSTEM (PP. 883–889)

InterActive Physiology®: Orientation

Art Labeling Activity: Alimentary Canal and Related Accessory Organs (Fig. 23.1, p. 883)

PART TWO: FUNCTIONAL ANATOMY OF THE DIGESTIVE SYSTEM (PP. 889–927)

InterActive Physiology®: Anatomy Review

Art Labeling Activity: Anatomy of the Stomach (Fig. 23.14, p. 899)

Art Labeling Activity: Microscopic Anatomy of the Stomach (Fig. 23.15, p. 901)

Art Labeling Activity: Gross Anatomy of the Large Intestine (Fig. 23.29, p. 923)

Memory: Digestive System Associated Structures

Memory: The Digestive System

PART THREE: PHYSIOLOGY OF CHEMICAL DIGESTION AND ABSORPTION (PP. 927–933)

InterActive Physiology®: Control of the Digestive System

InterActive Physiology®: Motility

InterActive Physiology®: Secretion

InterActive Physiology®: Digestion and Absorption

PhysioEx: Chemical and Physical Processes of Digestion

Case Study: Iron Deficiency Anemia

Section 23.4 Developmental Aspects of the Digestive System (pp. 933, 936–937)

Chapter Summary

Self-Study Quizzes

Art Labeling Quiz

Matching Quiz

Multiple-Choice Quiz (Level I)

Multiple-Choice Quiz (Level II)

True-False Quiz

Crossword Puzzles

Crossword Puzzle 23.1

Crossword Puzzle 23.2

Media

See Guide to Audio-Visual Resources in Appendix A for key to AV distributors.

Slides

1. *Digestive Tract Set* (CBS). Contains tissue samples from all major organs of the digestive tract.
2. *Human Organs and Glands of Digestion Set* (CBS). Represents all organs and glands in the digestive tract.

Video

1. *Breakdown* (FHS; 28 min., 1984). From the award-winning *The Living Body* series, this video investigates the digestive consequences of eating a meal, following the food through the entire alimentary canal.
2. *Digestion* (FHS; 20 min., 1995). From the award-winning *The New Living Body* series, this video provides a thorough introduction to the structures and functions of the digestive tract.
3. *The Digestive System: Down the Hatch!* (KV; 20 min., 2001). From the four-part series *Amazing Adventures Inside the Human Body*. This video explores the mechanical and chemical processes of digestion that turn food into nutrients and vitamins that the body can absorb.
4. *Digestive System: Your Personal Power Plant* (FHS/IM; 25 min., 2000). From *The Human Body: Systems at Work* series, this program examines the processes by which the digestive system acts as a power plant for the body by turning food into energy.
5. *The Food Machine* (NIMCO; 25 min., 1994). This video, from *The Body Atlas* series, follows the path of food through the alimentary canal and explains how the body separates useful substances from wastes.
6. *Gastrointestinal Disorders* (IM; 50 min., 1997). This video details diagnostic procedures and presents information about numerous GI diseases.
7. *The Human Digestive System Videotape* (BC; 33 min., 1998). This video provides an excellent overview of the human digestive system.

8. *Passage of Food Through the Digestive Tract* (WNS; 8 min.). A concise video that introduces the student to the digestive system. Students are able to relate each part of the digestive tract to the digestion of food through the use of X-ray motion photography.

Software

1. *A.D.A.M.® InterActive Anatomy® 4.0* (see p. 9 of this guide for full listing).
2. *A.D.A.M.® MediaPro* (see p. 9 of this guide for full listing).
3. *A.D.A.M.® Anatomy Practice* (see p. 86 of this guide for full listing).
4. *Bodyworks* (see p. 9 of this guide for full listing).
5. *The Human Digestive System* (IM; Win/Mac). Accesses endoscopic pictures and lab experiments to show the human digestive system at work.
6. *InterActive Physiology® 9-System Suite CD-ROM* (BC; Win/Mac). The Digestive System module walks students through animations that clearly and simply explain every part of the human digestive process, from basic anatomy to complete digestion and absorption. Like the rest of the CD, students learn at their own pace by pausing and/or replaying animations when needed, and test their knowledge with the worksheets and quizzes available at the end of the module.
7. *The Ultimate Human Body* (see p. 9 for full listing).

Lecture Enhancement Material

To view thumbnails of all of the illustrations for Chapter 23, see Appendix B.

Transparencies Index/Media Manager

Figure 23.1   Alimentary canal and related accessory digestive organs.
Figure 23.2   Gastrointestinal tract activities.
Figure 23.3   Peristalsis and segmentation.
Figure 23.4   Neural reflex pathways initiated by stimuli inside or outside the gastrointestinal tract.
Figure 23.5   The peritoneum and the peritoneal cavity.
Figure 23.6   Basic structure of the alimentary canal.
Figure 23.7   Anatomy of the oral cavity (mouth).
Figure 23.8   Dorsal surface of the tongue.
Figure 23.9   The salivary glands.
Figure 23.10   Human deciduous and permanent teeth of the lower jaw.
Figure 23.11   Longitudinal section of a canine tooth within its bony alveolus.
Figure 23.12   Microscopic structure of the esophagus.
Figure 23.13   Deglutition (swallowing).
Figure 23.14   Anatomy of the stomach.
Figure 23.15   Microscopic anatomy of the stomach.
Figure 23.16   Neural and hormonal mechanisms that regulate the release of gastric juice.
Figure 23.17   Regulation and mechanism of HCl secretion.
Figure 23.18   Peristaltic waves in the stomach.
Figure 23.19   Neural and hormonal factors inhibiting gastric emptying.
Figure 23.20   The duodenum of the small intestine, and related organs.
Figure 23.21   Structural modifications of the small intestine that increase its surface area for digestion and absorption.
Figure 23.22   Villi and microvilli of the small intestine.

Answers to End-of-Chapter Questions

Multiple Choice and Matching Question answers appear in Appendix G of the main text.

Short Answer Essay Questions

18. A drawing of the organs of the alimentary tube and labels can be found on page 883, Fig. 23.1.

19. The digestive system does contain local nerve plexuses known as the local (enteric) nervous system or the gut brain. This is essentially composed of nerve plexuses in the wall of the alimentary canal that extend the entire length of the GI tract. These plexuses respond to local stimuli in the GI tract by initiating both short and long reflexes. The gut brain solely mediates the short reflexes. Long reflexes are initiated by both external and local stimuli, and involve both the gut brain and the ANS. (Sympathetic nerves inhibit GI tract activity, whereas parasympathetic nerves, primarily the vagus nerve, stimulate it.) (pp. 885–886)

20. The basic alimentary canal wall structure consists of four tunics: the mucosa, submucosa, muscularis, and serosa. The mucosa consists of a surface epithelium underlain by a small amount of connective tissue called the lamina propria and a scanty amount of smooth muscle fibers, the muscularis mucosae. Typically, the epithelium of the mucosa is a simple columnar epithelium rich in mucus-secreting goblet cells and other types of glands. The mucus protects certain digestive organs from being digested themselves by the enzymes working within their cavities and eases the passage of food along the tract. In some digestive organs the mucosa contains both enzyme-secreting and hormone-secreting cells. The lamina propria, consisting of areolar connective tissue and containing lymph nodules, is important in the defense against bacteria and other pathogens. In the small intestine, the muscularis mucosae throw the mucosal tunic into a series of small folds that vastly increases its surface area for secretion and absorption.

The submucosa is areolar connective tissue containing blood vessels, lymphatic vessels, nerve endings, and epithelial glands. Its vascular network supplies surrounding tissues and carries away absorbed nutrients. Its nerve plexus is part of the enteric nerve supply of the gastrointestinal tube.

The muscularis externa mixes and propels food along the digestive tract. This muscular tunic usually has an inner circular layer and an outer longitudinal layer of smooth muscle cells, although there are variations in this pattern.

The serosa is formed of areolar connective tissue covered with mesothelium, a single layer of squamous epithelial cells. It is the protective outermost layer and the visceral peritoneum. (pp. 887–888)

21. The mesentery is a double peritoneal fold that suspends the small intestine from the posterior abdominal wall. The mesocolon is a special dorsal mesentery that secures the transverse colon to the parietal peritoneum of the posterior abdominal wall. The greater omentum is also a double peritoneal sheet that covers the coils of the small intestine and wraps the transverse portion of the large intestine. (pp. 886, 900)

22. The six functional activities of the digestive system are ingestion, propulsion, mechanical digestion, chemical digestion, absorption, and defecation. (pp. 884–885)

23. The boundaries of the oral cavity include the lips, cheeks, tongue, palate, and oropharynx. The epithelium is stratified squamous epithelium because the walls have to withstand considerable abrasion. (pp. 889–900)

24. a. The normal number of permanent teeth is 32; deciduous teeth, 20.

    b. Enamel covers the crown; cementum, the root.

    c. Dentin makes up the bulk of the tooth.

    d. Pulp is found in the central cavity in the tooth. Soft tissue structures (connective tissue, blood vessels, and nerve fibers) compose pulp. (pp. 893–895)

25. The two phases of swallowing are as follows:

    a. Buccal (voluntary) phase of swallowing: organs involved—tongue, soft palate; activities—tongue compacts food into a bolus, forces the bolus into the oropharynx via tongue contractions. The soft palate rises to close off the superior nasopharynx. (pp. 897–898)

    b. Pharyngeal-esophageal (involuntary) phase: organs involved—pharynx and esophagus; activities—motor impulses sent from the swallowing center to their muscles, which contract to send the food to the esophagus by peristalsis. Arrival of food/peristaltic wave at the gastroesophageal sphincter causes it to open. (p. 898)

26. The parietal cells secrete hydrochloric acid and intrinsic factor. Chief cells produce pepsinogen. Mucous neck cells produce mucus that helps shield the stomach wall from damage by gastric juices. Enteroendocrine cells secrete hormones into the lamina propria. (pp. 900–901)

27. Gastric secretion is controlled by both neural and hormonal mechanisms. The stimulation of gastric secretion involves three distinct phases: the cephalic, gastric, and intestinal phases.

    The cephalic phase occurs before food enters the stomach and is triggered by the sight, aroma, taste, or thought of food. Input is relayed to the hypothalamus, which stimulates the vagal nuclei of the medulla oblongata, causing motor impulses to be sent via vagal nerve fibers to the stomach. This reflex may be dampened during depression or loss of appetite.

    The gastric phase is initiated by neural and hormonal mechanisms once food reaches the stomach. Stomach distension activates stretch receptors and initiates reflexes that transmit impulses to the medulla and then back to the stomach, leading to acetylcholine release. Acetylcholine stimulates the output of gastric juice. During this phase, the hormone gastrin is more important in gastric juice secretion than neural influences. Chemical stimuli provided by foods directly activate gastrin-secreting cells. Gastrin stimulates the gastric glands to spew out even more gastric juice. Gastrin secretions are inhibited by high acidity.

The intestinal phase is set into motion when partially digested food begins to fill the duodenum. This filling stimulates intestinal mucosal cells to release a hormone (intestinal gastrin) that encourages the gastric glands to continue their secretory activity briefly; but as more food enters the small intestine, the enterogastric reflex is initiated, which inhibits gastric secretion and food entry into the duodenum to prevent the small intestine from being overwhelmed. Additionally, intestinal hormones (enterogastrones) inhibit gastric activity. (pp. 902–905)

28. a. The cystic and common hepatic ducts fuse to form the bile duct, which fuses with the pancreatic ducts just before entering the duodenum. (p. 912)

    b. The point of fusion of the common bile duct and pancreatic duct is called the hepatopancreatic ampulla. (p. 908)

29. The absence of bile (which causes fat emulsification) and/or pancreatic juice (which contains essentially the only important source of lipase) causes fat absorption to be so slow as to allow most of the fat to be passed into the large intestine. (p. 932)

30. The Kupffer cells function to remove debris such as bacteria from the blood. The hepatocytes function to produce bile, in addition to their many metabolic activities. (p. 912)

31. a. Brush border enzymes are intestinal digestive enzymes; these are part of the plasma membrane of the microvilli of the intestinal absorptive cells. (p. 910)

    b. Chylomicrons are fatty droplets consisting of triglycerides combined with small amounts of phospholipids, cholesterol, and free fatty acids, and coated with proteins. They are formed within the absorptive cells and enter the lacteals. (p. 932)

32. Common inflammatory conditions include appendicitis in adolescents, ulcers, and gallbladder problems in middle-age adults, and constipation in old age. (p. 937)

33. The effects of aging on digestive system activity include declining mobility, reduced production of digestive juice, less efficient absorption, and slowing of peristalsis. (p. 937)

Critical Thinking and Clinical Application Questions

1. If the agent promotes increased bowel motility without providing for increased bulk, diverticulosis is a possibility, because the rigor of the colonic contractions increases when the volume of residues is small. This increases the pressure on the colon wall, promoting the formation of diverticula. If the product irritates the intestinal mucosa, diarrhea will occur. Intestinal contents will be moved rapidly through both the small and large intestines, leaving inadequate time for absorption of water, which can result in dehydration and electrolyte imbalance. (pp. 926–927)

2. This patient has the classical symptoms of a gallbladder attack in which a gallstone has lodged in the cystic duct. The pain is discontinuous and colicky because it reflects the rhythm of peristaltic contractions (contract-relax-contract-relax, etc.). The stone can be removed surgically or by sound or laser treatment. If it is not removed, bile will back up into the liver, and jaundice will result. (p. 917)

3. The baby's blood would indicate acidosis due to the intestinal juice passing through the large intestine with little or no time for reabsorption of water and substances such as bicarbonate ions dissolved in water by the large intestine. (p. 927)

4. a. Most gastric ulcers are found to be caused by infection with *Helicobacter pylori*. This drug regimen successfully eradicates the infection.

b. Possible consequences of nontreatment could be surgical removal of the existing ulcer due to internal bleeding, or the occurrence of multiple ulcers. (p. 902)

5. An endoscope is an instrument used to visually inspect any cavity of the body and is composed of an illuminated fiber optic tube with a lens. The polyps seen were removed immediately because most colorectal cancers arise from initially benign polyps. Presently, colon cancer is the second largest cause of cancer death in males in the U.S. (p. 937)

6. Along with the risk of dehydration, severe diarrhea can result in loss of potassium, which could lead to an electrolyte imbalance that affects his neuromuscular function. His severe weakness may be a symptom of this. (p. 927)

Suggested Readings

Bansil, R., K.R. Bhaskar, J.D. Bradley, P. Garik, J.T. LaMont, H.E. Stanley, and B.S. Turner. "Viscous Fingering of HCl Through Gastric Mucin." *Nature* 360 (Dec. 1992): 458.

Barary, Nathan and Zon, Leonard I. "Endothelium—Chicken Soup for the Endoderm." *Science* 294 (5542) (Oct. 2001): 530–531.

Blaser, M. "The Bacteria Behind Ulcers." *Scientific American* 274 (Feb. 1996): 104–107.

Bnendia, M., and P. Tiollais. "Hepatitis B Virus." *Scientific American* 264 (Apr. 1991): 116.

Desai, K.M., W.C. Sessa, and J.R. Vane. "Involvement of Nitric Oxide in the Reflex Relaxation of the Stomach to Accommodate Food or Fluid." *Nature* 351 (June 1991): 477.

Fackelmann, K.A. "Nabbing a Gene for Colorectal Cancer." *Science News* 144 (Dec. 1993): 388.

Ferber, Dan. "Cracking Gut Bugs' Cell-Skewing Strategy." *Science* 294 (5550) (Dec. 2001): 2269.

Greenaugh, W.B., and N. Hirschhorn. "Progress in Oral Rehydration Therapy." *Scientific American* 264 (May 1991): 50.

Harder, Ben. "Germs That Do a Body Good." *Science News* 161 (5) (Feb. 2002): 72–74.

Koff, R. "Solving the Mysteries of Viral Hepatitis." *Scientific American: Science & Medicine* 1 (Mar./April 1994): 24–33.

Lambolez, Florence and Rocha, Benedita. "A Molecular Gut Reaction." *Science* 294 (5548) (Nov. 2001): 1848–1849.

Levine, D.S. "Barrett's Esophagus." *Scientific American: Science & Medicine* 1 (Nov./Dec. 1995): 16–25.

Raloff, J. "Housecleaning Cells May Become Assassins." *Science News* 143 (May 1993): 277.

Raloff, J. "Live Cancer: Homing in on the Risks." *Science News* 142 (Nov. 1992): 308.

Richardson, S. "Tongue Bugs." *Discover* (Oct. 1995): 44–46.

Turner, C.G. "Teeth and Prehistory in Asia." *Scientific American* 260 (Feb. 1989): 88–96.

Schiller, L.R. "Peristalis." *Scientific American: Science & Medicine* 1 (Nov./Dec. 1995): 38–47.

Seppa, N. "Immune Cells Rush to Gut in Food Allergy." *Science News* 159 (14) (April 2001): 214.

Stroh, M. "Exposing Salmonella's Gutsy Moves." *Science News* 141 (June 1992): 420.

Uvnas-Moberg, K. "The Gastrointestinal Tract in Growth and Reproduction." *Scientific American* 261 (July 1989): 78–83.

24 Nutrition, Metabolism, and Body Temperature Regulation

Objectives

Nutrition

1. Define a nutrient and list the six major nutrients of the body.

2. Discuss the dietary sources, uses in the body, and dietary requirements for carbohydrates, lipids, proteins, vitamins, and minerals.

3. Compare an essential amino acid and a nonessential amino acid, a complete and an incomplete protein.

4. Describe the difference between fat-soluble and water-soluble vitamins and the role of antioxidants.

Metabolism

5. Define metabolism, anabolism, catabolism, and oxidation-reduction reactions.

6. Explain the role of coenzymes in oxidation-reduction reactions.

7. Indicate the difference between substrate-level phosphorylation and oxidative phosphorylation.

8. Discuss carbohydrate metabolism and its three phases: glycolysis, Krebs cycle, and electron transport.

9. Compare glycogenesis and glycogenolysis.

10. Define gluconeogenesis.

11. Identify lipid metabolism, lipogenesis, and lipolysis.

12. Describe protein metabolism.

13. Discuss the catabolic and anabolic steady state of the body.

14. Explain the absorptive and postabsorptive states.

15. Discuss the metabolic roles of the liver.

Energy Balance

16. Define energy intake and energy output, and discuss their relationship.

17. Discuss the regulation of food intake and its theories.

18. Describe the body's metabolic rate, basal metabolic rate, and total metabolic rate.

19. Explain the regulation of body temperature, both heat generation and heat loss mechanisms.

Developmental Aspects of Nutrition and Metabolism

20. Discuss the consequences of poor nutrition in both the developing embryo and the elderly.

Suggested Lecture Outline

I. Nutrition (pp. 943–956; Figs. 24.1–24.2; Tables 24.1–24.3)

A. A nutrient is a substance in food that is used by the body to promote normal growth, maintenance, and repair. (pp. 943–944; Fig. 24.1)

   1. There are six categories of nutrients: carbohydrates, lipids, proteins, vitamins, minerals, and water.

2. Essential nutrients are those that cannot be made by the body and must be obtained in the diet.

B. Carbohydrates (p. 944; Table 24.1)

1. Except for milk sugar (lactose) and small amounts of glycogen found in meats, all the carbohydrates we ingest are derived from plants.

2. Glucose is the carbohydrate molecule ultimately used by the body as fuel to make ATP.

3. The current recommendation is 125–175 grams of carbohydrates daily with the emphasis on complex carbohydrates.

C. Lipids (pp. 944–946; Table 24.1)

1. The most common dietary lipids are the neutral fats, triglycerides or triacylglycerols, which occur as saturated fats and unsaturated fats.

2. Cholesterol is another dietary lipid that is found in egg yolk, meats, and milk products.

3. Dietary fats are essential as the major source of fuel for hepatocytes and skeletal muscle, for absorption of fat-soluble vitamins, and as components of the myelin sheaths and cellular membranes of the body.

D. Proteins (pp. 946–947; Fig. 24.2; Table 24.1)

1. Animal products contain the highest-quality proteins, those with the greatest amount and best ratio of amino acids.

   a. Proteins in eggs, milk, and meats are considered to be complete proteins that meet all the body's amino acid requirements for tissue maintenance and growth.

   b. Legumes, nuts, and cereals are protein-rich but not complete, but when cereal grains and legumes are ingested together they provide all the essential amino acids.

2. Proteins are important as structural materials of the body, enzymes, and hormones.

   a. All amino acids needed to make a particular protein must be present in a cell at the same time and in sufficient amounts for the protein to be made.

   b. For optimal protein synthesis the diet needs sufficient carbohydrate or fat calories for ATP production.

   c. The body is in nitrogen balance when the amount of nitrogen ingested in proteins is equal to the amount lost in urine and feces.

   d. Anabolic hormones accelerate protein synthesis and growth.

3. The amount of protein a person needs reflects his or her age, size, metabolic rate, and current state of nitrogen balance.

E. Vitamins are potent organic compounds needed in small amounts for growth and good health, most of which function as coenzymes. (pp. 947–952; Table 24.2)

1. Fat-soluble vitamins (A, D, E, and K) bind to ingested lipids and are absorbed along with their digestion products.

2. Water-soluble vitamins (B complex vitamins and vitamin C) are absorbed along with water from the gastrointestinal tract, and excess amounts are excreted from the body in urine.

3. Vitamins A, C, and E are antioxidants that disarm tissue-damaging free radicals.

F. The body requires moderate amounts of seven minerals and trace amounts of about a dozen others that are used by the body to add strength to structures or to act as ions in the blood and cells. (pp. 952–956; Table 24.3)

II. Metabolism (pp. 956–981; Figs. 24.3–24.22; Tables 24.4–24.7)

A. Overview of Metabolic Processes (pp. 956–959; Figs. 24.3–24.4; Table 24.4)

1. Anabolism is the general term for all reactions in which larger molecules or structures are built from smaller ones.

2. Catabolism refers to all processes that break down complex structures to simpler ones.

3. In oxidation-reduction reactions one substance is oxidized and loses energy by losing electrons, while another substance is reduced and gains energy and electrons that are transferred from the oxidized substance.

4. Our cells use two mechanisms to capture some of the energy liberated through oxidation-reduction reactions to make ATP.

    a. Substrate-level phosphorylation occurs when high-energy phosphate groups are transferred directly from phosphorylated substrates to ADP.

    b. Oxidative phosphorylation is carried out by electron transport, which occurs in the cristae of the mitochondria and couples the movement of substances across membranes to chemical reactions.

B. Carbohydrate Metabolism (pp. 959–967; Figs. 24.5–24.12)

1. Oxidation of glucose

    a. Glycolysis is a series of ten steps where glucose is converted into two pyruvic acid molecules in the cytosol of cells.

    b. Krebs cycle occurs in the matrix of the mitochondria where the pyruvic acid is passed through a series of reactions that generate reduced electron carrier molecules, $NADH + H^+$ and $FADH_2$.

    c. Electron transport chain passes electrons through a series of oxidative phosphorylation reactions that generate 28 ATP molecules.

2. Glycogenesis is the formation of glycogen, the animal storage form of glucose, that occurs when excess glucose is ingested.

3. Glycogenolysis is the breakdown of glycogen into individual glucose molecules that occurs when the blood sugar levels drop.

4. Gluconeogenesis is the process of forming new glucose from noncarbohydrate molecules that occurs in the liver using glycerol and amino acids.

C. Lipid Metabolism (pp. 967–970; Figs. 24.13–24.14)

1. Most body cells easily convert glycerol to glyceraldehyde phosphate, a glycolysis intermediate that enters the Krebs cycle.

2. Beta oxidation is the first phase of fatty acid metabolism where fatty acid chains are split into two carbon acetic acid fragments and coenzymes are reduced.

3. Lipogenesis is the reformation of triglycerides from unused glycerol and fatty acid chains for storage in the body.

4. Lipolysis is the breakdown of stored fats into glycerol and fatty acids to be used by the body for fuel.

D. Protein metabolism occurs whenever proteins have reached the end of their life span and must be broken down to replace the "aged" proteins. (pp. 970–971; Fig. 24.15)

1. Oxidation of Amino Acids
    a. Transamination is the process of transferring an amine group to alpha-ketoglutaric acid to make glutamic acid.
    b. Oxidative deamination occurs in the liver and removes the amine group of glutamic acid as ammonia and regenerates alpha-ketoglutaric acid.
    c. Keto acid modification is used to produce molecules that can be oxidized in the Krebs cycle or converted to glucose from keto acids produced through transamination.

E. The body exists in a dynamic catabolic-anabolic state, where substances are continually being broken down and rebuilt. (pp. 971–973; Figs. 24.16–24.17)

F. Absorptive and Postabsorptive States (pp. 973–978; Figs. 24.8–24.21; Tables 24.5–24.6)

1. Absorptive state is the time during and shortly after eating when nutrients are moving into the blood from the GI tract.
    a. Absorbed monosaccharides are delivered directly to the liver where they are converted into glucose and either used by the cells of the body, stored as glycogen, or converted into fats to be stored.
    b. Triglycerides are either used for anabolic purposes or stored in adipose tissue.
    c. Amino acids are delivered to the liver, which deaminates some and uses others to make plasma proteins, but most remain in the blood to be distributed to body cells.
    d. Insulin directs all events of the absorptive state.

2. Postabsorptive state is the period when the GI tract is empty and energy resources are supplied by the body reserves.
    a. Sources of blood glucose include glycogen in the liver, skeletal muscle cells, adipose tissues, and cellular proteins.
    b. Glucose sparing is the increased use of noncarbohydrate fuel molecules for energy to save glucose during times of fasting.
    c. The sympathetic nervous system and several hormones interact to control the postabsorptive state.

G. The Metabolic Role of the Liver (pp. 978–981; Fig. 24.22; Table 24.7)

1. The hepatocytes carry out over 500 metabolic functions.
2. Cholesterol serves as the structural basis for bile salts, steroid hormones, vitamin D; as a component of the plasma membrane; and as a signaling molecule in embryonic development.
3. About 85% of cholesterol is made in the liver and other body cells, and is lost from the body in bile salts in feces.
4. Cholesterol is insoluble in water and must be transported in the body bound to small lipid-protein complexes called lipoproteins.
5. Factors Regulating Plasma Cholesterol Levels
    a. Severe restriction of dietary cholesterol does not lead to a steep reduction in plasma cholesterol levels.
    b. Saturated fatty acids stimulate liver synthesis of cholesterol and inhibit its excretion from the body.
    c. Unsaturated fatty acids enhance excretion of cholesterol from the body.
    d. Trans fatty acids cause a greater increase in LDL levels and a greater reduction in HDL levels than saturated fatty acids.

   e. Smoking, coffee drinking, and stress increase LDL levels; regular aerobic exercise appears to reduce LDL levels and increase HDL levels.

III. Energy Balance (pp. 981–989; Figs. 24.23–24.26)

A. A dynamic exists within the body between the energy intake and energy output. (pp. 981–982)

   1. Energy intake is the energy liberated during food oxidation.

   2. Energy output includes energy lost as heat, energy used to do work, and energy that is stored as fat or glycogen.

B. Regulation of Food Intake (pp. 982–984; Fig. 24.23)

   1. When energy intake and energy output are balanced weight remains stable; when not balanced weight is either lost or gained.

   2. Factors that control eating include: neural signals from the digestive system, bloodborne signals related to body energy stores, hormones, body temperature, and psychological factors.

C. The body's rate of energy output is called the metabolic rate, which is the total heat produced by all the chemical reactions and mechanical work of the body. (pp. 984–985)

   1. The basal metabolic rate (BMR) reflects the energy the body needs to perform only its most essential activities.

   2. Factors influencing BMR include body surface area, age, gender, stress, and hormones.

   3. The total metabolic rate (TMR) is the rate of kilocalorie consumption needed to fuel all ongoing activities both involuntary and voluntary.

D. Body temperature regulation represents a balance between heat production and heat loss. (pp. 985–989; Figs. 24.24–24.26)

   1. The body's core (organs within the skull, thoracic and abdominal cavities) has the highest temperature and its shell (the skin) has the lowest temperature in most circumstances.

   2. Mechanisms of Heat Exchange

      a. Radiation is the loss of heat in the form of infrared waves (thermal energy).

      b. Conduction is the transfer of heat from a warmer object to a cooler one when the two are in direct contact with each other.

      c. Convection occurs when the warm air surrounding the body expands and rises and is replaced by cooler air molecules.

      d. Evaporation removes large amounts of body heat when water absorbs heat before vaporizing.

   3. The hypothalamus is the brain's main integrating center for thermoregulation, containing the heat-loss center and the heat-promoting center.

   4. Heat-promoting mechanisms are triggered when the external temperature is low, or blood temperature falls and the heat-promoting center is activated.

      a. Vasoconstriction of cutaneous blood vessels

      b. Increase in metabolic rate

      c. Shivering

      d. Enhanced thyroxine release

      e. Behavioral modifications

5. Heat-loss mechanisms protect the body from excessively high temperatures.
    a. Vasodilation of cutaneous blood vessels allows the body to lose heat through radiation, conduction, and convection.
    b. Enhanced sweating is used if the environment becomes so hot it cannot be lost by other means than evaporation.
6. Fever is controlled hyperthermia, usually resulting from an infection somewhere in the body.

IV. Developmental Aspects of Nutrition and Metabolism (pp. 989–992)

A. Embryological
    1. Good nutrition is essential *in utero* for the growth of fetal tissues and brain.
    2. Inadequate calories during the first three years of life, a time of brain growth, will lead to mental deficits or learning disorders.
    3. Proteins are needed for muscle and bone growth, and calcium is required for strong bones.
B. Aging
    1. By middle age and old age non-insulin-dependent diabetes mellitus becomes a problem, especially in the obese.
    2. Metabolic rate declines as we age.
    3. Muscle and bones deteriorate, and the efficiency of the endocrine system decreases.

Cross References

Additional information on topics covered in Chapter 24 can be found in the chapters listed below.

1. Chapter 2: Chemical bonding; carbohydrates; lipids; proteins; water; ATP; oxidation/reduction; chemical equations; patterns of chemical reactions; reversibility of reactions; enzymes
2. Chapter 3: Membrane transport; cytoplasm; mitochondria
3. Chapter 12: Hypothalamus
4. Chapter 13: Receptors
5. Chapter 16: Prostaglandins; growth hormone; sex steroids; glucocorticoids; diabetes; insulin; glucagon; thyroxine
6. Chapter 19: Blood flow regulation
7. Chapter 23: Chylomicrons; bile formation
8. Chapter 25: Ketone bodies as abnormal urine constituents

Lecture Hints

1. In order to fully understand the metabolic pathways, students should review the basic concepts of chemistry in Chapter 2 and cellular structure in Chapter 3. Refer the class to specific sections related to the lecture topic being discussed.
2. Point out that fatty acids perform several functions: structural (membranes), functional (prostaglandins), and as an energy source (enters the Krebs cycle as acetyl CoA).
3. Mention that cholesterol is responsible for membrane fluidity and is the structural basis of the steroid hormones.

4. As a point of interest, mention the logical meaning of the term *anabolic steroid*.

5. Point out the difference between vitamins and minerals.

6. The chemist's approach to the metabolic pathways is often very different than that of a biologist. One of the most effective methods for presenting the biochemical pathways of ATP synthesis (from the perspective of a physiologist) is to start with a quick review of cell structure related to the process (membranes, cytoplasm, mitochondria, etc.). Then give the overall outcome of each step (glycolysis, Krebs cycle, electron transport), followed by a more detailed examination of each step. It is essential that students see the "overall picture" in order to understand the significance of the metabolic pathways. Many students have previously studied the pathways and have never realized the relevance to life. You will often receive comments to the effect of: "I've memorized these pathways before, but never understood why until now!"

7. Point out that the Krebs cycle is often considered part of aerobic respiration, but that this step in the pathway does not use oxygen directly.

8. Emphasize that glycolysis occurs whether or not oxygen is present, so the term *anaerobic* must be used with caution.

9. Draw and project a diagram of the cell with a disproportionately large mitochondrion. Label the diagram with the locations of glycolysis, Krebs cycle, and electron transport. Give a brief summary of each step.

10. Mention possible alternate terms for Krebs cycle: *citric acid cycle* (citrate is the first substrate in the cycle), *tricarboxylic acid cycle* (several intermediates have three carboxyl groups).

11. A diagram of the chemiosmotic mechanism of ATP synthesis is very helpful in presenting electron transport. Draw (on a blank acetate) a diagram of the phospholipid bilayer, fill in electron carriers, and ATP synthetase complex, and trace the pathway of electron flow. It is helpful for the instructor to physically draw the diagram (if time allows), especially if the students are required to draw and analyze diagrams on the exam.

12. To measure student understanding, ask plenty of questions during discussion of the pathways. For example, ask: "What would happen to ATP production if $NADH + H^+$ reduced the cytochrome oxidase complex instead of the NADH dehydrogenase complex?"

13. Remind the class of the different ways that nutrients are absorbed and transported (lipids into lacteals, carbohydrates and proteins into blood capillaries). Small reminders help keep the chemistry tied to biological processes.

14. Remind the class that deamination of amino acids is necessary for the carbon "skeletons" to enter catabolic pathways. The nitrogenous compounds are metabolic waste products, the elimination of which is discussed in Chapter 25.

15. When discussing mechanisms of heat control, point out that one can think of heat flowing down its "concentration gradient."

16. Reinforce the concept of the reflex arc when presenting material on hypothalamic control of body temperature.

Activities/Demonstrations

1. Audio-visual materials listed under Multimedia in the Classroom and Lab.

2. Using the Dubois Body Surface Chart, students can make rough estimations of basal metabolic rate by calculating respiratory rate and body surface area.

3. Use a small portable fan and a container of water to demonstrate the mechanics of cooling the body.

4. Use laminated posters showing the various metabolic pathways as you discuss them.

Critical Thinking/Discussion Topics

1. Discuss the need for a balanced diet.

2. Explore the idea that more vitamins and minerals are lost in the urine of Americans than are in the diets of people in many other countries. Discuss overdosing from vitamins, etc., from health food store products and other sources, rather than getting vitamins and minerals only from the food we eat.

3. Discuss the various metabolic disorders and relate each one to the dietary deficiency that causes the disorder.

4. Examine the differences between the lipid- and water-soluble vitamins and why care should be taken when using vitamins as a food supplement.

5. Why are there so many steps in the complete oxidation of glucose (i.e., why not just one step)?

6. Discuss the consequences (in terms of ATP production) if $NADH + H^+$ reduced the cytochrome b-c1 complex instead of the NADH dehydrogenase complex.

Library Research Topics

1. Research the differences between and significance of low-density and high-density cholesterol.

2. Study the effects of the inability to sweat.

3. Research the effects of a liquid protein diet on the body.

4. Investigate the various types of popular diets currently being publicized. Note differences, similarities, and adverse effects, if any.

Multimedia in the Classroom and Lab

Online Resources for Students

The
Anatomy & Physiology Place   **MyA&P**
www.anatomyandphysiology.com   www.myaandp.com

The following shows the organization of the Chapter Guide page in both the Anatomy & Physiology Place and MyA&P™. The Chapter Guide organizes all the chapter-specific online media resources for Chapter 24 in one convenient location, with e-book links to each section of the textbook. Please note that both sites also give you access to other general A&P resources, like InterActive Physiology®, PhysioEx 6.0™, Anatomy 360°, Flashcards, a Glossary, a Histology Tutorial, *and much more.*

Objectives
Section 24.1 Nutrition (pp. 943–956)
Section 24.2 Metabolism (pp. 956–981)
Activity: Overview of Cellular Respiration
Activity: The Three Major Phases of Glycolysis
Case Study: Diabetes Mellitus
Memory: Nutrition and Metabolism

Memory: Processes of Metabolism
Section 24.3 Energy Balance (pp. 981–989)
Section 24.4 Developmental Aspects of Nutrition and Metabolism (pp. 989, 992)
Chapter Summary
Self-Study Quizzes
Art Labeling Quiz
Matching Quiz
Multiple-Choice Quiz (Level I)
Multiple-Choice Quiz (Level II)
True-False Quiz
Crossword Puzzles
Crossword Puzzle 24.1
Crossword Puzzle 24.2

Media

See Guide to Audio-Visual Resources in Appendix A for key to AV distributors.

Video

1. *Cellular Respiration* (FHS; 6-part series, 10 min. each). The series traces cellular respiration by examining the essential fuels and machinery that sustain life. It traces the breakdown of glucose through glycolysis, the Krebs cycle, and oxidative phosphorylation. Finally, it connects these processes with nutrition.
2. *Contemporary Nutrition* (FHS; 60 min., 1993). This program examines nutrition issues of the day. It shows physiological details critical to human nutrition, as well as explanations and demonstrations by experts.
3. *The Food Guide Pyramid: Contemporary Nutrition* (FHS; 30 min., 1993). Starting with a brief history of nutrition, this program illustrates how contemporary nutrition can improve how you look, feel, and live.
4. *Free Radicals* (FHS; 30 min., 1996). Free radicals are an important weapon in the immune system but they can also cause chemical reactions that lead to damage of fatty acids, DNA mutation, and protein destruction.
5. *Fundamental Human Nutrition* (IM; 36 min., 1996). Examines how nutrients aid in cell maintenance, metabolic regulation, and energy production. Explains the roles of carbohydrates, lipids, proteins, vitamins, minerals, and water in human nutrition.
6. *Nutrition and Cancer* (FHS; 21 min., 1997). This video focuses on the new field of nutritional oncology and efforts to prove the relationship between cancer and nutrition.
7. *Proteins* (FHS; 37 min., 1994). This program provides insights into the structure and several of the functions of proteins, including their role in catalytic biochemical reaction and reproduction.

Software

1. *Cellular Respiration* (CBS; Win/Mac). Includes both anaerobic and aerobic processes. Presents the newest model of ATP synthesis. An analysis of net gain of ATPs in fermentation and in aerobic respiration is fully detailed. Allows students to review involved concepts such as the electron transport chain until they fully comprehend the material.
2. *Cellular Respiration CD-ROM* (WNS; Win/Mac). Important and complicated cellular processes come to life with the special effects and colorful animation sequences that fill the program. Covers oxidation-reduction reactions, fermentation, and the Krebs cycle.

3. *Nutrition* (FHS; Win/Mac). Examines nutrition and the components of a healthy diet, and defines the problems and effects of deficient diets, harmful diets, and dietary imbalances in humans and animals. Food is broken down into its chemical products; carbohydrates, starches, proteins, and vitamins.

4. *Nutrition Interactive* (IM; Win/Mac). This CD-ROM provides an introduction to concepts in nutrition. It discusses digestion, metabolism, vitamins and minerals, and diet analysis with animation, hands-on exercises, and an audio glossary.

Lecture Enhancement Material

To view thumbnails of all of the illustrations for Chapter 24, see Appendix B.

Transparencies Index/Media Manager

Table 24.6   Summary of Normal Hormonal Influences on Metabolism
Table 24.7   Summary of Metabolic Functions of the Liver
A Closer Look   Obesity: Magical Solution Wanted*
Indicates images that are on the Media Manager only.

Answers to End-of-Chapter Questions

Multiple Choice and Matching Question answers appear in Appendix G of the main text.

Short Answer Essay Questions

16. Cellular respiration is a group of reactions that break down (oxidize) glucose, fatty acids, and amino acids in the cell. Some of the energy released is used to synthesize ATP. FAD and NAD$^+$ function as reversible hydrogen acceptors that deliver the accepted hydrogen to the electron transport chain. (pp. 956–958)

17. Glycolysis occurs in the cytoplasm of cells. It may be separated into three major events: (1) sugar activation, (2) sugar cleavage, and (3) oxidation and ATP formation. During sugar activation, glucose is phosphorylated, converted to fructose, and phosphorylated again to yield fructose-1,6-diphosphate; two molecules of ATP are used. These reactions provide the activation energy for the later events of glycolysis. During sugar cleavage, fructose-1,6-diphosphate is split into two 3-carbon fragments: glyceraldehyde 3-phosphate or dihydroxyacetone phosphate. During oxidation and ATP formation, the 3-carbon molecules are oxidized by the removal of hydrogen (which is picked up by NAD). Inorganic phosphate groups that are attached to each oxidized fragment by high-energy bonds are cleaved off, capturing enough energy to form four ATP molecules. The final products of glycolysis are two molecules of pyruvic acid, two molecules of reduced NAD, and a net gain of two ATP molecules per glucose molecule. (pp. 960–961)

18. Pyruvic acid is converted to acetyl CoA, which enters the Krebs cycle. For pyruvic acid to be converted to acetyl CoA, the following must take place: decarboxylation to remove a carbon, oxidation to remove hydrogen atoms, and combination of the resulting acetic acid with coenzyme A to produce acetyl CoA. (p. 961)

19. Glycogenesis is the process by which glucose molecules are combined in long chains to form glycogen. Gluconeogenesis is the formation of new sugar from noncarbohydrate molecules. Lipogenesis is the term for triglyceride synthesis. Glycogenesis (and perhaps lipogenesis) is likely to occur after a carbohydrate-rich meal. Gluconeogenesis is likely to occur just before waking up in the morning. (pp. 966–967)

20. Metabolic acidosis due to ketosis is the result of excessive amounts of fats being burned for energy. Starvation, unwise dieting, and diabetes mellitus can result in ketosis. (p. 969)

21.

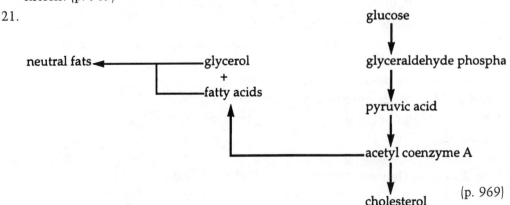

(p. 969)

22. HDLs function to transport cholesterol from the peripheral tissues to the liver. LDLs transport cholesterol to the peripheral tissues. (p. 980)

23. Factors influencing plasma cholesterol levels include diet (through intake of cholesterol and/or saturated fatty acids), smoking, drinking, and stress. Sources of cholesterol in the body include the intake of animal foods and production from acetyl coenzyme A in the liver (and intestinal cells). Cholesterol is lost from the body when it is catabolized and secreted in bile salts that are eventually excreted in feces. It is used by body cells in plasma membranes and in synthesizing vitamin D and steroid hormones. (pp. 978–980)

24. "Body energy balance" means that energy intake is equal to total energy output. If the body is not in exact balance, weight is either gained or lost. (p. 982)

25. Metabolic rate is increased with increased production of thyroxine. Eating increases metabolic rate, an effect called chemical thermogenesis. A higher ratio of body surface area to body volume requires a higher metabolic rate, because heat exchange surface area is greater. Muscular exercise and emotional stress increase metabolic rate. Starvation decreases metabolic rate. (pp. 984–985)

26. The body's core includes organs within the skull and the thoracic and abdominal cavities. The core has the highest temperature. The shell, or skin, has the lowest temperature. Blood serves as the heat transfer agent between the core and shell. (p. 986)

27. Heat-promoting mechanisms to maintain or increase body temperature include vasoconstriction in the shell, which inhibits heat loss via radiation; conduction and convection; increase in metabolic rate due to epinephrine release; and shivering. Heat-loss mechanisms include vasodilation of blood vessels in the skin and sweating (which enhances heat transfer via evaporation).

    Whenever core temperature increases above or decreases below normal, peripheral and central thermoreceptors send input to the hypothalamus. Much like a thermostat, the hypothalamus responds to the input by initiating the appropriate heat-promoting or heat-loss reflex mechanisms via autonomic effector pathways. (pp. 987–989)

Critical Thinking and Clinical Application Questions

1. The number of ATP molecules resulting from the complete oxidation of a particular fatty acid can be calculated easily by counting the number of carbon atoms in the fatty acid and dividing by two to determine the number of acetyl CoA molecules produced. For our example, an 18-carbon fatty acid yields 9 acetyl CoA molecules. Because each of these yield 12 ATP molecules per turn of the Krebs cycle, a total of 108 ATP molecules is provided from the oxidative pathways: 9 from electron transport oxidation of 3 NADH + H$^+$, 2 from the oxidation of 1 FADH$_2$, and a net yield of 1 ATP during the Krebs cycle. Also, for every acetyl CoA released during beta oxidation, an additional molecule each of NADH + H$^+$ and FADH$_2$ is produced, which, when reoxidized, yield a total of 5 ATP molecules more. In an 18-carbon fatty acid, this would occur 8 times, yielding 40 more ATP molecules. After subtracting the ATP needed to get the process going, this adds up to a grand total of 147 ATP molecules from that single 18-carbon fatty acid! (pp. 968, 965–966)

2. Hypothermia is abnormally depressed body temperature. It kills by dropping the body temperature below the relatively narrow range in which biochemical reactions can take place. The elderly have less subcutaneous tissue. Also, their metabolic rate (and heat-generating capacity) is slower. (p. 989)

3. With a diagnosis of high cholesterol and severe arteriosclerosis, he should avoid foods containing saturated fatty acids and avoid eating eggs and large amounts

of red meat. He should substitute foods containing unsaturated fatty acids and add fish to his diet. He should also stop smoking, cut down on his coffee, avoid stress situations when possible, and increase his amount of aerobic exercise. (pp. 978–981)

4. The chemiosmotic machinery concerns the operation of the electron transport chain and generation of the proton gradient during which most ATP is harvested in the mitochondria. If uncoupled, cells will use more and more nutrients in an effort to generate needed ATP, leaving fewer "calories" for protein synthesis and tissue maintenance. (pp. 958–959, 963–965)

5. Simon is exhibiting signs of vitamin C deficiency, otherwise known as scurvy. Although he has rich sources of many nutrients on his island, his diet is lacking fruits and green leafy vegetables as a source of vitamin C. (p. 949)

6. Gregor's blood tests probably revealed high cholesterol and high triglyceride levels. Cutting down on saturated fats such as steak and butter is a good idea. The fat in cottage cheese is also saturated and should be ingested in moderation. Gregor should increase his intake of the unsaturated fats such as olive oil and also add omega-3 fatty acids from fish. Gregor can replace the animal proteins with soy proteins to further lower his cholesterol levels. In addition to dietary changes Gregor needs to begin exercising to further lower his levels and help with his "bad" blood results.

Suggested Readings

Christensen, Damaris. "Fatty Findings." *Science News* 159 (15) (April 2001): 238–239.

Dulloo, Abdul G. "A Sympathetic Defense Against Obesity." *Science* 297 (5582) (Aug. 2002): 780–781.

Flier, Jeffrey S. "The Missing Link with Obesity?" *Nature* 409 (6818) (Jan. 2001): 292–293.

Friedman, Jeffrey. "Fat in All the Wrong Places." *Nature* 415 (6869) (Jan. 2002): 268–269.

Ioannou, Yiannis A. "Multidrug Permeases and Subcellular Cholesterol Transport." *Nature Reviews: Molecular Cell Biology* 2 (9) (Sept. 2001): 657–668.

Maeder, Thomas. "Down with the Bad, Up with the Good." *Scientific American* 286 (2) (Feb. 2002): 32–33.

Millington, David S. "Newborn Screening for Metabolic Diseases." *American Scientist* 9 (1) (Jan./Feb. 2002): 40–47.

Rader, Daniel J. "A New Feature on the Cholesterol-Lowering Landscape." *Nature Medicine* 7 (12) (Dec. 2001): 1282–1284.

Seppa, N. "Weak Appetite in Elderly Ties to Hormone." *Science News* 160 (Dec. 2001): 390.

Tatar, Marc and Rand, David M. "Dietary Advice on Q." *Science* 295 (5552) (Jan. 2002): 54–55.

Taubes, Gary. "The Soft Science of Dietary Fat." *Science* 291 (5513) (March 2001): 2536–2545.

Travis, John. "The Hunger Hormone?" *Science News* 161 (7) (Feb. 2002): 107–108.

Vidal-Puig, Antonio and O'Rahilly, Stephen. "Controlling the Glucose Factory." *Nature* 413 (6852) (Sept. 2001): 125–126.

Wang, L. "Veggies Prevent Cancer Through Key Protein." *Science News* 159 (14) (March 2001): 182.

Yoshida, M., Muneyuki, E., and Hisabori, T. "ATP Synthase—A Marvelous Rotary Engine of the Cell." *Nature Reviews: Molecular Biology* 2 (Sept. 2001): 669–677.

The Urinary System

Objectives

Kidney Anatomy

1. Describe the anatomy of the kidney and its placement in the body.
2. List the regions of the kidney and the structures found within each region.
3. Trace the vascular pathway through the kidney.
4. Name the structures and functions of the nephron and its elements.

Kidney Physiology: Mechanisms of Urine Formation

5. List the steps of urine formation.
6. Explain glomerular filtration and the mechanisms that control its pressure and rate.
7. Define tubular reabsorption; list the solutes that are reabsorbed and the mechanisms used to reclaim them from the filtrate.
8. Discuss the differences in solute reabsorption in each portion of the nephron tubules.
9. Explain tubular secretion, and list the solutes that are secreted.
10. Describe the countercurrent mechanism regulating urine concentration and volume.
11. Identify the roles of antidiuretic hormone and aldosterone in water and sodium reabsorption.

Urine

12. List the physical characteristics of urine and indicate its chemical composition.

Ureters

13. Describe the anatomy of the ureters.

Urinary Bladder

14. Explain the structure, location, and capacity of the urinary bladder.

Urethra

15. Identify the general location, structure, and function of the urethra and compare the male and female urethras.

Micturition

16. Define micturition and the events controlling it.

Developmental Aspects of the Urinary System

17. Explain the developmental events of the fetal urinary system.
18. Discuss the changes in control of micturition that occur during childhood.
19. List the age-related changes that occur in the urinary system.

Suggested Lecture Outline

I. Kidney Anatomy (pp. 998–1006; Figs. 25.1–25.7)

A. Location and External Anatomy (pp. 998–999; Figs. 25.1–25.2)

1. The kidneys are bean-shaped organs that lie retroperitoneal in the superior lumbar region.
2. The medial surface is concave and has a renal hilus that leads into a renal sinus, where the blood vessels, nerves, and lymphatics lie.

   3. The kidneys are surrounded by a fibrous, transparent renal capsule; a fatty adipose capsule that cushions the organ; and an outer fibrous renal fascia that anchors the kidney to surrounding structures.

B. Internal Anatomy (pp. 999–1001; Fig. 25.3)

   1. There are three distinct regions of the kidney: the cortex, the medulla, and the renal pelvis.

   2. Major and minor calyces collect urine and empty it into the renal pelvis.

C. Blood and Nerve Supply (p. 1001; Fig. 25.3)

   1. Blood supply into and out of the kidneys progresses to the cortex through renal arteries to segmental, lobar, interlobar, arcuate, and cortical radiate arteries, and back to renal veins from cortical radiate, arcuate, and interlobar veins.

   2. The renal plexus regulates renal blood flow by adjusting the diameter of renal arterioles and influencing the urine-forming role of the nephrons.

D. Nephrons are the structural and functional units of the kidneys that carry out processes that form urine (pp. 1001–1006; Figs. 25.4–25.7).

   1. Each nephron consists of a renal corpuscle composed of a tuft of capillaries (the glomerulus), surrounded by a glomerular capsule (Bowman's capsule).

   2. The renal tubule begins at the glomerular capsule as the proximal convoluted tubule, continues through a hairpin loop, the loop of Henle, and turns into a distal convoluted tubule before emptying into a collecting duct.

   3. The collecting ducts collect filtrate from many nephrons, and extend through the renal pyramid to the renal papilla, where they empty into a minor calyx.

   4. There are two types of nephrons: 85% are cortical nephrons, which are located almost entirely within the cortex; 15% are juxtamedullary nephrons, located near the cortex-medulla junction.

   5. The peritubular capillaries arise from efferent arterioles draining the glomerulus, and absorb solutes and water from the tubules.

   6. Blood flow in the renal circulation is subject to high resistance in the afferent and efferent arterioles.

   7. The juxtaglomerular apparatus is a structural arrangement between the afferent arteriole and the distal convoluted tubule that forms granular cells and macula densa cells.

   8. The filtration membrane lies between the blood and the interior of the glomerular capsule, and allows free passage of water and solutes.

II. Kidney Physiology: Mechanisms of Urine Formation (pp. 1007–1021; Figs. 25.8–25.16; Tables 25.1–25.2)

A. Step 1: Glomerular Filtration (pp. 1007–1011; Figs. 25.9–25.10)

   1. Glomerular filtration is a passive, nonselective process in which hydrostatic pressure forces fluids through the glomerular membrane.

   2. The net filtration pressure responsible for filtrate formation is given by the balance of glomerular hydrostatic pressure against the combined forces of colloid osmotic pressure of glomerular blood and capsular hydrostatic pressure exerted by the fluids in the glomerular capsule.

   3. The glomerular filtration rate is the volume of filtrate formed each minute by all the glomeruli of the kidneys combined.

4. Maintenance of a relatively constant glomerular filtration rate is important because reabsorption of water and solutes depends on how quickly filtrate flows through the tubules.

5. Glomerular filtration rate is held relatively constant through intrinsic autoregulatory mechanisms, and extrinsic hormonal and neural mechanisms.

   a. Renal autoregulation uses a myogenic control related to the degree of stretch of the afferent arteriole, and a tubuloglomerular feedback mechanism that responds to the rate of filtrate flow in the tubules.

   b. Extrinsic neural mechanisms are stress-induced sympathetic responses that inhibit filtrate formation by constricting the afferent arterioles.

   c. The renin-angiotensin mechanism causes an increase in systemic blood pressure and an increase in blood volume by increasing Na^+ reabsorption.

B. Step 2: Tubular Reabsorption (pp. 1011–1015; Figs. 25.11–25.12; Table 25.1)

   1. Tubular reabsorption begins as soon as the filtrate enters the proximal convoluted tubule, and involves near total reabsorption of organic nutrients, and the hormonally regulated reabsorption of water and ions.

   2. The most abundant cation of the filtrate is Na^+, and reabsorption is always active.

   3. Passive tubular reabsorption is the passive reabsorption of negatively charged ions that travel along an electrical gradient created by the active reabsorption of Na^+.

   4. Obligatory water reabsorption occurs in water-permeable regions of the tubules in response to the osmotic gradients created by active transport of Na^+.

   5. Secondary active transport is responsible for absorption of glucose, amino acids, vitamins, and most cations, and occurs when solutes are cotransported with Na^+ when it moves along its concentration gradient.

   6. Substances that are not reabsorbed or incompletely reabsorbed remain in the filtrate due to a lack of carrier molecules, lipid insolubility, or large size (urea, creatinine, and uric acid).

   7. Different areas of the tubules have different absorptive capabilities.

      a. The proximal convoluted tubule is most active in reabsorption, with most selective reabsorption occurring there.

      b. The descending limb of the loop of Henle is permeable to water, while the ascending limb is impermeable to water but permeable to electrolytes.

      c. The distal convoluted tubule and collecting duct have Na^+ and water permeability regulated by the hormones aldosterone, antidiuretic hormone, and atrial natriuretic peptide.

C. Step 3: Tubular Secretion (p. 1015)

   1. Tubular secretion disposes of unwanted solutes, eliminates solutes that were reabsorbed, rids the body of excess K^+, and controls blood pH.

   2. Tubular secretion is most active in the proximal convoluted tubule, but occurs in the collecting ducts and distal convoluted tubules, as well.

D. Regulation of Urine Concentration and Volume (pp. 1015–1021;
   Figs. 25.13–25.16)

   1. One of the critical functions of the kidney is to keep the solute load of body
      fluids constant by regulating urine concentration and volume.

   2. The countercurrent mechanism involves interaction between filtrate flow
      through the loops of Henle (the countercurrent multiplier) of juxtamedullary
      nephrons and the flow of blood through the vasa recta (the countercurrent
      exchanger).

      a. Since water is freely absorbed from the descending limb of the loop of
         Henle, filtrate concentration increases and water is reabsorbed.

      b. The ascending limb is permeable to solutes, but not to water.

      c. In the collecting duct, urea diffuses into the deep medullary tissue, con-
         tributing to the increasing osmotic gradient encountered by filtrate as it
         moves through the loop.

      d. The vasa recta aids in maintaining the steep concentration gradient of
         the medulla by cycling salt into the blood as it descends into the
         medulla, and then out again as it ascends toward the cortex.

   3. Since tubular filtrate is diluted as it travels through the ascending limb of
      the loop of Henle, production of a dilute urine is accomplished by simply
      allowing filtrate to pass on to the renal pelvis.

   4. Formation of a concentrated urine occurs in response to the release of
      antidiuretic hormone, which makes the collecting ducts permeable to water
      and increases water uptake from the urine.

   5. Diuretics act to increase urine output by either acting as an osmotic
      diuretic or by inhibiting Na^+ and resulting obligatory water reabsorption.

E. Renal Clearance (p. 1021)

   1. Renal clearance refers to the volume of plasma that is cleared of a specific
      substance in a given time.

   2. Inulin is used as a clearance standard to determine glomerular filtration
      rate since it is not reabsorbed, stored, or secreted.

   3. If the clearance value for a substance is less than that for inulin, then some
      of the substance is being reabsorbed; if the clearance value is greater than
      the inulin clearance rate, then some of the substance is being secreted. A
      clearance value of zero indicates the substance is completely reabsorbed.

III. Urine (pp. 1021–1023; Table 25.2)

A. Physical Characteristics (p. 1021)

   1. Freshly voided urine is clear and pale to deep yellow due to urochrome, a
      pigment resulting from the destruction of hemoglobin.

   2. Fresh urine is slightly aromatic, but develops an ammonia odor if allowed
      to stand, due to bacterial metabolism of urea.

   3. Urine is usually slightly acidic (around pH 6) but can vary from about
      4.5–8.0 in response to changes in metabolism or diet.

   4. Urine has a higher specific gravity than water, due to the presence of
      solutes.

B. Chemical Composition (pp. 1022–1023; Table 25.2)

   1. Urine volume is about 95% water and 5% solutes, the largest solute
      fraction devoted to the nitrogenous wastes urea, creatinine, and uric acid.

IV. Ureters (pp. 1023–1024; Fig. 25.17)

A. Ureters are tubes that actively convey urine from the kidneys to the bladder.

B. The walls of the ureters consist of an inner mucosa continuous with the kidney pelvis and the bladder, a double-layered muscularis, and a connective tissue adventitia covering the external surface.

V. Urinary Bladder (pp. 1024–1026; Figs. 25.18–25.19)

A. The urinary bladder is a muscular sac that expands as urine is produced by the kidneys to allow storage of urine until voiding is convenient.

B. The wall of the bladder has three layers: an outer adventitia, a middle layer of detrusor muscle, and an inner mucosa that is highly folded to allow distention of the bladder without a large increase in internal pressure.

VI. Urethra (p. 1026; Fig. 25.18)

A. The urethra is a muscular tube that drains urine from the body; it is 3–4 cm long in females, but closer to 20 cm in males.

B. There are two sphincter muscles associated with the urethra: the internal urethral sphincter, which is involuntary and formed from detrusor muscle; and the external urethral sphincter, which is voluntary and formed by the skeletal muscle at the urogenital diaphragm.

C. The external urethral orifice lies between the clitoris and vaginal opening in females, or occurs at the tip of the penis in males.

VII. Micturition (p. 1027; Fig. 25.20)

A. Micturition, or urination, is the act of emptying the bladder.

1. As urine accumulates, distention of the bladder activates stretch receptors, which trigger spinal reflexes, resulting in storage of urine.

2. Voluntary initiation of voiding reflexes results in activation of the micturition center of the pons, which signals parasympathetic motor neurons that stimulate contraction of the detrusor muscle and relaxation of the urinary sphincters.

VIII. Developmental Aspects of the Urinary System (pp. 1027–1030; Fig. 25.21)

A. In the developing fetus, the mesoderm-derived urogenital ridges give rise to three sets of kidneys: the pronephros, mesonephros, and metanephros. (pp. 1027–1028; Fig. 25.21)

1. The pronephros forms and degenerates during the fourth through sixth weeks, but the pronephric duct persists, and connects later-developing kidneys to the cloaca.

2. The mesonephros develops from the pronephric duct, which then is named the mesonephric duct, and persist until development of the metanephros.

3. The metanephros develops at about five weeks, and forms ureteric buds that give rise to the ureters, renal pelvises, calyces, and collecting ducts.

4. The cloaca subdivides to form the future rectum, anal canal, and the urogenital sinus, which gives rise to the bladder and urethra.

B. Newborns void most frequently, because the bladder is small and the kidneys cannot concentrate urine until two months of age. (p. 1030)

C. From two months of age until adolescence, urine output increases until the adult output volume is achieved. (p. 1030)

D. Voluntary control of the urinary sphincters depends on nervous system development, and complete control of the bladder even during the night does not usually occur before 4 years of age. (p. 1030)

E. In old age, kidney function declines due to shrinking of the kidney as nephrons decrease in size and number; the bladder also shrinks and loses tone, resulting in frequent urination. (p. 1030)

Cross References

Additional information on topics covered in Chapter 25 can be found in the chapters listed below.

1. Chapter 3: Hydrostatic pressure and membranes; membrane transport; microvilli
2. Chapter 4: Epithelial cells; dense connective tissue
3. Chapter 10: Levator ani
4. Chapter 14: Sympathetic control; parasympathetic pelvic splanchnic nerves; epinephrine
5. Chapter 16: Vitamin D activation; aldosterone; antidiuretic hormone; atrial natriuretic factor; epinephrine
6. Chapter 17: Erythropoietin; plasma
7. Chapter 19: Fenestrated capillaries; arterioles; autoregulation of blood flow; vascular resistance; fluid dynamics; renin-angiotensin
8. Chapter 26: Renin-angiotensin mechanism in control of extracellular fluid volume; electrolyte balance; glomerulonephritis; H^+ and HCO_3- and kidney function; hypoaldosteronism
9. Chapter 27: Male urethra and delivery of semen

Laboratory Correlations

1. Marieb, E. N. *Human Anatomy & Physiology Laboratory Manual: Cat and Fetal Pig Versions.* Eighth Edition Updates. Benjamin Cummings, 2006.
   Exercise 40: Anatomy of the Urinary System
   Exercise 41: Urinalysis
2. Marieb, E. N. *Human Anatomy & Physiology Laboratory Manual: Main Version.* Seventh Edition Update. Benjamin Cummings, 2006.
   Exercise 40: Anatomy of the Urinary System
   Exercise 41: Urinalysis

Histology Slides for the Life Sciences

Available through Benjamin Cummings, an imprint of Pearson Education, Inc. To order, contact your local Benjamin Cummings sales representative.

Slide 52	Transitional Epithelium, Bladder.
Slide 53	Renal Corpuscle, Kidney.
Slide 54	Wall of Urinary Bladder.
Slide 55	Cross Section of Ureter.

Lecture Hints

1. Emphasize the retroperitoneal location of urinary structures.

2. Stress the importance of maintaining the kidney in a normal position. Project slides showing kidneys in place and point out the difference in encasement between kidneys and other abdominal organs.

3. Use the analogy of a cone-shaped filter in a glass funnel to illustrate how a pyramid fits into its calyx. This gives students a 3-D structure to relate to kidney anatomy.

4. Emphasize that the "lines" pointing to the papilla are due to the large number of microscopic tubules oriented in that direction.

5. Poke a finger into a partially inflated balloon to illustrate how the glomerular capsule forms around the glomerulus.

6. Emphasize the unique microvasculature of the kidney: arterioles feed and drain the glomerulus. During the discussion of anatomy (before physiology has been covered), ask the students if they can come up with a logical function for this design (remind them of the function of arterioles).

7. Students will often confuse the different capillary beds of the kidney. Stress the difference between glomerulus, peritubular capillaries, and the vasa recta.

8. Figure 25.6 is an excellent schematic diagram of overall kidney function. Use this diagram to introduce the class to renal physiology.

9. Emphasize that the filtration membrane is actually composed of three layers, not a single phospholipid bilayer as some students imagine.

10. Introduce the control of glomerular filtration by presenting the overall logic of the system: Filtration is driven by hydrostatic pressure; therefore, control of the afferent arteriole (and possibly efferent arteriole) is the obvious means of pressure control to the nephron, and thereby control of glomerular filtration is achieved. Both extrinsic and intrinsic mechanisms of glomerular filtration regulation work toward the same goal: control of pressure in the glomerulus.

11. Establishing a point of reference is essential for student understanding of renal system terminology. Students often have problems with reabsorption versus secretion: "Is the tubule secreting into the blood?" Make sure the class establishes the epithelial cells of the tubule (or blood) as a reference point when using the terms *secretion* and *reabsorption*. Another possible source of confusion is secretion versus excretion.

12. Clearly distinguish between the effects of aldosterone and antidiuretic hormone. Although both result in decreased urine output (and increased blood volume), the mechanisms are different.

13. Emphasize that the backflow of urine into the ureters is prevented by means of a physiological sphincter; the ureters enter the bladder wall at an angle so that volume and pressure in the bladder increase; pressure forces the openings to the ureter to collapse, preventing retrograde movement of urine. Use a diagram to illustrate this mechanism since it is difficult for most students to visualize.

14. Mention the similar function of the rugae in the bladder to the rugae in the stomach.

15. Emphasize that the urinary system is one of the few locations in the body that contains transitional epithelium.

Activities/Demonstrations

1. Audio-visual materials listed under Multimedia in the Classroom and Lab.
2. If possible, arrange for someone from a local renal dialysis center to come and talk to the class about how the artificial kidney works and other aspects of the dialysis process.
3. Display a hydrometer and other materials used to perform a urinalysis. Discuss the importance of the urinalysis in routine physicals and in pathological diagnosis.
4. Use a torso model and/or dissected animal model to exhibit urinary organs.
5. Use a funnel and filter paper to demonstrate the filtration process in the renal corpuscle.
6. Set up a dialysis bag to show the exchange of ions based on osmolarity.
7. Use a model of a longitudinally sectioned kidney to identify the major anatomical features. If the nephron is part of the model or if one is available, demonstrate the anatomical regions of the nephron and describe the specific functions of each area.

Critical Thinking/Discussion Topics

1. Discuss the link between emotions and kidney function.
2. Explore the effects of certain drugs on kidney function.
3. Explain why physicians tell a sick individual to drink plenty of fluids and why fluid intake and output is so carefully monitored in hospital settings.
4. Discuss how kidney stones are formed, why they are formed, and how they can be treated.
5. Examine the thirst mechanism and relate it to renal physiology.
6. Identify the role of the kidneys in blood pressure regulation.
7. Discuss the different types of renal inflammation/infection and the consequences to other body systems.

Library Research Topics

1. Research the effects of common drugs such as penicillin, the myceins, etc., on kidney function.
2. Study the effects of hypertensive drugs on kidney function.
3. Research the effect of circulatory shock on kidney function and explain why the kidneys are affected.
4. Examine the link between the emotions and kidney function.
5. Investigate the available treatments for kidney stones.
6. Explore the process of dialysis.
7. Research the latest treatments for incontinence.
8. Study the latest updates in renal physiology.
9. Describe recent advances in the role of atrial natriuretic factor in fluid/electrolyte balance.
10. Research the urinary system implications for an infant born with congenital adrenal hyperplasia (CAH), and the treatment aimed at this specific problem.

Multimedia in the Classroom and Lab

Online Resources for Students

The
Anatomy & Physiology Place
www.anatomyandphysiology.com

MyA&P
www.myaandp.com

The following shows the organization of the Chapter Guide page in both the Anatomy & Physiology Place and MyA&P™. The Chapter Guide organizes all the chapter-specific online media resources for Chapter 25 in one convenient location, with e-book links to each section of the textbook. Please note that both sites also give you access to other general A&P resources, like InterActive Physiology®, PhysioEx 6.0™, Anatomy 360°, Flashcards, a Glossary, a Histology Tutorial, and much more.

Objectives
Section 25.1 Kidney Anatomy (pp. 998–1006)
InterActive Physiology®: Anatomy Review
Art Labeling Activity: The Urinary System (Fig. 25.1, p. 998)
Art Labeling Activity: Internal Anatomy of the Kidney (Fig. 25.3, p. 1000)
Art Labeling Activity: Location and Structure of Nephrons (Fig. 25.4, p. 1002)
Section 25.2 Kidney Physiology: Mechanisms of Urine Formation (pp. 1007–1021)
InterActive Physiology®: Glomerular Filtration
InterActive Physiology®: Early Filtrate Processing
InterActive Physiology®: Late Filtrate Processing
PhysioEx: Renal System Physiology
Case Study: Diabetic Nephropathy (Kidney Damage)
Case Study: Renal Failure
Section 25.3 Urine (pp. 1021–1023)
Section 25.4 Ureters (pp. 1023–1024)
Section 25.5 Urinary Bladder (pp. 1024–1026)
Section 25.6 Urethra (p. 1026)
Memory: The Urinary System In Situ
Section 25.7 Micturition (p. 1027)
Case Study: Urinary Frequency (Polyuria) and Excessive Thirst (Polydipsia)
Section 25.8 Developmental Aspects of the Urinary System (pp. 1027–1030)
Chapter Summary
Self-Study Quizzes
Art Labeling Quiz
Matching Quiz
Multiple-Choice Quiz (Level I)
Multiple-Choice Quiz (Level II)
True-False Quiz
Crossword Puzzles
Crossword Puzzle 25.1
Crossword Puzzle 25.2

Media

See Guide to Audio-Visual Resources in Appendix A for key to AV distributors.

Video

1. *Excretory System* (IM; 23 min., 1992). This video describes the work of the kidneys as regulators of the body's salt and fluid levels. This program traces the anatomy of the excretory system and explains the role of the endocrine system.
2. *The Human Urinary System* (BC; 23 min., 1999). This video provides an excellent overview of the workings of the human urinary system.
3. *The Kidney* (FHS; 15 min., 1996). From *The World of Living Organisms* series, this program discusses the structure and function of the kidneys and describes how they help maintain homeostasis.
4. *Kidney Disease* (FHS; 26 min., 1990). From *The Doctor Is In* series, this video looks at ESRD (end-stage renal disease), its causes, and the difficulties related to transplantation.
5. *Kidney Transplant* (FHS; 45 min., 1995). This video shows a live-related kidney transplant from a son to his tissue-matched father.
6. *The Urinary Tract: Water!* (FHS; 28 min., 1989). From the award-winning series *The Living Body*, this video shows the crucial part water plays in the body's functioning and how it keeps it in balance.
7. *Work of the Kidneys* (IM; 23 min., 1989). This program analyzes how a kidney regulates homeostasis.

Software

1. *A.D.A.M.® InterActive Anatomy® 4.0* (see p. 9 of this guide for full listing).
2. *A.D.A.M.® MediaPro* (see p. 9 of this guide for full listing).
3. *A.D.A.M.® Anatomy Practice* (see p. 86 of this guide for full listing).
4. *Bodyworks* (see p. 9 of this guide for full listing).
5. *Fluids and Electrolytes* (NIMCO; Windows). Teaches more than 200 fundamental principles in the field of fluids and electrolytes.
6. *Kidney Functions* (NIMCO; Win/Mac). Explores the numerous functions of the kidneys.
7. *InterActive Physiology® 9-System Suite CD-ROM* (BC; Win/Mac). Interactive software with sections on the urinary system and fluids and electrolytes that explore the physiology of the urinary system and its effect on fluid and electrolyte balance.
8. *The Ultimate Human Body* (see p. 9 of this guide for full listing).

Lecture Enhancement Material

To view thumbnails of all of the illustrations for Chapter 25, see Appendix B.

Transparencies Index/Media Manager

Figure 25.1   The urinary system.
Figure 25.2   Position of the kidneys against the posterior body wall.
Figure 25.3   Internal anatomy of the kidney.
Figure 25.4   Location and structure of nephrons.
Figure 25.5   Comparison of cortical and juxtamedullary nephron anatomy.
Figure 25.6   Juxtaglomerular apparatus (JGA) of a nephron.
Figure 25.7   The filtration membrane.
Figure 25.8   The kidney depicted schematically as a single, uncoiled nephron.
Figure 25.9   Forces determining glomerular filtration and filtration pressure.

*Indicates images that are on the Media Manager only.

Answers to End-of-Chapter Questions

Multiple Choice and Matching Question answers appear in Appendix G of the main text.

Short Answer Essay Questions

11. The perineal fat capsule helps to hold the kidney in place against the posterior trunk wall and cushions it against blows. (p. 999)

12. A creatine molecule travels the following route from a glomerulus to the urethra. It first passes through the glomerular filtration membrane, which is a porous membrane made up of a fenestrated capillary endothelium, a thin basement membrane, and the visceral membrane of the glomerular capsule formed by the podocytes. The creatine molecule then passes through the proximal convoluted tubule, the loop of Henle, and the distal convoluted tubule, and into the collecting duct in which it travels into the medulla through the renal pyramids. From the medulla the molecule enters the renal pelvis, and leaves the kidney via the ureter. Then it travels to the urinary bladder and then to the urethra. (pp. 1001–1003; 1023–1026)

13. Renal filtrate is a solute-rich fluid without blood cells or plasma proteins because the filtration membrane is permeable to water and all solutes smaller than plasma proteins. The capillary endothelium restricts passage of formed elements, whereas the anion-rich basement membrane holds back most protein and some smaller anionic molecules. (p. 1007)

14. The mechanisms that contribute to renal autoregulation are the myogenic mechanism and the tubuloglomerular feedback mechanism. The myogenic mechanism reflects the tendency of vascular smooth muscle to contract when it is stretched. An increase in systemic blood pressure causes afferent arterioles to constrict, which impedes blood flow into the glomerulus and prevents glomerular blood pressure from rising to damaging levels. Conversely, a decline in systemic blood pressure

causes dilation of afferent arterioles and an increase in glomerular hydrostatic pressure. Both responses help maintain a normal GFR.

The tubuloglomerular mechanism reflects the activity of the macula densa cells in response to a slow filtration rate or low filtrate osmolarity. When so activated they release chemicals that cause vasodilation in the afferent arterioles.

Renal autoregulation maintains a relatively constant kidney perfusion over an arterial pressure range from about 80 to 180 mm Hg, preventing large changes in water and solute excretion. (pp. 1008–1010)

15. Sympathetic nervous system controls protect the body during extreme stress by redirecting blood to more vital organs. Strong sympathetic stimulation causes release of norepinephrine to alpha adrenergic receptors, causing strong vasoconstriction of kidney arterioles. This results in a drop in glomerular filtration, and indirectly stimulates another extrinsic mechanism, the renin-angiotensin mechanism. The renin-angiotensin mechanism involves the release of renin from the granular juxtaglomerular cells, which enzymatically converts the plasma globulin angiotensinogen to angiotensin I. Angiotensin I is further converted to angiotensin II by angiotensin converting enzyme (ACE) produced by capillary endothelium. Angiotensin II causes vasoconstriction of systemic arterioles, increased sodium reabsorption by promoting the release of aldosterone, decreases peritubular hydrostatic pressure, which encourages increased fluid and solute reabsorption, and acts on the glomerular mesangial cells, causing a decrease in glomerular filtration rate. In addition, angiotensin II results in stimulation of the hypothalamus, which activates the thirst mechanism and promotes the release of antidiuretic hormone, which causes increased water reabsorption in the distal nephron. Other factors that may trigger the renin-angiotensin mechanism are a drop in mean systemic blood pressure below 80 mm Hg, and activated macula densa cells responding to low plasma sodium. (p. 1010)

16. In active tubular reabsorption, substances are usually moving against electrical and/or chemical gradients. The substances usually move from the filtrate into the tubule cells by secondary active transport coupled to Na^+ transport and move across the basolateral membrane of the tubule cell into the interstitial space by diffusion. Most such processes involve cotransport with sodium.

Passive tubular reabsorption encompasses diffusion, facilitated diffusion, and osmosis. Substances move along their electrochemical gradient without the use of metabolic energy. (pp. 1012–1015)

17. The peritubular capillaries are low-pressure, porous capillaries that readily absorb solutes and water from the tubule cells. They arise from the efferent arteriole draining the glomerulus. (p. 1003)

18. Tubular secretion is important for the following reasons: (a) disposing of substances not already in the filtrate; (b) eliminating undesirable substances that have been reabsorbed by passive processes; (c) ridding the body of excessive potassium ions; and (d) controlling blood pH. Tubular secretion moves materials from the blood of the peritubular capillaries through the tubule cells or from the tubule cells into the filtrate. (p. 1015)

19. Aldosterone modifies the chemical composition of urine by enhancing sodium ion reabsorption so that very little leaves the body in urine. (p. 1015)

20. As it flows through the ascending limb of the loop of Henle, the filtrate becomes hypotonic because it is impermeable to water, and because sodium and chloride are being actively pumped into the interstitial fluid, thereby decreasing solute concentration in the tubule. The interstitial fluid at the tip of the loop of Henle and the deep portions of the medulla are hypertonic because: (1) the loop of Henle serves as a

countercurrent multiplier to establish the osmotic gradient, a process that works due to the characteristics of tubule permeability to water in different areas of the tubule and ion transport to the interstitial areas; and (2) the vasa recta acts as a countercurrent exchanger to maintain the osmotic gradient by serving as a passive exchange mechanism that removes water from the medullary areas but leaves salts behind. The filtrate at the tip of the loop of Henle is hypertonic due to the passive diffusion of water from the descending limb to the interstitial areas. (pp. 1016–1018)

21. The bladder is very distensible. An empty bladder is collapsed and has rugae. Expansion of the bladder to accommodate increased volume is due to the ability of the transitional epithelial cells lining the interior of the bladder to slide across one another, thinning the mucosa, and the ability of the detrusor muscle to stretch. (pp. 1025–1026)

22. Micturition is the act of emptying the bladder. The micturition reflex is activated when distension of the bladder wall activates stretch receptors. Afferent impulses are transmitted to the sacral region of the spinal cord and efferent impulses return to the bladder via the parasympathetic pelvic splanchnic nerves, causing the detrusor muscle to contract and the internal sphincter to relax. (p. 1027)

23. In old age the kidneys become smaller, the nephrons decrease in size and number, and the tubules become less efficient. By age 70, the rate of filtrate formation is only about one half that of middle-aged adults. This slowing is believed to result from impaired renal circulation caused by arteriosclerosis. The bladder is shrunken, with less than half the capacity of a young adult. Problems of urine retention and incontinence occur. (p. 1030)

Critical Thinking and Clinical Application Questions

1. Diuretics will remove water from the blood and eliminate it in the urine. Consequently, water will move from the peritoneal cavity into the bloodstream reducing her ascites.

   (1) Osmotic diuretics are substances that are not reabsorbed or that exceed the ability of the tubule to reabsorb it. (2) Loop diuretics (Lasix) inhibit symporters in the loop of Henle by diminishing sodium chloride uptake. They reduce the normal hyperosmolality of the medullary interstitial fluid, reducing the effects of ADH, resulting in loss of NaCl and water. (3) Thiazides act on the distal convoluted tubule to inhibit water reabsorption.

   Her diet is salt-restricted because if salt content in the blood is high, it will cause her to retain water rather than allowing her to eliminate it. (pp. 1019–1021)

2. A fracture at the lumbar region will stop the impulses to the brain, so there will be no voluntary control of micturition and he will never again feel the urge to void. There will be no dribbling of urine between voidings as long as the internal sphincter is undamaged. Micturition will be triggered in response to bladder stretch by a reflex arc at the sacral region of the spinal cord as it is in an infant. (p. 1028)

3. Cystitis is bladder inflammation. Women are more frequent cystitis sufferers than men because the female urethra is very short and its external orifice is closer to the anal opening. Improper toilet habits can carry fecal bacteria into the urethra. (p. 1026)

4. Hattie has a renal calculus, or kidney stone, in her ureter. Predisposing conditions are frequent bacterial infections of the urinary tract, urinary retention, high concentrations of calcium in the blood, and alkaline urine. Her pain comes in waves because waves of peristalsis pass along the ureter at intervals. The pain results when the ureter walls close in on the sharp kidney stone during this peristalsis. (p. 1024)

5. The use of spermicides in females kills many helpful bacteria, allowing infectious fecal bacteria to colonize the vagina. Intercourse will drive bacteria from the vagina into the urethra, increasing the incidence of urinary tract infection in these females. (p. 1026)

6. Renal failure patients accumulate both phosphorus and water between dialysis appointments. Increased levels of phosphorus can lead to leaching of calcium from the bones. Increased water can lead to relatively decreased red blood cell counts. Calcium/magnesium supplements can offset calcium loss from bones, but water intake should be carefully monitored to prevent accumulation in the plasma. (p. 1023)

Suggested Readings

Bader, Michael. "Tissue Renin-Angiotensin Systems." *Science and Medicine* 8 (3) (May/June 2002): 128–137.

Borgnia, Mario, et al. "Cellular and Molecular Biology of Aquaporin Water Channels." *Annual Review of Biochemistry* 68 (1999): 425–458.

Hunter, Malcolm. "Accessory to Kidney Disease." *Nature* 414 (6863) (Nov. 2001): 502–503.

Lee, M. Douglas, et al. "The Aquaporin Family of Water Channel Proteins in Clinical Medicine." *Medicine* 76 (3) (May 1997): 141–156.

Steigerwalt, S.P. "Unraveling the Causes of Hypertension and Hypokalemia." *Hospital Practice* 30 (July 1995): 67–68.

Tajkhorshid, Emad, et al. "Control of the Selectivity of the Aquaporin Water Channel Family by Global Orientational Tuning." *Science* 296 (April 2002): 525–530.

Tanner, M.J. "The Acid Test for Band 3." *Nature* 382 (July 1996): 209–210.

Fluid, Electrolyte, and Acid-Base Balance

26

Objectives

Body Fluids

1. List the water content of males, females, and infants, and the factors contributing to differences in water content among these groups.
2. Name the fluid compartments and subcompartments of the body, and the relative amount of body fluid in each.
3. Differentiate between electrolytes and nonelectrolytes, and discuss the relative osmotic power of each.
4. Compare the relative solute concentration of specific solutes in the intracellular and extracellular compartments.
5. Describe the mechanisms of fluid movement between fluid compartments.

Water Balance and ECF Osmolality

6. Identify the routes of water intake and output to and from the body.
7. Explain the thirst mechanism and mechanism of cessation of thirst.
8. Indicate how shifts in water output by the body occur, and how the body compensates for such shifts.
9. Discuss the activity of antidiuretic hormone (ADH).
10. Describe imbalances of fluid homeostasis and their consequences.

Electrolyte Balance

11. Explain how salt is balanced in the body.
12. Describe how sodium regulates fluid and electrolyte balance.
13. Identify the mechanisms regulating sodium balance of the body fluids.
14. Examine the mechanisms regulating potassium, calcium, and phosphate balance of the body fluids.
15. Discuss the mechanism regulating anions in the body fluids.

Acid-Base Balance

16. Define acidosis and alkalosis, and describe the sources of hydrogen ions and how their concentration is regulated.
17. Describe the components and activity of chemical buffer systems.
18. Explain the mechanisms of the bicarbonate, phosphate, and protein buffer systems.
19. Discuss how the respiratory and renal systems regulate pH.
20. Differentiate between respiratory and metabolic acidosis and alkalosis.

Developmental Aspects of Fluid, Electrolyte, and Acid-Base Balance

21. Describe the changes in body water content and regulation during fetal development and throughout life.

Suggested Lecture Outline

I. Body Fluids (pp. 1036–1038; Figs. 26.1–26.3)

A. Body Water Content (p.1036)

1. Total body water is a function of age, body mass, and body fat.

a. Due to their low body fat and bone mass, infants are about 73% water.

b. The body water content of men is about 60%, but since women have relatively more body fat and less skeletal muscle than men, theirs is about 50%.

2. Body water declines throughout life, ultimately comprising about 45% of total body mass in old age.

B. Fluid Compartments (p. 1036; Fig. 26.1)

1. There are two main fluid compartments of the body: the intracellular compartment contains slightly less than two-thirds by volume; the remaining third is distributed in the extracellular fluid.

2. There are two subcompartments of the extracellular fluid: blood plasma and interstitial fluid.

C. Composition of Body Fluids (pp. 1036–1037)

1. Nonelectrolytes include most organic molecules, do not dissociate in water, and carry no net electrical charge.

2. Electrolytes dissociate in water to ions, and include inorganic salts, acids and bases, and some proteins.

3. Electrolytes have greater osmotic power because they dissociate in water and contribute at least two particles to solution.

4. The major cation in extracellular fluids is sodium, and the major anion is chloride; in intracellular fluid the major cation is potassium, and the major anion is phosphate.

5. Electrolytes are the most abundant solutes in body fluids, but proteins and some nonelectrolytes account for 60–97% of dissolved solutes.

D. Fluid Movement Among Compartments (pp. 1037–1038; Figs. 26.2–26.3)

1. Anything that changes solute concentration in any compartment leads to net water flows.

2. Nearly protein-free plasma is forced out of the blood by hydrostatic pressure, and almost completely reabsorbed due to colloid osmotic (oncotic) pressure of plasma proteins.

3. Movement of water between the interstitial fluid and intracellular fluid involves substantial two-way osmotic flow that is equal in both directions.

4. Ion fluxes between the interstitial and intracellular compartments are restricted; but movement of nutrients, respiratory gases, and wastes typically occur in one direction.

II. Water Balance and ECF Osmolality (pp. 1039–1043; Figs. 26.4–26.7)

A. For the body to remain properly hydrated, water intake must equal water output.

1. Most water enters the body through ingested liquids and food, but is also produced by cellular metabolism.

2. Water output is due to evaporative loss from lungs and skin (insensible water loss), sweating, defecation, and urination.

B. Regulation of Water Intake (pp. 1039–1040; Figs. 26.4–26.5)

1. The thirst mechanism is triggered by a decrease in plasma osmolarity, which results in a dry mouth and excites the hypothalamic thirst center.

2. Thirst is quenched as the mucosa of the mouth is moistened, and continues with distention of the stomach and intestines, resulting in inhibition of the hypothalamic thirst center.

C. Regulation of Water Output (pp. 1040–1041; Fig. 26.4)

1. Drinking is necessary since there is obligatory water loss due to the insensible water losses.

2. Beyond obligatory water losses, solute concentration and volume of urine depend on fluid intake.

D. Influence of ADH (p. 1041; Fig. 26.6)

1. The amount of water reabsorbed in the renal collecting ducts is proportional to ADH release.

   a. When ADH levels are low, most water in the collecting ducts is not reabsorbed, resulting in large quantities of dilute urine.

   b. When ADH levels are high, filtered water is reabsorbed, resulting in a lower volume of concentrated urine.

2. ADH secretion is promoted or inhibited by the hypothalamus in response to changes in solute concentration of extracellular fluid, large changes in blood volume or pressure, or vascular baroreceptors.

E. Disorders of Water Balance (pp. 1041–1043; Fig. 26.7)

1. Dehydration occurs when water output exceeds water intake, and may lead to weight loss, fever, mental confusion, or hypovolemic shock.

2. Hypotonic hydration is a result of renal insufficiency, or intake of an excessive amount of water very quickly.

3. Edema is the accumulation of fluid in the interstitial space, which may impair tissue function.

III. Electrolyte Balance (pp. 1043–1049; Figs. 26.8–26.10; Table 26.1)

A. The Central Role of Sodium in Fluid and Electrolyte Balance (p. 1043)

1. Sodium is the most important cation to regulation of fluid and electrolyte balance in the body due to its abundance and osmotic pressure.

2. Since all body fluids are in chemical equilibrium, any change in sodium levels causes a compensatory shift in water, affecting plasma volume, blood pressure, and intracellular and interstitial fluid volumes.

B. Regulation of Sodium Balance (pp. 1043–1048; Figs. 26.8–26.10)

1. When aldosterone secretion is high, nearly all the filtered sodium is reabsorbed in the distal convoluted tubule and the collecting duct.

2. The most important trigger for the release of aldosterone is the renin-angiotensin mechanism, initiated in response to sympathetic stimulation, decrease in filtrate osmolality, or decreased blood pressure.

3. Cardiovascular baroreceptors monitor blood volume so that blood pressure remains stable.

4. Atrial natriuretic peptide reduces blood pressure and blood volume by inhibiting release of ADH, renin, and aldosterone, and directly causing vasodilation.

5. Estrogens are chemically similar to aldosterone, and enhance reabsorption of salt by the renal tubules.

6. Glucocorticoids enhance tubular reabsorption of sodium, but increase glomerular filtration.

C. Regulation of Potassium Balance (pp. 1048–1049)

1. Potassium is critical to the maintenance of the membrane potential of neurons and muscle cells, and is a buffer that compensates for shifts of hydrogen ions in or out of the cell.

2. Potassium balance is chiefly regulated by renal mechanisms, which control the amount of potassium secreted into the filtrate.

3. Blood plasma levels of potassium are the most important factor regulating potassium secretion.

4. Aldosterone influences potassium secretion, since potassium secretion is simultaneously enhanced when sodium reabsorption increases.

D. Regulation of Calcium and Phosphate Balance (p. 1049)

1. Calcium ion levels are closely regulated by parathyroid hormone and calcitonin; about 98% is reabsorbed.

a. Parathyroid hormone is released when blood calcium levels decline, and targets the bones, small intestine, and kidneys.

b. Calcitonin is an antagonist to parathyroid hormone, and is released when blood calcium rises, targeting bone.

E. Regulation of Anions (p. 1049)

1. Chloride is the major anion reabsorbed with sodium, and helps maintain the osmotic pressure of the blood.

IV. Acid-Base Balance (pp. 1049–1057, 1060; Figs. 26.11–26.14; Table 26.2)

A. Because of the abundance of hydrogen bonds in the body's functional proteins, they are strongly influenced by hydrogen ion concentration. (pp. 1049–1050)

1. When arterial blood pH rises above 7.45, the body is in alkalosis; when arterial pH falls below 7.35, the body is in acidosis.

2. Most hydrogen ions originate as metabolic by-products, although they can also enter the body via ingested foods.

B. Chemical Buffer Systems (pp. 1050–1052; Fig. 26.11)

1. A chemical buffer is a system of one or two molecules that acts to resist changes in pH by binding H^+ when the pH drops, or releasing H^+ when the pH rises.

2. The bicarbonate buffer system is the main buffer of the extracellular fluid, and consists of carbonic acid and its salt, sodium bicarbonate.

a. When a strong acid is added to the solution, carbonic acid is mostly unchanged, but bicarbonate ions of the salt bind excess H^+, forming more carbonic acid.

b. When a strong base is added to solution, the sodium bicarbonate remains relatively unaffected, but carbonic acid dissociates further, donating more H^+ to bind the excess hydroxide.

c. Bicarbonate concentration of the extracellular fluid is closely regulated by the kidneys, and plasma bicarbonate concentrations are controlled by the respiratory system.

3. The phosphate buffer system operates in the urine and intracellular fluid similar to the bicarbonate buffer system: sodium dihydrogen phosphate is its weak acid, and monohydrogen phosphate is its weak base.

4. The protein buffer system consists of organic acids containing carboxyl groups that dissociate to release H^+ when the pH begins to rise, or bind excess H^+ when the pH declines.

C. Respiratory Regulation of H^+ (p. 1052)

1. Carbon dioxide from cellular metabolism enters erythrocytes and is converted to bicarbonate ions for transport in the plasma.

2. When hypercapnia occurs, blood pH drops, activating medullary respiratory centers, resulting in increased rate and depth of breathing and increased unloading of CO_2 in the lungs.

3. When blood pH rises, the respiratory center is depressed, allowing CO_2 to accumulate in the blood, lowering pH.

D. Renal Mechanisms of Acid-Base Balance (pp. 1052–1054; Figs. 26.12–26.14)

1. Only the kidneys can rid the body of acids generated by cellular metabolism, while also regulating blood levels of alkaline substances and renewing chemical buffer components.

   a. Bicarbonate ions can be conserved from filtrate when depleted, and their reabsorption is dependent on H^+ secretion.

   b. Type A intercalated cells of the renal tubules can synthesize new bicarbonate ions while excreting more hydrogen ions.

   c. Ammonium ions are weak acids that are excreted and lost in urine, replenishing the alkaline reserve of the blood.

   d. When the body is in alkalosis, type B intercalated cells excrete bicarbonate, and reclaim hydrogen ions.

E. Abnormalities of Acid-Base Balance (pp. 1054–1057, 1060; Table 26.2)

1. Respiratory acidosis is characterized by falling blood pH and rising P_{CO2}, which can result from shallow breathing or some respiratory diseases.

2. Respiratory alkalosis results when carbon dioxide is eliminated from the body faster than it is produced, such as during hyperventilation.

3. Metabolic acidosis is characterized by low blood pH and bicarbonate levels, and is due to excessive loss of bicarbonate ions, or ingestion of too much alcohol.

4. Metabolic alkalosis is indicated by rising blood pH and bicarbonate levels, and is the result of vomiting or excessive base intake.

5. Respiratory rate and depth increase during metabolic acidosis, and decrease during metabolic alkalosis.

6. In renal compensation for respiratory acidosis, blood P_{CO2} and bicarbonate ion concentrations are high; in respiratory alkalosis, blood pH is high, but P_{CO2} is low.

V. Developmental Aspects of Fluid, Electrolyte, and Acid-Base Balance (p. 1060)

A. An embryo and young fetus are more than 90% water, but as solids accumulate, the percentage declines to about 70–80% at birth.

B. Distribution of body water begins to change at 2 months of age, and takes on adult distribution by the time a child is 2 years of age.

C. At puberty, sex differences in body water content appear as males develop more skeletal muscle.

D. During infancy, problems with fluid, electrolyte, and acid-base balance are common, due to large-scale changes in P_{CO_2}.

E. In old age, body water loss is primarily from the intracellular compartment, due to decline in muscle mass, and increase in adipose tissue.

F. Increased insensitivity to thirst cues makes the elderly vulnerable to dehydration, and electrolyte or acid-base imbalances.

Cross References

Additional information on topics covered in Chapter 26 can be found in the chapters listed below.

1. Chapter 2: Ions; water; acid-base reactions and pH
2. Chapter 3: Sodium-potassium pump; membrane transport (osmosis, diffusion)
3. Chapter 12: Hypothalamus
4. Chapter 16: ADH (water conservation); diabetes (mellitus, insipidus); aldosterone (sodium conservation); atrial natriuretic factor; estrogens; glucocorticoids; parathyroid hormone/calcitonin
5. Chapter 17: Plasma
6. Chapter 19: Baroreceptors; capillary exchange
7. Chapter 22: Carbon dioxide and bicarbonate; hemoglobin and pH control
8. Chapter 24: Ketone bodies and metabolism
9. Chapter 25: ADH (water conservation); aldosterone (sodium conservation); atrial natriuretic factor; control of renal blood flow; glomerular filtration; glomerulonephritis; juxtaglomerular apparatus; renin-angiotensin mechanism; potassium reabsorption; H^+ and HCO_3^- and the kidney

Lecture Hints

1. Stress that fluid compartments are an abstract idea; draw a schematic diagram depicting the cell and its external environment. Stress that the plasma membrane is the structure separating these fluid compartments.
2. Clearly define the boundaries of each fluid compartment, and stress the dynamic nature of fluid movements in the body—fluid subcompartments are all "interconnected" and it is membrane selectivity that creates the different chemical environments.
3. Refer students to a review of osmosis and diffusion. A thorough understanding of the movements of solute and solvent are crucial for comprehension of fluid/electrolyte balance.
4. Stress the different solute compositions of intracellular and extracellular compartments. Remind students of the physiology of the action potential as an example of the importance of maintaining cellular boundaries (therefore the relative compositions of the fluid compartments).
5. Get the class involved by asking students questions: "What are some of the ways we lose water (water output)?" "What are the sources of body water (water intake)?"
6. Emphasize that water will always move with solutes whenever possible. Water cannot be actively transported, so balance is achieved by controlling solute movement and water permeability.

7. Remind the class of blood pressure control by nervous, renal, and hormonal mechanisms. All of these control systems are highly integrated, and this is an opportunity to illustrate the cooperative nature of body systems in maintaining homeostasis. Although we treat the body as having distinct systems, one must not forget that all systems are part of a functional individual.

8. Stress the importance of acid-base balance and levels of intracellular potassium, especially in excitable cells. Also point out that potassium is the major ion in the intracellular fluid and therefore is the major control of water balance within the cell. As a point of interest, mention the consequences of excessively high or low levels of potassium.

9. Emphasize the importance of acidity or basicity on all chemical reactions.

10. Start the discussion of acid-base balance by mentioning that the respiratory and renal systems are powerful pH control mechanisms.

11. Emphasize the difference between using strong acid-base combinations versus weak acid-base combinations as buffering systems. Relating the two makes it easier for students to realize the need for the latter.

12. Clearly distinguish between metabolic and respiratory acids and bases.

Activities/Demonstrations

1. Audio-visual materials listed under Multimedia in the Classroom and Lab.

2. Demonstrate the principles of osmosis and diffusion as a reminder to students about those processes.

3. Perform a simple titration to demonstrate how strong acids and bases can be neutralized by weaker acids and bases.

4. To help students visualize how solute imbalances affect cells, obtain some dialysis tubing and create "cells" by filling it with saline solution and tying off the ends. After weighing the "cells," immerse them in hypertonic and hypotonic solutions for a period of time and then reweigh them.

Critical Thinking/Discussion Topics

1. Discuss the effects of IV therapy on the fluid and electrolyte balance in the body; distinguish between the infant or small child and the adult.

2. Explain why a sodium bicarbonate IV is used in cases of cardiac arrest or circulatory shock.

3. Discuss the effects of alcoholism on acid-base balance.

4. Explore the effects of prolonged use of antacids on acid-base balance.

Library Research Topics

1. Research the rationale behind taking arterial blood gas values to help determine acid-base balance.

2. Investigate the reasons for and effects of IV therapy in cases of heart attack, surgery, chemotherapy, etc.

3. Study the roles in the body of the more common electrolytes such as Na^+, Mg^{++}, Ca^{++}, etc.

Multimedia in the Classroom and Lab

Online Resources for Students

The
Anatomy & Physiology Place
www.anatomyandphysiology.com

MyA&P
www.myaandp.com

The following shows the organization of the Chapter Guide page in both the Anatomy & Physiology Place and MyA&P™. The Chapter Guide organizes all the chapter-specific online media resources for Chapter 26 in one convenient location, with e-book links to each section of the textbook. Please note that both sites also give you access to other general A&P resources, like InterActive Physiology®, PhysioEx 6.0™, Anatomy 360°, *Flashcards, a Glossary, a Histology Tutorial, and much more.*

Objectives

Section 26.1 Body Fluids (pp. 1036–1038)

Section 26.2 Water Balance and ECF Osmolality (pp. 1039–1043)

InterActive Physiology®: Introduction to Body Fluids

InterActive Physiology®: Water Homeostasis

Activity: Mechanisms and Consequences of ADH Release

Section 26.3 Electrolyte Balance (pp. 1043–1049)

InterActive Physiology®: Electrolyte Homeostasis

Activity: Mechanisms and Consequences of Aldosterone Release

Case Study: Fluids and Electrolytes

Section 26.4 Acid-Base Balance (pp. 1049–1057, 1060)

InterActive Physiology®: Acid/Base Homeostasis

PhysioEx: Acid/Base Balance

Case Study: Renal Failure

Section 26.5 Developmental Aspects of Fluid, Electrolyte, and Acid-Base Balance (p. 1060)

Chapter Summary

Self-Study Quizzes

Art Labeling Quiz

Matching Quiz

Multiple-Choice Quiz (Level I)

Multiple-Choice Quiz (Level II)

True-False Quiz

Crossword Puzzles

Crossword Puzzle 26.1

Crossword Puzzle 26.2

Media

See Guide to Audio-Visual Resources in Appendix A for key to AV distributors.

Video

1. *Body Fluids: The Critical Balance, Part 2* (CM; 17 min., 1990). Describes the role of the renin-angiotensin system and the hormones aldosterone and ADH in maintaining homeostasis.

2. *Homeostasis* (FHS; 60 min.). Six-part series of videos. Each video is 10 minutes. The program presents a comprehensive definition of homeostasis. Uses computer animation to illustrate how the body deals with changing conditions.

3. *Homeostasis* (FHS; 20 min., 1995). From *The New Living Body* series. Contains the most up-to-date information with live action video, three-dimensional computer graphics, and current imaging technology.

Software

1. *InterActive Physiology® 9-System Suite CD-ROM* (BC; Win/Mac). The Fluid, Electrolyte, and Acid/Base Balance topic focuses on the processes involved in maintaining homeostasis. Contains excellent graphics and animations at both gross and cellular levels.

2. *Fluid Movement and Balance* (IM; Windows). Explains how solutions, solutes, and the semipermeable membrane interact in diffusion and osmosis, considering osmotic and hydrostatic pressures, filtration, and the effects of plasma proteins.

3. *Fluids and Electrolytes* (IM; Windows). Enables users to study and review fluids and electrolytes at any pace. Features case studies, self-assessment tools, and more than 150 animations.

4. *Fundamentals of Fluids and Electrolytes* (IM; Windows). Provides an introduction to fluids and electrolytes, exploring fluid compartments, distribution of body fluids, and fluid intake and output.

Lecture Enhancement Material

To view thumbnails of all of the illustrations for Chapter 26, see Appendix B.

Transparencies Index/Media Manager

Indicates images that are on the Media Manager only.

Answers to End-of-Chapter Questions

Multiple Choice and Matching Question answers appear in Appendix G of the main text.

Short Answer Essay Questions

14. The body fluid compartments include the intracellular fluid compartment, located inside the cells with fluid volume approximately 25 liters, and the extracellular fluid compartment (plasma and interstitial fluid), located in the external environment of each cell with fluid volume approximately 15 liters. (p. 1036)

15. It is believed that a decrease in plasma volume of 10% or more and/or an increase in plasma osmolality of 1 to 2% results in a dry mouth and excites the hypothalamic thirst or drinking center. Hypothalamic stimulation occurs because the osmoreceptors in the thirst center become irritable and depolarize as water, driven by the hypertonic ECF, moves out of them by osmosis. Collectively, these events cause a subjective sensation of thirst. The quenching of thirst begins as the mucosa of the mouth and throat are moistened and continues as stretch receptors in the stomach and intestine are activated, providing feedback signals that inhibit the hypothalamic thirst center. (pp. 1039–1040)

16. It is important to control the extracellular fluid (ECF) osmolality because the ECF determines the ICF volume and underlies the control of the fluid balance in the body. The ECF is maintained by both thirst and the antidiuretic hormone (ADH). A rise in plasma osmolality triggers thirst and the release of ADH, a drop in plasma osmolality inhibits thirst and ADH. (pp. 1038–1039)

17. Sodium is pivotal to fluid and electrolyte balance and to the homeostasis of all body systems since it is the principal extracellular ion. While the sodium content of the body may be altered, its concentration in the ECF remains stable because of immediate adjustments in water volume. The regulation of the sodium-water balance is inseparably linked to blood pressure and entails a variety of neural and hormonal controls: (1) aldosterone—increases the reabsorption of sodium from the filtrate; water follows passively by osmosis, increasing blood volume (and pressure). The renin-angiotensin mechanism is an important control of aldosterone release; the juxtaglomerular apparatus responds to: (a) decreased stretch (due to decreased blood pressure), (b) decreased filtrate osmolality, or (c) sympathetic nervous system stimulation resulting ultimately in aldosterone release from the adrenal cortex.
(2) ADH—osmoreceptors in the hypothalamus sense solute concentration in the ECF: increases in sodium content stimulate ADH release, resulting in increased water retention by the kidney (and increasing blood pressure). (3) Atrial natriuretic peptide—released by cells in the atria during high-pressure situations, has potent diuretic and natriuretic (sodium-excreting) effects; the kidneys do not reabsorb as much sodium (therefore water) and blood pressure drops. (pp. 1038, 1043–1046)

18. Respiratory system regulation of acid-base balance provides a physiological buffering system. Falling pH, due to rising hydrogen ion concentration or P_{CO_2} in plasma, excites the respiratory center (directly or indirectly) to stimulate deeper, more rapid respirations. When pH begins to fall, the respiratory center is depressed. (pp. 1055–1057)

19. Chemical acid-base buffers prevent pronounced changes in H^+ concentration by binding to hydrogen ions whenever the pH of body fluids drops and releasing them when pH rises. (p. 1050)

20. (a) The rate of H^+ secretion rises and falls directly with CO_2 levels in the ECF. The higher the content of CO_2 in the peritubular capillary blood, the faster the rate of H^+ secretion. (b) Type A intercalated cells secrete H^+ actively via a H^+-ATPase

pump and via a K^+-H^+ antiporter. The secreted H^+ combines with HPO_4^{2-}, forming $H_2PO_4^-$ which then flows out in urine. (c) The dissociation of carbonic acid in the tubule cells liberates HCO_3^- as well as H^+. HCO_3^- is shunted into the peritubular capillary blood. The rate of reabsorption of bicarbonate depends on the rate of secretion or excretion of H^+ in the filtrate. (p. 1052)

21. Factors that place newborn babies at risk for acid-base imbalances include very low residual volume of infant lungs, high rate of fluid intake and output, relatively high metabolic rate, high rate of insensible water loss, and inefficiency of the kidneys. (p. 1060)

Critical Thinking and Clinical Application Questions

1. This patient has diabetes insipidus caused by insufficient production of ADH by the hypothalamus. The operation for the removal of the cerebral tumor has damaged the hypothalamus or the hypothalamohypophyseal tract leading to the posterior pituitary. Because of the lack of ADH, the collecting tubules and possibly the convoluted part of the distal convoluted tubule are not absorbing water from the glomerular filtrate. The large volume of very dilute urine voided by this man and the intense thirst that he experiences are the result. (p. 1041)

2. Problem 1: pH 7.63, P_{CO2} 19 mm Hg, HCO_3^- 19.5 m Eq/L
   a. The pH is elevated = alkalosis.
   b. The P_{CO2} is low and is the cause of the alkalosis.
   c. The HCO_3^- is also low = compensating. This is a respiratory alkalosis, possibly due to hyperventilation, being compensated by metabolic acidosis.

   Problem 2: pH = 7.22, P_{CO2} 30 mm Hg, HCO_3^- 12.0 mEq/L
   a. The pH is below normal = acidosis.
   b. The P_{CO2} is low, therefore not the cause of the acidosis, but is compensating.
   c. The HCO_3^- is very low and is the cause of the acidosis. This is a metabolic acidosis. Possible causes include ingestion of too much acid (drinking too much alcohol), excessive loss of bicarbonate ion (diarrhea), accumulation of lactic acid during exercise, or shock, or by the ketosis that occurs in diabetic crises or starvation. (pp. 1055–1060)

3. Emphysema impairs gas exchange or lung ventilation, leading to retention of carbon dioxide and respiratory acidosis. Congestive heart failure produces oxygenation problems as well as edema and causes metabolic acidosis due to an increase in lactic acid. (pp. 1055–1057)

4. The patient has a normal sodium ion concentration; CO_2 is slightly low as is Cl^-. The potassium ion concentration is so abnormal that the patient has a medical emergency. The greatest danger is cardiac arrhythmia and cardiac arrest. (p. 1048)

5. Candace's right kidney is smaller due to decreased blood flow from the narrowing of her right renal artery. The right kidney's reduced blood flow is decreasing the glomerular filtration rate of the kidney which is responding by signaling to the body to increase blood pressure to increase blood flow to the kidney. You would expect to find her potassium levels low, and the levels of sodium, aldosterone, angiotensin II, and rennin to all be high. (pp. 1010, 1048)

Suggested Readings

Alpern, R.J. and Freisig, F.A. "Renal Acid-Base Transport." In *Diseases of the Kidney.* Boston: Little, Brown, 1997.

Barta, M.A. "Correcting Electrolyte Imbalances." *RN* (Feb. 1988).

Beauchamp, G.K. "The Human Preference for Excess Salt." *American Scientist* 75 (Jan./Feb. 1987): 27.

Gamble, J. L. Jr. "Moving More Closely to Acid-Base Relationships in the Body as a Whole." *Perspectives in Biological Medicine* 39 (1996): 593.

Halperin, M.L., and M. Goldstein. *Fluid, Electrolytes, and Acid-Base Emergencies.* Philadelphia: W.B. Saunders Co., 1988.

Horne, M.M., and P.L. Swearingen. *Pocket Guide to Fluids and Electrolytes.* St. Louis: C.B. Mosby Co., 1989.

Schwartz, M.W. "Potassium Imbalances." *American Journal of Nursing* 87 (Oct. 1987): 1292.

Simonson, M.S. "Endothelins: Multifunctional Renal Peptides." *Physiological Reviews* 73 (Jan. 1993): 375.

Wakabayashi, S. et al. "Molecular Physiology of Vertebrate Na^+/H^+ Exchangers." *Physiological Reviews* 77 (1997): 51.

The Reproductive System

27

Objectives

Anatomy of the Male Reproductive System

1. Explain the structure and function of the testes.
2. Describe the structure and function of the penis.
3. List and discuss the location, structure, and function of the male accessory ducts and glands.

Physiology of the Male Reproductive System

4. Define the male sexual response.
5. Describe the process of spermatogenesis.
6. Identify the hormonal regulation of the male reproductive function.
7. Name the male secondary sex characteristics and explain the role of testosterone in their formation.

Anatomy of the Female Reproductive System

8. Indicate the structure and function of the ovaries.
9. Describe the structure, function, and location of the female reproductive duct system.
10. Identify the structures of the female external genitalia.
11. Discuss the mammary glands and breast cancer.

Physiology of the Female Reproductive System

12. Explain the process of oogenesis.
13. Discuss the ovarian cycle including its three phases and their major events.
14. Indicate the hormonal interactions of the ovarian cycle.
15. Describe the uterine cycle.
16. Identify the effects of estrogen and progesterone on the development of structures and physiological processes other than the ovarian cycle.

Sexually Transmitted Diseases

17. Discuss the causative agents and modes of transmission of gonorrhea, syphilis, chlamydia, genital warts, and genital herpes.

Developmental Aspects of the Reproductive System: Chronology of Sexual Development

18. Identify what determines sex.
19. Discuss the process of sexual differentiation as it occurs in the developing embryo.
20. Explain the descent of the gonads.
21. Define and discuss puberty and menopause.

Suggested Lecture Outline

I. Anatomy of the Male Reproductive System (pp. 1066–1072; Figs. 27.1–27.4)

A. The scrotum is a sac of skin and superficial fascia that hangs outside the abdominopelvic cavity at the root of the penis and houses the testes. (p. 1067; Figs. 27.1–27.2)

1. Provides an environment three degrees below the core body temperature.

2. Responds to temperature changes.

B. The testes are the primary reproductive organ of the male, producing both sperm and testosterone. (pp. 1067–1069; Figs. 27.1–27.3)

1. The testes are divided into lobules with seminiferous tubules inside, where sperm are produced.

2. Interstitial cells are found in the connective tissue surrounding the seminiferous tubules and produce testosterone.

C. The penis is the copulatory organ, designed to deliver sperm into the female reproductive tract. (p. 1069; Figs. 27.1, 27.4)

1. The penis is made of an attached root, a free shaft or body that ends in the glans.

2. The prepuce, or foreskin, covers the penis and may be slipped back to form a cuff around the glans.

3. Internally the penis contains the corpus spongiosum and the corpora cavernosum, two erectile tissues.

D. The Male Duct System (pp. 1069–1071; Figs. 27.1, 27.4)

1. The epididymis consists of a highly coiled tube that provides a place for immature sperm to mature and to be expelled during ejaculation.

2. The ductus deferens, or vas deferens, carries sperm from storage sites in the epididymis, through the inguinal canal, over the bladder, and into the ejaculatory duct.

3. The urethra is the terminal portion of the male duct system and carries both urine and sperm (not at the same time) to the exterior environment.

E. Accessory Glands (pp. 1071–1072; Figs. 27.1, 27.4)

1. The seminal vesicles lie on the posterior bladder wall and their alkaline secretion accounts for 60% of the volume of semen consisting of fructose, ascorbic acid, a coagulating enzyme (vesiculase), and prostaglandins.

2. The prostate gland is responsible for producing a milky, slightly acidic fluid containing citrate, several enzymes, and prostate-specific antigen, making up about one-third of the semen.

3. The bulbourethral glands, or Cowper's glands, produce a thick, clear mucus prior to ejaculation that neutralizes any acidic urine in the urethra.

F. Semen is a milky white, somewhat sticky mixture of sperm and accessory gland secretions that provides a transport medium for sperm. (p. 1072)

II. Physiology of the Male Reproductive System (pp. 1072–1082; Figs. 27.5–27.10)

A. Male Sexual Response (pp. 1072–1073)

1. Erection, enlargement, and stiffening of the penis results from the engorgement of the erectile tissues with blood triggered during sexual excitement.

2. Ejaculation is the propulsion of semen from the male duct system triggered by the sympathetic nervous system.

B. Spermatogenesis is the series of events in the seminiferous tubules that produce male gametes (sperm or spermatozoa). (pp. 1073–1080; Figs. 27.5–27.9)

1. Meiosis consists of two consecutive nuclear divisions and the production of four daughter cells with half as many cells as a normal body cell.

    a. Meiosis I reduces the number of chromosomes in a cell from 46 to 23 by separating homologous chromosomes into different cells.

    b. Meiosis II resembles mitosis in every way, except the chromatids are separated into four cells.

2. Summary of Events in the Seminiferous Tubules

    a. Spermatogenesis begins when the spermatogonia divide to produce type A daughter cells that maintain the stem cell line, and type B daughter cells that get pushed toward the lumen to become primary spermatocytes and ultimately sperm.

    b. Each primary spermatocyte undergoes meiosis I to produce two secondary spermatocytes, which then undergo meiosis II to form spermatids.

    c. Spermiogenesis is a streamlining process that strips the spermatid of excess cytoplasm and forms a tail resulting in a sperm with a head, a midpiece, and a tail.

    d. The sustentacular cells, or Sertoli cells, form a blood-testis barrier that prevents membrane-bound antigens from escaping into the bloodstream.

C. Hormonal Regulation of Male Reproductive Function (pp. 1080–1082; Fig. 27.10)

1. Brain-testicular axis refers to the relationship and interactions between the hypothalamus, anterior pituitary gland, and the testes.

    a. The hypothalamus releases gonadotropin-releasing hormone (GnRH), which controls the release of the anterior pituitary hormones follicle-stimulating hormone (FSH) and luteinizing hormone (LH) in males.

    b. FSH indirectly stimulates spermatogenesis.

    c. LH, also called interstitial cell-stimulating hormone (ICSH), stimulates the interstitial cells to produce testosterone.

    d. Locally testosterone acts as a final trigger for spermatogenesis.

    e. Testosterone inhibits hypothalamic release of GnRH and acts directly on the anterior pituitary gland to inhibit gonadotropin release

    f. Inhibin is produced by the sustentacular cells and released when sperm count is high.

2. Mechanism and Effects of Testosterone Activity

    a. Testosterone is synthesized from cholesterol and exerts its effects by activating specific genes to be transcribed.

    b. Testosterone targets accessory organs (ducts, glands, and penis) causing them to grow and assume adult size and function.

    c. Testosterone induces male secondary sex characteristics: pubic, axillary, and facial hair, deepening of the voice, thickening of the skin and increase in oil production, and an increase in bone and skeletal muscle size and mass.

III. Anatomy of the Female Reproductive System (pp. 1082–1090, Figs. 27.11–27.18)

A. The ovaries are the primary reproductive organs of the female. (pp. 1082–1084; Figs. 27.11–27.13)

1. The ovaries produce the female gametes (ova or egg) and the sex hormones (estrogens and progesterone).

2. The paired ovaries are found on either side of the uterus and are held in place by several ligaments.

3. Saclike structures called ovarian follicles consist of an immature egg, called an oocyte, encased by one or more layers of different cells.

4. Follicles at different stages are distinguished by their structure as primordial follicles, primary follicles, secondary follicles, and Graafian or vesicular follicles.

5. Ovulation occurs each month in adult women when one of the maturing follicles ejects its oocyte from the ovary.

6. The ruptured follicle transforms into a glandular structure called the corpus luteum, which eventually degenerates.

B. The Female Duct System (pp. 1084–1088; Figs. 27.11, 27.14–27.15)

1. The uterine tubes, or fallopian tubes or oviducts, form the beginning of the female duct system, receive the ovulated oocyte, and provide a site for fertilization to take place.

2. The uterus is a hollow, thick-walled muscular organ that functions to receive, retain, and nourish a fertilized ovum.

   a. The uterus is supported by the mesometrium, the lateral cervical ligaments, the uterosacral ligaments, and the round ligaments.

   b. The wall of the uterus is composed of three layers: the perimetrium, the myometrium, and the endometrium.

3. The vagina provides a passageway for delivery of an infant and for menstrual blood, and also receives the penis and semen during sexual intercourse.

C. The external genitalia, also called the vulva or pudendum, include the mons pubis, labia, clitoris, and structures associated with the vestibule. (pp. 1088–1089; Figs. 27.11, 27.14)

D. Mammary glands are present in both sexes but usually function only in females to produce milk to nourish a newborn baby. (pp. 1089–1090; Figs. 27.17–27.18)

1. Mammary glands are modified sweat glands that are really part of the integumentary system.

2. Breast cancer usually arises from the epithelial cells of the ducts and grows into a lump in the breast from which cells eventually metastasize.

IV. Physiology of the Female Reproductive System (pp. 1091–1100; Figs. 27.19–27.22, Table 27.1)

A. Oogenesis is the production of female gametes called oocytes, ova, or eggs. (pp. 1091–1092; Fig. 27.19)

1. A female's total egg supply is determined at birth and the time in which she releases them extends from puberty to menopause.

2. In the fetal period the oogonia multiply rapidly by mitosis, become primordial follicles, and then become primary follicles that begin the first meiotic division.

3. After puberty a few oocytes are activated each month, but only one will continue meiosis I, ultimately producing two haploid cells, a polar body, and a secondary oocyte.

4. The secondary oocyte stops in metaphase II and if a sperm penetrates it, it will complete meiosis II, producing a second polar body and a large ovum.

B. The ovarian cycle is the monthly series of events associated with the maturation of the egg. (pp. 1093–1094; Fig. 27.20)

 1. The follicular phase is the period of follicle growth typically lasting from day 1 to 14.

 2. Ovulation occurs when the ovary wall ruptures and the secondary oocyte is expelled.

 3. The luteal phase is the period of corpus luteum activity, days 14–28.

C. Hormonal Regulation of the Ovarian Cycle (pp. 1094–1096; Fig. 27.21; Table 27.1)

 1. During childhood, the ovaries grow and secrete small amounts of estrogen that inhibit the release of GnRH until puberty, when the hypothalamus becomes less sensitive to estrogen and begins to release GnRH in a rhythmic manner.

 2. Hormonal Interactions During the Ovarian Cycle

    a. On day 1 of the cycle, levels of GnRH rise and stimulate increased production and release of FSH and LH.

    b. FSH and LH stimulate follicle growth and maturation, and estrogen secretion.

    c. Rising levels of estrogen in the plasma exert negative feedback on the anterior pituitary, inhibiting release of FSH and LH.

    d. Estrogen exerts positive feedback on the anterior pituitary resulting in a burst of LH triggering ovulation and transforming the ruptured follicle into the corpus luteum.

    e. Rising plasma levels of progesterone and estrogen exert a negative feedback on LH and FSH release.

    f. LH levels fall and luteal activity ends; the corpus luteum degenerates dropping the levels of estrogen and progesterone and the cycle starts again.

D. The uterine (menstrual) cycle is a series of cyclic changes that the uterine endometrium goes through each month in response to changing levels of ovarian hormones in the blood. (pp. 1096–1098; Fig. 27.22)

 1. The menstrual phase takes place on days 1–5 typically, and is the time when the endometrium is shed from the uterus.

 2. The proliferation phase (days 6–14) is the time in which the endometrium is rebuilt once again becoming velvety, thick, and well vascularized.

 3. The secretory phase (days 15–28) is the phase in which the endometrium prepares for implantation of an embryo.

E. Extrauterine Effects of Estrogens and Progesterone (p. 1098; Table 27.1)

 1. Rising estrogen levels promote oogenesis and follicle growth in the ovary, as well as growth and function of the female reproductive structures.

 2. Estrogens also cause the epiphyses of the long bones to close during growth spurts in puberty.

 3. The estrogen-induced secondary sex characteristics of females include growth of breasts, increased deposition of subcutaneous fat in the hips and

breast, widening and lightening of the pelvis, growth of pubic and axillary hair, and metabolic changes.

    4. Progesterone works with estrogen to establish and help regulate the uterine cycle, and promotes changes in cervical mucus.

F. In the female sexual response, the clitoris, vaginal mucosa, and breasts become engorged with blood; the nipples erect; vestibular glands increase in activity; and the final phase is orgasm. (pp. 1098–1100)

V. Sexually Transmitted Diseases (pp. 1100–1101)

A. Gonorrhea is caused by *Neisseria gonorrhoeae* bacteria, which invade the mucosae of the reproductive and urinary tracts.

B. Syphilis is caused by *Treponema pallidum*, a bacteria that easily penetrate intact mucosae and abraded skin, and enter the lymphatics and the bloodstream.

C. Chlamydia is the most common sexually transmitted disease in the U.S. and is caused by the bacteria *Chlamydia trachomatis*.

D. Genital warts are caused by a group of about 60 viruses known as the human papillomavirus (HPV).

E. Genital herpes is generally caused by the herpes simplex virus type 2, which is transferred via infectious secretions.

VI. Developmental Aspects of the Reproductive System: Chronology of Sexual Development (pp. 1101–1108; Figs. 27.23–27.25)

A. Embryological and Fetal Events (pp. 1101–1104; Figs. 27.23–27.25)

    1. Sex is determined by the sex chromosomes at conception; females have two X chromosomes and males have an X and a Y chromosome.

    2. Sexual Differentiation of the Reproductive System

        a. The gonads of both males and females begin to develop during week 5 of gestation.

        b. During week 7 the gonads begin to become testes in males, and in week 8 they begin to form ovaries in females.

        c. The external genitalia arise from the same structures in both sexes, with differentiation occurring in week 8.

    3. About two months before birth the testes begin their descent toward the scrotum, dragging their nerve supply and blood supply with them.

B. Puberty is the period of life, generally between the ages of 10 and 15 years, when the reproductive organs grow to adult size and become functional. (pp. 1104–1105)

C. Ovarian function declines gradually with age; menstrual cycles become more erratic and shorter until menopause, when ovulation and menstruation stop entirely. (pp. 1106–1108)

Cross References

Additional information on topics covered in Chapter 27 can be found in the chapters listed below.

1. Chapter 3: Cell division; tight junctions; organelles; microvilli
2. Chapter 4: Pseudostratified epithelium; tubuloalveolar glands
3. Chapter 9: Peristalsis (smooth muscle contraction)

4. Chapter 10: Male and female perineum; muscles of the pelvic floor
5. Chapter 12: Testosterone and brain anatomy
6. Chapter 13: Reflex activity
7. Chapter 14: Sympathetic and parasympathetic effects
8. Chapter 16: Brain-testicular axis; prostaglandins; testosterone; FSH and LH; ovaries and estrogen
9. Chapter 25: Male urethra
10. Chapter 28: Fertilization; vaginal environment and sperm viability; passage of sperm through the female reproductive tract in preparation of fertilization; relationship of spermatozoon and oocyte structure related to fertilization; uterine function in reproduction; interruption of uterine and ovarian cycles by pregnancy; completion of meiosis II
11. Chapter 29: Meiosis as related to genetics; importance of tetrad formation and recombination

Laboratory Correlations

1. Marieb, E. N. *Human Anatomy & Physiology Laboratory Manual: Cat and Fetal Pig Versions*. Eighth Edition Updates. Benjamin Cummings, 2006.
   Exercise 42: Anatomy of the Reproductive System
   Exercise 43: Physiology of Reproduction: Gametogenesis and the Female Cycles
2. Marieb, E. N. *Human Anatomy & Physiology Laboratory Manual: Main Version*. Seventh Edition Update. Benjamin Cummings, 2006.
   Exercise 42: Anatomy of the Reproductive System
   Exercise 43: Physiology of Reproduction: Gametogenesis and the Female Cycles

Histology Slides for the Life Sciences

Available through Benjamin Cummings, an imprint of Pearson Education, Inc. To order, contact your local Benjamin Cummings sales representative.

Slide 110 Seminiferous Tubules, Monkey Testis.
Slide 111 Active Lactating, Mammary Gland.
Slide 112 Mammalian (Primate) Uterus, Menstrual Phase.
Slide 113 Vesicular (Mature) Follicle, Ovary.
Slide 114 Mucosa of Ductus (Vas) Deferens.
Slide 115 Ductus (Vas) Deferens in Cross Section.
Slide 116 Ductus Epididymis, Primate.
Slide 117 Penis, Transverse Section.
Slide 118 Semen consisting of sperm and fluids secreted by the accessory glands.
Slide 119 The ovary and its follicles in various stages of development.
Slide 120 Prostate Gland.

Lecture Hints

1. Emphasize that sperm are not capable of fertilizing an egg immediately, but must first be naturally or artifically capacitated.
2. The duct system of the male reproductive system is difficult for most students to visualize. Use models and diagrams so that 3-D structure becomes apparent.

3. Emphasize the different secretions (and their functions) in the male reproductive tract.

4. Use cross-sectional and longitudinal diagrams of the anatomy of the penis. Both sections are necessary to establish the correct 3-D internal structure.

5. Emphasize the difference between mitosis and meiosis. Mitosis involves a single round of DNA synthesis followed by a single cytokinetic event to result in two diploid cells. Meiosis involves a single round of DNA synthesis followed by two successive cytokinetic events resulting in four haploid structures (four spermatozoa in the male, or two or three polar bodies and an egg in the female).

6. Students will have a clearer understanding if you draw a schematic diagram of spermatogenesis and relate it to a cross section of a seminiferous tubule.

7. Be sure to indicate the reasoning behind the terms *reduction* and *equatorial division*. Students often have difficulty with the concept of chromatid versus chromosome, and therefore have difficulty with these terms.

8. Clearly distinguish between spermatogenesis and spermiogenesis. Students are often confused by the similar-sounding names.

9. Point out that erection is a parasympathetic response and ejaculation is due to sympathetic reflex action.

10. Stress the importance of the blood-testis barrier in preventing immune action against sperm antigens.

11. Emphasize that testosterone has somatic effects as well as those involving reproductive functions.

12. Mention that the term *germinal epithelium* has nothing to do with ovum formation.

13. Show a diagram or slide of a mature follicle and primordial follicle to illustrate the size difference between the two.

14. It is often of benefit to compare and contrast spermatogenesis and oogenesis side-by-side to emphasize the similarities and differences.

15. Stress that the secondary oocyte (even when initially ovulated) does not complete meiosis II until fertilized by the spermatozoon, and therefore should technically not be called an ovum until fertilization has occurred.

16. Mention that the polar bodies are actually tiny nucleate haploid cells (that are not fertilizable) and that the size difference between polar bodies and oocyte is due to the amount of cytoplasm present.

17. A great deal of confusion can be generated during the presentation of ovarian and menstrual cycles. Regardless of the sequence of presentation, emphasize that both cycles occur concurrently and that both should be visualized as one continuous process even though different events occur at different times. At the end of the discussion, present a plot of hormone concentration versus day in the cycle, and review the function of each hormone as the level rises and falls. Be sure to indicate sources of hormones (follicle vs. corpus luteum) so that students will understand maintenance of pregnancy in Chapter 28.

18. Emphasize the difference between menstrual phase and menstrual cycle. Students will often confuse the two.

19. Clearly explain chromosomal determination of gender. Emphasize that it is the male that determines gender since the female only has one possible form of sex chromosome to contribute, but the male contributes one of two possible chromosomal options.

Activities/Demonstrations

1. Audio-visual materials listed under Multimedia in the Classroom and Lab.
2. Use a torso model, reproductive model, and/or dissected animal model to exhibit reproductive organs.
3. Display a large wall chart of the hormone levels during ovarian and uterine (menstrual) cycles.
4. Project a series of 2 × 2 color slides of the process of cell reproduction to refresh memories of the sequence of events.
5. Obtain and project slides of the effects of various sexually transmitted diseases.
6. Obtain or prepare a display of the various methods of birth control.
7. Use models showing the process of meiosis in spermatogenesis and oogenesis.

Critical Thinking/Discussion Topics

1. Discuss the need for mammograms and self-examination for early diagnosis of breast cancer.
2. Underscore the need for self-exam for testicular cancer.
3. Describe the current treatments available for breast cancer.
4. Explore the signs and symptoms of premenstrual syndrome and menopause.
5. Discuss the various treatments available for infertility.
6. Describe the consequences of a lack of the blood-testis barrier.
7. Examine the possible consequences of a lack of estrogen (or any other reproductive hormone) during the ovarian/menstrual cycles.

Library Research Topics

1. Research the current treatments for breast cancer.
2. Investigate the current prostate gland disorder treatments.
3. Research the disorders associated with the menstrual cycle.
4. Study the various causes of infertility in males and females and how fertility can be enhanced.
5. Explore the latest advances in birth control. How soon will a male oral contraceptive be available? What about the 5-year female contraceptive implant?
6. Research the current perspective in the medical community concerning hormone replacement therapy and menopause.

Multimedia in the Classroom and Lab

Online Resources for Students

The
Anatomy & Physiology Place   MyA&P
www.anatomyandphysiology.com   www.myaandp.com

The following shows the organization of the Chapter Guide page in both the Anatomy & Physiology Place and MyA&P™. The Chapter Guide organizes all the chapter-specific online media resources for Chapter 27 in one convenient location, with e-book links to each section of the textbook. Please note that both sites also give you access to other general A&P resources, like InterActive Physiology®, PhysioEx 6.0™, Anatomy 360°, Flashcards, a Glossary, a Histology Tutorial, and much more.

Objectives

Section 27.1 Anatomy of the Male Reproductive System (pp. 1066–1072)

Art Labeling Activity: Male Reproductive System (Fig. 27.1, p. 1066)

Case Study: Reproductive System

Activity: Male Reproductive Organs

Section 27.2 Physiology of the Male Reproductive System (pp. 1072–1082)

Section 27.3 Anatomy of the Female Reproductive System (pp. 1082–1091)

Art Labeling Activity: Female Reproductive System (Fig. 27.11, p. 1082)

Art Labeling Activity: The Ovary (Fig. 27.12, p. 1083)

Activity: Female Reproductive Organs

Section 27.4 Physiology of the Female Reproductive System (pp. 1091–1100)

Memory: Male and Female Reproductive Organs

Section 27.5 Sexually Transmitted Diseases (pp. 1100–1101)

Case Study: Sexually Transmitted Disease

Section 27.6 Developmental Aspects of the Reproductive System: Chronology of Sexual Development (pp. 1101–1105, 1108)

Chapter Summary

Self-Study Quizzes

Art Labeling Quiz

Matching Quiz

Multiple-Choice Quiz (Level I)

Multiple-Choice Quiz (Level II)

True-False Quiz

Crossword Puzzles

Crossword Puzzle 27.1

Crossword Puzzle 27.2

Media

See Guide to Audio-Visual Resources in Appendix A for key to AV distributors.

Video

1. *A Human Life Emerges* (FHS; 35 min., 1995). This program presents a close-up view of reproduction, beginning with the fertilization of the female egg, through gestation and the millions of cell divisions, culminating in the birth of a fully formed individual.

2. *The Human Female Reproductive System* (IM; 29 min., 1997). Describes the structures and functions of the female reproductive system and the hormones that regulate these functions. Explores medical conditions and how technology assists in treatment.

3. *The Human Male Reproductive System* (IM; 29 min., 1997). This video presents an overview of reproduction in vertebrates. It highlights the human male reproductive structures, and looks at the hormones involved in regulating male reproductive functions.

4. *Human Reproductive Biology* (FHS; 35 min., 1994). This program focuses on the processes that lead to normal impregnation, and the physical hindrances that can prevent it. Superb microscopy and computer animation illustrate the processes.

5. *The Human Reproductive System Videotape* (BC; 32 min., 1999). This video provides an excellent overview of the reproductive system in humans.

6. *Reproduction: Shares in the Future* (FHS; 26 min., 1989). From *The Living Body* series. Shows the characteristics of sperm and ova and how each contains a partial blueprint for the future offspring. The mechanism of cell division is shown through exceptional microphotography; the mechanisms of heredity are carefully described.

7. *The Reproductive System Video* (NIMCO; 18 min., 1998). From *The Human Body* series, explores the maturation of eggs and sperm and explains the genetic contribution that each makes to the fertilized egg.

8. *Unsafe Sex and Its Consequences* (FHS; 20 min., 1995). Identifies the most common sexually transmitted diseases other than HIV. Discusses their symptoms, treatments, and prevention.

Software

1. *A.D.A.M.® InterActive Anatomy®* 4.0 (see p. 9 of this guide for full listing).
2. *A.D.A.M.® MediaPro* (see p. 9 of this guide for full listing).
3. *A.D.A.M.® Anatomy Practice* (see p. 86 of this guide for full listing).
4. *Bodyworks* (see p. 9 of this guide for full listing).
5. *Meiosis* (CBS; Win/Mac). Topics include the prokaryotic and eukaryotic cell; genetic material within a eukaryotic cell, as well as spermatogenesis, oogenesis, meiosis I, meiosis II, and fertilization.
6. *The Ultimate Human Body* (see p. 9 of this guide for full listing).

Lecture Enhancement Material

To view thumbnails of all of the illustrations for Chapter 27, see Appendix B.

Transparencies Index/Media Manager

Figure 27.1   Reproductive organs of the male, sagittal view.
Figure 27.2   Relationships of the testis to the scrotum and spermatic cord.
Figure 27.3   Structure of the testis.
Figure 27.4   Male reproductive structures.
Figure 27.5   The human life cycle.
Figure 27.6   Comparison of mitosis and meiosis in a mother cell with a diploid number ($2n$) of 4.
Figure 27.7   Meiosis.
Figure 27.8   Spermatogenesis.
Figure 27.9   Spermiogenesis: transformation of a spermatid into a functional sperm.
Figure 27.10   Hormonal regulation of testicular function, the brain-testicular axis.
Figure 27.11   Internal organs of the female reproductive system, midsagittal section.
Figure 27.12   Structure of an ovary.
Figure 27.13   Ovulation.
Figure 27.14   Internal reproductive organs of a female.
Figure 27.15   The endometrium and its blood supply.
Figure 27.16   The external genitalia (vulva) of the female.
Figure 27.17   Structure of lactating mammary glands.
Figure 27.18   Mammograms.
Figure 27.19   Events of oogenesis.
Figure 27.20   Schematic view of the ovarian cycle: development and fate of ovarian follicles.

Answers to End-of-Chapter Questions

Multiple Choice and Matching Question answers appear in Appendix G of the main text.

Short Answer Essay Questions

18. In males, the urethra transports both urine and semen and thus serves both the urinary and reproductive systems; in females, the two systems are structurally and functionally separate. (p. 1071)

19. A spermatid is converted to a motile sperm by a process called spermiogenesis, during which most of the superfluous cytoplasmic "baggage" is sloughed off and a tail is fashioned. The sperm regions are the head: the genetic (DNA-delivering) region; the midpiece: the metabolizing (ATP-producing) region; and the tail: the locomotor region. (pp. 1077–1079)

20. Three tiny polar bodies, nearly devoid of cytoplasm, assure that the fertilized egg has enough nutrient reserves to support it during its journey to the uterus. (pp. 1091–1092)

21. Secondary sexual characteristics of the female include breasts; deposits of subcutaneous fat, especially in the hips and breasts; appearance of pubic hair; and widening and lightening of the pelvis. (p. 1098)

22. The events of menopause include a decline in estrogen production, an anovulatory ovarian cycle, and erratic menstrual periods that are shorter in length and eventually cease entirely. Possible consequences of menopause include atrophy of the reproductive organs and breasts, dryness of the vagina, painful intercourse, vaginal infections, irritability and mood changes, intense vasodilation of the skin's blood vessels ("hot flashes"), gradual thinning of the skin, loss of bone mass, and slowly rising blood cholesterol levels. (pp. 1105, 1108)

23. Menarche is the first menstrual cycle, occurring when the adult pattern of gonadotropin cycling is achieved. (p. 1094)

24. The pathway of a sperm from the male testes to the uterine tubule of a female is as follows: testis, epididymis, ductus deferens, male urethra, vagina, uterus, and uterine tube. (pp. 1069–1072, 1084–1088)

25. As luteinizing hormone blood levels drop, the corpus luteum begins to degenerate. Progesterone levels fall, depriving the endometrium of hormonal support, and the spiral arteries kink and go into spasms. Denied oxygen, endometrial cells die, and as their lysosomes rupture the functional layer "self-digests." (p. 1098)

26. The vaginal epithelium houses dendritic cells that act as antigen-presenting cells in the immune response, thus providing for early recognition of and attack against

invading bacteria and viruses. The cervical mucous glands secrete glycogen which is metabolized anaerobically by the vaginal mucosal cells to lactic acid providing low vaginal pH that is bacteriostatic. (pp. 1087–1088)

27. The mucus produced by these glands cleanses the urethra of traces of urine before ejaculation of semen occurs. (p. 1072)

28. His cremaster muscles had contracted to bring the testes closer to the warmth of the body wall. (p. 1067)

Critical Thinking and Clinical Application Questions

1. This patient has a prolapsed uterus, no doubt caused by the stress on the pelvic floor muscles during her many pregnancies. Since she also has keloids, one can assume that the central tendon to which those muscles attach has been severely damaged and many vaginal tears have occurred. (p. 1086)

2. The patient probably has a gonorrhea infection caused by the *Neisseria gonorrhoeae* bacterium. It is treated with penicillin and other antibiotics. If untreated, it can cause urethral constriction and inflammation of the entire male duct system. (p. 1100)

3. No, she will not be menopausal, because the ovaries will not be affected; they will continue to produce hormones. Tubal ligation is the cutting or cauterizing of the uterine tubes. (pp. 1099, 1129)

4. The man would be asked questions such as whether he has difficulty in urination or problems with impotence. The major test to be run would be to determine his sperm count. (p. 1080)

5. There is no continuity between the ovary and the uterine tube and the secondary oocytes are released into the peritoneal cavity. The ovulated oocyte is "coaxed" into the uterine tube by the activity of the fimbriae and tubal cilia. Though it is a longer journey, oocytes released on one side of the peritoneal cavity could ultimately enter the uterine tube on the opposite side. (pp. 1084–1086)

Suggested Readings

Alexander, N.J. "Barriers to Sexually Transmitted Diseases." *Scientific American: Science & Medicine* 3 (Mar./April 1996): 32–41.

Brainard, J. "HIV's Quiet Accomplice." *Science News* 154 (Sep. 1998): 158–159.

Cho, C., et al. "Fertilization Defects in Sperm from Mice Lacking Fertilin B." *Science* 281 (Sep. 1998): 1857–1859.

Christensen, Damaris. "Mammograms on Trial." *Science News* 161 (17) (April 2002): 264–266.

Fackelmann, K.A. "Medicine for Menopause." *Science News* 153 (June 1998): 392–393.

Garbers, David L. "Ion Channels: Swimming with Sperm." *Nature* 413 (6856) (Oct. 2001): 579–582.

Garnick, M.B. "Prostate Cancer." *Scientific American* 279 (Dec. 1998): 74–83.

Jegalian, Karin and Lahn, Bruce T. "Why the Y is So Weird." *Scientific American* 284 (2) (Feb. 2001): 56-61.

Jordan, V.C. "Designer Estrogens." *Scientific American* 279 (Oct. 1998): 60–67.

Kang-Decker, Ningling, et al. "Lack of Acrosome Formation in Hrb-deficient Mice." *Science* 294 (5546) (Nov. 2001): 1531–1533.

Kuiper, G.J.M., M. Carlquist, and J. Gustafsson. "Estrogen Is a Male and Female Hormone." *Science & Medicine* 5 (Jul/Aug 1998): 36–45.

Muramatsu, Takashi. "Carbohydrate Recognition in Spermatogenesis." *Science* 295 (5552) (Jan. 2002): 53–54.

Nantel, F., et al. "Spermiogenesis Deficiency and Germ-Cell Apoptosis in CREM-Mutant Mice." *Nature* 380 (Mar. 1996): 159–162.

Pollard, J. W. "Modifiers of Estrogen Action." *Science & Medicine* 6 (Jul./Aug. 1999): 38–47.

Raloff, J. "Common Pollutants Undermine Masculinity." *Science News* 155 (Apr. 1999): 213.

Raloff, Janet. "Hormones: Here's the Beef." *Science News* 161 (1) (Jan. 2002): 10–12.

Seppa, N. "Soy Estrogens: Too Much of a Good Thing?" *Science News* 159 (24) (June 2001): 375.

Smaglik, P. "Understanding the Language of Reproduction." *Science News* 151 (Feb. 1997): 85.

Tilly, Jonathan L. "Commuting the Death Sentence: How Oocytes Strive to Survive." *Nature Reviews: Molecular Cell Biology* 2 (11) (Nov. 2001): 838–848.

Wu, C. "Boning up on Postmenopausal Hormones." *Science News* 150 (Nov. 1996): 293.

Pregnancy and Human Development 28

Objectives

From Egg to Embryo

1. Define fertilization and discuss the limits of timing on its occurrence.
2. Describe the process of sperm capacitation and its importance.
3. Explain the need for blocks to polyspermy and how this is accomplished.
4. Identify cleavage divisions, and the cellular and embryonic products of cleavage divisions.
5. Discuss the events of implantation, and the role of human chorionic gonadotropin (hCG).
6. Explain the process of placentation.

Events of Embryonic Development

7. Describe the development and function of the embryonic membranes.
8. Define gastrulation and list the layers formed.
9. Identify organogenesis, and discuss the specialization that occurs within each germ layer.
10. Explain the development of the specialized structures of the fetal circulation, and the function of each.

Events of Fetal Development

11. Discuss the events of fetal development.

Effects of Pregnancy on the Mother

12. Describe the anatomical, metabolic, and physiological changes experienced by the mother during pregnancy.

Parturition (Birth)

13. Explain the triggers that initiate labor and discuss the three stages of labor.

Adjustments of the Infant to Extrauterine Life

14. List the factors considered in the Apgar score, and describe how the score is used to assess the newborn.
15. Describe the changes that occur to specialized fetal circulatory structures after birth.

Lactation

16. Define lactation, and describe the mechanism of hormones and neural stimuli involved.

Suggested Lecture Outline

I. From Egg to Embryo (pp. 1114–1122; Figs. 28.1–28.7)

A. Accomplishing Fertilization (pp. 1114–1117; Figs. 28.1–28.2)

1. Fertilization occurs when a sperm fuses with an egg to form a zygote.

2. Millions of sperm ejaculated into the female reproductive tract are lost due to leakage from the vaginal canal, destruction by the acidic environment of the vagina, inability to pass the cervical mucus, or destruction by defense cells of the uterus.

3. In order to fertilize an egg, sperm must be capacitated, a process involving weakening of the sperm cell membrane in order to allow release of acrosomal hydrolytic enzymes.

4. When sperm cells bind to the zona pellucida surrounding the egg, they undergo an acrosomal reaction, where acrosomal enzymes are released to the oocyte.

   a. Hundreds of sperm cells must release their acrosomal enzymes before fertilization can occur.

   b. Once a sperm cell binds to membrane receptors on the oocyte membrane, its nucleus is pulled into the cytoplasm of the oocyte.

5. Polyspermy, or fertilization by more than one sperm cell, leads to a lethal number of chromosomes, and must be prevented.

   a. The fast block to polyspermy occurs when the membrane of the oocyte depolarizes and prevents similar binding by other sperm cells.

   b. The slow block to polyspermy results in destruction of sperm receptors, and the formation of a swollen membrane that removes other sperm cells from the surface of the oocyte.

6. After a sperm enters an oocyte, it loses its tail and midpiece, and migrates to the center of the oocyte while the oocyte completes meiosis II.

   a. After meiosis II is completed, male and female pronuclei fuse and produce a zygote, which almost immediately enters into mitosis.

B. Preembryonic Development (pp. 1117–1122; Figs. 28.3–28.7)

   1. Preembryonic development begins with fertilization and continues with the movement of the preembryo to the uterus, where it implants in the uterine wall.

   2. The mitotic divisions after fertilization occur without much growth between divisions, resulting in progressively smaller cells, a process called cleavage.

      a. Cleavage forms two identical cells, blastomeres, which then form a morula, a hollow ball of cells, by 72 hours.

      b. After 4–5 days, the blastocyst escapes from the degrading zona pellucida to implant in the uterine wall.

   3. Implantation occurs after 6–7 days; the trophoblast adheres to the endometrium, and produces enzymes that irritate the endometrium.

      a. Uterine capillaries become permeable and leaky, and the trophoblast proliferates, forming the cytotrophoblast and the syncytiotrophoblast.

      b. Trophoblast cells secrete human chorionic gonadotropin (hCG), which acts on the corpus luteum.

   4. Placentation is the formation of the placenta, and is the process of proliferation of the trophoblast.

      a. The placenta is fully functional as a nutritive, respiratory, excretory, and endocrine organ by the end of the third month of gestation.

II. Events of Embryonic Development (pp. 1122–1132; Figs. 28.8–28.13; Tables 28.1–28.2)

A. Formation and Roles of the Embryonic Membranes (pp. 1122–1123)

1. While implantation is occurring, the blastocyst is being converted into a gastrula, in which three primary germ layers form and embryonic membranes develop.

   a. The amnion forms the transparent sac ultimately containing the embryo, and provides a buoyant environment that protects the embryo from physical trauma.

   b. The yolk sac forms part of the gut, produces the earliest blood cells and blood vessels, and is the source of germ cells that migrate into the embryo to seed the gonads.

   c. The allantois is the structural base for the umbilical cord that links the embryo to the placenta, and becomes part of the urinary bladder.

   d. The chorion helps to form the placenta, and encloses the embryonic body and all other membranes.

B. Gastrulation: Germ Layer Formation (p. 1123; Fig. 28.8)

1. Gastrulation is the process of transforming the two-layered embryonic disc to a three-layered embryo containing three germ layers: ectoderm, mesoderm, and endoderm.

2. Gastrulation begins with the appearance of the primitive streak, which establishes the long axis of the embryo.

   a. The endoderm gives rise to epithelial linings of the gut, respiratory, and urogenital systems, and associated glands.

   b. The mesoderm gives rise to all types of tissues not formed by ectoderm or endoderm, such as muscle tissue.

   c. The ectoderm gives rise to structures of the nervous system and the epidermis.

C. Organogenesis: Differentiation of the Germ Layers (pp. 1123–1132; Figs. 28.9–28.13; Tables 28.1–28.2)

1. Organogenesis is the formation of organs and organ systems; by the end of the embryonic period, all organ systems are recognizable.

   a. Neurulation, the formation of the brain and spinal cord, is the first event of organogenesis.

   b. As the embryo develops from a flat plate of cells, it rolls into a tube and the inferior endoderm becomes the lining of the primitive gut.

   c. Mesodermal specialization forms the notochord, and gives rise to the dermis, parietal serosa, bones, muscles, cardiovascular structures, and connective tissues.

   d. By 3 1/2 weeks, the embryo has a blood vessel system and a pumping heart.

   e. Vascular modifications include umbilical arteries and veins, a ductus venosus, and the foramen ovale and ductus arteriosus.

III. Events of Fetal Development (p. 1133; Fig. 28.14; Table 28.2)

A. The fetal period extends from weeks 9–38, and is a time of rapid growth of body structures established in the embryo.

B. During the first half of the fetal period, cells are still differentiating into specific cell types to form the body's distinctive tissues.

IV. Effects of Pregnancy on the Mother (pp. 1133–1135; Fig. 28.15)

A. Anatomical Changes (pp. 1133–1134; Fig. 28.15)

1. The female reproductive organs and breasts become increasingly vascular and engorged with blood.
2. The uterus enlarges dramatically, causing a shift in the woman's center of gravity and an accentuated lumbar curvature (lordosis).
3. Placental production of the hormone relaxin causes pelvic ligaments and the pubic symphysis to soften and relax.
4. There is a normal weight gain of around 28 pounds, due to growth of the fetus, maternal reproductive organs, and breasts, and increased blood volume.

B. Metabolic Changes (pp. 1134–1135)

1. As the placenta enlarges, it produces human placental lactogen, which woks with estrogen and progesterone to promote maturation of the breasts for lactation.
2. Human placental lactogen also promotes the growth of the fetus, and exerts a glucose-sparing effect on maternal metabolism.
3. Human chorionic thyrotropin from the placenta increases maternal metabolic rate.

C. Physiological Changes (p. 1135)

1. Many women suffer morning sickness during the first few months of pregnancy, until their systems adapt to elevated levels of estrogen and progesterone.
2. Heartburn often results from the displacement of the esophagus, and constipation may result due to the decreased motility of the digestive tract.
3. The kidneys produce more urine, since there is additional fetal metabolic waste.
4. Vital capacity and respiratory rate increases, but there is a decrease in residual volume, and many women suffer from difficult breathing, or dyspnea.
5. Blood volume increases to accommodate the needs of the fetus, so blood pressure and heart rate rise, increasing cardiac output.

V. Parturition (Birth) (pp. 1135–1137; Figs. 28.16–28.17)

A. Parturition is the process of giving birth, and usually occurs within 15 days of the calculated due date, which is 280 days from the last menstrual period.

B. Initiation of Labor (pp. 1135–1136; Fig. 28.16)

1. Estrogen levels peak, stimulating myometrial cells of the uterus to form abundant oxytocin receptors, and antagonizing the quieting effect of progesterone on uterine muscle.
2. Fetal cells produce oxytocin, which promotes the release of prostaglandins from the placenta, and further stimulates uterine contraction.
3. Increasing emotional and physical stresses activate the mother's hypothalamus, which signals the release of oxytocin.
4. Expulsive contractions are aided by a change that occurs in an adhesive protein, fetal fibronectin, converting it to a lubricant.

C. Stages of Labor (p. 1137; Fig. 28.17)

1. The dilation stage of labor extends from onset of labor to the time when the cervix is fully dilated by the baby's head, at about 10 cm in diameter.

2. The expulsion stage extends from full dilation until the time the infant is delivered.

    a. When the baby is in the vertex, or head first, position, the skull acts as a wedge to dilate the cervix.

    b. Crowning occurs when the baby's head distends the vulva, and once the head has been delivered, the rest of the baby follows much more easily.

    c. After birth, the umbilical cord is clamped and cut.

3. During the placental stage, uterine contractions cause detachment of the placenta from the uterine wall, followed by delivery of the placenta and membranes (afterbirth).

VI. Adjustments of the Infant to Extrauterine Life (pp. 1137–1138)

A. The Apgar score is an assessment of the infant's physiological status based on heart rate, respiration, color, muscle tone, and reflexes. (p. 1137)

B. Taking the First Breath (pp. 1137–1138)

1. Once the placenta is no longer removing carbon dioxide from the blood, it builds up in the infant's blood, resulting in acidosis that signals the respiratory control centers.

2. The transitional period is the 6–8 hours after birth characterized by intermittent waking periods in which the infant's heart rate, respiratory behavior, and body temperature fluctuate.

C. Occlusion of Special Fetal Blood Vessels and Vascular Shunts (p. 1138)

1. After birth, the umbilical arteries and veins constrict and become fibrosed, becoming the medial umbilical ligaments, superior vesical arteries of the bladder, and the round ligament of the liver, or ligamentum teres.

2. The ductus venosus closes, and is eventually converted to the ligamentum venosum.

3. A flap of tissue covers the foramen ovale, ultimately sealing it and becoming the fossa ovalis, while the ductus arteriosus constricts, becoming the ligamentum arteriosus.

VII. Lactation (pp. 1138–1139; Fig. 28.18)

A. Lactation is the production of milk by the hormone-prepared mammary glands.

1. Rising levels of placental estrogens, progesterone, and lactogen stimulate the hypothalamus to produce prolactin-releasing hormone (PRH), which promotes secretion of prolactin by the anterior pituitary.

2. Colostrum, a high-protein, low-fat product is initially secreted by the mammary glands, but after two to three days, true milk is produced.

3. Nipple stimulation during nursing sends neural signals to the hypothalamus, resulting in production of PRH and a burst of prolactin that stimulates milk production for the next feeding.

4. Oxytocin causes the let-down reflex, resulting in the release of milk from the alveoli of the mammary glands in both breasts.

5. Advantages of breast milk are: better absorption and more efficient metabolism of many components; antibodies and other chemicals that protect the infant; a natural laxative effect that helps to prevent physiological jaundice; and encouragement of the natural intestinal fauna.

VIII. Assisted Reproductive Technology and Reproductive Cloning (pp. 1139–1140; Fig 28.19)

   A. Hormones can be used to increase sperm or egg production and surgery can be used to open blocked tubes. (p. 1139)

   B. Assisted reproductive technology involves surgically removing oocytes from a woman's ovaries, fertilizing the eggs and returning them to the woman's body. (p. 1139)

   C. Cloning involves the placing of a somatic cell nucleus into an oocyte. (pp. 1139–1140)

Cross References

Additional information on topics covered in Chapter 28 can be found in the chapters listed below.

1. Chapter 2: Enzymes
2. Chapter 16: Hormones and hormone function; parathyroid hormone and calcium balance; oxytocin; prolactin
3. Chapter 18: Fetal heart
4. Chapter 19: Fetal blood vessels and shunts; varicose veins
5. Chapter 21: Antibodies
6. Chapter 22: Acidosis and respiratory drive
7. Chapter 27: Oogenesis; secondary oocyte; vaginal environment; semen; cervical mucus; spermatozoon structure; oocyte structure; hypothalamic-pituitary control of the ovarian cycle; uterus and uterine tubes; endometrium; corpus luteum and hCG; ovarian and menstrual cycles

Laboratory Correlations

1. Marieb, E. N. *Human Anatomy & Physiology Laboratory Manual: Cat and Fetal Pig Versions.* Eighth Edition Updates. Benjamin Cummings, 2006.
   Exercise 44: Survey of Embryonic Development
2. Marieb, E. N. *Human Anatomy & Physiology Laboratory Manual: Main Version.* Seventh Edition Update. Benjamin Cummings, 2006.
   Exercise 44: Survey of Embryonic Development

Lecture Hints

1. Emphasize the difference between the terms *conceptus*, *embryo*, and *fetus* (and the associated periods).
2. Stress that the early cell divisions of the conceptus increase total cell number but do not result in cell size increase. Cells become increasingly smaller until the zona ruptures.
3. When discussing the maintenance of the corpus luteum (which initially maintains pregnancy and is under hormonal control by the trophoblast cells), mention that a measurement of hCG levels would be an ideal indicator of pregnancy (EPT home tests, blood tests).
4. Point out that the blastocyst is actually embedded into the endometrial wall, not attached to the surface as some students first imagine.

5. Use plenty of models and/or wall charts illustrating the different stages of embryonic and fetal development. Students are often overwhelmed by the terminology of development.

6. Point out the dual origin of the placenta.

7. Emphasize that from the mother's point of view, the placenta is just another organ drawing resources from the mother's blood supply. This idea is helpful to establish the placenta as an exchange organ.

8. Stress that embryonic/fetal blood does not come into contact with maternal blood under normal circumstances, but that most substances (including the gamma class of immunoglobulins) cross the placental barrier to embryonic/fetal circulation.

9. Spend time emphasizing the embryonic/fetal membranes since the anatomical orientation of these membranes is difficult for many students to visualize.

10. Mention that the yolk sac is not the source of nutrients for the egg as it is in birds and reptiles, but instead is an early site of blood formation.

11. As a point of interest, reveal that "eating for two" is a popular belief that has no physiological basis.

12. Review hypothalamic and pituitary control of the ovarian cycle.

13. Point out the logic behind the various modifications of fetal circulation and how those shunts must be redirected when the umbilical cord is cut.

14. When discussing the changes that occur in the mother during pregnancy, emphasize each in a commonsense way: urinary output must increase because the fetus is adding a considerable amount of waste to the mother's blood; blood volume increases due to the excess draw on the mother's resources, etc.

15. The *Miracle of Life* video is one of the best available depicting developmental events from fertilization to birth. It is worthwhile to take time to present this videotape, especially if you do not use any other.

16. Clearly differentiate between the process of milk production and milk let-down into the ducts.

Activities/Demonstrations

1. Audio-visual materials listed under Multimedia in the Classroom and Lab.

2. Have the students bring in a recent article that deals with the effects of maternal drug-taking or disease (such as AIDS, herpes, etc.) on the well-being of the fetus.

3. Obtain a fresh placenta from a local hospital to demonstrate the anatomical features of this vital structure.

4. Use a pregnancy model to exhibit fetal development, placement, and birth.

5. Use a doll and a drawstring sack to illustrate the placement of the fetus for vaginal delivery and the turning movements that result in delivery.

6. Use a doll and a drawstring sack to illustrate abnormal placements for delivery.

7. Use a series of models to illustrate embryonic and fetal development.

8. If available, display embryos and fetuses in different stages of development.

Critical Thinking/Discussion Topics

1. Discuss the importance of folic acid to the prevention of neural tube defects.

2. Explore the drastic changes the fetus must undergo at birth and how those changes might be minimized.

3. Examine the pros and cons of determining when life begins (be sure to advance both sides of the issue).

4. Discuss the methods available to produce pregnancy (i.e., artificial insemination, in vitro fertilization, etc.) and what cautions should be given to those choosing these methods.

5. Student assignment for class discussion:

   a. Define *episiotomy* and explain why this procedure is performed.

   b. Define *Down syndrome* (trisomy 21) and indicate in which maternal age group it is most common.

Library Research Topics

1. Research the pros, cons, and contraindications of exercise during pregnancy.

2. Research the types of birth presentations and note the symptoms, prognosis, and difficulties encountered in each type.

3. Study several types of birth defects by symptom category, i.e., skeletal system, circulatory system, etc.

4. Investigate various environmental effects on embryological and fetal development, i.e., alcohol, drugs (legal and nonlegal), infectious diseases, etc.

5. Research the various methods of contraception, including those currently being used as well as projected methods.

6. Explore the benefits of breast-feeding to both child and mother.

7. Research the fetal and infant problems associated with the mother's lifestyle, i.e., sexually transmitted disease infections, infectious disease infections, alcoholism and DTs, AIDS, etc.

8. Examine the pros and cons concerning traditional delivery procedures versus underwater births or births in warm, dimly lit rooms, etc.

Multimedia in the Classroom and Lab

Online Resources for Students

The
Anatomy & Physiology Place
www.anatomyandphysiology.com

MyA&P
www.myaandp.com

The following shows the organization of the Chapter Guide page in both the Anatomy & Physiology Place and MyA&P™. The Chapter Guide organizes all the chapter-specific online media resources for Chapter 28 in one convenient location, with e-book links to each section of the textbook. Please note that both sites also give you access to other general A&P resources, like InterActive Physiology®, PhysioEx 6.0™, Anatomy 360°, Flashcards, a Glossary, a Histology Tutorial, and much more.

Objectives

Section 28.1 From Egg to Zygote (pp. 1114–1117)

Art Labeling Activity: The Placenta and Associated Structures (Fig. 28.7, p. 1121)

Activity: Embryonic Membranes and the Placenta

Memory: Embryonic Development

Section 28.2 Events of Embryonic Development: Zygote to Blastocyst Implantation (pp. 1117–1122)

Case Study: Genetics/Pregnancy and Human Development

Media

See Guide to Audio-Visual Resources in Appendix A for key to AV distributors.

Video

1. *A New Life* (FHS; 28 min., 1994). From the award-winning *The Living Body* series, this video looks at the events that led from fertilization of a cell to development of a human baby.

2. *Caring for Premature Babies* (FHS; 19 min.). Highlights the risks for pre-term labor, the problems of the premature infant, and the tools now available to save young lives. Helps students understand the problems associated with premature birth.

3. *Coming Together* (FHS; 28 min., 1989). From the award-winning *The Living Body* series, this video covers the physiological events underlying reproduction.

4. *Embryonic Development and Differentiation* (IM; 26 min., 1997). This video describes the events that follow fertilization of the human ovum.

5. *Infertility and IVF* (FHS; 19 min., 1995). Presents an update on in vitro fertilization and the subject of infertility in general. Covers the causes and controversies. Useful for allied health students.

6. *Infertility: New Treatments* (FHS; 25 min., 1995). Program explores the newest treatment for infertility and examines the difficulties involved with the process of in vitro fertilization. Explains how new technologies increase the odds for success.

7. *Into the World* (FHS; 28 min., 1984). From the award-winning *The Living Body* series, this video covers the events of birth using fetoscopy and shows what happens from the baby's viewpoint.

8. *NOVA® The Miracle of Life* (CBS; 60 min., 1986). Swedish photographer Lennert Nilsson takes you on a voyage to the human womb. Travel down the oviduct and observe the sperm and egg, then observe the development of the embryo and finally the birth of a child.

9. *Prenatal Development: A Life in the Making* (IM; 26 min., 1996). Traces the transformation of a one-celled zygote into a fully functioning human being in just 266 days. Explores the three stages of prenatal development and reviews the organs and structures that nourish and protect the fetus.

10. *Reproduction: Shares in the Future* (FHS; 26 min., 1989). From *The Living Body* series. Shows the characteristics of sperm and ova and how each contains a partial blueprint for the future offspring. The mechanism of cell division is shown through exceptional microphotography; the mechanisms of heredity are carefully described.

11. *Small Miracles: Curing Fatal Conditions in the Womb* (FHS; 51 min., 1995). An unprecedented introduction to the diagnosis and treatment of babies with fatal conditions who are still in the womb. Encourages class discussion.

Software

1. *The Embryonic Disk* (IM; Windows). Tracking the formation of the human embryo from fertilization to folding, this CD-ROM presents the first month of life on a page that links each day to an illustrated description of its major events

2. *Interactive Embryology: The Human Embryo Program* (IM; Win/Mac). Features a series of movies simulating development of the human embryo. It shows representations of developmental processes and tissue movements that are too complex to be easily understood from serial sections.

Lecture Enhancement Material

To view thumbnails of all of the illustrations for Chapter 28, see Appendix B.

Transparencies Index/Media Manager

Figure 28.1   Diagrams showing the relative size of a human conceptus from fertilization to the early fetal stage.

Figure 28.2   Sperm penetration and the cortical reaction (slow block to polyspermy).

Figure 28.3   Events immediately following sperm penetration.

Figure 28.4   Cleavage from zygote to blastocyst.

Figure 28.5   Implantation of the blastocyst.

Figure 28.6   Hormonal changes during pregnancy.

Figure 28.7   Events of placentation, early embryonic development, and embryonic membrane formation.

Figure 28.8   Formation of the three primary germ layers.

Figure 28.9   Neurulation.

Figure 28.10   Folding of the embryonic body.

Figure 28.11   Endodermal differentiation to form the epithelial linings of the digestive and respiratory tracts and associated glands.

Figure 28.12   Early mesodermal differentiation.

Figure 28.13   Circulation in fetus and newborn.

Figure 28.14   Photographs of a developing fetus.

Figure 28.15   Relative size of the uterus before conception and during pregnancy.

Figure 28.16   Hormonal induction of labor.

Figure 28.17   Parturition.

Figure 28.18   Positive feedback mechanism of the milk let-down reflex.

Figure 28.19   Brief summary of selected techniques of assisted reproductive technology (ART).

Table 28.1   Derivatives of the Primary Germ Layers
Table 28.2   Developmental Events of the Fetal Period
A Closer Look   Contraception: To Be or Not To Be*
*Indicates images that are on the Media Manager only.

Answers to End-of-Chapter Questions

Multiple Choice and Matching Question answers appear in Appendix G of the main text.

Short Answer Essay Questions

16. The process of fertilization involves numerous steps. First, sperm deposited in the vagina must be capacitated; that is, their membranes must become fragile so that the hydrolytic enzymes in their acrosomes can be released. The acrosomal reaction is the release of acrosomal enzymes (hyaluronidase, acrosin, proteases, and others) that occurs in the immediate vicinity of the oocyte. Hundreds of acrosomes must rupture to break down the intercellular cement that holds the granulosa cells together and to digest holes in the zona pellucida. Once a path has been cleared and a single sperm makes contact with the oocyte membrane receptors, its nucleus is pulled into the oocyte cytoplasm.

    As soon as the plasma membrane of one sperm makes contact with the oocyte membrane, sodium channels open and ionic sodium moves into the oocyte from the extracellular space, causing its membrane to depolarize. The depolarization causes ionic calcium to be released into the oocyte cytoplasm. This surge in intra-cellular calcium levels initiates the cortical reaction and activates the oocyte. The activated secondary oocyte completes meiosis II to form the ovum nucleus and ejects the second polar body. The ovum and sperm nuclei swell, becoming the female and male pronuclei, and approach each other as a mitotic spindle develops between them. The pronuclei membranes then rupture, releasing their chromosomes into the immediate vicinity of the spindle. Combination of the maternal and paternal chromosomes constitutes the act of fertilization and produces the diploid zygote. The effect of fertilization is the formation of a single cell (zygote) with chromosomes from the egg and sperm, and determination of the offspring's sex. (pp. 1114–1117)

17. In cleavage, daughter cells become smaller and smaller, resulting in cells with a high surface-to-volume ratio and providing a larger number of cells to serve as building blocks for constructing the embryo. (p. 1117)

18. a. Viability of the corpus luteum is due to human chorionic gonadotropin secreted by trophoblast cells of the blastocyst which bypasses the pituitary-ovarian controls, prompting continued production of estrogen and progesterone to main-tain the endometrium.

    b. The corpus luteum must remain functional following implantation until the placenta can assume the duties of hormone production; otherwise, the endometri-um will not be maintained and the conceptus will be sloughed off in menses. (p. 1120)

19. The placenta is formed from embryonic (trophoblastic) and maternal (endometrial) tissues. When the trophoblast acquires a layer of mesoderm it becomes the chorion. The chorion sends out chorionic villi, which come in contact with maternal blood. Oxygen and nutrients diffuse from the maternal to the embryonic blood; embryonic wastes diffuse from the embryo to the mother's circulation. (pp. 1120–1122)

20. As soon as the plasma membrane of one sperm makes contact with the oocyte membrane, sodium channels open and ionic sodium moves into the oocyte from the extracellular space, causing the membrane to depolarize. This "fast block to polyspermy" prevents other sperm from fusing with the oocyte. This is followed by the cortical reaction which constitutes the "slow block to polyspermy." (p. 1115)

21. The gastrulation process gives rise to the three primary germ layers, the ectoderm, mesoderm, and endoderm from which all tissues are formed. (p. 1123)

22. a. Breech presentation is buttocks-first presentation.

b. Two problems of breech presentation include a more difficult delivery and the baby's difficulty in breathing. (p. 1137)

23. The factors that bring about uterine contractions include high levels of estrogen; production of oxytocin by the fetus, which acts on the placenta to stimulate the production and release of prostaglandins; and activation of the hypothalamus to produce oxytocin for release by the posterior pituitary. (pp. 1135–1136)

24. The flat embryonic disc achieves a cylindrical body shape as its sides fold inward and it lifts up off the yolk sac into the amniotic cavity. At the same time, the head and tail regions fold under. All this folding gives the month-old embryo a tadpole shape. The sequence is illustrated in Figure 28.10 on p. 1126.

Critical Thinking and Clinical Application Questions

1. (c). Most major developmental events occur during the first three months of pregnancy, and events that are blocked for whatever reason never occur because development has a precise timetable. Assessment should be done to analyze possible problems. (pp. 1130, 1133)

2. An episiotomy is a midline incision from the vaginal orifice laterally or posteriorly toward the rectum. It is performed to reduce tissue tearing as the baby's head exits from the perineum. (p. 1137)

3. The woman was in labor, the expulsion stage. She probably would not have time to get to the hospital. Typically it takes 50 minutes in the first birth and 20 minutes in subsequent births for birth to occur once the expulsion stage has been reached. A 60-mile drive would take over an hour. (p. 1137)

4. Mary's fetus might have respiratory problems or even congenital defects due to her smoking, since smoking causes vasoconstriction, which would hinder blood (hence oxygen) delivery to the placenta. (p. 1133)

5. Segmentation is the presence of multiple, repeating units, lined up from head to tail along the axis of the body. The body's segmented structures, such as vertebrae, ribs, and the muscles between the ribs, are primarily derived from somites of mesoderm. (p. 1127)

6. It would be unlikely that the resulting cell could develop into a healthy embryo because the polar body lacks the needed cellular organelles and nutritional sources that are found in the oocyte. (p. 1091)

Suggested Readings

Barinaga, Marsha. "Cells Exchanged During Pregnancy Live On." *Science* 296 (5576) (June 2002): 2169–2172.

Couzin, Jennifer. "Quirks of Fetal Environment Felt Decades Later." *Science* 296 (5576) (June 2002): 2167–2169.

Duesbery, Nicholas S. and Vande Woude, George F. "An Arresting Activity." *Nature* 416 (April 2002): 804–805.

Holden, Constance. "Research on Contraception Still in the Doldrums." *Science* 296 (5576) (June 2002): 2172–2173.

Ivell, Richard. "This Hormone Has Been Relaxin' Too Long!" *Science* 295 (5555) (Jan. 2002): 637–638.

Paria, B. C., Reese, Jeff, Das, Sanjoy K., and Dey, S.K. "Deciphering the Cross-Talk of Implantation: Advances and Challenges." *Science* 296 (5576) (June 2002): 2185–2188.

Primakoff, Paul and Myles, Diana G. "Penetration, Adhesion, and Fusion in Mammalian Sperm-Egg Interaction." *Science* 296 (5576) (June 2002): 2183–2185.

Thisse, Christine and Zon, Leonard I. "Organogenesis—Heart and Blood Formation from the Zebrafish Point of View." *Science* 295 (5554) (Jan. 2002): 457–462.

Heredity

Objectives

The Vocabulary of Genetics

1. Define the following terms: sex chromosomes, autosomes, karyotype, alleles, heterozygous, homozygous, dominant, recessive, genotype, and phenotype.

Sexual Sources of Genetic Variation

2. Explain the processes of segregation, independent assortment, crossing over, and random fertilization.

Types of Inheritance

3. Discuss dominant-recessive inheritance, incomplete dominance, multiple-allele inheritance, sex-linked inheritance, and polygene inheritance.

4. Underscore why most genetic disorders are recessive traits.

5. Explain the difference between the X and the Y chromosomes.

Environmental Factors in Gene Expression

6. Discuss possible environmental factors influencing gene expression.

Nontraditional Inheritance

7. Explain genomic imprinting and mitochondrial inheritance.

Genetic Screening, Counseling, and Therapy

8. Indicate the significance of carrier recognition.

9. Describe two methods of fetal testing.

10. Discuss human gene therapy, how it is done, when it would be used, and the ethical concerns surrounding it.

Suggested Lecture Outline

I. The Vocabulary of Genetics (pp. 1146–1147; Fig. 29.1)

A. Introduction (p. 1146)

1. The nuclei of all human cells except gametes contain the diploid number of chromosomes (46) or 23 pairs of homologous chromosomes.

2. Two of the 46 chromosomes are the sex chromosomes, and the remaining 44 are the 22 pairs of autosomes that guide the expression of most other traits.

3. Homologous chromosomes are the two chromosomes that make up a pair in a diploid cell, one from the egg and one from the sperm.

4. The karyotype is the diploid chromosomal complement displayed in homologous pairs.

B. Chromosomes are paired, with one coming from each parent, and the genes on those chromosomes are also paired. (p. 1146)

1. Alleles are any two matched genes at the same locus (site) on homologous chromosomes.

2. Homozygous means that the two alleles are the same.

3. Heterozygous means the two alleles are different.

4. A dominant allele is one that will mask or suppress the expression of the other allele.

5. A recessive allele is the allele that is suppressed by the dominant allele and will only be expressed in the homozygous condition.

C. Genotype and Phenotype (p. 1147)

1. A person's genetic makeup is called his or her genotype.

2. The way the genotype is expressed in the body is that individual's phenotype.

II. Sexual Sources of Genetic Variation (pp. 1147–1149; Figs. 29.2–29.3)

A. During metaphase of meiosis I the alignment of the tetrads along the center of the cell is completely random, allowing for the random distribution of maternal and paternal chromosomes into the daughter cells. (pp. 1147–1148)

   a. In meiosis I the two alleles determining each trait are segregated, or distributed to different gametes.

   b. Alleles on different pairs of homologous chromosomes are distributed independently of each other.

   c. Independent assortment of homologues during meiosis I can be calculated as 2^n, where n is the number of homologous pairs.

B. During meiosis I homologous chromosomes may exchange gene segments, a process called crossing over, which gives rise to recombinant chromosomes that have contributions from each parent. (pp. 1148–1149)

C. Random fertilization occurs because a single human egg is fertilized by a single human sperm in a completely haphazard basis. (p. 1149)

III. Types of Inheritance (pp. 1149–1152; Figs. 29.4–29.5; Tables 29.1–29.2)

A. Dominant-Recessive Inheritance (pp. 1149–1150)

1. A Punnett square is used to determine the possible gene combinations resulting from the mating of parents of known genotypes.

2. Dominant traits include widow's peaks, dimples, freckles, and detached earlobes.

3. Genetic disorders caused by dominant genes are uncommon because lethal dominant genes are always expressed and result in the death of the embryo, fetus, or child.

4. Recessive traits include some desirable conditions such as normal vision, but they also include most genetic disorders.

B. Some traits exhibit incomplete dominance, where the heterozygote has a phenotype intermediate between those of the homozygous dominant and the homozygous recessive. (p. 1150)

C. Some genes exhibit more than two allele forms, such as blood type, leading to a phenomenon called multiple-allele inheritance. (p. 1151)

D. Inherited traits determined by genes on the sex chromosomes are said to be sex-linked. (p. 1152)

1. The Y chromosome is much smaller than the X chromosome and lacks many of the genes present on the X that code for nonsexual characteristics, such as red-green color blindness.

2. Genes found only on the X chromosome are said to be X-linked; those found only on the Y chromosome, such as those that code for maleness, are said to be Y-linked.

E. Polygene inheritance results in continuous or quantitative phenotypic variation between two extremes, and depends on several gene pairs at different locations acting in tandem (an example of this is skin color). (p. 1152)

IV. Environmental Factors in Gene Expression (pp. 1152–1153)

A. In many situations environmental factors override or at least influence gene expression. (p. 1152)

B. Phenocopies are environmentally produced phenotypes that mimic conditions that may be caused by genetic mutations. (p. 1152)

C. Environmental factors may also influence genetic expression after birth, such as the effect of poor infant nutrition on brain growth, body development, and height. (p. 1153)

V. Nontraditional Inheritance (pp. 1153–1154)

A. Nontraditional inheritance is the result of control mechanisms outside of the coding portion of DNA and of the chromosome entirely. (p. 1153)

B. Double-stranded RNAs, called microRNAs and short interfering RNAs, can help control transposons to disable or hyperactive genes. (p 1153)

C. Epigenetic marks, proteins, and chemical groups that bind to and around DNA determine which areas in the DNA are ready for transcription. (p. 1154)

D. Genomic imprinting somehow tags genes during gametogenesis as either paternal or maternal and confers important functional differences in the resulting embryo. (p. 1154)

E. Disorders have been traced to errors in mitochondrial genes that are transmitted to the offspring almost exclusively by the mother. (p. 1154)

VI. Genetic Screening, Counseling, and Therapy (pp. 1154–1157; Figs. 29.6–29.7)

A. When one of the parents of a developing embryo displays a recessive disorder it is important to determine if the other partner is a heterozygote and thus a carrier for that trait. (pp. 1154–1155)

1. One way to identify if an individual may be a carrier for a particular trait is to do a pedigree, which traces a genetic trait through several generations.

2. Blood tests, both simple and a more sophisticated blood chemistry test, and DNA probes can be used to detect the presence of unexpressed recessive genes.

B. Fetal testing is used when there is a known risk of a genetic disorder. (pp. 1155–1157)

1. The most common type of fetal testing is amniocentesis, where a needle is inserted into the amniotic sac to withdraw amniotic fluid for testing.

2. Chorionic villi sampling (CVS) suctions off bits of the chorionic villi from the placenta for examination.

C. Human gene therapy and genetic engineering have the potential to alleviate or even cure diseases, especially those traced to one defective gene. (p. 1157)

Cross References

Additional information on topics covered in Chapter 29 can be found in the chapters listed below.

1. Chapter 3: Mitosis; chromatin
2. Chapter 27: Meiosis; tetrad formation

Laboratory Correlations

1. Marieb, E. N. *Human Anatomy & Physiology Laboratory Manual: Cat and Fetal Pig Versions.* Eighth Edition Updates. Benjamin Cummings, 2006.
   Exercise 45: Principles of Heredity
2. Marieb, E. N. *Human Anatomy & Physiology Laboratory Manual: Main Version.* Seventh Edition Update. Benjamin Cummings, 2006.
   Exercise 45: Principles of Heredity

Lecture Hints

1. Stress that an individual receives a member of an allele from each parent.
2. Students often confuse the terms *genotype* and *phenotype*. Mention that the genotype is the entire genetic complement (geno) of an individual. It is sometimes easier for students to remember the difference between genotype and phenotype by this simple association.
3. Emphasize the importance of segregation and independent assortment.
4. Review the process of recombination and use diagrams to reinforce the concepts.
5. Remind the class of the structure and function of DNA.
6. Refer the class to a review of basic probability problem solving.

Activities/Demonstrations

1. Audio-visual materials listed under in the Multimedia Classroom and Lab.
2. Use pipe cleaners and craft balls (with holes in them) to form chromosomes. Then use those "chromosomes" to demonstrate various genotypes and other genetic patterns.
3. Use ice cream sticks with looped tape to form chromosomes and use them to demonstrate how dominant and recessive genes can be combined.

Critical Thinking/Discussion Topics

1. Describe the tests available to detect various genetic and/or development problems prior to birth.
2. Discuss the moral dilemma concerning terminating a pregnancy due to genetic disorders.
3. Explore the relationship between the age of the mother and the possibility of birth defects.

Library Research Topics

1. Research several types of birth defects by system category, i.e., skeletal system, circulatory system, etc.

2. Investigate the chromosomal aberrations that result in congenital disorders.

3. Study the multiple-allele inheritance disorders.

4. Research sex-linked traits and disorders.

5. Construct a pedigree for a genetic trait or disorder that you are aware of in your family.

Multimedia in the Classroom and Lab

Online Resources for Students

The
Anatomy & Physiology Place
www.anatomyandphysiology.com

MyA&P
www.myaandp.com

The following shows the organization of the Chapter Guide page in both the Anatomy & Physiology Place and MyA&P™. The Chapter Guide organizes all the chapter-specific online media resources for Chapter 29 in one convenient location, with e-book links to each section of the textbook. Please note that both sites also give you access to other general A&P resources, like InterActive Physiology®, PhysioEx 6.0™, Anatomy 360°, Flashcards, a Glossary, a Histology Tutorial, *and much more.*

Objectives

Section 29.1 The Vocabulary of Genetics (pp. 1146–1147)

Section 29.2 Sexual Sources of Genetic Variation (pp. 1147–1149)

Section 29.3 Types of Inheritance (pp. 1149–1153)

Case Study: Sickle Cell Anemia

Section 29.4 Environmental Factors in Gene Expression (p. 1153)

Section 29.5 Nontraditional Inheritance (pp. 1153–1154)

Section 29.6 Genetic Screening, Counseling, and Therapy (pp. 1154–1157)

Case Study: Genetics/Pregnancy and Human Development

Chapter Summary

Self-Study Quizzes

Art Labeling Quiz

Matching Quiz

Multiple-Choice Quiz (Level I)

Multiple-Choice Quiz (Level II)

True-False Quiz

Crossword Puzzles

Crossword Puzzle 29.1

Crossword Puzzle 29.2

Media

See Guide to Audio-Visual Resources in Appendix A for key to AV distributors.

Video

1. *After the Human Genome* (IM; 50 min., 2001). Although scientists have successfully read and published the three billion letters in the genetic code, there is still much speculation about its meaning. This video interviews those involved in the project to shed light on possible meanings and uses of this "book of life."

2. *Biologix Genetics Video Set* (WNS; 29 min. each). Series of six videos: *Introduction to Classical Genetics and Monohybrid Crosses; Dihybrid Crosses; Alternate Patterns of Inheritance; Chromosomal Basis of Inheritance;* and *Sex-linked Inheritance.*

3. *Breaking the Code: Applying Genetic Techniques to Human Disease* (IM; 38 min., 1997). This video explores how genetic engineering is applied to the study and treatment of inherited diseases.

4. *Cracking the Code of Life* (CBS; 120 min., 2001). NOVA follows corporate and academic scientists as they race to capture the complete, letter-by-letter sequence of the human genome.

5. *Ethical Issues and Considerations Surrounding Genetics* (IM; 53 min., 2002). This program discusses the strengths and limitations of genetic testing and counseling and considers the potential risks.

6. *Genetic Discoveries, Disorders, and Mutations* (FHS; 23 min., 1997). From the *Genetics: A Popular Guide to the Principles of Human Heredity* series. This program analyzes the contributions of Mendel and Darwin, the transmission of single- and multiple-gene disorders, and genetic mutation.

7. *Genetics and Heredity Video* (WNS; 29 min.). Basic concepts of genetics and heredity including homologous chromosomes, dominance and recessiveness, meiosis, Punnett squares, independent assortment, and more.

8. *Practical Applications and Risks of Genetic Science* (FHS; 24 min., 1997). From the *Genetics: A Popular Guide to the Principles of Human Heredity* series. This program discusses the Human Genome Project, gene-related medical research, and beneficial and potentially dangerous applications of genetic technology both to humans and to plants.

9. *Understanding the Basic Concepts of Genetics* (FHS; 28 min., 1997). From the *Genetics: A Popular Guide to the Principles of Human Heredity* series. After recapping the contributions of Schwann, Schleiden, Crick, Watson, and Wilkins, this program investigates the basic concepts of genetics.

Software

1. *Gene Pools: Changing Populations* (IM; Win/Mac). An introduction to the principles of population genetics, this CD-ROM examines how different factors influence the transmission of hereditary traits between parents and their children.

2. *Genetics* (FHS, IM; Win/Mac). This CD-ROM enables users to explore the mechanisms and consequences of new genetic technologies. It discusses cell function, teaches the nature of genes and heredity, and investigates advances in genetic engineering.

3. *Investigating Heredity* (WNS; Win/Mac). This multimedia program introduces the basic concepts of heredity and various human genetic disorders.

4. *Karyotypes and Genetic Disorders* (IM, NIMCO; Win/Mac). This CD-ROM contains an interactive simulation that allows users to explore human karyotypes and genetic disorders. It includes animated sequences of the major types of chromosomal errors.

5. *Pea Plant Genetics CD-ROM* (WNS; Windows). Conduct realistic breeding experiments that investigate five types of genetic inheritance including co- and complete dominance.

6. *Understanding Basic Genetics* (IM; Win/Mac). This CD-ROM features a comprehensive and humorous look at basic genetics, focusing on the Mendelian Model of Inheritance. It covers such fundamental concepts as dominance, fertilization, generation, genotype, phenotype, inheritance, probability, Punnett squares, segregation, and traits.

8. *WARD'S Investigating Genetics CD-ROM* (WNS; Win/Mac). Students analyze, measure, and karyotype several chromosome spreads to detect genetic defects. Contains illustrations, animation, video clips, and text with hyperlinks.

Lecture Enhancement Material

To view thumbnails of all of the illustrations for Chapter 29, see Appendix B.

Transparencies Index/Media Manager

Figure 29.1	Preparing a karyotype.
Figure 29.2	Gamete variability resulting from independent assortment.
Figure 29.3	Crossover and genetic recombination.
Figure 29.4	Genotype and phenotype probabilities resulting from a mating of two heterozygous parents.
Figure 29.5	Simplified model for polygenic inheritance of skin color based on three gene pairs.
Figure 29.6	Pedigree analysis to detect carriers of particular genes.
Figure 29.7	Fetal testing.
Table 29.1	Traits Determined by Simple Dominant-Recessive Inheritance
Table 29.2	ABO Blood Groups

Answers to End-of-Chapter Questions

Multiple Choice and Matching Question answers appear in Appendix G of the main text.

Short Answer Essay Questions

3. The mechanisms that lead to genetic variations in gametes are segregation and independent assortment of chromosomes, crossover of homologues and gene recombination, and random fertilization. Segregation implies that the members of the allele pair determining each trait are distributed to different gametes during meiosis. Independent assortment of chromosomes means that alleles for the same trait are distributed independently of each other. The net result is that each gamete has a single allele for each trait, but that allele represents only one of the four possible parent alleles. Crossover of homologues and gene recombination implies that two of the four chromatids in a tetrad take part in crossing over and recombination, but these two may make many crossovers during synapsis. Paternal chromosomes can precisely exchange gene segments with the homologous maternal ones, giving rise to recombinant chromosomes with mixed contributions from each parent. Random fertilization implies that a single human egg will be fertilized by a single sperm on a totally haphazard basis. (pp. 1147–1149)

4.

	T	t
T	TT	Tt
t	Tt	tt

a. 75% or 3/4 tasters possible —but any one or all of the three offspring could be or not be tasters. The chance that all three will be tasters is 27/64 or approximately 42%. The chance all will not be tasters is 1/64 or under 2%. The chance that two will be tasters and one will be a nontaster is 9/64 or slightly more than 14%.

	T	t
t	Tt	tt
t	Tt	tt

b. Percentage of tasters is 50%. Nontasters: 50%. Homozygous recessive: 50%. Heterozygous: 50%. Homozygous dominant: 0%. (pp. 1149–1151)

5. Both nonalbino parents carry the recessive gene for albinism, hence they are heterozygous for the trait. (p. 1151)

6. The mother's genotype is $I^A i$. The father's genotype is $I^B i$; his phenotype, B. Child number one has an ii genotype; child number two, $I^B i$. (p. 1150)

7. a. AABBCC × aabbcc

   (very dark) (very light)

   offspring genotype: AaBbCc

   offspring phenotype: medium range of color

   b. AABBCC × AaBbCc

   (very dark) (medium color)

   offspring: genotype phenotype

   AABBCC   very dark

   AaBbCc   medium to dark color

   c. AAbbcc × aabbcc

   (light) (very light)

   offspring: genotype Aabbcc

   offspring: phenotype lighter than AAbbcc parent, but not as light as aabbcc parent

   This is an example of polygenic inheritance. (p. 1152)

8. Amniocentesis is done after the 14th week. A needle is inserted through the mother's abdominal wall to remove fluid (or fetal cells) to be tested. Chorionic villi sampling can be done at 8 weeks. A tube is inserted through the vagina and cervical os. It is guided by ultrasound to an area where a piece of placenta can be removed. (pp. 1155–1156)

Critical Thinking and Clinical Application Questions

1. Maternal grandfather XcY

   Mother with normal vision XCXc

   Color-blind father XcY

	XC	Xc
Xc	XCXc	XcXc
Y	XCY	XcY

   a. One chance in two of the first child being a son. A son will either be color-blind or have normal vision. To determine the probability of two events happening in succession, we must multiply together the probabilities of the separate events happening. The probability of getting a son as the first child is 1/2. The probability of a son being color-blind is 1/2, hence the probability of the first child being a color-blind son is 1/4 (1/2 × 1/2). The combined probability will be the same for the first child being a color-blind daughter (1/4).

b. The probability that there will be one color-blind son is 1/4. The probability of two color-blind sons is 1/4 × 1/4 = 1/16, or slightly more than 6%. The production of each child is an independent event that does not influence the others. (pp. 1149–1152)

2.

(pp. 1149–1152)

3. Mrs. Lehman should be tested, since Tay-Sachs is a recessive disorder. The baby would have to get both recessive genes for the disease. If there is no incidence of the disease in her family, the recessive gene could be there but would always be masked by the dominant gene. If her husband carries one recessive gene and she carries a recessive gene, the baby would have a chance of getting two recessive alleles and having the disease. (p. 1151)

4. a. 1/4 × 1/4 × 1/4 = 1/64 = .020%

b. 3.4 × 3.4 × 3.4 = 27/64 = 0.42%

c. 1/4 or 25%

d. 3/4 or 75%

(pp. 1149–1150)

Suggested Readings

Anderson, W.F. "Gene Therapy." *Scientific American* 273 (Sept. 1995): 124–128.

Barlow, D.P. "Gametic Imprinting in Mammals." *Science* 270 (Dec. 1995): 1610–1630.

Brook, J.D. "Positional Cloning." *Scientific American: Science & Medicine* 1 (Nov./Dec. 1995): 48–57.

Cibelli, Jose B. et al. "The First Human Cloned." *Scientific American* 286 (1) (Jan. 2002): 44–51.

Cystal, R.G. "Transfer of Genes to Humans: Early Lessons and Obstacles to Success." *Science* 270 (Oct. 1995): 404–410.

Douglas, J.T., and D.T. Curiel. "In Utero Gene Therapy." *Science and Medicine* 5 (Jan./Feb. 1998): 4.

Frank, S.A., and L.D. Hurst. "Mitochondria and Male Disease." *Nature* 383 (Sep. 1996): 224.

Gardner, Thomas A. "Gene Therapy." *Science and Medicine* 8 (3) (May/June 2002): 124–125.

Hoprin, Karen. "Death to Sperm Mitochondria." *Scientific American* 280 (3) (March 1999): 21.

Marshall, E. "Gene Therapy's Growing Pains." *Science* 269 (Aug. 1995): 1050–1055.

Surani, M.A. "Immaculate Misconception." *Nature* 416 (6880) (April 2002): 491–493.

Taubes, G. "Ontogeny Recapitulated." *Discover* 19 (May 1998): 66.

Travis, J. "A Fantastical Experiment." *Science News* 151 (Apr. 1997): 214.

Wallace, D.C. "Mitochondrial DNA in Aging and Disease." *Scientific American* 277 (Aug. 1997): 40.

Wilmut, Ian. "Are There Any Normal Cloned Mammals?" *Nature Medicine* 8 (3) (March 2002): 215–216.

Guide to
Audio-Visual Resources

The following audio-visual resource distributors are referenced under Multimedia in the Classroom and Lab.

ADAM   A.D.A.M., Inc.
1600 RiverEdge Parkway, Suite 100
Atlanta, GA 30328
770-980-0888
http://www.adam.com

BC   Benjamin Cummings
1301 Sansome Street
San Francisco, CA 94111-2525
800-950-2665/415-402-2500
www.aw-bc.com

CBS   Carolina Biological Supply
Company
2700 York Road
Burlington, NC 27215
800-334-5551
www.carolina.com

CE   CyberEd, Inc.
P.O. Box 3480
Chico, CA 95927-3480
888-318-0700/530-899-1212
www.cybered.net

CM   Concept Media
P.O. Box 19542
Irvine, CA 92623-9542
800-233-7078
www.conceptmedia.com

ED   Edumatch, Inc.
d.b.a. Cambridge Development Lab
(CDL)
86 West Street
Waltham, MA 02451-1110
800-637-0047
www.edumatch.com

FHS   Films for the Humanities and
Sciences
P.O. Box 2053
Princeton, NJ 08453
800-257-5126
www.films.com

FSE   Fisher Scientific Education
3970 John's Creek Court, Suite 500
Suwanee, GA 30024
800-766-7000/770-871-4726
www.fishersci.com

HRM   HRM Video
41 Kensico Drive
Mount Kisco, NY 10549
800-431-2050
www.hrmvideo.com

IM   Insight Media
2162 Broadway
New York, NY 10024
800-233-9100/212-721-6316
www.insight-media.com

KV   Kinetic Video
255 Delaware Avenue
Buffalo, NY 14202
800-466-7631/716-856-7838
www.kineticvideo.com

LM   Landmark Media
3450 Slade Run Dr.
Falls Church, VA 22042
800-999-6645/800-889-3939
www.landmarkmedia.com

LP Laser Professor of Clear Lake, Inc.
351 Lakeside Lane, Suite 308
Houston, TX 77058
800-550-0335/281-333-5550
www.laserprofessor.com

NIMCO NIMCO, Inc.
P.O. Box 9
102 Highway 81 N
Calhoun, KY 42327-0009
800-962-6662
www.nimcoinc.com

RIL Riverdeep Interactive Learning
100 Pine Street, Suite 1900
San Francisco, CA 94111
888-242-6747
www.riverdeep.net

RSI Research Systems, Inc.
4990 Pearl East Circle
Boulder, CO 80301
303-786-9900/303-786-9909
www.rsinc.com

SIN Sinauer Associates, Inc., Publishers
23 Plumtree Road
P.O. Box 407
Sunderland, MA 01375-0407
413-549-4300/413-549-1118
www.sinauer.com

UL United Learning
1560 Sherman Avenue, Suite 100
Evanston, IL 60201
888-892-3484/847-328-6706
www.unitedlearning.com

WNS Ward's Natural Science
5100 West Henrietta Road
P.O. Box 92912
Rochester, NY 14692-9012
800-962-2660/585-334-6174
www.wardsci.com

Additional Audio-Visual Resources

Annenberg/CPB Project
The Corporation for Public Broadcasting
P.O. Box 2345
S. Burlington, VT 05407-2345
1-800-LEARNER
www.learner.org

Anatomical Chart Company
4711 Golf Road
Suite 650
Skokie, IL 60076
847-679-4700/800-621-7500
www.anatomical.com

AIMS Media
20765 Superior Street
Chatsworth, CA 91311-4409
800-367-2467
www.aimsmultimedia.com

Ambrose Video
145 West 45th Street, Suite 1115
New York, NY 10036
800-526-4663/212-768-7373
www.ambrosevideo.com

Bullfrog Films
P.O. Box 149
Oley, PA 19547
800-543-FROG (3674)
www.bullfrogfilms.com

Biodisc, Inc.
6963 Easton Court
Sarasota, FL 34238-2610
941-284-5122
www.biodisc.com

BrainViews, Ltd.
3175 Bird Drive
Ravenna, OH 44266
330-297-7043
www.brainviews.com

Connecticut Valley Biological Supply
82 Valley Road
P.O. Box 326
Southampton, MA 01073
800-628-7748/800-355-6813
www.ctvalleybio.com

Denoyer Geppert Company
P.O. Box 1727
Skokie, IL 60076-8727
800-621-1014/866-531-1221
www.denoyer.com

Educational Activities, Inc.
P.O. Box 87
Baldwin, NY 11510
800-645-3739/516-623-9282
www.edact.com

Encyclopedia Britannica Educational Corporation
Britannica Customer Support
331 North La Salle Street
Chicago, IL 60610
800-323-1229/312-294-2104
www.britannica.com

Educational Images, Ltd.
P.O. Box 3456 Westside Station
Elmira, NY 14905-0456
800-527-4264/607-732-1183
www.educationalimages.com

Eli Lilly & Company, Medical Division
Lilly Corporate Center
Indianapolis, IN 46285
317-276-2000
www.lilly.com

EME Corporation
581 Central Parkway
P.O. Box 1949
Stuart, FL 34995
800-848-2050/772-219-2206
www.emescience.com

EMT Skills
7 Summer Street, Unit #2
Chelmsford, MA 01824
888-408-5453
www.communicationskills.com

Frey Scientific
P.O. Box 8101
100 Paragon Parkway
Mansfield, OH 44903
800-225-FREY (3739)/877-256-FREY
www.freyscientific.com

Flinn Scientific, Inc.
P.O. Box 219
Batavia, IL 60510
800-452-1261/866-452-1436
www.flinnsci.com

Guidance Associates
100 South Bedford Road, Suite 120
Mt. Kisco, NY 10549
800-431-1242/914-666-5319
www.guidanceassociates.com

Gold Standard Multimedia
320 West Kennedy Blvd., Suite 400
Tampa, FL 33606
800-375-0943/813-259-1585
www.gsm.com

Hawkhill Associates, Inc.
125 East Gilman Street
Madison, WI 53703
800-422-4295/608-251-3924
www.hawkhill.com

Health Care Advances
A Division of NIMCO, Inc.
P.O. Box 9
102 Highway 81 North
Calhoun, KY 42327-0009
800-962-6662/270-273-5844
www.nimcoinc.com

HW Wilson Company
(publishes *Biological and Agricultural Index Plus, General Science Database*)
950 University Avenue
Bronx, NY 10452
800-367-6770/718-588-8400
www.hwwilson.com

Icon Learning Systems
Elsevier Customer Service
1180 Westline Industrial Drive
St. Louis, MO 63146
800-545-2522
www.netterart.com

Media Basics Video
16781 Chagrin Blvd, Box #130
Shaker Heights, OH 44120
800-542-2505/203-458-9816
www.mediabasicsvideo.com

Milner-Fenwick, Inc.
2125 Greenspring Drive
Timonium, MD 21093
800-432-8433
www.milner-fenwick.com

Nebraska Scientific
3823 Leavenworth Street
Omaha, NE 68105
800-228-7117/402-346-7214
www.nebraskascientific.com

National Geographic Film Library
1145 17th Street NW
Washington, D.C. 20036
877-730-2022/202-429-5755
www.natgeostock.com

National Geographic Society
P.O. Box 10041
Des Moines, IA 50340-0041
888 CALL NGS (888-225-5647)
www.nationalgeographic.com

Public Broadcasting Service
1320 Braddock Place
Alexandria, VA 22314
www.pbs.org

Phoenix Learning Group
2349 Chaffee Drive
St. Louis, MO 63146
800-221-1274
www.phoenixlearninggroup.com

Primal Pictures, Ltd.
2nd Floor, Tennyson House
159-163 Great Portland Street
London, W1W 5PA, U.K.
880-716-2475/020-7637-1010
www.primalpictures.com

Pyramid Media
P.O. Box 1048/WEB
Santa Monica, CA 90406
800-421-2304/310-453-9083
www.pyramidmedia.com

Queue, Inc.
One Controls Drive
Shelton, CT 06484
800-232-2224/800-775-2729
www.queueinc.com

RAmEx Ars Medica, Inc.
1714 S. Westgate Avenue, #2
Los Angeles, CA 90025-3852
800-633-9281/310-826-9674
www.ramex.com

Research Systems, Inc.
4990 Pearl East Circle
Boulder, CO 80301
303-786-9900/303-786-9909
www.rsinc.com

Scientific American
415 Madison Avenue
New York, NY 10017
800-333-1199/212-754-0550
www.sciam.com

Science Kit and Boreal Laboratories
777 East Park Drive
P.O. Box 5003
Tonawanda, NY 14150
800-828-7777/800-828-3299
www.sciencekit.com

CLEARVUE & SVE
6465 North Avondale Avenue
Chicago, IL 60631
800-253-2788/800-444-9855
www.svemedia.com

Thomson/Gale
(publishes *Video Source Book*)
27500 Drake Road
Farmington Hills, MI 48331
800-877-4253/248-699-4253
www.galegroup.com

Teacher's Media Company
P.O. Box 9120
Plainview, NY 11803-9020
800-431-1934/800-434-5638
www.teachersvideo.com

Videodiscovery, Inc.
920 N. 34th
Seattle, WA 98103
800-548-3472/206-285-5400
www.videodiscovery.com

Visible Productions
213 Linden Street, Suite 200
Fort Collins, CO 80524
800-685-4668/970-407-7248
http://visiblep.com

VWR International
1310 Goshen Parkway
West Chester, PA 19380
800-932-5000
www.vwr.com

Visual Resource Guide

This Visual Resource Guide presents a chapter-by-chapter guide to the art, photos, and tables available in the Image Library of the Media Manager for *Human Anatomy & Physiology*, Seventh Edition. Histology, bone, and soft tissue images from *A Brief Atlas of the Human Body* are also included on the Media Manager and are displayed at the end of this guide.

In addition to the thumbnails listed here, the Media Manager provides a number of other valuable resources for instructors. The Image Library includes every figure in unlabeled and leaders-only formats. The Multimedia Library contains animations that can be incorporated into presentations. The PowerPoint® Library includes customizable Label Edit Art and Step Edit Art. Download the Label Edit Art slides to edit, highlight, resize, create, and delete labels and leaders from any figure in the textbook. Complement your lectures with Step Edit Art, our new multi-slide PowerPoint presentations of selected complex figures that break the processes down into clearer, more manageable steps.

Chapter 1:
The Human Body: An Orientation

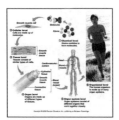

01-01Levels_L.jpg

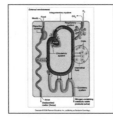

01-02Interrelation_L.jpg

01-03a-cOrganSys_L.jpg

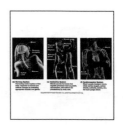

01-03d-fOrganSys_L.jpg

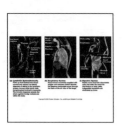

01-03g-iOrganSys_L.jpg

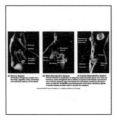

01-03j-lOrganSys_L.jpg

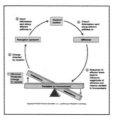

01-04EleHomeo_L.jpg

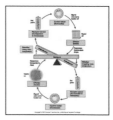

01-05_RoomNeg_0_L.jpg

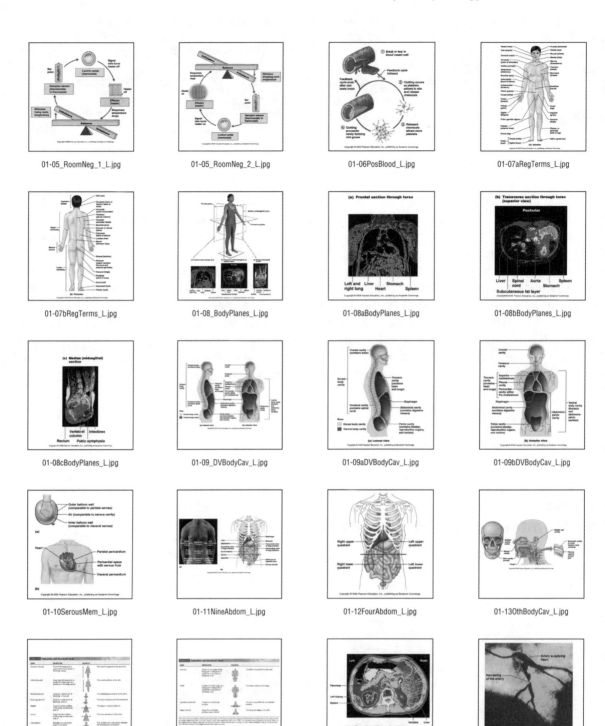

01-05_RoomNeg_1_L.jpg

01-05_RoomNeg_2_L.jpg

01-06PosBlood_L.jpg

01-07aRegTerms_L.jpg

01-07bRegTerms_L.jpg

01-08_BodyPlanes_L.jpg

01-08aBodyPlanes_L.jpg

01-08bBodyPlanes_L.jpg

01-08cBodyPlanes_L.jpg

01-09_DVBodyCav_L.jpg

01-09aDVBodyCav_L.jpg

01-09bDVBodyCav_L.jpg

01-10SerousMem_L.jpg

01-11NineAbdom_L.jpg

01-12FourAbdom_L.jpg

01-13OthBodyCav_L.jpg

01-T01aOrienDir_1_TAB.jpg

01-T01bOrienDir_2_TAB.jpg

01-UN01CTSupAbd_L.jpg

01-UN02DSAArteries_L.jpg

Chapter 2:
Chemistry Comes Alive

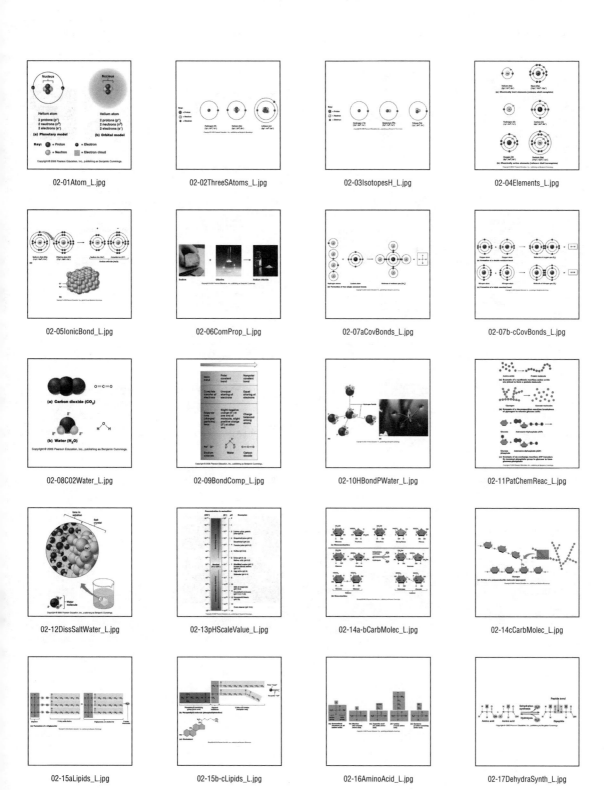

02-01Atom_L.jpg

02-02ThreeSAtoms_L.jpg

02-03IsotopesH_L.jpg

02-04Elements_L.jpg

02-05IonicBond_L.jpg

02-06ComProp_L.jpg

02-07aCovBonds_L.jpg

02-07b-cCovBonds_L.jpg

02-08CO2Water_L.jpg

02-09BondComp_L.jpg

02-10HBondPWater_L.jpg

02-11PatChemReac_L.jpg

02-12DissSaltWater_L.jpg

02-13pHScaleValue_L.jpg

02-14a-bCarbMolec_L.jpg

02-14cCarbMolec_L.jpg

02-15aLipids_L.jpg

02-15b-cLipids_L.jpg

02-16AminoAcid_L.jpg

02-17DehydraSynth_L.jpg

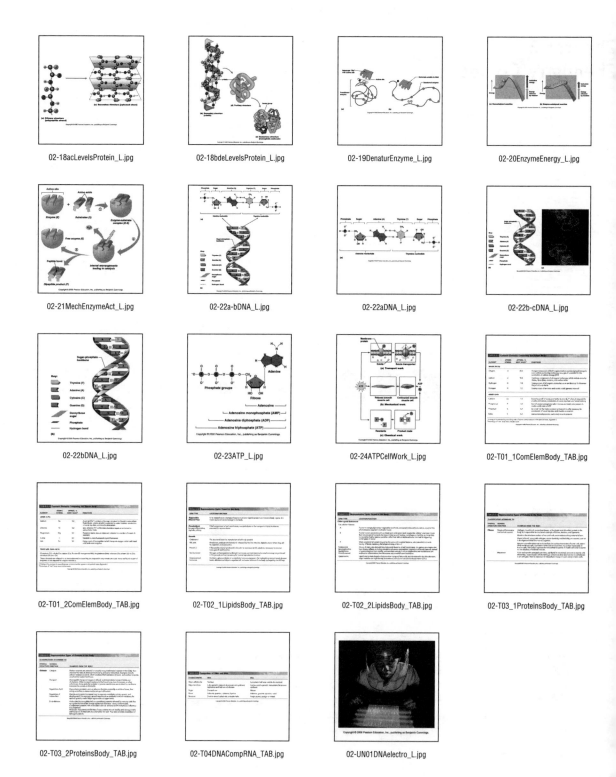

02-18acLevelsProtein_L.jpg

02-18bdeLevelsProtein_L.jpg

02-19DenaturEnzyme_L.jpg

02-20EnzymeEnergy_L.jpg

02-21MechEnzymeAct_L.jpg

02-22a-bDNA_L.jpg

02-22aDNA_L.jpg

02-22b-cDNA_L.jpg

02-22bDNA_L.jpg

02-23ATP_L.jpg

02-24ATPCellWork_L.jpg

02-T01_1ComElemBody_TAB.jpg

02-T01_2ComElemBody_TAB.jpg

02-T02_1LipidsBody_TAB.jpg

02-T02_2LipidsBody_TAB.jpg

02-T03_1ProteinsBody_TAB.jpg

02-T03_2ProteinsBody_TAB.jpg

02-T04DNACompRNA_TAB.jpg

02-UN01DNAelectro_L.jpg

Chapter 3:
Cells: The Living Units

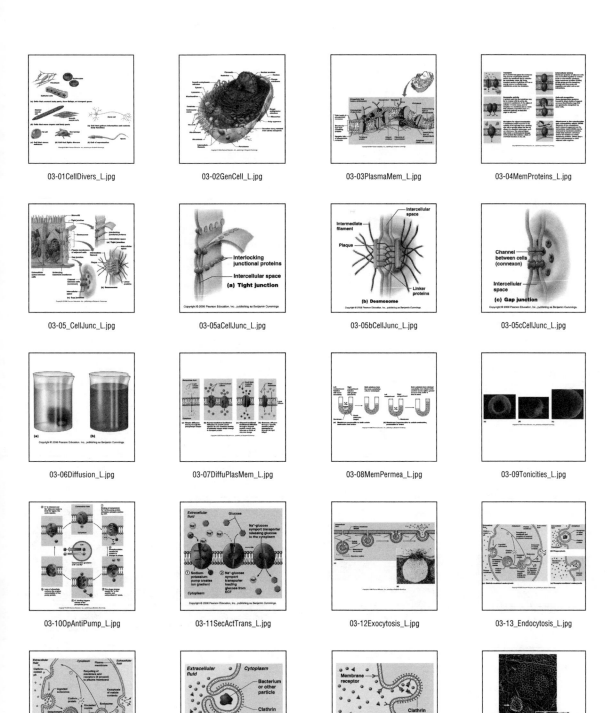

03-01CellDivers_L.jpg

03-02GenCell_L.jpg

03-03PlasmaMem_L.jpg

03-04MemProteins_L.jpg

03-05_CellJunc_L.jpg

03-05aCellJunc_L.jpg

03-05bCellJunc_L.jpg

03-05cCellJunc_L.jpg

03-06Diffusion_L.jpg

03-07DiffuPlasMem_L.jpg

03-08MemPermea_L.jpg

03-09Tonicities_L.jpg

03-10OpAntiPump_L.jpg

03-11SecActTrans_L.jpg

03-12Exocytosis_L.jpg

03-13_Endocytosis_L.jpg

03-13aEndocytosis_L.jpg

03-13bEndocytosis_L.jpg

03-13cEndocytosis_L.jpg

03-14Vesicles_L.jpg

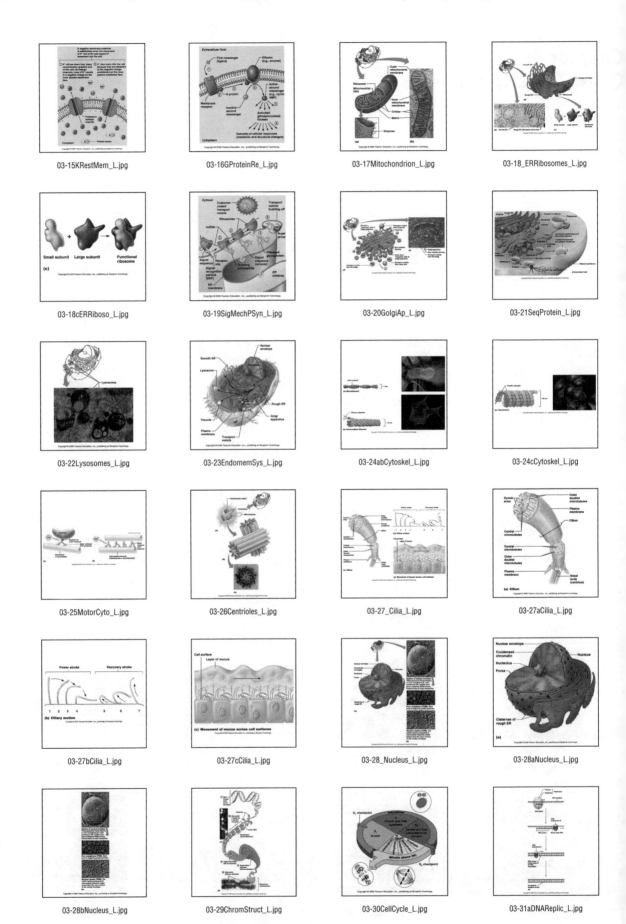

03-15KRestMem_L.jpg

03-16GProteinRe_L.jpg

03-17Mitochondrion_L.jpg

03-18_ERRibosomes_L.jpg

03-18cERRiboso_L.jpg

03-19SigMechPSyn_L.jpg

03-20GolgiAp_L.jpg

03-21SeqProtein_L.jpg

03-22Lysosomes_L.jpg

03-23EndomemSys_L.jpg

03-24abCytoskel_L.jpg

03-24cCytoskel_L.jpg

03-25MotorCyto_L.jpg

03-26Centrioles_L.jpg

03-27_Cilia_L.jpg

03-27aCilia_L.jpg

03-27bCilia_L.jpg

03-27cCilia_L.jpg

03-28_Nucleus_L.jpg

03-28aNucleus_L.jpg

03-28bNucleus_L.jpg

03-29ChromStruct_L.jpg

03-30CellCycle_L.jpg

03-31aDNAReplic_L.jpg

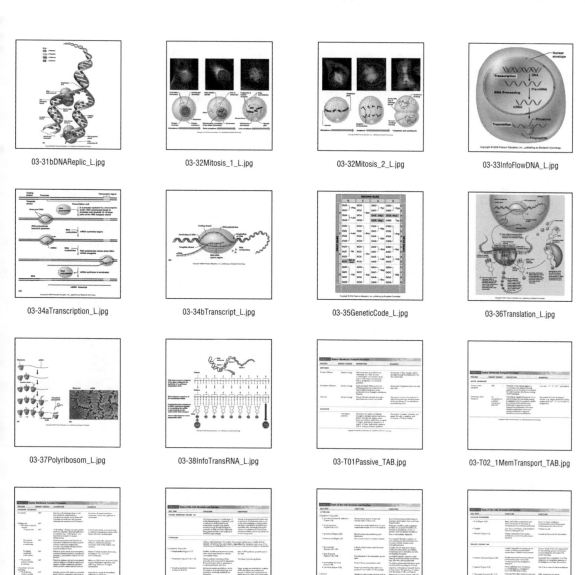

03-31bDNAReplic_L.jpg

03-32Mitosis_1_L.jpg

03-32Mitosis_2_L.jpg

03-33InfoFlowDNA_L.jpg

03-34aTranscription_L.jpg

03-34bTranscript_L.jpg

03-35GeneticCode_L.jpg

03-36Translation_L.jpg

03-37Polyribosom_L.jpg

03-38InfoTransRNA_L.jpg

03-T01Passive_TAB.jpg

03-T02_1MemTransport_TAB.jpg

03-T02_2MemTransport_TAB.jpg

03-T03_1CellParts_TAB.jpg

03-T03_2CellParts_TAB.jpg

03-T03_3CellParts_TAB.jpg

Chapter 4:
Tissue: The Living Fabric

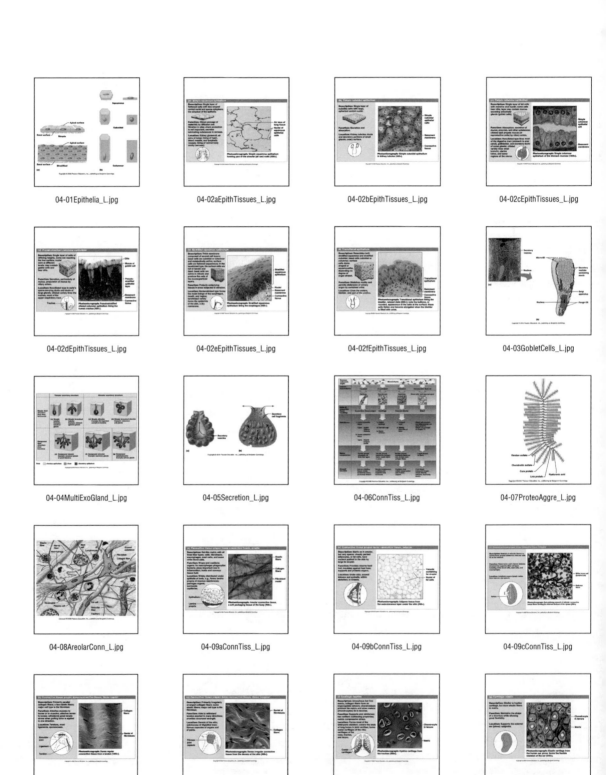

04-01Epithelia_L.jpg

04-02aEpithTissues_L.jpg

04-02bEpithTissues_L.jpg

04-02cEpithTissues_L.jpg

04-02dEpithTissues_L.jpg

04-02eEpithTissues_L.jpg

04-02fEpithTissues_L.jpg

04-03GobletCells_L.jpg

04-04MultiExoGland_L.jpg

04-05Secretion_L.jpg

04-06ConnTiss_L.jpg

04-07ProteoAggre_L.jpg

04-08AreolarConn_L.jpg

04-09aConnTiss_L.jpg

04-09bConnTiss_L.jpg

04-09cConnTiss_L.jpg

04-09dConnTiss_L.jpg

04-09eConnTiss_L.jpg

04-09fConnTiss_L.jpg

04-09gConnTiss_L.jpg

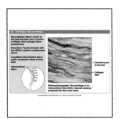

04-09hConnTiss_L.jpg

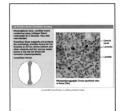

04-09iConnTiss_L.jpg

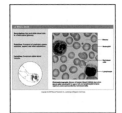

04-09jConTiss_L.jpg

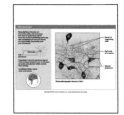

04-10NervTiss_L.jpg

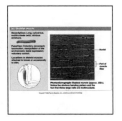

04-11aMuscTiss_L.jpg

04-11bMuscTiss_L.jpg

04-11cMuscTiss_L.jpg

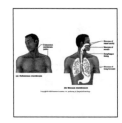

04-12a-bMembranes_L.jpg

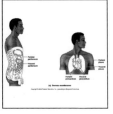

04-12cMembranes_L.jpg

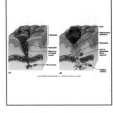

04-13a-bRegenFibro_L.jpg

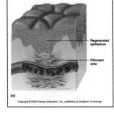

04-13cRegenFibro_L.jpg

04-14EmbryGerm_L.jpg

04-UN01ColonCancer_L.jpg

Chapter 5:
The Integumentary System

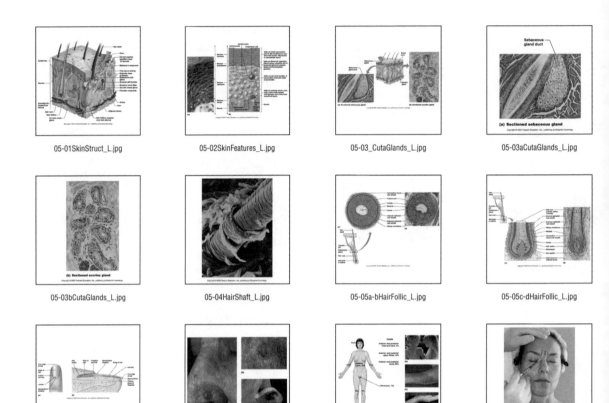

05-01SkinStruct_L.jpg

05-02SkinFeatures_L.jpg

05-03_CutaGlands_L.jpg

05-03aCutaGlands_L.jpg

05-03bCutaGlands_L.jpg

05-04HairShaft_L.jpg

05-05a-bHairFollic_L.jpg

05-05c-dHairFollic_L.jpg

05-06NailStruct_L.jpg

05-07SkinCancer_L.jpg

05-08Burns_L.jpg

05-UN01Botox_L.jpg

Chapter 6:
Bones and Skeletal Tissues

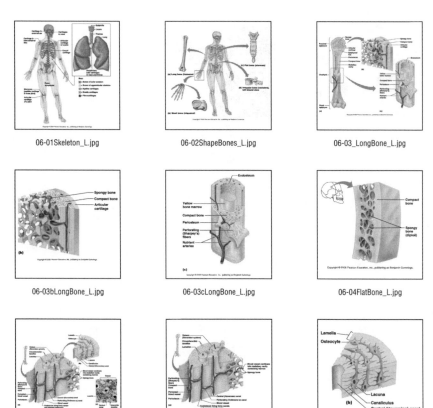

06-01Skeleton_L.jpg

06-02ShapeBones_L.jpg

06-03_LongBone_L.jpg

06-03aLongBone_L.jpg

06-03bLongBone_L.jpg

06-03cLongBone_L.jpg

06-04FlatBone_L.jpg

06-05Osteon_L.jpg

06-06_CompactBone_L.jpg

06-06aCompactBone_L.jpg

06-06bCompactBone_L.jpg

06-06cCompactBone_L.jpg

06-07IntraOssif_1_L.jpg

06-07IntraOssif_2_L.jpg

06-08EndoOssif_L.jpg

06-09GrowthLBone_L.jpg

06-10YouthLBone_L.jpg

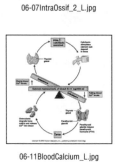

06-11BloodCalcium_L.jpg

06-12BoneAnatomy_L.jpg

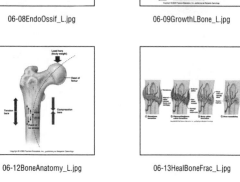

06-13HealBoneFrac_L.jpg

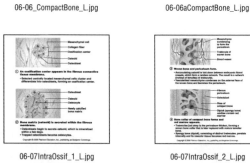
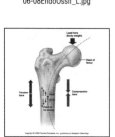

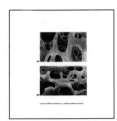

06-14ContrastBone_L.jpg

06-15FetusOssif_L.jpg

06-T01aBoneMark_TAB.jpg

06-T01bBoneMark_TAB.jpg

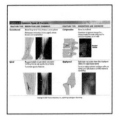

06-T02aFractures_1_TAB.jpg

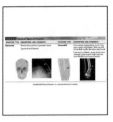

06-T02bFractures_2_TAB.jpg

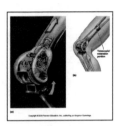

06-UN01Endoprosth_L.jpg

Chapter 7:
The Skeleton

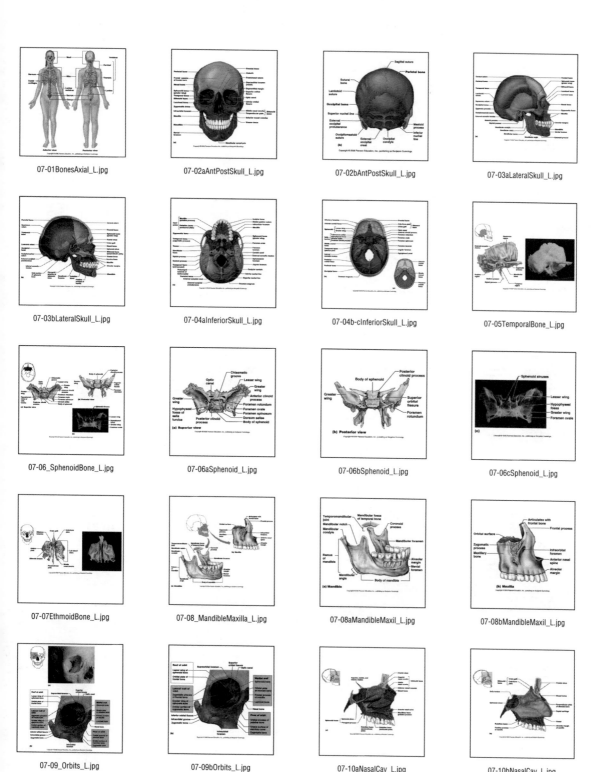

07-01BonesAxial_L.jpg

07-02aAntPostSkull_L.jpg

07-02bAntPostSkull_L.jpg

07-03aLateralSkull_L.jpg

07-03bLateralSkull_L.jpg

07-04aInferiorSkull_L.jpg

07-04b-cInferiorSkull_L.jpg

07-05TemporalBone_L.jpg

07-06_SphenoidBone_L.jpg

07-06aSphenoid_L.jpg

07-06bSphenoid_L.jpg

07-06cSphenoid_L.jpg

07-07EthmoidBone_L.jpg

07-08_MandibleMaxilla_L.jpg

07-08aMandibleMaxil_L.jpg

07-08bMandibleMaxil_L.jpg

07-09_Orbits_L.jpg

07-09bOrbits_L.jpg

07-10aNasalCav_L.jpg

07-10bNasalCav_L.jpg

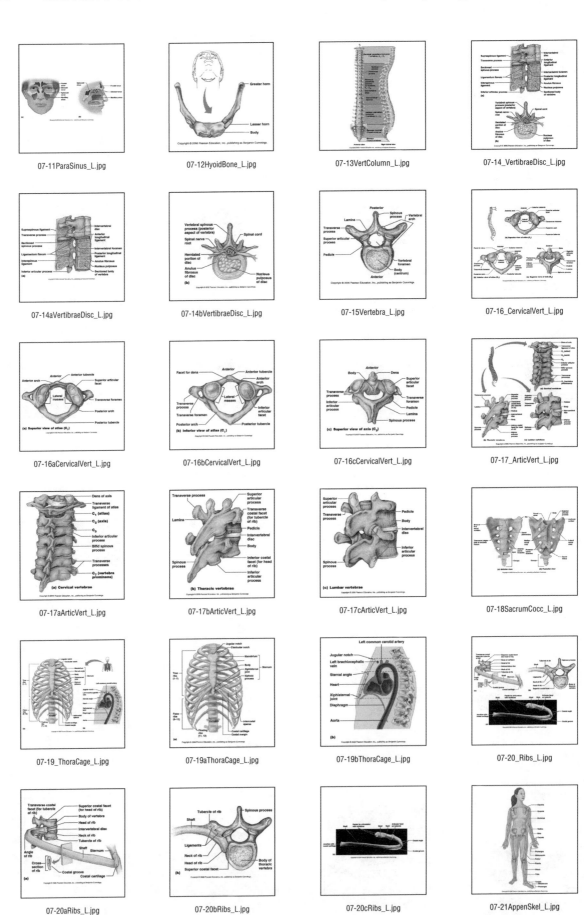

07-11ParaSinus_L.jpg

07-12HyoidBone_L.jpg

07-13VertColumn_L.jpg

07-14_VertibraeDisc_L.jpg

07-14aVertibraeDisc_L.jpg

07-14bVertibraeDisc_L.jpg

07-15Vertebra_L.jpg

07-16_CervicalVert_L.jpg

07-16aCervicalVert_L.jpg

07-16bCervicalVert_L.jpg

07-16cCervicalVert_L.jpg

07-17_ArticVert_L.jpg

07-17aArticVert_L.jpg

07-17bArticVert_L.jpg

07-17cArticVert_L.jpg

07-18SacrumCocc_L.jpg

07-19_ThoraCage_L.jpg

07-19aThoraCage_L.jpg

07-19bThoraCage_L.jpg

07-20_Ribs_L.jpg

07-20aRibs_L.jpg

07-20bRibs_L.jpg

07-20cRibs_L.jpg

07-21AppenSkel_L.jpg

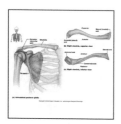

07-22a-cPecGirdle_L.jpg

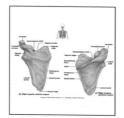

07-22d-ePecGirdle_L.jpg

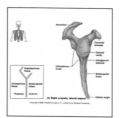

07-22fPecGirdle_L.jpg

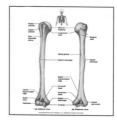

07-23Humerus_L.jpg

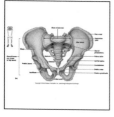

07-24RadiusUlna_L.jpg

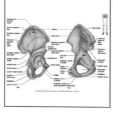

07-25aPecGirdUpper_L.jpg

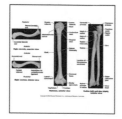

07-25bPecGirdUpper_L.jpg

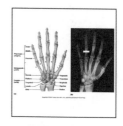

07-26HandBones_L.jpg

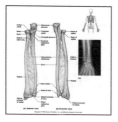

07-27aPelvisBones_L.jpg

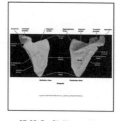

07-27b-cPelvisBones_L.jpg

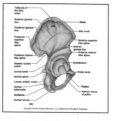

07-27bPelvisBones_L.jpg

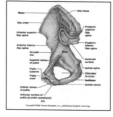

07-27cPelvisBones_L.jpg

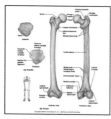

07-28ThighKneeBones_L.jpg

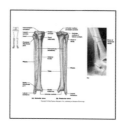

07-29TibulaFibula_L.jpg

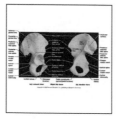

07-30aPelvicGird_L.jpg

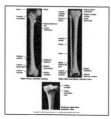

07-30bPelvicGird_L.jpg

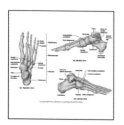

07-31_FootBones_L.jpg

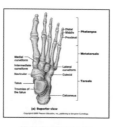

07-31aFootBones_L.jpg

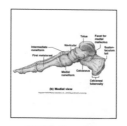

07-31bFootBones_L.jpg

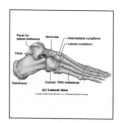

07-31cFootBones_L.jpg

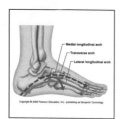

07-32FootArches_L.jpg

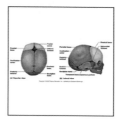

07-33FetalSkull_L.jpg

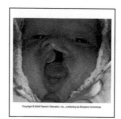

07-34CleftLipBaby_L.jpg

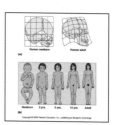

07-35DiffGrowRate_L.jpg

07-T01aSkullBones_1_TAB.jpg

07-T01bSkullBones_2_TAB.jpg

07-T01cSkullBones_3_TAB.jpg

07-T02aCTLVert_1_TAB.jpg

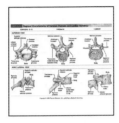

07-T02bCTLVert_2_TAB.jpg

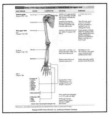

07-T03PecGirdUpLimb_TAB.jpg

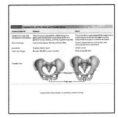

07-T04aComparePelv_1_TAB.jpg

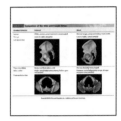

07-T04bComparePelv_2_TAB.jpg

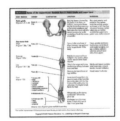

07-T05AppenBones_TAB.jpg

Chapter 8:
Joints

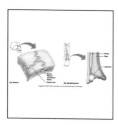

08-01FibrJoints_L.jpg

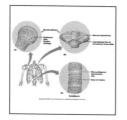

08-02CartJoints_L.jpg

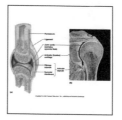

08-03SynovJoint_L.jpg

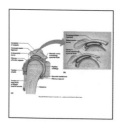

08-04BurTenSheath_L.jpg

08-05a-bMovement_L.jpg

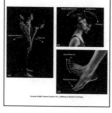

08-05c-eMovement_L.jpg

08-05f-gMovement_L.jpg

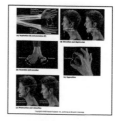

08-06SpecialMoves_L.jpg

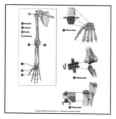

08-07a-cTypeSynoJnts_L.jpg

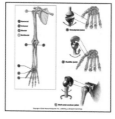

08-07d-fTypeSynoJnts_L.jpg

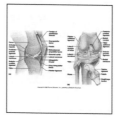

08-08_a-bKneeJoint_L.jpg

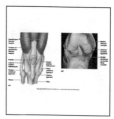

08-08_c-dKneeJoint_L.jpg

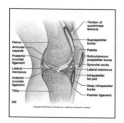

08-08aKneeJoint_L.jpg

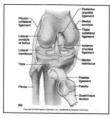

08-08bKneeJoint_L.jpg

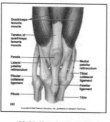

08-08cKneeJoint_L.jpg

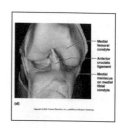

08-08dKneeJoint_L.jpg

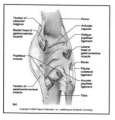

08-08eKneeJoint_L.jpg

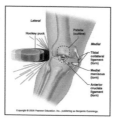

08-09ComKneeInjury_L.jpg

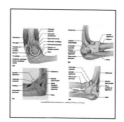

08-10_ElbowJoint_L.jpg

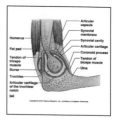

08-10aElbowJoint_L.jpg

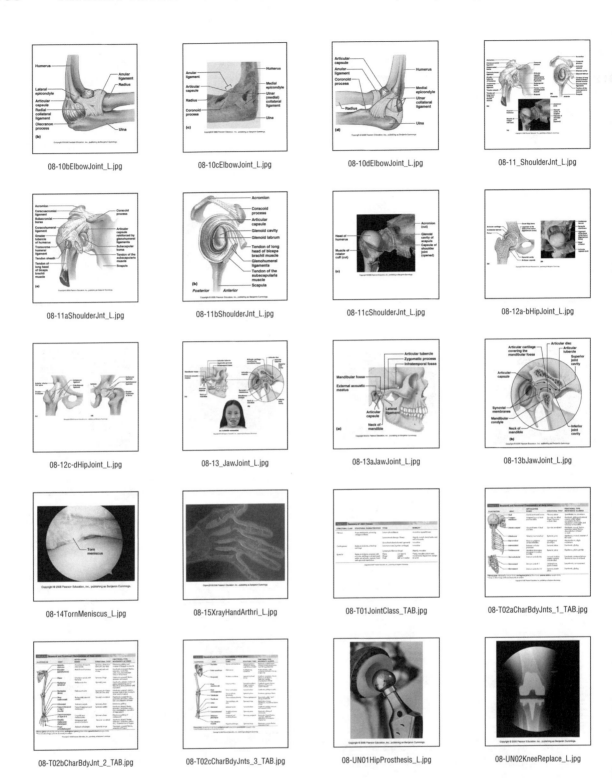

08-10bElbowJoint_L.jpg

08-10cElbowJoint_L.jpg

08-10dElbowJoint_L.jpg

08-11_ShoulderJnt_L.jpg

08-11aShoulderJnt_L.jpg

08-11bShoulderJnt_L.jpg

08-11cShoulderJnt_L.jpg

08-12a-bHipJoint_L.jpg

08-12c-dHipJoint_L.jpg

08-13_JawJoint_L.jpg

08-13aJawJoint_L.jpg

08-13bJawJoint_L.jpg

08-14TornMeniscus_L.jpg

08-15XrayHandArthri_L.jpg

08-T01JointClass_TAB.jpg

08-T02aCharBdyJnts_1_TAB.jpg

08-T02bCharBdyJnt_2_TAB.jpg

08-T02cCharBdyJnts_3_TAB.jpg

08-UN01HipProsthesis_L.jpg

08-UN02KneeReplace_L.jpg

Chapter 9:
Muscles and Muscle Tissue

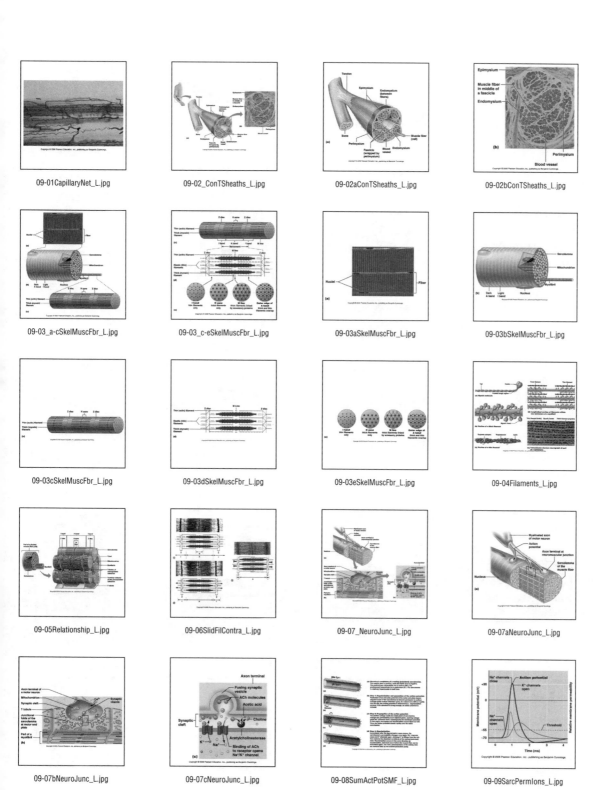

09-01CapillaryNet_L.jpg

09-02_ConTSheaths_L.jpg

09-02aConTSheaths_L.jpg

09-02bConTSheaths_L.jpg

09-03_a-cSkelMuscFbr_L.jpg

09-03_c-eSkelMuscFbr_L.jpg

09-03aSkelMuscFbr_L.jpg

09-03bSkelMuscFbr_L.jpg

09-03cSkelMuscFbr_L.jpg

09-03dSkelMuscFbr_L.jpg

09-03eSkelMuscFbr_L.jpg

09-04Filaments_L.jpg

09-05Relationship_L.jpg

09-06SlidFilContra_L.jpg

09-07_NeuroJunc_L.jpg

09-07aNeuroJunc_L.jpg

09-07bNeuroJunc_L.jpg

09-07cNeuroJunc_L.jpg

09-08SumActPotSMF_L.jpg

09-09SarcPermIons_L.jpg

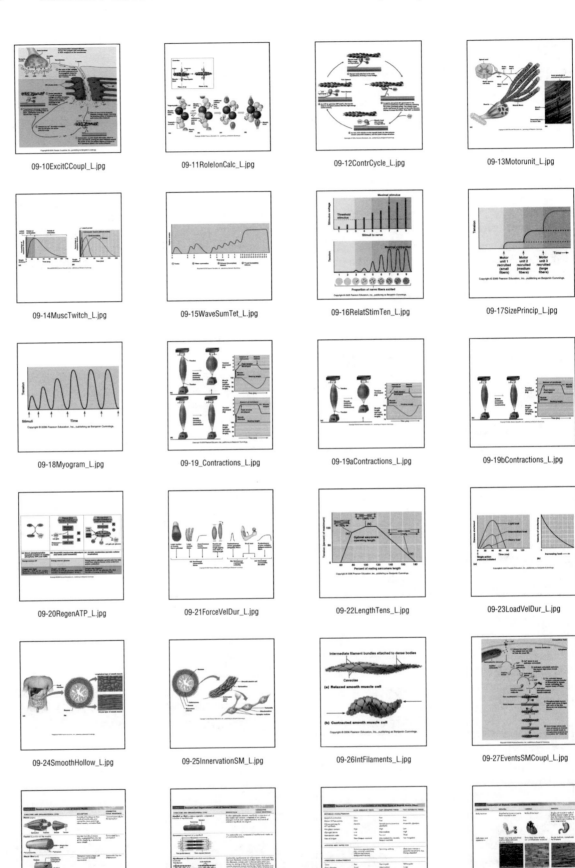

09-10ExcitCCoupl_L.jpg

09-11RoleIonCalc_L.jpg

09-12ContrCycle_L.jpg

09-13Motorunit_L.jpg

09-14MuscTwitch_L.jpg

09-15WaveSumTet_L.jpg

09-16RelatStimTen_L.jpg

09-17SizePrincip_L.jpg

09-18Myogram_L.jpg

09-19_Contractions_L.jpg

09-19aContractions_L.jpg

09-19bContractions_L.jpg

09-20RegenATP_L.jpg

09-21ForceVelDur_L.jpg

09-22LengthTens_L.jpg

09-23LoadVelDur_L.jpg

09-24SmoothHollow_L.jpg

09-25InnervationSM_L.jpg

09-26IntFilaments_L.jpg

09-27EventsSMCoupl_L.jpg

09-T01aLevelsSkel_TAB.jpg

09-T01bLevelsSkel_TAB.jpg

09-T02ThreeSkelMus_TAB.jpg

09-T03aMuscleComp_1_TAB.jpg

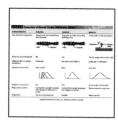

09-T03bMuscleComp_2_TAB.jpg

09-T03cMuscleComp_3_TAB.jpg

09-T03dMuscleComp_4_TAB.jpg

Chapter 10:
The Muscular System

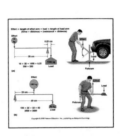

10-01FascArrang_L.jpg

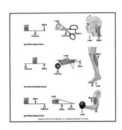

10-02LeverSysMech_L.jpg

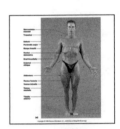

10-03LeverSys_L.jpg

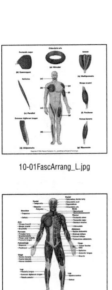

10-04aAntSupMuscl_L.jpg

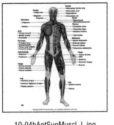

10-04bAntSupMuscl_L.jpg

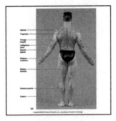

10-05aPosSupMuscl_L.jpg

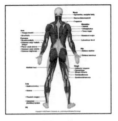

10-05bPosSupMuscl_L.jpg

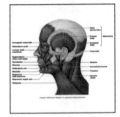

10-06LateralMuscles_L.jpg

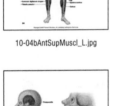

10-07_MasticaTongue_L.jpg

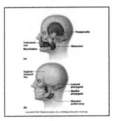

10-07a-bMastica_L.jpg

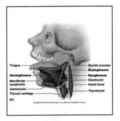

10-07cMastica_L.jpg

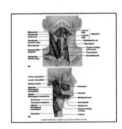

10-08_SwallowMuscle_L.jpg

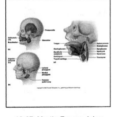

10-08aSwallowMuscle_L.jpg

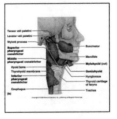

10-08bSwallowMuscle_L.jpg

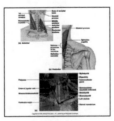

10-09_NeckHead_1_L.jpg

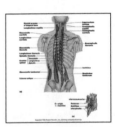

10-09_NeckHead_2_L.jpg

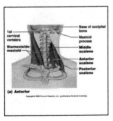

10-09aNeckHead_L.jpg

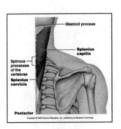

10-09bNeckHead_L.jpg

10-09cNeckHead_L.jpg

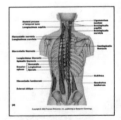

10-09dNeckHead_L.jpg

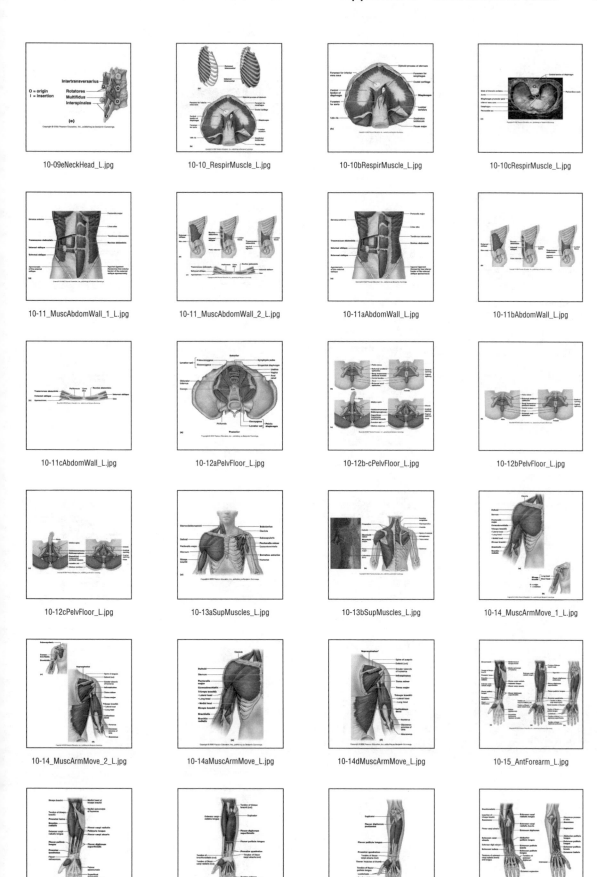

10-09eNeckHead_L.jpg

10-10_RespirMuscle_L.jpg

10-10bRespirMuscle_L.jpg

10-10cRespirMuscle_L.jpg

10-11_MuscAbdomWall_1_L.jpg

10-11_MuscAbdomWall_2_L.jpg

10-11aAbdomWall_L.jpg

10-11bAbdomWall_L.jpg

10-11cAbdomWall_L.jpg

10-12aPelvFloor_L.jpg

10-12b-cPelvFloor_L.jpg

10-12bPelvFloor_L.jpg

10-12cPelvFloor_L.jpg

10-13aSupMuscles_L.jpg

10-13bSupMuscles_L.jpg

10-14_MuscArmMove_1_L.jpg

10-14_MuscArmMove_2_L.jpg

10-14aMuscArmMove_L.jpg

10-14dMuscArmMove_L.jpg

10-15_AntForearm_L.jpg

10-15aAntForearm_L.jpg

10-15bAntForearm_L.jpg

10-15cAntForearm_L.jpg

10-16_PosForearm_1_L.jpg

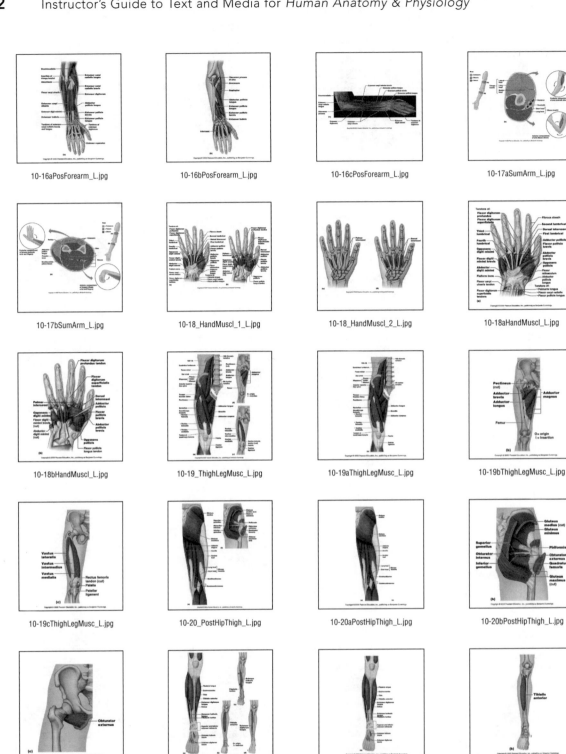

10-16aPosForearm_L.jpg

10-16bPosForearm_L.jpg

10-16cPosForearm_L.jpg

10-17aSumArm_L.jpg

10-17bSumArm_L.jpg

10-18_HandMuscl_1_L.jpg

10-18_HandMuscl_2_L.jpg

10-18aHandMuscl_L.jpg

10-18bHandMuscl_L.jpg

10-19_ThighLegMusc_L.jpg

10-19aThighLegMusc_L.jpg

10-19bThighLegMusc_L.jpg

10-19cThighLegMusc_L.jpg

10-20_PostHipThigh_L.jpg

10-20aPostHipThigh_L.jpg

10-20bPostHipThigh_L.jpg

10-20cPostHipThigh_L.jpg

10-21_MuscAntLeg_L.jpg

10-21aMuscAntLeg_L.jpg

10-21bMuscAntLeg_L.jpg

10-21cMuscAntLeg_L.jpg

10-21dMuscAntLeg_L.jpg

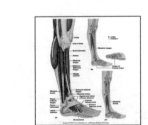

10-22_MuscLatLeg_L.jpg

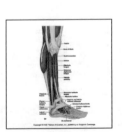

10-22aMuscLatLeg_L.jpg

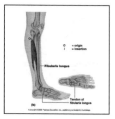

10-22bMuscLatLeg_L.jpg

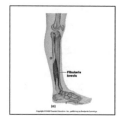

10-22cMuscLatLeg_L.jpg

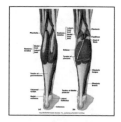

10-23a-bPostLeg_L.jpg

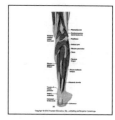

10-23cPostLeg_L.jpg

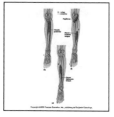

10-23d-fPostLeg_L.jpg

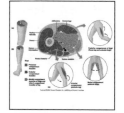

10-24aSumThighLeg_L.jpg

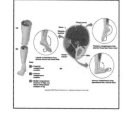

10-24bSumThighLeg_L.jpg

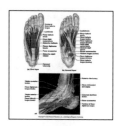

10-25_FootPlant_1_L.jpg

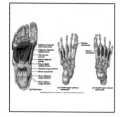

10-25_FootPlant_2_L.jpg

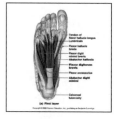

10-25aFootPlant_L.jpg

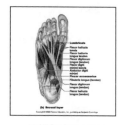

10-25bFootPlant_L.jpg

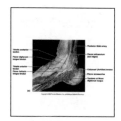

10-25cFootPlant_L.jpg

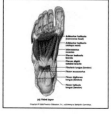

10-25dFootPlant_L.jpg

10-T01aFacialExpr_TAB.jpg

10-T01bFacialExpr_TAB.jpg

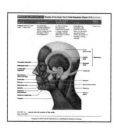

10-T01cFacialExpr_TAB.jpg

10-T02aMasTongue_TAB.jpg

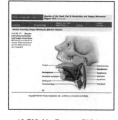

10-T02bMasTongue_TAB.jpg

10-T02cMasTongue_TAB.jpg

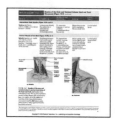

10-T03aSwallowing_TAB.jpg

10-T03bSwallowing_TAB.jpg

10-T03cSwallowing_TAB.jpg

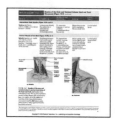

10-T04aHeadTrunk_TAB.jpg

10-T04bHeadTrunk_TAB.jpg

10-T04cHeadTrunk_TAB.jpg

10-T04dHeadTrunk_TAB.jpg

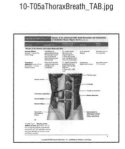

10-T04eHeadTrunk_TAB.jpg

10-T05aThoraxBreath_TAB.jpg

10-T05bThoraxBreath_TAB.jpg

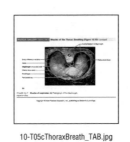

10-T05cThoraxBreath_TAB.jpg

10-T06aAbdomWall_TAB.jpg

10-T06bAbdomWall_TAB.jpg

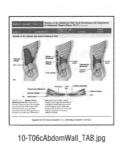

10-T06cAbdomWall_TAB.jpg

10-T07aPelvFlPeri_TAB.jpg

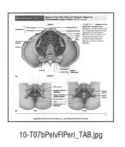

10-T07bPelvFlPeri_TAB.jpg

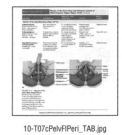

10-T07cPelvFlPeri_TAB.jpg

10-T08aScapula_TAB.jpg

10-T08bScapula_TAB.jpg

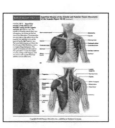

10-T08cScapula_TAB.jpg

10-T09aArmMove_TAB.jpg

10-T09bArmMove_TAB.jpg

10-T09cArmMove_TAB.jpg

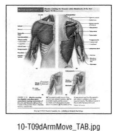

10-T09dArmMove_TAB.jpg

10-T10aFlexForearm_TAB.jpg

10-T10bFlexForearm_TAB.jpg

10-T11aWristFingrs_TAB.jpg

10-T11bWristFingrs_TAB.jpg

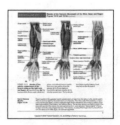

10-T11cWristFingrs_TAB.jpg

10-T11dWristFingrs_TAB.jpg

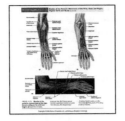

10-T11eWristFingrs_TAB.jpg

10-T12aSumArmHand_TAB.jpg

10-T12bSumArmHand_TAB.jpg

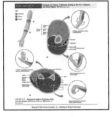

10-T12cSumArmHand_TAB.jpg

10-T13aFineFingrs_TAB.jpg

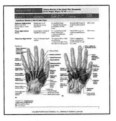

10-T13bFineFingrs_TAB.jpg

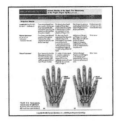

10-T13cFineFingrs_TAB.jpg

10-T14aThighLeg_TAB.jpg

10-T14bThighLeg_TAB.jpg

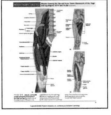

10-T14cThighLeg_TAB.jpg

10-T14dThighLeg_TAB.jpg

10-T14eThighLeg_TAB.jpg

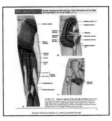

10-T14fThighLeg_TAB.jpg

10-T14gThighLeg_TAB.jpg

10-T14hThighLeg_TAB.jpg

10-T15aAnkleToes_TAB.jpg

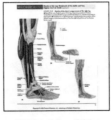

10-T15bAnkleToes_TAB.jpg

10-T15cAnkleToes_TAB.jpg

10-T15dAnkleToes_TAB.jpg

10-T15eAnkleToes_TAB.jpg

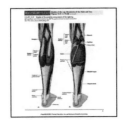

10-T15fAnkleToes_TAB.jpg

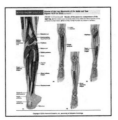

10-T15gAnkleToes_TAB.jpg

10-T16aSumThighFoot_TAB.jpg

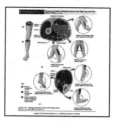

10-T16bSumThighFoot_TAB.jpg

10-T16cSumThighFoot_TAB.jpg

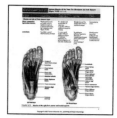

10-T17aToeMoveArch_TAB.jpg

10-T17bToeMoveArch_TAB.jpg

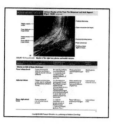

10-T17cToeMoveArch_TAB.jpg

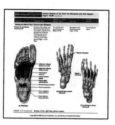

10-T17dToeMoveArch_TAB.jpg

Chapter 11:
Fundamentals of the Nervous System and Nervous Tissue

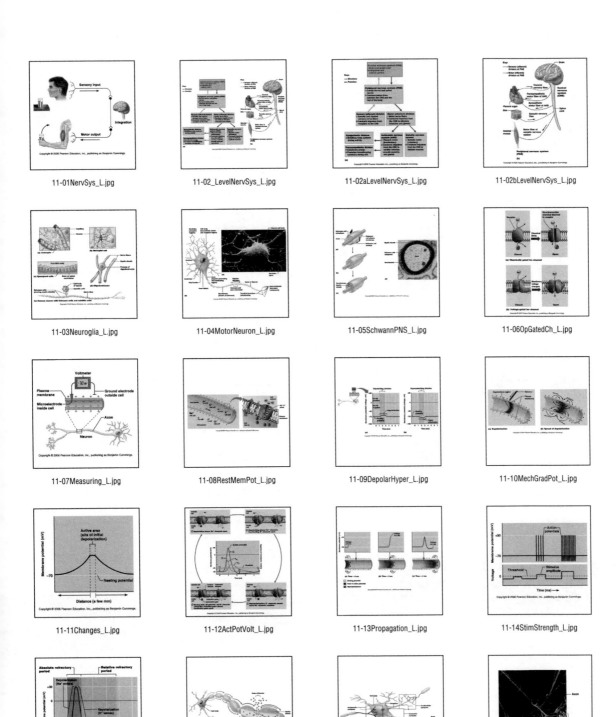

11-01NervSys_L.jpg

11-02_LevelNervSys_L.jpg

11-02aLevelNervSys_L.jpg

11-02bLevelNervSys_L.jpg

11-03Neuroglia_L.jpg

11-04MotorNeuron_L.jpg

11-05SchwannPNS_L.jpg

11-06OpGatedCh_L.jpg

11-07Measuring_L.jpg

11-08RestMemPot_L.jpg

11-09DepolarHyper_L.jpg

11-10MechGradPot_L.jpg

11-11Changes_L.jpg

11-12ActPotVolt_L.jpg

11-13Propagation_L.jpg

11-14StimStrength_L.jpg

11-15Recording_L.jpg

11-16Saltatory_L.jpg

11-17aSynapses_L.jpg

11-17bSynapses_L.jpg

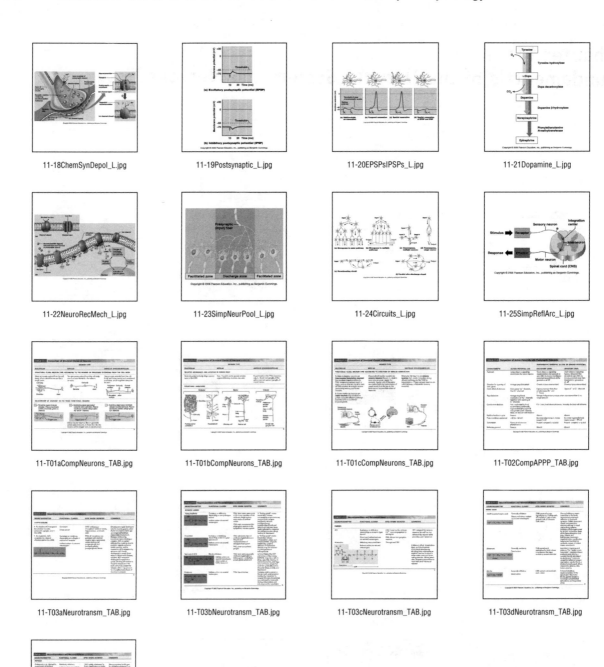

11-18ChemSynDepol_L.jpg

11-19Postsynaptic_L.jpg

11-20EPSPsIPSPs_L.jpg

11-21Dopamine_L.jpg

11-22NeuroRecMech_L.jpg

11-23SimpNeurPool_L.jpg

11-24Circuits_L.jpg

11-25SimpReflArc_L.jpg

11-T01aCompNeurons_TAB.jpg

11-T01bCompNeurons_TAB.jpg

11-T01cCompNeurons_TAB.jpg

11-T02CompAPPP_TAB.jpg

11-T03aNeurotransm_TAB.jpg

11-T03bNeurotransm_TAB.jpg

11-T03cNeurotransm_TAB.jpg

11-T03dNeurotransm_TAB.jpg

11-T03eNeurotransm_TAB.jpg

Chapter 12:
The Central Nervous System

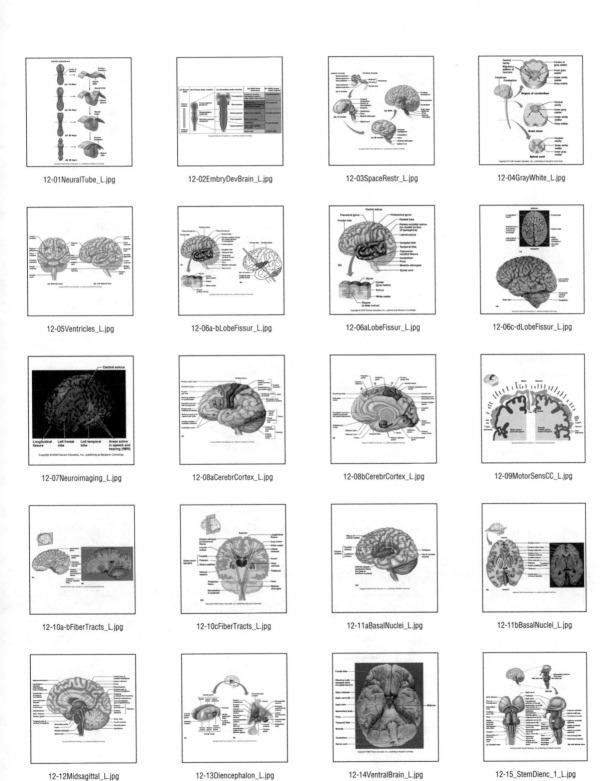

12-01NeuralTube_L.jpg

12-02EmbryDevBrain_L.jpg

12-03SpaceRestr_L.jpg

12-04GrayWhite_L.jpg

12-05Ventricles_L.jpg

12-06a-bLobeFissur_L.jpg

12-06aLobeFissur_L.jpg

12-06c-dLobeFissur_L.jpg

12-07Neuroimaging_L.jpg

12-08aCerebrCortex_L.jpg

12-08bCerebrCortex_L.jpg

12-09MotorSensCC_L.jpg

12-10a-bFiberTracts_L.jpg

12-10cFiberTracts_L.jpg

12-11aBasalNuclei_L.jpg

12-11bBasalNuclei_L.jpg

12-12Midsagittal_L.jpg

12-13Diencephalon_L.jpg

12-14VentralBrain_L.jpg

12-15_StemDienc_1_L.jpg

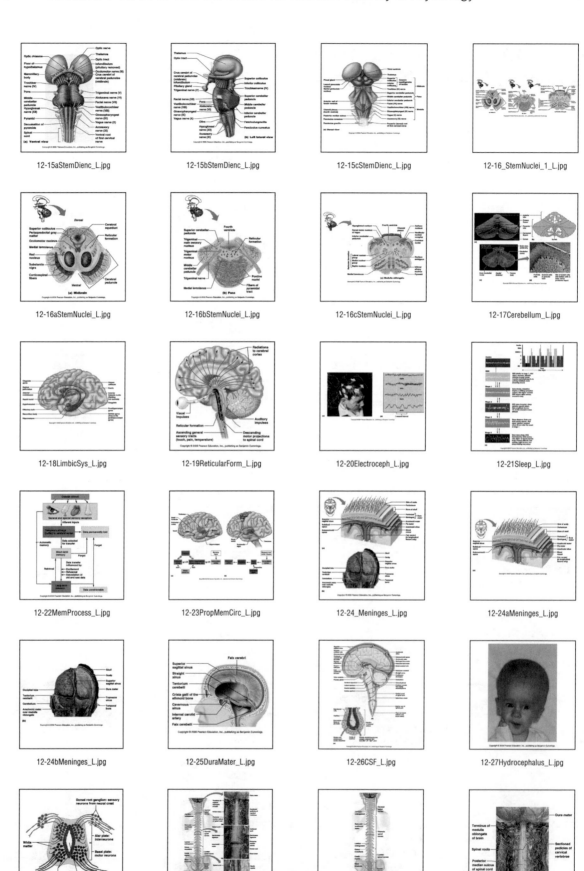

12-15aStemDienc_L.jpg

12-15bStemDienc_L.jpg

12-15cStemDienc_L.jpg

12-16_StemNuclei_1_L.jpg

12-16aStemNuclei_L.jpg

12-16bStemNuclei_L.jpg

12-16cStemNuclei_L.jpg

12-17Cerebellum_L.jpg

12-18LimbicSys_L.jpg

12-19ReticularForm_L.jpg

12-20Electroceph_L.jpg

12-21Sleep_L.jpg

12-22MemProcess_L.jpg

12-23PropMemCirc_L.jpg

12-24_Meninges_L.jpg

12-24aMeninges_L.jpg

12-24bMeninges_L.jpg

12-25DuraMater_L.jpg

12-26CSF_L.jpg

12-27Hydrocephalus_L.jpg

12-28EmbSpinalCord_L.jpg

12-29_GrossSpinal_L.jpg

12-29aGrossSpinal_L.jpg

12-29bGrossSpinal_L.jpg

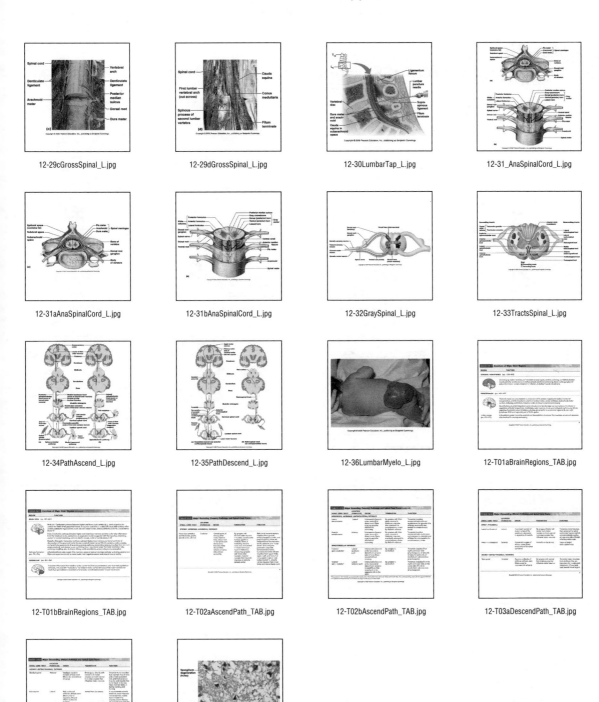

12-29cGrossSpinal_L.jpg

12-29dGrossSpinal_L.jpg

12-30LumbarTap_L.jpg

12-31_AnaSpinalCord_L.jpg

12-31aAnaSpinalCord_L.jpg

12-31bAnaSpinalCord_L.jpg

12-32GraySpinal_L.jpg

12-33TractsSpinal_L.jpg

12-34PathAscend_L.jpg

12-35PathDescend_L.jpg

12-36LumbarMyelo_L.jpg

12-T01aBrainRegions_TAB.jpg

12-T01bBrainRegions_TAB.jpg

12-T02aAscendPath_TAB.jpg

12-T02bAscendPath_TAB.jpg

12-T03aDescendPath_TAB.jpg

12-T03bDescendPath_TAB.jpg

12-UN01CreutzJak_L.jpg

Chapter 13:
The Peripheral Nervous System and Reflex Activity

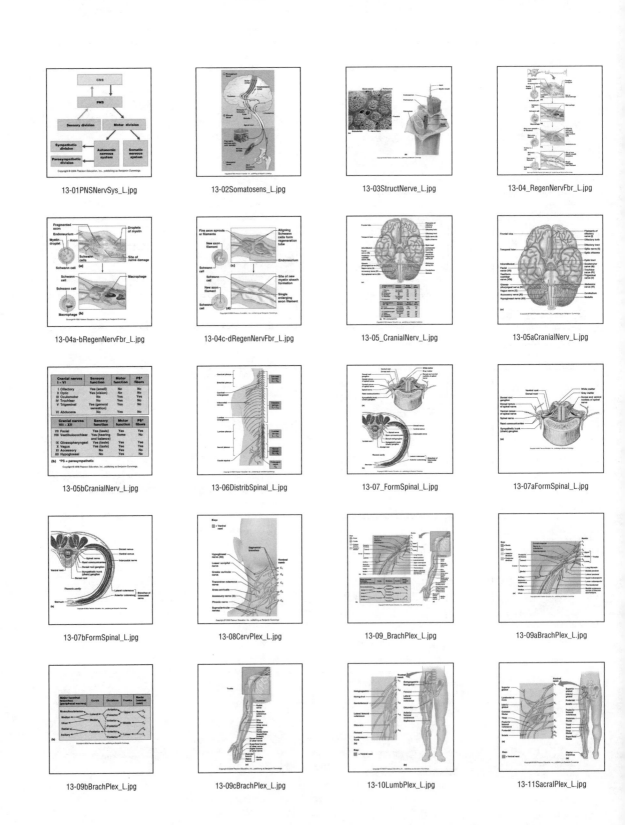

13-01PNSNervSys_L.jpg

13-02Somatosens_L.jpg

13-03StructNerve_L.jpg

13-04_RegenNervFbr_L.jpg

13-04a-bRegenNervFbr_L.jpg

13-04c-dRegenNervFbr_L.jpg

13-05_CranialNerv_L.jpg

13-05aCranialNerv_L.jpg

13-05bCranialNerv_L.jpg

13-06DistribSpinal_L.jpg

13-07_FormSpinal_L.jpg

13-07aFormSpinal_L.jpg

13-07bFormSpinal_L.jpg

13-08CervPlex_L.jpg

13-09_BrachPlex_L.jpg

13-09aBrachPlex_L.jpg

13-09bBrachPlex_L.jpg

13-09cBrachPlex_L.jpg

13-10LumbPlex_L.jpg

13-11SacralPlex_L.jpg

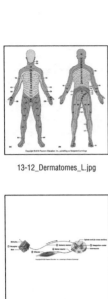

13-12_Dermatomes_L.jpg

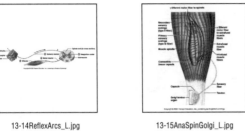

13-12aDermatomes_L.jpg

13-12bDermatomes_L.jpg

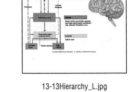

13-13Hierarchy_L.jpg

13-14ReflexArcs_L.jpg

13-15AnaSpinGolgi_L.jpg

13-16StretchReflex_L.jpg

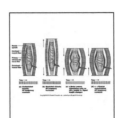

13-17OpMuscSpin_L.jpg

13-18GolgiTendRe_L.jpg

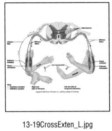

13-19CrossExten_L.jpg

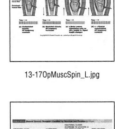

13-T01aGenSensRec_TAB.jpg

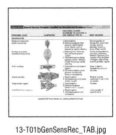

13-T01bGenSensRec_TAB.jpg

13-T02aCranialNerv_TAB.jpg

13-T02bCranialNerv_TAB.jpg

13-T02cCranialNerv_TAB.jpg

13-T02dCranialNerv_TAB.jpg

13-T02eCranialNerv_TAB.jpg

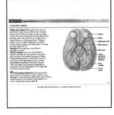

13-T02fCranialNerv_TAB.jpg

13-T02gCranialNerv_TAB.jpg

13-T02hCranialNerv_TAB.jpg

13-T02iCranialNerv_TAB.jpg

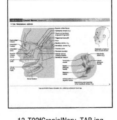
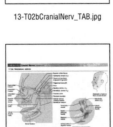

13-T02jCranialNerv_TAB.jpg

13-T02kCranialNerv_TAB.jpg

13-T02lCranialNerv_TAB.jpg

13-T02mCranialNerv_TAB.jpg

13-T02nCranialNerv_TAB.jpg

13-T03CervicalPlex_TAB.jpg

13-T04BrachialPlex_TAB.jpg

13-T05LumbarPlex_TAB.jpg

13-T06SacralPlex_TAB.jpg

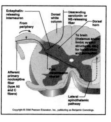

13-UN01Pain_L.jpg

Chapter 14:
The Autonomic Nervous System

14-01PlaceANS_L.jpg

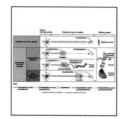

14-02Compare_L.jpg

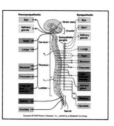

14-03SubdivANS_L.jpg

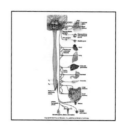

14-04ParasymDiv_L.jpg

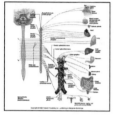

14-05SympathDiv_L.jpg

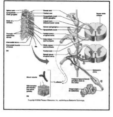

14-06SympTrunkPath_L.jpg

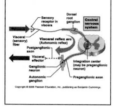

14-07ViscReflex_L.jpg

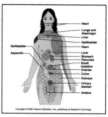

14-08ReferredPain_L.jpg

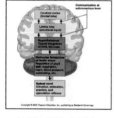

14-09LevANSControl_L.jpg

14-T01DiffParaSym_TAB.jpg

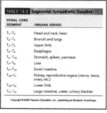

14-T02Segment_TAB.jpg

14-T03CholinAdren_TAB.jpg

14-T04DrugClasses_TAB.jpg

14-T05aEffects_TAB.jpg

14-T05bEffects_TAB.jpg

Chapter 15:
The Special Senses

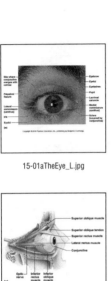

15-01aTheEye_L.jpg

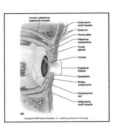

15-01bTheEye_L.jpg

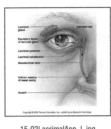

15-02LacrimalApp_L.jpg

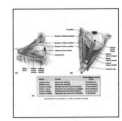

15-03_ExtrinEyeMusc_L.jpg

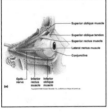

15-03aExtrinEyeMusc_L.jpg

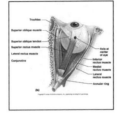

15-03bExtrinEyeMusc_L.jpg

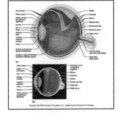

15-04_InternalEye_L.jpg

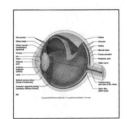

15-04aInternalEye_L.jpg

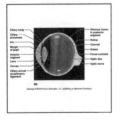

15-04bInternalEye_L.jpg

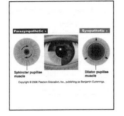

15-05PupilDilation_L.jpg

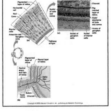

15-06_MicroRetina_L.jpg

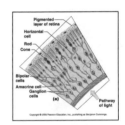

15-06aMicroRetina_L.jpg

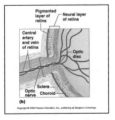

15-06bMicroRetina_L.jpg

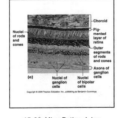

15-06cMicroRetina_L.jpg

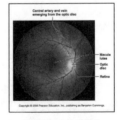

15-07PosteriorWall_L.jpg

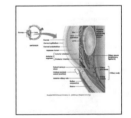

15-08Circulation_L.jpg

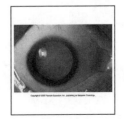

15-09Cataract_L.jpg

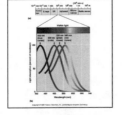

15-10ElectroSpec_L.jpg

15-11Spoon_L.jpg

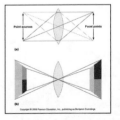

15-12BendingLight_L.jpg

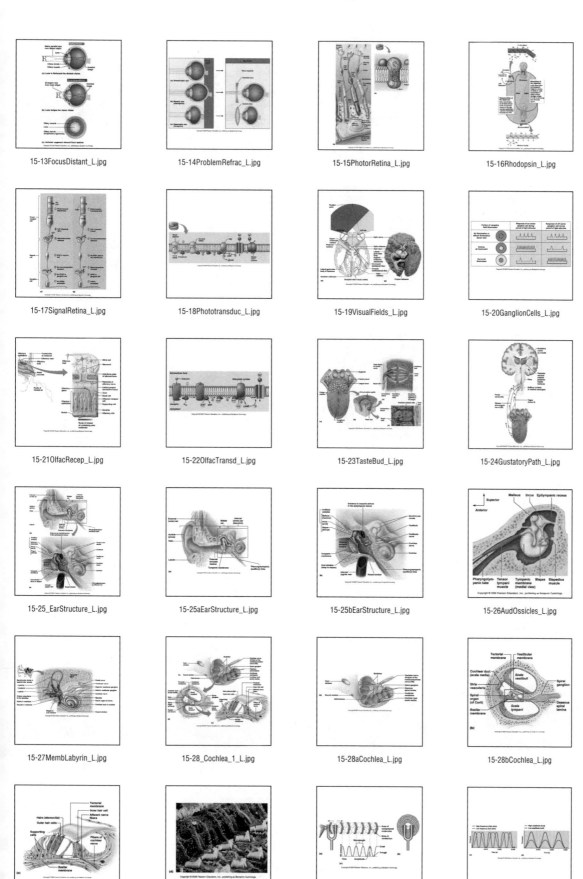

15-13FocusDistant_L.jpg

15-14ProblemRefrac_L.jpg

15-15PhotorRetina_L.jpg

15-16Rhodopsin_L.jpg

15-17SignalRetina_L.jpg

15-18Phototransduc_L.jpg

15-19VisualFields_L.jpg

15-20GanglionCells_L.jpg

15-21OlfacRecep_L.jpg

15-22OlfacTransd_L.jpg

15-23TasteBud_L.jpg

15-24GustatoryPath_L.jpg

15-25_EarStructure_L.jpg

15-25aEarStructure_L.jpg

15-25bEarStructure_L.jpg

15-26AudOssicles_L.jpg

15-27MembLabyrin_L.jpg

15-28_Cochlea_1_L.jpg

15-28aCochlea_L.jpg

15-28bCochlea_L.jpg

15-28cCochlea_L.jpg

15-28dCochlea_L.jpg

15-29Sound_L.jpg

15-30FreqSoundWav_L.jpg

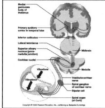

15-31RouteWaves_L.jpg

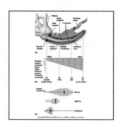

15-32_Resonance_L.jpg

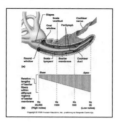

15-32a-bResonance_L.jpg

15-33CochlearHair_L.jpg

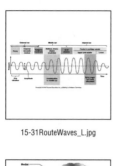

15-34AuditoryPath_L.jpg

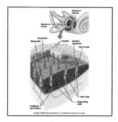

15-35Macula_L.jpg

15-36GravPullMacula_L.jpg

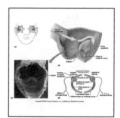

15-37_CristaAmp_L.jpg

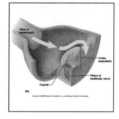

15-37bCristaAmp_L.jpg

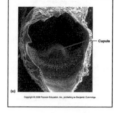

15-37cCristaAmp_L.jpg

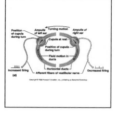

15-37dCristaAmp_L.jpg

15-38PathBalance_L.jpg

Chapter 16:
The Endocrine System

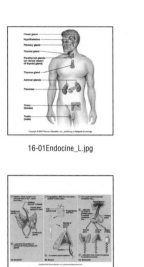

16-01Endocine_L.jpg

16-02CyclicAMP_L.jpg

16-03PIPMech_L.jpg

16-04DirectGene_L.jpg

16-05EndocrStim_L.jpg

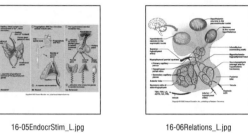

16-06Relations_L.jpg

16-07Metabolic_L.jpg

16-08_GrossThyroid_L.jpg

16-08aGrossThyroid_L.jpg

16-08bGrossThyroid_L.jpg

16-09SynThyroid_L.jpg

16-10ThyDisorder_L.jpg

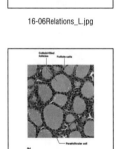

16-11Parathyroid_L.jpg

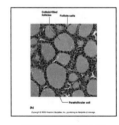

16-12EffectParathy_L.jpg

16-13MicroAdrenal_L.jpg

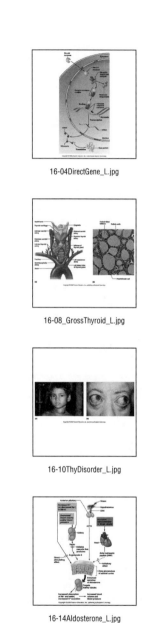

16-14Aldosterone_L.jpg

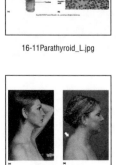
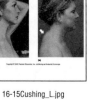

16-15Cushing_L.jpg

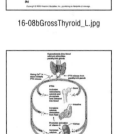
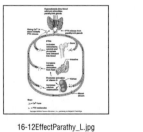

16-16StressAdrenal_L.jpg

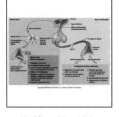

16-17Pancreatic_L.jpg

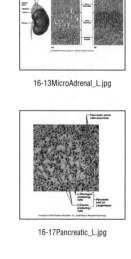

16-18_Regulation_L.jpg

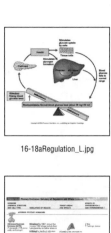

16-18aRegulation_L.jpg

16-18bRegulation_L.jpg

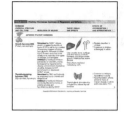

16-19Symptomatic_L.jpg

16-T01aPituitary_TAB.jpg

16-T01bPituitary_TAB.jpg

16-T01cPituitary_TAB.jpg

16-T01dPituitary_TAB.jpg

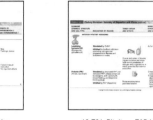

16-T02aThyroid_TAB.jpg

16-T02bThyroid_TAB.jpg

16-T03aAdrenal_TAB.jpg

16-T03bAdrenal_TAB.jpg

16-T04aOtherOrgans_TAB.jpg

16-T04bOtherOrgans_TAB.jpg

16-UN01DM_L.jpg

Chapter 17: Blood

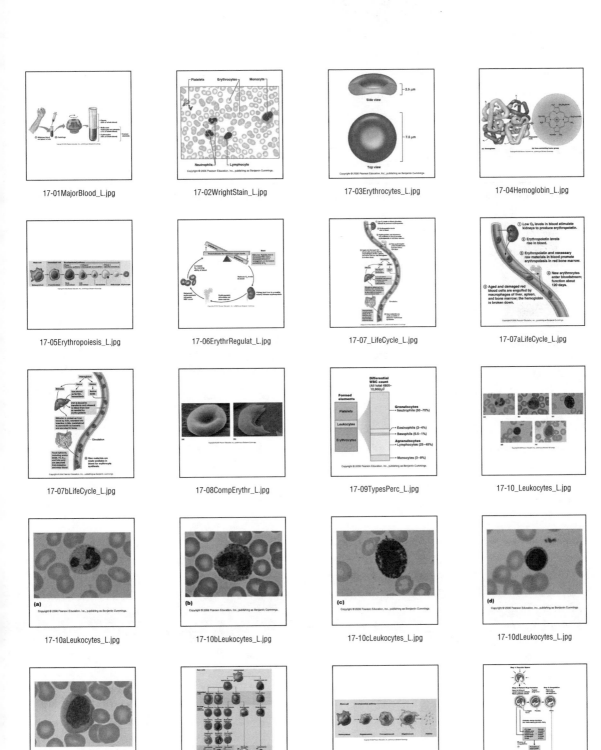

17-01MajorBlood_L.jpg

17-02WrightStain_L.jpg

17-03Erythrocytes_L.jpg

17-04Hemoglobin_L.jpg

17-05Erythropoiesis_L.jpg

17-06ErythrRegulat_L.jpg

17-07_LifeCycle_L.jpg

17-07aLifeCycle_L.jpg

17-07bLifeCycle_L.jpg

17-08CompErythr_L.jpg

17-09TypesPerc_L.jpg

17-10_Leukocytes_L.jpg

17-10aLeukocytes_L.jpg

17-10bLeukocytes_L.jpg

17-10cLeukocytes_L.jpg

17-10dLeukocytes_L.jpg

17-10eLeukocytes_L.jpg

17-11LeukocForm_L.jpg

17-12GenesisPlate_L.jpg

17-13aHemostasis_L.jpg

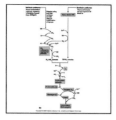

17-13bHemostasis_L.jpg

17-14ErythFibrin_L.jpg

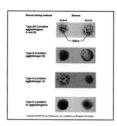

17-15BloodTyping_L.jpg

17-T01CompoPlasma_TAB.jpg

17-T02aSumElement_TAB.jpg

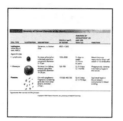

17-T02bSumElement_TAB.jpg

17-T03Clotting_TAB.jpg

17-T04ABOBlood_TAB.jpg

17-UN01ArtifBlood_L.jpg

Chapter 18:
The Cardiovascular System: The Heart

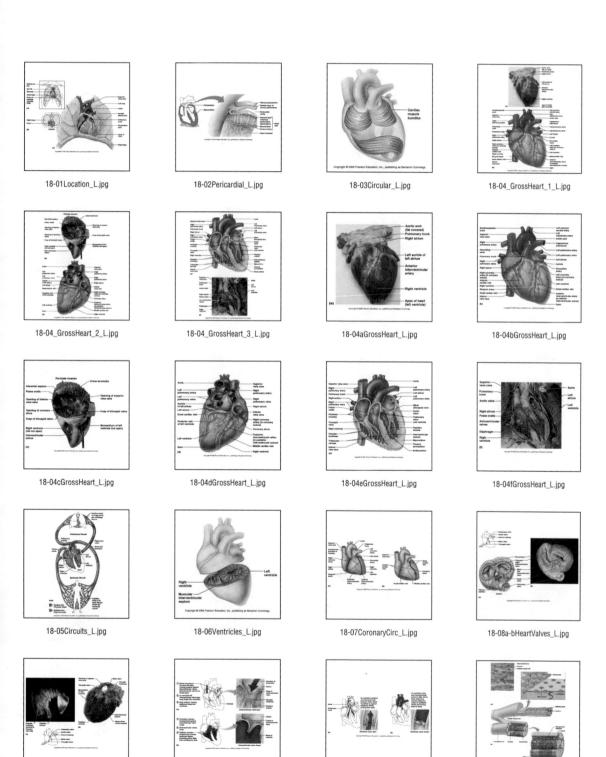

18-01Location_L.jpg

18-02Pericardial_L.jpg

18-03Circular_L.jpg

18-04_GrossHeart_1_L.jpg

18-04_GrossHeart_2_L.jpg

18-04_GrossHeart_3_L.jpg

18-04aGrossHeart_L.jpg

18-04bGrossHeart_L.jpg

18-04cGrossHeart_L.jpg

18-04dGrossHeart_L.jpg

18-04eGrossHeart_L.jpg

18-04fGrossHeart_L.jpg

18-05Circuits_L.jpg

18-06Ventricles_L.jpg

18-07CoronaryCirc_L.jpg

18-08a-bHeartValves_L.jpg

18-08c-dHeartValves_L.jpg

18-09Atrioventricul_L.jpg

18-10Semilunar_L.jpg

18-11_CardiacMuscle_L.jpg

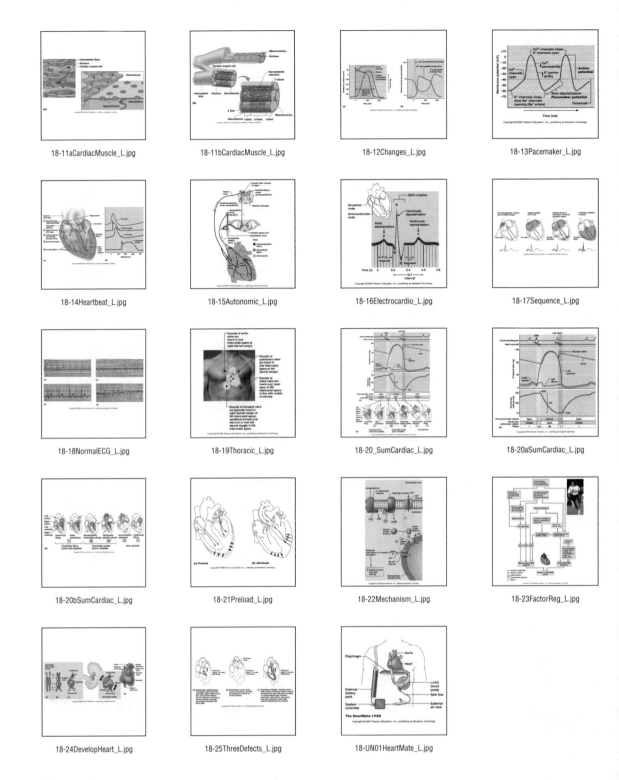

18-11aCardiacMuscle_L.jpg

18-11bCardiacMuscle_L.jpg

18-12Changes_L.jpg

18-13Pacemaker_L.jpg

18-14Heartbeat_L.jpg

18-15Autonomic_L.jpg

18-16Electrocardio_L.jpg

18-17Sequence_L.jpg

18-18NormalECG_L.jpg

18-19Thoracic_L.jpg

18-20_SumCardiac_L.jpg

18-20aSumCardiac_L.jpg

18-20bSumCardiac_L.jpg

18-21Preload_L.jpg

18-22Mechanism_L.jpg

18-23FactorReg_L.jpg

18-24DevelopHeart_L.jpg

18-25ThreeDefects_L.jpg

18-UN01HeartMate_L.jpg

Chapter 19:
The Cardiovascular System: Blood Vessels

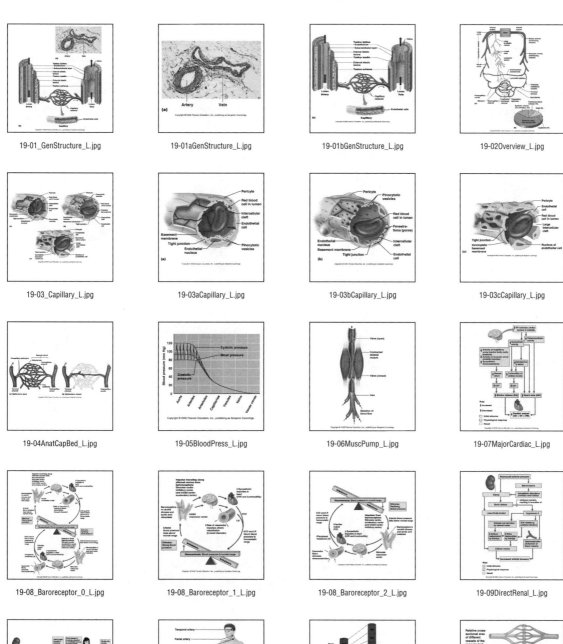

19-01_GenStructure_L.jpg

19-01aGenStructure_L.jpg

19-01bGenStructure_L.jpg

19-02Overview_L.jpg

19-03_Capillary_L.jpg

19-03aCapillary_L.jpg

19-03bCapillary_L.jpg

19-03cCapillary_L.jpg

19-04AnatCapBed_L.jpg

19-05BloodPress_L.jpg

19-06MuscPump_L.jpg

19-07MajorCardiac_L.jpg

19-08_Baroreceptor_0_L.jpg

19-08_Baroreceptor_1_L.jpg

19-08_Baroreceptor_2_L.jpg

19-09DirectRenal_L.jpg

19-10FactorsMAP_L.jpg

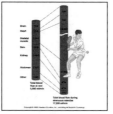

19-11BodySites_L.jpg

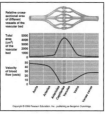

19-12Distribution_L.jpg

19-13Relationship_L.jpg

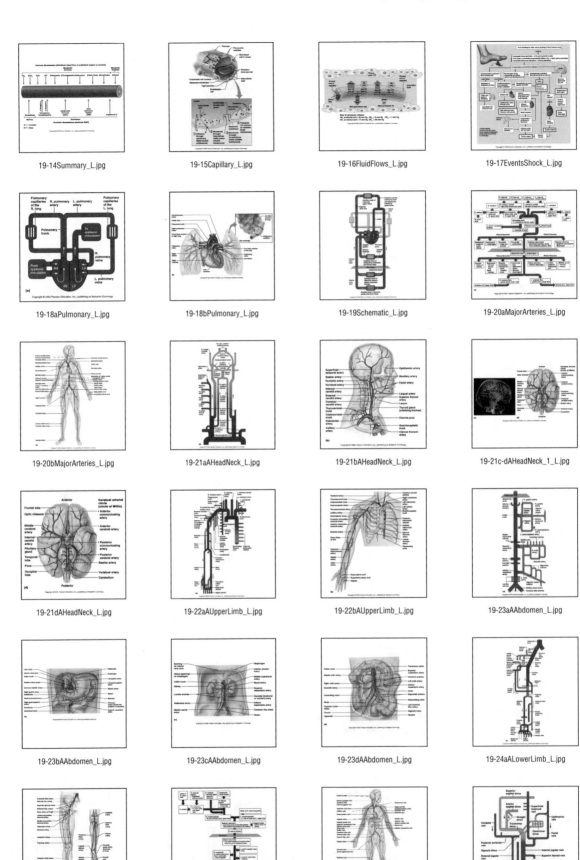

19-14Summary_L.jpg

19-15Capillary_L.jpg

19-16FluidFlows_L.jpg

19-17EventsShock_L.jpg

19-18aPulmonary_L.jpg

19-18bPulmonary_L.jpg

19-19Schematic_L.jpg

19-20aMajorArteries_L.jpg

19-20bMajorArteries_L.jpg

19-21aAHeadNeck_L.jpg

19-21bAHeadNeck_L.jpg

19-21c-dAHeadNeck_1_L.jpg

19-21dAHeadNeck_L.jpg

19-22aAUpperLimb_L.jpg

19-22bAUpperLimb_L.jpg

19-23aAAbdomen_L.jpg

19-23bAAbdomen_L.jpg

19-23cAAbdomen_L.jpg

19-23dAAbdomen_L.jpg

19-24aALowerLimb_L.jpg

19-24b-cALowerLimb_L.jpg

19-25aMajorVeins_L.jpg

19-25bMajorVeins_L.jpg

19-26aVDrainage_L.jpg

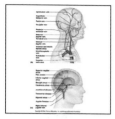

19-26b-cVDrainage_L.jpg

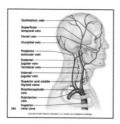

19-26bVDrainage_L.jpg

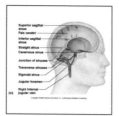

19-26cVDrainage_L.jpg

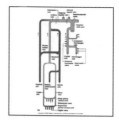

19-27aVUpperLimb_L.jpg

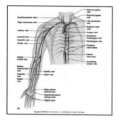

19-27bVUpperLimb_L.jpg

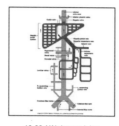

19-28aVAbdomen_L.jpg

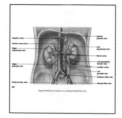

19-28bVAbdomen_L.jpg

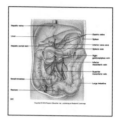

19-28cVAbdomen_L.jpg

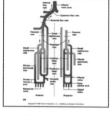

19-29aVLowerLimb_L.jpg

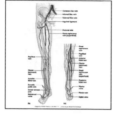

19-29b-cVLowerLimb_L.jpg

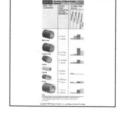

19-T01SumAnatomy_TAB.jpg

19-T02Influence_TAB.jpg

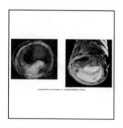

19-UN01Artherioscle_L.jpg

Chapter 20:
The Lymphatic System

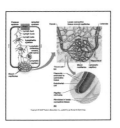

20-01Distribution_L.jpg

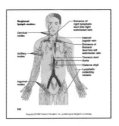

20-02aLymphatic_L.jpg

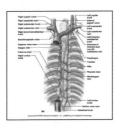

20-02bLymphatic_L.jpg

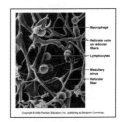

20-03Reticular_L.jpg

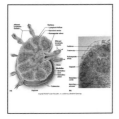

20-04_LymphNode_L.jpg

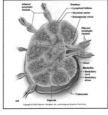

20-04aLymphNode_L.jpg

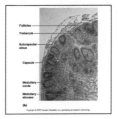

20-04bLymphNode_L.jpg

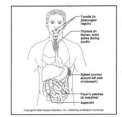

20-05Lymphoid_L.jpg

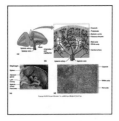

20-06Spleen_L.jpg

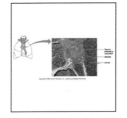

20-07Thymus_L.jpg

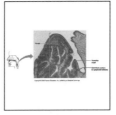

20-08PalaTonsil_L.jpg

20-09PeyersPatch_L.jpg

Chapter 21:
The Immune System: Innate and Adaptive Body Defenses

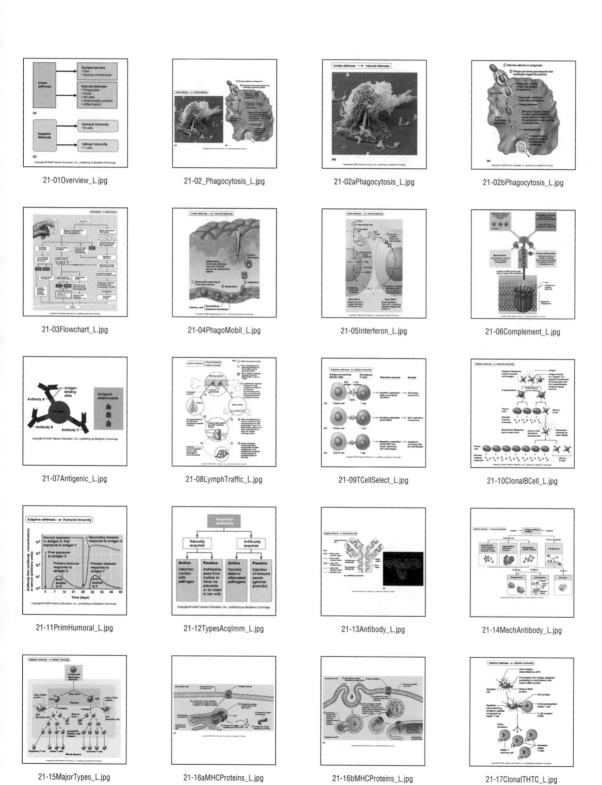

21-01Overview_L.jpg

21-02_Phagocytosis_L.jpg

21-02aPhagocytosis_L.jpg

21-02bPhagocytosis_L.jpg

21-03Flowchart_L.jpg

21-04PhagoMobil_L.jpg

21-05Interferon_L.jpg

21-06Complement_L.jpg

21-07Antigenic_L.jpg

21-08LymphTraffic_L.jpg

21-09TCellSelect_L.jpg

21-10ClonalBCell_L.jpg

21-11PrimHumoral_L.jpg

21-12TypesAcqImm_L.jpg

21-13Antibody_L.jpg

21-14MechAntibody_L.jpg

21-15MajorTypes_L.jpg

21-16aMHCProteins_L.jpg

21-16bMHCProteins_L.jpg

21-17ClonalTHTC_L.jpg

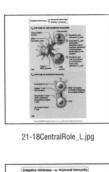

21-18CentralRole_L.jpg

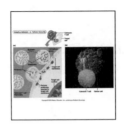

21-19Cytotoxic_L.jpg

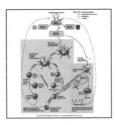

21-20PrimImmune_L.jpg

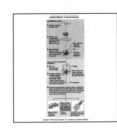

21-21_MechAllergic_L.jpg

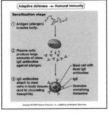

21-21aMechAllergic_L.jpg

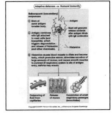

21-21bMechAllergic_L.jpg

21-T01Inflammatory_TAB.jpg

21-T02aSumDefenses_TAB.jpg

21-T02bSumDefenses_TAB.jpg

21-T03aImmunoglob_TAB.jpg

21-T03bImmunoglob_TAB.jpg

21-T04aCellsAdapt_TAB.jpg

21-T04bCellsAdapt_TAB.jpg

21-T04cCellsAdapt_TAB.jpg

21-UN1Comic_L.jpg

Chapter 22:
The Respiratory System

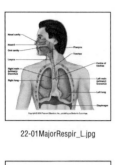

22-01MajorRespir_L.jpg

22-02ExternalNose_L.jpg

22-03aUpperRespir_L.jpg

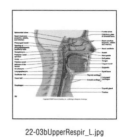

22-03bUpperRespir_L.jpg

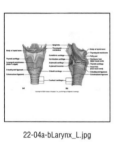

22-04a-bLarynx_L.jpg

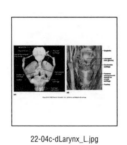

22-04c-dLarynx_L.jpg

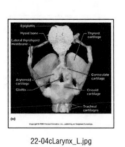

22-04cLarynx_L.jpg

22-04dLarynx_L.jpg

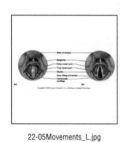

22-05Movements_L.jpg

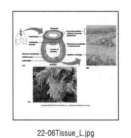

22-06Tissue_L.jpg

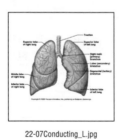

22-07Conducting_L.jpg

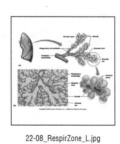

22-08_RespirZone_L.jpg

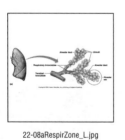

22-08aRespirZone_L.jpg

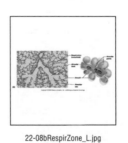

22-08bRespirZone_L.jpg

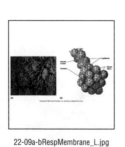

22-09a-bRespMembrane_L.jpg

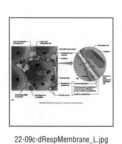

22-09c-dRespMembrane_L.jpg

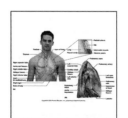

22-10a-bAnatomical_L.jpg

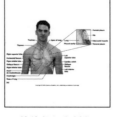

22-10aAnatomical_L.jpg

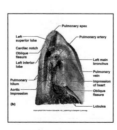

22-10bAnatomical_L.jpg

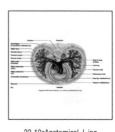

22-10cAnatomical_L.jpg

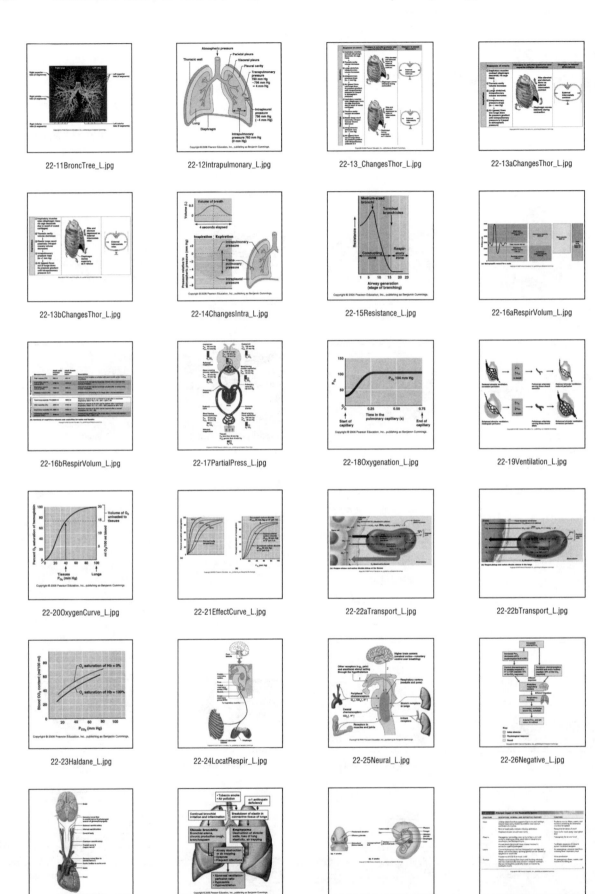

22-11BroncTree_L.jpg

22-12Intrapulmonary_L.jpg

22-13_ChangesThor_L.jpg

22-13aChangesThor_L.jpg

22-13bChangesThor_L.jpg

22-14ChangesIntra_L.jpg

22-15Resistance_L.jpg

22-16aRespirVolum_L.jpg

22-16bRespirVolum_L.jpg

22-17PartialPress_L.jpg

22-18Oxygenation_L.jpg

22-19Ventilation_L.jpg

22-20OxygenCurve_L.jpg

22-21EffectCurve_L.jpg

22-22aTransport_L.jpg

22-22bTransport_L.jpg

22-23Haldane_L.jpg

22-24LocatRespir_L.jpg

22-25Neural_L.jpg

22-26Negative_L.jpg

22-27LocatPeriph_L.jpg

22-28COPD_L.jpg

22-29Embryonic_L.jpg

22-T01aPrincipalOrg_TAB.jpg

22-T01bPrincipalOrg_TAB.jpg

22-T02EffectBreath_TAB.jpg

22-T03NonrespirAir_TAB.jpg

22-T04Comparison_TAB.jpg

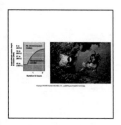

22-UN1Decomp_L.jpg

Chapter 23:
The Digestive System

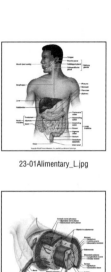

23-01Alimentary_L.jpg

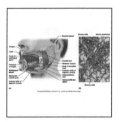

23-02Gastrointest_L.jpg

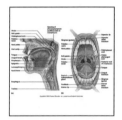

23-04NeuralReflex_L.jpg

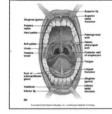

23-05Peritoneum_L.jpg

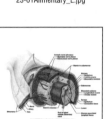

23-06BasicStruct_L.jpg

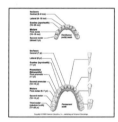

23-07_AnatomyOral_L.jpg

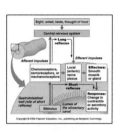

23-07aAnatomyOral_L.jpg

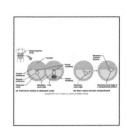

23-07bAnatomyOral_L.jpg

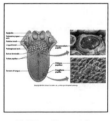

23-08DorsalTongue_L.jpg

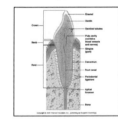

23-09Salivary_L.jpg

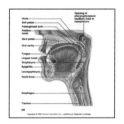

23-10Deciduous_L.jpg

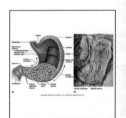

23-11Longitudinal_L.jpg

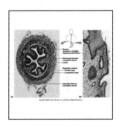

23-12Esophagus_L.jpg

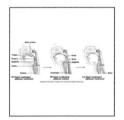

23-13a-cDeglutition_L.jpg

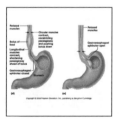

23-13d-eDeglutition_L.jpg

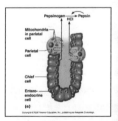

23-14AnatoStomach_L.jpg

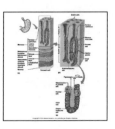

23-15_MicroStomach_L.jpg

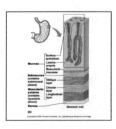

23-15aMicroStomach_L.jpg

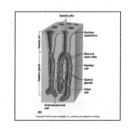

23-15bMicroStomach_L.jpg

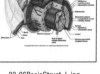

23-15cMicroStomach_L.jpg

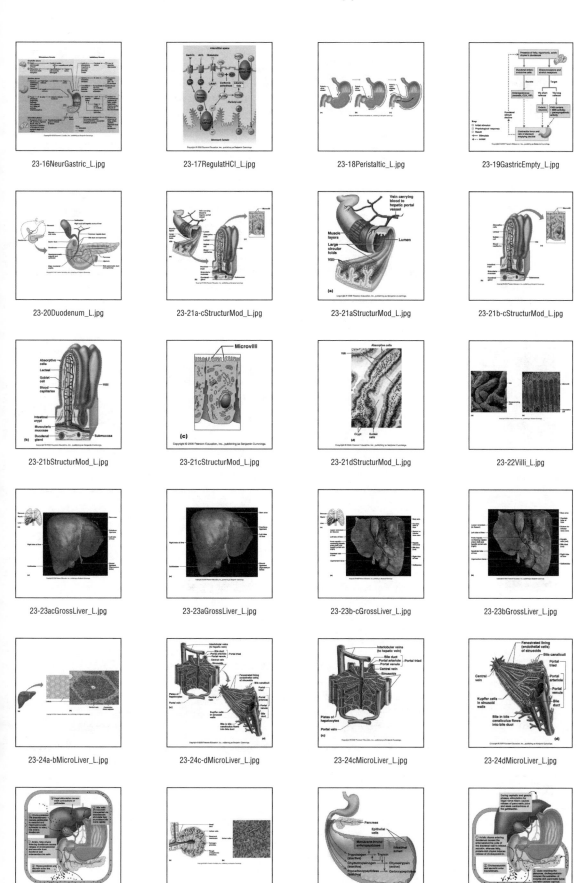

23-16NeurGastric_L.jpg

23-17RegulatHCl_L.jpg

23-18Peristaltic_L.jpg

23-19GastricEmpty_L.jpg

23-20Duodenum_L.jpg

23-21a-cStructurMod_L.jpg

23-21aStructurMod_L.jpg

23-21b-cStructurMod_L.jpg

23-21bStructurMod_L.jpg

23-21cStructurMod_L.jpg

23-21dStructurMod_L.jpg

23-22Villi_L.jpg

23-23acGrossLiver_L.jpg

23-23aGrossLiver_L.jpg

23-23b-cGrossLiver_L.jpg

23-23bGrossLiver_L.jpg

23-24a-bMicroLiver_L.jpg

23-24c-dMicroLiver_L.jpg

23-24cMicroLiver_L.jpg

23-24dMicroLiver_L.jpg

23-25MechBile_L.jpg

23-26Pancreas_L.jpg

23-27Activation_L.jpg

23-28RegulPancrea_L.jpg

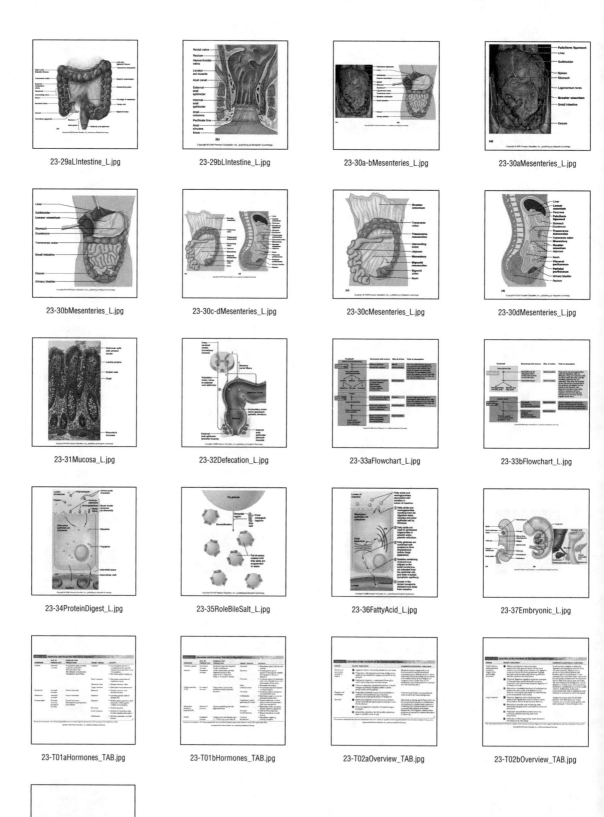

23-29aLIntestine_L.jpg

23-29bLIntestine_L.jpg

23-30a-bMesenteries_L.jpg

23-30aMesenteries_L.jpg

23-30bMesenteries_L.jpg

23-30c-dMesenteries_L.jpg

23-30cMesenteries_L.jpg

23-30dMesenteries_L.jpg

23-31Mucosa_L.jpg

23-32Defecation_L.jpg

23-33aFlowchart_L.jpg

23-33bFlowchart_L.jpg

23-34ProteinDigest_L.jpg

23-35RoleBileSalt_L.jpg

23-36FattyAcid_L.jpg

23-37Embryonic_L.jpg

23-T01aHormones_TAB.jpg

23-T01bHormones_TAB.jpg

23-T02aOverview_TAB.jpg

23-T02bOverview_TAB.jpg

23-T03ControlSmall_TAB.jpg

Chapter 24:
Nutrition, Metabolism, and Body Temperature Regulation

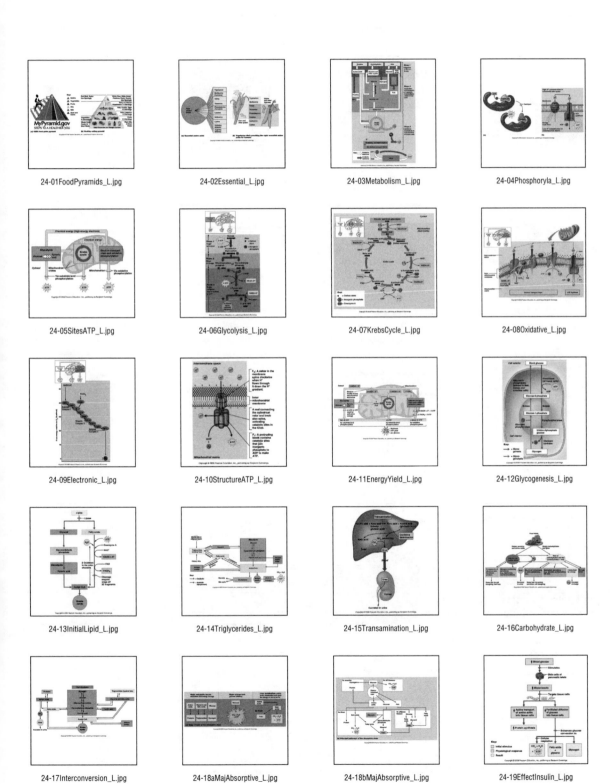

24-01FoodPyramids_L.jpg

24-02Essential_L.jpg

24-03Metabolism_L.jpg

24-04Phosphoryla_L.jpg

24-05SitesATP_L.jpg

24-06Glycolysis_L.jpg

24-07KrebsCycle_L.jpg

24-08Oxidative_L.jpg

24-09Electronic_L.jpg

24-10StructureATP_L.jpg

24-11EnergyYield_L.jpg

24-12Glycogenesis_L.jpg

24-13InitialLipid_L.jpg

24-14Triglycerides_L.jpg

24-15Transamination_L.jpg

24-16Carbohydrate_L.jpg

24-17Interconversion_L.jpg

24-18aMajAbsorptive_L.jpg

24-18bMajAbsorptive_L.jpg

24-19EffectInsulin_L.jpg

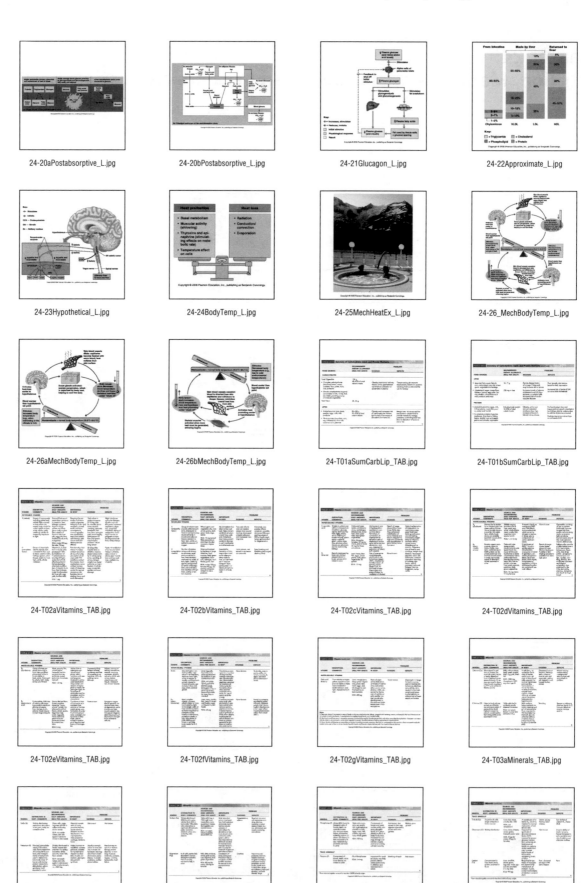

24-20aPostabsorptive_L.jpg

24-20bPostabsorptive_L.jpg

24-21Glucagon_L.jpg

24-22Approximate_L.jpg

24-23Hypothetical_L.jpg

24-24BodyTemp_L.jpg

24-25MechHeatEx_L.jpg

24-26_MechBodyTemp_L.jpg

24-26aMechBodyTemp_L.jpg

24-26bMechBodyTemp_L.jpg

24-T01aSumCarbLip_TAB.jpg

24-T01bSumCarbLip_TAB.jpg

24-T02aVitamins_TAB.jpg

24-T02bVitamins_TAB.jpg

24-T02cVitamins_TAB.jpg

24-T02dVitamins_TAB.jpg

24-T02eVitamins_TAB.jpg

24-T02fVitamins_TAB.jpg

24-T02gVitamins_TAB.jpg

24-T03aMinerals_TAB.jpg

24-T03bMinerals_TAB.jpg

24-T03cMinerals_TAB.jpg

24-T03dMinerals_TAB.jpg

24-T03eMinerals_TAB.jpg

24-T03fMinerals_TAB.jpg

24-T03gMinerals_TAB.jpg

24-T04Thumbnail_TAB.jpg

24-T05Profiles_TAB.jpg

24-T06SumNormal_TAB.jpg

24-T07aSumMetabolic_TAB.jpg

24-T07bSumMetabolic_TAB.jpg

Chapter 25:
The Urinary System

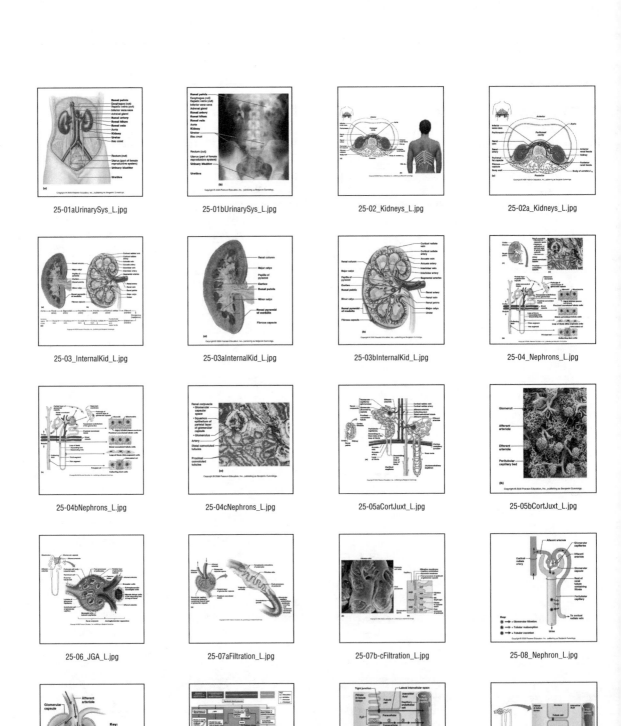

25-01aUrinarySys_L.jpg

25-01bUrinarySys_L.jpg

25-02_Kidneys_L.jpg

25-02a_Kidneys_L.jpg

25-03_InternalKid_L.jpg

25-03aInternalKid_L.jpg

25-03bInternalKid_L.jpg

25-04_Nephrons_L.jpg

25-04bNephrons_L.jpg

25-04cNephrons_L.jpg

25-05aCortJuxt_L.jpg

25-05bCortJuxt_L.jpg

25-06_JGA_L.jpg

25-07aFiltration_L.jpg

25-07b-cFiltration_L.jpg

25-08_Nephron_L.jpg

25-09_Forces_L.jpg

25-10_Regulating_L.jpg

25-11_Transcellular_L.jpg

25-12_ReabsorpPCT_L.jpg

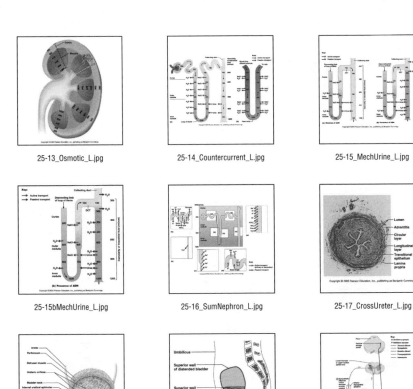

25-13_Osmotic_L.jpg

25-14_Countercurrent_L.jpg

25-15_MechUrine_L.jpg

25-15aMechUrine_L.jpg

25-15bMechUrine_L.jpg

25-16_SumNephron_L.jpg

25-17_CrossUreter_L.jpg

25-18aUrinBladder_L.jpg

25-18bUrinBladder_L.jpg

25-19_EmptyBladd_L.jpg

25-20aNeuralCirc_L.jpg

25-20bNeuralCirc_L.jpg

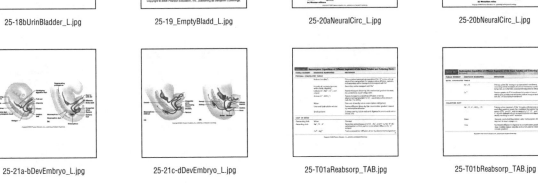

25-21a-bDevEmbryo_L.jpg

25-21c-dDevEmbryo_L.jpg

25-T01aReabsorp_TAB.jpg

25-T01bReabsorp_TAB.jpg

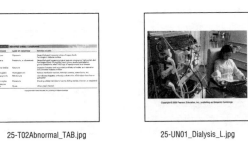

25-T02Abnormal_TAB.jpg

25-UN01_Dialysis_L.jpg

Chapter 26:
Fluid, Electrolyte, and Acid-Base Balance

26-01_MajorFluid_L.jpg

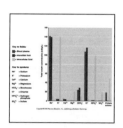

26-02_ElectroComp_L.jpg

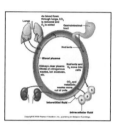

26-03_MixingFluid_L.jpg

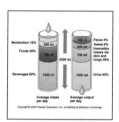

26-04_SourceWater_L.jpg

26-05_ThirstMech_L.jpg

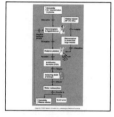

26-06_ADHrelease_L.jpg

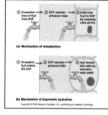

26-07_Disturbances_L.jpg

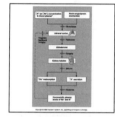

26-08_Aldosterone_L.jpg

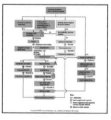

26-09_MechSodium_L.jpg

26-10_ANPrelease_L.jpg

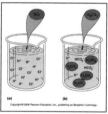

26-11_Dissociation_L.jpg

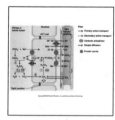

26-12_ReabsorFilter_L.jpg

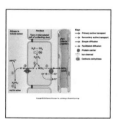

26-13_GenBuffer_L.jpg

26-14_GenGlutamine_L.jpg

26-T01aElectrolyte_TAB.jpg

26-T01bElectrolyte_TAB.jpg

26-T02aAcidBase_TAB.jpg

26-T02bAcidBase_TAB.jpg

Chapter 27:
The Reproductive System

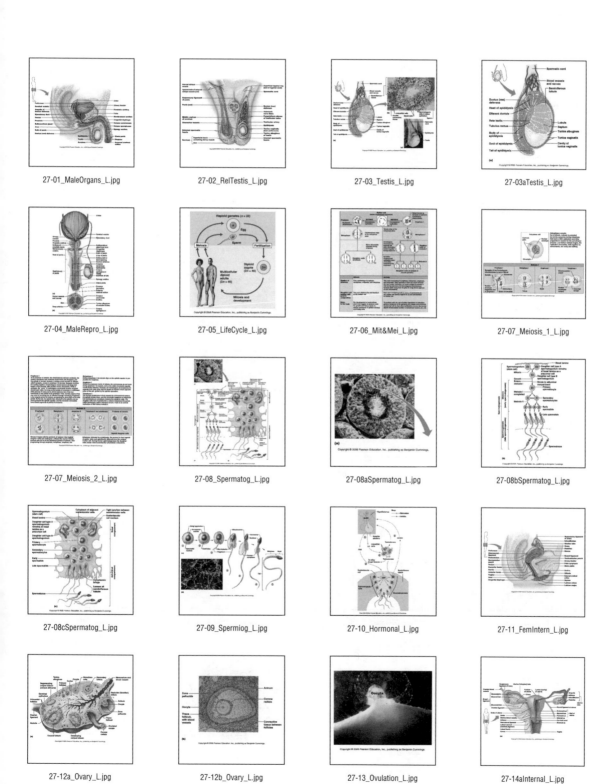

27-01_MaleOrgans_L.jpg

27-02_RelTestis_L.jpg

27-03_Testis_L.jpg

27-03aTestis_L.jpg

27-04_MaleRepro_L.jpg

27-05_LifeCycle_L.jpg

27-06_Mit&Mei_L.jpg

27-07_Meiosis_1_L.jpg

27-07_Meiosis_2_L.jpg

27-08_Spermatog_L.jpg

27-08aSpermatog_L.jpg

27-08bSpermatog_L.jpg

27-08cSpermatog_L.jpg

27-09_Spermiog_L.jpg

27-10_Hormonal_L.jpg

27-11_FemIntern_L.jpg

27-12a_Ovary_L.jpg

27-12b_Ovary_L.jpg

27-13_Ovulation_L.jpg

27-14aInternal_L.jpg

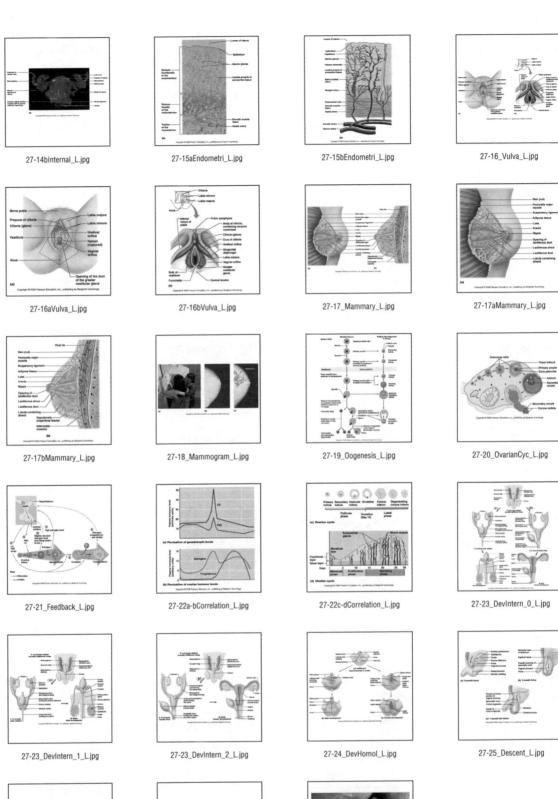

27-14bInternal_L.jpg

27-15aEndometri_L.jpg

27-15bEndometri_L.jpg

27-16_Vulva_L.jpg

27-16aVulva_L.jpg

27-16bVulva_L.jpg

27-17_Mammary_L.jpg

27-17aMammary_L.jpg

27-17bMammary_L.jpg

27-18_Mammogram_L.jpg

27-19_Oogenesis_L.jpg

27-20_OvarianCyc_L.jpg

27-21_Feedback_L.jpg

27-22a-bCorrelation_L.jpg

27-22c-dCorrelation_L.jpg

27-23_DevIntern_0_L.jpg

27-23_DevIntern_1_L.jpg

27-23_DevIntern_2_L.jpg

27-24_DevHomol_L.jpg

27-25_Descent_L.jpg

27-T01aHormon_TAB.jpg

27-T01bHormon_TAB.jpg

27-UN01_Viagra_L.jpg

Chapter 28:
Pregnancy and Human Development

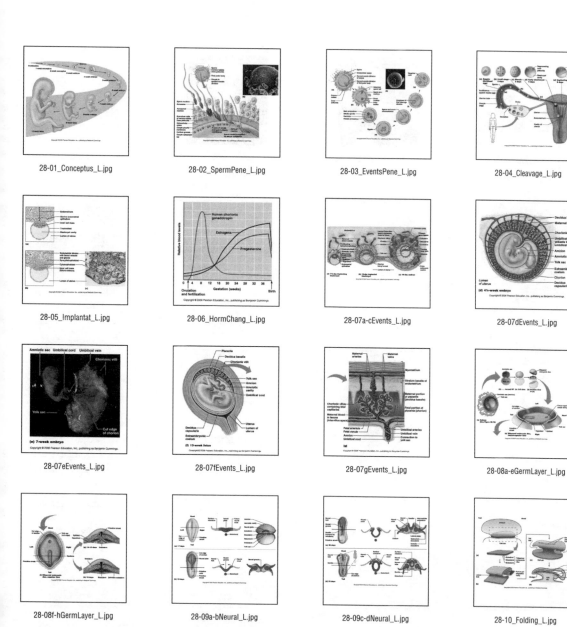

28-01_Conceptus_L.jpg

28-02_SpermPene_L.jpg

28-03_EventsPene_L.jpg

28-04_Cleavage_L.jpg

28-05_Implantat_L.jpg

28-06_HormChang_L.jpg

28-07a-cEvents_L.jpg

28-07dEvents_L.jpg

28-07eEvents_L.jpg

28-07fEvents_L.jpg

28-07gEvents_L.jpg

28-08a-eGermLayer_L.jpg

28-08f-hGermLayer_L.jpg

28-09a-bNeural_L.jpg

28-09c-dNeural_L.jpg

28-10_Folding_L.jpg

28-10a-bFolding_L.jpg

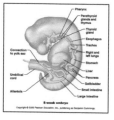

28-10c-dFolding_L.jpg

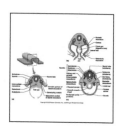

28-11_Endoderm_L.jpg

28-12_Mesoderm_L.jpg

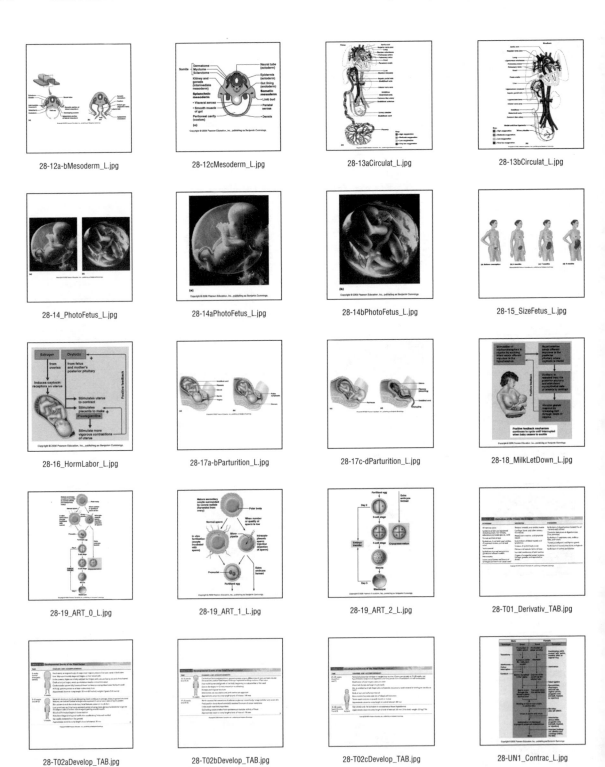

28-12a-bMesoderm_L.jpg

28-12cMesoderm_L.jpg

28-13aCirculat_L.jpg

28-13bCirculat_L.jpg

28-14_PhotoFetus_L.jpg

28-14aPhotoFetus_L.jpg

28-14bPhotoFetus_L.jpg

28-15_SizeFetus_L.jpg

28-16_HormLabor_L.jpg

28-17a-bParturition_L.jpg

28-17c-dParturition_L.jpg

28-18_MilkLetDown_L.jpg

28-19_ART_0_L.jpg

28-19_ART_1_L.jpg

28-19_ART_2_L.jpg

28-T01_Derivativ_TAB.jpg

28-T02aDevelop_TAB.jpg

28-T02bDevelop_TAB.jpg

28-T02cDevelop_TAB.jpg

28-UN1_Contrac_L.jpg

Chapter 29: Heredity

29-01_Karyotype_L.jpg

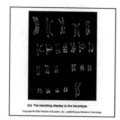

29-01cKaryotype_L.jpg

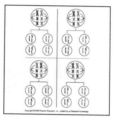

29-02_Gamete_L.jpg

29-03_Crossover_L.jpg

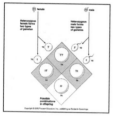

29-04_GenePhen_L.jpg

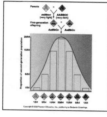

29-05_Polygenic_L.jpg

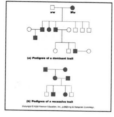

29-06_Pedigree_L.jpg

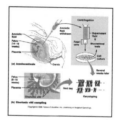

29-07_FetalTest_L.jpg

29-T01_Traits_TAB.jpg

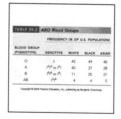

29-T02_ABO_TAB.jpg

A Brief Atlas of the Human Body, Second Edition

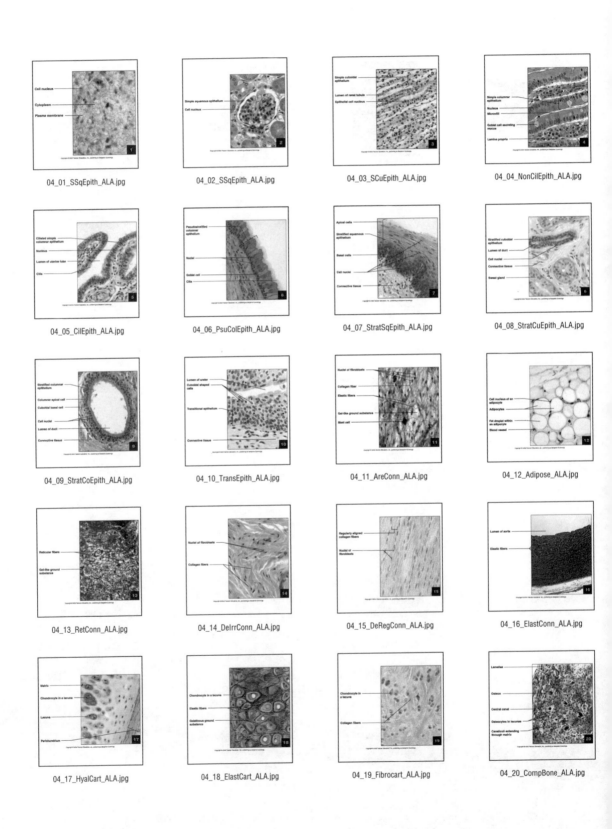

04_01_SSqEpith_ALA.jpg

04_02_SSqEpith_ALA.jpg

04_03_SCuEpith_ALA.jpg

04_04_NonCilEpith_ALA.jpg

04_05_CilEpith_ALA.jpg

04_06_PsuColEpith_ALA.jpg

04_07_StratSqEpith_ALA.jpg

04_08_StratCuEpith_ALA.jpg

04_09_StratCoEpith_ALA.jpg

04_10_TransEpith_ALA.jpg

04_11_AreConn_ALA.jpg

04_12_Adipose_ALA.jpg

04_13_RetConn_ALA.jpg

04_14_DeIrrConn_ALA.jpg

04_15_DeRegConn_ALA.jpg

04_16_ElastConn_ALA.jpg

04_17_HyalCart_ALA.jpg

04_18_ElastCart_ALA.jpg

04_19_Fibrocart_ALA.jpg

04_20_CompBone_ALA.jpg

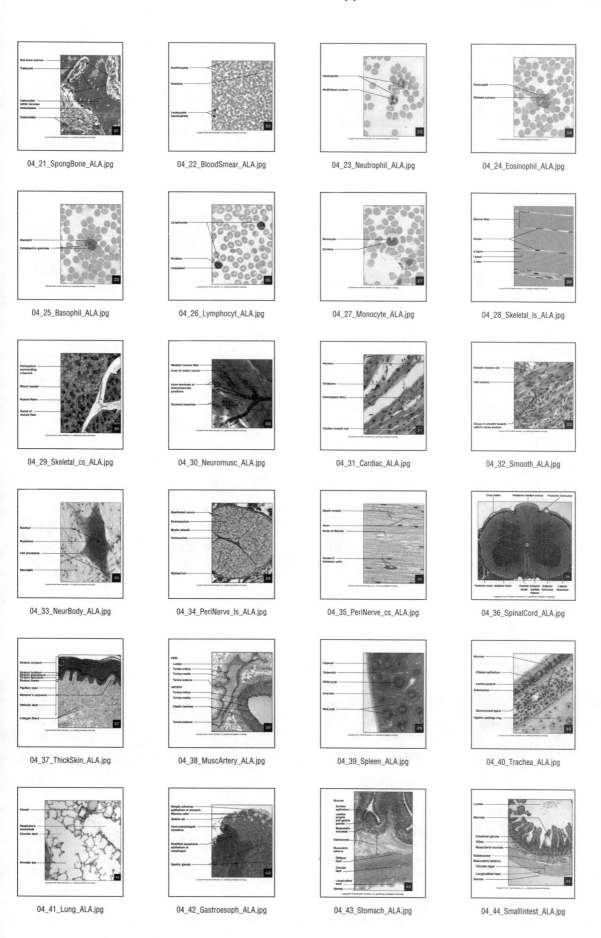

04_21_SpongBone_ALA.jpg

04_22_BloodSmear_ALA.jpg

04_23_Neutrophil_ALA.jpg

04_24_Eosinophil_ALA.jpg

04_25_Basophil_ALA.jpg

04_26_Lymphocyt_ALA.jpg

04_27_Monocyte_ALA.jpg

04_28_Skeletal_ls_ALA.jpg

04_29_Skeletal_cs_ALA.jpg

04_30_Neuromusc_ALA.jpg

04_31_Cardiac_ALA.jpg

04_32_Smooth_ALA.jpg

04_33_NeurBody_ALA.jpg

04_34_PeriNerve_ls_ALA.jpg

04_35_PeriNerve_cs_ALA.jpg

04_36_SpinalCord_ALA.jpg

04_37_ThickSkin_ALA.jpg

04_38_MuscArtery_ALA.jpg

04_39_Spleen_ALA.jpg

04_40_Trachea_ALA.jpg

04_41_Lung_ALA.jpg

04_42_Gastroesoph_ALA.jpg

04_43_Stomach_ALA.jpg

04_44_SmallIntest_ALA.jpg

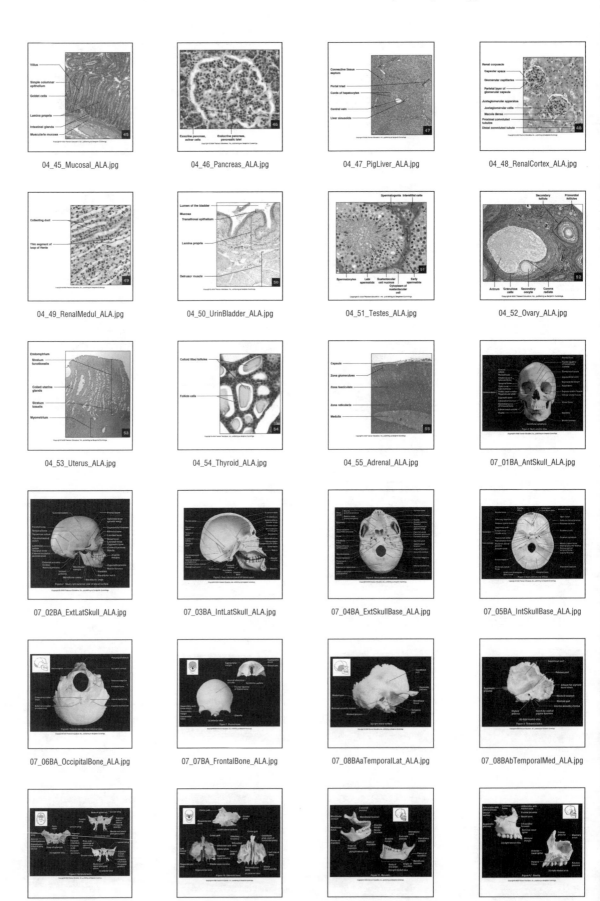

04_45_Mucosal_ALA.jpg

04_46_Pancreas_ALA.jpg

04_47_PigLiver_ALA.jpg

04_48_RenalCortex_ALA.jpg

04_49_RenalMedul_ALA.jpg

04_50_UrinBladder_ALA.jpg

04_51_Testes_ALA.jpg

04_52_Ovary_ALA.jpg

04_53_Uterus_ALA.jpg

04_54_Thyroid_ALA.jpg

04_55_Adrenal_ALA.jpg

07_01BA_AntSkull_ALA.jpg

07_02BA_ExtLatSkull_ALA.jpg

07_03BA_IntLatSkull_ALA.jpg

07_04BA_ExtSkullBase_ALA.jpg

07_05BA_IntSkullBase_ALA.jpg

07_06BA_OccipitalBone_ALA.jpg

07_07BA_FrontalBone_ALA.jpg

07_08BAaTemporalLat_ALA.jpg

07_08BAbTemporalMed_ALA.jpg

07_09BA_SphenoidBone_ALA.jpg

07_10BA_EthmoidBone_ALA.jpg

07_11BA_Mandible_ALA.jpg

07_12BA_Maxilla_ALA.jpg

07_13BA_PalatineBone_ALA.jpg

07_14BA_BonyOrbit_ALA.jpg

07_15BA_NasalCavity_ALA.jpg

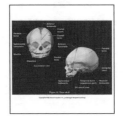

07_16BA_FetalSkull_ALA.jpg

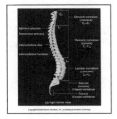

07_17BAaVertColRight_ALA.jpg

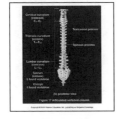

07_17BAbVertColPost_ALA.jpg

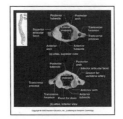

07_18BAa-bAtlas_ALA.jpg

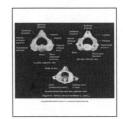

07_18BAc-eAxis_ALA.jpg

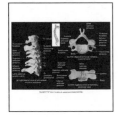

07_19BAa-cCervicalVert_ALA.jpg

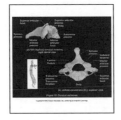

07_19BAd-eCervicalVert_ALA.jpg

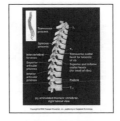

07_20BAaThoracicVert_ALA.jpg

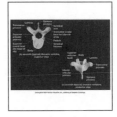

07_20BAb-cThoracicVert_ALA.jpg

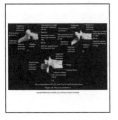

07_20BAdThoracicVert_ALA.jpg

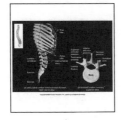

07_21BAa-bLumbarVert_ALA.jpg

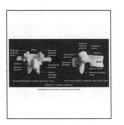

07_21BAc-dLumbarVert_ALA.jpg

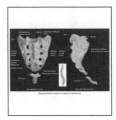

07_22BAa-bSacrumCoccyx_ALA.jpg

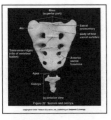

07_22BAcSacrumCoccyx_ALA.jpg

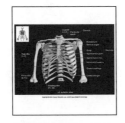

07_23BAaAntBonyThorax_ALA.jpg

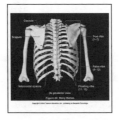

07_23BAbPosBonyThorax_ALA.jpg

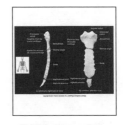

07_23BAc-dSternum_ALA.jpg

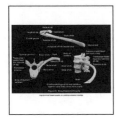

07_23BAe-fRibVertebra_ALA.jpg

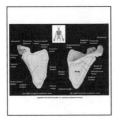

07_24BAa-bScapula_ALA.jpg

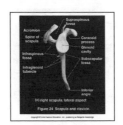

07_24BAcScapClavicl_ALA.jpg

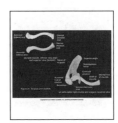

07_24BAd-eScapClavicl_ALA.jpg

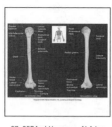

07_25BAa-bHumerus_ALA.jpg

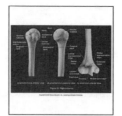

07_25BAc-eHumerus_ALA.jpg

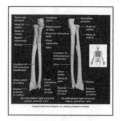

07_26BAa-bUlnaRadius_ALA.jpg

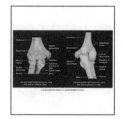

07_26BAc-dUlnaRadius_ALA.jpg

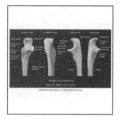

07_26eBA_Ulna_ALA.jpg

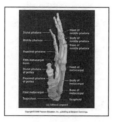

07_27BAaHand_ALA.jpg

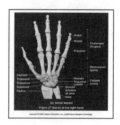

07_27BAbHand_ALA.jpg

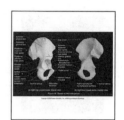

07_28BAa-bMalePelvis_ALA.jpg

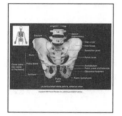

07_28BAcMalePelvis_ALA.jpg

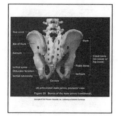

07_28BAdMalePelvis_ALA.jpg

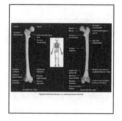

07_29BAa-bFemur_ALA.jpg

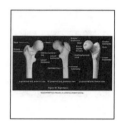

07_29BAc-eFemur_ALA.jpg

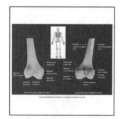

07_29BAf-gFemur_ALA.jpg

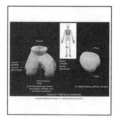

07_29BAh-iFemur_ALA.jpg

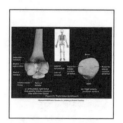

07_29BAj-kFemur_ALA.jpg

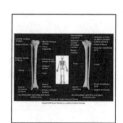

07_30BAa-bTibiaFibula_ALA.jpg

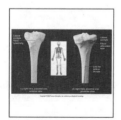

07_30BAc-dTibiaFibula_ALA.jpg

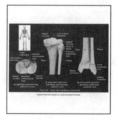

07_30BAe-gTibiaFibula_ALA.jpg

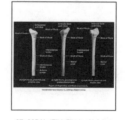

07_30BAh-jTibiaFibula_ALA.jpg

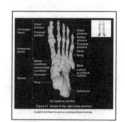

07_31BAaAnkleFoot_ALA.jpg

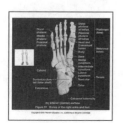

07_31BAbAnkleFoot_ALA.jpg

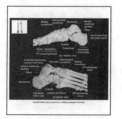

07_31BAc-dAnkleFoot_ALA.jpg

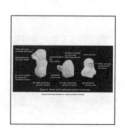

07_31BAe-gAnkleFoot_ALA.jpg

10_32BA_PosThoraxMusc_ALA.jpg

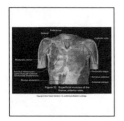

10_33BA_AntThoraxMusc_ALA.jpg

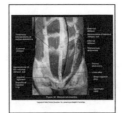

10_34BA_Abdominal_ALA.jpg

10_35BA_Shoulder_ALA.jpg

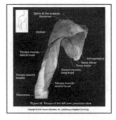

10_36BA_Triceps_ALA.jpg

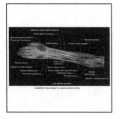

10_37aBA_ForearmWrist_ALA.jpg

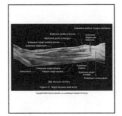

10_37bBA_ForearmWrist_ALA.jpg

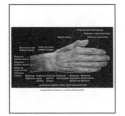

10_38BAaWristHand_ALA.jpg

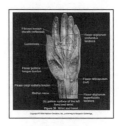

10_38BAbWristHand_ALA.jpg

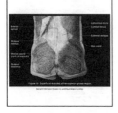

10_39BA_GlutealRegion_ALA.jpg

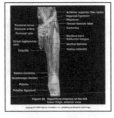

10_40BA_LowerThigh_ALA.jpg

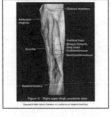

10_41BA_UpperThigh_ALA.jpg

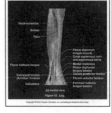

10_42BAaMedialLeg_ALA.jpg

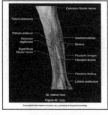

10_42BAbLateralLeg_ALA.jpg

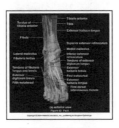

10_43BAaAntFoot_ALA.jpg

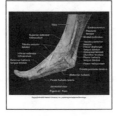

10_43BAbAntFoot_ALA.jpg

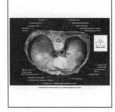

10_63BA_Diapgragm_ALA.jpg

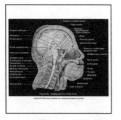

12_46BA_SagittalHead_ALA.jpg

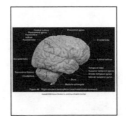

12_48BA_CerebralHemis_ALA.jpg

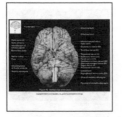

12_49BA_VentralBrain_ALA.jpg

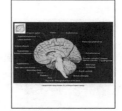

12_50BA_MidsagBrain_ALA.jpg

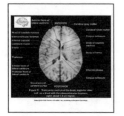

12_51BA_TransversBrain_ALA.jpg

12_52BA_Brainstem_ALA.jpg

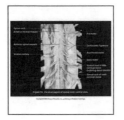

12_53BA_SpinalCord_ALA.jpg

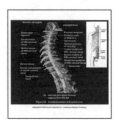

12_54BAaVertebColumn_ALA.jpg

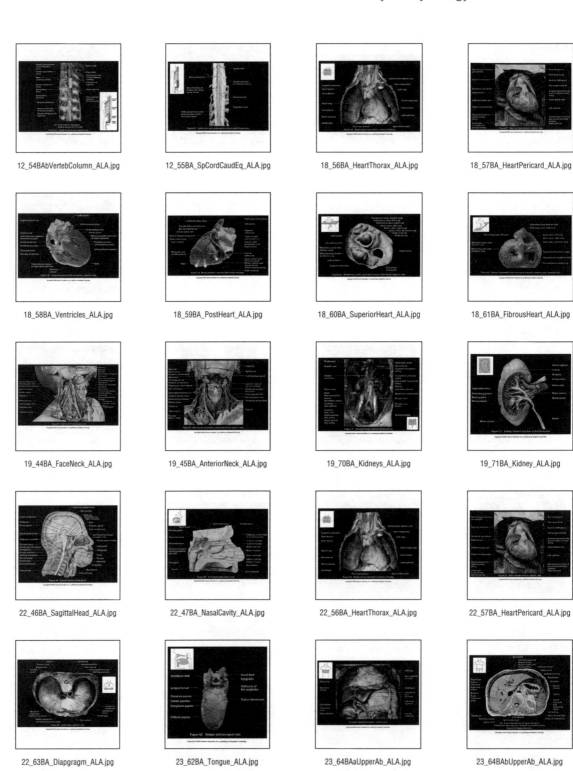

12_54BAbVertebColumn_ALA.jpg

12_55BA_SpCordCaudEq_ALA.jpg

18_56BA_HeartThorax_ALA.jpg

18_57BA_HeartPericard_ALA.jpg

18_58BA_Ventricles_ALA.jpg

18_59BA_PostHeart_ALA.jpg

18_60BA_SuperiorHeart_ALA.jpg

18_61BA_FibrousHeart_ALA.jpg

19_44BA_FaceNeck_ALA.jpg

19_45BA_AnteriorNeck_ALA.jpg

19_70BA_Kidneys_ALA.jpg

19_71BA_Kidney_ALA.jpg

22_46BA_SagittalHead_ALA.jpg

22_47BA_NasalCavity_ALA.jpg

22_56BA_HeartThorax_ALA.jpg

22_57BA_HeartPericard_ALA.jpg

22_63BA_Diapgragm_ALA.jpg

23_62BA_Tongue_ALA.jpg

23_64BAaUpperAb_ALA.jpg

23_64BAbUpperAb_ALA.jpg

23_65BA_Liver_ALA.jpg

23_66BA_LowerAb_ALA.jpg

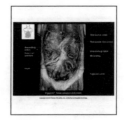

23_67BA_Smallintest_ALA.jpg

23_68BA_GastroVessels_ALA.jpg

23_69BAaStomach_ALA.jpg

23_69BAbSmallintest_ALA.jpg

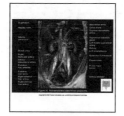

25_70BA_Kidneys_ALA.jpg

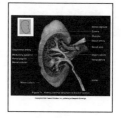

25_71BA_Kidney_ALA.jpg

27_72BA_MalePelvis_ALA.jpg

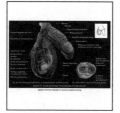

27_73BA_MaleRepro_ALA.jpg

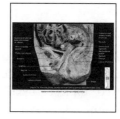

27_74BA_FemalePelvis_ALA.jpg

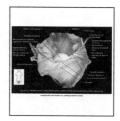

27_75BA_Uterus_ALA.jpg

InterActive Physiology®
Exercise Sheets

The *InterActive Physiology® 9-System Suite* CD-ROM, packaged free with each new copy of *Human Anatomy & Physiology*, Seventh Edition, is a successful study tool that uses detailed animations and engaging quizzes to help students advance beyond memorization to a genuine understanding of complex A&P topics. Covering nine body systems, this tutorial series encourages active learning through quizzes, activities, and review exercises, which are oriented toward making the difficult task of learning A&P more interesting and fun. This appendix contains exercise sheets, written by Dr. Shirley Whitescarver and Brian Witz, that assess students' knowledge of essential topics covered in IP. The CD-ROM body systems and their corresponding topics are listed below, followed by the IP exercise sheets.

Muscular System

Neuromuscular Junction; Sliding Filament Theory; Contraction of Whole Muscle

Nervous System I

Ion Channels; Membrane Potential; The Action Potential

Nervous System II

Ion Channels; Synaptic Transmission; Synaptic Potentials and Cellular Integration

Cardiovascular System: The Heart

Intrinsic Conduction System and Cardiac Action Potential; Cardiac Cycle; Cardiac Output

Cardiovascular System: Blood Vessels

Factors That Affect Blood Pressure; Blood Pressure Regulation; Autoregulation and Capillary Dynamics

Respiratory System

Pulmonary Ventilation; Gas Exchange; Control of Respiration

Urinary System

Glomerular Filtration; Early Filtrate Processing; Late Filtrate Processing

Fluid, Electrolyte, and Acid-Base Balance

Introduction to Body Fluids; Water Homeostasis; Acid-Base Homeostasis

Endocrine System

Endocrine System Review; Biochemistry, Secretion and Transport of Hormones; The Actions of Hormones on Target Cells; The Hypothalamic-Pituitary Axis; Response to Stress

Digestive System

Anatomy Review; Control of the Digestive System; Motility; Secretion; Digestion and Absorption

Muscular System:
Neuromuscular Junction

1. What insulates each muscle cell? _____

2. Synaptic vesicles in the axon terminal of a motor neuron contain what

   neurotranmitter? _____

3. An action potential in the axon terminal of a motor neuron opens what type of ion

   channels? _____

4. By what means of membrane transport does the neurotransmitter leave the

   axon terminal? _____

5. Binding of neurotransmitter to the receptors on the motor endplate open

   what type of ion channels? _____

6. Opening of these channels leads to _____ of the motor endplate.

7. How is the neurotransmitter removed from the synaptic cleft?

8. As a result of question 6, an action potential is propagated along the

   _____ of the muscle cell and down the _____

   into the cell.

9. The result of this action potential releases what ion from the terminal cisternae?

   _____

10. a. What effect did molecule "X" in the quiz have on the muscle contraction?

    b. Explain its mechanism of action.

    c. What drug did molecule "X" act like? _____

11. a. What effect did molecule "Y" have on the muscle contraction?

   b. Explain its mechanism of action.

   c. What drug did molecule "Y" act like? _____

12. a. What effect did molecule "Z" have on the muscle contraction?

   b. Explain its mechanism of action.

   c. What drug did molecule "Z" act like? _____

Muscular System:
Sliding Filament Theory

1. a. The thick filament is composed of what molecule? _____

   b. Flexing the head of this molecule provides what is known as the

      _____.

2. The cross bridge (myosin head) contains binding sites for what two molecules?

   a.

   b.

3. Three molecules make up the thin filament.

   a. Which molecule has a binding site for myosin cross bridges? _____

   b. Which molecule covers this binding site? _____

   c. Which molecule has a binding site for calcium ions? _____

4. What molecule must bind to the cross bridge in order for it to disconnect with

   actin? _____

5. Hydrolysis of the molecule in question 4 returns the myosin molecule to the

   _____ confirmation.

6. Binding of the cross bridges sequentially prevents _____ of the

   thin filament.

7. Name three roles for ATP in the contraction of muscle.

   a.

   b.

   c.

8. What molecule is connected to the Z line? _____

9. Which of the following shorten during contraction? (may be more than one)

   a. Thin filament

   b. Sarcomere

   c. H zone

   d. Thick filament

10. a. What is the name of the condition in which muscles become rigid after

    death? _____

    b. What is this condition due to?

Muscular System:
Contraction of Whole Muscle

1. Which of the following contract in an all or none fashion?

   a. Whole muscle   b. Single muscle fiber

2. The development of tension in a muscle, in response to a stimulus above

   threshold, is called a _____.

3. Identify the three phases of a muscle twitch from the following definitions:

   a. Sarcomeres shorten _____

   b. Sarcomeres return to resting length _____

   c. Sarcomeres at resting length _____

4. a. Temporal summation results from:

   b. In temporal summation, you must _____ (↑or↓) the time interval between

      stimuli.

5. Below is a list of the five phases of temporal summation. Put in the correct order
   and describe each stage.

Order	Stage	Description
	Fatigue	
	Incomplete tetanus	
	Treppe	
	Complete tetanus	
	Temporal summation	

6. In the Motor Unit Summation section, how many motor units were required to lift
   the weights when:

   a. the weight was 160? _____

   b. the weight was 80? _____

7. In the next lab simulation, what was:

    a. the threshold stimulus? _____ V

    b. voltage when recruitment was obvious? _____ V

    c. voltage when all motor units were recruited? _____ V

8. a. In the Length-Tension Relationship experiment, at what degree of stretch was the maximum tension developed? _____

    b. What would congestive heart failure be an example of?

    _____

Nervous System I: Ion Channels

1. What structures in the cell membrane function as ion channels?

2. Ion channels are selective for specific ions. What three characteristics of the ions are important for this selectivity?

   a.

   b.

   c.

3. Channels can be classified as either active or passive channels. A sodium channel

   that is always open would be classified as a/an _____ channel.

4. Would sodium ions move into or out of the neuron through these channels?

   _____

5. Voltage-gated potassium channels open at what voltage? _____ mV

6. Acetylcholine (ACh) and GABA are neurotransmitters that open chemically-gated channels. What ions pass into the cell when these channels are activated?

   a. ACh: _____ ions

   b. GABA: _____ ions

7. Ion channels are regionally located and functionally unique. List all the areas on the neuron and the type of potential dependent on the following types of ion channels:

Channels	Areas on the neuron	Type of potential
Passive		
Chemically-gated		
Voltage-gated		

8. From the quiz, place an "X" by the characteristics of voltage-gated sodium channels.

   _____ Always open

   _____ Found along the axon

   _____ Important for action potential

   _____ Opened and closed by gates

   _____ Found on the dendrites and cell bodies

   _____ Important for resting membrane potential

9. Name two channels (active or passive) through which chloride ions could pass into the cell.

   a.

   b.

10. a. The Japanese puffer fish contains a deadly toxin (tetrodotoxin). What type of channels does this toxin block? _____

   b. What potential would this toxin block? _____

   c. What specifically would cause death? _____

Nervous System I: Membrane Potential

1. Record the intracellular and extracellular concentrations of the following ions (mM/L):

	Intracellular	Extracellular
Sodium (Na$^+$)		
Potassium (K$^+$)		
Chloride (Cl$^-$)		

2. Excitable cells, like neurons, are more permeable to _____ than to _____ .

3. How would the following alterations affect the membrane permeability to K$^+$? Use arrows to indicate the change in permeability.

   a. An increase in the number of passive K$^+$ channels _____

   b. Opening of voltage-gated K$^+$ channels _____

   c. Closing of voltage-gated K$^+$ channels _____

4. a. What acts as a chemical force that pushes K$^+$ out of the cell? _____

   b. What force tends to pull K$^+$ back into the cell? _____

5. When the two forces listed above are equal and opposite in a cell permeable only to

   K$^+$, this is called the _____ potential for K$^+$ which is _____ mV.

6. In an excitable cell, also permeable to Na$^+$ and Cl$^-$, the gradients mentioned

   in question 4 would both tend to move Na$^+$ _____ the cell.

7. Would the gradients in question 4 promote or oppose the movement of Cl$^-$ into the cell?

   a.

   b.

8. Since the neuron is permeable to Na$^+$ as well as K$^+$, the resting membrane poten-

   tial is not equal to the equilibrium potential for K$^+$, instead it is _____ mV.

9. What opposes the movement (leakage) of Na^+ and K^+ ions?

    _____

10. What will happen to the resting membrane potential of an excitable cell if: (Write pos or neg to indicate which way the membrane potential would change.)

    a. ↑ extracellular fluid concentration of K^+ _____

    b. ↓ extracellular fluid concentration of K^+ _____

    c. ↑ extracellular fluid concentration of Na^+ _____

    d. ↑ number of passive Na^+ channels _____

    e. open voltage-gated K^+ channels _____

    f. open voltage-gated Na^+ channels _____

Nervous System I: The Action Potential

1. a. The action potential changes the membrane potential from _____ mV (resting)

   to _____ mV and back again to the resting membrane potential.

   b. This results from a change in membrane permeability first to _____ then to

   _____ due to the opening of what type of ion channels? _____

2. a. Where is the density of voltage-gated Na$^+$ channels the greatest?

   _____

   b. What areas of the neuron generate signals that open these voltage-gated

   channels? _____

   c. Opening of these channels causes the membrane to _____ (voltage

   change).

3. a. If the membrane reaches the trigger point, known as _____, what

   electrical potential will be generated? _____

   b. During the depolarization phase, voltage-gated _____ channels open and

   _____ enters the cell.

4. What are the two processes that stop the potential from rising above +30 mV?

   a.

   b.

5. a. The opening of voltage-gated K$^+$ channels cause the membrane to

   _____.

   b. Does K$^+$ move into or out of the cell? _____

   c. If the membrane potential becomes more negative than −70 mV, this is called

   _____.

   d. This potential is caused by what characteristic of K$^+$ permeability? _____

   _____.

6. a. After an action potential, the neuron cannot generate another action potential

   because _____ channels are inactive. This period is called the _____

   period.

   b. During the _____ period, the cell can generate another action

   potential but only if the membrane is _____ (more or less) depolarized.

7. a. Conduction velocity along the axon is increased by what two characteristics?

   1. _____

   2. _____

   b. Conduction along a myelinated axon is called _____

   conduction.

8. a. Name the disease whose symptoms include loss of vision and increasing muscle

   weakness: _____ (from the quiz section)

   b. What does this disease destroy? _____

   c. How does this stop an action potential?

Nervous System II: Ion Channels

1. List four neurotransmitters that bind to ion channels; these neurotransmitters

   are called _____-acting neurotransmitters.

   a.

   b.

   c.

   d.

2. a. The binding of ACh opens ion channels in the dendrites or cell body that

   permits both _____ and _____ to move through them.

   b. Which ion would move into the cell? _____ out of the cell? _____

   c. Which ion has the greatest electrochemical gradient? _____

   d. The net movement of these two ions would do what to the cell? _____

   e. This would be called an _____ postsynaptic potential,

   or _____.

3. a. An inhibitory postsynaptic potential (IPSP) causes a neuron to _____.

   b. An example of a neurotransmitter that causes an IPSP is _____.

   c. What type of ions move into the cell in response to this neurotransmitter?

   _____.

4. a. Norepinephrine binds to a receptor that is separate from the ion channel.

   This is known as a/an _____ -acting neurotransmitter.

   b. Norepinephrine is known as the _____ messenger.

   c. The receptor is coupled to the ion channel by a _____.

5. a. This activates an enzyme which induces the production of a _____

     messenger.

    b. An intracellular enzyme is activated and _____ the ion channel.

    c. As a result of this sequence of events, what channels are closed? _____

    d. What does this do to the neuron? _____

6. Name three neurotransmitters that can only act indirectly.

    a.

    b.

    c.

7. Which of the four neurotransmitters mentioned in question 1 can also act indirectly?

    a.

    b.

    c.

8. Which one of the four neurotransmitters mentioned in question 1 can only act

     directly? _____

Nervous System II: Synaptic Transmission

1. What channels in the presynaptic neuron open up in response to an action

   potential? _____

2. The presence of what ion inside the cell causes the synaptic vesicles to

   fuse with the membrane? _____

3. a. What is the name for the chemicals stored in the synaptic vesicles? _____

   b. What do these chemicals diffuse across? _____

   c. Where do these chemicals bind to receptors? _____

4. What type of gated channels do these chemicals open? _____

5. Name two ways these chemicals can be removed from the synaptic cleft.

   a.

   b.

6. The response on the postsynaptic cell depends on two factors:

   a.

   b.

7. Name the two types of cholinergic receptors and indicate where these are found.

Type	Found
	excitatory: inhibitory:

8. Indicate where the following three adrenergic receptors are found:

α1	
β1	
β2	

9. Autonomic nerves innervate what three things?

10. The most common excitatory neurotransmitter in the CNS is _____.

11. Two major inhibitory neurotransmitters in the CNS are:

    a.

    b.

12. Name a drug that alters synaptic transmission in the following ways:

    a. blocks the action of the neurotransmitter at the postsynaptic membrane

       _____.

    b. blocks the reuptake of the neurotransmitter at the presynaptic membrane

       _____.

    c. blocks the release of the neurotransmitter _____ and

       _____.

Nervous System II:
Synaptic Potentials and Cellular Integration

1. Enhanced postsynaptic potentials are due to increased _____ entering the

   terminal as a result of _____.

2. Presynaptic inhibition is due to decreased _____ entering the terminal as

   a result of _____.

3. a. Synaptic potentials are also known as _____ potentials.

   b. They _____ as they travel away from the synapse.

4. a. Increasing the number of action potentials on an axon in a given period

      of time would cause _____ summation.

   b. Increasing the number of synapses from different neurons would cause

      _____ summation.

5. The magnitude of the EPSPs may be reduced (thus affecting their ability to generate

   and their action potential) by adding _____

   potentials, or _____s.

6. Inhibitory synapses would have the maximum effect if located where?

   _____

7. From the quiz, how many impulses did it take to cause an action potential:

   a. From the axon the furthest away from the cell body? _____

   b. From the axon located on the cell body? _____

8. Pulses from how many neurons were required to stimulate the postsynaptic

   neuron? _____

9. Compare action potentials and synaptic potentials:

	Action Potential	**Synaptic Potential**
Function		
Depolarization/ hyperpolarizations		
Magnitude		

Cardiovascular System, the Heart: Intrinsic Conduction System and Cardiac Action Potential

1. List the functions for the following parts of the intrinsic conduction system:

   a. SA node _____

   b. AV node _____

   c. AV bundle (bundle of His) _____

   d. Purkinje fibers _____

2. On an ECG, what do the following wave forms reflect?

   a. P wave _____

   b. QRS complex _____

   c. T wave _____

3. A left bundle branch block would have a wider than normal _____.

4. How do the waves of depolarization, generated by the autorhythmic cells spread to the muscle cells?

5. Name the three channels essential for generating an action potential. Which way do the ions move? (Circle *into* or *out of*)

   a. _____ channels into / out of the cell

   b. _____ channels into / out of the cell

   c. _____ channels into / out of the cell

6. The pacemaker potential is due to a _____ efflux of _____ ions compared

   to a normal influx of _____ ions.

7. Threshold for the SA node is at _____ mV. What channels open causing

   depolarization? _____

8. The reversal of membrane potential causes the _____ channels to open

   causing the _____ of the membrane.

9. Gap junctions allow what cations to pass into the cardiac contractile cells causing the opening of voltage gated sodium channels?

10. State the voltage-gated channels responsible for the following stages of the action potential in cardiac contractile cells.

   a. Depolarization _____

   b. Plateau _____

   c. Repolarization _____

Cardiovascular System, the Heart: Cardiac Cycle

1. Valves open in response to _____ on their two sides.

2. List the chambers/vessels that the four valves connect:

Chamber		Chamber/Vessel
	Pulmonary Semilunar	
	Aortic Semilunar	
	Tricuspid	
	Bicuspid	

3. a. Ventricular filling occurs during _____ ventricular _____.

   b. Blood flows through the _____ or _____ valves into the ventricles.

4. During Ventricular Systole, what closes the AV valves?

5. During Ventricular Systole, what opens the semilunar valves?

6. During Isovolumetric Relaxation, what closes the semilunar valves?

7. During Isovolumetric Relaxation, what opens the AV valves?

8. Why is hypertension hard on the heart?

9. Looking at the ventricular volume graph, the stroke volume is approximately how

   many ml? _____

10. During the four phases listed below, state whether the AV and semilunar valves are open or closed:

	AV valves	Semilunar valves
Ventricular Filling		
Isovolumetric Contraction		
Ventricular Ejection		
Isovolumetric Relaxation		

Cardiovascular System, the Heart: Cardiac Output

1. Define Cardiac Output (CO).

2. Write the equation for CO.

3. Define Stroke Volume (SV).

4. Write the equation for SV.

5. Write the normal values (include correct units) for the following:

   a. HR (heart rate) = _____

   b. SV (stroke volume) = _____

   c. EDV (end diastolic volume) = _____

   d. ESV (end systolic volume) = _____

6. Given the values for HR and SV, calculate cardiac output:

   CO =

7. Explain how the following factors affect HR, SV, and CO by placing arrows (↑, ↓, or ↔ for no change) under them.

	HR	SV	CO
a. ↑ SNS	___	___	___
b. ↑ Venous return	___	___	___
c. Exercise	___	___	___
d. ↑ Calcium	___	___	___
e. ↓ HR	___	___	___

8. Why would stroke volume increase with an increase in the sympathetic nervous system or an increase in calcium?

9. Why would stroke volume increase when heart rate slows down?

10. If stroke volume is 75 ml/beat and heart rate is 80 beats/min, how many of the soda bottles would equal the correct volume (from the quiz)? _____

Cardiovascular System, Blood Vessels: Factors That Affect Blood Pressure

1. What are the three main factors that influence total peripheral resistance (TPR)?

   a.

   b.

   c.

2. Name three hormones that act as vasoconstrictors.

   a.

   b.

   c.

3. Name two hormones that directly increase blood volume.

   a.

   b.

4. Track the effect on blood pressure by reducing venous return. Go through all the steps.

   ↓ VR →

5. Categorize the following into:

   A. Factors that increase blood pressure

   B. Factors that decrease blood pressure

   ____ ↓ arterial diameter   ____ ↑ total vessel length

   ____ ↑ vessel elasticity   ____ ↓ plasma epinephrine

   ____ ↓ blood volume   ____ ↓ plasma angiotensin

   ____ ↑ stroke volume   ____ ↑ plasma ADH

   ____ ↓ blood viscosity   ____ ↑ vagus nerve stimulation

   ____ ↑ blood volume   ____ ↑ sympathetic stimulation

Use arrows in the spaces for questions 6 through 10.

6. A ↓ in hematocrit will result in ____ blood viscosity and ____ blood pressure.

7. An ↑ in fatty tissue will result in ____ total vessel length and an ____ blood pressure.

8. Arteriosclerosis will result in ____ vessel elasticity and an ____ blood pressure.

9. Excessive sweating will result in a short-term ____ in blood volume and a ____ in blood pressure.

10. An ↑ in epinephrine will result in ____ vessel diameter and an ____ in blood pressure.

Cardiovascular System, Blood Vessels: Blood Pressure Regulation

1. a. Short-term mechanisms for regulating blood pressure include regulating what three things?

    1.

    2.

    3.

    b. Long-term mechanisms will regulate _____.

2. Two major arterial baroreceptors are located where?

    a.

    b.

3. Using up and down arrows, show the effect of increased blood pressure (BP) on the impulses sent to the brain, the effect on the parasympathetic (PNS) and sympathetic (SNS) nervous systems and the resulting change in blood pressure.

    ↑BP → _____ impulses → _____ PNS and _____ SNS → _____ BP

4. As a result of these changes in the PNS and SNS, list two effects on the heart and one on blood vessels.

    Heart:

    Blood vessels:

5. Similar to question 3, show the effect of decreasing blood pressure.

    ↑BP → _____ impulses → _____ PNS and _____ SNS → _____ BP

6. In addition to effects on the heart and blood vessels, what hormones were

    released from the adrenal gland? _____ and

    _____

7. a. What cells in the kidney monitor low blood pressure? _____

    b. What enzyme is released as a result of low blood pressure? _____

    c. What does this enzyme act on in the blood? _____

8. Name two effects of Angiotensin II.

    a. _____

    b. _____

9. a. The main effect of aldosterone is: _____

    b. How does this increase blood volume? _____

10. a. What other hormone will increase water reabsorption from the kidney?

       _____

    b. What is the major stimulus for this hormone? _____

Cardiovascular System, Blood Vessels:
Autoregulation and Capillary Dynamics

1. a. What regulates the flow of blood into true capillaries? _____

   b. If all sphincters are closed, blood is _____ to the venules through

      _____ capillaries.

2. Use arrows to show whether high or low levels of the following would cause the feeder arterioles to dilate and the sphincters to relax:

   a. O_2 _____   c. pH _____

   b. CO_2 _____   d. nutrients _____

3. Physical factors also act as regulatory stimuli. How would the following affect arterioles?

   a. Decreased blood pressure _____

   b. Increased blood pressure _____

4. Name three structural characteristics of capillaries that allow for passage of materials out of the capillaries.

   a.

   b.

   c.

5. a. Diffusion accounts for the passage of _____.

   b. Non-lipid soluble molecules move by _____.

   c. Water-soluble solutes, such as amino acids and sugars, move through

      _____.

6. Bulk fluid flows cause _____ at the arterial end and _____ at

   the venous end of the capillary.

7. a. In a capillary, what is equivalent to hydrostatic pressure?

    b. Why is hydrostatic pressure low in the interstitial fluid?

    c. Net hydrostatic pressure tends to move fluid _____ the capillary.

8. a. Osmotic (or Colloid Osmotic) pressure in the capillaries is _____

    compared to the interstitium.

    b. Net osmotic pressure tends to move fluid _____ the capillaries.

9. Given a net hydrostatic pressure of 34 mmHg and a net osmotic pressure

    of 22 mmHg, the force favoring filtration would equal _____ mmHg.

10. Indicate which of the following move through the capillary walls by diffusion and
    which move through fenestrations and/or clefts:

    a. Butter:

    b. Fish:

    c. Cola:

    d. Potatoes:

Respiratory System: Pulmonary Ventilation

1. a. The relationship between pressure and volume is known as _____ Law.

   b. Indicate the relationship with arrows below

      1. ↑ volume → ____ pressure

      2. ↓ volume → ____ pressure

2. Mark "I" for the muscles that control inspiration and "E" for the muscles that control forceful expiration.

   a. ____ Diaphragm

   b. ____ Internal intercostals

   c. ____ External oblique and rectus abdominus

   d. ____ External intercostals

3. Intrapulmonary pressure ____s (↑ or ↓) during inspiration.

4. a. What pressure is always negative and helps to keep the lungs inflated?

      _____ pressure

   b. It is most negative during _____.

5. a. If transpulmonary pressure equals zero, what will happen to the lungs?

      _____

   b. This is known as a _____.

6. a. When the bronchiole constricts, what will happen to resistance?

      ____ (use arrows)

   b. To airflow? ____ (use arrows)

7. Name two other important factors that play roles in ventilation:

   a.

   b.

For questions 8 through 10, fill in constrict *or* dilate, *then* ↑ *and* ↓ *arrows:*

8. Histamine will _____ bronchioles → ____ resistance → ____ airflow

9. Epinephrine will _____ bronchioles → ____ resistance → ____ airflow

10. Acetylcholine will _____ bronchioles → ____ resistance → ____ airflow

11. Fibrosis will (↑ or ↓) ___ compliance making it _____ to inflate the lungs.

12. A decrease in surfactant will result in a ____ (↑ or ↓) in compliance.

Respiratory System: Gas Exchange

1. The atmosphere is a mixture of gases. Write down the percentages for:

   a. O_2 _____

   b. CO_2 _____

   c. N_2 _____

   d. H_2O _____

2. Calculate the partial pressures of the following gases at both atmospheric pressures:

               760 mmHg   747 mmHg

   a. O_2 _____ _____

   b. CO_2 _____ _____

   c. N_2 _____ _____

   d. H_2O _____ _____

3. What is the atmospheric pressure on the top of Mt. Whitney? _____

4. Calculate the partial pressure of O_2 on the top of Mt. Whitney. _____ mmHg

5. a. Why does more CO_2 than O_2 dissolve in liquid when both gases are at the same pressure?

   b. Name the law that explains this. _____

6. Efficient external respiration depends on three main factors; list them.

   a.

   b.

   c.

7. What three factors cause the partial pressures of gases in the alveoli to differ from pressures in the atmosphere?

   a.

   b.

   c.

8. When airflow is restricted so that the partial pressure of O_2 is low and CO_2 is high, what happens to the:

   a. arterioles? _____

   b. bronchioles? _____

9. Internal respiration depends on three factors; list them.

   a.

   b.

   c.

10. The planet Pneumo has a total atmospheric pressure of 900 mmHg. Oxygen and carbon dioxide each constitute 30% of the atmosphere.

    a. What is the partial pressure of oxygen on the planet Pneumo? _____

    b. Which gas would be found in the highest concentration in your blood?

Respiratory System: Control of Respiration

1. a. Where is the inspiratory center located in the medulla?

   _____

   b. Where is the expiratory center located in the medulla?

   _____

2. What modifies these medullary centers?

   a.

   b.

3. What is the most important stimulus controlling ventilation? _____

4. What ion directly stimulates the central chemoreceptors? _____

5. Arterial P_{O_2} must drop below what to stimulate the peripheral

   chemoreceptors? _____

6. If a person hyperventilates, what will happen to the following in the blood?

   a. P_{CO_2} _____

   b. pH _____

7. If a person hypoventilates, what will happen to the following in the blood?

   a. P_{O_2} _____

   b. P_{CO_2} _____

8. a. What does lung hyperinflation stimulate? _____

   b. The effect on inspiration is _____.

   c. What is this reflex called? _____

9. Dust, smoke, and noxious fumes will stimulate receptors in airways.

   a. Name the receptors. _____

   b. Explain the protective reflexes.

10. Name four of the six factors that probably increase ventilation during exercise.

a.

b.

c.

d.

Urinary System: Glomerular Filtration

1. What force drives filtration at the glomerulus? _____

2. Glomerular filtration is a process of _____ driven

   by the _____ of the blood.

3. Common components of the filtrate are divided into four categories on the
   CD program. These include:

   a.

   b.

   c.

   d.

4. Blood pressure in the glomerulus is about _____ mmHg.

5. What two pressures oppose filtration and what are their values?

   a.

   b.

6. What is the normal net filtration pressure? _____ mmHg

7. With a glomerular filtration rate of 125 ml/min, how much plasma would

   be filtered per day? _____ in 24 hours

8. In an exercising individual the afferent arteriole will <u>dilate</u> or <u>constrict</u>
   (circle one) to avoid excess fluid loss.

9. Two mechanisms that provide autoregulatory control over renal processes include:

   a.

   b.

10. High osmolarity (or high Na^+ and Cl^-) in the ascending loop of Henle will

    cause afferent arterioles to <u>dilate</u> or <u>constrict</u> (circle one) by releasing

    _____.

11. In periods of extreme stress, the sympathetic nervous system will override autoregulation. An increase in sympathetic flow to the kidney will result in what two important effects that will aid maintenance of blood pressure?

    a.

    b.

Urinary System: Early Filtrate Processing

1. What are the two reabsorption pathways through the tubular cell barrier?

   a.

   b.

2. How can we cause water to diffuse from the lumen into the interstitial space?

3. Transport of what ion could cause the diffusion in question 2?

4. Summarize reabsorption in the proximal tubule.

5. What percent of the filtrate is reabsorbed in the proximal tubule? _____%

6. The simple squamous cells of the thin descending loop are permeable to

   _____ but impermeable to _____.

7. The ascending limb of the loop of Henle is permeable to

   _____ but impermeable to _____.

8. What is the role of the loop of Henle?

9. What is the role of the vasa recta?

10. From the quiz section, what does furosemide do?

11. If you increase furosemide, what would happen to the following? (↑ or ↓)

    a. ____ $Na^+/K^+/2Cl^-$ cotransport

    b. ____ $Na^+/K^+/2Cl^-$ retained in tubule

    c. ____ interstitial osmolarity

    d. ____ water reabsorption in descending limb

    e. ____ filtrate and volume flow

    f. ____ urine output

    g. ____ loss of body water and electrolytes

Urinary System: Late Filtrate Processing

1. Name the two types of cells in the late distal tubules and cortical collecting ducts and describe their function.

   a.

   b.

2. a. Aldosterone is stimulated by an increase or decrease in what ions?

   1. _____   2. _____

   b. What does aldosterone increase in the basolateral membrane?

3. What does antidiuretic hormone (ADH) increase in the luminal membrane?

4. In dehydration and overhydration, what would be the levels of:

   a. ADH? _____ dehydration _____ overhydration (↑ or ↓)

   b. Aldosterone? _____ dehydration _____ overhydration (↑ or ↓)

5. Describe what moves out of the tubule and what the osmolarity would be in the following nephron segments:

   a. Proximal tubule   _____ moves out   _____ mOsm

   b. Descending limb   _____ moves out   _____ mOsm

   c. Ascending limb   _____ moves out   _____ mOsm

   d. Late distal tubule   _____ moves out   _____ mOsm

6. a. By the medullary collecting duct, only _____% of the filtrate remains.

   b. Under the following conditions, report the levels of ADH and subsequent urine osmolarity and flow rate:

Hydration	ADH	Urine Osmolarity	Urine Volume
Normal			
Dehydration			
Overhydration			

7. a. Urine with a "high normal osmolarity" and containg RBC's and protein

   would indicate: _____

   b. Urine with a very high osmolartiy and glucose would indicate: _____

   c. Urine with a very low osmolarity and high volume would indicate:

   _____

8. An increase in plasma potassium levels would lead to what changes in the following? (↑ or ↓)

   a. _____ Aldosterone levels

   b. _____ Potassium excretion

   c. _____ Sodium excretion

   d. _____ Interstitial osmolarity

   e. _____ Urine volume

Fluid, Electrolyte, and Acid-Base Balance: Introduction to Body Fluids

1. a. Where are fluids absorbed? _____

   b. Where are excess fluids and electrolytes lost? _____

2. Name four of the six functions of water.

   a.

   b.

   c.

   d.

3. a. The amount of water in the body depends on the amount of _____.

   b. From the CD, list the person with the highest and lowest percentage of water and give the percentage.

   1. Highest _____   _____%

   2. Lowest _____   _____%

4. List the three fluid compartments and the percentage of total body water in each.

   a. _____   _____%

   b. _____   _____%

   c. _____   _____%

5. Give an example of each of the following solutes:

   a. Ions/electrolytes _____

   b. Colloids _____

   c. Nonelectrolytes _____

6. List the major extracellular and intracellular cations and anions

   a. Extracellular cations: _____   anions: _____

   b. Intracellular cations: _____   anions: _____

7. Within a fluid compartment, the total number of _____

   must be equal to the total number of _____.

8. Name four of the seven functions given for electrolytes:

   a.

   b.

   c.

   d.

9. Osmosis: When more solute particles are added to one side of a container with a semipermeable membrane, which way will the water move?

10. What happens to a patient's red blood cells when the following solutions are given?

   a. Hypotonic solution _____

   b. Hypertonic solution _____

   c. Isotonic solution _____

Fluid, Electrolyte, and Acid-Base Balance: Water Homeostasis

1. Below are listed the four examples of disturbances in water homeostasis. Indicate if there is an increase (↑), decrease (↓), or no change (↔) in volume and osmolarity. Give an example of each.

Disturbance	Volume	Osmolarity	Example
Hypervolemia			
Hypovolemia			
Overhydration			
Dehydration			

2. What are the four primary mechanisms to regulate fluid homeostasis?

   a.

   b.

   c.

   d.

3. Answer the following questions on antidiuretic hormone (ADH):

   a. What is the major stimulus? _____

   b. What is the direct effect of the hormone? _____

   c. What effect will this have on plasma volume and osmolarity?

   _____

   d. What effect will this have on urine volume and osmolarity?

   _____

4. List three ways dehydration leads to increased thirst:

   a.

   b.

   c.

5. Answer the following questions on the Renin-Angiotensin-Aldosterone System.

   a. What enzyme is released from the kidney in response to decreased blood

   pressure? _____

   b. What enzyme converts angiotensin I to angiotensin II? _____

   c. What are two effects of angiotensin II?

   d. How does aldosterone cause more sodium to be reabsorbed in the kidney?

   e. As a result, what happens to blood volume and blood pressure? _____

6. a. A decrease in blood volume and blood pressure will lead to a/an _____

   in the sympathetic nervous system (SNS).

   b. This will result in a decrease ($\downarrow$), and increase ($\uparrow$), or no change ($\leftrightarrow$) in the following:

   1. _____ Afferent arteriolar constriction

   2. _____ Blood flow to the glomerulus

   3. _____ Urine loss

   4. _____ Renin release

7. a. Diabetes insipidus is due to _____.

   b. What will happen to the following?

   1. _____ Urine output

   2. _____ Plasma sodium

   3. _____ Plasma osmolarity

   4. _____ Thirst

Fluid, Electrolyte, and Acid-Base Balance: Acid-Base Homeostasis

1. List the three important buffer systems in the body:

   a.

   b.

   c.

2. Write the equation showing the relationship of CO_2 and H_2O levels with bicarbonate and hydrogen ion levels:

   $CO_2 + H_2O \leftrightarrow$ _____ $\leftrightarrow$ _____

3. A decrease in respiration will result in _____ CO_2 and will shift the equation

   to the _____, resulting in an increase in _____ ions, making the plasma

   more _____.

4. When body pH is decreased, what are the three compensatory renal mechanisms to restore pH?

   a.

   b.

   c.

5. a. Normal arterial pH is _____ to _____.

   b. What is the pH in alkalosis? _____

   c. What is the pH in acidosis? _____

6. With ketoacidosis, show what happens to the following:

   a. _____ Plasma pH

   b. _____ (*Left* or *right*) shift of the carbonic acid/bicarbonate system

   c. _____ Bicarbonate levels

   d. _____ Respiratory rate

   e. _____ Renal excretion of H^+

7. With metabolic alkalosis, show what happens to the following:

    a. _____ Plasma pH

    b. _____ (*Left* or *right*) shift

    c. _____ Bicarbonate levels

    d. _____ Respiratory rate

    e. _____ Renal excretion of bicarbonate

8. With respiratory acidosis, show what happens to the following:

    a. _____ Plasma pH

    b. _____ (*Left* or *right*) shift

    c. _____ Respiratory rate

    d. _____ Renal excretion of bicarbonate

    e. _____ Renal excretion of H^+

9. With respiratory alkalosis, show what happens to the following:

    a. _____ Plasma pH

    b. _____ (*Left* or *right*) shift

    c. _____ Respiratory rate

    d. _____ Renal excretion of bicarbonate

    e. _____ Renal excretion of H^+

Endocrine System: Endocrine System Review

1. Hormones act at specific target organs because these organs contain _____ specific for the hormones.

2. Growth hormone, secreted by the _____ _____ gland, stimulates growth of bones and muscle by activating intermediary proteins called _____.

3. _____ (hormone) from the anterior pituitary stimulates secretion of cortisol from the _____ _____ (gland). The anterior pituitary consists of _____ tissue.

4. The parafollicular or C-cells of the _____ gland produce _____, a peptide hormone that lowers plasma calcium levels.

5. Hormones secreted by the pancreatic islets of the pancreas include _____ from the α cells and _____ from the β cells. Which of these hormones raise blood glucose levels?

6. Specialized muscle cells in the atria of the heart produce _____ (hormone), which increases excretion of _____ (electrolyte) by the kidneys.

7. _____ (hormone) promotes the final conversion of vitamin D to _____ in the kidney.

8. _____ (hormone) produced by G-cells in the pyloric antrum stimulates _____ secretion in the stomach.

9. One ventral hypothalamic hormone (_____) is essential for the stress response and another (_____) inhibits release of prolactin.

10. _____ (hormone) is a stimulus for sperm production in the male and maturation of ovarian follicles in the female.

11. _____, secreted by the pineal gland, helps regulate body activities with the light-dark cycle.

12. The zona glomerulosa of the adrenal cortex primarily produces the hormone

    _____, which acts on the _____ (organ) to increase _____ (electrolyte)

    reabsorption.

13. The _____ _____ (gland) is a modified sympathetic ganglion producing the

    amine hormones known as _____. This category of amine hormones

    includes both _____ and _____ (two hormones).

14. The _____ (organ) produces a steroid hormone called _____ in the

    interstitial cells and a peptide hormone called _____ that inhibits FSH.

15. Large follicles in this gland (_____) contain a protein colloid called

    _____ from which the hormones _____ and _____ are made. These hor-

    mones regulate many metabolic functions and are important for nervous system

    development and growth.

16. Nuclei in the ventral hypothalamus produce two hormones that are stored in the

    posterior pituitary. The two nuclei that produce these hormones are _____ and

    _____; the hormones stored in the posterior pituitary are _____ and _____.

    _____ is important for water balance.

Endocrine System: Biochemistry, Secretion and Transport of Hormones

1. Place the following hormones into one of the three categories of hormones (peptides, amines or steroids): T_4 (thyroxin), estradiol, norepinephrine, insulin, aldosterone, glucagon, cortisol, growth hormone, T_3 (triiodothyronine), epinephrine, testosterone and vasopressin (ADH).

Peptides	Amines	Steroids

2. Peptide hormones are synthesized as large precursor hormones called

    _____. The hormones (or prohormones) are stored in _____ _____

    and released from the cell by _____. Do peptide hormones require a carrier in

    the bloodstream?

3. Catecholamines are produced in the _____ of the adrenal gland and are classi-

    fied as _____ hormones since they are derived from _____.

    Stimulation of the chromaffin cells causes an influx of _____ ions, which causes

    the vesicles to merge with the plasma membrane and release the hormone by

    _____. Are catecholamines water-soluble or lipid-soluble?

4. Thyroid hormones include two molecules called _____ and ____. T_3 consists of two

    _____ molecules plus ____ iodine molecules and is (*more* or *less*) abundant than

    T_4. Are carriers required for the transport of thyroid hormones?

5. All steroid hormones are derived from _____; which steroid hormone is pro-

    duced is determined by the _____ present in the cell. The common precursor

    molecule for all steroid hormones is _____, which itself is not a

    hormone. Steroid hormones enter the bloodstream by _____ and _____ (*do* or *do not*) require a carrier. The rate of secretion of steroid hormones is (*faster* or *slower*) than catecholamines because steroid hormones are not _____.

6. Preganglionic sympathetic fibers trigger the release of _____ and _____ (hormones) from the _____ _____ (gland), this is an example of neural regulation of hormone secretion.

7. Two examples of hormonal regulation of hormone secretion include: (1) the negative feedback of T_3 & T_4 to decrease _____ levels; and (2) the negative feedback of cortisol which decreases both _____ and _____ levels.

8. Besides increased levels of plasma glucose and amino acids (humoral regulation), increased levels of both _____ (hormone) and the _____ nervous system increase plasma insulin levels.

9. Some hormones are released in rhythmic 24-hour patterns known as _____ rhythms. _____ is a hormone where stressful stimuli can override this pattern and increase the plasma hormone levels. In contrast, _____ (amine hormones) are an example where large amounts of the hormones are bound to carrier proteins in the plasma forming a large circulating reservoir. Thus, acute changes do not produce large changes in the plasma level of this hormone.

10. The _____ and _____ are the major organs that metabolize hormones. The type of hormone determines how fast that hormone is metabolized. _____ and _____ are rapidly metabolized, while _____ and _____ take longer to metabolize.

Endocrine System:
The Actions of Hormones on Target Cells

1. The receptor is activated by the input signal that is the _____. This signal

   causes a biochemical change in the cell. Name three of the five possible changes.

   _____

   _____

   _____

2. Water soluble proteins such as _____ and _____ bind to receptors

   located where on the cell? _____

3. G proteins:

   a. What is bound to the G protein in the inactive state? _____

      In the active state? _____

   b. What catalyzes the conversion of ATP to cAMP? _____ _____

   c. What is known as the first messenger? _____Second messenger? _____

   d. A molecule of cAMP activates _____ _____ ____, which can

      phosphorylate many proteins.

   e. A single molecule of a hormone can have a large effect on the cell due to this

      process called _____.

   f. What is the enzyme that inactivates cAMP? _____

4. Insulin:

   a. Insulin decreases plasma glucose, amino acids and fatty acids by stimulating the
      conversion of them to their storage form. Name these storage forms.

      glucose   → _____

      amino acids → _____

      fatty acids → _____

b. Conversion to the storage form is known as _____ metabolism.

c. After a meal, high levels of glucose, amino acids and fatty acids lead to a/an (*decrease* or *increase*) in insulin secretion.

d. The autonomic nervous system also regulates insulin secretion. What effects would the sympathetic and parasympathetic system have on insulin secretion?

Sympathetic   → _____

Parasympathetic → _____

e. Insulin travels in the blood and binds to what type of receptors on the cell membrane? _____

f. What is the approximate half-life of insulin? _____

g. What hormone increases plasma glucose levels? _____ This hormone breaks down the storage forms and this is known as _____ metabolism.

5. Diabetes:

a. Type (*1* or *2*) diabetes is characterized by a resistance of the target cells to insulin. Plasma insulin levels are normal or high.

b. In type 1 diabetes, the lack of insulin and glycogenolysis in the liver leads to (*hypoglycemia* or *hyperglycemia*).

c. With the increase in filtration of glucose at the kidneys, the carriers become _____, which causes glucose to appear in the urine, also known as _____.

d. Glucose acts as an _____ _____ leading to increased urine flow.

e. Increased lipolysis produces an increase in _____ _____, which when used as fuel produces _____.

f. The presence of these in plasma and urine is known respectively as _____ and _____.

6. a. Lipid soluble hormones such as _____ and _____ hormone bind to

   receptors located _____.

   b. Once the hormone binds to the receptor, the _____ dissociates from the

   receptor complex.

   c. The hormone receptor complexes act as _____ _____.

   d. The receptor-hormone complex then binds to _____.

   e. The mRNA produces _____ that catalyze biochemical reactions in

   the cell.

7. a. Cortisol is classified as a _____ hormone.

   b. Name four major actions of cortisol.

   _____

   _____

   _____

   _____

   These actions are important for the stress response.

8. a. The main function of thyroid hormones is: _____.

   b. Three other specific functions include:

   _____

   _____

   _____

Endocrine System: The Hypothalamic-Pituitary Axis

1. The anterior pituitary is composed of _____ tissue. Name the six classic hormones whose functions are well known.

   a.

   b.

   c.

   d.

   e.

   f.

2. TRH, GNRH, CRH, etc., are known as _____ hypothalamic hormones which regulate the function of the _____ pituitary. These hormones are released into capillary beds and carried directly to the pituitary by the _____ _____ _____ located in the _____.

3. _____ and _____, the posterior pituitary hormones, are synthesized in the _____ and _____ nuclei of the hypothalamus. They are stored in the axon terminals located in the _____ pituitary. Similar to neurotransmitters, an _____ _____ in the neuron causes their release.

4. In negative feedback, the target hormone feeds back to alter the release of the anterior or hypothalamic hormones thus (*increasing* or *decreasing*) its own release.

5. Give an example of a hormone that has negative feedback mainly to the anterior pituitary. _____

   Give an example of a hormone that has negative feedback to both the anterior pituitary and the ventral hypothalamus. _____

6. Prolactin is unique in that the main ventral hypothalamic hormone regulating its secretion (_____) inhibits its release. _____ (hormone) increases prolactin release. Very high levels of this hormone during pregnancy actually block the effect of prolactin on milk production.

7. _____ hormones are necessary for the release of _____ hormone. This is

an example of modulation of a hormone by a target hormone of another series.

8. Suckling of an infant causes milk letdown by stimulating what hormone?

_____

Changes in osmolarity detected by chemically sensitive neurons in the hypothala-

mus will alter what hormone's level? _____

9. Cortisol release is synchronized by the light/dark cycle and has a 24-hour pattern of

secretion known as a _____ rhythm. Levels are highest at what part of the

day? _____

10. Besides controlling levels of T_3 and T_4, TSH also promotes _____ of the thy-

roid gland. T_3 and T_4 are carried in the bloodstream bound to _____ _____

because they are (*hydrophilic* or *lipophilic*).

11. T_3 and T_4 enter the target cells by _____ and bind to receptors located

_____. T_3 and T_4 are synthesized from _____ and _____.

12. Which of the following would be symptoms of hypothyroidism also known as

_____?

lethargy	or	hyperexcitability
high BMR	or	low BMR
high heart rate	or	low to normal heart rate
feeling cold	or	sweating
weight loss	or	weight gain

13. Lack of dietary iodine would cause (*primary* or *secondary*) hypothyroidism and the

patient would probably get an iodine-deficient _____.

14. Graves' disease is the most common cause of primary _____. The

body secretes _____ _____ _____, which mimics the action of

TSH and thus may cause a _____ as well as high levels of thyroid hormones.

Endocrine System: Response to Stress

1. What two body systems work together to provide well-coordinated, generalized, nonspecific responses to combat stress? _____ and _____

2. Increased levels of what three hormones indicate that an individual is experiencing stress? _____, _____ and _____

3. In the nervous system's response to stress, _____ and _____ exert many effects on the body. Choose the correct response in the pairs listed.

   ↑ or ↓CO   ↑ or ↓ sweating
   ↑ or ↓ventilation   ↑ or ↓ insulin
   ↑ or ↓ BP   ↑ or ↓ blood flow to digestive system
   ↑ or ↓ plasma levels of glucose,
      fatty acids, etc.

4. In response to stress, the hypothalamus increases the release of CRH, which increases _____ from the anterior pituitary and _____ from the adrenal cortex. These hormones prolong the response to stress provided by the nervous system.

5. Cortisol enhances _____ (in vessels) to help maintain blood pressure and also (*increases* or *inhibits*) the inflammation and immune response.

6. Besides cortisol, the adrenal cortex releases _____, which promotes salt and water retention, which helps maintain blood volume and blood pressure.

7. _____ (posterior pituitary hormone) also aids in the stress response by promoting water retention and at high levels it is also a potent _____. Both of these hormones help maintain blood pressure.

8. Epinephrine is a (*lipophilic* or *hydrophilic*) hormone. Thus it (*does* or *does not*) require a protein carrier and the receptors at the target cell are located _____. Epinephrine is synthesized from _____ and has a very short half-life of _____.

9. _____ is a condition in which there is hypersecretion of catecholamines

   by a tumor in the adrenal medulla. Which of the following symptoms would be

   present in a patient with this condition?

sweating	or	cool dry skin
↓ BP	or	↑ BP
↓ blood glucose	or	↑ blood glucose
↑ HR	or	↓ HR
↑ TPR	or	↓ TPR

10. Cortisol is a (*lipophilic* or *hydrophilic*) hormone. Thus it (*does* or *does not*) require

    a protein carrier and the receptors on the target organ are located _____.

    Cortisol is synthesized from _____ and has a half-life of _____.

11. Hypercortisolism is better known as _____ _____, which is due to a

    hypersecreting tumor in the anterior pituitary. What hormone is being

    hypersecreted? _____. Hypercortisolism from all other causes, such as

    glucocorticoid drugs, is known as _____ _____.

12. Primary adrenal insufficiency is better known as _____ _____. What two

    hormones are deficient? _____ and _____

13. The following symptoms would be characteristic of which disease? _____

    Low blood pressure, decreased plasma sodium and hypoglycemia

14. The following symptoms would be characteristic of which disease? _____

    high blood pressure, poor wound healing and hyperglycemia

15. Classify the following as either part of the rapid response (R) to stress mediated by the sympathetic nervous system, the prolonged (P) response of the endocrine system, or both:

maintains gas exchange _____

maintains fuel levels _____

maintains body defenses _____

redirects blood flow _____

makes fuel available _____

maintains high BP _____

Digestive System: Anatomy Review

1. List two main divisions of the digestive system.

   a. _____

   b. _____

2. The four main layers of the digestive tract wall are:

   a. _____

   b. _____

   c. _____

   d. _____

3. Label the diagram below with the four main layers you listed in the previous question.

4. The mucosa includes a type of columnar _____that forms the inner lining of the

   lumen.

5. Blood and lymph vessels of the mucosa are found in its _____ _____ connective

   tissue layer.

6. The smooth muscle layer of the mucosa is called the _____ _____.

7. The function of epithelial goblet cells is to secrete _____.

8. _____ cells of the mucosa secrete hormones into the blood.

9. Absorption of nutrients occurs through the mucosal epithelium and into either

   _____ or _____ vessels.

10. Using the following diagram, label the vessels you listed in the previous question.

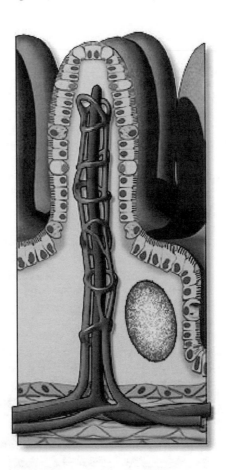

11. The muscularis mucosa has both _____ and _____ fibers that function in

    moving the villi to aid in digestion and absorption.

12. The built-in (intrinsic) network of nerve cells in the submucosa is the _____

    _____.

13. The two types of movements produced by contractions of the muscularis externa

    are _____ and _____.

14. The network of neurons in between the two muscle layers of the muscularis

    externa is the _____ _____.

15. The mouth, with its ____ ____ epithelium, is involved in both chemical and ____

    digestion.

16. List the four regions of the stomach:

   a. _____

   b. _____

   c. _____

   d. _____

17. List the three sheets of muscle in the stomach's muscularis externa:

   a. _____

   b. _____

   c. _____

18. Label the three sheets of muscle in the stomach's muscularis externa in the diagram below.

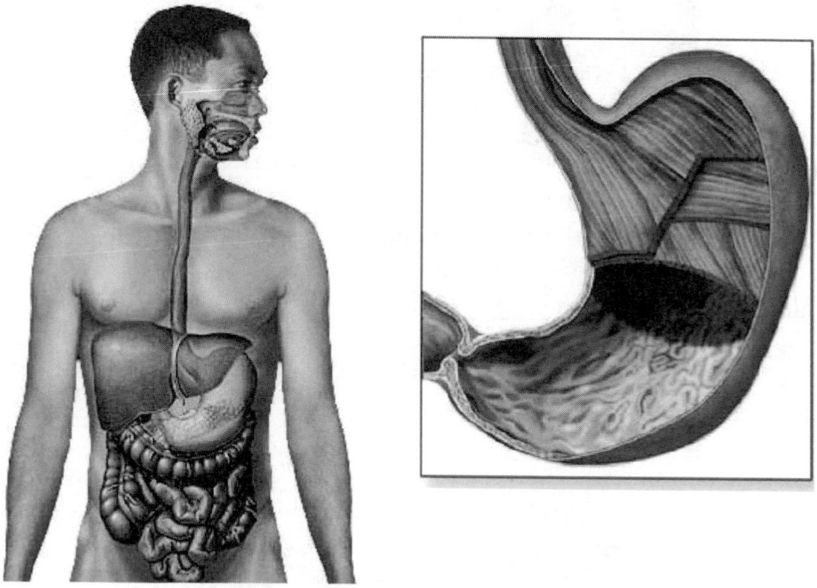

19. In order from the pylorus to the colon, list the three regions of the small intestine:

   a. _____

   b. _____

   c. _____

20. From largest to smallest, list the three modifications of the small intestine's inner wall that function to increase surface area:

    a. _____

    b. _____

    c. _____

21. Label two of the modifications of the intestine to increase surface area in the following diagram.

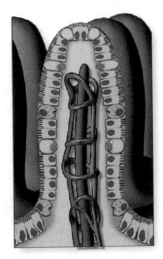

22. The microvilli of the small intestine's epithelial cells form the _____ border.

23. The large intestine absorbs _____, _____, and _____.

24. Starting from the ileocecal valve, trace the path of undigested material through the large intestine.

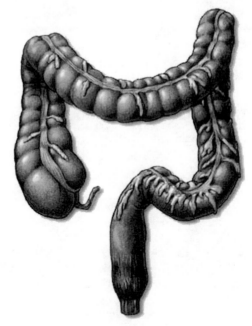

25. The anus is lined with _____ _____ epithelium.

26. List the six sphincters of the digestive tract:

    a. _____

    b. _____

    c. _____

    d. _____

    e. _____

    f. _____

27. The single digestive function of the liver is to produce _____.

28. The main digestive enzyme-producing organ in the body is the _____.

29. Three pairs of _____ _____ function to moisten food in the mouth.

Digestive System: Control of the Digestive System

1. List the primary two mechanisms that control the motility and secretion of the digestive system.

    a. _____

    b. _____

2. List the three phases of digestive system processes.

    a. _____

    b. _____

    c. _____

3. The _____ nerve triggers the responses during the cephalic phase of digestion.

4. The stimulation of _____ receptors triggers the gastric phase of digestion.

5. List the four main responses during the intestinal phase of digestion.

    a. _____

    b. _____

    c. _____

    d. _____

6. The small intestine typically_____.

    a. slows gastric emptying
    b. accelerates gastric emptying
    c. has no effect on gastric emptying

7. The _____ and _____ _____ nerves carry parasympathetic impulses to the enteric nervous system.

8. Sympathetic nervous system innervation of the digestive tract is via_____ fibers.

    a. preganglionic
    b. postganglionic

9. The _____ and _____ plexuses are the two components of the

enteric nervous system.

10. Digestive system reflexes that involve the brain are called _____ _____.

11. A meal consisting largely of fatty foods will take _____ to digest than a meal

consisting mainly of starchy foods.

   a. a longer time
   b. a shorter time
   c. the same time

12. All preganglionic ANS fibers release _____ while only postganglionic fibers of the

sympathetic division release _____.

13. Which of the following neurotransmitters stimulates smooth muscle contraction in
   the digestive tract?

   a. VIP
   b. norepinephrine
   c. NO
   d. ACh

14. _____ slow intestinal motility and cause the pyloric sphincter to contract.

15. List five peptide hormones of the GI tract:

   a. _____

   b. _____

   c. _____

   d. _____

   e. _____

16. List four functions of duodenal CCK.

   a. _____

   b. _____

   c. _____

   d. _____

17. Secretin stimulates gastric HCl secretion.

   a. True
   b. False

18. GIP stimulates the pancreas to secrete_____.

19. _____ stimulates motility of the intestine, thereby moving its contents toward the

   terminal ileum.

20. _____ occurs when the combined action of two hormones is greater than the sum

   of their individual effects.

Digestive System: Motility

1. The process by which food is received into the GI tract via the mouth is called

   _____.

2. The esophagus is digestive in function.

   a. True
   b. False

3. Swallowing has both voluntary and involuntary components.

   a. True
   b. False

4. The function of the epiglottis is to prevent a bolus from entering the _____.

5. The first wave of contraction of the esophageal muscles is called _____ _____.

6. If a food bolus does not make it all the way to the stomach, _____ peristalsis

   forces the bolus the remainder of the way.

7. Peristaltic contractions of the stomach occur about _____ times per minute when

   food makes it into the body and fundus.

8. The frequency of peristaltic contractions is regulated by _____ cells.

9. Gastric emptying would be slowed by which of the following:

   a. Fats in the duodenum
   b. Acids in the duodenum
   c. Hypertonic solutions in the duodenum
   d. Distention of the duodenum
   e. All of the above

10. _____ regulate gastric juice secretion during the cephalic phase.

11. The cephalic phase of digestion is regulated by short reflexes.

    a. True
    b. False

12. The _____ nerve carries electrical signals from the medulla oblongata to the

    stomach.

13. The hormone _____ regulates gastric secretion during the gastric phase of digestion.

14. Gastric motility _____ as the stomach begins to receive food.

15. The hormone _____ released by the duodenum causes gastric motility to decrease when fats are present in the duodenum.

16. The hormone _____ causes the gallbladder to contract and release bile into the small intestine.

17. The _____ reflex describes the communication between the intestine and the stomach.

18. Sympathetic nervous system stimulation _____ digestive system activity.

19. The motility process illustrated below is _____.

20. Segmentation moves chyme in only one direction.

    a. True
    b. False

21. The frequency of segmentation contractions is greatest in the _____.

22. _____ reflexes stimulate the ileum to increase activity when food is in the stomach.

23. The hormone _____ causes the ileocecal sphincter to relax during the gastric phase.

24. During the inter-digestive period, _____ _____ _____ occur about once every 90 minutes to move undigested materials toward the terminal ileum.

25. Migrating motility complexes are controlled by the central nervous system.

    a. True
    a. False

26. List the two major functions of the large intestine.

    a. _____

    b. _____

27. Pockets formed by the contractions of the transverse and descending colon musculature are called _____.

28. Sustained, intense propulsive peristaltic contractions of the large intestine (colon) are called _____ _____.

29. Which of the following is under voluntary control?

    a. internal anal sphincter
    b. external anal sphincter

30. Only about _____ ml of the 500 ml of chyme that entered the colon is voided as feces.

31. Place the following labels on the large intestine figure below:

    cecum, ascending colon, transverse colon, descending colon, sigmoid colon, rectum, haustra, appendix

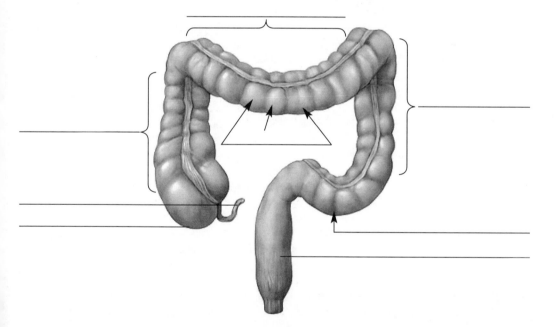

32. The _____ reflex stimulates mass movements of the colon.

33. List three emotions that may produce constipation.

    a. _____

    b. _____

    c. _____

34. The vomiting reflex is coordinated in the _____.

35. Which of the following is not typically a stimulus for the vomiting reflex?

    a. Noxious chemicals
    b. Abnormal vestibular stimulation
    c. Sudden injury to the testes
    d. Sleep

Digestive System: Secretion

1. Of the approximately 9.0 L of fluids contained in the digestive tract daily, only

   _____ L are eliminated with the feces.

2. Of the approximately 800 g of food ingested during a typical day, only about ____ g

   are eliminated as undigested food in the feces.

3. Label the parotid, submandibular, and sublingual salivary glands in the figure below:

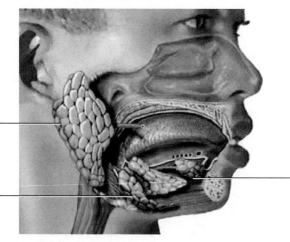

4. List the four major functions of saliva.

   a. _____

   b. _____

   c. _____

   d. _____

5. Parasympathetic innervation to the salivary glands is transmitted by cranial nerves

   number _____ and _____.

6. Both the sympathetic and parasympathetic divisions of the ANS stimulate the sali-

   vary glands.

   a. True
   b. False

7. _____ division innervation stimulates watery, enzyme-rich saliva secretion, whereas _____ division innervation stimulates a mucus-rich, more viscous saliva secretion.

8. Label the figure below with the terms ***parasympathetic*** and ***sympathetic***.

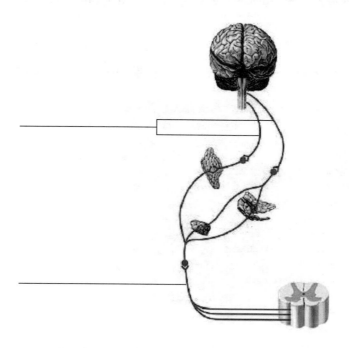

9. The esophagus secretes digestive enzymes.

   a. True
   b. False

10. The four main components of gastric juice are:

   a. _____

   b. _____

   c. _____

   d. _____

11. Place the following labels on the figure below:

parietal cell: HCl + IF, chief cell: pepsinogen, paracrine cell: histamine, mucus neck cells

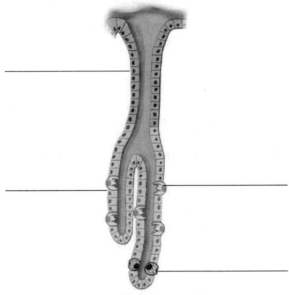

12. Gastrin-producing G-cells are found in the gastric glands located in the _____ region of the stomach.

13. List the only two substances that are absorbed across the stomach's mucosal epithelium.

   a. _____

   b. _____

14. HCl in the stomach produces a pH of between _____ in the luminal fluid.

15. Which of the following is a function of HCl in the stomach?

   a. Activates pepsinogen
   b. Breaks down cell walls
   c. Kills most bacteria
   d. Denatures proteins in food
   e. All of the above are functions of HCl

16. Without _____ _____, vitamin B_{12}, necessary for normal RBC development, cannot be absorbed by the intestine.

17. List the two secretions that stimulate HCl release from parietal cells.

   a. _____

   b. _____

18. During the cephalic phase _____, neural reflexes stimulate an increased production of gastric juice.

19. Lipids in the intestine cause the release of the hormone_____, while acid in the intestine causes the release of _____.

20. Match the following pairs of terms:

    CCK   bicarbonate pancreatic juice
    secretin   enzyme-rich pancreatic juice

21. List the three major proteases (inactive forms) secreted by the exocrine pancreas.

    a. _____

    b. _____

    c. _____

22. Intestinal _____ converts (activates) trypsinogen into trypsin.

23. The endocrine pancreatic hormone _____ regulates the absorptive state, while _____ regulates the post-absorptive state.

24. List the four organic components of bile.

    a. _____

    b. _____

    c. _____

    d. _____

25. Intestinal digestive enzymes that are embedded in the epithelial microvilli membranes are called _____ _____ enzymes.

26. The intestinal hormone _____ causes contraction of the gallbladder and release of bile into the duodenum.

27. _____ _____ protects the wall of the large intestine from mechanical damage and from damage by bacterial acid.

Digestive System: Digestion and Absorption

1. List the three major nutrient classes (a.k.a. macronutrients).

   a. _____

   b. _____

   c. _____

2. Which of the following carbohydrates is NOT a disaccharide?

   a. maltose
   b. lactose
   c. starch
   d. sucrose

3. Match the following pairs of molecules with their monomers by placing the number next to the matching letter:

   a. Sucrose _____

   b. Maltose _____

   c. Starch _____

   d. Lactose _____

   The monomers:

      1. many glucose monomers
      2. glucose + fructose
      3. glucose + galactose
      4. glucose + glucose

4. The breakdown products (monomers) of proteins are _____ _____.

5. The breakdown products of triglycerides include monoglycerides and _____

   _____.

6. Place the following labels on the diagram below:

maltose, maltotriose, limit dextrin

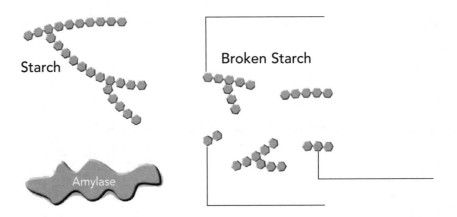

7. Once food is acidified in the stomach, amylase continues to digest starch.

   a. True
   b. False

8. The digestive enzyme _____ begins the breakdown of proteins in the stomach.

9. Pepsin is inactivated in the duodenum.

   a. True
   b. False

10. Pancreatic _____ is responsible for the majority of fat digestion.

11. Most water and salt are absorbed in the colon.

    a. True
    b. False

12. The active transport of sodium is necessary for water absorption in the small intestine.

    a. True
    b. False

13. The final digestion of carbohydrates is accomplished with _____ _____ enzymes.

14. Which of the following is NOT a brush border enzyme?

    a. Amylase
    b. Sucrase
    c. Dextrinase
    d. Glucoamylase

15. Place the following labels on the figure below:

    luminal side, facilitated diffusion transporter, basolateral side

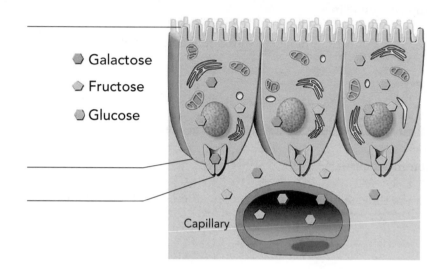

16. List the three major pancreatic proteases.

    a. _____

    b. _____

    c. _____

17. Only single amino acids are absorbed in the small intestine.

    a. True
    b. False

18. List the two main brush border proteases.

    a. _____

    b. _____

19. List the two mechanisms that help to increase the surface area of lipids for subsequent digestion with pancreatic lipase.

    a. _____

    b. _____

20. Bile salts surround monoglycerides and free fatty acids to form tiny droplets called

    _____.

21. Triglycerides combine with lipoproteins inside the intestinal epithelial cells to form

    _____.

22. Chylomicrons exit the intestinal epithelial cells and then enter the _____

    lymphatic capillaries.

23. The colon epithelium produces substantial amounts of digestive enzymes.

    a. True
    b. False

24. Colic bacteria produce substantial quantities of _____ ___ as a by-product of

    their metabolism.

25. List the three main substances that are absorbed in the large intestine.

    a. _____

    b. _____

    c. _____

InterActive Physiology®
Exercise Sheet Answers

Answers for Muscular System: Neuromuscular Junction

1. Endomysium
2. Acetylcholine (ACh)
3. Voltage-regulated Ca^{++} (same as voltage-gated)
4. Exocytosis
5. Chemically-regulated (chemically-gated)
6. Depolarization
7. By the enzyme – Acetylcholinesterase (AChE)
8. Sarcolemma, T-tubules
9. Ca^{++}
10. a. Decreased muscle contractions
    b. Competed with ACh by blocking receptor sites on channel
    c. Curare
11. a. Increased muscle contractions
    b. Prevented breakdown of ACh
    c. Neostigmine
12. a. Increased muscle contractions
    b. Binds to ACh receptor but is not broken down by AChE
    c. Nicotine

Answers for Muscular System: Sliding Filament Theory

1. a. Myosin
   b. Power stroke
2. a. ATP
   b. Actin
3. a. Actin
   b. Tropomyosin
   c. Troponin
4. ATP
5. high energy
6. backsliding
7. a. Energize the power stroke
   b. Disconnect the myosin cross bridge
   c. Actively transport Ca^{++} into the sarcoplasmic reticulum

8. Actin
9. b, c
10. a. Rigor mortis
    b. Lack of ATP after death

Answers for Muscular System: Contraction of Whole Muscle

1. b
2. muscle twitch
3. a. Contraction
   b. Relaxation
   c. Latent
4. a. second stimulus applied before complete relaxation
   b. ↓
5.

Order	Stage	Description
5	Fatigue	↓ tension due to ↓ ATP and ↑ buildup of lactic acid
3	Incomplete Tetanus	Rapid cycles but some relaxation seen
1	Treppe	↑ tension due to warming and ↑ enzyme efficiency
4	Complete Tetanus	Smooth sustained contraction
2	Temporal Summation	↑ tension due to repeated stimulation prior to complete relaxation

6. a. Many
   b. Few
7. a. 0.3 V
   b. 0.4 V
   c. 1.5 V
8. a. Moderate
   b. Overstretched

Answers for Nervous System I: Ion Channels

1. Integral proteins
2. a. Charge
   b. Size
   c. How much water the ion holds around it
3. passive
4. Into
5. 130
6. a. Sodium
   b. Chloride
7.

Channels	Areas on the neuron	Type of potential
Passive	dendrites, cell body, axon	resting membrane potential
Chemically-gated	dendrites and cell body	synaptic potential
Voltage-gated	axons	action potential

8. Found along the axon, Important for action potential, Opened and closed by gates
9. a. Passive chloride
   b. Chemically-gated (GABA)
10. a. Voltage-gated sodium
    b. Action
    c. Respiratory failure

Answers for Nervous System I: Membrane Potential

1.

	Intracellular	Extracellular
Sodium (Na^+)	15	150
Potassium (K^+)	150	5
Chloride (Cl^-)	10	125

2. K^+, Na^+
3. a. ↑
   b. ↑
   c. ↓
4. a. Concentration gradient
   b. Electrical gradient
5. equilibrium, –90
6. into
7. a. Concentration gradient—promote
   b. Electrical gradient—oppose
8. –70
9. Na^+–K^+ pump

10. a. pos
    b. neg
    c. pos
    d. pos
    e. neg
    f. pos

Answers for Nervous System I: The Action Potential

1. a. –70, +30
   b. Na^+, K^+, Voltage-gated
2. a. Axon hillock
   b. Dendrites, cell body
   c. Depolarize
3. a. Threshold, Action potential
   b. Na^+, Na^+
4. a. Inactivation of voltage-gated Na^+ channels
   b. Opening of voltage-gated K^+ channels
5. a. repolarize
   b. Out of
   c. hyperpolarization
   d. Slow decline
6. a. Na^+, absolute refractory
   b. relative refractory, more
7. a. 1. Increased diameter
      2. Presence of myelin
   b. Saltatory
8. a. Multiple sclerosis
   b. Myelin sheaths of CNS axons
   c. Too few voltage-gated Na^+ channels between the nodes of Ranvier

Answers to Nervous System II: Ion Channels

1. directly
   a. ACh
   b. Glutamate
   c. GABA
   d. glycine
2. a. Na^+, K^+
   b. Na^+, K^+
   c. Na^+
   d. Depolarize
   e. excitatory, EPSP
3. a. hyperpolarize
   b. GABA
   c. Cl^-
4. a. Indirectly
   b. first
   c. G protein
5. a. Second
   b. Phosphorylates

c. K^+
d. depolarizes
6. a. Norepinephrine
   b. Epinephrine
   c. Dopamine
7. a. ACh
   b. Glutamate
   c. GABA
8. Glycine

Answers for Nervous System II: Synaptic Transmission

1. voltage-gated Ca^{++}
2. Ca^{++}
3. a. Neurotransmitters
   b. Synaptic cleft
   c. Postsynaptic cell membrane
4. Chemically-gated
5. a. Pumped back into presynaptic terminals
   b. Broken down by enzymes
6. a. Specific neurotransmitter released
   b. Type of receptor on the postsynaptic cell
7.

Type	Found
Nicotinic	Neuromuscular junction
Muscarinic	excitatory: target organ in most cases inhibitory: heart and CNS

8.

α1	Blood vessels
β1	Heart (kidney) – excitatory
β2	Most sympathetic target organs – inhibitory

9. Smooth muscle, cardiac muscle, glands
10. glutamate
11. a. GABA
    b. glycine
12. a. Strychnine
    b. Cocaine
    c. Botulinus toxin, tetanus toxin

Answers for Nervous System II: Synaptic Potentials and Cellular Integration

1. Ca^{++}, rapid firing of action potentials
2. Ca^{++}, an axoaxonic synapse
3. a. graded
   b. decay
4. a. temporal
   b. spacial

5. inhibitory postsynaptic, IPSP
6. Cell body
7. a. 5
   b. 2
8. 2
9.

	Action Potential	Synaptic Potential
Function	Release neurotransmitters	Generate/inhibit action potentials
Depolarization/ hyperpolarizations	Depolarizations only	Both
Magnitude	100 mV	Varies with strength of stimulus

Answers for Cardiovascular System, the Heart: Intrinsic Conduction System and Cardiac Action Potential

1. a. Sets the pace for the entire heart
   b. Delay occurs allowing atria to contract
   c. Link between atria and ventricles
   d. Convey the depolarizations throughout the ventricular walls
2. a. Atrial depolarization
   b. Ventricular depolarization
   c. Ventricular repolarization
3. QRS complex
4. through gap junctions
5. a. Sodium, into
   b. Potassium, out of
   c. Fast calcium, into
6. reduced, potassium, sodium
7. –40, Fast calcium channels
8. potassium, repolarization
9. Sodium, calcium, potassium
10. a. Fast sodium channels
    b. Slow calcium channels
    c. Potassium channels

Answers for Cardiovascular System, the Heart: Cardiac Cycle

1. differences in blood pressure
2.

Chamber		Chamber/Vessel
Right ventricle	Pulmonary semilunar	Pulmonary trunk
Left ventricle	Aortic semilunar	Aorta
Right atrium	Tricuspid	Right ventricle
Left atrium	Bicuspid	Left ventricle

3. a. mid to late, diastole

   b. atrioventricular, AV

4. Intraventricular pressure is greater than atrial pressure

5. Intraventricular pressure is greater than pressure in the pulmonary trunk and aorta

6. Blood flow back toward the heart (due to aortic pressure being greater than intraventricular pressure)

7. Atrial pressure is greater than intraventricular pressure

8. With hypertension, the ventricular pressure must rise higher to open the semilunar valves. For the same increase in pressure in a normotensive person, less blood is ejected in a hypertensive person. Thus, the heart of someone with hypertension must work harder to eject the same stroke volume.

9. 70

10.

	AV Valves	Semilunar Valves
Ventricular filling	Open	Closed
Isovolumetric contraction	Closed	Closed
Ventricular ejection	Closed	Open
Isovolumetric relaxation	Closed	Closed

Answers for Cardiovascular System, the Heart: Cardiac Output

1. The amount of blood pumped out by each ventricle in one minute

2. CO = HR × SV

3. The amount of blood ejected from each ventricle in one heartbeat

4. SV = EDV − ESV

5. a. 75 beats/minute (bpm)

   b. 70 ml/beat

   c. 120 ml

   d. 50 ml

6. CO = HR × SV

   = 75 beats/minute × 70 ml/beat

   = 5250 ml/minute or 5.25 L/minute

7.

	HR	SV	CO
a. ↑ SNS	↑	↑	↑
b. ↑ Venous return	↔	↑	↑
c. Exercise	↑	↑	↑
d. ↑ Calcium	↑	↑	↑
e. ↓ HR	↓	↑	↔

8. An increase in contractility leads to an increase in the force of contraction

9. An increase in filling time leads to an increase in end diastolic volume—Frank Starling Mechanism

10. 3 bottles (6 liters)

Answers for Cardiovascular System, Blood Vessels: Factors That Affect Blood Pressure

1. a. Vessel diameter

   b. Blood viscosity

   c. Total vessel length

2. a. Epinephrine

   b. Angiotensin II

   c. Vasopressin (ADH)

3. a. Aldosterone

   b. Vasopressin (ADH)

4. ↓ VR → ↓ SV → ↓ CO → ↓ BP

5.

A. Factors that increase blood pressure	B. Factors that decrease blood pressure
↓ arterial diameter	↓ plasma epinephrine
↑ total vessel length	↑ vessel elasticity
↑ stroke volume	↓ plasma angiotensin
↑ blood volume	↓ blood viscosity
↑ plasma ADH	↑ vagus nerve stimulation
↑ sympathetic stimulation	↓ blood volume

6. ↓, ↓

7. ↑, ↑

8. ↓, ↑

9. ↓, ↓

10. ↓, ↑

Answers for Cardiovascular System, Blood Vessels: Blood Pressure Regulation

1. a. Short term mechanisms:

      1. Vessel diameter

      2. Heart rate

      3. Contractility

   b. blood volume

2. a. Aortic arch

   b. Carotid sinus

3. ↑ BP → ↑ impulses → ↑ PNS and ↓ SNS → ↓ BP

4. Heart → ↓ heart rate

   → ↓ cardiac output

   Blood vessels → vasodilation (increased arterial diameter due to relaxation of smooth muscle)

5. ↓ BP → ↓ impulses → ↓ PNS and ↑ SNS → ↑ BP

6. Epinephrine, norepinephrine

7. a. Juxtaglomerular

   b. Renin

   c. Angiotensinogen

8. a. ↑ Aldosterone

   b. Vasoconstriction

9. a. $\uparrow$ Na$^+$ reabsorption in kidney
   b. Water follows Na$^+$
10. a. ADH
    b. $\uparrow$ in plasma osmolarity

Answers for Cardiovascular System, Blood Vessels: Autoregulation and Capillary Dynamics

1. a. Precapillary sphincters
   b. Shunted, thoroughfare
2. a. $\downarrow$
   b. $\uparrow$
   c. $\downarrow$
   d. $\downarrow$
3. a. more perfusion
   b. less perfusion
4. a. fenestrations
   b. clefts
   c. cytoplasmic vesicles
5. a. O$_2$ and CO$_2$
   b. exocytosis
   c. clefts or fenestrations
6. filtration, reabsorption
7. a. Blood pressure
   b. Excess fluid is picked up by lymphatics
   c. out of
8. a. high
   b. into
9. 12 mmHg (34−22)
10. a. diffusion
    b. fenestrations or clefts
    c. fenestrations or clefts
    d. fenestrations or clefts

Answers for Respiratory System: Pulmonary Ventilation

1. a. Boyle's
   b. 1. $\uparrow$ volume → $\downarrow$ pressure
      2. $\downarrow$ volume → $\downarrow$ pressure
2. a. I
   b. E
   c. E
   d. I
3. $\downarrow$
4. a. Intrapleural
   b. inspiration
5. a. Lungs collapse
   b. pneumothorax
6. a. $\uparrow$
   b. $\downarrow$
7. a. resistance within the airways
   b. lung compliance

8. constrict, $\uparrow$, $\downarrow$
9. dilate, $\downarrow$, $\uparrow$
10. constrict, $\uparrow$, $\downarrow$
11. $\downarrow$, harder
12. $\downarrow$

Answers for Respiratory System: Gas Exchange

1. a. 20.9%
   b. 0.04%
   c. 78.6%
   d. 0.46%
2. a. 159 mmHg, 156 mmHg
   b. 0.3 mmHg, 0.3 mmHg
   c. 597 mmHg, 587 mmHg
   d. 3.5 mmHg, 3.4 mmHg
3. 440 mmHg
4. 92
5. a. CO$_2$ is much more soluble in liquid than O$_2$
   b. Henry's Law
6. a. surface area and structure of the respiratory membrane
   b. partial pressure gradients
   c. matching alveolar airflow to pulmonary capillary blood flow
7. a. humidification of air
   b. gas exchange between alveoli and capillaries
   c. mixing of new and old air
8. a. vasoconstriction (CO$_2$ effect)
   b. dilation (O$_2$ effect)
9. a. available surface area
   b. partial pressure gradients
   c. rate of blood flow varies
10. a. P$_{O_2}$ = 270 mmHg
    b. CO$_2$ would be found in the highest concentration in blood

Answers for Respiratory System: Control of Respiration

1. a. Dorsal respiratory group (DRG)
   b. Ventral respiratory group (VRG)
2. a. Central and peripheral chemoreceptors
   b. Pons
3. CO$_2$
4. H$^+$
5. 60 mmHg
6. a. $\downarrow$ P$_{CO_2}$,
   b. $\uparrow$ pH
7. a. $\downarrow$ P$_{O_2}$
   b. $\uparrow$ P$_{CO_2}$
8. a. Pulmonary Stretch Receptors (PSRs)
   b. inhibition
   c. Inflation reflex or Hering-Breuer reflex

9. a. Irritant receptors
    b. Remove irritants from the airways by invoking coughing and sneezing
10. a. Learned responses
    b. Neural input from motor cortex
    c. Receptors in muscles and joints
    d. Increased body temperature
    e. Epinephrine and norepinephrine
    f. pH changes due to lactic acid

Answers for Urinary System: Glomerular Filtration

1. Blood pressure
2. bulk flow, hydrostatic pressure
3. a. Water
    b. Ions (Na^+, K^+)
    c. Nitrogenous waste (urea, uric acid)
    d. Organic molecules (glucose, amino acids)
4. 60
5. a. Capsular hydrostatic pressure (15 mmHg)
    b. Osmotic pressure of blood (28 mmHg)
6. 17
7. 180 L
8. constrict
9. a. Myogenic mechanism
    b. Tubuloglomerular feedback
10. constrict, vasoconstrictor chemicals
11. a. Blood is shunted to other vital organs
    b. GFR reduction causes minimal fluid loss from blood

Answers for Urinary System: Early Filtrate Processing

1. a. transcellular through luminal and basolateral membranes (most substances)
    b. paracellular—through tight junctions
2. Increased osmolarity of the interstitium
3. Transport of Na^+ from the cell into the interstitium
4. Basolateral transport of Na^+: Interstitial osmolarity increases causing diffusion of water. Decreased intracellular Na^+ leads to additional Na^+ reabsorption through the luminal membrane.
5. 65%
6. water, NaCl
7. Na^+, Cl^-, and K^+; water
8. Forms and maintains the interstitial osmolarity gradient
9. Delivers nutrients without altering osmotic gradient
10. It causes dilution of the filtrate because transport in ascending loop will be impaired. It blocks the $Na^+/K^+/2Cl^-$ cotransporter. Furosemide is a potent loop diuretic.

11. a. ↓
    b. ↑
    c. ↓
    d. ↓
    e. ↑
    f. ↑
    g. ↑

Answers for Urinary System: Late Filtrate Processing

1. a. Intercalated cells—secrete hydrogen ions
    b. Principal cells—perform hormonally regulated water and sodium reabsorption and potassium secretion
2. a. 1. decreased sodium
        2. increased potassium
    b. the number of sodium/potassium ATPase pumps
3. Water channels
4. a. ↑, ↓
    b. ↑, ↓
5. a. water and solutes, 300
    b. water, increasing
    c. solutes, decreasing
    d. water and solutes, 100–300
6. a. 5
    b.

Hydration	ADH	Urine Osmolarity	Urine Volume
Normal	Moderate	600 mOsm	1.1 ml/min
Dehydration	High	1400 mOsm	0.25 ml/min
Overhydration	Low	100 mOsm	16 ml/min

7. a. Renal disease
    b. Diabetes mellitus
    c. Diabetes inspidus
8. a. ↑
    b. ↑
    c. ↓
    d. ↑
    e. ↓

Answers for Fluid, Electrolyte, and Acid-Base Balance: Introduction to Body Fluids

1. a. Intestines
    b. In urine
2. a. Maintain body temperature
    b. Protective cushioning
    c. Lubricant
    d. Reactant
    e. Solvent
    f. Transport

3. a. fat tissue
   b. 1. Newborns, 73%
      2. Heavier persons, 40%
4. a. Intracellular fluid, 62%
   b. Interstitial fluid, 30%
   c. Plasma, 8%
5. a. Na^+, K^+
   b. Proteins
   c. Glucose
6. a. Cations: Na^+ (K^+, Ca^{++}, Mg^{++}), anions: Cl^- (proteins, HCO_3^-)
   b. intracellular cations: K^+ (Na^+, Mg^{++}), anions: proteins, phosphates (Cl^-, SO_4^-)
7. positive charges, negative charges
8. a. Cofactors for enzymes
   b. Contribute to membrane and action potential
   c. Secretion and action of hormones
   d. Muscle contraction
   e. Acid/base balance
   f. Secondary active transport
   g. Osmosis
9. Water moves toward the side with more particles (hypertonic side)
10. a. cells expand/swell—hemolysis
    b. cells shrink—crenate
    c. Volume remains constant

Answers for Fluid, Electrolyte, and Acid-Base Balance: Water Homeostasis

1.

Disturbance	Volume	Osmolarity	Example
Hypervolemia	↑	↔	Infusion of isotonic fluid
Hypovolemia	↓	↔	Blood loss
Overhydration	↑	↓	Drinking too much water
Dehydration	↓	↑	Sweating

2. a. Antidiuretic Hormone (ADH)
   b. Thirst
   c. Aldosterone
   d. Sympathetic Nervous System
3. Antidiuretic Hormone (ADH):
   a. Increased plasma osmolarity
   b. Increased reabsorption of water
   c. ↑ volume and ↓ plasma osmolarity
   d. ↓ volume and ↑ osmolarity
4. a. Dry mouth
   b. Increased plasma osmolarity—osmoreceptors
   c. Decreased blood volume

5. a. renin
   b. Angiotensin converting enzyme (ACE)
   c. Increased aldosterone and increased vasoconstriction
   d. Increases the number of sodium/potassium ATPase pumps
   e. Both increase
6. a. increase
   b. 1. ↑
      2. ↓
      3. ↓
      4. ↑
7. a. decreased ADH secretion
   b. 1. ↑
      2. ↑
      3. ↑
      4. ↑

Answers for Fluid, Electrolyte, and Acid-Base Balance: Acid-Base Homeostasis

1. a. Carbonic acid—bicarbonate buffer system
   b. Phosphate buffer system
   c. Protein buffer system
2. $CO_2 + H_2O \leftrightarrow H_2CO_3 \leftrightarrow H^+ + HCO_3^-$
3. ↑, right, H^+, acidic
4. a. Reabsorption of filtered bicarbonate
   b. Generation of new bicarbonate
   c. Secretion of hydrogen ions
5. a. 7.35, 7.45
   b. pH > 7.45
   c. pH < 7.35
6. a. ↓
   b. left
   c. ↓
   d. ↑
   e. ↑
7. a. ↑
   b. right
   c. ↑
   d. ↓
   e. ↓
8. a. ↓
   b. right
   c. ↔
   d. ↓
   e. ↑
9. a. ↑
   b. left
   c. ↔
   d. ↑
   e. ↓

Answers for Endocrine System: Endocrine System Review

1. receptors
2. anterior pituitary, somatomedins or insulin-like growth factors (IGFs)
3. ACTH (adrenocorticotropic hormone), adrenal cortex, glandular
4. thyroid, calcitonin
5. glucagon, insulin, glucagon
6. ANP (atrial natriuretic peptide), sodium (Na^+)
7. PTH (parathyroid hormone), calcitriol
8. Gastrin, HCl (hydrochloric acid)
9. CRH (corticotropin-releasing hormone), dopamine
10. FSH (follicle stimulating hormone)
11. Melatonin
12. aldosterone, kidneys, sodium (Na^+)
13. adrenal medulla, catecholamines, epinephrine and norepinephrine
14. testes, testosterone, inhibin
15. thyroid, thyroglobulin, T_3 and T_4 (triiodothyronine and thyroxine)
16. supraoptic nucleus and the paraventricular nucleus, oxytocin and vasopressin, Antidiuretic hormone (ADH)

Answers for Endocrine System: Biochemistry, Secretion and Transport of Hormones

1.

Peptides	Amines	Steroids
insulin	T_4 (thyroxin)	estradiol
glucagon	norepinephrine	aldosterone
growth hormone	T_3 (triiodothyronine)	cortisol
vasopressin (ADH)	epinephrine	testosterone

2. preprohormones, secretory vesicles, exocytosis, no carrier required—water-soluble (hydrophilic)
3. medulla, amine, tyrosine, calcium, exocytosis, water-soluble—no carrier required
4. T_3 and T_4 (triiodothyronine and thyroxin), tyrosine, 3 (iodine molecules), less abundant, carriers are required—lipid-soluble (lipophilic)
5. cholesterol, enzymes, pregnenolone, diffusion, do require a carrier, slower, stored (in secretory vesicles)
6. epinephrine and norepinephrine, adrenal medulla
7. TSH, ACTH and CRH
8. GIP, parasympathetic
9. circadian, cortisol, thyroid hormones (T_3 & T_4)
10. liver and kidneys, Peptide hormones and catecholamines, thyroid hormones and steroid hormones

Answers for Endocrine System: The Actions of Hormones on Target Cells

1. hormone, any three of the following are correct: contraction, secretion, transport, synthesis, breakdown
2. peptides and catecholamines, on the cell membrane
3. a. GDP (guanosine diphosphate), GTP
   b. adenylate cyclase
   c. hormone, cAMP
   d. protein kinase A
   e. amplification
   f. phosphodiesterase
4. a. glucose → glycogen, amino acids → proteins, fatty acids → triglycerides
   b. anabolic (metabolism)
   c. increase (in insulin)
   d. sympathetic → decrease, parasympathetic → increase
   e. tyrosine kinase
   f. 10 minutes
   g. glucagons, catabolic (metabolism)
5. a. Type 2
   b. hyperglycemia
   c. saturated, glucosuria
   d. osmotic diuretic
   e. plasma lipids, ketones
   f. ketosis (ketonemia) and ketonuria
6. a. steroids and thyroid (hormone), in the cell (cytoplasm or nucleus)
   b. chaperone
   c. transcription factors
   d. DNA
   e. enzymes (proteins)
7. a. steroid hormone
   b. ↑ gluconeogenesis and glycogenolysis
      ↑ lipolysis and protein breakdown
      enhances vasoconstriction
      inhibits inflammation and immune response
8. a. main regulator of metabolic rate
   b. alter carbohydrate, lipid and protein metabolism
      essential for growth
      essential for nervous system development and function

Answers for Endocrine System: The Hypothalamic-Pituitary Axis

1. endocrine, epithelial (tissue)
   a. TSH
   b. FSH
   c. LH
   d. ACTH
   e. GH
   f. PRL
2. ventral, anterior, hypophyseal portal veins, infundibulum

3. Oxytocin and vasopressin (ADH), supraoptic and paraventricular, posterior, action potential
4. decreasing
5. T_3 and T_4—negative feedback to TSH in anterior pituitary, Cortisol—negative feedback to both the anterior pituitary (ACTH) and hypothalamus (CRH)
6. dopamine (DA), estrogen
7. Thyroid (T_3 and T_4), growth (GH)
8. oxytocin, vasopressin (ADH)
9. circadian (rhythm), early morning
10. growth (of thyroid gland), carrier proteins, lipophilic
11. diffusion, mainly in the nucleus, tyrosine and iodine
12. myxedema, lethargy, low BMR, low to normal heart rate, feeling cold, weight gain
13. primary, goiter
14. hyperthyroidism, thyroid stimulating immunoglobulin, goiter

Answers for Endocrine System: Response to Stress

1. endocrine and nervous systems
2. epinephrine, norepinephrine, cortisol
3. epinephrine and norepinephrine
   ↑ CO
   ↑ ventilation
   ↑ BP
   ↑ plasma levels of glucose, fatty acids, etc.
   ↑ sweating
   ↓ insulin
   ↓ blood flow to digestive system
4. ACTH, cortisol
5. vasoconstriction, inhibits
6. aldosterone
7. Vasopressin (ADH), vasoconstrictor
8. hydrophilic, does not, on the membrane, tyrosine, 10 seconds
9. Pheochromocytoma
   symptoms: sweating
              ↑ BP
              ↑ blood glucose
              ↑ HR
              ↑ TPR
10. lipophilic, does, inside the cell, cholesterol, 90 minutes
11. Cushing's disease, ACTH, Cushing's syndrome
12. Addison's disease, cortisol and aldosterone
13. Addison's disease
14. Cushing's disease
15. R: maintains gas exchange
    makes fuel available
    redirects blood flow

R+P: maintains high BP
P: maintains body defenses
     maintains fuel levels

Answers for Digestive System: Anatomy Review

1. a. Digestive (alimentary) tract
   b. Accessory organs
2. a. Mucosa
   b. Submucosa
   c. Muscularis Externa
   d. Serosa
3.

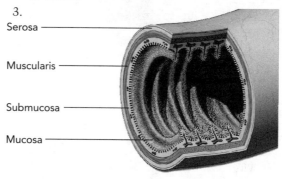

Serosa ——————
Muscularis ——————
Submucosa ——————
Mucosa ——————

4. epithelium
5. lamina propria
6. muscularis mucosa
7. mucin
8. Enteroendocrine
9. blood, lymphatic (lacteal)
10.

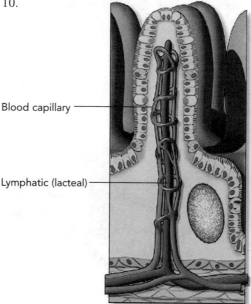

Blood capillary ——————
Lymphatic (lacteal) ——————

11. circular, longitudinal
12. submucosal plexus
13. peristalsis, segmentation
14. myenteric plexus
15. stratified squamous, mechanical

16. a. Cardia
    b. Fundus
    c. Body
    d. Pylorus
17. a. Circular
    b. Longitudinal
    c. Oblique
18.

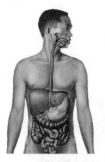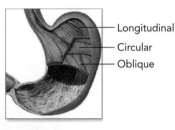

— Longitudinal
— Circular
— Oblique

19. a. Duodenum
    b. Jejunum
    c. Ileum
20. a. Plicae circularis
    b. Villi
    c. Microvilli
21.

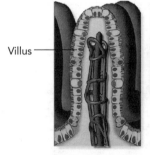

Microvillus

Villus

22. brush
23. water, salt, vitamin K
24.

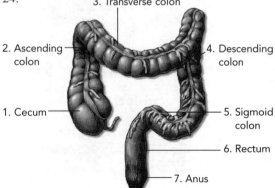

3. Transverse colon
2. Ascending colon
4. Descending colon
1. Cecum
5. Sigmoid colon
6. Rectum
7. Anus

25. stratified squamous
26. a. UES   d. Ileocecal sphincter
    b. LES   e. Internal anal sphincter
    c. Pyloric   f. External anal sphincter

27. bile
28. pancreas
29. salivary glands

Answers for Digestive System: Control of the Digestive System

1. a. Autonomic nervous system
   b. Hormones
2. a. Cephalic
   b. Gastric
   c. Intestinal
3. vagus
4. stretch
5. a. Bicarbonate secretion
   b. Enzyme secretion
   c. Bile release
   d. Segmenting contractions
6. (a) slows gastric emptying
7. vagus, pelvic splanchnic
8. (b) postganglionic
9. submucosal, myenteric
10. long reflexes
11. (a) a longer time
12. acetylcholine, norepinephrine
13. (d) ACh
14. Enkephalins
15. a. Gastrin
    b. CCK
    c. Secretin
    d. GIP
    e. Motilin
16. a. Causes gall bladder to contract and release bile
    b. Causes pancreas to release digestive enzymes
    c. Inhibits gastric emptying
    d. Stimulate growth of pancreas & gall bladder mucosa
17. False
18. insulin
19. Motilin
20. Potentiation

Answers for Digestive System: Motility

1. ingestion
2. False
3. True
4. trachea
5. primary peristalsis
6. secondary
7. 3–5
8. pacemaker
9. (e) All of the above

10. Nerves
11. False
12. vagus
13. gastrin
14. increases
15. CCK
16. CCK
17. enterogastric
18. decreases
19. segmentation
20. False
21. duodenum
22. Long
23. gastrin
24. mass motility complexes
25. False
26. a. Storage/concentration of feces
    b. Absorption of water, salts, vitamin K
27. haustra
28. mass movements
29. (b) external anal sphincter
30. 150
31.

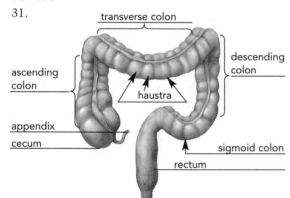

32. Gastroileal
33. a. Pain
    b. Fear
    c. Depression
32. Brainstem
33. (d) Sleep

Answers for Digestive System: Secretion

1. 0.15
2. 50
3.

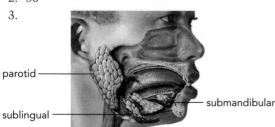

4. a. Protraction
   b. taste
   c. lubrication
   d. digestion
5. VII, IX
6. True
7. Parasympathetic, sympathetic
8.

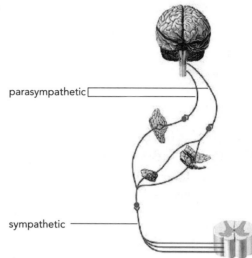

9. False
10. a. mucus
    b. pepsinogen
    c. HCl
    d. intrinsic factor
11.

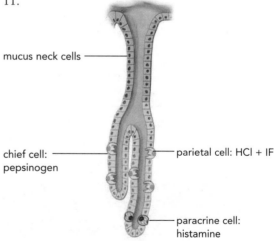

12. pyloric
13. a. aspirin
    b. alcohol
14. 1.5–2.0
15. (e) All of the above are functions of HCl
16. intrinsic factor
17. a. gastrin
    b. histamine
18. long
19. CCK, secretin

20. CCK: enzyme-rich pancreatic juice; secretin: bicarbonate pancreatic juice
21. a. trypsinogen
    b. chymotrypsinogen
    c. procarboxypeptidase
22. enterokinase
23. insulin, glucagon
24. a. bile salts
    b. lecithin
    c. cholesterol
    d. bilirubin
25. brush border
26. CCK
27. Alkaline mucus

Answers for Digestive System: Digestion and Absorption

1. a. carbohydrates
   b. proteins
   c. lipids (fats)
2. (c) Starch
3. a. 2
   b. 4
   c. 1
   d. 3
4. amino acids
5. fatty acids
6.

limit dextrin

Broken Starch

Starch

Amylase

maltose   maltotriose

7. False
8. pepsin
9. True
10. lipase
11. False
12. True
13. brush border
14. (a) Amylase
15. luminal side

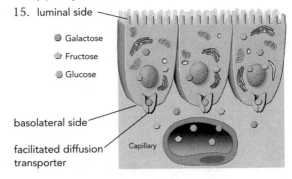

- Galactose
- Fructose
- Glucose

basolateral side

facilitated diffusion transporter

Capillary

16. a. trypsin
    b. chymotrypsin
    c. carboxypeptidase
17. False
18. a. aminopeptidase
    b. dipeptidase
19. a. segmentation
    b. emulsification
20. Micelles
21. Chylomicrons
22. Lacteal
23. False
24. vitamin K
25. a vitamin K
    b. water
    c. salts

Correlation Guide to A.D.A.M.® Interactive Anatomy (AIA)

As visual learners, many students find it easier to answer questions using AIA. This brief guide is intended to provide links to specific anatomical images in AIA that will help answer selected questions on anatomy found in the Review Questions section of *Human Anatomy & Physiology*, Seventh Edition.

After launching AIA and pulling up the **Open** dialog window (on the **File** menu, click **Open Content...**), you may begin by checking the reference list on the following page, which is organized by chapter, to determine the suggested **LINK** you wish to open. Click the appropriate **LINK**, by selecting either the *Dissectible Anatomy* button or *Atlas Anatomy* button. (Note that once you are in either of these viewers, you may move back and forth between them as the situation demands.)

If you are using *Dissectible Anatomy*, follow these steps:

- Click the appropriate gender option by selecting either the **Male** or **Female** option.
- Select the view you want to open by clicking the appropriate preview icon (Anterior, Lateral, etc.).
- Click the **Open** button or press **Enter** on your keyboard (you may also double-click the selected icon).
- If a **Layer** is suggested on your reference list, use the **Depth Bar** and move it up or down to find the suggested layer number. Now you are ready to explore the image structure at the appropriate layer to answer the question.

If you are using *Atlas Anatomy,* follow these steps:

- Select the appropriate option under **Show Images For:** by **Body Region**, **Body System**, **View Orientation**, or **Image Type** as suggested on your reference list.
- Now choose an image by selecting the appropriate preview icon (in **Thumbnail** mode) or selecting the appropriate **Title** (in **Details** mode). Click the **Open** button or press **Enter** on your keyboard (you may also double-click the highlighted icon or image title).

Chapter 1

Review Question 6 **LINK**: Dissectible Anatomy: Male: Medial.

Scroll and click on the visible organs to identify.

Review Question 9 **LINK**: Atlas: System: Skeletal: Abdominal Quadrants (Post).

Chapter 7

Review Question 3 **LINK**: Dissectible Anatomy: Male: Anterior: Layer 329.

Scroll vertically and horizontally to identify bones.

Review Question 9 **LINK**: Atlas Anatomy: System: Skeletal: Bones of the Trunk (Lat).

Chapter 8

Review Question 5 **LINK**: Atlas Anatomy: Region: Lower Limb: Knee Joint (Post).

Chapter 10

Review Question 3 **LINK**: Dissectible Anatomy: Male: Anterior: Layers: 8, 10, 12.

Review Question 5 **LINK**: Dissectible Anatomy: Male: Anterior: Layer 20.

Scroll to upper arm.

Review Question 6 **LINK**: Dissectible Anatomy: Male: Lateral: Layers: 51, 115, 122, 124.

Scroll to head. Click to identify muscles.

Review Question 7 **LINK**: Dissectible Anatomy: Male: Lateral: Layers: 42, 43, 242.

Scroll to neck. Click to identify muscles.

Review Question 9 **LINK**: Dissectible Anatomy: Male: Posterior: Layer 11.

Scroll to upper back.

Review Question 10 **LINK**: Dissectible Anatomy: Male: Anterior: Layers: 191, 192.

Scroll to lower leg. Click to identify components of the quadriceps.

Chapter 12

Review Question 12 **LINK**: Atlas Anatomy: System: Nervous: Brain (Lat).

Chapter 15

Review Question 1 **LINK**: Atlas Anatomy: System: Nervous: Olfactory Nerve in Nasal Cavity.

Review Question 3 **LINK**: Atlas Anatomy: System: Digestive: Surface of Tongue (Dorsal).

Review Question 10 **LINK**: Atlas Anatomy: System: Nervous: Sagittal Section of Eyeball.

Chapter 16

Review Question 18 **LINK**: Dissectible Anatomy: Male: Anterior: Layer 232.

Scroll to abdomen.

Chapter 18

Review Question 10 **LINK**: Dissectible Anatomy: Male: Anterior: Layer 170.

Scroll to Thoracic area of the body.

Review Question 13 **LINK**: Atlas Anatomy: System: Cardiovascular: Coronary Arteries (Ant).

Chapter 19

Review Question 11 **LINK**: Dissectible Anatomy: Male: Anterior: Layer 88.

Scroll to upper limb.

Review Question 12 **LINK**: Dissectible Anatomy: Male: Anterior: Layer 238.

Scroll to abdomen.

Review Question 25 **LINK**: Atlas Anatomy: System: Cardiovascular: Hepatic Portal Vein.

Chapter 22

Review Question 17 **LINK**: Dissectible Anatomy: Male: Medial. (What is the review question to determine where to direct the end user to go?)

Review Question 18 **LINK**: Atlas Anatomy: System: Respiratory: Bronchial Tree (Post).

Chapter 23

Review Question 11 **LINK**: Dissectible Anatomy: Male: Anterior: Layer 205.

Scroll to abdomen.

Review Question 18 **LINK**: Clinical Illustrations: System: Digestive: Digestive system.

Review Question 20 **LINK**: Dissectible Anatomy: Male: Anterior: Layer 195.

Scroll to abdomen.

Chapter 25

Review Question 21 **LINK**: Atlas Anatomy: System: Urinary: Male Pelvic Organs (Med) 1.